Lecture Notes in Computer Science 1542

Edited by G. Goos, J. Hartmanis and J. van Leeuwen

Springer
Berlin
Heidelberg
New York
Barcelona
Hong Kong
London
Milan
Paris
Singapore
Tokyo

Henrik I. Christensen (Ed.)

Computer Vision Systems

First International Conference, ICVS'99
Las Palmas, Gran Canaria, Spain,
January 13-15, 1999
Proceedings

Springer

Series Editors

Gerhard Goos, Karlsruhe University, Germany
Juris Hartmanis, Cornell University, NY, USA
Jan van Leeuwen, Utrecht University, The Netherlands

Volume Editor

Henrik I. Christensen
Royal Institute of Technology
Department of Numerical Analysis
and Computing Science
S-100 44 Stockholm, Sweden
E-mail: hic@nada.kth.se

Cataloging-in-Publication data applied for

Die Deutsche Bibliothek - CIP-Einheitsaufnahme

Computer vision systems : first international conference ;
proceedings / ICVS '99, Las Palmas, Gran Canaria, Spain, January
13 - 15, 1999. Henrik I. Christensen (ed.). - Berlin ; Heidelberg ;
New York ; Barcelona ; Hong Kong ; London ; Milan ; Paris ;
Singapore ; Tokyo : Springer, 1998
  (Lecture notes in computer science ; Vol. 1542)
  ISBN 3-540-65459-3

CR Subject Classification (1998): I.4, I.2.9-10, I.3.1, C.3

ISSN 0302-9743
ISBN 3-540-65459-3 Springer-Verlag Berlin Heidelberg New York

Typesetting: Camera-ready by author
SPIN 10693033   06/3142 – 5 4 3 2 1 0   Printed on acid-free paper

Preface

Computer Vision has now reached a level of maturity that allows us not only to perform research on individual methods but also to build fully integrated computer vision systems of a significant complexity. This opens up a number of new problems related to architectures, systems integration, validation of systems using benchmarking techniques, and so on. So far, the majority of vision conferences have focused on component technologies, which has motivated the organization of the First International Conference on Computer Vision Systems (ICVS). It is our hope that the conference will allow us not only to see a number of interesting new vision techniques and systems but hopefully also to define the research issues that need to be addressed to pave the way for more wide-scale use of computer vision in a diverse set of real-world applications.

ICVS is organized as a single-track conference consisting of high-quality, previously unpublished, contributed papers on new and original research on computer vision systems. All contributions will be presented orally. A total of 65 papers were submitted for consideration by the conference. All papers were reviewed by three reviewers from the program committee. Thirty-two of the papers were selected for presentation.

ICVS'99 is being held at the Alfredo Kraus Auditorium and Convention Centre, in Las Palmas, on the lovely Canary Islands, Spain. The setting is spring-like, which seems only appropriate as the basis for a new conference.

I would like to thank all the members of the program committee for their help in the reviewing process. It is their competence and hard work which has enabled the organizing committee to put together a high-quality conference.

I would like to thank our sponsors: the Spanish Ministry of Education, Cabildo de Gran Canaria, Excmo. Ayuntamiento de Las Palmas de Gran Canaria, University of Las Palmas de Gran Canaria, El Corte Ingles, and the EU TMR Networks SMART-II and CAMERA. Without their support this conference would not have been possible. I would also like to thank Springer-Verlag in Heidelberg, for their support of this conference through the proceedings.

Finally, I would like to thank member of the Computer Vision and Active Perception group and especially Emma Gniuli and Jan-Olof Eklundh for their never ending patience and support.

I wish all participants a successful and inspiring conference and a pleasant stay on the Canary Islands.

October 1998   Henrik Iskov Christensen
                                                          Program Chair
                                                              ICVS'99

Organization

Organizing Commitee

Conference Chair:	James L. Crowley (INPG, Grenoble, F)
Program Chair:	Henrik I. Christensen (KTH, Sweden)
Local Chair:	Jorge Cabrera (ULP, Spain)
Publication:	Claus S. Andersen (Aalborg University, DK)

Programme Committee

Claus S. Anderssen, (AAU)
Ruzena Bajcsy, (UPENN)
Aaron Bobeck, (MIT)
Kevin Bowyer, (USF)
Chris Brown, (Rochester)
Jorge Cabrera, (ULP)
Henrik I. Christensen (KTH)
Patrick Courtney (Visual Automation)
James L. Crowley, (INPG)
Ernst Dickmann, (UBW)
Rudiger Dillmann, (Karlsruhe)
Bruce Draper, (Colarado)
Jan-Olof Eklundh, (KTH)
Robert Fisher (Edinburgh)
Catherine Garbay (IMAG)
Erik Granum, (AAU)
Domingo Guinea (IAI)

Hirochika Inoue, (Univ. of Tokyo)
David Kortenkamp, (JSC, NASA)
Kurt Konolige, (SRI)
Claus Madsen, (AAU)
Bernd Neumann, (Hamburg)
Ehud Rivlin, (Technion)
Giulio Sandini, (Univ Genoa)
Bernt Schiele, (MIT)
Chris Taylor, (Univ. of Manchester)
Mohan Trivedi, (UCSD)
John Tsotsos, (Toronto)
David Vernon, (Maynooth College)
Jose Santos Victor (IST, Lisbon)
Thierry Vieville, (INRIA)
Jordi Vitria (Barcelona)

Sponsoring Institutions

Spanish Ministry of Education
Cabildo de Gran Canaria
Excmo. Ayuntamiento de Las Palmas de Gran Canaria
University of Las Palmas de Gran Canaria
The TMR Network SMART-II
The TMR Network CAMERA
El Corte Ingles

Table of Contents

Knowledge Based Methods/Systems

Architectures

Integrating Vision Based Behaviours with an Autonomous Robot *

Christian Schlegel, Jörg Illmann, Heiko Jaberg, Matthias Schuster, and Robert Wörz

Research Institute for Applied Knowledge Processing (FAW)
Helmholtzstraße 16, D-89081 Ulm, Germany
<last-name>@faw.uni-ulm.de

Abstract. Although many different vision algorithms and systems have been developed so far, integration into a complex intelligent control architecture of a mobile robot is in most cases an open problem. In this paper we describe the integration of different vision based behaviours into our architecture for sensorimotor systems. By means of different scenarios like person tracking and searching of different objects, the structure of the vision system and the interaction with the overall architecture is explained. Especially the interaction of vision based modules with the task level control and the symbolic world model is an important topic. The architecture is successfully used on different mobile robots in natural indoor environments.

1 Introduction

Integration of vision modules into a control architecture for an autonomous mobile robot is more difficult than just adding the vision components. This is due to the high bandwidth of vision sensors which require a task specific configuration of vision based behaviours. Another important aspect is lack of processing power on a mobile robot. This often prevents the use of existing powerful algorithms or requires to adjust them to the specific needs for use on a mobile platform. Therefore integrating vision based behaviours into an intelligent architecture for mobile robots is not only adding different components but affects many parts of the architecture itself.

The mobile robot described in this paper is used as demonstrator within the SFB 527. The SFB (collaborative research center) is a basic research project on "Integration of Symbolic and Subsymbolic Information Processing in Adaptive Sensorimotor Systems".

The paper is organized as follows. First we describe the main parts of the currently used architecture and the integration of vision based behaviours into the overall system. Then we describe two main vision based behaviours in more detail. The first one is used to detect and locate different objects within a natural indoor environment. It is used e.g. within a cleanup procedure to put different objects into waste baskets etc. The second behaviour is able to track and follow a person. This behaviour is especially useful for service robotic applications where a person is guided by a mobile robot or where a person shows the robot where to execute a specific task.

* This work is part of project C3 (http://www.uni-ulm.de/SMART/Projects/c3.html) of the SFB 527 sponsored by the Deutsche Forschungsgemeinschaft

1.1 System Overview

The basic idea of the system architecture is described in [14]. At the implementation level this architecture currently comprises three layers as shown in figure 1. The sub-symbolic level consists of continuously working modules. These modules work on raw sensor data and generate commands for the actuators. Realtime capabilities are an important topic at this level. Many skills of the robot are implemented at this level. In some sense, they contain no state and just build a reactive system which has to be configured appropriately. Algorithms for motion control and map building for example are at this layer. The second layer is the execution layer which is responsible for appropriate configuration and synchronization of the activities of the subsymbolic level. It supervises tasks performed on the subsymbolic level. In particular it selects appropriate parameters for skills taking into account the current execution context. It only works on discrete states which are used to synchronize real world execution with the symbolic task description. Since the outcome of a selected behaviour could be different to the expected one, a simple linear sequence of primitive behaviours is not sufficient. The execution layer must conditionally select appropriate behaviours for the current situation. The third layer contains time-consuming algorithms. Normally different transitions occur at the execution layer while the deliberation layer tries to generate a solution. One of the modules at this layer contains the symbolic planner. The generated plans describe the desired plot only at a very abstract level and constrain the selection of execution possibilities at the execution layer. The subsymbolic level is often called the skill layer and the intermediate level the sequencing layer.

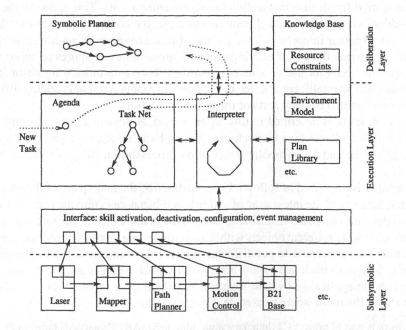

Fig. 1. Architecture overview

1.2 Related Work

Since in this paper both the architecture of the mobile robot and the vision component is part of the reported work, we describe related work in both areas. Due to space restrictions we concentrate on person following approaches in the area of vision because the algorithms used in the other vision modules are mainly off-the-shelf.

Architecture The kind of architecture we use is very similar to 3T [2]. This is not surprising because this kind of architecture seems to be extremely well suited to implement an intelligent control architecture for a mobile robot. The main strength of this kind of architecture is that by dividing the whole system into three layers, each layer is significantly easier to implement than the whole system. Another important topic is that the sequencing layer allows to abstract from details that would complicate the planning layer. This is the key to bridge the gap between the skill layer and the deliberative layer. Implementations of multilayer architectures are different with respect to the used algorithms at each layer. The sequencing layer often consists of a variant of the RAP system [7]. Recently, new programming languages like ESL [8] have been proposed, but they are not especially designed to be used with a symbolic planner. A very good overview on multilayer architectures is given in [13]. An unsolved topic, however, is the kind of interaction between different layers. Therefore many existing layered architectures are different with respect to this point.

Person Following Much work in the field of person detection and tracking is based on vision systems using stationary cameras [19]. Many of the approaches assume a stationary background because moving objects are detected by subtracting two frames [15, 4]. Other methods require that the tracked person is never occluded by other objects [1]. Therefore they are typically not suitable for person following on a mobile robot since at the same time the robot tracks the person, it has to move into the person's direction to stay close enough.

Many approaches can be classified regarding the kind of models that are used. Models range from complex 3D models [9] to simpler 2D models [15, 19]. The basic idea is to use deformable models to represent the boundary of the segmented body. Even those approaches assume one or more static cameras.

Several approaches use color-based image segmentation for object-ground separation [1, 3]. Persons to be tracked are represented by a collection of color blobs. A color-based system which is able to track colored blobs in real-time is presented in [20]. It is implemented on a mobile robot which locates a person in dynamic environments but requires to wear a uni-colored shirt with one of four predefined colors. Drawbacks are that the approach is not adaptive to illumination changes and, since it relies solely on the color and does not consider any shape, it requires that the person can be uniquely identified by its color. Therefore the person's color should not occur in the background.

A model-based approach for object tracking using two-dimensional geometrical models can be found in [11]. A binary contour model is matched against the current edge image using the Hausdorff distance. A successive match leads to an update of the contour model. This approach adapts to continuous deformations of the person's image during movement. Thus, it overcomes the difficulties which person tracking imposes on rigid-model based approaches. The main drawback of this approach is its computational complexity. Without any restrictions in the search space, it seems not to be suitable for real-time application.

2   Details of the Architecture

Although the basic architecture is based on a well-known three-layer model, there are significant differences. These concern mainly the interaction between different layers and are described in more detail in this section.

The basic entity of the robot software is a *module*. A module is equivalent to a process and consists of different threads. The external interface of a module is built using predefined communication templates. The software framework SMARTSOFT [18] also defines the basic internal structure of each module. This allows to completely hide any communication details from the module implementation and ensures standardized module interfaces. This includes a configuration interface for each module which is used for example by the execution layer to coordinate module activations. The modules form a client-server architecture and can be distributed transparently over different computers.

The execution layer is very similar to the RAP-system [7]. It has knowledge about default execution of different tasks. By appropriately configuring the modules at the subsymbolic level, different behaviours can be realized using the available modules. This allows to build different behaviours based on a limited set of skills. The configuration of a behaviour not only consists of activating and deactivating skills. Moreover, since the whole system is based on a client-server architecture, module interconnections can be changed online. We do not use a precompiled wiring of data flow between modules.

Events are not standalone or equivalent to skills but part of a skill. This allows to include extended status information about the situation which fired the event. Furthermore, only inside a module sufficient details are accessible to decide whether to fire an event. If events are separated from skills, many private details of modules have to be exported to events.

The currently used syntax to represent task networks is very close to the RAP notation. The main differences are the kind of interface to the subsymbolic level and the structure of the knowledge base. The knowledge base is organized as a frame system with single inheritance of object features. This allows a more structured representation which is important as soon as the knowledge base grows. The knowledge base is separated from the agenda interpreter and is accessed by a very simple tell-and-ask interface. Therefore, different kinds of knowledge representations can be used without reimplementing the whole execution layer. The agenda interpreter has been extended to handle some more ordering constraints in task nets like *try-in-order* etc. These modifications allow a more convenient formulation of task nets.

Another important detail concerns transient conditions. They can occur when switching between configurations and have to be avoided. For example, having activated the path planner together with the event *no path available* before the mapper can provide the requested part of the map, would fire the event unmeant. Therefore, the skill interface has been redesigned to provide more options to specify the order of skill activation and deactivation than the original RAP system.

As interface to the symbolic planner, an abstract STRIPS-like [6] description of the tasks available at the execution layer is used. With the current implementation, the planner is called from the execution layer for specific predefined problems. Whenever the *planner operator* occurs within a task net, the agenda interpreter calls the symbolic planner together with the appropriate part of the knowledge base. Because we know, for which problems we call the symbolic planner, we can also predefine, which part of the knowledge base has to be transformed into the planners representation for each problem instance. The generated plan defines the expansion of the planner operator and substitutes it in the task net. A typical subproblem solved by the planner is generating a sequence to get a specific box out of a stack of boxes. The currently used planner is IPP [12]. Of course, this kind of planner interface is one of the simplest ones, but it has specific advantages as well. By preselecting only problem relevant parts of the knowledge base and hiding as many details as possible from the symbolic planner, the planner is at all able to produce plans within a reasonable time.

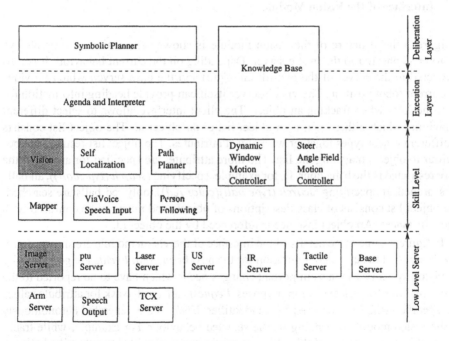

Fig. 2. Modules at different layers

Some of the currently implemented modules at different layers are shown in figure 2. Many modules at the subsymbolic layer deal with motion control and map building. Another important module e.g. is self localization, which ensures that the position error of the robot stays within certain boundaries [10]. Details of the motion control skills can be found in [16]. The vision system consists of two different modules. The first module is able to search and locate different objects, whereas the second module is able to track a person. The execution layer, the knowledge base and the symbolic planner are each implemented in a separate module.

3 Model Based Object Recognition

The vision component is used to detect and locate different objects in a natural indoor environment. One task, e.g., includes cleaning up an area. That means while moving around and exploring the workspace, objects have to be recognized on the fly. Significant difficulties arise from the moving robot and the movements of the pan-tilt-unit, that are necessary to fully explore the actual workspace. The following section describes details of the object recognition process, which is specifically adjusted to the requirements of a mobile robot.

3.1 Interface of the Vision Module

In figure 3 the structure of the vision module is shown. The vision module always has to be connected to the image server. Depending on the current behaviour it is also connected to the server of the pan-tilt unit (ptu) and the base server, which provides the current robot position. The vision server itself can provide heading information for other modules when tracking an object. The client interface allows to select different behaviours which either require an object list or an object id. The object list consists of different object types together with object attributes. The object list restricts the behaviour to objects matching the list. The more attributes are specified for an object the more restricted is the behaviour. If, for example, specifying *(search (type ball))*, all balls are searched. If specifying *(search (type ball)(color red))*, only red balls are searched. The object list consists of class descriptions of objects and must not be confused with object instances. An object instance is referenced by the object id.

In figure 4 some more details of the interface of the vision module are shown. *Commands* are used to set the configuration for the next behaviour. *Events* are generated by the vision system as soon as important changes occur which have to be reported to the execution layer for task execution purposes. *Requests* are used to ask for attribute values of a specific instance referenced by its identifier. *Updates* are generated autonomously by the vision module depending on the selected behaviour. For example, while tracking an object the position of this object is continuously provided to subscribed clients. Normally the motion control uses this information to move the robot into the desired direction. In figure 5 the configuration sequence for searching red balls and blue trashcans is shown in detail. After being activated, the behaviour quits as soon as one matching object is found. In this case an event is generated reporting the object id of the object found.

The following behaviours are implemented in the vision server. They provide basic capabilities which can be used to realize more complex vision based tasks.

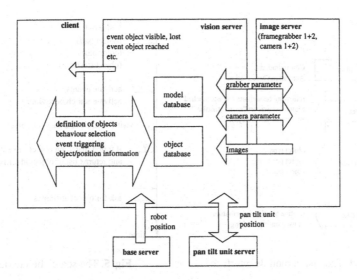

Fig. 3. Structure of the vision module

search *objectlist*	Search the specified objects and stop searching as soon as one matching object is found.
track *objectid*	Track the specified object but without providing heading information for motion control.
follow *objectid*	Follow the specified object, stop the robot if the object is reached or lost. If lost, search for it.
fullsearch *objectlist*	Use the ptu to fully explore the visible area without moving the robot. This behaviour reports all matching objects.
reset	Reset the vision module.

3.2 Object Classification

The vision module uses a model base to perform object recognition. Each object type is specified by a set of feature values. Features used to describe objects include form descriptors (rule based form classifiers) and color (color thresholds, color histograms). Since the object recognition has to work fast and robust on a mobile platform, we can use only computational inexpensive features. However, these have to be discriminant with respect to the occuring objects. Approved features are:

size	number of pixels belonging to the object
realsize	real visible area of the object
boundingbox	image coordinates of the upper left and the lower right corner of the color blob
eccentricity	eccentricity of the object
theta	angle between the major axis
fill	size(bounding box)/size(blob)

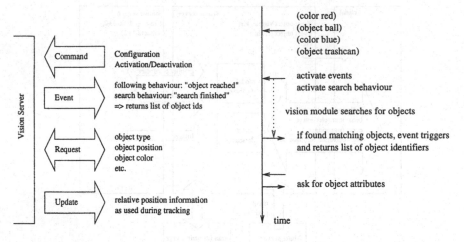

Fig. 4. The vision module interface   **Fig. 5.** The search behaviour

It depends on the object, which features are necessary for classification. Not all features are used with all objects. According to the tasks to be performed by the robot, the following objects are currently supported:

object bottle, ball, trashcan, cylinder, balloon, block, door, doorlabel, palette, table, notype

color red, green, blue, yellow, brown, orange, pink, lightgreen, white, black, lightorange, turquoise, lightblue, nocolor

The classification process now works as follows. If an object is specified, the corresponding feature values are looked up in the model base. These values form an object specific classifier which decides whether this object is in the image. In our scenario there exist only colored objects. The colortype *nocolor* means, that the object can have any of the above colors. Therefore, if an object is only specified by type, all supported colors are checked. Colors can be defined in different ways, e.g. as upper and lower bounds in RGB or in NCC color space. Classification consists of three steps which are also shown in figure 6.

1. color segmentation
2. feature extraction
3. classification with object specific classifiers based on extracted features

If the command *(search (type ball)(color red), (type trashcan)(color yellow))* is given, a new image is shot. First all red color blobs are detected by a simple color thresholding. After thresholding, the shape features for these blobs are computed. If a blob is smaller or bigger than a given threshold, it is deleted. If the shape of the blobs fulfil the criteria for balls, a ball with its attributes and coordinates is added to the object database. After that the same procedure starts from the beginning for all other objects specified in the objectlist.

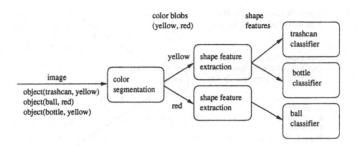

Fig. 6. Procedure of object classification

3.3 Object Database

In the object database – maintained by the vision module – each object instance has a unique object identifier. An entry in the object database contains the following information.

objectclass id for the objectclass
objectcolor id for the object color
features all computed features
pos3d cartesian 3d world coordinates
pos2d polar coordinates
distance distance to the camera
refpoint location of the spatial reference point in relation to the floor

If a behaviour with an object list is executed, the vision system normally generates a new unique identifier for each matching object. The only exception is when an already known object falls into an object dependent circular region around the object's position. If the object type and the attributes besides position are compatible, the old identifier is reused and the object's position is updated. If the objects are not compatible, the old identifier is deleted and a new entry is generated.

Figure 7 shows an example of the update process when performing a *fullsearch* for balls. The object database assumes a red ball at position A and a blue ball at position B. The current situation is a red ball at position A, a yellow ball at position B and a green ball at position C. The object at position D is not inside the field of view and is therefore not considered. Because the object type and attributes at position A are compatible, the red ball is kept in the object database and only its position is updated. Although the object type at position B is compatible, the color attribute does not match. Therefore, the object id 2 is deleted and the new id 3 is introduced. Since the object at position C is new, the object id 4 is introduced.

Each assertion or deletion in the object database is reported to the knowledge base. In the above example, one has to delete the entry with the vision object id 2 and assert new entries for the objects with the vision object identifiers 3 and 4. The knowledge base only maintains references to objects and symbolic descriptions of object attributes. The geometric model, e.g., of a bottle as it is used at the vision system, is private to the vision system and of no use at the symbolic level. The model of a bottle is totally different in

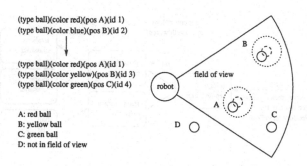

Fig. 7. Update of the object data base

the module which has to plan grasping operations. The symbolic level only maintains the links to the distributed representations.

4 Person Following

Since the person following behaviour includes a moving platform, the person tracking approach has to cope with varying illumination conditions and a changing background. It must also be able to track different persons. Furthermore, the available processing power is limited and has to be shared with other modules. To fulfil these requirements, we use a combination of a fast color-based approach with a contour-based method. The color-based method provides regions where the computationally expensive contour-based approach is applied. A startup phase is used to generate both the color and the contour model of the person to be tracked. During the tracking phase these models are continuously updated.

4.1 Color Based Person Tracking

We developed two color based methods which can be used interchangeably. Further details can be found in [17]. Both methods are based on the NCC color space, where the intensity information is removed. They are different with respect to the representation of the person-specific color model.

Modified NCC Method We first extended the approach presented in [20] to allow tracking of any uni-colored shirt. As shown in figures 8 and 9, the person presents itself to the robot and a predefined region is used to generate the person-specific color model. The thresholds (r_l, r_h, g_l, g_h) for the red and green color band are computed as $r_{l/h} = \mu_r \mp \sigma_r$ and $g_{l/h} = \mu_g \mp \sigma_g$. We assume a normal distribution of the color values of each color band. The thresholds define a rectangular area in the NCC color space describing the color distribution to be tracked.

During the tracking phase, the current image is transformed into a binary image. A pixel is set to 1 in the binary image if the corresponding NCC color value is within the rectangular area specifying the color model. The center of gravity of the largest blob in the binary image determines the position of the person to be tracked.

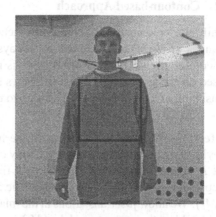

Fig. 8. Startup following behaviour

Fig. 9. Predefined region to extract color model

Histogram Based Method Since the modified NCC method can only track uni-colored shirts, we introduced color histograms. Based on an image representation in the NCC color space, we compute a two dimensional histogram h_{2D} where $h_{2D}(\hat{r}, \hat{g})$ specifies the number of image pixels with the color value $(\hat{r}, \hat{g})$ (figure 10). To detect and locate the person in the image, the histogram values are backprojected on the image. The pixel value $p(x, y)$ in the backprojection image with the color value $(\hat{r}, \hat{g})$ is set to the histogram value of $(\hat{r}, \hat{g})$: $p_{\hat{r}, \hat{g}} = h_{2D}(\hat{r}, \hat{g})$. The resulting image specifies the frequency that the image point $p(x, y)$ belongs to the tracked person. Subsequently, pixels with low probability values are eliminated. The target position is estimated by a weighted center of gravity in the backprojection image. This is shown in figure 11 where the person is wearing a two-colored shirt.

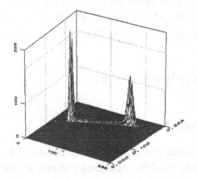

Fig. 10. Normalized 2D-histogram of red and green color bands

Fig. 11. Backprojection image

4.2 Contour-based Approach

While the presented color-based approaches are fast and fairly robust against shape changes of the person, they are not always sufficient. If different persons wear similar colored dresses, further information is needed. Therefore, we developed a method based on the approach in [11], that allows to track non-rigid objects. A contour model consisting of a set of edge pixels allows to describe the shape of a person.

Detection of the Seeked Object In the first step, the RGB-image is converted to a greylevel image which is fed into a Canny operator [5] to generate a binary edge image. Let I_t be the binary edge image taken at time step t and M_t be the model at time step t represented by a binary edge image. The model may undergo certain transformations $g(M_t)$. We allow just translations in the image space. Then the seeked object is detected by matching the current model $g(M_t)$ against the next image I_{t+1}. To estimate the similarity between model and edge image we use the generalized Hausdorff-distance [11] as a distance measure.

$$h_k(g(M_t), I_{t+1}) = K_{p \in M_t}^{th} \min_{q \in I_{t+1}} \|g(p) - q\| \tag{1}$$

Minimizing h_k over all transformations $g(.)$ provides the translation of the model M_t which leads to the best match. Let g^* be the transformation which minimizes (1) and d be the minimal distance.

$$d = min_{g \in G} h_k(g(M_t), I_{t+1}) \tag{2}$$

Descriptively this means that at least K points of the transformed model $g(M_t)$ lie at most at a distance d away from any point of the image I_t.

Contour Model Generation and Update The initial contour model is generated by a startup step. All edges within a predefined rectangular area are defined to belong to the initial contour model of the presented person. To be able to handle shape changes, the model has to be updated. The new model M_{t+1} is built from the points of the image I_{t+1} whose distance to a point of the transformed model $g(M_t)$ do not exceed a threshold δ. The parameter δ controls which shape changes are allowed within one timestep. That also covers small rotations and size variations.

$$M_{t+1} = \{q \in I_{t+1} | \min_{p \in M_t} \|g^*(p) - q\| \le \delta\} \tag{3}$$

4.3 Combination of Color-based and Contour-based Approach

Since the contour-based approach is computational too expensive we combine it with the color-based one. The color-based approach is used for detecting regions where it is reasonable to apply the contour-based approach. Figure 12 depicts our concept.

To update the contour model, the result of the color segmentation is used to mask the edge image. A binary image representing the blob belonging to the detected person is first dilated (figure 13 shows the dilated blob image) and a rectangular region

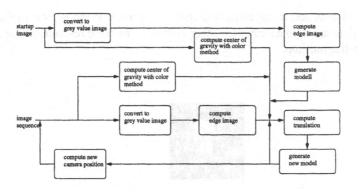

Fig. 12. Combined color- and contour-based approach

is added for the persons head. This considers the characteristic shape of the head and shoulder part when generating the initial model though the color distribution is generated only from the body. This binary mask is used to eliminate edge pixels belonging to the background. In figure 14 the updated contour model is shown. By masking the edge image before updating the contour model, unlimited growing of the contour model is prevented. This has been a problem with the original contour based approach.

Fig. 13. Mask image

Fig. 14. Model update

4.4 Implementation

To implement the behaviour person-following on our mobile robot, control commands for the robots actuators have to be generated. After detecting and locating the seeked person within the image, we use a very simple camera model to implement a reactive following-behaviour. The video cameras of our robot are mounted on a pan-tilt unit (ptu) which owns two degrees of freedom. The ptu is used to implement a gaze holding behaviour, i.e. steadily holding the person in the center of the image. To compute the control commands for the ptu, we assume a known focal length f and size of the CCD-Chip. A camera's field of view γ is computed as $\gamma_x = 2\arctan\left(\frac{ccdsize(x)}{2f}\right)$ horizontally and vertically. The ptu-angles are modified by $\alpha_x = \frac{\frac{x_B}{2} - x}{x_B}\gamma_x$ where x_B denotes the number of columns and x the estimated center of gravity of the person in the image. These directions are used as input for other modules which are responsible for generating collision free motions.

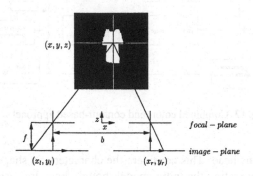

Fig. 15. Distance calculation

For holding a given distance between target and robot, we use a method based on the disparity between two simultaneously shot images. The conjugate pair we use are the centers of gravity of the segmented color blobs in both images. Our model is shown in figure 15. The distance z can be computed to $z = \frac{bf}{x_l - x_r}$. This is precise enough for a simple distance-estimation in order to decide if the robot has to accelerate or to decelerate. If the person is lost more than three times in sequence a stop command is sent to the motion control. After redetection the motion control gets new goal information.

5 Integration on the Robot

5.1 Person Following

At the execution layer, the capabilities of the person following module are modeled as two different behaviours. A behaviour can be executed by putting it on the agenda of the execution layer. The startup behaviour allows to build the model of the person (figure 8). The task net for this behaviour provides the following individual steps: First, speech output is used to ask the person to stand in front of the camera and to acknowledge this by speech input. Now the startup step is executed within the person following module. An event reports the result and speech output is used to inform the person. In case of success, an unique identifier to reference the person is provided and the startup step is finished.

The person following behaviour expects the identifier of the person presented before. Executing the person following behaviour includes a more complicated configuration at the skill level. The person following module gets images from the image server and provides the ptu with control commands. The motion controller is provided with the distance to and direction of the person relative to the robot. This module gets laser

Fig. 16. Person following

scans and tries to move into the proposed direction without collision. The speed is adjusted to the distance between the person and the robot. Different events are used to synchronize with the execution layer. The person following module can report whether the person has been lost. In this case the robot stops but tries to reacquire the person. The motion controller, e.g., can report that no path is available. The appropriate event handling procedure is invoked within the task net at the execution layer. The person following behaviour is shown in figure 16, the data flow between involved modules in figure 17.

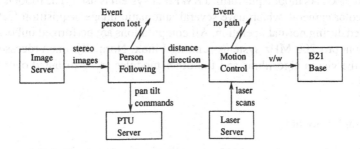

Fig. 17. Data flow during person following

5.2 Vision Module

The capabilities of the vision module are also represented by different behaviours at the execution layer. Each behaviour includes a task net and a description of the configuration of the skill level. The task net describes the different execution steps and specifies how to handle events reported from the skill level. Depending on the behaviour different skills are involved and different events can occur.

```
(define-rap (goto-object ?objectid)
  (method
    (context (object ?type ?objectid ?color ?approach-distance))
    (task-net
      (sequence
        (t1 (follow-object ?objectid))
        (t2 (search-object ?type ?color => ?object))
        (t3 (move-to-object-blind ?object ?approach-distance))
))))
```

Fig. 18. Task net for approaching an object

As example, figure 18 shows the task net of the vision based object approaching behaviour. The error handling code is not included in this example. The behaviour requires to specify an object id, which references a knowledge base entry. As first step, the `follow-object`-behaviour moves close to the expected object location as provided by the knowledge base. Then, the `search-object`-behaviour is used to confirm the expected object. If the object is near the expected position, the current object position is updated in the knowlegde base. Since the object is out of sight when the robot has to move very close to it, the last step is a blind move to the updated position.

6 Experiments

The overall system is being used in our everyday office environment, where it has to fulfil different tasks. As mobile platform, a RWI B21 system is used. The robot is equipped with two color cameras which have several automatic image acquisition features that are activated during normal operation. All computations are performed onboard by two dual pentium pro 200 MHz systems running Linux. Normally, one processor is used to handle the vision algorithms and the other modules are distributed over the other processors.

6.1 Person Following

Using 192×144 sized images for person following, cycle time is approximately 1 second for the combined color and contour based approach. This cycle time is achieved with the integrated system where different other tasks of the robot are running in parallel. It is fast enough to provide comfortable walking speed. Our robot successfully tracked different persons through our institute building at speeds up to 400 mm/s. The average speed normally is about 300 mm/s, the average length of a run is 5 minutes. Varying illumination conditions due to passing beneath lamps or moving next to window fronts have been handled robustly as long as the startup step is done accurately. If the acquired color distribution and contour model is quite exact, tracking and online adaptation is done fairly robust. Because the person following behaviour is monitored by the execution layer, the loss of the person to be tracked can be handled. In such a case speech output is used to ask the person to present itself once more to acquire a new model. The coordination is done by task nets, where context dependent execution orders can be expressed comfortably.

6.2 Vision Module

Typical tasks involving the vision module are collecting objects (figure 19) in a certain area and putting them in appropriate trashcans (figure 20). The vision module has to look for objects and trashcans during exploration of the area. Each recognized trashcan is stored in the knowledge base. This allows to move to the nearest trashcan as soon as an object has been found and picked up. The robot drives with 200 mm/s when searching for objects. To be able to pick up an object, the robot has to approach it in such a way that the gripper is placed correctly. This is done by a tracking behaviour, where the vision module provides heading information for the motion controller. An event signals when the object has been reached and can be picked up. The coordination of the different steps is done by the execution layer guided by the task net. Depending on the required behaviour, different configurations of the vision module and other skills are selected and synchronized by events.

Fig. 19. Some example objects   **Fig. 20.** Putting a ball into a trashcan

Some of the objects detectable by the vision system are shown in figure 19. The object classification mainly relies on color. In many cases only two other features like object size and eccentricity are necessary. The discrimination performance of the used features with respect to our objects is now discussed in more detail. Since we assume that all objects rest on a flat floor (ground-plane-constraint), the tilt-angle corresponds to the distance between object and camera. Therefore, the interval for the feature values can be defined dependent on the tilt angle. This allows for example to cope with size variations. A feature therefore provides useful discrimination information, if the feature value curve has a big distance to curves of other objects over all tilt angles. The

18

correlation between the tilt-angle and the object size for different objects (bottle, trash-can, ball, cylinder) is shown in figure 21. The object size is defined as the size of the color blob after the color segmentation and is measured in pixels. For many objects, the size is besides color already sufficient for classification. However, further information is needed to distinguish balls and bottles. As shown in figure 22, the eccentricity allows this distinction. Figure 22 shows the dependence of the object eccentricity upon the tilt-angle. Noticeable is the strong fluctuation of the bottles' eccentricity curve. This results from reflexions on the glass bottle which cause strong differences from one angular step to the next. Nevertheless, both features size and eccentricity allow to discriminate balls and bottles. Using the pan-tilt unit to scan the workspace, it takes about 6 seconds to inspect an area of 30 sqm.

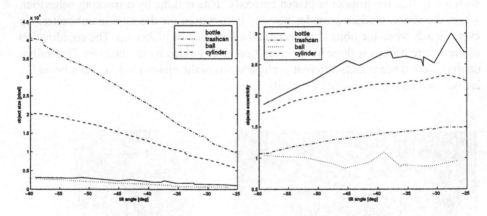

Fig. 21. Size depending upon tilt-angle   **Fig. 22.** Eccentricity depending upon tilt-angle

7   Conclusion

We have described the vision modules on our mobile robot together with the currently used overall system architecture. The three layer architecture well supports the integration of different modules to form a complex system which can execute a wide variety of different tasks. Practical experience showed that the requirements of a mobile platform and the necessity to build an integrated system make specific demands on the vision component. These requirements are best met by using simple but robust approaches. Due to the high bandwidth needed by vision systems, task dependent behaviour selection is crucial. By a context dependent configuration of vision based behaviours, limited ressources can be shared adequately. Therefore, the vision components have to be highly modularized and have to provide a configuration facility.

The kind of integration described in this paper provides a very close integration at the level of task execution and behaviour coordination. However, the interaction between the symbolic environment model and the vision components has to be further extended. Currently, expected objects can be confirmed by the vision system as long as they are within the field of view. Also newly seen objects or incompatibilities between object attributes can be reported. The more difficult problem is to decide whether an expected object has disappeared. This can be done only for objects in the field of view. For objects lying outside the field of view, nothing can be said. Therefore, a close interaction with a geometric model which allows to decide which objects are expected to be visible is required. Hence, current work within the SFB aims at a deeper integration of vision at the level of map building and representation of the environment.

References

1. A. Azarbayejani, C. Wren, and A. Pentland. Real-time 3-d tracking of the human body. In *Proceedings of IMAGE'COM 96*, 1996.
2. R.P. Bonasso, R.J. Firby, E. Gat, D. Kortenkamp, D. Miller, and M. Slack. Experiences with an architecture for intelligent reactive agents. *Journal of Experimental and Theoretical Artificial Intelligence*, 9(2), 1997.
3. S.A. Brock-Gunn, G.R. Dowling, and T.J. Ellis. Tracking using colour information. In *3rd ICCARV*, pages 686–690, 1994.
4. Q. Cai, A. Mitchie, and J.K. Aggarwal. Tracking human motion in an indoor environment. In *2nd International Conference on Image Processing*, Oct. 1995.
5. J. Canny. Finding edges and lines in images. Technical Report AI-TR-720, MIT Artificial Intelligence Lab, 1983.
6. R.E. Fikes and N.J. Nilsson. STRIPS: a new approach to the application of theorem proving to problem solving. *Artificial Intelligence*, 2:189–208, 1971.
7. R.J. Firby. *Adaptive Execution in Complex Dynamic Worlds*. PhD thesis, Yale University, 1989.
8. E. Gat. ESL: A language for supporting robust plan execution in embedded autonomous agents. In *Proceedings of the IEEE Aerospace Conference*, Los Alamitos, California, 1997. IEEE Computer Society Press.
9. D.M. Gavrila and L.S. Davis. Towards 3-d model-based tracking and recognition of human movement: a multi-view approach. In *Int. Workshop on Face and Gesture Recognition*, 1995.
10. J.S. Gutmann and C. Schlegel. AMOS: Comparison of scan matching approaches for self-localization in indoor environments. In *IEEE Proceedings of the 1st Euromicro Workshop on Advanced Mobile Robots*, pages 61–67, 1996.
11. D. Huttenlocher, J.J. Noh, and W.J. Ruckli. Tracking non-rigid objects in complex scenes. Technical Report TR92-1320, Department of Computer Science, Cornell University, 1992.
12. J. Koehler, B. Nebel, J. Hoffmann, and Y. Dimopoulos. Extending planning graphs to an ADL subset. In *Proc. European Conference on Planning*, pages 273–285. Springer Verlag, 1997.
13. D. Kortenkamp, R.P. Bonasso, and R. Murphy. *Artificial Intelligence and Mobile Robots - Case Studies of Successful Robot Systems*. AAAI Press and The MIT Press, Menlo Park, CA, 1998.
14. F.J. Radermacher. Cognition in systems. *Cybernetics and Systems*, 27:1–41, 1996.
15. C. Richards, C. Smith, and N. Papanikolopoulos. Detection and tracking of traffic objects in IVHS vision sensing modalities. In *Proc. Fifth Annual Meeting of ITS America*, 1995.
16. C. Schlegel. Fast local obstacle avoidance under kinematic und dynamic constraints for a mobile robot. In *Proc. IEEE/RSJ International Conference on Intelligent Robots and Systems (IROS)*, Victoria, Canada, 1998.

17. C. Schlegel, J. Illmann, H. Jaberg, M. Schuster, and R. Wörz. Vision based person tracking with a mobile robot. In *Proc. British Machine Vision Conference*, volume 2, pages 418–427, 1998.
18. C. Schlegel and R. Wörz. SmartSoft software architecture. http://www.faw.uni-ulm.de/deutsch/bereiche/autonomsys/c3-main-e.html.
19. M. Sullivan, C. Richards, C. Smith, O. Masoud, and N. Papanikolopoulos. Pedestrian tracking from a stationary camera using active deformable models. In IEEE Industrial Electronics Society, editor, *Proc. of Intelligent Vehicles*, pages 90–95, 1995.
20. C. Wong, D. Kortenkamp, and M. Speich. A mobile robot that recognizes people. In *IEEE International Joint Conference on Tools with Artificial Intelligence*, 1995.

Topological Maps for Visual Navigation*

José Santos-Victor[1], Raquel Vassallo[2] and Hans Schneebeli[2]

[1] Instituto de Sistemas e Robótica, Instituto Superior Técnico,
Lisboa Portugal, jasv@isr.ist.utl.pt
[2] Dept. Engenharia Elétrica, Universidade Federal do Espírito Santo,
Vitoria/ES - Brasil, {raquel,hans}@ele.ufes.br

Abstract. We address the problem of visual-based indoors navigation based on a single camera that provides the required visual feedback information. The usual approach relies on a map to relocate the robot with respect to the environment. Once the robot position and orientation are known, a suitable trajectory is defined according to the mission goals and the structure of the environment. However, one could argue that it should be possible to perform most missions without a precise knowledge of the robot position and orientation. This is indeed the case for many living beings when they navigate in complex environments. We propose to represent the environment as a *topological map* that is tightly related to the system perceptual and motion capabilities. The map should contain environmental information that can easily be extracted by the system and the mission should be described in terms of a set of available *behaviors* or *primitive* actions. We present results that merge visual servoing and appearance based methods. Servoing is used locally when a continuous stream of visual information is available. Appearance based methods offer a means of providing a topological description of the environment, without using odometry information or any absolute localization method. Preliminary tests are presented and discussed.

1 Introduction

Increasing the autonomy of a robot is intimately connected to its ability to perceive the surrounding environment and react to dynamic changes while performing a specified task. Examples in navigation include controlling the robot orientation and velocity, detecting obstacles, going to a point, etc.

Although vision can provide a rich description of the working space of a robot, earlier research was focused on partial or full reconstruction of the 3D structure of the scene before taking any action. In spite the fact that we have witnessed an impressive increase of the available computational power in the past few years, together with the advance of new vision algorithms and techniques, the reconstruction approach is still a difficult, demanding problem, hardly suitable for real-time navigation.

Since the early days of active vision [1, 3] it became clear that for some visual tasks one could profit from exploiting the structure of the specific problem to

* This research has been partially funded by projects PRAXIS/2/2.1/TPAR/2074/95.

handle, together with the definition of *customized* algorithms to increase both the system robustness and speed. Typically it corresponds to sacrificing the generality of the reconstruction paradigm for specific visual measurements (in some cases imprecise or qualitative) relevant to a precise problem. Additionally, vision is used in a more *continuous* way [14] to control the actions of a mobile agent.

This line of research has been used in various working systems (see [18] for example) and a suitable theoretical framework was defined to study some of these problems [5] at a more conceptual level. However, as there is no *map* of the environment it is difficult to deal with problems involving global tasks or coordinate systems, like going to a distant destination.

On the other extreme one finds navigation systems that rely heavily on an environment map. Such systems usually include a map building module (using vision, sonars or laser) and a localization system that determines the robot position and orientation as a function of a set of *landmarks* or environmental features. A certain degree of accuracy has been achieved with such systems but map building (in metric terms) and localization are computationally expensive (and may require special sensing devices) and one can argue if this is absolutely necessary.

Indeed, map building or localization are not really the ultimate goals of the navigation system. Instead, a common mission is usually specified (or could be) in terms of *qualitative/topological* relationships between the robot and the environment. When telling someone to go to the center of our home town, the path may be described like, "go down, find the square, take a left, then turn on the second road on your right hand side and look for the phone booth on your left."

If, instead, we rely on a metric description/map of the environment one could also specify the way as "go ahead 32.15m; rotate 34.78 degrees clockwise, then move on for 45.8m, etc.". Although valid as a mission description, this is hardly the best way to accomplish the mission of going to a specific point.

These two examples illustrate what we refer to as the difference between *metric* and *topological* maps. We believe that it is advantageous if the map used for a navigation can be defined in terms that are easily related to the robot perceptual capabilities and a set of motion or available behaviors.

In this paper, we focus on indoors environments, and represent the environment as a *topological map* that is both related to the robot perceptual and action capabilities. We combine two methodologies to achieve the overall flexibility and robustness of the navigation system: visual servoing and appearance based methods.

Visual servoing uses prior knowledge about the 3D scene where the robot operates, together with a purposive definition of the navigation task to be solved. This mode is used whenever a continuous stream of image features can be extracted from the video sequence. In the example shown in the paper, this is done by servoing on the vanishing point defined by the intersection of the corridor guidelines observed by the robot camera [12]. As discussed earlier, visual servoing alone can hardly cope with more global navigation tasks that require the existence of some kind of map or internal representation of the environment.

Appearance based techniques offer an alternative solution for transforming pre-stored images in motion commands [13, 2]. Here we use such techniques as an *implicit* topological description of the environment, that is used to monitor the robot progress along the task. In an indoors environment, one can build a graph-like structure representing the hallways, office doors, lifts, and other relevant environmental features. Links in the graph correspond to trajectory segments where visual features are available for visual servoing (as the corridor guidelines). Progression can be monitored using appearance based methods, simply by comparing previously stored images against acquired views. Nodes in the graph occur whenever decisions need to be taken like turning left, entering a door or picking an object.

Similar methods have been proposed in the past. In some cases it was assumed that image features were **always** available thus providing the necessary input to the visual servoing system (see [16, 11, 4], for example). In other cases, the use of appearance methods alone does not exploit the full geometric structure available for servoing [2] and may impose heavier computational requirements on the whole system.

From the point of view of building systems, most approaches shift a significant effort from the mission/navigation goals to the underlying localization module. Here, the approach is different from a conceptual point of view. The question is to find the minimum requirements (on the localization system) necessary to perform a given mission. It is often the case that some tasks do not really need an accurate knowledge of the robot position and orientation. Hence, this approach allows a more parsimonious use of resources in a number of navigation problems and, therefore, contribute for the design of simpler and yet robust navigation systems.

While the robot is moving along a corridor, with the camera pointing forward, the navigation system must control the angular velocity based on the images acquired by the vision system. Meanwhile, the appearance based system provides *qualitative* measurements of the position of the robot, thus monitoring the progress of the overall mission. Once certain *relevant* positions are attained, other navigation behaviors are launched. This is done by an onboard computer, that runs the tasks of image processing and determines the changes of the robot angular velocity. The control sequence consists of the following operations:

- Image acquisition.
- Detection of the corridor guidelines.
- Calculation of the vanishing point and lines orientation.
- Use image based error signals to determine angular velocity commands.
- Monitor the robot progress along the task relying on appearance based methods and determine if special decisions need to be taken.

All the experiments described in the paper were made with a TRC Labmate platform from HelpMate Robotics Inc. The processing was done in 192x144 grayscale images captured from a Sony pan-tilt camera installed on the robot, and a DT3852 frame grabber. Communication between the base motion controller and the main computer is done via a serial link.

This paper is organized as follows: in Section 2, we show how appearance based methods can be used for topological maps representation, thus extending the autonomy achieved by servoing methods alone. Section 3 describes the geometric foundations related to the vanishing point determination and the servoing strategy. The main experimental results are also included in Section 4. Finally, in Section 5, we draw some conclusions and final remarks.

2 Topological Maps for Visual Navigation

As mentioned earlier, by servoing on image features alone it is hard to tackle navigation problems involving a more global representation of the environment.

We extend the robot autonomy by implicitly embedding a topological representation of the environment based on appearance based methods. The representation should be adequate both in terms of the set of available behaviors (e.g go along the corridor, turn left, enter the door, dock to a point) and the perceptual capabilities for evaluating the mission progress. Such a map can be represented as a graph. Links correspond to trajectory segments where visual servoing can be used. Nodes correspond to locations where special actions need to take place like turning, entering a door, launching another navigation behavior, etc.

Figure1 shows an example of such a map. It contains information regarding qualitative spatial relations between points or regions in the environment. In this case, we represent corridors and special sites like office doors, bars, etc.

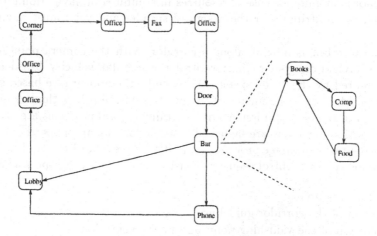

Fig. 1. Topological map of an indoors environment, showing offices, rooms, etc. Links correspond to the hallways where servoing can be applied.

The assumption is that we have a set of available behaviors that can be used to navigate in the map. In the example of this paper we use servoing strategies for navigating along corridors (links in the graph). In the past we have built several visual behaviors for tasks like obstacle avoidance, docking, centering and wall-following, etc [15, 17, 18].

The map can contain multiple sub-graphs. For instance, when entering the bar area one could also go to the bookshop, computer shop, etc, following the various graph links.

The progress along the links is monitored by using a set of reference images acquired at *meaningful* positions along the path. Hence, each link has an associated sequence of images. During normal operation, the current image is compared to the reference images and the best matching indicates the approximate position of the robot. Similarly, special sites (landmarks) requiring specific actions or decisions correspond to nodes in the graph identified by a pre-stored image. Figure 2 shows a reference image set acquired along a corridor at the Instituto Superior Técnico, in Lisbon, Portugal.

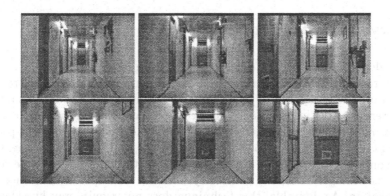

Fig. 2. Reference images $\{1^{st}, 3^{rd}, 5^{th}, 7^{th}, 9^{th}, 11^{th}\}$ used for the appearance based method (clockwise, starting at the upper left image).

Figure 3 shows an image acquired during the robot operation and the result of the comparison (using the SSD - *sum of squared differences* metric) against the reference image set.

The comparison of the current image and the reference set is supported by the causality constraint, i.e the reference positions are ordered according to the direction of motion. The aim of the appearance based method is not to obtain accurate position or orientation estimates. Instead, we need *qualitative* information regarding the robot status along the task that is sufficient to trigger further actions. As an example, the final images in the corridor are used to realize that the robot is located in a corner (node) and perform and adequate turn to proceed. Similarly, one of such images could indicate that the robot is close to the final destination, thus eliciting another operating mode.

In the next section, we describe the servoing strategy adopted to navigate along corridors.

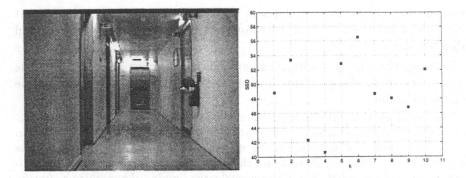

Fig. 3. Left: Image acquired along the trajectory. Right: Result of the SSD computed between the candidate images and the reference image set. The best match is obtained against the 4th image.

3 Servoing on the vanishing point

In an indoors environment one has often to navigate along corridors to move between rooms to perform a task. For this reason, the ability to extract the visual information required to navigate along corridors is quite important [12]. Our system uses the information on the corridor guidelines for motion control.

In terms of projective geometry, the corridor guidelines intersect at a point in the line at infinity belonging to the ground plane [9, 6]. If the camera orientation is kept constant relative to the guidelines, this point at infinity should be remain fixed in the image. Thus, the control system has to keep the vanishing point under fixation. As desirable, this technique does not require any knowledge of the camera calibration parameters. Figure 4 illustrates the view of a corridor captured by the on-board camera.

We consider the robot and ground coordinate frames as shown in Figure 4. The robot has 3 degrees of freedom defined by its position on the ground plane and the heading direction.

As shown in Figure 4, the corridor guidelines can be defined by the points:

$$\text{line } r_1: \quad (x_1, y_1) = (0,0); \quad (x_2, y_2) = (0,1)$$
$$\text{line } r_2: \quad (x_3, y_3) = (d,0); \quad (x_4, y_4) = (d,1) \tag{1}$$

where d denotes the corridor width. Any point ^{W}P expressed in the world coordinate frame $\{W\}$ can be expressed in the robot coordinate frame $\{R\}$ through a rotation matrix $^{R}R_W$ and a translation $^{W}P_{OR}$:

$$^{R}P = {}^{R}R_W({}^{W}P - {}^{W}P_{OR}) \quad \text{with} \quad {}^{R}R_W = \begin{bmatrix} \cos\theta & \sin\theta \\ -\sin\theta & \cos\theta \end{bmatrix} \tag{2}$$

where θ is the robot heading direction. We can then define a collineation on the projective space relating points expressed in the world coordinate frame and the

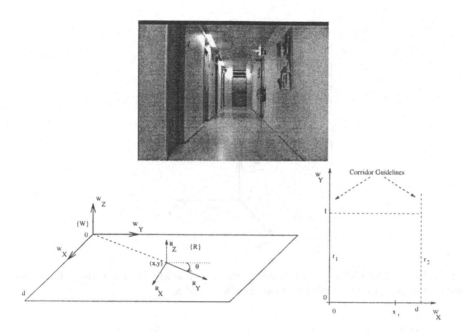

Fig. 4. Top: The corridor guidelines intersect at the vanishing point at the horizon line. Bottom left: Robot and World (ground) coordinate frames, and the degrees of freedom identifying the robot position and orientation relative to the world frame. Bottom right: Definition of the corridor guidelines.

same points expressed in the robot coordinate frame[3]:

$$
{}^R T_W = \begin{bmatrix} c_\theta & s_\theta & 0 & -x_r c_\theta \\ -s_\theta & c_\theta & 0 & x_r s_\theta \\ 0 & 0 & 1 & 0 \\ 0 & 0 & 0 & 1 \end{bmatrix} \tag{3}
$$

where we denote the position of robot coordinate frame along the corridor x direction by x_r. The position along the y axis is irrelevant for this analysis and, therefore, we consider $y = 0$.

We further assume that the camera coordinate frame $\{C\}$ differs from the robot coordinate frame by a *pitch*-angle, p, measured downwards, and a vertical translation by h (height), as shown in Figure 5.

In this way ,we can now introduce another coordinate transformation from the robot frame to the camera frame, ${}^C T_R$:

$$
{}^C T_R = \begin{bmatrix} 1 & 0 & 0 & 0 \\ 0 & -s_p & -c_p & h c_p \\ 0 & c_p & -s_p & h s_p \\ 0 & 0 & 0 & 1 \end{bmatrix} \tag{4}
$$

---

[3] To simplify the notation we use (s_α, c_α) to denote $(\sin\alpha, \cos\alpha)$

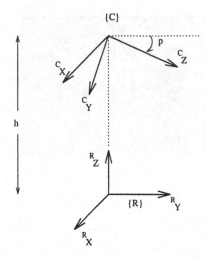

Fig. 5. Robot and Camera coordinate frames differ solely by a rotation about that camera x axis - pitch, p, and a vertical translation of h.

Now that we have all the information to express the points on the ground plane on the camera coordinate frame, we can determine the image projections using the pin-hole camera model. The projection is achieved by the following camera matrix ^iT_C:

$$^iT_C = \begin{bmatrix} S_u & 0 & u_0 & 0 \\ 0 & S_v & v_0 & 0 \\ 0 & 0 & 1 & 0 \end{bmatrix} \tag{5}$$

where S_u, S_v, u_o and v_o are the usual camera intrinsic parameters. On the remaining part of the paper, we assume that the image coordinate system is centered on the principal point, i.e. $(u_0, v_0) = (0, 0)$.

Using all the coordinate transformations defined above, one can express the overall coordinate transformation from the ground plane points (^wx, ^wy, ^wz) to the image projections (^ix, ^iy):

$$\begin{bmatrix} \lambda\,^ix \\ \lambda\,^iy \\ \lambda \end{bmatrix} = {}^iT_W \begin{bmatrix} ^wx \\ ^wy \\ ^wz \\ 1 \end{bmatrix} \qquad \text{with} \quad ^iT_W = {}^iT_C\,{}^CT_R\,{}^RT_W$$

Noting that all the points of interest lie on the ground plane and therefore $^wz = 0$, we can define a homography ^iH_W relating ground plane points and their image projections:

$$\begin{bmatrix} \lambda\,^ix \\ \lambda\,^iy \\ \lambda \end{bmatrix} = {}^iH_W \begin{bmatrix} ^wx \\ ^wy \\ 1 \end{bmatrix}, \tag{6}$$

$$\text{with} \quad ^iH_W = \begin{bmatrix} S_u c_\theta & S_u s_\theta & -S_u c_\theta x_r \\ -S_v s_\theta s_p & S_v s_p c_\theta & S_v(s_p s_\theta x_r - h c_p) \\ -s_\theta c_p & c_p c_\theta & c_p s_\theta x_r + h s_p \end{bmatrix}$$

The transformation ^iH_W depends on the robot heading and position, (θ, x_r), and on the camera intrinsic and extrinsic parameters. The corridor guidelines equations can now be determined and the corresponding image projections found. The projective coordinates of both lines $\tilde{r}_1, \tilde{r}_2$ are given by the vector product of the supporting points:

$$\tilde{r}_1 \sim \tilde{u}_1 \times \tilde{u}_2 \sim [1 \ 0 \ 0]^T$$
$$\tilde{r}_2 \sim \tilde{u}_3 \times \tilde{u}_4 \sim [1 \ 0 \ d]^T$$

where $\sim$ denotes equality up to scale, and $\tilde{u}_1$ to $\tilde{u}_4$ are the homogeneous coordinates of the points defined in equation (1). Similarly, the point at infinity $\tilde{u}_\infty$ where these lines intersect can be determined in projective coordinates by the vector product of the lines representation:

$$\tilde{u}_\infty \sim \tilde{r}_1 \times \tilde{r}_2 \sim [0 \ 1 \ 0]^T$$

We can project $\tilde{u}_\infty$ on the image plane using equation (6) to get the vanishing point coordinates $(^ix_v, {}^iy_v)$:

$$(^ix_v, {}^iy_v) = (S_u \frac{\tan \theta}{c_p}, \ S_v \tan p) \tag{7}$$

Equation (7) shows that the horizontal coordinate of the vanishing point depends on the robot heading, θ, on the horizontal pixel size and on the camera pitch angle. It does not depend on the robot position, x_r. Therefore, it can be extracted from images and when servoed to zero, we ensure that the vehicle heading is parallel to the corridor direction.

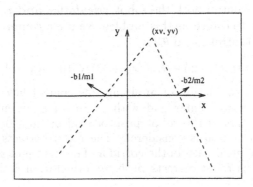

Fig. 6. Image projection of the corridor guidelines, showing the vanishing point and parameterization.

To extract information regarding the robot position, x_r, we need to look at the image projection of corridor guidelines again and use information about the lines slope, m_i, and intercept b_i. In particular the image point where the lines cross the row $y = 0$ are quite meaningful, as shown in Figure 6 :

$$\frac{b_1}{m_1} = S_u \frac{s_p x_r - s_\theta c_p h}{h c_\theta} \qquad\qquad \frac{b_2}{m_2} = S_u \frac{s_p (x_r - d) - s_\theta c_p h}{h c_\theta}$$

If we take the average between these two coordinates, it yields:

$$\delta_x = \frac{1}{2}(\frac{b_1}{m_1} + \frac{b_2}{m_2})$$

$$= S_u \frac{s_p (x_r - d/2)}{h c_\theta} - S_u \tan \theta c_p$$

$$= S_u \frac{s_p (x_r - d/2)}{h c_\theta} - {}^i x_v \cos^2 p$$

The equations above show that the signal δ_x, that can be extracted from the image projection of the corridor guidelines, conveys information regarding the robot position error relative to the corridor center $(x_r - d/2)$. However, it is also dependent on a second term influenced by the robot heading. This coupled effect can be removed either if the camera pitch angle p or the camera parameter S_v, are known. The parameter S_v can be used to determine the camera pitch angle, p, from ${}^i y_v$ defined in equation (7).

Figure 7 shows the evolution of the vanishing point coordinate ${}^i x_v$, when the robot is centered in the corridor and the orientation changes. Similarly, the same figure shows how δ_x varies when the robot is suitably oriented in the corridor (i.e. $\theta = 0$) and its transversal position changes (when the robot is centered in the corridor, we have $x_r = 0.5$).

In some cases, when the robot is located away from the central trajectory in the corridor, using the vanishing point alone to control the robot heading can result in further deviating the robot from the central path. This is due to the fact that we need to control both the robot *orientation* **and** *position* with only a single error signal. To overcome this problem we use a combination of ${}^i x_v$ and δ_x to determine the control signal θ_c:

$$\theta_c(k) = \theta_c(k - 1) - K_p ({}^i x_v + \delta_x), \text{with} \quad K_p \sim 0.3 \qquad (8)$$

Figure 8 shows a simulation of applying this control law when the robot is started off the corridor center and with an incorrect orientation. The left plot shows the evolution of the robot position and orientation when only the vanishing point information is considered. The robot corrects the orientation but fails to follow a central path in the corridor. The right plot shows the results of introducing δ_x. The robot corrects both the orientation and the position in the corridor.

3.1 Extracting the vanishing point data

The corridor guidelines are extracted using the Sobel gradient operator [9, 10] and by imposing a set of constraints to select the points of interest belonging to the guidelines. The procedure used is as follows:

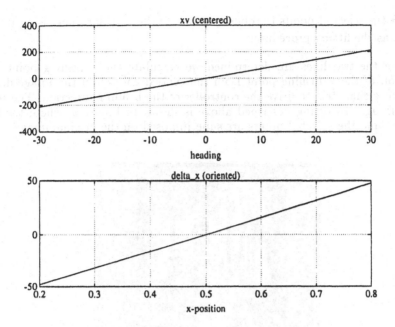

Fig. 7. Top: change of $^{i}x_{v}$ when the robot orientation changes. Bottom : δ_{x} as a function of the robot position.

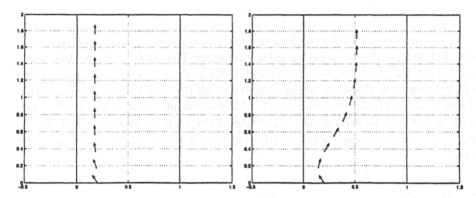

Fig. 8. Simulation of the robot control when only the vanishing point is used (left) or when δ_{x} is also included (right).

- Extract the vertical and horizontal image gradient components;
- Select the points that have significant horizontal **and** vertical gradient information. This procedure keeps only edge points that have diagonal directions.
- Separate this point set in the subsets of positive gradient orientation and negative gradient orientation. Each set corresponds to one of the corridor lines.
- Erode each image with a mask corresponding to diagonal lines, to further eliminate data outliers in the previous point sets.

– Use the selected points to robustly estimate the corridor lines, using Ransac [7], as the fitting procedure.

Once the two lines are determined we calculate the vanishing point. The deviation of the vanishing point from the central column of the image defines the error signal, ^ix_v, to drive the controller of the heading direction. The result of the image processing described above is shown in Figure 9, where the lines detected and the selected points are superimposed on the original image.

Fig. 9. Results of the line detection process.

So far we use a PID for the heading control, while the linear velocity is kept constant independently of the visual information. The current control frequency is about 1 Hz. Another relevant aspect is that we propagate the uncertainty information from the edge localization errors all the way till the determination of the vanishing point coordinates [8]. This uncertainty measurement, $\sigma^2_{ix_v}$, can be used not only to validate the extraction of the corridor guidelines but also to modulate the control gains as a function of the reliability of the visual measurements.

4 Results

We have tested the system in a simple indoor office environment to show the potential of integrating these two methodologies. The environment consists in a set of corridors with office doors on the sides. We have set the navigation goal to making a complete tour of all corridors. Hence, the topological map can be represented as in Figure 10.

There are 5 nodes in the graph: the start and end positions and 3 intermediate corners of the corridors. In each corridor we use the servoing strategy as defined in the previous section. Simultaneously, the *indicative* robot position is inferred from the appearance based sub-system. The corners (nodes) correspond to special sites where a specific action must be taken. In this case these actions correspond to a clock-wise turn of 90 degrees.

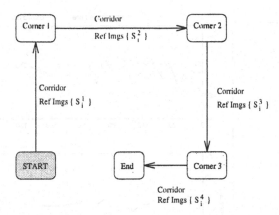

Fig. 10. Topological map of the office environment. Nodes correspond to points where the robot must turn to another corridor. Navigation along the corridors is done using the servoing strategy and progress monitored by the appearance based approach.

This idea can be extended to missions like entering a given office. It would only require the appearance based system to identify the door and then a suitable servoing strategy would be launched. A complex environment can be mapped in such a way, considering various levels of the graph. A node could then be expanded to another sub-graph and the robot pursue to the following goal.

Figure 11 shows some results obtained while maneuvering in one corridor. We can observe the robot trajectory recovered from odometry measurements. The figure also shows the temporal evolution of $^i x_v$ and the corresponding standard deviation estimate $\sigma_{^i x_v}$; and the heading angle over time.

Figure 12 shows the result of the integrated navigation control system on our office floor. The images identifying the corners are also shown. The full path length is about 50 meters and the mission was accomplished without requiring accurate positioning or odometry information. For visualization purposes alone we plot the robot trajectory recovered from odometry. We have used a simple linear model to correct odometry errors along the corridors. This information is only need for displaying.

5 Concluding Remarks

We have addressed in this paper the problem of visual-based mobile robot navigation using a single camera and processing a sequence of grayscale images captured during the robot motion.

The main argument here is about the nature of a suitable *map* to support global navigation tasks. Vision based control can accomplish local tasks but fails to address more global navigation problems. We argue that it is advantageous to have a *map* representation that can be easily related to the robot perceptual and navigation capabilities, and not necessarily in metric terms. This is what we call a *topological map* that embeds qualitative relationships between the robot

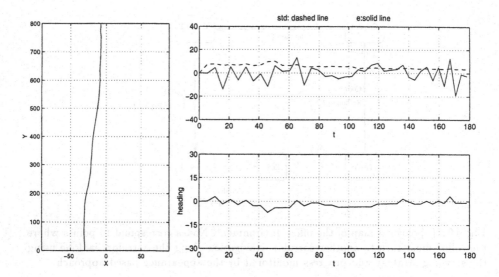

Fig. 11. Left: Robot trajectory during the maneuver (cm). Top right : horizontal coordinate of the vanishing point and propagated standard variation estimate (both in pixels). Bottom right: robot heading (degrees) during the experiment.

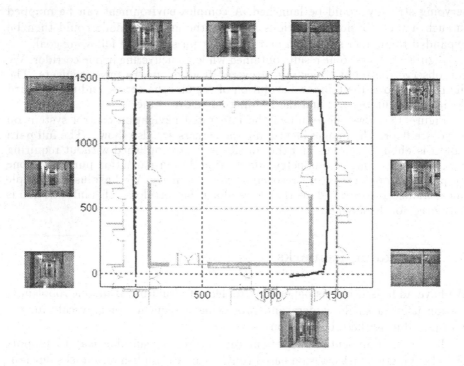

Fig. 12. Navigation results on an office floor. The full path consists of about 50 meters. The integrated navigation system does not require accurate position information or odometry information.

and the environment that can be used to specify a mission, as humans usually do when describing the path to a given location.

The control strategy combines two different approaches. On one hand we servo on the vanishing point defined by the corridor guidelines as captured in the image. This mode is suitable when a continuous stream of image features can be extracted from the video sequence, but it does not provide a means with dealing with environment representation or global tasks.

The topological map is a qualitative representation of the environment that is implicitly embedded in the system by using appearance based methods for navigation. Images acquired in relevant positions along the path are stored initially. Then, during normal operation the system compares the current image with the reference set to approximately determine its position.

The environment "map" can then be seen as a graph structure whose links correspond to paths where visual servoing can be applied. Nodes indicate sites where decisions are to be taken: turning, entering a door, grasping an object, etc. The task execution is monitored by means of the appearance based methods. Visual servoing provides a robust way to perform *local* tasks while appearance based methods embed the environment representation required for more general tasks. Preliminary tests have shown encouraging results. We believe that by combining these two powerful approaches, one can significantly extend the robot autonomy without requiring accurate measurements of the robot position and orientation.

One problem to address in the future is the definition of methods to automatically extract the reference images that will be used as landmarks. Right now, these images are acquired off-line at pre-defined positions. Another aspect for future research is to find more efficient image representations and associated comparison metrics to improve both the speed and robustness of the appearance based method. We have done early experiments using image projections in order to reduce the processing time, without jeopardizing the system performance.

References

1. Y. Aloimonos, I. Weiss, and A. Banddophaday. Active vision. *International Journal of Computer Vision*, 1(4):333–356, January 1988.
2. C. Andersen, S.D. Jones, and J.L. Crowley. Appearance based processes for navigation. In *Proc. of the 5th International Symposium on Intelligent Robotic Systems - SIRS97*, Stockholm, Sweden, July 1997.
3. R. Bajcsy. Active perception. *Proceedings of the IEEE*, 76(8):996–1005, August 1988.
4. C. Carreira and J. Santos-Victor. Vision based teleoperated cellular robots. In *Proc. of the 5th International Symposium on Intelligent Robotic Systems - SIRS97*, Stockholm, Sweden, July 1997.
5. B. Espiau, F. Chaumette, and Patrick Rives. A new approach to visual servoing in robotics. *IEEE Transactions on Robotics and Automation*, 8(3):313–326, June 1992.
6. O. Faugeras. *Three-Dimensional Computer Vision- A Geometric Viewpoint*. MIT Press, 1993.

7. M. A. Fischler and R. C. Bolles. Random sample consensus: A paradigm for model fitting with applications to image analysis and automated cartography. *Communications of ACM*, 24(6), 1981.
8. R. Haralick. Propagating covariance in computer vision. In *Proc. ECCV Workshop of Performance Characteristics of Vision Algorithms*, Cambridge, UK, April 1996.
9. B. Horn. *Robot Vision*. MIT Press, 1986.
10. R. Jain, R. Kastwi, and B.G. Schunck. *Machine Vision*. McGraw-Hill, 1995.
11. J. Kosecka. Visually guided navigation. *Robotics and Autonomous Systems*, 21(1):37–50, July 1997.
12. X. Lebegue and J.K. Aggarwal. Significant line segments for an indoor mobile robot. *IEEE Transactions on Robotics and Automation*, 9(6):801–806, December 1993.
13. J. Nielsen and G. Sandini. Learning mobile robot navigation: A behavior-based approach. In *IEEE Int. Conf. on Systems, Men and Cybernetics*, San Antonio, Texas, USA, October 1994.
14. G. Sandini, F. Gandolfo, E. Grosso, and M. Tistarelli. Vision during action. In Y. Aloimonos, editor, *Active Perception*. Lawrence Erlbaum Associates, 1993.
15. J. Santos-Victor and G. Sandini. Uncalibrated obstacle detection using the normal flow. *Machine Vision and Applications*, 9(3):130–137, 1996.
16. J. Santos-Victor and G. Sandini. Embedded visual behaviors for navigation. *Robotics and Autonomous Systems*, 19(3-4):299–313, March 1997.
17. J. Santos-Victor and G. Sandini. Visual behaviors for docking. *Computer Vision and Image Understanding*, 67(3):223–238, September 1997.
18. J. Santos-Victor, G. Sandini, F. Curotto, and S. Garibaldi. Divergent stereo in autonomous navigation : From bees to robots. *International Journal of computer Vision*, 14:159–177, 1995.

Vision-Aided Outdoor Navigation of an Autonomous Horticultural Vehicle

B Southall[1,2], T Hague[1], J A Marchant[1], and B F Buxton[2]

[1] Silsoe Research Institute, Wrest Park, Silsoe,
Bedfordshire, MK45 4HS, UK

[2] Department of Computer Science, University College London, Gower Street,
London, WC1E 6BT, UK
B.Southall@cs.ucl.ac.uk

Abstract. An autonomous outdoor vehicle has been developed at the Silsoe Research Institute as a testbed to investigate precise crop protection. The vehicle is able to navigate along rows of crop by using a Kalman filter to fuse information from proprioceptive sensing (odometry and inertial sensors) with data from an on-board computer vision system to generate estimates of its position and orientation. This paper describes a novel implementation of a previously proposed vision algorithm which uses a model of the crop planting pattern to extract vehicle position and orientation information from observations of many plants in each image. It is demonstrated that by implementing the vision system to compress the multiple plant observations into a single "pseudo observation" of vehicle position and orientation, it is possible to separate the vision system from the main body of the vehicle navigation Kalman filter, thus simplifying the task of fusing data from different sources. The algorithm is also used to segment the image sequences into areas of crop and weed, thus providing potential for targeting treatment. The implementation is tested on the vehicle, and results are shown from trials both in an indoor test area and outdoors on a field of real crop. Segmentation results are given for images captured from the vehicle.

1 Introduction

Previous work [16] proposed and demonstrated the potential of an algorithm to provide navigation information for an autonomous crop protection vehicle which has been developed at the Silsoe Research Institute [8]. The vehicle has been designed for the task of *plant scale husbandry* which aims to treat farmed crop at the level of the individual plant rather than at the level of large patches of field. To achieve this task, the vehicle must be able to steer itself along the crop rows and perform a segmentation between crop and weed plants. This paper describes the implementation of the algorithm on the vehicle hardware, along with experiments conducted to test the performance of the algorithm in the field. The algorithm of [16] made use of a grid-like model (see section 2 below) of crop planting position to exploit the known planting geometry of the crop in the field.

This model allows navigation of the vehicle relative to the crop and segmentation of the image into crop and weed features by virtue of feature position – features supporting the crop planting grid are taken to be plants, whereas outliers to the model are assumed to be weeds.

At the heart of the vehicle controller is an extended Kalman filter (EKF) which allows the fusion of data from many sources into estimates of vehicle position and velocity. The data sources include proprioceptive sensors (wheel odometry and accelerometers), delivering information at 50 Hz, and the vision system, an exteroceptive sensor providing information about the outside world, which currently runs at 10 Hz. These two separate data rates, along with the parallel architecture of the vehicle's on-board computing, encourage a modular approach to the data fusion problem. To this end, the vehicle control EKF incorporates the proprioceptive data for the majority of the time, periodically passing a prior estimate to the vision system EKF which returns a "pseudo observation" of the crop model position derived from the set of observed plant positions in each video image. This pseudo observation is then fused with the vehicle controller's estimate; a correction to the dead-reckoning estimate based on external sensing.

The algorithm described here provides estimates of the vehicle bearing and lateral offset from the crop rows and also a forward displacement along the field; as such it replaces and enhances the functionality of a Hough transform based algorithm [12] which was previously implemented on the vehicle. The Hough transform algorithm did not estimate forward distance, and as such could not provide the segmentation that will be demonstrated by the new algorithm below. Furthermore, the very nature of the Hough method means that its output estimates are quantized, and also that no assessment of estimate quality is given, unlike the estimate variance of the Kalman filter. Another advantage of the Kalman filtering technique over the Hough transform is its computational simplicity; there is no Hough space to load, nor a search to perform for the peak result.

A brief review of related work is presented and then, after introducing the crop planting pattern model and stating the Kalman filter technique of [16], the new "pseudo observation" implementation of the vision system is given, which illustrates how the vision data is fused with proprioceptive information. Finally, results are given which show the performance of the vehicle both on an indoor test-bed and outside with real crop.

1.1 Related Work

The Kalman filter has found numerous applications in robotics and machine vision, with examples from world geometry modelling both indoors [3] and outdoors [9], control of road vehicles [4] and mobile robot localization and map-building [11, 2]. In [6, 5], the visually-aided navigation of a small mobile platform is described, along with the Kalman filter based fusion of vision and odometric information. Their robot operates in a simplified indoor environment, using two

39

sets of illuminated co-planar points whose fixed position in space is known *a priori* for localization in an absolute reference frame. This contrasts with the task of navigation in a less constrained outdoor environment where the landmarks (crop plants) are less distinctive and not in a known position.

The work presented in the following sections concentrates on the formulation of a Kalman filter which allows easy separation of the proprioceptive sensing and the vision system. Both [10] and [15] propose methods for distributing the computational load of the Kalman filter, resulting in networks of communicating nodes. The topologies of these networks are shown in figure 1 (copied from [15]). Referring to the left-hand side of figure 1, it can be seen that the system ar-

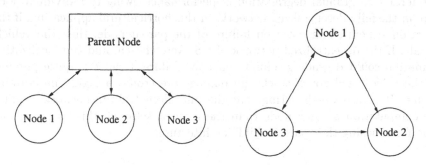

Fig. 1. Network topologies. Left: That described in [10]. Right: The topology from [15]. The double headed arrows represent two-way communication connections.

rangement of [10] has a central "parent" node which communicates with "child" nodes. The parent node carries out the bulk of the computation, with the child nodes either returning sensor data alone, or perhaps performing some local computation to produce a result which is then fused with the state estimate held in the parent node. The architecture of the system used in the horticultural vehicle, illustrated in figure 3 below, is of this form; the vehicle navigation Kalman filter takes the place of the parent node, which receives sensor information from the odometers and inertial sensors, along with processed information from the vision system. The vision system compresses observations of the crop taken from each image into a single "pseudo-observation" of the vehicle position relative to the crop rows. By taking a group of observations in image space and compressing them into a single pseudo-observation of the vehicle's relative world position, this work in a sense generalizes the data compression filter of [17], where a set of observations are compressed into a single observation, where both the original set and final compressed observation occupy the same space.

In [15] each node in the network consists of a sensor along with local computation, as seen on the right-hand side of figure 1; this kind of network is described as being fully decentralized. Each node computes the filter's plant model (prediction) and takes local measurements from the sensor to correct predictions. Information relating to state (and estimate covariance) corrections is then communicated between nodes to further correct and synchronize the state estimates between nodes. In short, each node carries its own state model, estimate of global state and covariance, and uses local measurements along with information from the other nodes to keep accurate global state estimates. A claimed advantage of such a system is robustness to individual node failure; if one node malfunctions, then the rest of the network is able to continue operating, although perhaps less effectively owing to the loss of one of its components. The network assumes a degree of redundancy if it is to tolerate individual node failure. Evidently in the "parent-child" network where the bulk of computation occurs in the parent node, the whole network would cease to function if the parent node fails. However, this kind of catastrophic failure of the central processing node may be preferable to gradual degradation of performance owing to individual node failure in the fully decentralized network. In this horticultural application, if the navigation system shuts down on failure of the parent node, then the vehicle will halt. If the decentralized network of [15] were chosen, and the localization information could degrade gradually on node failure, then it is quite possible that the vehicle will go off track and damage the crop – a highly undesirable outcome. It is also worth noting that the fully decentralized network requires more computation at each node than the method selected; this was a second reason for choosing the "parent-child" architecture.

2   The crop pattern model

Figure 2 shows a schematic view of a patch of crop, with the plants being represented by black circles. There are two sets of axes in the figure, (x_w, y_w) and (x_c, y_c, z_c) which represent the world and camera co-ordinate systems respectively, with the world z_w axis projecting out of the page, and camera axis z_c projecting into the page. It can be seen that the world y axis is coincident with the middle plant row. The model of the crop consists of the two measurements; r, the spacing between the rows and l the space between plants in the row. Three parameters $(t_x, Y$ and $\Psi)$, specify the position of the model relative to the camera as shown in the diagram. The measurement Y is the offset in world co-ordinates from the world origin of the plant in the central row at the bottom of the image. The offset of the camera y_c axis from the world origin is given by t_x. It can be seen then that the t_x and Ψ parameters may be used to provide navigation information in terms of a heading angle and offset of the camera (and hence the vehicle) relative to the rows, and the parameter Y can yield the position of individual plants via (1) and (2) below.

$$x_w = nr \tag{1}$$

$$y_w = ml + Y \tag{2}$$

The quantities $n \in \{-1, 0, 1\}$ and $m \in \{0, -1, -2, \ldots, -(m_{max} - 1)\}$ index into the $3 \times m_{max}$ grid formed by the planting pattern, and each plant may be described by a unique index i corresponding to a single m, n pair. It should be

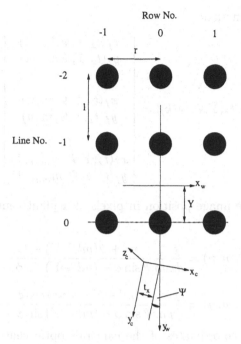

Fig. 2. The crop planting model

noted that the plant centres are assumed to be on the ground plane ($z_w = 0$). It is stressed that the model describes the grid on which individual plants should lie, rather than the actual location of the individual plants.

2.1 Estimating model position

In [16], the model position parameters, t_x, Y and Ψ are estimated using an extended Kalman filter. The standard update equations for the EKF [1] are given by:

$$\mathbf{W}(k{+}1) = \mathbf{P}(k{+}1|k)\mathbf{H}'(k{+}1)[\mathbf{H}(k{+}1)\mathbf{P}(k{+}1|k)\mathbf{H}'(k{+}1) + \mathbf{R}(k{+}1)]^{-1} \quad (3)$$

$$\hat{\mathbf{x}}(k{+}1|k{+}1) = \hat{\mathbf{x}}(k{+}1|k) + \mathbf{W}(k{+}1)[\mathbf{z}(k{+}1) - \mathbf{h}(\hat{\mathbf{x}}(k{+}1|k))] \quad (4)$$

$$\mathbf{P}(k{+}1|k{+}1) = \mathbf{P}(k{+}1|k) - \mathbf{W}(k{+}1)[\mathbf{H}(k{+}1)\mathbf{P}(k{+}1|k)\mathbf{H}'(k{+}1) +$$
$$\mathbf{R}(k{+}1)]\mathbf{W}'(k{+}1) \quad (5)$$

Where $\mathbf{W}$ is the Kalman gain, $\mathbf{P}(k{+}1|k)$ the predicted state covariance estimate, $\mathbf{H}$ the Jacobian of the state observation equations evaluated at the state prediction point $\hat{\mathbf{x}}(k{+}1|k)$, $\hat{\mathbf{x}}(k{+}1|k{+}1)$ is the corrected state vector, $\mathbf{z}$ is the observation, $\mathbf{R}$ the covariance of observation noise $\mathbf{w}(k)$, and $\mathbf{P}(k{+}1|k{+}1)$ is the corrected state covariance estimate.

In the crop pattern tracking filter, the state vector $\mathbf{x} = [t_x \; Y \; \Psi]'$ (this vector is seen again below as the pseudo observation $\hat{\mathbf{z}}$), and the Jacobian $\mathbf{H}$ is of the batch observation function:

$$\mathbf{z}(k) = \mathbf{f}[k, t_x, Y, \Psi, \mathbf{w}(k)] = \begin{bmatrix} x_f(t_x, Y, \Psi, 0, -1) \\ y_f(t_x, Y, \Psi, 0, -1) \\ \vdots \\ x_f(t_x, Y, \Psi, m, n) \\ y_f(t_x, Y, \Psi, m, n) \\ \vdots \\ x_f(t_x, Y, \Psi, m_{max}, 1) \\ y_f(t_x, Y, \Psi, m_{max}, 1) \end{bmatrix} + \mathbf{w}(k) \qquad (6)$$

where (x_f, y_f) is the image position in pixels of a plant centre on the ground plane:

$$x_f(t_x, Y, \Psi, m, n) = \frac{f}{dx} \frac{nr + \Psi(ml + Y) + t_x}{nr\Psi \sin\phi - (ml + Y)\sin\phi + t_z} + C_x \qquad (7)$$

$$y_f(t_x, Y, \Psi, m, n) = \frac{f}{dy} \frac{(ml + Y - \Psi nr)\cos\phi}{nr\Psi \sin\phi - (ml + Y)\sin\phi + t_z} + C_y \qquad (8)$$

C_x and C_y are the co-ordinates of the camera's optic centre on the CCD in pixels, f the focal length of the camera, and dx and dy the side-lengths of the pixels.

It can be seen that the batch observation $\mathbf{z}$ is constructed by stacking the i positions of the $3 \times m_{max}$ individual plants into a composite entity. Each position has an individual observation function dependent on t_x, Y and Ψ and the indices for plant i (m_i, n_i). A nearest neighbour policy is used to associate features extracted from the image (via a simple thresholding then chain-coding) with plant positions; a validation gate is used at this stage to perform outlier rejection. More detail is given below, once the Kalman filter formulation has been outlined.

Along with $\mathbf{x}$ and $\mathbf{H}$, the quantity $\mathbf{R}$, the observation covariance matrix must also be defined. This is also a batch quantity, in fact a block diagonal matrix with the covariance matrices associated with each observation i, $\mathbf{R}_i$ forming the diagonal. Each matrix $\mathbf{R}_i$ is given by the first order projection of the matrix $\mathbf{R_w}$ from the world plane (where it represents the uncertainty in position of the plant i) into the image plane, with the centre of projection being the world co-ordinate of observation i. For details, refer to [16].

3 Modular EKF formulation

Above, multiple observations of plant locations were combined in one parallel update of the state estimate by stacking the observations. Here we propose an alternative formulation, the principle of which is to compress the set of plant position observations from one video image into a single pseudo observation of forward position, lateral offset and orientation.

This alternative formulation has a number of advantages. Firstly, it is a modular approach, which allows much of the processing of vision derived observations to be separated cleanly from the main body of the Kalman filter used for vehicle navigation – the vehicle Kalman filter simply passes its state estimate to the vision system, which returns the pseudo observation. This is particularly important for our application where the filter used for navigation is complex with inputs from several sensors, and a multi processor architecture has been adopted. A second benefit is that the method is computationally simpler, requiring less costly matrix operations. Finally, a recursive scheme rather than a batch update is used to combine the observations into one pseudo observation; this eliminates the need for variable sizes of matrix to hold the stacked observations and thus removes the overhead of dynamic memory allocation.

The conventional extended Kalman filter equations $(3 \cdots 5)$ can be written in the *inverse covariance* form [13] (noting that here $\hat{x}$ refers to the vehicle control Kalman filter state estimate):

$$\mathbf{P}^{-1}(k{+}1|k{+}1) = \mathbf{P}^{-1}(k{+}1|k) + \mathbf{H}'(k{+}1)\mathbf{R}^{-1}(k{+}1)\mathbf{H}(k{+}1) \tag{9}$$

$$\mathbf{P}^{-1}(k{+}1|k{+}1)\hat{\mathbf{x}}(k{+}1|k{+}1) = [\mathbf{P}^{-1}(k{+}1|k) + \mathbf{H}'(k{+}1)\mathbf{R}^{-1}(k{+}1)\mathbf{H}(k{+}1)]\hat{\mathbf{x}}(k{+}1|k)$$
$$+\mathbf{H}'(k{+}1)\mathbf{R}^{-1}[\mathbf{z}(k{+}1) - \mathbf{h}(\hat{\mathbf{x}}(k{+}1|k))] \tag{10}$$

Assume that the observation model $\mathbf{z}(k) = \mathbf{h}(\mathbf{x}(k))$ can be functionally decomposed thus:

$$\mathbf{z}(k{+}1) = \mathbf{f}(\tilde{\mathbf{z}}(k{+}1)) \tag{11}$$

$$\tilde{\mathbf{z}}(k{+}1) = \mathbf{g}(\mathbf{x}(k{+}1)) \tag{12}$$

Where $\tilde{\mathbf{z}}(k) = [t_x \ Y \ \Psi]'$ is the combined pseudo observation, $\mathbf{f}(\cdot)$ is that given by (6) and $\mathbf{g}(\cdot)$ describes the transformation between the vehicle state vector and the pseudo observation vector. Denoting the Jacobians

$$\mathbf{F}(k{+}1) = [\nabla_{\tilde{\mathbf{z}}}\mathbf{f}'(\tilde{\mathbf{z}})]'_{\tilde{\mathbf{z}}=\mathbf{g}(\hat{\mathbf{x}}(k{+}1|k))}$$

$$\mathbf{G}(k{+}1) = [\nabla_{\mathbf{x}}\mathbf{g}'(\mathbf{x})]'_{\mathbf{x}=\hat{\mathbf{x}}(k{+}1|k)}$$

Substituting $\mathbf{h}(\hat{\mathbf{x}}(k{+}1|k)) = \mathbf{f}(\mathbf{g}(\hat{\mathbf{x}}(k{+}1|k)))$ and $\mathbf{H}(k{+}1) = \mathbf{F}(k{+}1)\mathbf{G}(k{+}1)$ in equations $(9 \cdots 10)$ and rearranging yields:

$$\mathbf{P}^{-1}(k{+}1|k{+}1) = \mathbf{P}^{-1}(k{+}1|k) + \mathbf{G}'(k{+}1)\tilde{\mathbf{R}}^{-1}(k{+}1)\mathbf{G}(k{+}1) \tag{13}$$

$$\mathbf{P}^{-1}(k{+}1|k{+}1)\hat{\mathbf{x}}(k{+}1|k{+}1) = [\mathbf{P}^{-1}(k{+}1|k) + \mathbf{G}'(k{+}1)\tilde{\mathbf{R}}^{-1}(k{+}1)\mathbf{G}(k{+}1)]\hat{\mathbf{x}}(k{+}1|k)$$
$$+\mathbf{G}'(k{+}1)\tilde{\mathbf{R}}^{-1}[\tilde{\mathbf{z}}(k{+}1) - \mathbf{g}(\hat{\mathbf{x}}(k{+}1|k))] \tag{14}$$

Where pseudo observation $\tilde{\mathbf{z}}(k{+}1)$ and its covariance $\tilde{\mathbf{R}}(k{+}1)$ are given by

$$\tilde{\mathbf{R}}^{-1}(k{+}1) = \mathbf{F}'(k{+}1)\mathbf{R}^{-1}(k{+}1)\mathbf{F}(k{+}1) \tag{15}$$

$$\tilde{\mathbf{R}}^{-1}(k{+}1)\tilde{\mathbf{z}}(k{+}1) = \tilde{\mathbf{R}}^{-1}(k{+}1)\mathbf{g}(\hat{\mathbf{x}}(k{+}1|k))$$
$$+\mathbf{F}'(k{+}1)\mathbf{R}^{-1}(k{+}1)[\mathbf{z}(k{+}1) - \mathbf{f}(\mathbf{g}(\hat{\mathbf{x}}(k{+}1|k)))] \tag{16}$$

The equations $(15 \cdots 16)$ are in fact a first order approximate least squares solution for $\tilde{z}(k{+}1)$ in the non-linear equation (11). Rewriting this batch least-squares estimator in the summation form gives formulae for sequential update:

$$\tilde{R}^{-1}(k{+}1) = \sum_{i=1}^{N} F'_i(k{+}1) R_i^{-1}(k{+}1) F_i(k{+}1) \tag{17}$$

$$\tilde{R}^{-1}(k{+}1)\tilde{z}(k{+}1) = \tilde{R}^{-1}(k{+}1)g(\hat{x}(k{+}1|k))$$

$$+ \sum_{i=1}^{N} F'_i(k{+}1) R_i^{-1}(k{+}1)[z_i(k{+}1) - f_i(g(\hat{x}(k{+}1|k)))] \tag{18}$$

where R_i is the covariance matrix associated with plant i from the $3 \times m_{max}$ crop grid. In summary, it has been shown that a set of $N(= 3 \times m_{max})$ observations $z_i(k{+}1), (1 \leq i \leq N)$ taken from an image captured at time step $k{+}1$ can be compressed into a single pseudo observation $\tilde{z}(k{+}1)$ with inverse covariance $\tilde{R}^{-1}(k{+}1)$, using a recursive least squares method [equations $(17 \cdots 18)$]. This pseudo observation may then be used in the normal way in an extended Kalman filter, replacing z and R in equations $(3 \cdots 5)$.

Figure 3 illustrates the operation of the modular pseudo observation system, showing the vision subsystem and its relation to the spray system and vehicle navigation and control. It can be seen that, as described above, the vision system returns the pseudo observation and the pseudo observation covariance to the vehicle navigation EKF, whilst it receives two quantities from the navigation system; a prior prediction of crop pattern position, in the form of $g(\hat{x}(k{+}1|k))$ and a variance for this estimate, $G(k{+}1)P(k{+}1)G'(k{+}1)$. These are used for linearisation of the observation equations and feature association and validation, as explained below.

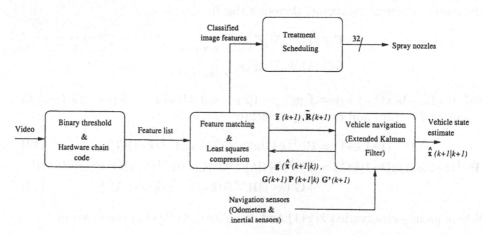

Fig. 3. The system architecture

Feature matching, validation and classification

As outlined above, features are derived from the image by imposing a binary threshold on the infra-red image to highlight areas of plant matter which are then extracted from the image using a chain coding algorithm [7] (contrast between plant and soil is more pronounced in the near infra-red wavelengths). These areas of plant matter will fall into three classes; areas of crop alone, weed alone and some areas of both crop and weed which are merged in the chain-coding process. Using the geometrical information provided by the crop planting model, it is possible to categorize these three classes into two types, either crop or weed. To obtain a better segmentation of the areas containing both crop and weed will require techniques operating on the visual appearance of the different types of plant, a topic currently under investigation.

Essentially, the classification is performed at the same time as feature matching and validation. There are two criteria for feature matching; the first is the size of the feature, and the second the position (i.e. the centre of area) of the feature. It is assumed that the crop plants are generally larger than the weeds; this assumption is based on the fact that the crop are transplanted into the soil, so are already a few centimetres high before the weeds start to grow. This information is used to reject (i.e. classify as weed) any feature whose area in pixels falls beneath a threshold level. The criterion of position is then used to match and classify the remaining features (i.e. those which exceed the size threshold).

To perform feature matching, i.e. associating image features with predicted crop positions, an adaptation of the nearest-neighbour strategy [14] is used. The nearest-neighbour data association policy chooses to associate with the predicted feature position (given by $\mathbf{g}(\hat{\mathbf{x}}(k{+}1|k))$, along with m and n) the observed feature which has the least Mahalanobis distance (calculated using $\mathbf{G}(k{+}1)\mathbf{P}(k{+}1)\mathbf{G}'(k{+}1)$) from the prediction. The Mahalanobis distance may be used to calculate the probability that the observation and prediction belong to the same parent distribution; this measure is used to validate and merge features. If the probability of the nearest neighbour observation belonging to the same distribution as the prediction is less than 5%, the feature is rejected (this is the standard validation gate technique [1]). If the probability lies between 5 and 50%, then that observation is associated with the prediction point, and classified as plant. If several observations lie within the 50–100% range then these are merged by associating their mean position with the prediction, and each merged feature is classified as plant. This merging mechanism has been adopted because the regions between leaves on some plants are dark, and when the binary threshold is applied, such plants fracture into a group of features corresponding to separate leaves. One further strategy is used to reduce the number of features input to the matching/validation procedure; any features in the image which lie outside the chassis width of the vehicle are ignored; such features do not lie in the planting bed currently under inspection.

4 Experiments

Experiments have been conducted to analyze the algorithm's performance in terms of both navigation and segmentation ability. The navigation experiments were performed both on an indoor test bed and outside with real crop. The segmentation experiments have been conducted on image sequences gathered in the Summer of 1997.

Navigation

Initial tests have been conducted to assess the performance of the vehicle in two situations. In the first, the vehicle was run indoors for approximately 12 metres along a black mat which has had a set of white circles marked on a grid to simulate the planting of crop in the field. A device was attached to the vehicle which leaves a marker trail, so that the path of the vehicle relative to the central row could be measured. The purpose of the indoor test was to run the vehicle in controlled surroundings with known inputs; markings on the mat enable a ground truth measurement to be taken, and the input images are simple, with large white objects simulating crop on a black background. The results of the run can be seen on the left in figure 4. The root mean square error between the measured and logged data has been calculated as $6mm$. A second experiment

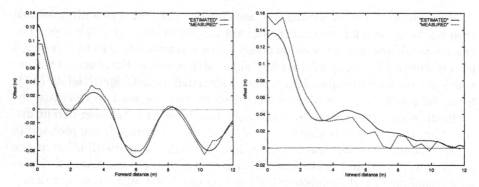

Fig. 4. Field trials. **Left**: Indoor test on mat. **Right**: Outdoor trial in field.

was then conducted in the outdoor environment of a field of crop. Once more, the vehicle was set to run a length of 12 metres, and a trail was left for measurement comparison. In this case, when the plants do not have the precise positioning of the circles on the mat, judging where the centre of the plant row lies is more subjective; this is reflected in the noisier measurements shown in the right hand side of figure 4; in this case, the r.m.s. error measure is $14mm$; this is larger than that measured on the mat, but is perfectly adequate for control purposes. Similar experiments conducted to analyze the previous Hough transform method yielded a figure of 13.5mm, which is marginally better, although for practical purposes this small difference is negligible. The advantages of using the EKF outweigh such as small performance difference, because the algorithm also allows segmentation of the image and estimation of forward distance.

Figure 5 plots estimated forward distance *vs.* time; the left-hand graph shows the result for the indoor run, the right-hand graph for the outdoor test. Both graphs show the same basic behaviour; a short period of acceleration followed by a longer period of approximately constant velocity and finally deceleration to rest. To assess the accuracy of the forward distance estimation, the distance travelled along the mat was measured and compared with the estimated distance travelled; the two figures were 12.07 and 12.02 metres respectively, an error of only 5cm.

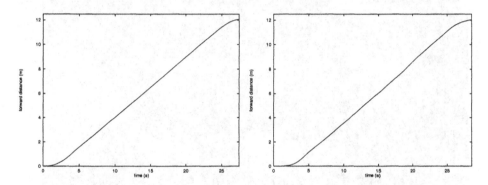

Fig. 5. Estimated forward distance *vs.* time. **Left**: Indoors. **Right**: Outdoors.

Segmentation

Figure 6 shows a typical image from a sequence collected from the vehicle during the Summer of 1997. Features lying between the vehicle "wheelings" (the width of the vehicle) have been classified into crop (white features) and weed (in black), using the matching and classification procedures described above. The image shows an area of crop which has several weeds, some of which are in the position of a missing plant (the second from the bottom in the left-most row). A plant that is out of position (to the right of the second plant from the bottom in the central row), has been classified as weed, and will therefore be scheduled for herbicide treatment; this is in fact a desirable course of action, because a plant out of position will simply be taking nutrients away from surrounding crop, thus decreasing yield. Close inspection of the image also reveals that some plant leaves have been classified as weed -- the feature merging process is not always successful.

Analysis of a sequence of 40 images (containing a total of 649 features belonging to the plant class and 1691 weeds) allows the segmentation performance of the algorithm to be assessed, and the classification rates are given in table 1. It should be noted that the percentages relate the the percentage of *features* classified, not the percentage of area. Most of the misclassifications of crop features as weed features are caused by single leaves becoming "detached" from the main body of the plant during the thresholding process. The majority of the misclassifications of weed as crop are caused by the weeds being close enough to the plants to be merged into a single feature by the chain-coder, although some do occur during the feature selection/merging process.

Fig. 6. Segmented image – features in white are classified as plants, those in black as weeds. Crosses show the predicted crop positions. Only features lying between the vehicle's wheel tracks have been segmented.

Crop—Crop	Weed—Weed	Crop—Weed	Weed—Crop
89.2%	94.8%	10.8%	5.2%

Table 1. Percentage classification rates of the segmentation algorithm. Key: A—B means type A classified as type B.

49

5 Conclusions and further work

A previously described algorithm has been adapted for implementation on an outdoor autonomous vehicle, replacing a previous method based upon the Hough transform. Results are given not only for estimates of navigation information, but also for segmentation of the image into crop and weed based upon the planting geometry of the crop. The new algorithm not only provides more information than the Hough method (the image segmentation and estimate of forward displacement) but is more computationally economical, whilst retaining the estimation accuracy required for navigation and control purposes.

Future work will involve implementation of a spray control system, to target chemical application on to the different classes of plant, and also improved feature segmentation, using optical properties of the plants (for example texture) to improve the segmentation given using planting geometry alone.

Acknowledgement

This work was funded by the BBSRC.

References

1. Y Bar-Shalom and T Fortmann. *Tracking and Data Association*. Academic Press, New York, 1988.
2. K S Chong and L Kleeman. Sonar based map building for a mobile robot. In *Proc. IEEE Int. Conf. Robotics and Automation*, pages 1700–1705. IEEE, April 1997.
3. R Deriche and O Faugeras. Tracking line segments. *Image and Vision Computing*, 8(4):261 – 270, November 1990.
4. E D Dickmanns. Expectation-based dynamic scene understanding. In A Blake and A Yuille, editors, *Active Vision*, Artificial Intelligence, chapter 18, pages 303–335. MIT Press, 1992.
5. T D'Orazio, M Ianigro, E Stella, F P Lovergine, and A Distante. Mobile robot navigation by multi-sensory integration. In *Proc. IEEE Int. Conf. Robotics and Automation*, pages 373–379, May 1993.
6. T D'Orazio, F P Lovergine, M Ianigro, E Stella, and A Distante. Mobile robot position determination using visual landmarks. *IEEE Trans. Industrial Electronics*, 41(6):654–661, December 1994.
7. H Freeman. On the encoding of arbitrary geometric configurations. *IEEE Trans. Elec. Computers*, EC-10:260–268, 1961.
8. T Hague and N D Tillett. Navigation and control of an autonomous horticultural robot. *Mechatronics*, 6(2):165–180, 1996.
9. C Harris. Geometry from visual motion. In A Blake and A Yuille, editors, *Active Vision*, Artificial Intelligence, chapter 16, pages 263–284. MIT Press, 1992.
10. H R Hashemipour, S Roy, and A J Laub. Decentralized structures for parallel Kalman filtering. *IEEE Trans. Auto. Control*, 33(1):88–93, 1988.
11. J J Leonard and H F Durrant-Whyte. Mobile robot localization by tracking geometric beacons. *IEEE Trans. Robotics and Automation*, 7(3):376–382, June 1991.

12. J A Marchant and R Brivot. Real time tracking of plant rows using a Hough transform. *Real Time Imaging*, 1:363–371, 1995.

13. P S Maybeck. *Stochastic Models, Estimation, and Control*, volume 1. Academic Press, 1979.

14. B Rao. Data association methods for tracking systems. In A Blake and A Yuille, editors, *Active Vision*, chapter 6. MIT Press, 1992.

15. B S Y Rao, H F Durrant-Whyte, and J A Sheen. A fully decentralized multi-sensor system for tracking and surveillance. *International Journal of Robotics Research*, 12(1):20–44, February 1993.

16. B Southall, J A Marchant, T Hague, and B F Buxton. Model based tracking for navigation and segmentation. In H Burkhardt and B Neumann, editors, *Proceedings 5th European Conference on Computer Vision*, volume 1, pages 797–811, June 1998.

17. D Willner, C B Chang, and K P Dunn. Kalman filter algorithms for a multi-sensor system. In *Proc. IEEE Int. Conf. Decision and Control*, pages 570–574, 1976.

An Interactive Computer Vision System DyPERS: Dynamic Personal Enhanced Reality System

Bernt Schiele, Nuria Oliver, Tony Jebara, and Alex Pentland

Vision and Modeling Group
MIT Media Laboratory, Cambridge, MA 02139, USA
{bernt,nuria,jebara,sandy}@media.mit.edu
http://www.media.mit.edu/vismod/demos/dypers

Abstract. DyPERS, 'Dynamic Personal Enhanced Reality System', uses augmented reality and computer vision to autonomously retrieve 'media memories' based on associations with real objects the user encounters. These are evoked as audio and video clips relevant for the user and overlayed on top of real objects the user encounters. The system utilizes an adaptive, audio-visual learning system on a tetherless wearable computer. The user's visual and auditory scene is stored in real-time by the system (upon request) and is then associated (by user input) with a snap shot of a visual object. The object acts as a key such that when the real-time vision system detects its presence in the scene again, DyPERS plays back the appropriate audio-visual sequence. The vision system is a probabilistic algorithm which is capable of discriminating between hundreds of everyday objects under varying viewing conditions (view changes, lighting, etc.). Once an audio-visual clip is stored, the vision system automatically recalls it and plays it back when it detects the object that the user wished to use to remind him of the sequence. The DyPERS interface augments the user without encumbering him and effectively mimics a form of audio-visual memory. First results on performance and usability are shown.

1 Introduction

Research in computer vision has been focusing around the idea to create general purpose computer vision algorithms. The spirit of these algorithms has been manifested in Marr's book [Mar82] where vision is essentially defined as a reconstruction process which maps the visual data into representations of increasing abstraction. However, it has been realized that computer vision algorithms are only part of a larger system with certain goals and tasks at hand possibly changing over time. This observation has led to the emergence of research fields such as active [Baj85,Baj88], animate [Bal91], purposive vision [Alo90] as well as dynamic vision [Dic97]. Whereas the main concern of Marr's paradigm might be summarized as *generality* of computer vision algorithms, active vision research has been concentrated on the *adaptability* of algorithms directed by goals, resources and environmental conditions.

Using computer vision algorithms in the context of human computer interfaces adds at least one further criterium which we summarize as *usability*. Usability refers to the need to design algorithms in such a way that they can be used in a beneficial way in a human-computer interaction scenario. In other words, a computer vision algorithm is usable only if the human user gains an advantage in using the overall system. Even though this seems like an obvious requirement it has deeper implications: first of all the system's response time has to be reasonable (ideally real-time). Furthermore, the system has to be robust and reliable enough in order to be usable in changing environments. On the other hand in a human-computer interaction scenario the user may assist the system to overcome limitations or to help bootstrap, if the user feels a real benefit using the system.

In this paper we propose a system which uses computer vision in a human-computer interaction scenario. An advantage of human-computer interaction scenarios is that as we can actually enclose the human in the overall system loop. In order to do so the human has to be able to influence the system's behavior. In addition to this, it is highly important that the user obtains feedback from the system in order to understand the calculated results of the system. More specifically for the system described here, the human uses a simple input device in order to teach the system. By observing the system's results he may understand limitations of the systems and may be able to assist the system in order to overcome them.

Obviously we do not want the user to adapt entirely to the system which is the case for traditional human-computer interfaces using only keyboard, mouse and screen. Furthermore, the user should not be obliged to know how the system works or even any implementation details. Rather, we are looking for scenarios where the user may benefit from using the system versus not using the system. Therefore, we always have to keep in mind the usability of the system or, in other words, that future users of the system are only interested in a beneficial use of the system and not in the system in itself.

In the following we will motivate the described system from an augmented reality point of view. Section 2 discusses related systems. Section 3 outlines the overall system while section 4 discusses the generic object recognition system. Section 5 lists several scenarios where a system like DyPERS might be used. Section 6 gives some experimental results of a museum tour scenario where DyPERS has been used to record and recall explanations of a guide about each painting.

1.1 Motivation for DyPERS: Dynamic Personal Enhanced Reality System

As computation becomes widely accessible, transparent, wearable and personal, it becomes a useful tool to augment everyday activities. Certain human capabilities such as daily scheduling need not remain the responsibility of a user when they can be easily transfered to personal digital assistants. This is especially important for tasks that are excessively cumbersome to humans yet involve little computational overhead. An important one is memory or information storage. It is well-known that some things are better stored using external artifacts (such as handwritten or electronic notes) than in a human brain. However, it is also critical that the transfer of information to be processed (i.e. by a digital assistant) proceeds in a natural, seamless way. Often, it is more cumbersome for a user to input data and functionality into a computer than to manually perform a task directly. In other words, the *transfer* from reality into a virtual space is often too distracting to the user and reduces a digital assistant's effectiveness. In such cases it would be helpful that the assistant operates autonomously without user intervention. DyPERS is a 'Dynamic Personal Enhanced Reality System' which is motivated by the above issues. It acts as an audio-visual memory assistant which reminds the user at appropriate times using perceptual cues as opposed to direct programming. Using a head-mounted camera and a microphone, DyPERS sees and hears what the user perceives to collect a fully audio-visual memory. The resulting multimedia database can be indexed and played back in real-time. The user then indicates to DyPERS which visual objects are important memory cues such that it learns to recognize them in future encounters and associate them with the recorded memories.

When a cue is recognized at some later time, DyPERS automatically overlays the appropriate audio-video clip on the user's world through a heads-up-display (HUD) [FMS92], as a reminder of the content. This process is triggered when a relevant object is detected by the video camera system which constantly scans the visual field to detect objects which are associated with the memories.

2   Background and Related Work

This section describes related areas, compares other systems to DyPERS, and describes some new contributions emphasized by the proposed system.

Ubiquitous vs. Wearable Computing: Both wearable/personal computing and ubiquitous computing present interesting routes to augmenting human capabilities with computers. However, wearable computers attempt to augment the user directly and provide a mobile platform while ubiquitous computing augments the surrounding physical environment with a network of machines and sensors. Weiser [Wei91] discusses the merits of ubiquitous computing while Mann [Man97] argues in favor of mobile, personal audio-visual augmentation in his wearable platform.

Memory Augmentation: Memory augmentation has evolved from simple pencil and paper paradigms to sophisticated personal digital assistants (PDAs) and beyond. Some closely related memory augmentation systems include the "Forget-me not" system [LF93], which is a personal information manager inspired by Weiser's ubiquitous computing paradigm, and the Remembrance Agent [RS96], which is a text-based context-driven wearable augmented reality memory system. Both systems collect and organize data that is relevant to the human user for subsequent retrieval.

Augmented Reality: Augmented reality systems form a more natural interface between user and machine which is a critical feature for a system like DyPERS. In [KVB97] a virtually documented environment system is described which assists the user in some performance task. It registers synthetic multimedia data acquired using a head-mounted video camera. However, information is retrieved explicitly by the user via speech commands.

On the other hand, the retrieval process is automated in [Lev97], a predecessor of DyPERS. This system used machine vision to locate 'visual cues,' and then overlaid a stabilized image, messages or clips on top of the users view of the cue object (via a HUD). The visual cues and the images/messages had to be prepared offline and the collection process was not automated. In addition, the machine vision algorithm used, was limited to 2D objects viewed from head-on and at appropriate distance. An earlier version, described in [SMR+97], further simplified the machine vision by using colored bar code tags as the visual cue.

In [RN95] the NaviCam system is described as a portable computer with video camera which detects pre-tagged objects. Users view the real-world together with context sensitive information generated by the computer. NaviCam is extended in the Ubiquitous Talker [RN95] to include a speech dialogue interface. Other applications include a navigation system, WalkNavi [NR96]. Audio Aura [MBWF97] is an active badge distributed system that augments the physical world with auditory cues. Users passively trigger the transmission of auditory cues as they move through their workplace. Finally, Jebara [JEW+97] proposes a vision-based wearable enhanced reality system called Stochasticks for augmenting a billiards game with computer generated shot planning.

Perceptual Interfaces: Most human-computer interaction is still limited to keyboards and pointing devices. The usability bottleneck that plagues interactive systems lies not in performing the processing task itself but rather in communicating requests and results between the system and the user [JLMP93]. Faster, more natural and convenient means for users to exchange information with computers are needed. This communication bottleneck has spurred increased research in providing perceptual capabilities (speech, vision, haptics) to the interface. These *perceptual interfaces* are likely to be a major model for future human-computer interaction [Tur97].

3 System Overview

The system's building blocks are depicted in Figure 1. The following describes the audio-visual association module and gives a short overview of the hardware. The generic object recognition algorithm is described in section 4.

3.1 Audio-Visual Associative Memory System

The audio-visual associative memory operates on a record-and-associate paradigm. Audio-visual clips are recorded by the push of a button and then associated

55

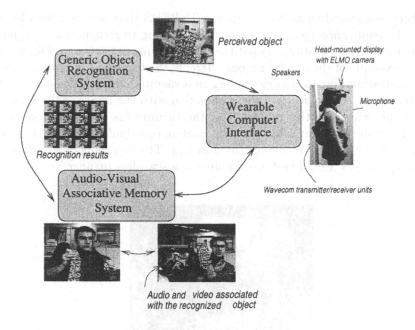
Perceived object

Head-mounted display
with ELMO camera

Speakers

Microphone

Wavecom transmitter/receiver units

Recognition results

Audio and video associated
with the recognized object

Fig. 1. System's architecture

to an object of interest. Subsequently, the audio-visual associative memory module receives object labels along with confidence levels from the object recognition system. If the confidence is high enough, it retrieves from memory the audio-visual information associated with the object the user is currently looking at and overlays this information on the user's field of view.

The audio-visual recording module accumulates buffers containing audio-visual data. These circular buffers contain the past 2 seconds of compressed audio and video. Whenever the user decides to record the current interaction, the system stores the data until the user signals the recording to stop. The user moves his head mounted video camera and microphone to specifically target and *shoot* the footage required. Thus, an audio-video clip is formed. After recording such a clip, the user selects the object that should trigger the clip's playback. This is done by by directing the camera towards an object of interest and triggering the unit (i.e. pressing a button). The system then instructs the vision module to add the captured image to its database of objects and associate the object's label to the most recently recorded A/V clip. Additionally, the user can indicate negative interest in objects which might get misinterpreted by the vision system as trigger objects (i.e. due to their visual similarity to previously encountered trigger-objects). Thus, both positive and negative reinforcement can be used in forming these associations. Therefore the user can actively assist the system to learn the differences between uninteresting objects and important cue objects.

Whenever the user is not recording or associating, the system is continuously running in a background mode trying to find objects in the field of view which have been associated to an A/V sequence. DyPERS thus acts as a parallel perceptual remembrance agent that is constantly trying to recognize and explain – by remembering associations – what the user is paying attention to. Figure 2 depicts an example of the overlay process. Here, in the top of the figure, an 'expert' is demonstrating how to change the bag on a vacuum cleaner. The user records the process and then associates the explanation with the image of the vacuum's body. Thus, whenever the user looks at the vacuum (as in the bottom of the figure) he or she automatically sees an animation (overlaid on the left of his field of view) explaining how to change the dust bag. The recording, association and retrieval processes are all performed online in a seamless manner.

Fig. 2. Sample Output Through heads-up-display (HUD)

3.2 Wearable Computer Interface

As pointed out in the beginning, a system such as DyPERS has to be useful and usable by the person wearing it. Ideally we would like a non-intrusive system that did not require new infrastructure to be incorporated in the environment –such as tags, infrared transmitters, etc– and which can be used in a seamless way by its user.

Using a camera attached to the user's HUD and the generic real-time computer vision object recognition system described in section 4 DyPERS is able to perceive, identify and recognize the objects that the user is looking at. Using such a vision system circumvents many problems associated with tagging technologies, such as cost, size, range, power consumption and flexibility. From a perceptual viewpoint, DyPERS (in the same way as some other wearable systems [JEW+97,SMR+97,RN95]) sees what the user sees and hears what the user hears, being closer to the user's perception of the world.

The primary functionality of DyPERS is implemented in a simple 3 button interface (via a wireless mouse or a notebook PC with a wireless WaveLan). The user can select from a record button, an associate button and a garbage button. The record button stores the A/V sequence. The associate button merely

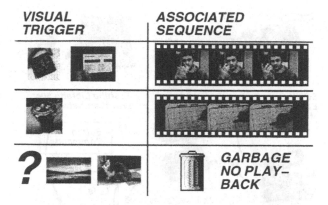

Fig. 3. Associating A/V Sequences to Objects

makes a connection between the currently viewed visual object and the previously recorded sequence. The garbage button associates the current visual object with a NULL sequence indicating that it should not trigger any play back. This helps resolve errors or ambiguities in the vision system. This association process is shown in Figure 3. In the current implementation of the system the interface is literately a three button interfaces. However, we are interfacing a small vocabulary speech recognizer in order to be replace the three buttons with spoken words.

3.3 Hardware

Currently, the system is fully tetherless with wireless radio connections allowing the user to roam around a significant amount of space (i.e. a few office rooms). Plans for evolving the system into a fully self-sufficient, compact and affordable form are underway. More powerful video processing in commercial units such as the PC104 platform or the VIA platform would eventually facilitate this process. However, for initial prototyping, a wireless system linked to off board processing was acceptable.

Figure 4 depicts the major components of DyPERS which are worn by the user during operation. The user dons a Sony GlassTron heads-up display with a semi-transparent visor and headphones. Attached to the visor is an ELMO video camera (with wide angle lens) which is aligned as closely as possible with the user's line of sight [SMR+97]. Thus the vision system is directed by the user's head motions to interesting objects. In addition, a nearby microphone is incorporated. The A/V data captured by the camera and microphone is continuously broadcast using a wireless radio transmitter. This wireless transmission connects the user and the wearable system to an SGI O2 workstation where the vision and other aspects of the system operate. The workstation collects the A/V data into clips, scans the visual scene using the object recognition system, and transmits the appropriate A/V clips back to the user. The clips are then rendered

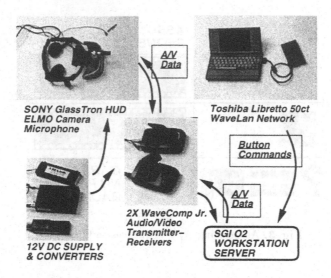

Fig. 4. The Wearable Hardware System

as an overlay via the user's GlassTron. Two A/V wireless channels are used at all times for a bidirectional real-time connection (user to SGI and SGI to user) [Man96].

4 Generic Object Recognition System

The video camera used by DyPERS is aligned with the line of sight of the user (see figure 8). Therefore, by gazing at interesting objects, the user directs the input to the recognition system which tries to recognize previously recorded objects. The recognition results are then sent to the audio-visual associative memory system which plays the appropriate clip.

The generic object recognition system used by DyPERS has been recently proposed by Schiele and Crowley [SC96]. A major result of their work is that a statistical representation based on local object descriptors provides a reliable means for the representation and recognition of object appearances.

Objects are represented by multidimensional histograms of vector responses from local neighborhood operators. Figure 5 shows two examples of two-dimensional histograms. Simple matching of such histograms (using χ^2-statistics or intersection [Sch97]) can be used to determine the most probable object, independent of its position, scale and image-plane rotation. Furthermore the approach is considerably robust to view point changes. This technique has been extended to probabilistic object recognition [SC96], in order to determine the probability of each object in an image only based on a small image region. Experiments (briefly described below) showed that only a small portion of the image (between 15% and 30%) is needed in order to recognize 100 objects correctly. In the following we summarize the probabilistic object recognition technique used. The current system runs at approximately 10Hz on a Silicon Graphics O2 machine using the OpenGL extension library for real-time image convolution.

Fig. 5. Two-dimensional histograms of two objects corresponding to a particular viewpoint, image plane rotation and scale. The image measurement is given by the Magnitude of the first derivative and the Laplace operator. The resolution of each histogram axis is 32.

Multidimensional receptive field histograms are constructed using a vector of arbitrary linear filters. Due to the generality and robustness of Gaussian derivatives, we selected multidimensional vectors of Gaussian derivatives (e.g. the magnitude of the first derivative and the Laplace operator at two or three different scales).

It is worthwhile to point out that the object representation is very general and can be used for a wide variety of objects. The objects most suited for the representation contain enough local texture and structure to be coded by the multidimensional histograms. A useful feature of the recognition system is that it often matches visually similar objects such as two business cards from the same company. In order to discriminate these cards a more specific system such as a character recognition system should be used. Since the response time of the system is only in the order of 100ms we are planning to use the result of the system to trigger more specific recognition systems as appropriate.

4.1 Probabilistic Object Recognition

In order to recognize an object, we are interested in computing the probability of the object O_n given a certain local measurement M_k (here a multidimensional vector of Gaussian derivatives). This probability $p(O_n|M_k)$ can be calculated using Bayes rule:

$$p(O_n|M_k) = \frac{p(M_k|O_n)p(O_n)}{p(M_k)}$$

with

- $p(O_n)$ the a priori probability of the object O_n,
- $p(M_k)$ the a priori probability of the filter output combination M_k, and
- $p(M_k|O_n)$ the probability density function of object O_n, which differs from the multidimensional histogram of an object O_n only by a normalization factor.

Having K independent local measurements $M_1, M_2, \ldots, M_K$ we can calculate the probability of each object O_n by:

$$p(O_n|M_1,\ldots,M_k) = \frac{\prod_k p(M_k|O_n)p(O_n)}{\prod_k p(M_k)} \tag{1}$$

M_k corresponds to a single multidimensional receptive field vector. Therefore K local measurements M_k correspond to K receptive field vectors which are typically from the same region of the image. To guarantee independence of the different local measurements we choose the minimal distance $d(M_k, M_l)$ between two measurements M_k and M_l to be sufficiently large (in the experiments below we chose the minimal distance $d(M_k, M_l) \geq 2\sigma$).

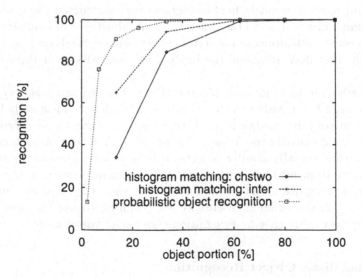

Fig. 6. Experimental results for 103 objects. Comparison of probabilistic object recognition and recognition by histogram matching: χ^2_{qv} (chstwo) and $\cap$ (inter). 1327 test images of 103 objects have been used.

Fig. 7. 25 of the 103 database objects use in the experiments.

In the following we assume all objects to be equally probable: $p(O_n) = \frac{1}{N}$ with N the number of objects. We use $p(M_k) = \sum_i p(M_k|O_i)p(O_i)$ for the calculation of the a priori probability $p(M_k)$. Since the probabilities $p(M_k|O_n)$ are directly given by the multidimensional receptive field histograms, Equation (1) shows a calculation of the probability for each object O_n based on the multidimensional receptive field histograms of the N objects. Perhaps the most remarkable property of Equation (1) is that no correspondence needs to be calculated. That means that the probability can be calculated for arbitrary points in the image. Furthermore the complexity is linear in the number of image points used.

Equation (1) has been applied to a database of 103 objects. Figure 7 shows some of the objects used. In an experiment 1327 test images of the 103 objects have been used which include scale changes up to ±40%, arbitrary image plane rotation and view point changes. Figure 6 shows results which were obtained for six-dimensional histograms, e.g. for the filter combination $Dx - Dy$ (first Gaussian derivatives in x- and y-direction) at three different scales ($\sigma = 2.0$, $= 4.0$ and $= 8.0$). A visible object portion of approximately 62% is sufficient for the recognition of all 1327 test images (the same result is provided by histogram matching). With 33.6% visibility the recognition rate is still above 99% (10 errors in total). Using 13.5% of the object the recognition rate is still above 90%. More remarkably, the recognition rate is 76% with only 6.8% visibility of the object. See [SC96,Sch97] for further details.

5 Scenarios

This section briefly describes some applications of DyPERS using the record-and-associate paradigm:

- Daily scheduling and to-do list can be stored and associated with the user's watch or other personal trigger object.
- An important conversation can be recorded and associated with the individual's business card.
- A teacher records names of objects in a foreign language and associates them with the visual appearance of the object. A student could then use the system to learn the foreign language.
- A story teller could read a picture book and associate each picture with its text passage. A child could then enjoy hearing the story by triggering the audio clips with different pages in the picture book.
- The system could be used for online instructions for an assembly task. An expert associates the image of the fully packaged item with animated instructions on how to open the box and lay out the components. Subsequently, when the vision system detects the components placed out as instructed, it triggers the subsequent assembly step.
- A person with poor vision could benefit by listening to audio descriptions of objects in his field of view.
- The visual appearance of an object can be augmented with relevant audio and video or messages. For instance, the contents of a container could be virtually exposed after it is sealed.

Many of the listed scenarios are beyond the scope of this paper. However, the list should convey to the reader the practical usefulness of a system such as DyPERS. In the following we describe one application in further depth and show test results.

6 A Sample Test Scenario

Evidently, DyPERS has many applications and it is unlikely to evaluate its performance in all possible situations. A *usability* study in a sample environment was selected to gain insight on real-world performance of the system as a whole. Since the system features audio-visual memory and significant automatic computer vision processing, test conditions involved these aspects in particular.

DyPERS was evaluated in a museum-gallery scenario. Audio-only augmented reality in a museum situation was previously investigated by [Bed95]. The museum constitutes a rich visual environment (paintings, sculptures, etc.) which is accompanied by many relevant facts and details (usually from a guide or text). Thus, it is an audio-visual educational experience and well-suited for verifying the system's usefulness as an educational tool.

A small gallery was created in our lab using 20 poster-sized images of various famous works ranging from the early 16th century to contemporary art. Three classes of human participants (types A, B, and C) were tested in a walk-through of the gallery while a guide was reading a script describing the paintings. The guide presented biographical and stylistic information about each painting while the subjects either used DyPERS (group A), took notes (group B) or simply listened attentively (group C). The subjects knew that they would be tested after the tour. Figure 8 shows a subject wearing DyPERS while listening to the museum guide.

Fig. 8. A DyPERS user listening to a guide during the gallery tour

After the completion of the tour, the subjects were given a 20-question multiple-choice test containing one query per painting presented. In addition, the users had visual access to the paintings since these were printed on test sheets or still visible in the gallery. Thus, the subjects could refer back to the images while being tested. For each test session, subjects of all three types described above were present and examined (i.e. A, B, and C were simultaneously present and, thus, variations in the guide's presentation do not affect their relative performance). Table 1 contains the accuracy results for each of the user groups. The results suggest that the subjects using DyPERS had an advantage over subjects without any paraphernalia or with standard pencil and paper notes. Currently, arrangements are being made with the List Visual Arts Center[1] for attempting the above test in their publically accessible contemporary art gallery.

---

[1] 20 Ames Street, MIT, Cambridge, MA 02139

Group	Description	Range	Average Accuracy
A	DyPERS	90%-95%	92.5 %
B	Note Pad	75%-95%	83.8%
C	No Aid	65%-95%	79.0%

Table 1. Subject Classes Accuracy

7 Summary and Conclusions

We have introduced an interactive computer vision system called DyPERS ('Dynamic Personal Enhanced Reality System'). The system combines computer vision and augmented reality to autonomously provide media memories related to real-world objects via a wearable platform. It allows a user to collect audio-visual clips in a seamless way and to retrieve them for playback automatically and meaningfully. The generic object recognition system has been described and its performance characteristics have been summarized. We have also discussed the two remaining building blocks of the system, namely the wearable hardware and interface, and the audio-visual associative memory. In addition, several application examples that DyPERS could span were enumerated.

Experiments in a visual arts gallery environment suggest that subjects using the computer vision system DyPERS would benefit of higher accuracy and more complete responses than participants using paper notes or no tools for information retention. These preliminary results are encouraging although more work is being planned to establish a final usability and performance evaluation. Nevertheless, the platform does provide interesting arguments for ways augmented reality and artificial perception can enrich the user and play a fundamental role in building a natural, seamless and intelligent interface.

Acknowledgments

Thanks to the participants involved in the experiment and to Nitin Sawhney, Brian Clarkson, Pattie Maes and Thad Starner for help and comments.

References

[Alo90] Y. Aloimonos. Purposive and qualitative active vision. In *Image Understanding Workshop*, pages 816–828, 1990.

[Baj85] R. Bajcsy. Active perception vs. pasive perception. In *IEEE Workshop on Computer Vision*, pages 55–59, 1985.

[Baj88] R. Bajcsy. Active perception. *Proceedings of the IEEE*, 296:996–1005, 1988.

[Bal91] D. Ballard. Animate vision. *Aritifcal Intelligence*, 48:57–86, 1991.

[Bed95] B.B. Bederson. Audio augmented reality: A prototype automated tour guide. In *ACM SIGCHI*, pages 210–211, 1995.

[Dic97] E.D. Dickmanns. Vehicles capaple of dynamic vision. In *15th International Joint Conference in Artificial Intelligence*, 1997.

[FMS92]   S. Feiner, B. MacIntyre, and D. Seligmann. Annotating the real world with knowledge-based graphics on see-through head-mounted display. In *Proc. of Graphics Interface*, pages 78–85, 1992.

[JEW⁺97] T. Jebara, C. Eyster, J. Weaver, T. Starner, and A. Pentland. Stochasticks: Augmenting the billiards experience with probabilistic vision and wearable computers. In *Intl. Symp. on Wearable Computers*, 1997.

[JLMP93] R.J.K. Jacob, J.J. Leggett, B.A. Myers, and R. Pausch. Interaction styles and input/output devices. *Behaviour and Information Technology*, 12(2):69–70, 1993.

[KVB97]   S. Kakez, C. Vania, and P. Bisson. Virtually documented environment. In *Intl. Symp. on Wearable Computers*, 1997.

[Lev97]   J. Levine. Real-time target and pose recognition for 3-d graphical overlay. Master's thesis, EECS Dept., MIT, June 1997.

[LF93]   M. Lamming and Flynn. Forget-me-not: intimate computing in support of human memory. In *Proceedings of FRIEND21 Intl. Symp. on Next Generation Human Interface*, 1993.

[Man96]   S. Mann. Wearable, tetherless computer-mediated reality. Technical Report 361, M.I.T. Media Lab, 1996.

[Man97]   S. Mann. Wearable computing: A first step toward personal imaging. *IEEE Computer; http://wearcam.org/ieeecomputer.htm*, 30(2), February 1997.

[Mar82]   D. Marr. *Vision*. W.H. Freeman and Company, 1982.

[MBWF97] E.D. Mynatt, M. Back, R. Want, and R. Frederik. Audio aura: Light weight audio augmented reality. In *UIST*, pages 211–212, 1997.

[NR96]   K. Nagao and J. Rekimoto. Agent augmented reality: a software agent meets the real world. In *Proc. of Intl. Conf. on Multiagent Sys.*, 1996.

[RN95]   J. Rekimoto and K. Nagao. The world through the computer: computer augmented interaction with real world environments. *UIST*, pages 29–36, 1995.

[RS96]   B. Rhodes and T. Starner. Remembrance agent: a continuously running automated information retrieval system. In *Intl. Conf. on the Practical Application of Intelligent Agents and Multi Agent Technology*, pages 487–495, 1996.

[SC96]   B. Schiele and J.L. Crowley. Probabilistic object recognition using multidimensional receptive field histograms. In *13th Intl. Conf. on Pattern Recognition, Volume B*, pages 50–54, August 1996.

[Sch97]   B. Schiele. *Object Recognition using Multidimensional Receptive Field Histograms*. PhD thesis, I.N.P.Grenoble, July 1997. English translation.

[SMR⁺97] T. Starner, S. Mann, B. Rhodes, J. Levine, J. Healey, D. Kirsch, R.W. Picard, and A.P. Pentland. Augmented reality through wearable computing. *Presence, Special Issue on Augmented Reality*, 1997.

[Tur97]   M. Turk, editor. *Perceptual User Interfaces Workshop Proceedings*, 1997.

[Wei91]   M. Weiser. The computer of the twenty-first century. *Scientific American*, 1991.

Using Computer Vision to Control a Reactive Computer Graphics Character in a Theater Play

Claudio Pinhanez and Aaron Bobick

Perceptual Computing Group – MIT Media Laboratory
20 Ames St. – Room E15-368C – Cambridge, MA 02139 – USA
{pinhanez,bobick}@media.mit.edu

Abstract

It/I is a two-character theater play where the human character *I* is taunted and played by a vision-based, autonomous computerized character — called *It* — which controls computer-graphics, sound, and stage lights. Unlike previous immersive interactive systems, the computer vision system recognizes the human character's actions by considering not only tracking and gestural information and the character's internal variables but also the context provided by the current situation in the story. This paper focuses on a methodology to represent and recognize the human and computer characters' actions that is based on *interval scripts*, a paradigm that uses Allen's temporal primitives to describe the relationships among the different actions and reactions. The system was tested in six public performances held at the MIT Media Laboratory in 1997, when the computer graphics character ran automatically during the 30-minute duration of the play.

1   Introduction

This paper reports our experience in producing a theater play — called *It/I* — which featured, probably for the first time ever, a computer-graphics character autonomously controlled by a computer. All the computer character's reactions during the play were based on the human actor's actions as detected by a 3-camera visual segmentation system invariant to lighting changes (based on [10]).

The play *It/I* was written considering the sensory limitations of computer vision. The actions of the human character — called *I* — were restricted to those that the computer could recognize automatically through image processing and computer vision techniques. In many ways, the understanding of the world by the computer character — named *It* — reflects the state-of-art of real-time automatic vision: the character's reaction is mostly based on tracking *I*'s movements and position and on the recognition of some specific gestures (using techniques similar to [7]).

However, the result of the low-level tracking system is considerably augmented by incorporating knowledge about the expected actions to happen in each moment of the play. Unlike other vision-based interactive systems (e.g. [14]), the actor's position and gestures are interpreted according to the current context provided by the script. When *I* moves towards one the stage screens, that is interpreted as "paying attention to the computer character" in the initial moments of one scene, but, some time later, as "trying to catch the computer character".

The main focus of this paper is on a paradigm called *interval scripts* to represent both the contextual elements required to recognize high-level *actions* (as defined by Bobick in [4]) and the behavior of the computer character. In this particular application — as well as in other interactive, immersive spaces like [5] — the context is largely set up by the actions of the computerized characters, justifying thus that the context for action recognition and the computer behavior to be unified in a sole structure or script.

Interval scripts have been first proposed in [23], and constitute a scripting paradigm rooted in the AI technique of temporal constraint propagation to enhance action recognition and context switching. The research presented in this paper extends the initial proposal of interval scripts by providing a well-defined scripting language and by using the paradigm to represent context for vision-based systems.

1.1 *It/I*: a Computer Theater Play

Computer theater is a term referring to live theatrical performances involving the active use of computers in the artistic process. Pinhanez [19] details the concept of computer theater, the origins of the term, and related works.

Our research in computer theater has concentrated on building automatic, story-aware computer-actors able to interact with human actors on camera-monitored stages. However, automatic control must not mean pre-timed response: computer-actors should be built as reactive autonomous systems that sense the world, consider the current place in the script, and find the appropriate line of action. Otherwise the magic of live performance is lost as the actors are not responsive to each other or to the audience.

An interesting aspect of having autonomous computer actors on stage is that we can have audience interaction in a truly novel way: if a character is controlled automatically by computers, it is possible to transform the stage into an interactive space where members of the audience can re-enact the story of the play in the role of the main characters.

Figure 1: Scene from *It/I*. The computer graphics object on the screen is autonomously controlled by the computer character *It*.

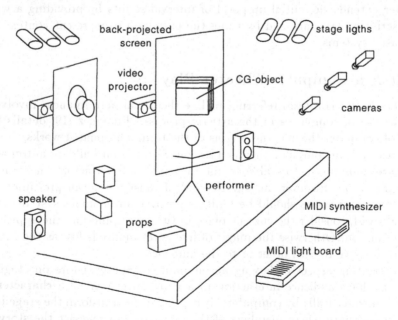

Figure 2: Diagram of the physical structure employed in *It/I*.

With these ideas in mind, one of the authors of this paper, Claudio Pinhanez, wrote the computer theater play *It/I*. The play is a pantomime where one of the characters, *It*, has a non-human body composed of CG-objects projected on screens (fig. 1). The objects are used to play with the human character, *I*. *It* "speaks" through images and videos projected on the screens, through sound played on stage speakers, and through the stage lights.

Figure 2 depicts a diagram of the different components of the physical setup of *It/I*. The sensor system is composed by three cameras rigged in front of the stage. The computer controls different output devices: two large back-projected screens; speakers connected to a MIDI-synthesizer; and stage lights controlled by a MIDI light-board.

The play is composed of four scenes, each being a repetition of a basic cycle where *I* is lured by *It*, is played with, gets frustrated, quits, and is punished for quitting. For example, the second scene of the play starts with *I* sitting on the stage, indifferent to everything, bathed by blue light. To attract his attention, *It* projects a vivid image of a sun on the stage screen. When *I* pays attention to the picture, the image is removed from the screen, the lights change, and a CG-object similar to a photographic camera appears on the other screen, following *I* around. When *I* makes a pose, the camera shutter opens with a burst of light and the corresponding clicking sound. Following, a CG-television appears on the other screen and, when *I* gets close, it starts to display a slide show composed by silhouette images "taken" by the camera. After some pictures are shown, the camera "calls" *I* to take another picture. This cycle is repeated until *I* refuses to continue to play with the machine and remains in front of the television; this refusal provokes an irate reaction from *It*, which throws CG-blocks at *I* while storming the stage with lights and playing harsh loud noises.

The above segment exemplifies the complexity of the interaction in a typical scene of *It/I*. The scenes have a complexity level that are quite beyond previous full-body interactive systems. For example, in *ALIVE* [14], although the main character (the dog-like CG-character *Silus*) had quite a complex internal structure, the meaning of the user's gestures remains constant as the interaction proceeds. In addition, *It/I* has a clear dramatic structure not present in most previous interactive, immersive systems as, for instance, the spaces designed by Krueger [11] and Sommerer and Mignonneau [24].

2   System Architecture

Figure 3 displays the control architecture used in the performances of *It/I*. It is a 2-layer architecture in which the upper layer contains information specific to the computer character and the bottom layer is comprised of modules directly interacting with the actual input and output devices. This control model is a simplification of a more elaborate 3-layered architecture, called *story-character-device* architecture, or *SCD*, which we are developing considering more difficult

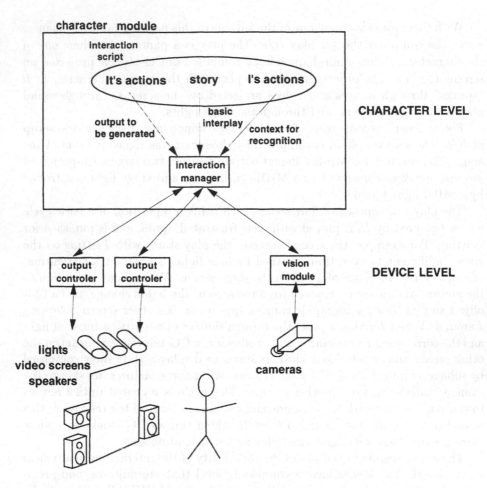

Figure 3: System architecture of *It/I*.

problems of controlling stories in immersive environments (see [22]).

As shown in fig. 3, the computer character control system is composed of one active element, the *interaction manager*, that process the interaction script (described in detail in [20]). The interaction script contains three types of information: the description of the *story* in terms of actions to be performed by the computer and the human characters; specification of *It's actions*, that is, what the computer character actually does when trying to perform the actions needed by the story; and the description of how the human actor's movements are recognized according to the current moment in the story, or of *I's actions*.

For instance, in a scene where the computer attracts the attention of the human character by displaying images on the screen, the basic interplay is the goal of attracting *I*'s attention. As part of the description of *It*'s actions there is a method that associates attracting the human character's attention with the displaying of particular images, each moving with a particular trajectory on the screen, accompanied by music and warm light. This is how "attract I's attention" is translated into output to be generated. At the same time, the story sets up the context for recognition of a movement of I walking towards the screen as "I is paying attention"; in most other situations of the play, such movement is not recognized as so.

We examine in the next section the vision module which uses a non-standard technique to segment the actor from the background. Following, we focus on the discussion of the various components of the computer character module.

3   The Vision System

The vision module shown in fig. 3 performs basic tracking and gesture recognition. The tracking module answers queries about the position (x,y,z coordinates) and size of the actor and three large blocks; the number of persons on stage (none, one, more than one); and the occurrence of the five pre-trained gestures.

In the performance setup we employed a frontal 3-camera stereo system able to segment the actor and the blocks and to compute a silhouette image that is used to track and recognize gestures. The stereo system, based on [10], constructs off-line a depth map of the background — stage, backdrops, and screens. Based on the depth map, it is possible to determine in real-time whether a pixel in the central camera image belongs to the background or to the foreground, in *spite of lighting or background screen changes*. This is an considerable improvement over vision systems based on background subtraction used before in many previous interactive environments [14, 5, 24], since it enables lighting change, an important dramatic element. The segmentation part of the vision system runs currently at 15 frames per second in a SGI Indy 5000 (although during the performances of *It/I* it ran at 8 frames/second). The analog video signals from the three cameras are compressed into a single video stream using a quad-splitter[1] and then digitized into 640x480 images.

Figure 4 shows a typical visual input to the system and the silhouette found. Using the silhouette, a tracking system analyses the different blobs in the image to find the actor. The analysis is performed under assumptions about the continuity and stability of movement, position, and shape of the actor. Smaller blobs are labeled as blocks only when isolated from the person's silhouette.

The vision system is trained to recognize the five different gestures shown in fig. 5. To perform gesture recognition we employ a simplification of the technique described by Davis and Bobick in [7]. During the performances we also employed manual detection of some of the gestures that could not be detected

---

[1]A video quad-splitter takes 4 input analog video streams and produces a single signal composed of the four images in half-size and tiled.

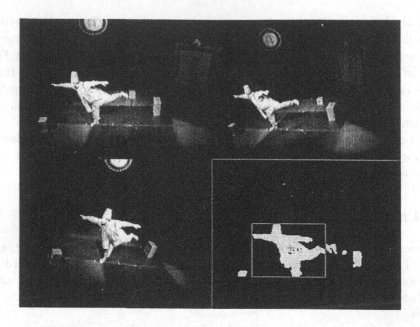

Figure 4: The 3-camera input to the vision module and the computed silhouette of the human actor (enclosed in the rectangle).

STOP   CUBE DOWN   CUBE UP

HANGING   SHOOTING

Figure 5: The 5 gestures used in *It/I*.

by the system with enough reliability. We had to resort to manual detection due to an absolute lack of time to improve the reliability to performance levels (which are very high, since during a performance accuracy is essential to avoid confusion in the actor or breaking the *suspension of disbelief* in the audience). Because the recognition of this type of gesture has already been demonstrated in computer vision (see [7]) and in real-time environments [5], we believe that there are no real technical obstacles for a fully autonomous run of the play.

4   From Tracking to Action Recognition

As described above, the vision module outputs only the position of the actor and the occurrence of some pre-defined gestures. How can this information be used by an interactive system based on a story script whose primitives refer to high-level actions such as "paying attention", "refusing to play with the machine", "posing for a picture"?

The fundamental problem has been addressed by Bobick [4] who distinguishes three categories of problems in recognizing human motion, according to an increasing use of knowledge: *movements*, *activities*, and *actions*. Basically, a *movement* is "... a space-time trajectory in some configuration space." (as defined in [4]) whose recognition is independent of contextual information, except for viewing conditions. An *activity* is a sequence of movements that can be recognized based on the statistical properties of their temporal relationships. Finally, an *action* is a movement or set of movements in a context, and its recognition requires the inclusion of knowledge about the context and the domain and the hypothesizing and verification of goal achievement.

Most attempts of performing action recognition have relied in choosing very restricted domains where the needed contextual knowledge can be codified without explicit inclusion of knowledge (for example, [15, 17]). Our approach in the *It/I* project differs from those because the action context is obtained from the story: different movements are recognized as different actions according to when they happen. For example, if the actor gets close to the screen when the computer character is showing attractive images, the movement is labeled as "paying attention"; or if the human character does not move immediately after the computer called him to play, the system recognizes the situation as "refusing to play".

Basically, our approach relies on setting up a situation where only some actions are expected, each of them with different spatial-temporal signatures. The idea has been used before in, among others, *The KidsRoom* [5], an interactive story-based bedroom for children. But unlike those cases, the *It/I* project specifically focused on the development of technology to easily and explicitly represent the story, the context, and the structure of the actions to be recognized, through the use of *interval scripts* as described in the next section.

5 Script Representation

The major technical novelty in *It/I* is the scripting language used to describe the story, the interaction with the human actor, the actions of the human actor, and the behavior of *It*. The 30-minute interaction between *It* and *I* is written as an *interval script*, a language for interaction based on the concept of time intervals and temporal relationships. Interval scripts have been first proposed by Pinhanez, Mase, and Bobick in [23], but in *It/I* we employed a new, revised, and improved version of the concept.

Previous scripting languages (for example, *Director* [13], or [6, 9]) lack appropriate ways to represent the duration and complexity of human action in immersive environments: hidden in the structure is an assumption that actions are pin-point events in time (coming from the typical point-and-click interfaces those languages are designed for) or a simple sequence of basic commands.

Also, unlike some previous reactive autonomous characters like *Silas* [3] or *NeuroBaby* [25], the interaction script of *It/I* contains the story of the play and *It*'s role in it. In this sense, *It* is more a *computer-actor* (as defined in [19]) than an autonomous creature. Specifically, *It* is pro-active in relation to a story, instead of reactive to human interaction or to internalized, creature-like goals [3]. Pro-active computer characters require scripting methods that allow representation of complex story patterns, including parallel actions, multiple paths, and some sense of cause and consequence.

5.1 Interval Scripts

An *interval script* associates a temporal interval with every action in the script. During run-time a label, `past`, `now`, or `fut`, or a disjunction of them, is dynamically assigned to each interval corresponding to the situations where the action has occurred, is occurring, or have not yet occurred, characterizing what we call the `PNF`-*state of the interval.*

The interval script paradigm allows two modes of definition of actions: a *descriptive* mode and a *constraint-based* mode. In the descriptive mode, the semantics of each interval is defined by three functions: `STATE`, a method to compute the current `PNF`-state of the interval; `START`, a function to start the action or sensing corresponding to the interval; and `STOP`, a function to end it. In the constraint-based mode, temporal constraints can be defined between different intervals, limiting their possible `PNF`-states during the run of script.

An interval script is a computer file containing the description of each action and statements about how the intervals are related temporally. Interval script files are converted into C++ code through a special compiler that encapsulates the different intervals and their functions into C++ functions attached to the interval control structure. A complete description of the syntax and semantics of interval scripts is beyond the scope of this paper (see [22]). We opted instead to present here some examples which illustrate some of the main features of the

```
             "bring sun image"=
             { START:
                 [>
                  ScreenCoord centerSmall (0.0,0.0,-1.0);
                  ScreenCoord startFrom (0.0,0.0,-40.0);
                  leftScreen.move (sunimageId,centerSmall,
                          startFrom,NULL,0,40,"decrescendo");
                 <].
                STOP:
                  [> leftScreen.stopMove (sunimageId);<].
                STATE:
                  [> return leftScreen.moveState (); <].
             }.
             "remove sun image"=
             {  ....  (similar to "bring sun image") ....      }.

             "sun image on screen"={}.

             "bring sun image" START "sun image on screen".

             "remove sun image" FINISH "sun image on screen".
```

Figure 6: Example of an interval script from the first scene of *It/I*. The five intervals described here control the movements of an image of the sun on the stage screen.

paradigm, followed by a basic description of the temporal formalism used in interval scripts and its run-time processing.

Figure 6 shows the definition of three intervals occurring in the beginning of the first scene of *It/I*. They control a short segment of the scene where *It* brings an image of the sun to the screen and moves it away when *I* shows interest on it by getting close to the screen. The first two intervals, **"bring sun image"** and **"remove sun image"** exemplify the descriptive mode of interval scripts. In an interval script, the **START**, **STOP**, and **STATE** functions can either be written as C++ code (inside the special symbols [> and <]) or as a combination of previously defined intervals. In the case of these two intervals, the interval functions call methods of the C++-object **leftScreen**, sending requests to the CG module of the left screen to move the sun image appropriately.

The interval **"sun image on screen"** defined in fig. 6 is a case where the interval is defined solely as a function of others through temporal constraints. Although the interval's own definition is empty, the two last lines of the fig. 6 define two temporal constraints determining that **"sun image on screen"** is started by **"bring sun image"** and finished by **"remove sun image"**. That is,

```
"I is close to big screen"=
{ STATE:
    [> if (close(vision.wherePerson(),bigScreeen.where))
        return NOW; else return PAST-OR-FUTURE;
    <];
}.

"I pays attention to sun image"=
{ STATE: IF "I is close to big screen" IS NOW
    AND "sun image on screen" IS NOW
    ASSERT NOW.
}.

"bring sun image" BEFORE OR MEET OR OVERLAP
  "I pays attention to sun image".

"I pays attention to sun image" BEFORE
  "remove sun image".
```

Figure 7: Part of the interval script from the first scene of *It/I*, showing an example of a mapping of a movement into a higher level action through the use of the story's context.

although the interaction script does not provide any computational definition of the state of the interval **"sun image on screen"**, during run-time its state is determined as a result of the current state of the two other intervals.

Figure 7 contains a simple example of the process of mapping a sensor element into a higher level action through the use of contextual elements from the story. It basically states that if the character *I* is close to the screen while the image of the sun is there, then *I* is paying attention to the screen. Of course under everyday circumstances proximity can not be immediately mapped into attention. However, the development of the play on the stage (or in its user-interactive version) creates surprise elements in this scene that propel the actor or user towards the screen when he is interested in exploring the new image.

This is expressed in the segment of interval scripts depicted in fig. 7. As in the preceding example, the interval **"I is close to big screen"** determines its PNF-state by calling a method of a C++-object, **vision**, that queries the vision module at the device level and compares that information to the position of the big screen as obtained through a class function.

The interval **"I pays attention to sun image"** shows another feature of interval scripts: the possibility of defining interval functions based on the state and interval functions of other intervals. As defined by its STATE function, the state of the interval is now if both **"I is close to big screen"** and **"sun image on screen"** are also now, and undetermined otherwise. How-

```
"sun image scene"=
{ START: TRYTO START "bring sun image".
  STOP: TRYTO START "remove sun image".
  WHEN "I pays attention to sun image" IS NOW
    TRYTO START "remove sun image".
}.
"sun image on screen" FINISH "sun image scene".

"I pays attention to sun image" ONLY-DURING
  "sun image scene".

WHEN "sun image scene" IS PAST
  TRYTO RESET "I is close to big screen".
```

Figure 8: Example of definition by an interval script of an interval solely based on previously declared intervals (from the first scene of *It/I*).

ever, this indeterminacy is constrained temporally by the two following statements that declare that **"bring sun image"** starts before **"I pays attention to sun image"**, and that the interval happens before **"remove sun image"**. Moreover, the temporal constraints assure that the action **"I pays attention to sun image"** is recognized only in the context of the presence of the sun image on the screen.

Figure 8 shows a third segment of the script of the first scene of *It/I* in which the previously defined intervals are combined. As noted before, the syntax of interval scripts allows the definition of start and stop functions in terms of previously defined intervals. For example, the **START** and **STOP** functions in fig. 8 are defined by calls to the **START** functions of **"bring sun image"** and **"remove sun image"**, respectively. When the interval **"sun image scene"** is set to start (by an interval not shown in the figure), the executed action is to call the **START** function of the **"bring sun image"** interval, executing its corresponding C++ code.

The definition of interval **"sun image scene"** also includes a **WHEN** statement that works as a trigger: when the character *I* starts paying attention to the image on the screen, the image is removed. **WHEN** statements are in fact macros of the language, being translated into an interval where the **STATE** and **START** functions are generated automatically such as to perform the "triggering" function. **WHEN** statements proved to be an intuitive way to include event-triggered intervals.

The last line of fig. 8 shows another mechanism allowed by interval scripts, the **RESET** function. To facilitate scripting, intervals can be "recycled" by the invocation of the **RESET** function of an interval. In this example, the end of the interval **"sun image scene"** triggers via a **WHEN** statement the process of reseting the sensing interval **"I is close to big screen"**[2].

---

[2]From a formal point of view, a call to a reset function does not reset but instead produces a new instance of the interval with identical temporal constraints.

5.2 Temporal Relationships

One of the major concerns of our work on scripting languages is to provide a structure which can handle complex temporal relationships. Human actions take variable periods of time; also, the order of the performance of actions to achieve a goal is often not strict. In other words, actions — and thus, interaction — can not be fully described neither by events (as *Director* does), nor by simple tree-forking structures as proposed in [18, 2], nor by straight encapsulation such as suggested by structured programming.

We adopted Allen's *interval algebra* [1] as the temporal model of interval scripts. Temporal relationships between intervals can be described as disjunctions of Allen's primitives and easily incorporated into an interval script. For instance, the statement of fig. 6 declares that "I pays attention to sun image" can only happen during "sun image scene", through the macro ONLY-DURING[3]. This statement creates a temporal constraint linking the PNF-state of the two intervals and preventing, for instance, the "I pays attention to sun image" interval from happening if "sun image scene" is in the past state, even if all the conditions listed in the STATE declaration apply.

Events, tree-structures, and encapsulated actions and other basic elements from other scripting languages are subsumed by Allen's algebra temporal relationships [1, 16]. Therefore, with explicit declaration of temporal constraints, the interval script paradigm allows the description of complex relations that occur in real interaction, like parallel and mutually exclusive actions, and even causality.

During the compilation of the interval script, those temporal constraints are pre-processed using Allen's path-consistency algorithm [1]. But to achieve speed during run-time constraint propagation, the resulting network is converted into a PNF-valued constraint network called a PNF-network. In [21] the PNF-theory and algorithms are explained in detail in the context of action detection.

5.3 Run-Time Processing

During run-time, the control cycle starts by gathering the state of all sensors and the previous PNF-state state of all intervals. An arc-consistency algorithm [12] is then run on the PNF-network, what, according to [21] determines an approximation of the minimal domain of the constraint network. Through this reduction process the PNF-state of an interval becomes more specific: for example, an interval whose end was undetermined (past-or-now state) can go to a a past state if, for instance a successor interval (defined through an exclusive *after* constraint between the two), is happening now.

Start and stop functions are called directly by intervals, as shown in fig.8, or by the run-time system when certain changes in the PNF-state of an interval is detected. Start functions are called automatically whenever an interval changes

---

[3]The macro ONLY-DURING represents the disjunction of the Allen relationships START, FINISH, EQUAL, or DURING. That is, ONLY-DURING establishes that the interval starts and ends during the other interval, including possibly its extremities.

Figure 9: Audience playing with the computer character *It*.

from the **fut** state to the **now** state. Similarly, stop functions are called by the run-time system if an interval goes from **now** to **past**.

6 Performances and Audience Participation

It/I was produced in the summer/fall of 1997 with direction of Claudio Pinhanez, art direction of Raquel Coelho, and actor Joshua Pritchard. The control of the computer graphics, sound, and lights was performed automatically by a system composed of four SGI workstations. The script of each scene comprised between 100 and 200 intervals describing the behavior of *It* according to the story and the human actor's actions. Supporting the upper level character module were seven lower layer modules running the controllers of specific interfaces, such as the low-level and middle-level vision modules, two CG-generators, movie and sound players, and the interface to the light-board.

The play was performed six times at the MIT Media Laboratory for a total audience of about 500 people. Each performance was followed by an explanation of the workings of the computer-actor. After that members of the audience were invited to go up on stage and play a scene from the play, first in front of the audience, and individually afterwards (see fig. 9).

When the spectators went on the stage to re-enact the scene of the play, they displayed a variety of reactions. Some of them could easily remember the sequence of actions in the play and could navigate through the scene without external help, but others were partially confused about what to do. From this experience, we believe that it is necessary to adapt the computer character to interact with non-actors: among the improvements, *It* must be scripted to provide some kind of help or suggestions when it is detected that the user is confused.

7 Conclusion

In this paper we describe how *interval scripts* can be used to describe story-based context to be provided to a vision system. In this paradigm, context switching is achieved naturally as a result of the story development, and different high-level labels for actions are determined according to current and past events. The core mechanism is Pinhanez and Bobick's PNF-propagation algorithm for action recognition that can be viewed as a fast specialization of general temporal constraint propagation (see [21]).

The concept was tested in real performances of a computer theater play. Although having an actor instead of an user simplifies the recognition task (the actor knows how an action can be more easily recognized), live performance conditions are extremely intolerant to errors, especially to system mistakes that break or violate the dramatic structure of the story. Moreover, we have also run successfully the system with non-actors from the audience who had quite diverse ways to move and act on the stage.

We see *It/I* as part of a continuing work of understanding and developing technology for story-based, interactive, immersive environments. which started with *SingSong* [23], followed by *The KidsRoom* [5], and after *It/I*, by *PAT*, a virtual aerobics personal trainer [8]. To our knowledge, *It/I* is the first play ever produced involving a character automatically controlled by a computer that was truly interactive. We believe that this was possible only because a flexible scripting system was developed to describe the story interplay and the computer and human characters' actions.

Acknowledgments

The research presented in this paper was partially sponsored by DARPA contract DAAL01-97-K-0103. *It/I* was sponsored by the Digital Life Consortium of the MIT Media Laboratory. We thank to all members of the crew, in particular Prof. Janet Sonenberg, John Liu, Chris Bentzel, Raquel Coelho, Leslie Bondaryk, Freedom Baird, Richard Marcus, Monica Pinhanez, Nathalie van Bockstaele, and Joshua Pritchard.

References

[1] James F. Allen. Towards a general theory of action and time. *Artificial Intelligence*, 23:123–154, 1984.

[2] Joseph Bates, A. Bryan Loyall, and W. Scott Reilly. An architecture for action, emotion, and social behavior. In *Proceedings of the Fourth European Workshop on Modeling Autonomous Agents in a Multi-Agent World*, S. Martino al Cimino, Italy, July 1992.

[3] Bruce Blumberg. *Old Tricks, New Dogs: Ethology and Interactive Creatures.* PhD thesis, M.I.T. Media Arts and Sciences Program, 1996.

[4] Aaron F. Bobick. Movement, activity, and action: The role of knowledge in the perception of motion. *Phil. Trans. Royal Society London B*, 352:1257–1265, 1997.

[5] Aaron F. Bobick, Stephen Intille, Jim Davis, Freedom Baird, Claudio Pinhanez, Lee Campbell, Yuri Ivanov, Arjan Schutte, and Andy Wilson. The KidsRoom: A perceptually-based interactive and immersive story environment. Technical Report 398, M.I.T. Media Laboratory Perceptual Computing Section, November 1996.

[6] M. Cecelia Buchanan and Polle T. Zellweger. Automatic temporal layout mechanisms. In *Proc. of ACM Multimedia'93*, pages 341–350, Ahaheim, California, August 1993.

[7] James W. Davis and A. Bobick. The representation and recognition of human movement using temporal templates. In *Proc. of CVPR'97*, pages 928–934, June 1997.

[8] James W. Davis and Aaron F. Bobick. Virtual PAT: a virtual personal aerobics trainer. Technical Report 436, M.I.T. Media Laboratory Perceptual Computing Section, January 1998.

[9] Rei Hamakawa and Jun Rekimoto. Object composition and playback models for handling multimedia data. In *Proc. of ACM Multimedia'93*, pages 273–281, Ahaheim, California, August 1993.

[10] Yuri Ivanov, Aaron Bobick, and John Liu. Fast lighting independent background subtraction. In *Proc. of the IEEE Workshop on Visual Surveillance – VS'98*, pages 49–55, Bombay, India, January 1998.

[11] Myron W. Krueger. *Artificial Reality II.* Addison-Wesley, 1990.

[12] A. K. Mackworth. Consistency in networks of relations. *Artificial Intelligence*, 8(1):99–118, 1977.

[13] MacroMind Inc. *Director's User Manual.* 1990.

[14] Pattie Maes, Trevor Darrell, Bruce Blumberg, and Alex Pentland. The ALIVE system: Full-body interaction with autonomous agents. In *Proc. of the Computer Animation '95 Conference*, Geneva, Switzerland, April 1995.

[15] R. Mann, A. Jepson, and Jeffrey Siskind. The computational perception of scene dynamics. In *Proc. of Fourth European Conference in Computer Vision*, April 1996.

[16] Itay Meiri. Combining qualitative and quantitative constraints in temporal reasoning. *Artificial Intelligence*, 87(1–2):343–385, November 1996.

[17] Hans-Hellmut Nagel. A vision of 'vision and language' comprises action: An example from road traffic. *Artificial Intelligence Review*, 8:189–214, 1995.

[18] Ken Perlin and Athomas Goldberg. Improv: A system for scripting interactive actors in virtual worlds. In *Proc. of SIGGRAPH'96*, August 1996.

[19] Claudio S. Pinhanez. Computer theater. In *Proc. of the Eighth International Symposium on Electronic Arts (ISEA'97)*, Chicago, Illinois, September 1997.

[20] Claudio S. Pinhanez and Aaron F. Bobick. Fast constraint propagation on specialized Allen networks and its application to action recognition and control. Technical report # 456, M.I.T. Media Laboratory Perceptual Computing Section, January 1998.

[21] Claudio S. Pinhanez and Aaron F. Bobick. Human action detection using PNF propagation of temporal constraints. In *Proc. of CVPR'98*, pages 898–904, Santa Barbara, California, June 1998.

[22] Claudio S. Pinhanez and Aaron F. Bobick. "It/I": A theater play featuring an autonomous computer graphics character. Technical report # 455, M.I.T. Media Laboratory Perceptual Computing Section, January 1998.

[23] Claudio S. Pinhanez, Kenji Mase, and Aaron F. Bobick. Interval scripts: A design paradigm for story-based interactive systems. In *CHI'97*, pages 287–294, Atlanta, Georgia, March 1997.

[24] Christa Sommerer and Laurent Mignonneau. Art as a living system. *Leonardo*, 30(5), October 1997.

[25] Naoko Tosa, Hideki Hashimoto, Kaoru Sezaki, Yasuharu Kunii, Toyotoshi Yamada, Kotaro Sabe, Ryosuke Nishino, Hiroshi Harashima, and Fumio Harashima. Network-based neuro-baby with robotic hand. In *Proc. of IJCAI'95 Workshop on Entertainment and AI/Alife*, Montreal, Canada, August 1995.

Sassy: A Language and Optimizing Compiler for Image Processing on Reconfigurable Computing Systems

Jeffrey P Hammes, Bruce A Draper, and A P Willem Böhm

Colorado State University, Fort Collins CO 80523, USA,
(hammes|draper|bohm)@cs.colostate.edu

Abstract. This paper presents Sassy, a single-assignment variant of the C programming language developed in concert with Khoral Inc. and designed to exploit both coarse-grain and fine-grain parallelism in image processing applications. Sassy programs are written in the Khoros software development environment, and can be manipulated inside Cantata (the Khoros GUI). The Sassy language supports image processing with true multidimensional arrays, sophisticated array access and windowing mechanisms, and built-in reduction operators (e.g. histogram). At the same time, Sassy restricts C so as to enable compiler optimizations for parallel execution environments, with the goal of reducing data traffic, code size and execution time.

In particular, the Sassy language and its optimizing compiler target reconfigurable systems, which are fine-grain parallel processors. Reconfigurable systems consist of field-programmable gate arrays (FPGAs), memories and interconnection hardware, and can be used as inexpensive co-processors with conventional workstations or PCs. The compiler optimizations needed to generate highly optimal host, FPGA, and communication code, are discussed. The massive parallelism and high throughput of reconfigurable systems makes them well-suited to image processing tasks, but they have not previously been used in this context because they are typically programmed in hardware description languages such as VHDL. Sassy was developed as part of the Cameron project, with the goal of elevating the programming level for reconfigurable systems from hardware circuits to programming language.

1 Introduction

A common programming methodology in image processing and computer vision uses a graphical programming environment where application programs are constructed by graphically interconnecting the outputs of one primitive operator to the inputs of another. One of the most widely used graphical programming environments for image processing and computer vision is Khoros(tm) [22], but other environments exist or are being developed for this purpose as well, including the Image Understanding Environment (IUE) [17] and CVIPtools [23]. These programming environments are advantageous in that they separate application programming, where domain knowledge may be required, from low-level image processing and/or computer vision programming, and even lower level machine dependent parallel programming. Also, they allow application programs to be distributed across multiple processors, or to be assigned to special-purpose co-processors.

This paper presents Sassy, a programming language based on C that has been developed in concert with Khoral Research Inc. (KRI). This work is part of the Cameron project, which seeks to create a high-level programming environment for image processing and computer vision that is targeted for fine-grain parallel processors. The goal is for low-level image processing algorithms to be written in Sassy inside the Khoros software development environment. Sassy programs can then be manipulated as glyphs inside Cantata (the Khoros GUI) just like any other program. Sassy programs can be executed on parallel architectures, and in particular on reconfigurable (a.k.a. adaptive) computing systems using field programmable gate arrays (FPGAs). Such reconfigurable systems are used in conjunction with a host processor, as shown in figure 1; the reconfigurable hardware has one or more FPGA chips and local memories that hold FPGA configurations and can be used as local memory.

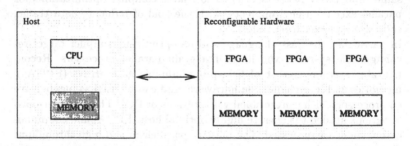

Fig. 1. General diagram of host and reconfigurable hardware.

Image processing (IP) applications feature large, regular image data structures and regular access patterns and hence can benefit from parallel implementations. Past attempts to exploit this regular parallelism, for instance with vector or pipelined co-processors, have suffered from communication bottlenecks between the host and co-processor, because of their fixed computation / communication behavior. The programmable nature of FPGA based parallel systems allows greater flexibility, and still promises massive parallelism and high throughput. Reconfigurable systems are therefore interesting candidates for special purpose IP acceleration hardware. Currently, FPGAs are not used in this context, because they are programmed using hardware description languages. The goal of Sassy is to make FPGAs available to IP experts, as opposed to circuit designers.

In many respects, Sassy is similar to other parallel, C-based (or C++-based) languages for image processing such as C\\ [6] or C_T++ [1], in that it parallelizes loops that operate over large arrays (e.g. images). Sassy offers a powerful set of language facilities for supporting image operations, including windowing facilities (with or without padding at the image boundaries), the ability to select array "sections" (rows, columns, windows, etc.), and reduction operators such as histogram and accumulation primitives. Sassy also supports true multidimensional arrays.

Unlike these other languages, however, Sassy supports fine-grain instruction-level parallelism. Sassy is a single assignment language, meaning that each variable can be assigned only once. Sassy also forbids recursion and pointer manipulation. These restrictions allow data dependencies in Sassy programs to be analyzed, enabling compiler optimizations, such as partial evaluation, strip-mining and loop reordering. The Sassy compiler can combine code from two or more loops, scheduling as many operations as possible on a selected window of pixels before moving on to the next window. This minimizes the number of times image data must be transferred between the host and the parallel co-processor, easing the primary bottleneck in many parallel image processing applications.

The Sassy program parts that are to be executed on the FPGA are converted into dataflow graphs that map directly onto FPGA configurations (circuits) to exploit the flexibility of reconfigurable hardware.

2 Reconfigurable Systems

The Sassy language is able to exploit coarse-grain, loop-level parallelism that should be useful for a variety of parallel architectures. It is also able to use the fine-grain, instruction-level parallelism that can be exploited on reconfigurable computing systems based on integrated circuits called field-programmable gate arrays (FPGAs). These chips, made by manufacturers such as Xilinx and Altera, are used along with optional on-board memory and/or co-processors in boards such as Wildfire(tm) by Annapolis Microsystems.

Field programmable devices, including FPGAs, already enjoy an established market and have been used extensively in digital devices of many kinds. They offer the manufacturer or user quick turnaround, low start-up costs and ease of design changes. Their speed of programming has improved, and it now is feasible to supplement a conventional CPU with one or more FPGAs and not only to configure them with custom functionality for each program that is run, but even to change the configuration during a program's execution.

Figure 2 shows the structure of a typical FPGA [2]. It consists of a grid of logic cells interspersed with wires to connect them. The perimeter has I/O cells that interface with the external pins of the chip. One example of a currently available FPGA is the Xilinx XC4085XL [29]. It is made up of 3,136 Configurable Logic Blocks (CLBs) and 448 I/O Blocks (IOBs). Each CLB has two 16-bit static random access memories (SRAMs), two D flip-flops, and a small number of miscellaneous multiplexors and gates. A CLB can function as RAM

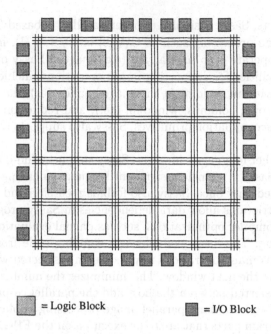

■ = Logic Block   ■ = I/O Block

Fig. 2. Structure of an FPGA

or as combinational logic. Each IOB controls one external pin of the chip, and contains two D flip-flops and associated buffer-driver circuits. The chip supports system speeds up to 80 MHz. Reconfigurable systems are programmed through configuration codes, which specify the functions of the cells and their interconnections within the FPGA.

Although the clock speeds of current FPGAs are lower than RISC processor clocks, the potential massive parallelism in an FPGA makes them good candidates for many real-time image processing tasks. Dehon calculates that, even with their lower clock speeds, FPGAs may have an order of magnitude better *computational density* (the number of bit operations a device can perform per unit of area-time) as compared with RISC CPUs [5]. Petersen and Hutchings specifically consider digital signal processing tasks, and also calculate a ten-fold speed-up [21]. More importantly, Hartenstein et al. demonstrate a ten-fold speed-up for *jpeg* image compression, a common image processing task [8]. Also, new investments in reconfigurable systems seem destined to increase their clock speeds and make inexpensive fine-grain parallel processors available for a wider range of applications.

Reconfigurable computing presents new challenges to language designers and compiler writers. The task of programming and compiling applications will consist of partitioning the algorithm between a host processor and reconfigurable modules, and devising ways of producing efficient FPGA configurations for each piece of code. Presently, FPGAs are programmed in hardware description languages, such as VHDL [20]. While such languages are suitable for programming chips that are used as "glue" logic in digital circuits, they are poorly suited for the kind of algorithmic expression that takes place in applications programming.

The Cameron project provides Khoros with a programming language for expressing IP applications, an optimizing and parallelizing Sassy compiler, and a run-time system for FPGA based, reconfigurable systems. This will enable IP programmers to exploit this desirable new hardware, by using a well known programming interface, and writing high level language code. This paper presents the first component of this trio, the Sassy programming language. A prototype Sassy implementation, generating C code, is available; work on the optimizing compiler for FPGAs continues.

3 Related Work

3.1 State of the Art: DataCube and Transputers

Most current real-time image processing applications run on either DataCube pipeline processors or Transputers. DataCube [4] produces a number of special-purpose image acquisition and processing boards that communicate with a host processor over a VME or PCI bus. Each DataCube board contains interconnected special-purpose processors designed for specific image processing operations, such as image capture, image arithmetic (addition/subtraction), or taking a histogram. DataCube programmers use a graphical interface to route data through sequences of these special-purpose processors, essentially drawing a small data-flow graph. Unfortunately, programmers are limited to the set of image operations (and interconnections) provided, and must learn a new (albeit graphical) programming language in order to use them. DataCube boards are also clocked at lower speeds than current general-purpose processors (for example, the MaxVideo 250 is clocked at 40MHz).

Transputers, on the other hand, represent an approach to parallelism that is more fine-grain than DataCube boards, but less fine-grain than reconfigurable systems. Each Transputer is a small general-purpose processor on a chip, with four high-speed input/output channels. Transputers can be connected together easily, and while the clock speeds of individual Transputers are typically low (50MHz or less), the speed-up comes via parallelism. Researchers in Munich, for example, have built a real-time image processing system out of three fast (Power-PC-based) Transputers and six slower (T4 or T8) Transputers for high-speed mobile robotics [13]. Unfortunately, it is difficult to program large networks of Transputers in MIMD style, so most Transputer systems for image processing use fewer than a dozen processors.

3.2 Parallel Languages for Image Processing

Compared to DataCubes or Transputers, reconfigurable systems offer two orders of magnitude more parallelism: thousands of functional units vs. tens. High-level parallel languages will be needed, however, if this advantage is to be exploited.

Most parallel languages for image processing are based on C or C++, and most are designed to parallelize loops over images or large arrays. C\\ [6], for example, is a parallel language for image processing based on C++ and targeted for the GFLOPS multiprocessor [9]. Variables are declared to be either scalar or parallel; scalar variables are kept on the host, while parallel variables are distributed across processors. A `forall` loop is introduced that allows distributed variables to be processed in parallel. Synchronization commands (*barrier*, *wait*, and *sync*) are also available to allow a programmer to control program threads explicitly.

Other parallel languages for image processing are designed for SIMD, rather than MIMD, programming environments. C_T++, for example, defines an array class that allows operations in parallel over the elements of the array [1]. The Image Understanding Architecture (IUA) programming environment used a similar mechanism for programming the IUA [27].

Two other parallel C-related languages, not targeted specifically to image processing, are SAC (Single Assignment C) [24] and Handel-C [19]. SAC emphasizes powerful array operations, for use in scientific numerical codes. Handel-C is designed to target synchronous, mostly FPGA-based hardware, and the language includes bit-precision specifications in its data types.

3.3 Functional Languages

Functional languages date back to the early 1960s when John McCarthy designed the Lisp language [15]. A variety of functional languages have been created since then, all built around a central idea: a computation is specified in terms of *pure*, i.e. non-side effecting, expressions [7]. The result of a function's evaluation is based only on its arguments, and the evaluation cannot change the state of the computation outside of the function. This guarantees that a function call's return value on a given set of arguments must be the same regardless of *when* the call takes place. This leads to inherent concurrency. For example, in the expression $f1(a, b) + f2(a, c)$, the calls of $f1$ and $f2$ can be evaluated in parallel since neither can alter a global state or cause side effects to its arguments. Examples of pure functional languages are Sisal [16] and Haskell [12]. Some languages are built around a functional core, but include side effecting extensions that make the language *impure*. An example of such a language is ML [14].

Early functional languages tended to omit loop constructs, relying instead on recursion to express iterative execution, and they emphasized recursive data structures such as lists and trees instead of arrays. However, some modern functional languages include loops and arrays for reasons of efficiency. A loop in a pure functional language is an expression, meaning that it returns one or more values. Arrays in pure functional languages are typically *monolithic*, meaning that the entire array is defined at once. The storage space for the array is dynamically allocated from the heap when the array is created, and the array is automatically garbage collected when it is no longer needed. An array carries its extents (or bounds) with it. Since a pure language is free of side effects, it is not possible to overwrite an array element with a new value. Semantically, updating an array requires copying the current array and replacing the desired value with a new one. However, compilers often can optimize this with *update-in-place* analysis, giving performance on a par with imperative languages [3].

The clean semantics, automatic garbage collection and inherent parallelism of functional languages make them appealing vehicles for high performance parallel computing. Their side effect-free nature makes compiler analysis much easier than that which is required for imperative languages. In spite of this, performance of functional languages often has been disappointing [10, 11]. Features of some very high level general purpose functional languages, such as higher order functions and lazy evaluation, have created new challenges for compiler writers and have prevented these languages from attaining the performance that some imperative languages achieve.

Sassy is designed to exploit the useful and efficiently implementable aspects of functional languages, while avoiding those aspects that have caused performance problems. This is done by integrating it in C, and restricting the functional aspects of the language to those features that are appropriate for image processing.

4 Sassy

Sassy (short for single-assignment C) attempts to take the best features of existing imperative and functional languages and combine them into a language that is amenable to compiler analysis and optimization, and that is well suited for image processing. The language is intended to exploit both coarse-grain (loop-level) and fine-grain (instruction-level) parallelism, as appropriate to the target architecture. The language should be suitable for conventional Symmetric Multiprocessors (SMPs), networks of workstations (NOWs), and vector computers, but the target of interest to the Cameron group is reconfigurable (a.k.a. adaptive) computing systems using field programmable gate arrays (FPGAs). Sassy is based on C in order to be as intuitive as possible to image processing experts, most of whom program in C or C++, but it differs from C in some important ways:

– It is an *expression-oriented*, pure functional language, not imperative.
– Its scalar types include signed and unsigned integers with specified bit widths. For example, the type **uint12** represents a twelve-bit unsigned integer.
– It has no explicit pointers.
– It is non-recursive.
– It has true multi-dimensional arrays, including array sections similar to those in Fortran 90. For instance, "**int10** V[:,:]" declares a two dimensional array of ten-bit integers.
– It has powerful loop generators and return operators similar to those in the Sisal language.
– It has multiple-value returns and assignments.

The elimination of pointers and recursion, and the single-assignment restriction, enable important compiler code optimizations. In compensation for these restrictions, Sassy programmers are given powerful high-level constructs to create and access arrays in concise ways. As an example, figure 3 shows Sassy code that smoothes an image with a median filter and then convolves it with an edge detection mask. In the discussion that follows, Sassy code examples will be shown with their C or Fortran 90 equivalents.

```
P1[:,:] = for window W[7,7] in Image {
          uint12 m = array_median (W);
        } return (array (m));

P2[:,:] = for window W[24,24] in P1 {
          uint12 ip = array_sum (W, M);
        } return (array (ip));
```

Fig. 3. Sassy code showing image smoothing with a median filter, followed by convolution with an edge detection mask.

Loops and arrays are at the heart of the language, and the two are closely interrelated. Loops have special forms designed to work with arrays, and arrays are easily created as return values of loops. The Sassy parallel **for** loop is the source of coarse-grain parallelism, and has three parts: one or more *generators*, a loop *body*, and one or more *return* values. The structure is:

for *generator(s)* { *body* } **return** *returns*.

for | *generator(s)* | { | *body* | } return | *return(s)* |

4.1 Loop Generators

There are three kinds of loop generators: *scalar*, *array-component* and *window*. The scalar generator produces a linear sequence of scalar values, similar to Fortran's do loop. The array-component and window generators extract components of arrays in various ways.

Two simple examples illustrate array component extraction:

```
for val in M                for (i=0; i<n; i++)
   ...                         for (j=0; j<m; j++)
                                 val = M[i][j];
                               ...

for V(~,:) in M             do i = 1, n
   ...                         V = M(i,:)
                               ...
```

The first extracts scalar values from M; the second extracts row vectors. Note that these loops automatically access the extents of M, making it unnecessary for the programmer to reference them explicitly. The '$\sim$' indicates a dimension over which iterations are indexed, whereas the ':' indicates an array section. The second example shows a Fortran 90 equivalent, since array section capability does not exist in C.

Window generators allow a rectangular window to traverse the source array, as in:

```
for window W[3,3] in M {          do i = 1, n-2
    ...                             do j = 1, m-2
                                      W = M(i:i+2,j:j+2)
                                    ...
```

Each iteration produces a 3x3 sub-array from the source matrix M. In general, windows always extract arrays with a rank equal to the rank of the source, but with smaller extents. The language includes a built-in function that pads values around an array's perimeter. This is useful with window generators so that the number of generated windows will be the same as the number of elements in the source array.

When a loop needs to extract values from more than one array, the Sassy programmer can use **dot** and **cross** products to combine generators. The **dot** product runs the generators in lock step, whereas cross products produce all combinations of components from the generators, producing the effect of nested loops. The following two examples demonstrate these two operators:

```
for a in A dot b in B {          for (i=0; i<n; i++) {
    uint8 p = a * b;               p = A[i] * B[i]
    ...                          ...

for a in A cross b in B {        for (i=0; i<n; i++)
    uint8 p = a * b;               for (j=0; j<m; j++) {
    ...                              p = A[i] * B[j]
                                     ...
```

Loop generators are important for two reasons. First, they give the programmer a simple and concise way of processing arrays in regular patterns, often making it unnecessary to create loop nests to handle multi-dimensional arrays or to refer explicitly to the array's extents or the loop's index variables. Second, they make compiler analysis of array access patterns significantly easier. In C or Fortran, the compiler must look at index variables generated by the loop nest and relate these indices to their uses in array references. In Sassy the index generators and the array references have been unified; the compiler can reliably infer the patterns of array access.

4.2 Loop Returns

Since Sassy is a functional language, every loop returns one or more values. In addition to returning scalar values, a Sassy loop can return arrays and reductions built from values that are produced in the loop iterations. In its simplest form, an array returned from a loop is built out of scalar values that are created in the loop generator or loop body. For example, the following loop creates an array A that has the same shape as matrix M, but with each value doubled:

<table>
<tr>
<td>

uint8 A[:,:] = **for** val **in** M
    return (**array** (2 * val));

</td>
<td>

for (i=0; i<n; i++)
  for (j=0; j<m; j++)
    A[i][j] = 2 * M[i][j];

</td>
</tr>
</table>

This example illustrates that the shape of the return array is determined by the shape of the generator. A generator that extracts scalars from a source array has the same shape as that array, so the returned array A has the same shape as M. Also, a Sassy loop body may be empty; this example shows a loop that has only a generator and a return. Arrays may also be built out of other array components, as well as by concatenating array components.

A variety of built-in operators are available to reduce scalar values that occur in loops. Many of these operators reduce to a scalar value, including **sum**, **product**, **min**, and **max**. For example, a loop to compute the dot product of two vectors can expressed as:

    for a **in** A **dot** b **in** B
        return (**sum** (a * b));

Other interesting reductions exist: **min_indices** and **max_indices** return an array of index locations of the min/max values, while **histogram** returns a histogram of the reduced values as a one-dimensional array. Any of the reduction operators can be used in an **accum** operation where a label value is used to partition the scalars into regions. For example,

    for a **in** A **dot** lab **in** L
        return (**accum** (**min** (a), lab, 4),
            accum (**max** (a), lab, 4))

will find the min and max value in each region of A, where the regions are defined by array L, as shown in Figure 4.

4.3 Sequential Loops

Sassy has sequential (non-parallel) **for** and **while** loops for use when loop-carried dependencies exist. A loop-carried dependency occurs when the value given to a variable in one iteration of a loop uses (directly or indirectly) that variable's value from the previous iteration. The assignment of a new value to a previously

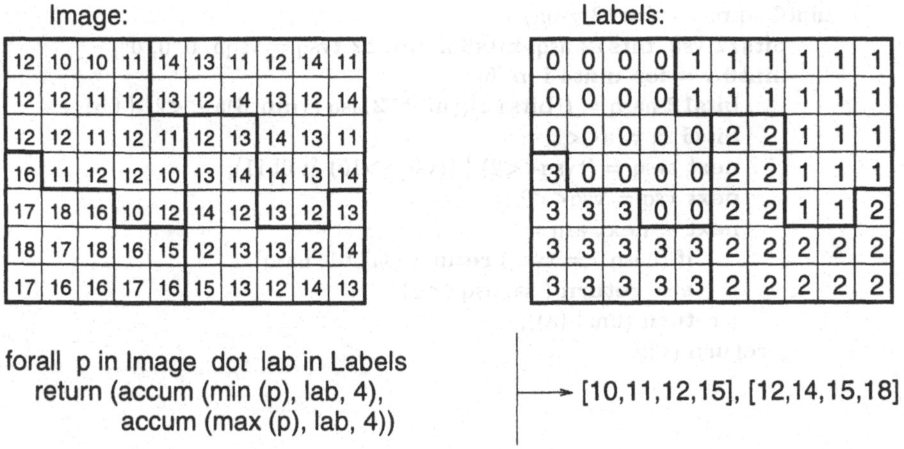

Image:

12	10	10	11	14	13	11	12	14	11
12	12	11	12	13	12	14	13	12	14
12	12	11	12	11	12	13	14	13	11
16	11	12	12	10	13	14	14	13	14
17	18	16	10	12	14	12	13	12	13
18	17	18	16	15	12	13	13	12	14
17	16	16	17	16	15	13	12	14	13

Labels:

0	0	0	0	1	1	1	1	1	1
0	0	0	0	1	1	1	1	1	1
0	0	0	0	0	2	2	1	1	1
3	0	0	0	0	2	2	1	1	1
3	3	3	0	0	2	2	1	1	2
3	3	3	3	3	2	2	2	2	2
3	3	3	3	3	2	2	2	2	2

```
forall p in Image dot lab in Labels
  return (accum (min (p), lab, 4),
          accum (max (p), lab, 4))
```

$\longrightarrow$ [10,11,12,15], [12,14,15,18]

Fig. 4. Example of accum operator, finding the min and max values in each region.

defined variable is counter to the idea of single-assignment, so Sassy treats these cases in a special way, as have other functional languages such as Sisal [16] and Id [18]. The keyword **next** allows a current loop variable be to computed based on its previous value. Conway's Life demonstrates an array variable A with a loop-carried dependence. It also shows how a window generator, combined with a mask, can implement general stencil-type operations.

```
uint1[:,:] main (uint1 A[:,:], uint16 n) {
    bool M[:,:] = array_def (bool, [3,3], {
                        {true, true, true},
                        {true, false, true},
                        {true, true, true}});
    uint1 res[:,:] =
        for _ in [n] {
            next A =
                for window W[3,3] in array_conperim (A, 1, 0) {
                    uint3 c = array_sum (W, M);
                    uint1 v = (c==3 || c==2 && W[1,1]==1) ? 1 : 0;
                    } return (array (v));
            print (true, A);
            } return (final (A));
    } return (res);
```

Another example of a sequential loop is the following square root function, designed to use only addition and bit-manipulation operators. It uses four variables with loop carried dependencies:

```
uint6 sq_root (uint12 vsqn) {
    bits12 vsq, bits12 asq, bits6 a, bits12 tvsq = vsqn, 0, 0, 0;
    uint6 v = for uint4 i in [6] {
        bits12 nasq = ((bits12)((uint12)asq+(uint6)a)<<2) | 0b1;
        bits6 sa = a<<1;
        next tvsq = (tvsq<<2) | ((vsq>>10) & 0b11);
        next vsq = vsq<<2;
        next a, next asq =
            if (nasq <= tvsq) return (sa|0b1, nasq)
            else return ( sa, asq<<2);
    } return (final (a));
} return (v);
```

5 Parallelism and Performance

Currently, high performance and throughput in FPGAs are achieved by manually optimizing circuit descriptions, using hardware design tools. To avoid this, Sassy is designed so that it can be automatically parallelized and optimized. Sassy exposes both coarse- and fine-grain parallelism. Its parallel for loop is a source of coarse-grain parallelism that should be useful across a wide variety of parallel architectures, while single assignment exposes expression parallelism. This allows Sassy procedures to be compiled into dataflow graphs and mapped directly into circuit diagram specifications.

The Sassy compiler will use an intermediate form called "Data Dependence and Control Flow" (DDCF) graphs, similar to the Sisal compiler's IF1 form [25]. This exposes data dependencies and opens up a wide range of loop-related optimization opportunities. The for loop generators are attractive because their "outputs" can be viewed as streams, making the transition from a memory-reading execution model to a data-driven stream model that is much closer to the execution that will take place on FPGAs. Similarly, the array loop-return operator produces array elements in storage order, making it easy to stream the results back into memory in a straightforward way.

Important DDCF-graph optimizations include

- Loop unrolling, which replicates a loop body one or more times, resulting in pipeline parallelism.
- Loop strip-mining, which splits a parallel loop into a pair of nested loops. The outer loop produces chunks of work; the inner loop performs the work in each chunk.
- Loop fusion, which takes two adjacent loops and fuses them into one loop. This can produce better coupling of array producers and consumers, sometimes completely eliminating intermediate arrays.
- Partial evaluation, which involves statically evaluating parts of an expression where some array references are constant. For example, the inner loop of the

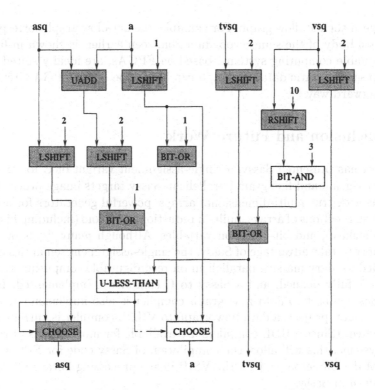

Fig. 5. Dataflow graph of square root loop body.

example in figure 3 uses a mask which may be known at compile time. If so, the loop can be fully unrolled and the constant mask values can be substituted in place, with subsequent expression simplification through constant folding.

- Flow control reordering, which is designed to tightly couple producers and consumers, promote data reuse and minimize host-FPGA data movement. In figure 3, array $P1$ can be eliminated; image data can be streamed to the FPGAs in appropriate-size chunks and the median values pipelined directly into the convolution loop.

These optimizations, as well as others, will be applied with the overall goal of streaming arrays into and out of FPGAs and reducing data movement between host and FPGAs. Evaluation order is crucial here, since the FPGA boards typically have limited ability to store temporary data close by; data will be streamed in chunks that are sized such that all necessary data can fit in the FPGA cache memories.

Sassy's single-assignment, functional semantics makes fine-grain, instruction-level parallelism easy to exploit on architectures such as FPGA-based reconfigurable systems. Since each Sassy variable is assigned exactly once, it is possible to create a static dataflow graph of a loop body in which each variable corresponds to an edge in the dataflow graph. For example, the dataflow graph corresponding to the loop body of the square root function, seen earlier, is shown in figure 5. Reconfigurable computing systems, based on FPGAs, are ideally suited to this approach since a static dataflow graph can be mapped onto FPGA circuits in a straightforward way.

6 Conclusion and Future Work

The paper has presented Sassy, a single-assignment variant of C for exploiting both coarse-grain and fine-grain parallelism. Sassy targets image processing applications with true multi-dimensional arrays, powerful generators for accessing elements and sections of arrays, built-in reduction operators (including histogram and accumulate), and bit-precision variables. Although many types of parallel processors can take advantage of Sassy, the single-assignment semantics of Sassy is intended to allow massive parallelism on reconfigurable computing systems.

Sassy is fully defined, and a Sassy to C compiler is implemented. In addition, a Sassy subset to data flow graph compiler is also implemented. As part of the Cameron project, a data flow graph to VHDL compiler is currently being implemented. (Since VHDL compilers are available for most brands of reconfigurable systems, this will allow the compilation of Sassy code for FPGAs.) Also as part of the Cameron project, the VSIP image processing library [26] is being programmed in Sassy.

References

1. F. Bodin, H. Essafi and M. Pic. A Specific Compilation Scheme for Image Processing Architecture. *Computer Architectures for Machine Perception*, Cambridge, MA, 1997, pp. 56-60.
2. S. Brown and J. Rose. Architecture of FPGAs and CPLDs: A Tutorial. *IEEE Design and Test of Computers*, Vol 12, number 2, pages 42-57, Summer 1996.
3. D. C. Cann. *Retire Fortran? A Debate Rekindled*. Communications of the ACM, Vol 35(8), 1992.
4. DataCube: http://www.datacube/com (or http://robocop.anu.edu.au/docs/MaxVideo250)
5. A. DeHon. Dynamically Programmable Gate Arrays: A Step Toward Increased Computational Density. *Proc of Fourth Canadian Workshop of Field-Programmable Devices*, Toronto, Canada, May 1996.
6. A. Fatni, D. Houzet and J. Basille. The C\\ Data Parallel Language on a Shared Memory Multiprocessor. *Computer Architectures for Machine Perception*, Cambridge, MA, 1997, pp. 51-55.
7. A. J. Field and P. G. Harrison. *Functional Programming*. Addison-Wesley, 1988.
8. R. Hartenstein, J. Becker, R. Kress, H. Reinig and K. Schmidt. A Reconfigurable Machine for Applications in Image and Video Compression. *Conf. on Compression Technologies and Standard for Image and Video Compression*, Amsterdam, 1995.
9. D. Houzet and A. Fatni. A 1-D Linearly Expandable Interconnection Network Performance Analysis. *IEEE Int. Conf. On Application Specific Array Processors*, Venice, 1993, pp. 572-582.

10. J. Hammes, O. Lubeck, and A. P. W. Böhm. Comparing Id and Haskell in a Monte Carlo photon transport code. *Journal of Functional Programming*, Vol. 5, Part 3, pp 283-316, July 1995.

11. J. Hammes, S. Sur, and A. P. W. Böhm. On the effectiveness of functional language features: NAS benchmark FT. *Journal of Functional Programming*, Vol. 7, Part 1, pp 103-123, January 1997.

12. P. Hudak, S. Peyton Jones and P. Wadler eds. Report on the Programming Language Haskell, A Non-strict Purely Functional Language (Version 1.2). *ACM SIGPLAN Notices*, vol 27, number 5, 1992.

13. M. Maurer, R. Behringer, S. Fürst, F. Thomanek, E.D. Dickmanns. A Compact Vision System for Road Vehicle Guidance, *International Conference on Pattern Recognition*, Vienna, 1996. Vol. C, pp. 313–317.

14. D. MacQueen, R. Harper, R. Milner, et al. *Functional Programming in ML*. Lfcs education, University of Edinburgh, 1987.

15. J. McCarthy, et al. *LISP 1.5 programmers manual*. MIT Press, 1962.

16. J. McGraw et.al., SISAL: Streams and Iteration in a Single Assignment Language: Reference Manual Version 1.2, Lawrence Livermore National Laboratory, Memo M-146, Rev. 1, 1985.

17. J. Mundy. The Image Understanding Environment Progam. *IEEE Expert*, 10(6):64-73, 1995.

18. R. S. Nikhil. Id Version 90.0 Reference Manual. Computational Structures Group Memo 284-1, Massachusetts Institute of Technology, 1990.

19. Oxford Hardware Compilation Group. The Handel Language. Technical report, Oxford University, 1997.

20. D. Perry. VHDL. McGraw-Hill, 1993.

21. R. Petersen and B. Hutchings. An Assessment of the Suitability of FPGA-Based Systems for use in Digital Signal Processing. *5th Int. Workshop on Field-Programmable Logic and Applications*, Oxford, 1995.

22. J. Rasure and S. Kubica. The KHOROS Application Development Environment. In H. I. Christenses and J. L. Crowley, editors, *Experimental Environments for Computer Vision and Image Processing*. World Scientific, New Jersey, 1994.

23. S. Umbaugh. *Computer Vision and Image Processing: A Practical Approach using CVIPtools*. Prentice Hall, New Jersey, 1998.

24. S. B. Scholz. Single Assignment C – Functional Programming Using Imperative Style. In *Proc. of the 6th International Workshop on th Implementation of Functional Languages*. University of East Anglia, 1994.

25. S. K. Skedzielewski, J. R. W. Glauert. IF1, an Intermediate Form for Applicative Languages. Refernce Manual, M-170, Lawrence Livermore National Laboratory, July 1985.

26. http://www.vsip.org/

27. C. Weems and J. Burrill. "The Image Understanding Architecture and its Software Development Tools," *Applied Imagery and Pattern Recognition Workshop*, McLean, VA, 1991.

28. M. Wolfe. *High Performance Compilers for Parallel Computing*. Addison-Wesley Publishing Company, 1996.

29. Xilinx. *The Programmable Logic Data Book*. Xilinx, Inc., San Jose, California, 1998.

30. H. Zima. *Supercompilers for Parallel and Vector Computers*. Addison-Wesley Publishing Company, 1990.

Simulation and Scheduling of Real-Time Computer Vision Algorithms

F.Torres[1], F.A.Candelas[1], S.T.Puente[1], L.M.Jiménez[2], C.Fernández[2], and R.J.Agulló[2]

[1] Physics, Systems Engineering and Signal Theory Department. University of Alicante, Spain
[2] Science and Technology Dept. System Engineering and Automation Div. University Miguel Hernández, Spain

Abstract. A fully integrated development tool for computer vision systems has been built in the framework of this paper.

There are many applications that help the user in the design of such systems, using graphical interfaces and function libraries. Even in some cases, the final source code can be generated by these applications.

This paper goes a step beyond; it allows the development of computer vision systems from a distributed environment. Besides, and as a distinctive characteristic with regard to other similar utilities, the system is able to automatically optimize task scheduling and assignment, depending on the available hardware.

1 Introduction

The proposed tool establishes a mechanism for the development of general computer vision applications from the posing stage until codification, scheduling and the necessary hardware selection to its execution. This process is complex, and usually causes time charges in the scheduling problem resolution and in the debugging of a specific codification for each equipment.

The exposed system integrates all the tasks and automates great part of the work that must be carried out by the programmer, who in this way can think in the problem analysis and the solution exposition. The debugging and scheduling tasks are analyzed depending on the accumulated experience in the applications design for specific hardware environments, being implemented in well-defined and robust modules.

The application structure establishes two main modules that are the visual workspace and the processing task scheduler. A database works as a link between both modules collecting the necessary information about the nature of the tasks designed by the programmer.

Standard systems as *Khoros* (Khoral Research) have been considered prior to this development. *Khoros* with his visual environment *Cantata* is highly modular and extensible with distributed processing capabilities. Other systems as *Gargoyle* (Univ. Chicago) are focused on active vision applications. Our system adds capability of distributed development (not jus distributed execution) and interface with scheduling algorithms.

1.1 Scheme of the Application

In the Fig. 1 the basic system architecture is schematically shown. The two main modules can be observed: the visual workspace (together with its associated database) and the scheduling module. Also, the interrelations between the different elements and the information flow are exposed.

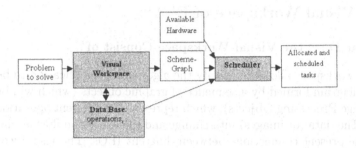

Fig. 1. Scheme of the application

In short, the objectives of the principal components of the application can be deduced from its input and output data (Table 1, Table 2).

Table 1. Data flow of Visual Workspace

Input data	Ouput data	Database contents
Ploblem to be solved	Scheme	Blocks description

Table 2. Data flow of Scheduler

Input data	Ouput data
Task graph (from a sheme)	Allocated and scheduled task
Blocks description	
Available hardware	

The first section of the article explains what the visual workspace consists of and which are its main functionalities. It makes a special point of the different characteristics in relation to other similar environments.

Next, the interface module is described in detail. All the required operations to obtain a task graph (required input in the scheduler) from a scheme (visual workspace output) are specified.

Finally, the third section focuses on the scheduler subsystem, describing all the offered possibilities and the different output information that can be obtained.

An example is added in order to offer a general view of the system, and to show the integration level obtained. A reconstruction process from images acquired by a pair of stereoscopic cameras has been chosen for this purpose.

2 The Visual Workspace of EVA[1]

2.1 What Does the Visual Workspace Consist of?

The visual workspace allows to specify the algorithm or application to be developed as a diagram formed by a sequence of graphic objects (which will be called IPOs – Image Processing Objects), which represent the different operations to be executed. The data (or images) interchange and the execution flow are indicated through the present connections between different IPOs. The visual workspace provides tools to create a scheme, that is to say, to draw IPOs that represent the operations and to interconnect them, as well as the tools to be able to execute the program.

The environment by itself does not execute a scheme, but it works as an interface or front-end application between the user and the processing software modules[2]. The way to operate is to convert the graphic representation into a scheme of commands for the software modules interpreter to refresh the state of the scheme in the screen.

In addition to a communication to the software modules interpreter, the visual workspace can reach remote applications like image servers or viewers. Actually it is not the application which connects to the viewer, but an special kind of IPO, viewer IPO, which is able to ask the interpreter for an image and to send its data to a server.

The EVA application is designed in a distributed way. It consists of different applications: an interpreter of the software modules server, a visual workspace for computer vision systems, and a viewer. Whichever of these applications can be executed several times and in several machines, provided that a TCP-IP connection between them is established.

Figure 2 represents a situation with four machines. Two of them, 3 and 4, work as servers. The other two, 1 and 2, have the visual workspace and the viewers, and are specifically assigned to users.

2.2 Visual Workspace Appearance

Hereafter, the components of the visual workspace are detailed. Figure 3 shows a scheme the way it is represented in the environment.

---

[1] EVA (Computer Vision Environment). This application belongs to a CICYT project coordinated by different Spanish Universities.

[2] In this paper the development of the software modules is not presented.

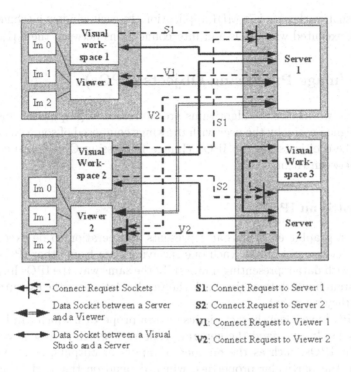

◄▌⫶ ⫶ Connect Request Sockets	**S1**: Connect Request to Server 1
◄▬► Data Socket between a Server and a Viewer	**S2**: Connect Request to Server 2
	V1: Connect Request to Viewer 1
◄▬► Data Socket between a Visual Studio and a Server	**V2**: Connect Request to Viewer 2

Fig. 2. EVA Architecture

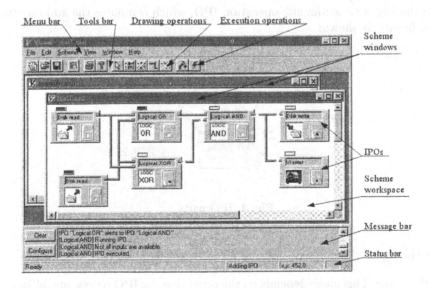

Fig. 3. Layout of the visual workspace

The visual workspace is a MDI application. In each window a scheme can be drawn and executed with IPOs and interconnections between them.[1].

3 The Image Processing Objects (IPOs)

In the visual workspace the algorithms are expressed as graphic schemes, which can be designed easily by the user with drawings composed of some basic graphic objects. These objects are the IPOs (Image Processing Objects) and the connections between them.

3.1 What is an IPO?

An IPO is a graphic element that represents an operation to be executed in a scheme. It has several inputs, each one receiving data from other IPOs (mainly they work with data representing images). In the same way, the IPOs have several outputs through which they give back the results data after the execution of the operation they represent.

Each IPO have some characteristics or own properties, which can be divided in two groups. In one hand the general properties, which represent values that have all the IPOs, such as the number of inputs or outputs, etc.; and on the other hand the particular properties, which depend on the kind of operations the IPO performs. An example of particular property can be the selection of a certain operation or function that the IPO must execute between all the possible operations of a type.

In the Fig. 4 an arithmetic operation IPO, which computes the add function of two inputs, is shown:

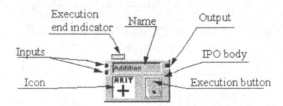

Fig. 4. IPO parts

In the figure the different parts of an IPO can be observed:

- IPO name. This name depends on the operation the IPO represents, although it can be modified by the user.
- IPO icon. It's a small drawing that helps to easily identify the operation the IPO represents.

- Execution button. The user can switch on or off the button. When the button is on, the IPO starts its execution, and the operation will be carried out provided all its inputs are available. When the button is off, the IPO resets.
- Execution indicator. It is the small indicator that is on top of the IPO, and points out whether its associated operation has been executed.
- Input and output connections. They are the square points that are on the sides of the IPO. On the left side there are the input connections, and on the right side there are the output ones. The number of inputs or outputs connections can be chosen depending on the IPO kind. There are IPOs that, because of its nature, have no input or output, IPOs that necessarily have a certain number of inputs or outputs, IPOs that have maximum and minimum limits in the inputs or outputs, etc.

3.2 Considerations of IPO Execution

The execution of each IPO of a scheme can be controlled manually through the execution button each IPO has. To execute an IPO and to operate input data, the execution button must be activated. This operation can be performed manually by the user, switching on the IPO button with the mouse, or automatically when the automatic execution mode is activated. Besides, before executing an IPO, the previous IPOs should have been correctly executed, so that their outputs are available.

When the execution of an IPO is achieved, this activates its execution indicator, operates input data according to specific properties, and, if the execution is correct, generates output data, that is sent to other IPOs which are connected. There are also IPOs as the viewer one or the disk writer (from the kind of IPO disk access) which don't produce any output data to other IPOs, and that only represent graphically or save the results. This kind of IPOs can be considered as outputs schemes, where the data flow ends.

The IPOs pass its data through some objects called connections.

3.3 IPOs connections

The connections are the way in which the dependence between input data of an IPO and output data generated by other IPOs is represented. A connection is represented in a scheme as a pipe that starts in an output IPO and stops, through possible ramifications, in the inputs of another IPOs.

When a IPO has not yet been executed (either it has been added recently to the scheme, or it has been reseted), the connections that start from this one are drawn as broken pipes to indicate that new data have not yet reached its destination. On the contrary, when an IPO is correctly executed and sends the data to its destination IPOs, the output connections appear as continuous pipes, without any cut, so representing circulation of the data to destination IPOs. This can be observed in the scheme of Fig. 5, where the XOR IPO has not yet been executed, and that's why the pipe to the AND IPO is broken. The same happens with the pipe between AND and the Disk Writer IPO.

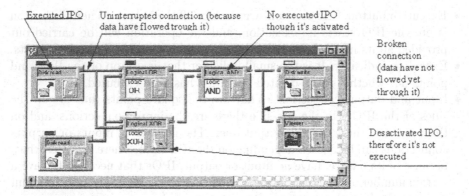

Fig. 5. A scheme example

4 Results Viewer: Viewer IPO

4.1 Viewer IPO Performance

A viewer IPO is not able to create by itself a window where to show the image received by the input connection. Instead, if it knows how to communicate to a server.

In this way, to be able to see images that arrive at the viewer IPOs, the viewer can reside in the same machine than the visual workspace, or in a machine which can be accessed through a network from the machine where the visual workspace is being executed.

4.2 Communication with IP Sockets

The connection between the visual workspace application and the server can be achieved through sockets, some objects to communicate between applications of a same machine or machines that coexist in a TCP-IP based network. A server will have assigned an IP address (the machine address where it is being executed in a network) and a port number that identifies it.

5 Visual Workspace / Scheduler Interface

It constitutes one of the main contributions of the present project. Its mission is to serve as an union link between the two applications.

The visual workspace that is described in the previous sections offers as a result a scheme of operations to be executed. As it has already been explained, these schemes are composed of elementary blocks (the so-called IPOs) interconnected between them.

Therefore, the elements that will be served as inputs for the interface are:

- Used IPOs.
- Connections between IPOs.
- Environment database.

The database contains detailed information about each one of the IPOs that can take part in the scheme. This information will be essential to convert the input data (scheme of operations) to a task graph (set of tasks, precedence relations and computation times required by the scheduling subsystem).

More in detail, the output interface must contain the following elements:

- List of elementary subtasks that take part in the process (generally, an IPO will be composed by several tasks of lower level).
- Data relative to the computation time for the subtasks.
- Precedence and exclusion relations (they will be described later).
- Information about preemptive and non preemptive tasks.
- Communication requirements and their associated costs.

5.1 Information about IPOs

We will study in depth which are the contents of the IPOs database required by the interface.

Subtasks Each IPO in the environment constitutes an artificial vision operation. It's possible, therefore, to split it in elementary blocks at many different levels. A high level division would represent a small number of operations and a high complexity degree; while a low level division would require more operations each one showing less complexity.

A multilevel representation has been used for the environment, so the user can work with elementary operations or, if he wish, he can use higher level operators. This way, he does not need to know the internal performance of each one of the algorithms he uses. For example, he can add in the system a block that carries out a certain morphological filter, instead of adding blocks for each one of the elementary operations of erosion and dilation. It's always possible, as it has been mentioned before, to use elementary blocks for very specific algorithms.

On the contrary, the task scheduler requires a representation at the lowest possible level, to be able to get an efficient implementation. Whichever algorithm is capable to be executed faster if we use the maximum parallelism of the system; if we use at the same time different processors to execute each subtask. On the other hand, the fact of executing in a certain order each one of the steps in an algorithm can also produce a speed improvement. But to achieve that point, it's necessary to know in detail the process. And the first data to be known are the subtasks in which a task can be divided. Besides, the more detailed this subdivision, the better the results.

Processor First of all, each one of the subtasks mentioned before must be characterized by the kind of function or kind of processors that can execute it.

First, in an artificial vision system there will be mainly two kinds of processor: CPUs and image processing boards (IAPBs). Most tasks will be carried out using whichever of these two elements. But there will be operations (for example image acquisition) that will be only executed by the processing board. In the same way, there will be complex algorithms that will be only implementable using CPUs.

This way, it's necessary to specify the kind or kinds of processors able to execute each subtask. This information will be used as a restriction in order to get a feasible scheduling.

Execution Time This value must also be specified for each subtask. A standard measure is used: the number of operations required. This way it will be possible to consider the different processor speeds in task assignment and scheduling.

Depending on the processors, there will be fixed or variable execution times. In the latter case, times will be represented by a formula according to the input image size and depth, or in general, according to whichever variable related to the block.

Possible Parameters Finally, the blocks also admits the possibility to be characterized according to:

- Different possibilities to perform the same operation.
- Image kind and size.
- Etc.

Most information is used at present by the scheduling system. The remaining data has been added anticipating possible new scheduler features.

5.2 Interface process

As it has been mentioned before, the output that must produce this interface is a task group. The information contained in this graph is organized in two lists:

- **Task and associated data list**
  Each task is described in terms of:
  - Execution time.
  - Preemption.
  - Communication requirements.
- **Precedence relations list**
  Considers task pairs in a fixed order:
  - Source task.
  - Destination task.

To obtain these lists a top-down procedure, which starts from a rough general description to refine it step by step, has been designed.

The necessary stages in this process are specified:

- **Obtaining the initial graph**
  A first graph is created assigning one task to each IPO. In this way, a tasks list and precedence list is generated. The precedence list is generated according to the present connections in the scheme.
- **Exploding the initial graph**
  Sequentially, each task (so far representing only one IPO) is exploded in its elemental components. This operation requires the following modifications in the lists:
  - Elimination of the task corresponding to the IPO and creation of as many new tasks as components it has.
  - Creation of new elements in the precedence relation list, binding each one of the IPO components.

  The final result of this process is a completely defined graph, to the detail specified in the visual workspace database.

6 Task Scheduler

It constitutes the last stage in the resolution of vision problems. Depending on the available hardware, an optimized space-time scheduling is calculated.

The system is generic and realistic: a static scheduler has been designed that, on one hand, considers subtasks interruption and, besides, takes into account precedence relations. In this way, we can assure that the offered solution is a feasible solution and therefore can be implemented in practice.

6.1 Characteristics of a static scheduling

In static scheduling the processor assignment, as well as start execution times for each subtask, are calculated before its real execution.

One of the main objectives of this scheduler is to reduce the final execution time of a subtasks group, as well as to obtain information about the possibility of executing it within certain time limits. [2] [3] [4] [5]. The algorithms that perform static scheduling can be classified in two groups: first of all, those that give an heuristic solution. This solution is usually based according to a cost weighted by the subtasks to be executed or another important information, so an exhaustive search of solutions is performed, and it tries to calculate the better possible one. On the other hand we have the algorithms that search an approximated solution, and they will stop in the moment that the achieved solution is acceptable. These algorithms are usually based on a solution and refine it in following iterations.

The major advantage of a static scheduling is that the required calculation time to perform the scheduling is spent in the subtasks compilation, what results to be more efficient at the execution time than the dynamic scheduling.

We must also have in mind that these systems do not always give an optimal solution because its calculation, practically in all cases, is a NP-hard problem [6]. An NP-hard ploblem is a seemingly intractable decision ploblem for which the only known solutions are exponential funcions of the ploblem size. Furthermore, there is not tolerance to treat with extern events that could appear during the system execution.

For the application, we have adopted static scheduling methods because they perfectly fit in the system nature: either the tasks to be executed or the available hardware are known a priori, what means that unexpected events will never appear. Moreover, the user needs to know in a reliable way the execution time associated to a certain scheme. Systems using dynamic scheduling are not able to offer such data.

6.2 Relations between Subtasks

Two kinds of relationship between subtasks can been established, one according to their creation instant and the other according to the capacity of being or not being able to be blocked between them [7][8].

Def. *Precedence relations:* a subtask i precedes another, j if and only if j can not start execution until the i subtask has been finished. The precedence relations can be expressed with a guided graph where the nodes are the subtasks to be executed and the edges represent the actual precedence relations. Independent subtasks can be executed concurrently.

Def. *Exclusion relations:* a subtask i excludes another j, when the i subtask is being executed the j subtask can not be executed. This condition serves to guarantee the access to shared resources, as input/output ports or printers.

6.3 Kinds of Subtasks

To perform the system scheduling we need to know the subtasks graph in which this system is divided. The interface module generates this information from the scheme coming from the artificial vision system editor.

The subtasks of this graph can be divided in three groups:

CPU This kind of subtask is to be executed only in a processor of CPU kind, and having in mind the characteristics of it, they will be able to be preemptive. The main purpose in vision systems will be to execute high level operations not available in hardware; as well as synchronizing execution with the rest of processors when necessary.

IAPB Low level subtasks that are only executed in a IAPB processor, as for example the image acquisition, filtering, etc. They will be able to be preemptive. To execute such a task in a certain IAPB, a CPU processor should have sent previously the proper order. These orders can be sent in packets, so making a better use of the available broadband. Therefore, before executing a IAPB subtask, a CPU task and a communication one called CPU/IAPB will be required.

CPU/IAPB They permit to send data between CPU and IAPB processors. This data can be, from single instructions to execute a certain process, to the results achieved in a certain processing. These subtasks can not be stopped and require the two implied processors to be available during the transmission; it's to say, we can consider that they are being executed in the two processors at the same time.

6.4 Scheduling and Allocation

The exposed development allows multiple possibilities of task scheduling/assignment, the user can choose among them according to the results he wishes to obtain:

1. Temporal scheduling using only one processor of each kind.
2. Temporal scheduling provided a previous spatial assignment has been performed manually.
3. Spatial assignment based on a temporal scheduling previously calculated for only one processor.
4. Simultaneous assignment and scheduling. These methods give the better results because they consider the possible interrelations between spatial and temporal distributions.
5. Information about the maximum number of processors of each kind necessary for a minimum time execution.

For the algorithms of kind 2, 3 and 4, it's necessary to know how many processors of each kind are available. This is part of the information required by the scheduler: the available hardware.

The scheduler gives, whichever the chosen algorithm, the following information about the scheduling results:

1. Spatial and temporal distribution graph: shows graphically which subtasks are executed in each processor and their start and finish times. Besides, a color code allows to distinguish between subtasks types.
2. Processor usage: indicates how busy each processor is (percentage of time the processor is not idle).
3. System usage: average time for all the available processors.
4. System Execution time: time necessary to fully execute the scheme.
5. Subtasks graph: graph used to obtain the scheduling.
6. Information about the subtasks: it allows to view the information relative to each subtask, displaying only those groups selected by the user.

Finally, we must emphasize that once the initial simulation has been performed, it's possible to obtain another simulation with the same data using a different algorithm or modifying the available hardware.

7 Example of the System Performance

To evaluate the functionality of the presented system, an example is outlined below showing a stereo correspondence algorithm. The example algorithm calculates the stereo correspondence between edge features obtained as the zero-crossings of the convolution of each image with the $\nabla^2 G$ (Laplacian of Gaussian) operator [9]. The algorithm implements the cross-channel coherence between filters tuned to different spatial frequencies [10].

Without deepening in the algorithm, whose details can be found in the previously indicated references, the images obtained from a stereo pair of parallel axis [10] are filtered at three different spatial frequency channels. The correspondence at each channel establishes a set of candidates based on the similarity constrains of sign and direction, within a maximum disparity interval. The last module establishes a coherence checkup between channels to accomplish a classification of matching candidates.

The following figures show step by step how the system behaves. Figure 6 represents the first step where the algorithm is represented as a visual workspace scheme. Figure 7 shows the task graph obtained from the scheme. Task procedures computation times and other data are available at this level. Figure 8 outlines the automatic allocation and scheduling results provided there are 3 CPUs and 2 IAPBs in the system. Figure 9 shows an alternative schedule using manual assignment. Finally, Fig. 10 represents the automatic allocation and scheduling provided there are no hardware restrictions.

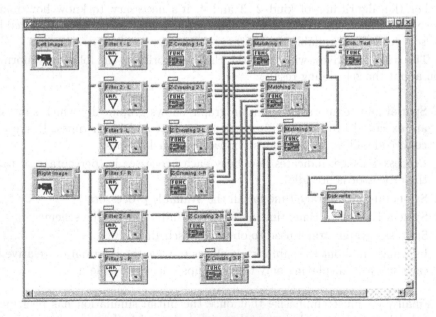

Fig. 6. Stereo algorithm scheme (Visual workspace view)

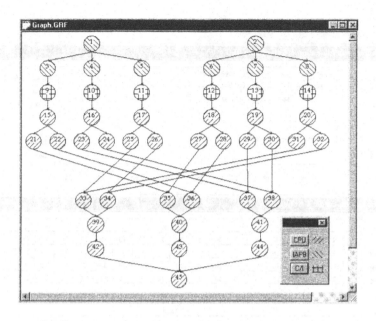

Fig. 7. Stereo algorithm task graph (Scheduler view)

8 Conclusions

The visual workspace becomes a powerful tool in the development of applications in computer vision, with the added possibility of hierarchical design in complex processes.

The application offers a huge amount of information to the user, as compared to other similar tools. Particularly, hardware selection becomes an easy task once the time requirements are fixed. And it is also possible to check for the feasibility of a certain real time processing algorithm by just simulating the system with no hardware restrictions.

The general algorithm (simultaneous assignment and scheduling) does not always find the optimal solution. In fact, on complex systems like those we are dealing with, it can not be assured that the optimal solution has been found without checking all the possible schedules, which in most cases is an unaffordable work (references on this point can be found on [6] and [11]). What the system gives is a pseudo-optimal schedule based on a heuristic algorithm. The performance evaluation of our algorithm in comparison with other scheduling techniques is not easy as most of these techniques can not be applied to scenarios as complex as those our algorithm deals with (preemption, etc.).

On the other side, the 'no hardware restrictions algorithm' (hardware requirements for optimal performance: figure 10) does give an optimal solution in terms of execution time, as it uses as many processors as needed.

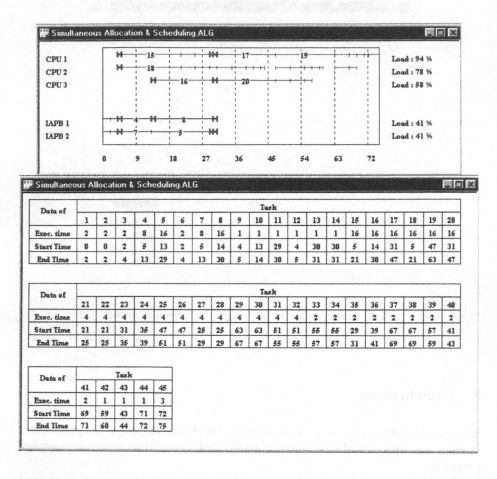

Fig. 8. Automatic task allocation and scheduling (Hardware: 3 CPU's, 2 IAPB's)

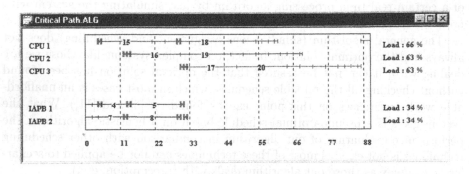

Fig. 9. Automatic scheduling (Hardware: 3CPU's, 2 IAPB's)

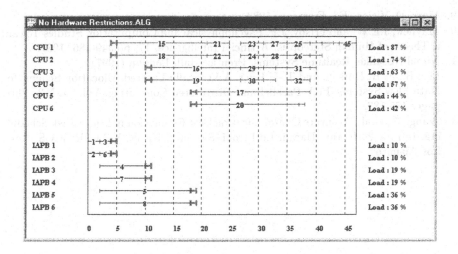

Fig. 10. Hardware requirements for optimal performance

Future improvements include the consideration of communication costs in order to make the simulations even more realistic. New scheduling techniques [12][13]are being investigated at present with promising results.

9 Acknowledgments

This work was supported by the Spanish Government through CICYT in the framework of project TAP-96-0629-C04-01.

References

1. Ben Shneiderman, Designing the User Interface, Addison Wesley, 1998.
2. Lo, V.M., Heuristic Algorithms for Task Assignment in Distributed systems. IEEE Trans. Computers, Vol C-37, N 11, Nov, 1988, pages 1384-1397.
3. Sarkar, V., and J. Hennesy, Compile-Time Partitioning and Scheduling of Parallel Programs. Symp. Compiler Constructrion, ACM Press, New York, N.Y., 1986, pages 17-26.
4. Shirazi, B., M. Wang and G. Pathak, Analysis and Evaluation of Heuristic Methods for Static Task Scheduling. In Parallel and Distributed Computing, Vol,. 10, 1990, pages 222-232.
5. Stone, H. S. Multiprocessor Scheduling with the Aid of Network Flow Algorithms. IEEE Trans. Software Eng, Vol. SE-3 N 1, Jan 1977, pages 85-93
6. Phillip A. Laplante, Real-Time Systems Design and Analysis. IEEE Press, New York (1997).
7. F. Torres Medina, Arquitectura paralela para el procesado de imgenes de alta resolucin. Aplicacin a la inspeccin de impresiones en tiempo real. PhD. ETSII, Polytechnic University of Madrid, 1995.
8. C.M. Krishna, Kang G. Shin, Real-time systems. McGraw-Hill, New York (1997).

9. Marr, D. Vision, Ed. Freeman, 1982
10. Mayhew, J.E.W. and Frisby, J.P. Psychophysical and Computation Studies Towars a Theory of Human Stereopsis, Artificial Intelligence, 17, pp.349-386, 1981.
11. Nimal Nissanke, Realtime Systems. Prentice Hall, London (1997).
12. Lee, B., A. R. Hurson, and T.-Y Feng, A Vertically Layered Allocation Scheme for Data Flow Systems. In J. Parallel and Distributed Computing. Vol. 11, N 3, 1991, pages 175-187.
13. Wang, M., et al,. Accurate Communication Cost Estimation in Static Task Scheduling. In Proc 24th Ann. Hawaii Int'l Conf. System Sciences. Vol I, IEEE CS Press, Los Alamitos

Real-Time Maintenance of Figure-Ground Segmentation

Peter Nordlund and Jan-Olof Eklundh

Computational Vision and Active Perception Laboratory (CVAP)
Department of Numerical Analysis and Computing Science
Royal Institute of Technology, S-100 44 Stockholm, Sweden
petern@nada.kth.se

Abstract. An approach to figure-ground segmentation based on a 2-dimensional histogram in feature space is presented. The histogram is then analyzed with a peak-finding algorithm designed with real-time performance in mind. The most significant peaks in the histogram are back-projected to the image to produce an object mask.
The method is applied to segmentation based on a 2-D color space and also on a combination of motion and stereo disparities.
Experiments with a system grabbing images direct from a CCD-camera with real-time performance having typical frame-rates of about 10 Hz is presented.

Keywords: real-time, image motion, segmentation, cue-integration

1 Introduction

A person that moves around in the world, while looking at various locations and things in his way, will experience that objects will enter and leave his field of view, due to his ego-motion or the motion of the objects. He will sometimes shift his gaze to such objects to find out, e.g. if their trajectory crosses his path, or, to determine what kind of things they are. In fact, he may be looking for specific types or instances of objects, for example they may be obstacles to avoid, or something he needs.

Certain capabilities that this observer displays are also of importance for a seeing robot acting in a real environment. First, the observer is capable of singling out things that stand out from their immediate surroundings. Secondly, he can hold these things in his field of view long enough to identify and derive various properties of them.

The first problem constitutes what is commonly referred to as the figure-ground problem. In this paper we will consider some aspects of that problem. The focus is on bottom-up methods, i.e. methods that allow a system to detect and segment out an object because it stands out from its immediate surroundings in some way. We have earlier argued [16] that such approaches should rely on multiple cues, since it is difficult to predict which cues are informative in a realistic cluttered and changing environment. Here we will in particular consider a specific method for fusing multiple cues. More precisely we will investigate a simple way to exploit the coincidence, or, consistency between cues. The approach will be based on conjunctions of two features and result in the classical problem of finding peaks in a 2-D histogram. An important aspect here is that we are considering dynamic situations where a seeing system is reacting in closed loop with the environment. Real-time and complexity issues are therefore central, as well as the system perspective: we are not looking for an algorithm functioning for offline processing of images but for a *system* that can perform figure-ground segmentation.

The main emphasis of this paper is on how to perform the segmentation using 2-D histograms. We will apply this to two somewhat different situations. The first one could simply be regarded as color based segmentation, although in a dynamic case and with coupling to using color for maintaining figure-ground segmentation. By this we mean the following: when an object has been segmented out it forms an entity to which properties can be ascribed. These characteristics can then be used to compute and maintain information about e.g. its shape and motion or recognizing it, but also to establish that it is the same object when it stops or changes motion pattern, or when only a fraction of it is seen due to occlusion: The target that's singled out forms its own model. It should be added, that what is used to analyze it further, in principle can be independent of what was used to identify it as being an object. In particular, it can often be assumed that the statistics of a target singled out in this way is simpler than that of the whole scene, and that an analysis of it therefore also could be simpler. What we in fact do in this case, is to use a 2-D color space as feature space. In the second case we use depth disparities and motion, this work has been treated earlier in [16]. Here we mainly show that our new simplified method for analyzing the histogram applies to this case also.

Our objective is to design a real-time algorithm integrating several modalities or features. That is: we want to be able to switch between a few methods depending on what is appropriate at the moment. For example: if the observer is not moving, it could be enough with some simple frame-differencing algorithm. When observer motion is present, (this could be detected by some image processing algorithm or by knowledge about vestibular parameters) a more sophisticated or motion-invariant algorithm must be used. As a trade-off for computational speed we have chosen a 2-dimensional color space, a linear projection on a plane perpendicular to the diagonal of the RGB color cube [21].

1.1 Related Work

Considerable work has been devoted to the general problem of image segmentation. Examples of methods using multispectral (usually color) images can be found in [23, 19, 7] These methods are computationally demanding and presently hardly useful in real-time systems with high frame-rate.

Color is frequently used a a cue to segmentation in recent work on retrieval from image databases, see e.g. [14, 2]. The goal in this case is however somewhat different from ours, and the output generally consists of candidate regions offered to a human user.

The work by Altunbasak et al. [1] is more closely related to ours. They are using color segmentation as a first step towards motion segmentation. They make the observation that object boundaries most often coincide with color boundaries. Their approach is to use a color segmentation method which they do not describe, for a first crude initialization step for motion segmentation. The idea is to use the color segmentation as a "seed" for for further iterative flow and clustering calculations. How the actual color segmentation is performed is not mentioned in the paper. Darrel et al. [5] present a tracking system using stereo and color to extract the outline of people appearing in front of the camera in real-time. The segmentation is achieved in a serial manner, first the stereo is used for an initial coarse segmentation, this to not confuse the color algorithm, which performs a refined segmentation, with a cluttered background. They use a 3-D color space and a two-sided classifier. I.e. they segment into one "skin" class and one "non-skin" class. Such an approach is not applicable in an unknown environment with potentially more than one colored object to segment out.

1.2 Outline of the Paper

We will first describe our peak detection scheme. Then we present some experiments, including a few comparing experiments with a method that we used in [16]. We will then briefly mention somewhat on different color space representations, thereafter we will show some experiments with our real-time implementation. The experiment section is finished with a description of performance figures achieved.

2 Computational Approach

Since our objective is to design a real-time algorithm integrating several modalities or features, the included components are of quite simple nature.

By experimenting we have found 2-d histogramming of different features to be a reasonable trade off between calculation accuracy and speed.

2.1 2-D Histogramming

Having 2 independent dense feature domains it is possible to produce a 2-D histogram. The feature domains could be e.g. a dense depth map and a dense 1-D motion map, as in [16]. If also confidence maps are available a weighted 2-D histogram can be produced. In most of the experiments here we have used as the 2 feature domains the 2 color components obtained by projecting the RGB color cube onto a plane, but in Fig. 3 we have an example of using depth and motion as the two feature domains. We will return to the color space representation in Section 3.

118

To efficiently exploit the computational resources it is important how to chose ranges for the histogram carefully. In the discrete case (which we have) both the ranges and sampling in the two dimensions affect the appearance of the histogram. This topic is not further addressed here but it is important to note that. We have chosen ranges adaptively based on statistics of the feature domains. For our color experiments we have used maximum and minimum values. In the depth-motion example shown in Fig. 3 we also used min and max values, but earlier performed experiments gave at hand that some method more robust to outliers should be used. In the case where computed feature domains have outliers or an uneven distribution other methods of choosing ranges must be considered.

Analyzing the Histogram. Peaks in the histogram reflect areas in the image which have approximately constant values in both feature domains at the same time. To decide which peaks are significant one needs to account for noise and quantization effects. This can be done by using a multiscale approach. Lindeberg [11] has proposed a method to handle this problem based on "The Scale-Space Primal Sketch", (see also [13]). 2-D histograms at different scales can be seen in Fig. 1. Note that the numbers of peaks is decreasing with coarser scale.

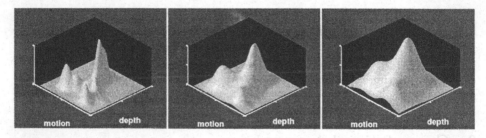

Fig. 1. Example of a 2-D histogram with different amounts of blurring. Coarser scale rightwards.

This method is a multiscale method which detect peaks at different scales. The detected peaks are given a significance measure and the peaks are also tracked over scale. The method has been considered as too computationally demanding experimentally, so a simplified peak-detection scheme has been developed.

The Simplified Peak Detection Scheme. First the histogram is blurred some predefined amount. We have chosen to blur until a predefined number of peaks remain (usually arbitrarily chosen to 8 peaks, during experiments, we know that 8 is significantly greater than the number of objects we can handle in the end). The 2-D histogram is sliced up giving a binary image in each slice. For each connected region in a slice, the bounding box is computed, see Fig. 2 for a graphical illustrating example.

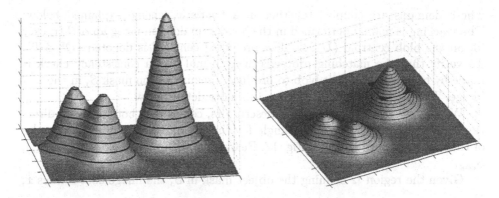

Fig. 2. Leftmost image shows level contours of a 2-D histogram to illustrate how the histogram is sliced up. Rightmost image illustrates the bounding box approximation for the same histogram seen from a slightly different angle. The black rectangle is the bounding-box approximation of one of the (in this particular example elliptical) slices of the highest peak.

The bounding boxes are matched from the bottom of the histogram and upwards to create blobs (which will be the simplified correspondence to the scale space blobs) by the following scheme: If a bounding box from a level below overlaps with a bounding box on the next level a match has been found. This matching gives us three categories of matches:

1. No match.
2. A single match
3. Multiple matches

When case 1 or 3 occurs, the blob is terminated as "no match" or "split". When a split occurs new blobs are created, starting on the level where the split occurred. After this matching we have a number of blobs which are represented by:

1. Their bounding box from their start level (bottom level).
2. Their start and end level.

The blobs can simply and fast be backprojected to the original image, see Figs. 3 and 5 for examples.

2.2 Tracking the Histogram Blob Over Time

After the blobs has been detected we track them over time in two different domains:

- In the histogram domain.
- In the backprojected 2-D image.

These domains are coupled together in a heuristic scheme explained below: The tracking is mainly performed in the histogram domain using an α-β-tracker [6] on the blob centroid $(\bar{D}, \bar{M})$. The predicted centroid is denoted $(\bar{D}^{\mathrm{P}}, \bar{M}^{\mathrm{P}})$. To verify that the matching proceeds in a normal way a consistency check is made by backprojecting the blob to produce a segmentation mask S, in the 2-D image. The matching will be explained in more detail below.

We compute an ellipse with the descriptors, centroid in both x and y direction, major axis, minor axis and angle for the backprojection mask. Examples of these ellipses can be seen in Fig. 17. Below denoted for S: $S_{\bar{x}}$, $S_{\bar{y}}$, $S_{\min}$, S_{maj}, S_{ang}.

Given the region Ω defining the object mask in S, the image coordinates x, y:

$$\sigma = \sum_{(x,y) \in \Omega} 1, \quad S_{\bar{x}} = \bar{x} = \frac{1}{\sigma} \sum_{(x,y) \in \Omega} x, \quad S_{\bar{y}} = \bar{y} = \frac{1}{\sigma} \sum_{(x,y) \in \Omega} y$$

$$\mu_{\mathrm{xx}} = \frac{1}{\sigma} \sum_{(x,y) \in \Omega} (x - \bar{x})^2, \quad \mu_{\mathrm{yy}} = \frac{1}{\sigma} \sum_{(x,y) \in \Omega} (y - \bar{y})^2$$

$$\mu_{\mathrm{xy}} = \frac{1}{\sigma} \sum_{(x,y) \in \Omega} (x - \bar{x})(y - \bar{y})$$

$$S_{\mathrm{maj}} = \left[8 \left(\mu_{\mathrm{xx}} + \mu_{\mathrm{yy}} + [(\mu_{\mathrm{xx}} - \mu_{\mathrm{yy}})^2 + 4\mu_{\mathrm{xy}}^2]^{1/2} \right) \right]^{1/2}$$

$$S_{\mathrm{min}} = \left[8 \left(\mu_{\mathrm{xx}} + \mu_{\mathrm{yy}} - [(\mu_{\mathrm{xx}} - \mu_{\mathrm{yy}})^2 + 4\mu_{\mathrm{xy}}^2]^{1/2} \right) \right]^{1/2}$$

$$S_{\mathrm{ang}} = \tan^{-1} \left[\frac{-2\mu_{\mathrm{xy}}}{\mu_{\mathrm{xx}} - \mu_{\mathrm{yy}} + [(\mu_{\mathrm{xx}} - \mu_{\mathrm{yy}})^2 + 4\mu_{\mathrm{xy}}^2]^{1/2}} \right]$$

Matching The matching consists of two steps. In both steps we compute a weighted distance measure, but with different weights.

On all of the descriptors mentioned above we apply α-β-trackers. The predicted values are denoted with a superscript P, so the predicted value of S_{maj} is S_{maj}^{p}, and so on.

The distance measure looks as follows:

$$w_1(\bar{M} - \bar{M}^{\mathrm{P}})^2 + w_2(\bar{D} - \bar{D}^{\mathrm{P}})^2 + w_3(S_{\bar{x}} - S_{\bar{x}}^{\mathrm{p}})^2 + w_4(S_{\bar{y}} - S_{\bar{y}}^{\mathrm{p}})^2 +$$
$$w_5(S_{\mathrm{maj}} - S_{\mathrm{maj}}^{\mathrm{p}})^2 + w_6(S_{\min} - S_{\min}^{\mathrm{p}})^2 + w_7(S_{\mathrm{ang}} - S_{\mathrm{ang}}^{\mathrm{p}})^2$$

In the first step w_1 and w_2 are much higher than the rest of the weights, thus raising the significance of a good histogram blob match. All matching candidates with a distance over a threshold are disregarded in this step. In the second matching/verification step the significance of the segmentation mask descriptors are raised, and if below a threshold, the candidate with shortest distance is chosen as a match. If no distance is below the threshold the tracked object is considered lost, the main hypothesis is that the object has been occluded, and a predict mode is entered, where the histogram blob centroid is remembered. In this mode the histogram blob centroid is used for matching, if a blob with a centroid within a small tolerance compared to the remembered centroid, appears in view, this is considered to be the object which now have entered the field of view again. If the blob detection step fails for occasional frames, this will be handled by the α-β-tracker.

This tracking approach is very similar to the one used in [16] where we performed tracking over long sequences using a depth-motion histogram. Here we have applied our tracking method to the 2-D color histogram where we can track colored objects with a typical frame-rate of 10-18 Hz over long sequences. See experiments 1-4 for results.

2.3 Comparison Between the Scale-Space Method and the New Method

Results from our new method can be seen in Fig. 3. Compare with the results using the method by Lindeberg [11] which can be seen in Fig. 4. For both methods we used a histogram of the size 75×75. For the scale-space method we used 20 different scales for the peak detection. The processing time is typically 3 seconds on a SparcStation Ultra, excluding the backprojection. For our new method we have used 20 slices of the histogram and we get a processing time including backprojection of 0.1 s using a Silicon Graphics Octane workstation (for hardware details, see Section 4). As can be seen in the Figures, the new method gives a somewhat less accurate result in this example, but the speedup is so significant that the method can be used in real-time applications.

In Figs. 5 and 6 similar results but for a 2-D color histogram can be seen. The color space used will be explained in the following section.

3 Color Space Representation

Extensive reviews/discussions of different 3-dimensional color spaces can be found in [18, 20]. Perez and Koch [20] argue that hue is a high level variable due to electophysciological experiments performed on monkeys. They also state that the motivation for using hue in image segmentation is that material boundaries correlate more strongly with hue than intensity differences. They state that segmentation in the 1-D hue space is computationally less expensive than in the 3-D RGB space. Of course this is true, but clearly some information is lost by not taking the saturation into account.

By projecting on a plane perpendicularly to the diagonal of the RGB color cube the intensity dependency can be cancelled. This has been practiced by among others Shuster [21], and we will use that idea.

In [8] it is mentioned that the two most important factors affecting the efficiency of any algorithm using color space processing are the *color space* chosen and its *quantization*. They state that they have tested a number of different

(a) The found blobs from analysis of a 2-D histogram of horizontal motion and binocular depth disparities. In the sliced histogram shown, motion is in the horizontal direction and relative depth in the vertical direction. The bounding box blob approximation that we use is circumferring the peaks in the histogram. Shown in grey is the histogram slice at the start level of each blob.

(b) Back-projection of the the vertical dimension of the peaks shown in Fig. 3(a).

(c) Back-projection of the the horizontal dimension of the peaks shown in Fig. 3(a).

(d) The final backprojection. The backprojections shown in Figs. 3(b) and 3(c) combined with logical AND.

Fig. 3. Figure-ground segmentation masks from our method. Each column corresponds to one segmentation.

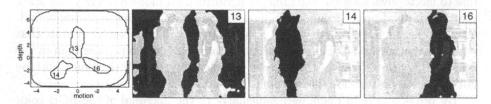

Fig. 4. Results from [16], where a method using much heavier calculations was used. Labels in upper right corners of figures refers to blob labels in the leftmost frame. Compare with Fig. 3.

(a) The found blobs from analysis of the 2D colorspace for the image in Fig. 18(e). The bounding box blob approximation that we use is circumferring the peaks in the histogram. Shown in grey is the sliced histogram at the start level of each blob.

(b) Back-projection of the the vertical dimension of the peaks shown in Fig. 5(a).

(c) Back-projection of the the horizontal dimension of the peaks shown in Fig. 5(a).

(d) The final backprojection. The backprojections shown in Figs. 5(b) and 5(c) combined with logical AND.

Fig. 5. Color segmentation masks from our method. Each column corresponds to one segmentation. (See Fig. 18(e) for original color image used.)

Fig. 6. Color segmentation using the scale-space primal sketch for blob detection in histogram over twodimensional chroma information in the CIE$u^* v^*$ color space [3]. Results from [11, 12]. (See Fig. 18(e) for original color image used.)

spaces and found that using the RGB space is "quite good". They also found that more buckets are needed in the case of using a 2-D color space compared to a 3-D space for equivalent results.

3.1 A Comparison Between Segmenting Different Color Spaces

In Fig. 7 is shown clustering result using the k-means algorithm [9], for clustering the colors in the 3-D RGB-space and also for a reduced 2-D space [21]. As seen in Fig. 7 the much more computationally efficient 2-D color space seems to perform at least as good as the RGB-space in this test example.

By reducing the dimensionality of the color segmentation from 3 dimensions to 2 dimensions a substantial speedup for the clustering can be achieved.

(a) Segmentation using 2-D color space [21].

(b) Segmentation using 3-D RGB color-space.

Fig. 7. Color segmentation using k-means clustering. In leftmost column the number of clusters is 2. Then the number of clusters are incremented by 1 for each column. Each cluster is visualized by a distinct gray-scale. See Fig. 18(e) for the color image used.

4 Experimental Setup

All algorithms were implemented in C++[1]. The hardware used was a Silicon Graphics Octane[2] with 1 Gbyte RAM and a SSI graphics board. The camera used was a CCD camera[3]. The analog RGB-signal from the camera was converted to a digital CCIR601 signal by a analog component to serial digital converter[4].

---

[1] We used the Silicon Graphics mipspro 7.20 compiler.

[2] The machine has two 195 MHZ IP30 Processors, CPU: MIPS R10000, but we only use one of the processors.

[3] A Hitachi KP-D50 1 chip color camera equipped with a Cosmicar Television Lens 6 mm 1:1.2 lens.

[4] An Ensemble Designs, Serial Box III.

Our system has a capacity to operate continuously on images coming direct from the camera, but the experimental results presented here come from prerecorded sequences, since, at present, this is the only way to store image-result from experiments on disk. The prerecorded sequences were grabbed using the program "mediarecorder" provided by SGI. Mediarecorder was set to grab images with a resolution of a quarter of a frame, which gives us images the size 320×243. The images were further cropped to a size of 176×112 pixels.

5 Experiments

In this section we present a few experiments. In Experiment 1 we only use color segmentation. In Experiment 2–4 we initialize the segmentation by a motion detection step. Thereafter an initial feature selection step decides on which cue to maintain.

5.1 Color Segmentation

Experiment 1. This experiment illustrates how a colored object is segmented out and tracked over time. When the object dissapears out of view the system remembers the centroid of the color space blob and is waiting until an object with a color blob centroid within a small error tolerance appear in view. The sequence contains of 200 images. In the images shown here the sampling is every 10th frame. The original sequence can be seen in Figs. 8 and 18(a). In Fig. 9 segmentation results can be seen. The segmentation mask in black is overlayed on the original image. When tracking fails the original image is shown. This happens in frame 110–140 since the object dissapears out of view. When the object appears in view again in frame 150 the tracking catches up. During this sequence all different colored objects found, are matched and tracked over time. When we start tracking one particular object we have a region of interest around the object, this facilitates the tracking, since the peak-detection is easier when only a narrow area around the actual object has to be analyzed, example of how this looks can be seen in Fig. 17(a). An example of segmentation with the whole image as region of interest can be seen in Fig. 17(b).

5.2 Combining Motion Cues, Color and Texture Segmentation

These experiments illustrates how a motion disparity cue is used to initialize a figure ground segmentation based on different features, either color or two different "textures". We have not managed to make any real-time texture segmentation using conventional texture segmentation algorithms, so we have taken the approach to simply use high magnitude of the x and y-gradients as two different and discriminating "textures". Having altogether three algorithms to choose from (color, "x-texture", "y-texture"), we can sketch on a method to choose which single one out of the three algorithms to apply.

Fig. 8. Experiment 1. Original sequence in grayscale. (See Fig. 18(a) for color images.) Numbers in the corners of images represent frame numbers in the sequence.

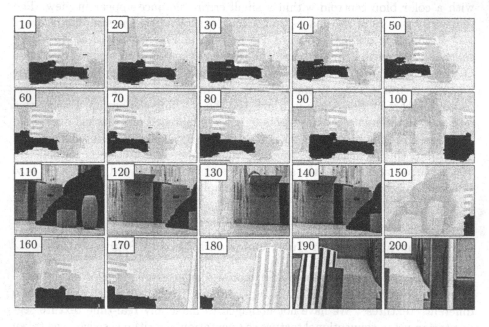

Fig. 9. Color segmentation mask from Experiment 1.

We threshold the x and y-derivatives to get the two different textures. A textured area is considered found if it is connected and has an area larger than a threshold. We only detect the largest area for the respective derivative in each image.

In all of the experiments the scene is static and the camera is translating and rotating. An object is singled out from the background due to motion parallax. We here use a simple motion detection algorithm based on an affine fit of the image from frame to frame, see e.g. [10, 17, 4]. When the affine fit has been performed a residual is produced. Next the residual image is thresholded. In the thresholded image objects with a motion not consistent with the dominat motion in the image will appear. This is a rather coarse approximation with the resolution we have used: 44×28 pixels.

In Fig. 16 can be seen the detected motion which is used to initialize the segmentation. A centroid for the area with motion is computed. The found area is further investigated. In the figure the centroid is marked with a brighter rectangle. We initilize the segmentation maintenance by chosing the feature with the shortest distance between the motion detection centroid, and

1. Color mask centroids.
2. An eventually found x-derivative mask centroid.
3. An eventually found y-derivative mask centroid.

The initially chosen feature is then maintained over time.

Experiment 2. A green toy-block has been placed in the foreground to create motion parallax when the camera is moving sidewards. In Fig. 16(a) the motion detection can be seen.

In Fig. 11 can be seen how the segmentation maintenace goes to the color tracking state. The object dissapears out of view in frame 60, in frame 70 it appears again and the tracking catches up in frame 80. One reason why the tracking does not catch up already in frame 70 can be that the background has such a distribution of colors that the object needs to occupy a large portion of the image to produce a peak that is detectable in the histogram.

Experiment 3. A vertically striped paper-sheet has been placed in the foreground to create motion parallax when the camera is moving sidewards.

In Fig. 13 the segmentation maintenace goes to the x-derivative tracking state. As can be seen in Fig. 16(b) the motion detection mask looks very good, this is not surprising since the motion in the image is basically in the horizontal direction and the motion detection is based on residuals for an affine fit between 2 consecutive images. The vertically striped object will generate high residuals.

Experiment 4. A horizontally striped paper-sheet has been placed in the foreground to create motion parallax when the camera is moving sidewards.

In Fig. 15 the segmentation maintenace goes to the y-derivative tracking state. As can be seen in Fig. 16(b) the motion detection mask is quite poor which is not surprising c.f. disussion above.

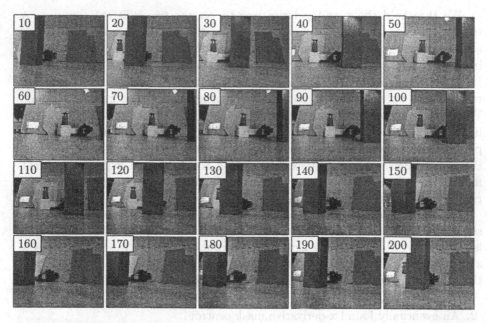

Fig. 10. Experiment 2. Original sequence in grayscale. (See Fig. 18(b) for a color image.) Numbers in the corners of images represent frame numbers in the sequence.

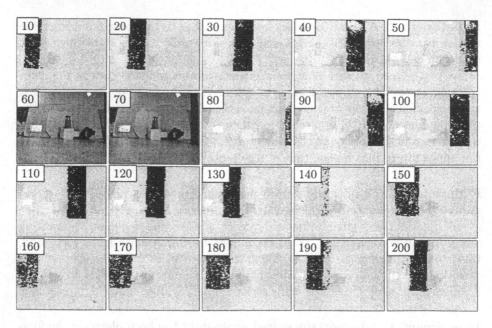

Fig. 11. Color segmentation mask from Experiment 2.

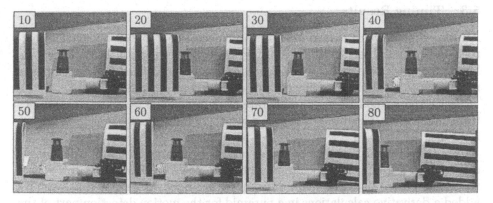

Fig. 12. Experiment 3. Original sequence in grayscale. (See Fig. 18(c) for a color image.) Numbers in the corners of images represent frame numbers in the sequence.

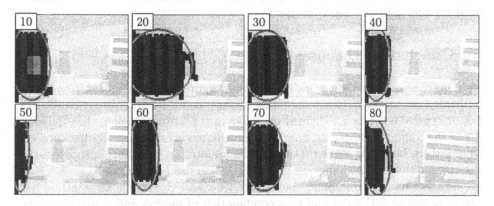

Fig. 13. "texture" segmentation mask from Experiment 3. In the first figure the motion detection centroid is marked with a brighter rectangle.

Fig. 14. Experiment 4. Original sequence in grayscale. (See Fig. 18(d) for a color image.) Numbers in the corners of images represent frame numbers in the sequence.

5.3 Timing Results

All experiments were performed with an image size 176×112 pixels. The histogram had a size of 50×50. The histogram was sliced in 15 levels. After the histogram was calculated it was smoothend until a predefined number of peaks remained. In all of the experiments this number was set to 8.

For Experiment 1 we get a frame-rate of 18 frames/s if we grab images direct from the camera. The frame-rate goes down to 15 frames/s if we read the images from disc.

For Experiment 2 we get a frame-rate of 9.5 frames/s if we grab images direct from the camera. The frame-rate goes down to 8 frames/s if we read the images from disc. The main difference from Experiment 1 is that we have added a derivative calculations in a pyramid for the motion detection part of the algorithm.

For Experiment 3 and Experiment 4 we get a frame-rate of 8 frames/s if we grab images direct from the camera. The frame-rate goes down to 7 frames/s if we read the images from disc. The difference from Experiment 2 is that we have added thresholding and morphology operations on the x and y derivative images used for the "texture" segmentation.

6 Concluding Discussion

As a part of our ongoing work on dynamic figure-ground segmentation using multiple cues we have considered a fast method based on 2-D histogramming in feature space. Objects are defined by peaks in the feature domain that indicate areas that differ significantly from the immediate surroundings. By backprojection and tracking, the segmentation can be maintained over time, also when the visibility of the object changes. The segmentation can be maintained both for an object that changes from being moving to static and vice versa. The method has been applied to 2-D color and to a combination of motion and disparities. The aim is to incorporate this in a general framework for figure-ground segmentation based on multiple cues and coupled to attentional and fixational processes, see [15].

7 Open Issues

An interesting issue is how the feedback for a system should be designed. There are various levels of feedback in a system, and how these feedback loops should be designed is an open question. E.g. should disparity fields be fed back from the last frame when computing a new disparity field? The answer is probably yes, but if the disparity field is totally wrong, subsequent computations will be corrupted. The right amount of feedback should be used, not more than that the system manages to recover if calculations are getting wrong. Such problems can be coped with to some extent by having a layered architecture like the one proposed in [22].

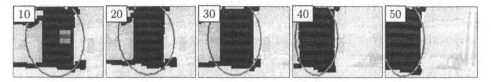

Fig. 15. "texture" segmentation mask from Experiment 4. In the first figure the motion detection centroid is marked with a brighter rectangle. (See Fig. 18(d) for color image from the sequence shown in Fig. 14.)

(a) From Experiment 2.   (b) From Experiment 3.   (c) From Experiment 4.

Fig. 16. Motion detection masks. The centroid is marked with a grey rectangle. (See Figs. 10, 12 and 14 for original sequences.)

(a) Example of   (b) Example of having the whole image as region of interest.
region of inter-
est.

Fig. 17. Color segmentation masks with fitted ellipses overlayed in white. Each segmentation mask is visualized with a distinct grayscale. (See Fig. 10 for original sequence.) Numbers in the corners of images represent frame numbers in the sequence.

Temporal aspect of the algorithms could be further investigated. Today most motion-based algorithms, including ours, only use a few frames for computing temporal derivatives. It would also be interesting to include texture based algorithms for segmentation, but so far we have not managed to get a real-time performance on such approaches. This holds also for shape cues in general.

An interesting topic to further investigate is how many different features that should be used in conjunction. Should features be integrated in parallel or in series. The answer is probably both. But much work remains to be done in this area, especially when it comes to having complete systems operating in interaction with the environment, since this puts much harder restrictions both concerning the computational cost and the general robustness of the included algorithms.

Finally it is still an open question how one should evaluate the efficiency of algorithms. How should we know how much time to spend on certain tasks? Should we chose high frame-rate or high resolution? These questions can probably be answered only by implementing complete systems where it is easier to judge the overall performance instead of looking on included algorithms in part. After all, the interesting question is the performance of a *complete system*.

Acknowledgement

We would like to thank Mårten Björkman for programming efforts and Tony Lindeberg for providing us with the experimental results in Fig. 6. The support from The Swedish Research Council for Engineering Science (TFR) is gratefully acknowledged.

References

1. Y. Altunbasak, P. E. Eren, and A. M. Tekapl. Region-based parametric motion segmentation using color information. *Graphical Models and Image Processing*, 60(1):13–23, January 1998.
2. S. Belongie, C. Carson, H. Greenspan, and J. Malik. Color- and texture-based image segmentation using the expectation-maximization algorithm and its application to content-based image retrieval. In *Proc. 6th International Conference on Computer Vision*, pages 675–682, Bombay, India, January 1998. IEEE Computer Society Press.
3. F. Billmeyer and M. Saltzman. *Principles of Colour Technology*. John Wiley and Sons, 1982.
4. M. Black and A. D. Jepson. Estimating optical flow in segmented images using variable-order parametric models with local deformations. *IEEE Trans. Pattern Analysis and Machine Intell.*, 18(10):972–986, 1996.
5. T. Darrel, G. Gordon, J. Woodfill, H. Baker, and M. Harville. Robust, real-time people tracking in open environments using integrated stereo, color, and face detection. In *IEEE Workshop on Visual Surveillance*, pages 26–32, Bombay, India, January 1998. IEEE Computer Society Press.

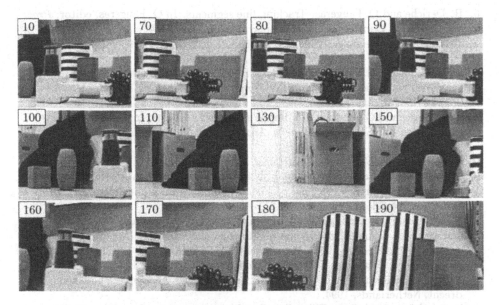

(a) Excerpt from sequence in Experiment 1. (Observe the odd sampling.)

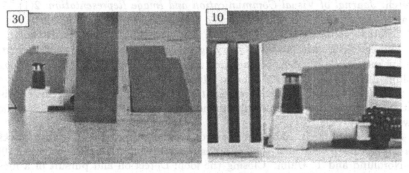

(b) One frame from Experiment 2.   (c) One frame from Experiment 3.

(d) One frame from Experiment 4.   (e) Fruit image.

Fig. 18. Color images. Numbers in upper left corners are the frame-numbers in a sequence.

6. R. Deriche and O. Faugeras. Tracking line segments. In O. Faugeras, editor, *Proc. 1st European Conference on Computer Vision*, volume 427 of *Lecture Notes in Computer Science*, pages 259–268, Antibes, France, April 1990. Springer Verlag, Berlin.

7. J. O. Eklundh, H. Yamamoto, and A. Rosenfeld. A relaxation method for multispectral pixel classification. *IEEE Trans. Pattern Analysis and Machine Intell.*, 2(1):72–75, January 1980.

8. F. Ennesser and G. Medioni. Finding Waldoo, or focus of attention using local color information. *IEEE Trans. Pattern Analysis and Machine Intell.*, 17(8):805–809, August 1995.

9. J. A. Hartigan. *Clustering Algorithms*. John Wiley and Sons, New York, 1975.

10. M. Irani and S. Peleg. Motion analysis for image enhancement: Resolution, occlusion, and transparency. *Journal of Visual Communication and Image Representation*, 4(4):324–335, December 1993.

11. T. Lindeberg. Detecting salient blob-like image structures and their scales with a scale-space primal sketch: A method for focus-of-attention. *Int. J. of Computer Vision*, 11(3):283–318, 1993. Also ISRN KTH/NA/P--93/33--SE.

12. T. Lindeberg. *Scale-Space Theory in Computer Vision*. The Kluwer International Series in Engineering and Computer Science. Kluwer Academic Publishers, Dordrecht, Netherlands, 1994.

13. T. Lindeberg and J.-O. Eklundh. On the computation of a scale-space primal sketch. *Journal of Visual Communication and Image Representation*, 2(1):55–78, March 1991.

14. W. Niblack, R. Barber, W. Equitz, M. Flickner, D. Glasman, D. Petkovic, and P. Yanker. The qbic project: Querying image by content using color, texture, and shape. In *Proc. SPIE: Storage and Retrieval for Image and Video Databases*, volume 1908, pages 173–187, February 1993.

15. P. Nordlund. *Figure-Ground Segmentation Using Multiple Cues*. Ph. D. dissertation, Dept. of Numerical Analysis and Computing Science, KTH, Stockholm, Sweden, May 1998.

16. P. Nordlund and J.-O. Eklundh. Towards a seeing agent. In *First Int. Workshop on Cooperative Distributed Vision*, pages 93–123, Kyoto, Japan, November 1997.

17. P. Nordlund and T. Uhlin. Closing the loop: Detection and pursuit of a moving object by a moving observer. *Image and Vision Computing*, 14(4):265–275, May 1996.

18. C. L. Novak and S. A. Shafer. Color vision. *Encyclopedia of Artificial Intelligence*, pages 192–202, 1992.

19. R. Ohlander. *Analysis of Natural Scenes*. PhD thesis, Carnigie-Mellon Univ. Pittsburgh, PA, December 1976.

20. F. Perez and C. Koch. Towards color image segmentation in analog VLSI: Algorithm and hardware. *Int. J. of Computer Vision*, 12(1):17–42, 1994.

21. R. Shuster. Color object tracking with adaptive modeling. In *Proc. Worshop on Visual Behaviors*, pages 91–96, Seattle, Washington, June 1994.

22. K. Toyama and G. D. Hager. Incremental focus of attention for robust visual tracking. In *Proc. IEEE Comp. Soc. Conf. on Computer Vision and Pattern Recognition, 1996*, pages 189–195, San Francisco, California, June 1996. IEEE Computer Society Press.

23. Y. Yakimovsky. On the recognition of complex structures: Computer software using artificial intelligence applied to pattern recognition. In *Proc. 2nd International Joint Conference on Pattern Recognition*, pages 345–353, Copenhagen, Denmark, August 1974.

An Integrating Framework for Robust Real-Time 3D Object Tracking

Markus Vincze, Minu Ayromlou, Wilfried Kubinger

Institute of Flexible Automation, Vienna University of Technology,
Gusshausstr. 27-29/361, 1040 Vienna, Austria,
{vm, ma, wk}@flexaut.tuwien.ac.at,
WWW home page: http://infa.tuwien.ac.at

Abstract. Vision-based control of motion can only be feasible if vision provides reliable control signals and when full system integration is achieved. In this paper we will address these two issues. A modular system architecture is built up around the basic primitives of object tracking, the features of the object. The initialisation is partly automated by using search functions to describe the task. The features found and tracked in the image are contained in a wire-frame model of the object as seen in the image. This model is used for feature tracking and continuous pose determination. Of particular need is a method of robust feature tracking. This is achieved using EPIC, a method of Edge-Projected Integration of Cues. A demonstration shows how the robot follows the pose of an object moved by hand in common room lighting at frame rate using a PC.

1 Introduction

In every day life humans keep tracking a multitude of objects to fulfil a series of tasks. Examples are, orientation in the environment, recognising persons and initiating contact, or locating, recognising, and handling objects. In all these cases the human eyes execute the needed gathering of information for a task in a time span, such that processes like walking, talking, and grasping are not limited by the performance of the perceptual system. Technical systems refer to this capability of operating without limiting system performance as *real-time*. It is an essential quality if a vision, robotic, or integrated system operate successfully in industrial or service applications.

A considerable number of works present systems to control a mechanism via visual input (e.g., see the Workshops at IROS'97, ICRA'98, and ECCV'98 on visual servoing). Analysing the present state-of-the-art, two major roadblocks are commonly identified [2].

1. The *integration of system components* is often neglected. However, integration of mechanism, control, and visual sensing and processing is essential to achieve good performance of the system and to take the step towards commercial applications.

2. Of all components assembled in a vision-based control system, the versatility of the vision system seems to be a limiting factor. In particular, the *robustness of the visual input* is the weakest element. A strong indication is the observation that applications are commonly restricted to special environments (results for autonomous car driving are impressive [6], however visual processing is tailored to the specific task) or prepared objects (markers, high contrast to background, manual initialisation).

The authors take the view that there is a need to build a robust, integrating system to track objects in three-dimensional space in real-time. This paper presents steps into this direction. A vision system is outlined which integrates

- a framework of image search functions for easy description of the task,
- automated initialisation procedures,
- real-time object tracking,
- robust feature tracking using edge projected integration of cues (EPIC),
- the ability to recover after loss of features or object, and
- modules to provide an extendible system architecture.

The advance of this work is seen primarily in two aspects. The first aspect is to build a visual system integrating all the functions needed to deliver control signals for steering a mechanism. The second advance is the robustness obtained in feature tracking. This paper will therefore focus on these two aspects.

1.1 Related Work

The integration of system components from vision over control to the mechanisms (robot, platform, active head) has been developed in the course of the project Vision as Process [5]. As one experience of this project Christensen and Vieville postulated a lack of standard hardware, software, and general methods for cue integration, recognition and description to integrate components of vision-based control systems [2]. Other work to obtain integrated visual servoing system is summarised in [12] and workshop notes of IROS'97, ICRA'98, and ECCV'98.

Robustness has been approached in recent years by adding some form of redundancy to the vision system (e.g., using multiple cameras, images, resolutions, models, and features, or temporal constraints [3, 14, 10]). Filtering and prediction are the common methods to improve robustness [28]. However, if the underlying visual process is not reliable, quality of prediction is limited. One method of improving robustness of 3D object tracking is to use a model [20, 15, 11, 25]. The main problem is changing background and high computational demands. For example, a space application where the object consists of parts of different surface characteristics, edge detection is more reliable but still requires dedicated hardware to run at frame rate [30].

In humans the integration of cues has been found as a likely source of the excellent ability to cope with changing conditions ([18], INSIGHT II project of the EC P-6019). Active vision research was the first to utilise cue integration. In

[16] focus is adjusted using three different cues from one image. Other early vision modules such (depth, motion, texture, and color) are coupled to the detection of sharp changes in brightness using an energy function in [9]. Regarding systems that detect objects and features, present state of the art in integration handles two cues to enhance robustness, such as edge and motion [23], edge and colour ([24] though not in real-time), or colour and image position [29]. Integration can be also used to enhance functional capabilities, as one cue (optical flow) is used for fast motion detection, and edge and corner detection are used for pose determination [25, 19]. Colour provides another series of features that can be exploited. Detection of specular points and perfect segmentation is presented in [1] though requires enormous computing power. However, the robustness of motion estimation [21] could be improved using colour information at reasonable processing times.

A different approach to attacking robustness is taken in [26]. It is the first work to analyse robust visual behaviour and the issue of initial robustness versus recovery after failure. Robustness is added by introducing a framework that can switch between single cue extraction methods. Several cue extraction modules [13] are used as selectors (to select a region of interest) and trackers (to keep tracking the object found) in a multilayer network. The layers of the network correspond to increasing accuracy. Top level trackers then lock on only to the target object, e.g., using SSD-tracking. If tracking at one level fails, less accurate levels are evoked to re-find the target. This post-failure recovery adds robustness to tracking. However, uninterrupted operation prefers to increase the initial robustness of tracking such that failure can be avoided from the beginning.

The review illustrates that methods for robust visual processing, performance evaluation, and general applicability are missing. Robustness is insofar a difficult problem, as robustness is hard to define and therefore evades a standardised characterisation. Although the lack of these methods has been postulated, research is still limited. A possible cause is the difficulty to evaluate robustness and hence project progress.

The remainder of the paper is organised as follows. The next section describes the modules integrated in our approach. Formulating a task description (section 3), tracking a wire-frame (section 4), and using EPIC for robust feature detection (section 5) are outlined in more detail. Details of the operation of the approach gives Section 6 with an experiment of following the motion of a cube in 6 degrees of freedom. The paper is concluded with a critique of the approach and an outlook to future work.

2   System for 3D Object Tracking

The goal of this work is to track an object in three-dimensional space. Using the results of tracking a control signal is derived to steer a mechanism, for example, to navigate a mobile platform or to handle parts with a robot arm. The tracking process itself operates on a sequence of images. In each image tracking is the process of re-finding the object. Commonly the object can be separated into a series of features, which are re-found at each tracking cycle. As a consequence, the *features* of the object constitute the central component of our system architecture for 3D object tracking (see Fig. 1).

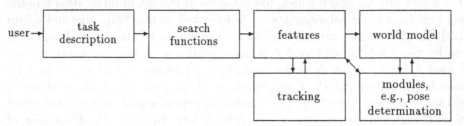

Fig. 1. Block diagram of principle strategy.

One goal of the tracking system is to continuously track the pose (position and orientation) of the object. Therefore the features tracked are selected accordingly. In our present implementation the object features which are tracked include lines, corners, and circles.

All features are tracked separately by the *tracking* module. The particular tracking method depends on the feature. The robust line tracking method is outlined in section 5. Corners are tracked as intersections of lines. Circles use a similar algorithm to find edgels as line tracking and additionally utilise the geometric constraint that edgels need to form an ellipse.

Tracking is the vital component of a system for vision-based control of motion. Fundamental investigations of the dynamic performance of such a system lead to the requirement for tracking to operate at the highest possible cycle rate of the control system [17]. Using common CCD-cameras cycle rate is restricted by image acquisition to *field rate* ($50Hz$). To obtain field rate of the visual process, a windowing technique has been adopted. This is founded in the following considerations: if tracking of a feature/object can be obtained on-the-fly [4] (that is, at the same time with image acquisition and without causing any further delay), then the entire image can be used. As this is not possible for any reasonable processing method, for example the method of robust feature tracking presented in section 5, the window size is adjusted to obtain field rate of the processing step.

A critical issue of a continuously operating system is the *initialisation*. Based on the feature-centred approach, high level *search functions* have been implemented that allow the user to specify a task in the form of a simple *task description*. The task description uses the search functions to incorporate task and object knowledge (section 3). To provide a general purpose visual tool kit, the description is a simple interface using object appearance and/or geometry. This methodology separates the details of image search from the object description. Given a description, the objective is to search the image for objects or targets fitting that description while retaining (through tracking) current information.

The *world model* keeps track of the state of the features. The model is image-based and therefore stores the topological model of the object found in the image. Using line, corner, and circle features the model is a wire-frame model. The advantage is the direct relation of the world model to a database of object models, which is commonly available from CAD-systems in wire-frame format. How features are tracked using the wire-frame model is described in section 4.

The system architecture of Fig. 1 is modular. The goal is to render adding new *modules* as easy as possible. For example, pose determination is linked to the world model and the features. Similarly, prediction can update features and/or world model data. Pose determination can be further exploited to set preferences for feature search. For example, pose determination is more reliable if a larger number of intersecting lines or circles is available. Therefore the pose determination module can be used to bias the search towards features which are best suited.

As both feature tracking and feature search (driven by the visual search functions and the need of pose determination) operate in parallel, feature dependencies and new search results are constantly incorporated into the model while targets are in motion.

The next three sections present in detail the use of the task description (3), formalise the tracking of a wire-frame model (4), and present the approach to robust line tracking (5).

3   Search Functions as Primitives of Visual Descriptions

The heart of the initialisation procedure is an object description based on a set of search functions. These functions can be thought of as a high-level description language for search. The description also contains a goal, e.g., pose determination or object identification, which can direct and terminate the search. Executing the search program generates features which are entered into the world model.

The search language primitives are a small set of functions operating on images. Table 1 gives a list of basic functions. These functions operate at different levels of resolution, from coarse level "pop-out" operators [13] to high resolution edge detection.

For example, a task specification may be to determine the pose of a stapler with a red bar on top. One possible description of the task is as follows. The fact that a red item is searched for is used as a clue to quickly find a candidate feature.

```
find_region(red)
find_at_border_of_region(line(mode right), direction: towards left)
repeat
    find_end_of_line(line_itself)
    if (end_of_line found)
        find_lines_at_end_of_line(line_itself, new_neighbor_lines)
until (structure_for_pose_found)
determine_pose
```

Fig. 2 illustrates the search pattern. Five possible lines are found. Using mode (see 5) to validate the lines, only one line remains, the front top line. The line

generic search strategies
find_line(line_type or attributes)
find_region(region_type)

search strategies relative to lines
find_end_of_line(line_itself)
find_lines_at_end_of_line(line_end, line_types)
find_along_line(line_itself, direction)
find_in_direction_from_line(line_itself, direction)

search strategies relative to regions
find_within_region(line_type or region_type)
find_at_border_of_region(line_type or region_type)
find_around_region(line_type or region_type)
find_in_direction_from_region(line_type, direction)

Table 1. A set of basic search functions for image exploration.

is added to the wire-frame model. As tracking proceeds the four lines of the top surface are found (at cycle 16), though not closed yet. At cycle 19 the front right corner is found. One of the found lines is the elongation of one of the top surface lines and the rectangle is finally closed. The vertical line is the second line of the side surface (Fig. 2).

4 Tracking a Wire-Frame Structure

During the execution of the task description the wire-frame model containing the features of the object found in the image is built up. An example of a wire-frame model is given in Fig. 3. The right part of this figure shows the graph structure corresponding to a side surface of a cube shaped object. The search functions use this graph-based model as database, and for adding or deleting lines and corners.

Tracking the wire-frame model found in the image means the updating of all features and feature relations at each cycle. In detail, tracking proceeds as follows. The wire-frame contains a set of N lines $\mathcal{L}$ and a set of M corners $\mathcal{C}$. A line l_i is denoted by its states in the image, location x, y, orientation o and length len: $l_i(x, y, o, len) \in \mathcal{L}$ for $i = \{0, \cdots, N\}$. Similarly, a corner is given by $c_j(x, y) \in \mathcal{C}$ with $j = \{0, \cdots, M\}$. The relations between lines and corners in a wire-frame model are then given by

$$f_1 : \mathcal{L} \mapsto \mathcal{C}^m \qquad m = \{0, \cdots, 2\} \tag{1}$$
$$f_2 : \mathcal{C} \mapsto \mathcal{L}^n \qquad n = \{2, \cdots, \infty\} \tag{2}$$

where m indicates that a line can exist without any or up to two corners and n indicates the number of lines intersecting at a corner. A wire-frame $\mathcal{WF}$ is the union of lines and corners, that is $\mathcal{WF} = \mathcal{L} \cup \mathcal{C}$.

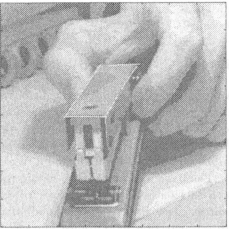

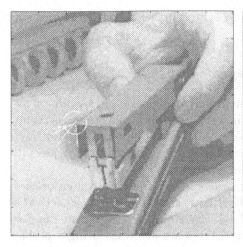

Fig. 2. Left, cycle 4: the edges found at the front end of the original line at the left of the red region. Right, cycle 19: top surface and the first line of the side surface found. The front four lines are sufficient to uniquely determine pose. For a monocular image the side length of the front line must be known.

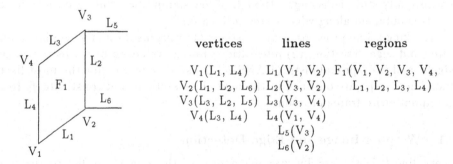

vertices	lines	regions
$V_1(L_1, L_4)$	$L_1(V_1, V_2)$	$F_1(V_1, V_2, V_3, V_4,$
$V_2(L_1, L_2, L_6)$	$L_2(V_3, V_2)$	$L_1, L_2, L_3, L_4)$
$V_3(L_3, L_2, L_5)$	$L_3(V_3, V_4)$	
$V_4(L_3, L_4)$	$L_4(V_1, V_4)$	
	$L_5(V_3)$	
	$L_6(V_2)$	

Fig. 3. Storing lines, corners (vertices), and regions (faces) in a graph-based model.

Updating the wire-frame at each tracking cycle using the data from the image **I** is then described by the following procedure:

```
update Wire-Frame WF:
    update Line L: ∀lᵢ ∈ L    f₃ : L × I ↦ L

        if   f₃(L, I) = lᵢ           // line found
        else f₃(L, I) = ∅           // mistrack

    update Corner C: ∀cⱼ ∈ C    f₄ : f₁(C) ↦ C
```

where f_3 is the result (line found or not found) of the tracking function outlined in section 5 and f_4 is the function of finding the intersection between all lines intersecting at one corner [8]. Tracking the features using the wire-frame update procedure is executed at each cycle before further search functions can be called.

5 EPIC: Edge-Projected Integration of Cues

A basic need of a vision-based control system that shall operate in a common indoor environment is robustness of visual image processing. Robustness indicates the ability to resist variations in the appearance of the object, the lighting, and the environment. This section will outline how the integration of a few cues can improve classical edge finding and tracking methods.

The basic idea of EPIC to obtain robustness is to project the values of cues such as intensity, colour, texture, or optical flow, shortly called *modes*, to the nearest edgel. Using the likelihood for these edgels renders subsequent line (or ellipse) detection more robust and effective. Lines are identified using a probabilistic [7] verification step, which adds the geometric constraint to obtain further robustness, as extensive tests on real images demonstrate [27]. The resulting line tracker shows stable behaviour when lighting conditions vary (as edgels will still form a line although mode values change, unless the edge becomes indistinguishable) and when background comes close to foreground intensity or colour (as the discontinuity still yields edgels though of low significance, but again a series of edgels is obtained along what seems to be a line).

Tracking a line proceeds in three steps: (1) warping an image window along a line and edge detection, (2) integration of mode values to find a list of salient edgels, and (3) a probabilistic (RANSAC [7]) scheme to vote for the most likely line. These steps are outlined in the next three sections and constitute f_3 from the update wire-frame procedure.

5.1 Warping Image and Edge Detection

Every line l_i is tracked by warping a part of the image parallel to the line. Warping cuts out of the image a window oriented parallel to the edge (using the same principle as [13]). As the object moves, the edge must be re-found in the new window. Each line tracker holds an associated *state vector* comprising the basic line parameters (x, y, o, len) and two mode values m_{left} and m_{right}, here representing intensity. These values are extracted from the image $\mathbf{I}(x)$ from search lines orthogonal to the line, in direction of the x-axis, as outlined below. The indices *left* and *right* are denoted with respect to the orientation of the line when standing on the line and looking from the origin outward. In this denotation lines have a direction and can have an angle o varying from 0 to 360 degrees.

In a first step edgels are found by computing the first derivative of the intensity, $grad\ \mathbf{I}(x)$, using a Prewitt filter of size 8×1 [13] (other common filters give similar results, the Prewitt filter can be implemented effectively as it uses only ones). The positions of the k local maxima x_{Mk} define intervals along the line. The two ends of the tracker line are used as limits of the leftmost and the rightmost intervals.

5.2 Integrating Edge and Mode Information

The second step is to project the modes values onto the edgel to find a likelihood value for each edgel. The mode value m for each interval is calculated using a histogram technique[1]. The mode value of an interval is the value of the bin containing the maximum counter value. Depending on the side of the interval relative to the maximum gradient x_{Mk}, the mode value is assigned to m_{left} or m_{right} for each edgel k.

The likelihood l_k that an edgel k is the correct edgel along the line to be tracked is evaluated to

$$l_k = \frac{1}{W} \sum_{i=1}^{n} w_i C_i \quad \text{with } i = 1, 2, 3, 4, \text{ and } W = \sum_{i=1}^{n} w_i, \qquad (3)$$

where the w_i are weights for the cues C_i. In the present implementation the following four cues have been found to be most significant. (Other cues have been tested, such as maximum gradient, the type of transition at the edge location, and the distance to previously found edge. However these cues do not improve robustness.)

$$C_1 = \begin{cases} 1 : x_{Mk} > 8 \text{ [pixel values]} \\ 0 : \text{ otherwise} \end{cases} \qquad (4)$$

$$C_2 = 1 - x_{Mk}^t / \max_k (x_{Mk}^t) \qquad (5)$$

$$C_3 = 1 - (m_{left}^t - m_{left}^{t-1})/255 \qquad (6)$$

$$C_4 = 1 - (m_{right}^t - m_{right}^{t-1})/255 \qquad (7)$$

where the superscripts t and $t-1$ refer to the mode values at the present and previous tracking cycle, respectively.

The functionality of the cues is as follows. C_1 (weight $w_1 = 1$) selects practically all edges above a (very small) threshold. Its sole purpose is to eliminate edges caused by noise. C_3 and C_4 select edgels with similar mode values as the edgels in the previous step. It can be easily seen that identical and similar mode values at cycles t and $t-1$ result in a high contribution to the likelihood.

At this point it is necessary to explain the use of the modes in more detail. Mode values are an effective means to find the edgels belonging to the object (ellipse) tracked. The scheme can be exploited most effectively if it is known on which side of the edge there is the object respectively the background. If the edge is a contour edge, the object can be only on one side and the respective weight is set to one (that is, the background is to the left $w_3 = 0$ & $w_4 = 1$ or to the right $w_3 = 1$ & $w_4 = 0$). In case the edge is not a contour edge, e.g., the edge between two visible surfaces of the object, then both weights are set to one. In this way edge detection is made robust to background changes (see experiments in Section 6).

---

[1] Experiments with median values gave results of similar robustness, however median computations increase strongly with larger intervals.

Appropriately using the three cues C_1, C_3, and C_4, selects all edgels with good mode values. However, C_1 uses a low threshold to find all edgels. The result is that edgels inside the object could be selected, too, although the edge is only caused by noise. These (noisy) edgels have the correct mode values since it is assumed that the entire surface of the object has practically one mode value.

An effective means to bias the likelihood of detecting the most significant edge is cue C_2. C_2 biases the selection of the correct edgel towards the strongest edge and weighs it slightly (the weight w_2 is 0.3 compared to 1 for the other weights) more than the other edgels. The rationale is that the contour edge or edge between surfaces of different orientation is likely to be stronger than a noisy edge inside the object. Experiments confirm that robustness in selecting the correct edgel is increased by adding cue C_2. Therefore the likelihood to select the correct edge among all edgels of one tracker line is increased.

The advantage of EPIC is that, based on the localisation of edgels, cues can be easily integrated and the list of cues given above can be completed using local cue operators. The principle idea is to use these cues to confirm the existence and the correctness of the edgel. First trials to incorporating colour added robustness to shadows and highlights.

5.3 Voting for Most Likely Line

In the final step, the edgels are used as input to the RANSAC voting scheme [7] for edge finding. The RANSAC idea is to randomly select two points to define a line and to count the votes given by the other edgels to this line. The line obtaining the highest number of votes is most likely the line searched for. The new states of the edge location and the mode values are calculated for this line and stored in the state vectors.

The investigation of the likelihood to find the correct line is the best justification for the combination of eq. (3) with the RANSAC scheme. A good line is found if two good edgels are selected to define the line. If the likelihood that an edgel is "good" is given by g, a good line is found with likelihood g^n with $n = 2$ [7]. As edgels are searched locally in each line of the warped window, the two events are independent. Repeating the random selection of n edgels to define a line k times gives the likelihood of finding the correct line l to

$$l = 1 - (1 - g^n)^k. \tag{8}$$

This relationship depends strongly on g. Therefore limiting the number of "good" edgels using EPIC is extremely effective to reduce k (exponentially for the same l). The result is the capability to find lines more robustly and at real-time (a few ms are needed for a line in a 40×40 window on a Pentium PC). The same method can be used to robustly track ellipses as shown in Fig. 4.

6 Experiments

The feasibility and robustness of the approach is demonstrated with a robot grasping a cube. Fig. 5 shows the robot, camera head and a workpiece on the

Fig. 4. Tracking a laddle in front of an office scene. The two top image show mistracking when using only gradient information. The bottom line uses EPIC for robust finding of edgels.

plate. There is no specific finishing or black cloth, the plate is particularly rough and has stains of rust. Lighting comes from two overhead neon lights and through the window behind the viewer.

A Pentium PC 133MHz executes image acquisition, image processing, and the short processing to determine relative pose to move the robot. A 486-PC runs RTLinux, a Linux version that provides Real-Time capabilities. An interface to the robot has been written in C++ such that the robot can be operated directly from the PC at a rate of 32 milliseconds [22]. RTLinux provides the utility to supply signals to the robot when requested. The two PCs communicate the control signals over a link using TCP/IP protocol.

The cube is found using the task description (for details please see [27]). The procedure is automatic. First cube coloured regions are searched for in the image at low resolution. By searching for the outline of this region, the top surface of the cube is found in a few steps. With the top surface four corners are available, which is sufficient information to determine the 6D pose. Using an extended Kalman filter the signal is smoothed and the control signal to steer the motion of the robot calculated. Fig. 6 shows snapshots from a descent motion. Fig. 7 plots the relative pose values (object set pose relative to gripper pose) in millimetres for position and degrees for orientation. The left graph is the

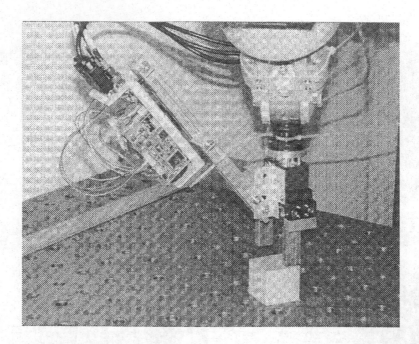

Fig. 5. The set-up in the lab. The sensor head is a SONY colour camera including zoom, controllable via interface, auto-focus and auto-iris.

approach to a fixed pose. The right graph gives the relative pose values when manually displacing the cube. The robot corrects the pose immediately. Each plot depicts a time of about five seconds.

Presently a simple proportional control low is used for the top level visual servoing loop. Simulations show that optimised PID control can highly increase performance [17]. Implementation will take some more months. The simple control law is the reason for the slight oscillations at the end of the motion. However, performance obtained is quite good considering that only one camera is used (see table 2). Stereo information would render the visual process more accurate.

	position mm			orientation deg		
	x	y	z	α	β	γ
mean	-0.188	-0.2218	-0.1336	0.2831	-0.2317	0.08
std	0.5473	0.5626	0.2421	0.6040	0.072	0.1913

Table 2. Mean and standard deviation of position and orientation accuracy obtained with one camera.

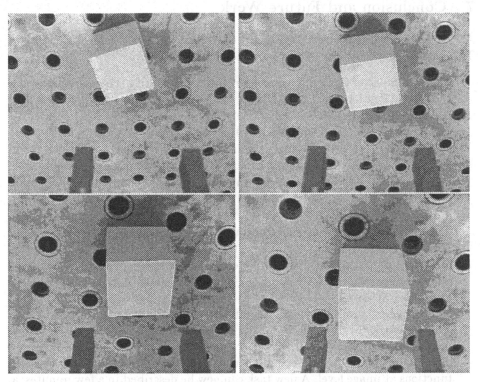

Fig. 6. Snapshots during the descent to grasp the cube. Note the changing light intensity, due to the shadow from the approaching robot, that causes no problem for the robust line trackers as long as a minimum edge remains visible.

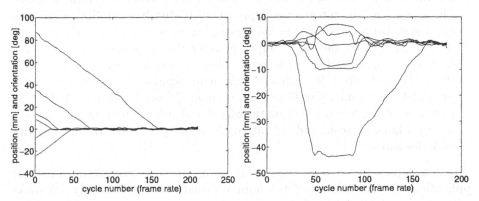

Fig. 7. Left: Plot of the 6 components of pose (from top to bottom: $z, y, \theta, \phi, \psi, x$) during the descent. The entire motion depicted is slightly longer than 5 seconds. Right: Motion when cube is displaced manually in all 6 DOF (from top at maximum displacement: $x, y, \psi, \phi, z, \theta$).

7 Conclusion and Future Work

An integrated approach to vision-based control of motion has been presented. The particular advantages of this approach are the following.

- The advantage of the approach is its *real-time* capability. The demonstration runs on a Pentium PC 133 MHz at field or frame rate for up to ten line features or two ellipses.
- The system architecture is based on the finding that there exists an *optimal system architecture* for a visual servoing (as well as a visual tracking) system [17]. It states that the system needs to operate at the highest possible rate and should use a certain number of pipelining steps depending on the overall latencies in vision and the mechanism. It is a guideline for system design for other researchers.
- The approach uses features as tracking primitives. It is the basis for a *modular architecture* that allows simple extensions. Due to the very nature of the modular approach, tracking of different features is independent. Thus parallel processes can be fully exploited by dividing individual trackers among available processors.
- The *image processing system* integrates tracking and detection in real-time. The system is totally modular using a wire frame model for what is found in the image as wells as for the object model.
- The approach uses a simple and efficient *task description*, which uses search functions at image level. A new task can now be described in a few minutes, a big improvement over common "hard-coded" programming. The descriptions are topological, thus allowing categorical models, e.g., a cube of any size or colour.
- The system is the dedicated to tackle the issue of *robustness* of the visual sensing system, an issue of major relevance for successful commercial applications. The cue integration approach EPIC (outlined in Section 5) is a good step forward to apply visual servoing in manufacturing environments. The demonstration object is simple, however the environmental conditions handled reach beyond previous work. The following conditions can be handled: (1) gradually (6% each step) changing lighting conditions, (2) foreground/background separation at a minimum of 8 pixel values (= 3.2%), (3) partly occlusion without loosing the object and still calculating pose as long as any 4 lines are seen, and (4) automatic recovery after occlusion using the task description.

Although improvements have been achieved, it is a long way from industrial applications or the abilities of the human visual system. Presently colour is utilised to speed up the initial search for the target. The use of colour within EPIC further increases robustness. A deficiency is still object recognition, as it is not real-time and needs an initialisation step. Reflections on metallic surfaces, significant changes in appearance, and bad conditioning from the monocular approach are further directions of improvement. However, the layout of the system is modular and is ready to be improved by integrating these extensions.

References

1. R. Bajcsy, S.W. Lee, and A. Leonardis: *Detection of diffuse and specular interface reflactions and inter-reflections by color image segmentation;* Int. J. of Computer Vision 17, pp. 241-272, 1996.

2. Christensen, H.I., Vieville, T.: *System Design and Control;* ECVNet webpage, http://pandora.inrialpes.fr/ECVNet/Policy/System.Design.Control.html#RTFToC4, 1996.

3. Cox, I.J., Hingorani, S.L.: *An Efficient Implementation of Reid's Multiple Hypothesis Tracking Algorithm and Its Evaluation for the Purpose of Visual Tracking;* IEEE Trans. PAMI Vol.18(2), 1996, S.138-150.

4. Corke, P.I., Good, M.C.: *Dynamic Effects in Visual Closed-Loop Systems;* IEEE Trans. on RA Vol.12(5), pp.671-683, 1996.

5. Crowley, J.L., Christensen, H.I.: *Vision as Process;* Springer Verlag, 1995.

6. Dickmanns, D.E.: *The 4D-Approach to Dynamic Machine Vision;* Conf. on Decision and Control, pp. 3770-3775, 1994.

7. Fischler, M.A., Bolles, R.C.: *Random Sample Consensus: A Paradigm for Model Fitting;* Communications of the ACM Vol.24(6), pp.381-395, 1981.

8. Förstner, W., Gülch, E.: *A Fast Operator for Detection and Precise Location of Distinct Points, Corners and Centers of Circular Features;* ISPRS Intercommission Workshop, Interlaken, 1987.

9. Gamble, E.B., Geiger, D., Poggio, T., Weinshall, D.: *Integration of Vision Modules and Labeling of Surface Discontinuities;* IEEE SMC Vol.19(6), pp.1576-1581, 1989.

10. Gee, A., Cipolla, R.: *Fast Visual Tracking by Temproal Consensus;* Image and Vision Processing 14, pp. 105-114, 1996.

11. Gennery, D.B.: *Visual Tracking of Known Three-Dimensional Objects;* Int. J. of Computer Vision Vol.7(3), pp.243-270, 1992.

12. Hashimoto, K.: *Visual Servoing;* World Scientific, 1993.

13. G. Hager, K. Toyama, *The XVision-System: A Portable Substrate for Real-Time Vision Applications,* Computer Vision and Image Understanding 69(1), pp.23-37, 1998.

14. Heuring, J.J., Murray, D.W.: *Visual Head Tracking and Slaving for Visual Telepresence;* ICRA, pp.2908-2914, 1996.

15. Kosaka, A., Nakazawa, G.: *Vision-Based Motion Tracking of Rigid Objects Using Prediction of Uncertainties;* ICRA, pp.2637-2644, 1995.

16. Krotkov, E., Bajcsy, R.: *Active Vision for Reliable Ranging: Cooperating Focus, Stereo, and Vergence;* Int. J. of Computer Vision Vol.11(2), pp.187-203, 1993.

17. Krautgartner, P., Vincze, M.: *Performance Evaluation of Vision-Based Control Tasks;* accepted for publication at IEEE ICRA, Leuven, 1998.

18. Landy, Maloney, Johnston, Young: *Vision Research*, 35, 389-412.

19. Lanser, S., Zierl, C.: *On the Use of Topological Constraints within Object Recognition Tasks;* 13th ICPR, Vienna 1996.

20. Lowe, D.G.: *Robust Model-Based Motion Tracking Through the Integration of Search and Estimation;* Int. J. of Computer Vision Vol.8(2), pp.113-122, 1992.

21. Magarey, J., Kokaram, A., Kingsbury, N.: *Robust Motion Estimation Using Chrominance Information in Colour Image Sequences;* Lecture Notes in Computer Science, Springer Vol.1310, pp.486-493, 1997.

22. Schaber, L.: *Echtzeit-Sensorschnittstelle zur Ansteuerung eines Roboters unter Linux;* Diploma Thesis, Inst. of Flexible Automation, Vienna University of Technology, 1997.

23. Y. Shirai, Y. Mae, S. Yamamoto: *Object Tracking by Using Optical Flows and Edges;* 7th Int. Symp. on Robotics Research, pp. 440-447, 1995.

24. T. F. Syeda-Mahmood: *Data and Model-Driven Selection Using Color Regions;* Int. Journal of Computer Vision, Vol.21 (1/2), pp.9-36, 1997.

25. Tonko, M., Sch"fer, K., Heimes, F., Nagel, H.H.: *Towards Visually Servoed Manipulation of Car Engine Parts;* ICRA, pp.3166-3171, 1997.

26. K. Toyama, G.D. Hager: *If at First You Don't Succeed...,* Study of Pre- and Post Failure Handling; Int. Conf. AAAI, Providence, pp. A3-9, August 1997.

27. Vincze, M., Ayromlou, M.: *Robust Vision for Pose Control of a Robot;* Proc. 22nd Workshop of the Austrian Association for Pattern Recongition ÖAGM '98, pp. 135-144, 1998.

28. Wilson, W.J., Williams Hulls, C.C., Bell, G.S.: *Relative End-Effector Control Using Cartesian Position Based Visual Servoing;* IEEE Trans. on RA Vol.12(5), pp.684-696, 1996.

29. Wren, C.R., Azarbayejani, A., Darrell, T., Pentland, A.P.: *Pfinder: Real-Time Tracking of the Human Body;* IEEE Transactions on Pattern Analysis and Machine Intelligence Vol.19(7), pp.780-785, 1997.

30. Wunsch, P., Hirzinger, G.: *Real-Time Visual Tracking of 3D-Objects with Dynamic Handling of Occlusion;* IEEE ICRA, 1997.

Face-Tracking and Coding for Video Compression

William E. Vieux[1]*, Karl Schwerdt[2]**, and James L. Crowley[2]***

[1] Department of Electrical and
Computer Engineering
University of Oklahoma
202 West Boyd, Room 219
Norman, OK 73019 USA
[2] Project PRIMA, Lab. GRAVIR - IMAG
INRIA Rhone-Alpes
655, ave. de l'Europe
38330 Montbonnot St. Martin
France

Abstract. While computing power and transmission bandwidth have both been steadily increasing over the last few years, bandwidth rather than processing power remains the primary bottleneck for many complex multimedia applications involving communication. Current video coding algorithms use intelligent encoding to yield higher compression ratios at the cost of additional computing requirements for encoding and decoding. The use of techniques from the fields of computer vision and robotics such as object recognition, scene interpretation, and tracking can further improve compression ratios as well as provide additional information about the video sequence being transmitted. We used a new face tracking system developed in the robotics area to normalize a video sequence to centered images of the face. The face-tracking allowed us to implement a compression scheme based on Principal Component Analysis (PCA), which we call Orthonormal Basis Coding (OBC). We designed and implemented the face tracker and video codecs entirely in software. Our current implementation of OBC operates on recorded video sequences, making it appropriate for applications such as video email.
Key words: video coding, face tracking, computer vision, principal component analysis

1 Introduction

Availability of high-performance computers at reasonable price levels has led to the development of complex multimedia applications for teleconferencing, video telephony, visual data exchange, and other video communications. As these new applications are developed, the bottleneck of limited transmission bandwidths and storage space becomes a critical problem. In general, researchers must make

---

* billv@ou.edu
** Karl.Schwerdt@imag.fr
*** Jim.Crowley@imag.fr

the encoding and decoding of video data more complex in order to lower bandwidth and space requirements. A common approach today is to develop systems and algorithms using computer vision techniques, often for modeling [1], but also for tracking [2] and combinations of both.

Previous research in our group has been devoted to exploring new ways for Man-Machine Interaction [3], [4] and the interpretation of scenes in images or video sequences. This research has produced results that are easily applied to communication applications. While their theoretical feasibility has been demonstrated [5], these techniques yet have to be integrated into a system comparable to current standards (H.323/H.263, MPEG) and applications (PitureTel [2]) to prove their practical use for video communication. We have recently started a project to tackle the task of building a video communication system in order to compare our algorithms with other standards and developments. This video communication system integrates a face tracker and a standard video codec, as well as an Orthonormal Basis Coding (OBC) compression scheme for face-tracked video sequences. The standard video codec was implemented according to the ITU-T (Telecommunication Sector of the International Telecommunication Union) recommendation H.263 [6].

Actual video coding standards from the ITU-T and ISO (International Organization for Standardization) rely mainly on the statistical relation between images and pixels. Intuitively, the use of additional a priori information, if wisely applied, should further increase compression ratios. Today, face trackers are commonly used in model-based applications. That is, they directly interact with the video codec. We are not targeting a model-based algorithm. Instead, we present in this paper a new, low-complexity face tracker, which has been combined with a standard video codec, as well as a OBC compression scheme. The OBC compression scheme currently operates on face-tracked sequences and is appropriate for applications such as video email. The face tracker is based on techniques that have been used in the robotics area, and has a fast, robust, and modular structure. The robustness comes from parallel use of partially redundant modules.

We will discuss the face tracker in more detail in section 2. Section 3 then discusses the integration and setup of the entire video processing system. Performance evaluation and results are presented in section 4, and finally, section 5 concludes the paper, giving an outlook on further research.

2 Face Tracking

The goal of visual tracking is to always keep a moving target centered in the field of view of one or more cameras. This is useful in application areas such as robotics (assembly, navigation) and surveillance. Using tracking as a pre-processing step for video image encoding provides the coder with images normalized to the object being tracked, e.g., a human head. This reduces the diversity of the most important image content: the face. In addition, it gives us the position and size of the face. Our system uses this information in two ways. Firstly, by adapting the quantizer step-size and maintaining motion vectors, the standard video codec

(H.263) can be measurably improved. Secondly, a video sequence with the head normalized in the center of the image can be generated for use with the OBC compression scheme.

The face tracker has been built with a modular structure. It automatically detects a face, keeps track of its position, and steers a camera to keep the face in the center of the image. This offers a user the possibility to freely move in front of the camera while the video image will always be normalized to his face. Figure 1 contains the block diagram of the face tracking system as it is implemented today.

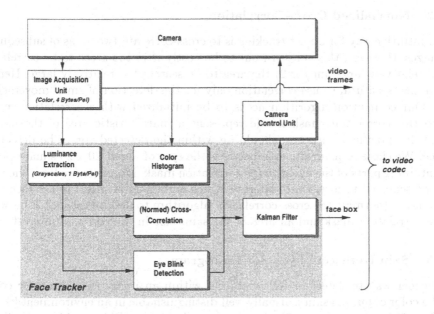

Fig. 1. Block diagram of the face tracker

We follow a face by maintaining a rectangle which frames the face, and call this rectangle the face box. There are three modules that actually do the tracking: Eye Blink Detection, Cross-Correlation, and Color Histogram. They have similar functions and are thus partially redundant. This redundancy guarantees that the face tracker is robust [5]. Since the modules of the face tracker have already been well-documented [5], we do not need to go into detail about the techniques involved. In the following subsection we rather briefly discuss the modules' features.

2.1 Eye Detection

The Eye or Blink Detection module is used for a quick initialization or recovery (re-initialization) of the face tracker. While appearance of different people can be extremely different (skin color, beard, hair, etc.), they all have to blink every ten seconds or so to keep their eyes moist. Blink duration is relatively short, well under a second. We have found that it is possible to detect eyes by taking the difference between two images with a time lag of approximately 200 milliseconds. This has shown to give good and reliable results.

Eye blinking does not occur frequently enough for use for permanent face tracking at a rate of 10 to 25 images per second. We therefore use the cross-correlation and color histogram modules for permanent tracking, and the eye detection module for the initialization of those modules.

2.2 Normalized Cross-Correlation

An intuitive way for object tracking is to cross-correlate two areas of subsequent images. However, this can turn out to be costly if 1) the areas to be correlated are relatively large and/or 2) the area to be searched is relatively large. Hence, it appears natural to use correlation only for the detection of small movements.

Our correlation algorithm needs to be initialized with a correlation mask, and this correlation mask should represent a characteristic area of the image, and, for practical purposes, should lie within the detected (or to be detected) face. We chose a quadratic area between the eyes of about 20 x 20 square pixels containing parts of the eyebrows as correlation mask. Moreover, we limit the area to be searched to a region of interest, which is roughly identical to the face box. We use a (normalized) cross-correlation algorithm to find a best match between the correlation mask and an area of the same size in the region of interest.

2.3 Skin Detection by Color Histogram

Another way to detect or follow objects within an image is to use their color. The color of human skin is usually well distinguishable in an environment like an office. It has been shown [7], that faces can be detected in a stable and reliable manner using a joint histogram of the color components of a pixel normalized by the pixel luminance. The color histogram module searches the entire image and returns the biggest area of skin. Once properly initialized, it can recover the face-box quickly and reliable.

2.4 Kalman Filtering

All three modules above output a face box, but the coordinates of the face boxes are generated differently. Therefore we added a zeroth order Kalman filter in order to smooth out jerky face box transitions and to keep the face-box at approximately the same size.

2.5 Confidence Factors

While all three modules return a result once they are run, those results have to be qualified in order to react properly to what is going on in front of the camera.

One possibility is the use of a confidence factor. Confidence factors are a normed quality measure between zero and one. An empirically determined threshold is then applied to decide if the face box found by a particular module is good.

2.6 Camera Control

The detected and filtered face box is eventually fed into the camera control unit. This unit calculates the distance between the actual position of a face and the center of the image. Then, a PD- controller has the camera pan, tilt, and/or zoom accordingly. We use a PD-controller because it dynamically reacts to the speed of head movement.

2.7 Performance

The face tracking system has been improved over the version of [5] to work faster and more stable at a frequency of about 12 Hz with, and 18 Hz without automatic camera control. The video sequences recorded for use with the PCA compression are recorded at approximately 5 to 6 Hz. This is due to the use of the Silicon Graphics Digital Media Library for writing out the file containing the video sequence. Code improvements, such as saving the images in memory or other techniques should allow recording at a much higher rate.

3 Adding face tracking to video coding

4 Overview

Today, there are four video coding standards being used for commercial systems: The ITU-T recommendations: H.261 [8] and H.263 [6], plus the ISO standards 11172 [9] (MPEG-1) and 13818 [10] (MPEG-2). H.261 is intended for low-motion video communication over p x 64 kbit/s ISDN lines, H.263 for low bit rate communication, MPEG-1 for full-motion video coding at up to 1.5 Mbit/s, MPEG-2 for up to 10 Mbit/s. We chose the H.263 recommendation as the standard video codec for our system since it comes closest to our purpose.

Our second codec approach, Orthonormal Basis Coding, was developed with a video email application in mind. A face tracked video sequence is cropped in order to provide a sequence of images with the face normalized and centered in each image. Then selected frames from the sequence are used to create a basis space into which new images can be mapped. Each mapped image can then be represented as a vector of coefficients; the number of coefficients is equal to the number of images in the original "basis space." By only storing and transmitting the vectors, extremely high compression rates can be achieved, especially for long sequences.

4.1 Integrating face tracking and video coding

The purpose of using a face tracker is to normalize the video stream images to an object, in our case a face. In other words, our face tracker can be seen as a camera control device, without direct interaction with any part of a video codec. It is a pre-processing stage, and its optional use under real-time constraints solely depends on the computer it is to be run on. This is very practical from a system integration point of view, because we do not need to alter the video codec and thus stay compatible.

Figure 2 shows the block diagram of our video processing system with face tracker and video codecs as separate modules. Both video codecs consist of three parts, a control unit, an encoder and a decoder. The only interaction between the face tracker and the codec is that the face tracker is providing the coding control unit with the face box.

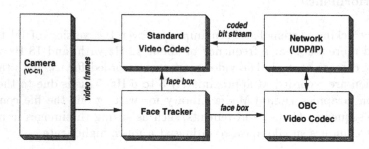

Fig. 2. Block diagram of the modules of the video processing system

MPEG-1 Basic algorithm of MPEG-1, as well as H.261, H.263, and MPEG-2, is the three step compression scheme: 1) energy compaction by Discrete Cosine Transform (DCT), 2) entropy reduction by Differential Pulse Code Modulation (DPCM), and 3) redundancy reduction by Variable Length Coding (VLC). Depending on their intended use, the different standards enhance this compression scheme by forward prediction, backward prediction, motion compensation, and other additional features.

Orthonormal Basis Coding The Orthonormal Basis Coding scheme operates as follows: 1) a limited set of images is chosen from the sequence to form the basis, 2) a Karhunen-Loeve expansion is performed to generate an orthonormal basis space from the images, 3) each image in the sequence is mapped into this basis space resulting in a small set of coefficients, 4) the images used to create the basis space and the sets of coefficients are stored in a file for later decoding [11] [12]. An image mapped into the basis space will produce a number of coefficients equal to the number of images used to create the basis space. We have obtained good results using only fifteen basis images for a 400-frame video sequence. Thus, each frame was represented by only fifteen coefficients.

Due to processing constraints, a full Principal Component Analysis cannot be done in a reasonable time. That is to say, a basis space cannot be generated using every image in the sequence and keeping only the most representative eigenvectors for a basis. Thus, we explored two algorithms for choosing the images for our basis. The threshold method assumes that similar frames are likely to be located sequentially in the video sequence. This is not necessarily the case when each image contains only a face talking. The most-representative method attempts to find similar images anywhere in the sequence.

The threshold method has a complexity of O(n) and works as follows. The normalized cross correlation is computed between image zero and subsequent images until it drops below a certain threshold. At that point in the sequence, the current image is added to the basis and subsequent images are cross correlated with that image until the threshold is crossed again. The most-representative method has a best case complexity of O(n) and a worst case of O(n2) although neither are very likely. It takes image zero and cross correlates it with all the other images in the sequence, all of the images that are very similar to image zero are put in set A, the others are put in a "to do" set. The first image of the "to do" set is cross correlated with all the others in the "to do" set and the most similar are put in set B. The rest stay in the "to do" set. This continues until all similar images are grouped in sets. One image from each of the biggest sets is taken to form the basis. In general, the most-representative method produced superior results at the cost of slightly more computing time. This is due to the fact that while the subject is talking, the mouth and facial features return to common positions at different times in the sequence.

5 Performance Evaluation

The system described above was developed and run on a Silicon Graphics INDY workstation in a common configuration and under normal working conditions. That is, the computer was used in a network with several users logged in. As evaluation criteria for image quality, we use the well known Peak-Signal-to-Noise-Ratio (PSNR). The PSNR of the k-th frame is defined as

$$PSNR(k) = 10 \cdot \log_{10} \left[\frac{255^2}{\frac{1}{MN} \sum_{m,n} \left[f_k(m, n) - \hat{f}_k(m, n) \right]^2} \right],$$

where M and N are the width and height of the image, m and n the pixel indices, $f()$ the original pixel values, $\hat{f}()$ the decoded pixel values. Note that the term in the denominator is the mean squared error.

5.1 Reconstruction

Various sequences were compressed and reconstructed using the *threshold*, *most-representative*, and MPEG methods. *The most-representative* method produced

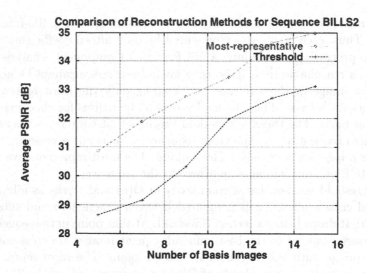

Fig. 3. PSNR vs. Number of basis images for both methods

better reconstructions than the threshold method in every case. In fact, it always averaged over 2 dB higher PSNR. See Figure 3.

In Figure 4, there is a noticeable improvement in the reconstruction quality as the number of basis frames is increased. Images included in the original basis space have no error in their reconstruction, thus PSNR has no meaning and is ignored in the following graphs.

Using the standard compression options with the Berkeley mpeg encode program [10], we found an average PSNR of approximately 27 dB for the BillS2 sequence. The MPEG reconstruction errors were due to artifacts in the images, while the reconstructed images from the OBC codec were slightly blurred, as can be seen in Figure 5. The closed mouth in Figure 5b is due to the fact that there were no images with a fully opened mouth among the fifteen basis images. This is a problem that could be rectified by better selection of the basis images, as discussed in the Conclusions and Future Work section.

5.2 Compression

The BillS2 video clip contains 418 frames and lasts 69 seconds (6 FPS). The various file sizes are shown in Table 1. It is important to note however, that the basis images are stored in the OBC file in raw YCrCb format. We used the GZIP utility [7] on the OBC to do simple compression (redundancy elimination) on the file. As explained in the Conclusions and Future Work section, specific compression (e.g., JPEG) of these images would significantly reduce file size. Each additional frame for the 15-basis-frame reconstruction would have added 60 bytes to the OBC file size. Additional frames for the 5-basis-frame reconstruction would have added only 20 bytes, while additional frames for the MPEG would have added significantly more.

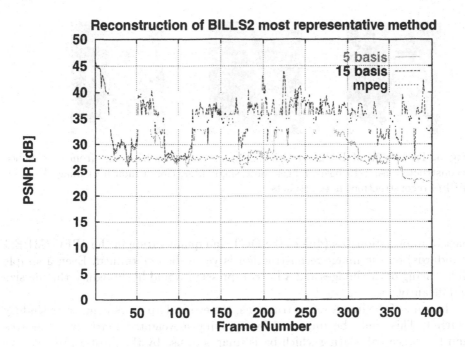

Fig. 4. PSNR for each frame of BillS2

6 Conclusions and Future Work

There are several areas that would benefit from additional research. The current system stores the original basis images in the file to transmit along with the coefficients for each frame. The coefficients are relatively small byte-wise compared to the images, and somewhat benefit from a variable length compression (VLC) scheme. The images are stored in raw YCrCb format, and we can further exploit a priori information about the images; they are all images of a normalized face. Either through JPEG compression of each basis image or an MPEG-like compression of the sequence, the file size could be significantly reduced. The im-

Table 1. File Size Comparison (kB) for BillS2

Video Stream	File Size [kB]
Original Video (Uncompressed)	12550
MPEG	72
OBC (5 basis frames)	71
OBC (5 basis frames) with GZIP	58
OBC (15 basis frames)	217
OBC (15 basis frames) with GZIP	178

Fig. 5. Frame 136 of BillS2 a) Original Image: no error b) Image from a sequence reconstructed using 15 basis images: note slight blur, closed mouth c) Image from an MPEG reconstruction: note artifacts

pact of information loss (due to the DCT and quantization in the JPEG/MPEG standards) on the image reconstruction is yet to be determined. Even a simple differencing of the images and VLC compression would likely reduce the file size significantly.

In some of the image reconstructions, the eye and lip movements were slightly blurred. This could be improved by applying a weighted mask over the eyes and lips when calculating which basis images to use by the most-representative method. A greater variety of eye and lip configurations would then be placed in the basis space allowing for better reconstruction of important facial expressions. Various techniques from computer vision have been used to create a fast and robust face tracking system, which in turn was used to improve the compression ratio of a standard video codec and our OBC compression scheme. The face tracker also enhances the usability of the entire video communication system by allowing the user to freely move in front of the camera while communicating. It is crucial however, that the face-tracking system be stable and accurate in order to provide the best results for OBC compression. An important question when enhancing any video coding system is, if the results in terms of image quality and compression ratio make up for the added complexity. The system described in this paper gives provides a positive outlook on further development of low-bandwidth video communication.

References

1. T. S. Huang and R. Lopez, "Computer vision in next generation image and video coding," *Lecture Notes in Computer Science*, vol. 0, no. 1035, pp. 13–22, 1996.
2. "La visioconférence sur IP selon PictureTel et Intel," *01 Reseaux*, pp. 64–65, January 1998.
3. J. L. Crowley, "Integration and control of reactive visual processes," *Robotics and Autonomous Systems*, vol. 16, no. 1, pp. 17–28, 1995.
4. J. L. Crowley, "Vision for man-machine interaction," *Robotics and Autonomous Systems*, vol. 19, no. 3-4, pp. 347–358, 1997.
5. J. L. Crowley, "Multi-modal tracking of faces for video communications," *IEEE Computer Society Conference on Computer Vision and Pattern Recognition*, pp. 640–645, June 1997.

6. ITU-T Study Group XV, "*Recommendation H.263*: Video coding for low bit rate communication," tech. rep., Telecommunication Standardization Sector of the International Telecommunication Union, Geneva, Switzerland, "http://www.itu.ch", 1996.

7. "The GZIP home page," *http://www.gzip.org*, May 1998.

8. ITU-T Study Group XV, "*Recommendation H.261*: Video codec for audiovisual services at px64 kbit/s," tech. rep., Telecommunication Standardization Sector of the International Telecommunication Union, Geneva, Switzerland, "http://www.itu.ch", 1993.

9. ISO/IEC 11172-2, "Information technology – coding of moving pictures and associated audio for digital storage media at up to about 1,5 mbit/s – part 2: Video," tech. rep., International Organization of Standardization, Geneva, Switzerland, "http://www.iso.ch/cate/d22411.html", 1993.

10. "Berkeley MPEG research," *http://bmrc.berkeley.edu/projects/mpeg*, 1997.

11. M. J. Turk and A. Pentland, "Eigenfaces for recognition," in *IFIP Working Conference on Engineering for Human-Computer Interaction*, vol. 3, pp. 71–86, 1991.

12. M. Kirby and L. Sirovich, "Application of the karhunen-loeve procedure for the characterization of human faces," *IEEE Transactions on Pattern Analysis and Machine Intelligence*, vol. 12, pp. 103–108, 1990.

Tracking People in a Railway Station During Rush-Hour

E. Prassler[1], J. Scholz[1] and A. Elfes[2]

[1] Research Institute for Applied Knowledge Processing (FAW), P.O. Box 2060
D-89010 Ulm, Germany
Phone: +49 731 501-621 Fax: +49 731 501-999
{prassler,scholz}@faw.uni-ulm.de
[2] Automation Institute Informatics Technology Center (CTI), P.O. Box 6162
13089-500 Campinas, SP, Brazil
Phone: +55 19 746-6115 Fax: +55 19 746-6167
elfes@ia.cti.br

Abstract. We propose a method for detecting and tracking the motion of a large number of moving objects in crowded environments, such as concourses in railway stations or airports, shopping malls, or convention centers. Unlike many methods for motion detection and tracking, our approach is not based on vision but uses 2D range images from a laser rangefinder. This facilitates the real-time capability of our approach, which was a primary goal. The time-variance of an environment is captured by a sequence of temporal maps, which we denoted as time stamp maps. A time stamp map is a projection of a range image onto a two-dimensional grid, where each cell which coincides with a specific range value is assigned a time stamp. Based on this representation we devised two very simple algorithms for motion detection and motion tracking. Our approach is very efficient, with a complete cycle involving both motion detection and tracking taking 6 ms on a Pentium 166Mhz.

Keywords: motion detection, real-time motion tracking, multiple moving objects, range images, temporal maps

1 Introduction

We consider the problem of observing a crowded spatial scene and detecting and tracking the motion of any moving object in the scene such as people, animals, or vehicles. No information is available in advance about the environment and its dynamics. It is neither known how many objects are present in the scene, nor is there any information about the shape of the objects, their intended motion direction, velocity or acceleration. Examples of such environments are shopping malls or concourses in airports or railway stations where typically tens or hundreds of objects move around. To travel through such an environment any object which may affect ones own locomotion must be identified and their motion must be tracked in order to discover and avoid potential collisions.

The problem becomes even more difficult, as we assume that the sensor is not stationary but also moves around while observing the environment. Accordingly, changes in the perception of the environment may not only be due to the actual motion of an object but also to a change of the view point. It is not a trivial problem to distinguish between these two cases only based on the perceived images of the environment. Distinguishing between a moving object and an unknown but stationary object is an important matter, if it comes to planning a collision-free locomotion through the surrounding environment.

The design requirements of our system include real-time obstacle avoidance with motion detection and tracking, and the use of off-the-shelf computer and sensor components.

The motion detection and tracking problem is studied in the context of a research project which is concerned with the development of a guidance system for an intelligent wheelchair MAid [11]. This guidance system should enable the wheelchair to maneuver autonomously in a shopping mall or a railway station and cross an area with many moving people. Such a system is particularly tailored for disabled persons who have lost most of their motion control capabilities and are physically unable to operate an electrical wheelchair.

2 Related Work

A large body of work in real-time tracking of moving objects exists in the field of computer vision. The approaches can be subdivided into *model based* methods, which require an exact object model, and *motion based* methods. The latter group can be further divided into *optical flow* and *motion energy* methods.

Model based object tracking methods allow to track the object's translational and rotational components [13], but they are not applicable if a description of the objects to be tracked is not available. Motion based methods use information about motion in the image to infer a corresponding motion in the real world. A well-established approach is the computation of *optical flow* [6]. Since this is a computational expensive and often ill–posed problem, many variants of optical flow have been explored. An example is SSD-optical flow [10], which requires the depth information to be known.

The *motion energy* method in general uses the image derivative to detect regions of activity. In most cases, image subtraction approximates the derivative and is combined with additional information like edge locations [7, 8] or dynamic background recovery [3].

Problems arise when the camera itself moves and the image motion induced by the camera motion must be separated from that induced by the object motion. While this can be accomplished for pure rotational movements of the camera [8], translational movements are practically not tractable. A recent approach by Nordlund and Uhlin [9] addresses this problem but is limited to one moving object in the scene. The approach is also computationally very expensive.

A different class of approaches to tracking moving objects refers to the data provided by range sensors instead of video images. A large portion of the work in this area deals with the special application of target tracking in radar scans [2]. Kalman filtering is used as a common technique in these applications. We have chosen not to use a Kalman filter approach as we would not be able to take advantage of the full power of the Kalman filter, since human purposive locomotion cannot be easily characterized using kinematic an dynamic models. Instead, we have chosen to approach our motion detection and tracking problem by matching individual points or clusters in consecutive range images on the basis of a *nearest–neighbor* (NN) measurement [12].

3 Fast Motion Detection

A rather obvious approach to identify changes in the surrounding environment is to consider a sequence of single observations and to investigate where these observations differ from each other. A discrepancy between two subsequent observations is a strong indication for a potential change in the environment. Either an unknown object has been discovered due to the egomotion of the observer or an already discovered object has moved by some distance. In the following sections we will discuss how this obvious and trivial idea can be translated into a fast motion detection and tracking system.

3.1 Sensors for Fast Motion Detection

We considered a variety of sensors for our task: vision, laser rangefinder, sonar, infrared, and tactile sensors. Not all of these sensors are equally useful for detecting and tracking motion. Infrared and tactile sensors can be excluded because of their limited range. Sonar has a very limited angular resolution and in our case provides sensor images which are too poor to reliably track a number of distinct objects. This reduces the selection of an appropriate type of sensor to vision or laser rangefinding systems.

Although there is quite a body of literature about motion detection in sequences of video images, we chose the laser range finder. Our choice is motivated as follows. Standard methods for motion detection in video images such as *optical flow* or *motion energy* allow to discover motion in the image plane. It is not straightforward, however, to infer from this the motion parameters of a moving object in the real 3D space, such as its motion direction, velocity, or acceleration. Stereo vision, which allows to infer the position of an object in the three-dimensional space, appears to be too expensive and too little robust for rapidly changing environments. As our experiments have shown, it is easier, more robust, and computationally less expensive to extract motion from the range images of a 2D laser rangefinder.

The sensor which we use for our application is a SICK PLS 200 laser rangefinder. The device works on a time-of-flight principle. It has a maximum range of $d = 50\,\mathrm{m}$ with an accuracy of $\sigma_d \approx 50\,\mathrm{mm}$. The sensor has an angular range of $\pm 90\,\mathrm{deg}$ with a resolution of $0.5\,\mathrm{deg}$. Accordingly, a full scan comprises 361 range measurements. The device is currently operated at a frequency of 3 Hz providing three range images per second.

3.2 Estimation of Sensor Motion

The range data provided by the laser rangefinder are naturally related to the local frame of reference attached to the sensor. In order to compare two subsequent local range images and to compute a differential image we have to transform the images into the same frame of reference in a first step. For this, it is necessary to know precisely which motion the sensor has undergone between two observations, how far it has moved from one viewpoint to the next and how far it has turned. In stationary environments the information about translation and rotation of the sensor might be inferred from the images themselves by some type of matching algorithm. In time-varying environments such an approach is excluded.

We obtain the information about the current position and orientation of the vehicle and the sensor, respectively, from a so-called *dead-reckoning* system, which our wheelchair is equipped with. This dead-reckoning system enables the wheelchair to keep track of its position and orientation over a limited travel distance with some accuracy. In our experiments, we measured a position error of $\sigma_{x,y} \approx 15\,\mathrm{cm}$ after a traveled distance of $10\,\mathrm{m}$. The dead-reckoning system utilizes a fibre-optical gyroscope to observe changes in the wheelchair's orientation. Because of this, the orientation information is of good quality even with unfavorable ground conditions.

The information from the dead-reckoning system is used to label each local range image with a stamp describing the position and orientation of the sensor at the observation point. With this information it is straightforward to transform the local range images from earlier measurements into the actual frame of reference.

Only the relative position and orientation offset between successive scans is needed for the presented tracking algorithm. Because of this, the accumulation of errors over time, which is typical for odometry, does not matter in this case. Also, if the position error between two scans is so large that the tracking system fails, for example in rough terrain, it recovers as soon as the position update becomes stable again, independent from any error in the absolute position. In case of such situations, the tracking system still recognizes the objects and their position relative to the vehicle, so that the navigation system still can avoid collisions. During the testing of MAid such situations occured very seldom.

3.3 Representations of Time-varying Environments

Next we have to consider which representation of the sensor data is the most suitable one for a motion detection algorithm. There are reasons which do not suggest using the raw range data. Range data, even if they are smoothed, are affected by noise. Unless we use an ideal sensor we will always discover variations in two subsequent range images, even if the environment and measurement conditions have not changed at all. This noise will affect any further operations on the range data, which are essentially point sets in the 2D plane, and will disturb the reliable detection of motion.

Furthermore, algorithms for relating and matching those point sets are computationally expensive. Minimizing the Hausdorff distance for two point sets, for example, has a complexity worse than $O(nm^4)$ [1], where n and m is the number of points in the point sets. With such a complexity the algorithm may not be apt in a real-time application.

In the following we present an alternative representation of range data of a time-varying environment which seems to be somewhat more suitable for motion detection. The representation involves a projection of the range data on a two-dimensional rectangular grid, where each grid element describes a small region in the real-world.

While investigating the performance of grid based mapping procedures such as suggested in [4] we noticed that most of the time was spent for mapping free space. Particularly, the further away the observed objects were, the more time it naturally cost to map the free space between the sensor and the object. Also, before a range image could be assimilated into a grid, the grid had to be completely initialized, that is, each cell had to be set to some default value. For grids with a typical size of several tens of thousands of cells these operations became quite expensive.

Now, mapping large areas of free space is rather dispensable for detecting and tracking moving objects. To avoid this, we devised an alternative representation where only those cells are mapped which were observed as occupied at time t while all other cells in this grid remain untouched. We call this representation a *time stamp map*.

Compared to the assimilation of a range image into an occupancy grid the generation of a time stamp map is rather simplified. Mapping of a range measurement involves only one single step. The cell which coincides with the range measurement gets a time stamp t. This stamp means the cell was *occupied at time t*. No other cell is involved in this operation. Particularly, we do not mark any cell as *free* which lies between the origin of the map and the cell corresponding to the range measurement.

The time-variance of an environment is captured by a sequence TSM_t, TSM_{t-1}, ..., TSM_{t-n} of those time stamp maps. An example of such a sequence is shown in Fig. 1 a) - c). The pictures there show three snapshots of a time-varying simple environment with a moving and a stationary object in a time stamp map representation. The age of the observation is indicated through different gray levels where darker regions indicate more recent observations. Note that the maps are already aligned so that they have the same orientation. A translation by a corresponding position offset finally transforms the maps into the same frame of reference. The aligned maps are shown in Fig. 1 d). The assimilation of a range image consisting of 361 measurements into a time stamp map takes 1.5 ms on a Pentium 166Mhz.

3.4 An Approach to Fast Motion Detection

Motion detection in a sequence of time stamp maps is based on a simple heuristic. We consider the set of cells in TSM_t which carry a time stamp t (*occupied at*

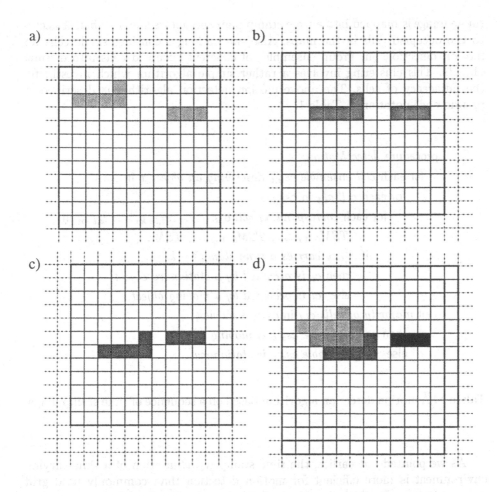

Fig. 1. A sequence of time stamp maps describing a toy-environment. The age of the observation is indicated through different gray levels. The more recent the observation the darker is the gray level which marks the object contours.

time t) and test whether the corresponding cells in TSM_{t-1} were occupied too, i.e., carry a time stamp $t-1$. If corresponding cells in TSM_t, TSM_{t-1} carry time stamps t and $t-1$, respectively, then we interpret this as an indication that the region in the real world, which is described by these cells has been occupied by a stationary object. If, however, the cells in TSM_{t-1} carry a time stamp different from $t-1$ or no time stamp at all, then the occupation of the cells in TSM_t must be due to a moving object.

Note that we consider only the two most recent maps, TSM_t and TSM_{t-1}, for detecting moving objects. Furthermore, we do not consider any cell in TSM_t but confine our search to those cells which carry a stamp *occupied at time t*. To make this search for moving object as efficient as possible, any cell *occupied at time t* is additionally entered into an ordered list. This list can be build up while a range image is mapped into a time stamp map and allows a more efficient access to the occupied cells in the maps. Also, we no longer consider single cells for motion detection but group ensembles of coherent occupied cells into distinct objects. This clustering involves a rather simple algorithm which investigates the adjacency of cells. The above motion detection algorithm is described in pseudo-code notation in Table 1.

procedure *detectMotion;*
    for each *cell ensemble $cs_{x,t}$ describing an object x in TSM_t*
        for each *cell $c_{i,t}$ in $cs_{x,t}$*
            for each *corresponding cell $c_{i,t-1}, \ldots, c_{i,t-k}, \ldots, c_{i,t-n}$ in*
                    $TSM_{t-1}, \ldots, TSM_{t-k}, \ldots, TSM_{t-n}$
                if *$c_{i,t-k}$ carries a time stamp $t - k$*
                    then *c_i is occupied by a stationary object*
                    else *c_i is occupied by a moving object*
    if *majority of cells $c_{i,t}$ in $cs_{x,t}$ is moving*
        then *cell ensemble $cs_{x,t}$ is moving*
        else *cell ensemble $cs_{x,t}$ is stationary*

Table 1. A motion detection algorithm based on a sequence of time stamp maps.

As we pointed out earlier, the time stamp representation of a time-varying environment is more efficient for motion detection than commonly used grid representations. Particularly, the time stamp representation allows us to use a sequence of maps in a round robin mode without a need to clear and initialize the map which is used to assimilate the new sensor image. Outdated time stamps which originate from the mapping of previous sensor images do not have to be deleted but are simply overwritten. This seems to be a very ugly procedure because the map which is supposed to receive a new sensor image may be polluted by outdated information. This procedure, however, is not only efficient - as we save an expensive initialization operation - but is also correct. Cells which are marked by an outdated time stamp are simply considered as free space, which has the same effect as assigning some default value.

The time stamp representation has one disadvantage, though. It does not make a difference between the discovery of a new stationary part of the environment and the observation of a moving object. That means, if we discover a new stationary object in an area which was formerly occluded, the above algorithm falsely reports a motion in that area. This is not a severe problem, however, since at the next time step the new object is already recognized as stationary.

It should be further mentioned that the motion detection algorithm described above discovers only motion of the observable part of a moving object, that is, in that part of the object which is facing the motion direction. This is due to our simple representation and to the heuristic which we use for motion detection. Luckily this effect does not cause any severe problems either. It neither affects the tracking of a moving object, as we will see below, nor does it affect the computation of a collision-free locomotion.

3.5 Motion tracking

To model the dynamics of a moving object and to track its motion ideally requires to know the values of the parameters such as the mass of the object, its acceleration, kinematic constraints and so forth. Now consider the task of detecting and tracking moving objects in a crowded waiting hall in a train station. Obviously, none of the parameters necessary to set up an analytical model of such a scene is available. Although kinematic and dynamic models of human walking mechanisms and gaits have been developed, there are no analytical models of human purposive locomotion, which would allow us to make inferences about the motion of a person over longer distances.

So the best we can do to track a moving object is to collect information about its past motion and to extrapolate this past motion into the near future, if necessary. For this purpose we consider the sequence of recent sensor images and extract the information about motion direction, velocity, or acceleration describing the motion history of moving objects from the spatial changes which we find in the mappings of these sensor images.

Note that while it is sufficient for motion detection to investigate only the mapping of two subsequent sensor images, provided the objects move at a sufficient speed, establishing a motion history requires to consider more extended sequences of sensor images. We assume that the cells which describe distinct objects are grouped into cell ensembles and we also assume that these cell ensembles and the corresponding objects are classified either as *moving* or as *stationary* by the motion detection algorithm described above.

The first step in establishing the motion history of a moving object is to identify the object in a sequence of mappings. Once we have found this correspondence it is easy to derive the motion direction and the velocity of a moving object from its previous positions. To find a correspondence between the objects in the mappings of two subsequent sensor images we use a nearest-neighbor criterion. This criterion is defined over the Euclidean distance between the centers of gravity of cell ensembles representing distinct objects. For each cell ensemble representing an object at time t we determine the nearest cell ensemble in terms of the Euclidean distance in the map describing the environment at the preceding time step $t - 1$. Obviously, this operation requires the objects to be represented in the same frame of reference.

If the distance to the nearest neighbor is smaller than a certain threshold then we assume that both cell ensembles describe the same object. The threshold depends on whether the considered objects and cell ensembles are stationary or moving. For establishing a correspondence between the two cell ensembles describing a stationary object we choose a rather small threshold since we expect the cell ensembles to have very similar shapes and to occupy the same space. Currently, we use a threshold of 30 cm for stationary objects. For a correspondence between the cell ensembles describing a moving object this value is accordingly larger. Here we use a threshold of 1 m which is approximately the distance which a person moving at fast walking speed covers between two sensor images.

A description of the above algorithm in pseudo-code notation is given in Table 2. On a Pentium 166MHz a complete cycle involving both detecting and tracking any moving objects takes approximately 6 ms.

```
procedure findCorrespondence;
    for each object o_{i,t} in TSM_t
        for each object o_{j,t-1} in TSM_{t-1}
            CorrespondenceTable[i,j] = corresponding(o_{i,t}, o_{j,t-1});

    function corresponding(o_{i,t}, o_{j,t-1});
        if o_{i,t} is stationary and o_{j,t-1} is stationary
            then ϑ = ϑ_s; (threshold for stationary objects)
            else ϑ = ϑ_m; (threshold for moving objects)
        if d(o_{i,t}, o_{j,t-1}) < ϑ
                and not_exists o_{k,t} :    d(o_{k,t}, o_{j,t-1}) < d(o_{i,t}, o_{j,t-1})
                and not_exists o_{l,t-1} :  d(o_{i,t}, o_{l,t-1}) < d(o_{i,t}, o_{j,t-1})
            then return true;
            else return false;
```

Table 2. An algorithm for tracking moving objects in a crowded environment.

Establishing a correspondence between the centers of gravity of cell ensembles is a very simple and efficient but not extremely reliable method for object tracking. Assume, for example, the view of an object has changed between two observations due to occlusion effects. If the parts of an object which are perceived at time t differ considerably from the parts which are perceived at time $t - 1$ then considering the centers of gravity is not sufficient and our tracking algorithm would fail to establish a correct correspondence. For efficiency reasons we accept this shortcoming and refrain from using shape matching methods which might improve the reliability but are also more time consuming. An additional source of errors is the use of thresholds. Whichever values we choose for these thresholds, there will be always cases were the choice was false.

Generally, we distinguish two types of errors which may occur while establishing a correspondence between objects in the representations of subsequent sensor images. First, a correspondence is established between two cell ensembles which do not correspond to each other and do not describe the same object in reality. Second, there are cell ensembles in the mapping of the environment at time t for which we do not find corresponding cell ensembles in the mapping at time $t - 1$. The first type of error occurs if two cell ensembles which actually correspond to each other do not satisfy the nearest-neighbor criterion, that is, the cell ensemble which would actually correspond to the considered ensemble is farther away than a cell ensemble which describes a different object. The probability of such an error depends on the velocity of the objects and on the density of the objects in the environment, the faster the objects and the more crowded the environment the more likely is such a false association. The probability of those false associations may be reduced by more sophisticated shape matching methods but cannot eliminated due to the limited shape information provided by a 2D range image.

The second type of error may have several reasons: The considered cell ensemble describes an object which has just entered the visibility range of our sensor and which was not visible at time $t - 1$. In that case it is natural that we do not find a corresponding cell ensemble in the mapping of the sensor image at time $t - 1$. Another reason may be that the considered object moves at a speed at which its distance to its position at time $t - 1$ exceeds the threshold discussed above. This error can be remedied by raising the value for this maximum distance. One has to be aware, however, that raising this threshold also raises the risk of a false association. A third reason may be that the nearest neighbor-criterion has already lead to a false association and that the cell ensemble at time $t - 1$ which would actually correspond to the one considered has been erroneously associated with a different object.

Although we have chosen a rather simple approach, our algorithm for tracking a large number of moving objects has not only proven to be very fast and efficient but in practice also works sufficiently reliably, as we will see in the experiments described in the following section.

4 Experimental results

Our approach was tested and validated in two series of experiments. The first series took place under more or less simplified and controlled lab conditions. The sensor (mounted on the wheelchair) was placed at a fixed position in an experimental area with a size of approximately $4 \times 7\text{m}^2$. The environment did not contain any stationary objects. The experiments were recorded by a video camera which was synchronized with the rangefinder and the motion detection and tracking algorithm. In each experiment we asked a number of people to move along prescribed trajectories in the experimental area at comfortable walking speed.

The results of this first series of experiments are shown in Fig. 2 a) - d). In the first experiment a test person walked along a given rectangular trajectory in the front area of the sensor. After several laps along this trajectory the test person headed back to its initial position. Our algorithm tracked the motion of the test person in real time without any problems. The trajectory estimated by the tracking algorithm is shown in Fig. 2 a).

In the experiment shown in Fig. 2 b) three people moved along more or less parallel straight lines away from the sensor with one person making a sudden left turn and heading back to the sensor. The people moved at slightly different velocities, so that nobody was occluded during the experiment. As the figure indicates, the algorithm could easily track the motion of these three persons. In the experiment in Fig. 2 c) we tracked again the motion of three test persons which moved along more or less parallel straight lines away from the sensor. This time the people moved at a similar speed.

The last experiment in this series deserves a more detailed discussion. We let two test persons move along straight lines which crossed each other. Accordingly, for a short period of time one person was occluded by the other from the view point of the sensor. Apparently, our algorithm was unable to track the occluded persons during this period of time. In Fig. d) this is reflected by the interruption of one of the trajectories. Our algorithm lost the person for two time steps. It detected and continued to track the motion after the person became visible again.

Tracking moving objects whose trajectories cross each other is a very general problem (see [2]) and is not a specific problem of our algorithm. Problems of this type cannot be eliminated even by more sophisticated methods such as described in [2], which assume that there is a model of the motion of the objects which are to be tracked. As mentioned above, we have to refrain from such an assumption since those models are not available in our application.

In this experiments the tracking system had to deal with only a few objects moving on clearly seperated trajectories. Due to this, all the trajectories where completely recognized (except for occluded parts). An object speed of up to 2 m/s was handled without problems. Additional testing showed that an object speed of more than 2 m/s sometimes lead to gaps in the tracked trajectories if the distance between objects in consecutive scans is larger than the threshold. Objects slower than 50 cm/sec where sometimes taken as stationary objects if they occupy too many overlapping cells. Anyhow the tracking system can find the correct correspodence for these objects. To determine the accuracy of the object position, we let another robot move in front of the sensor and compared the robots trajectory to the one provided by the tracking system and found an average position error of about 10 cm. The position error is caused by the fact that only the center of gravity of the visible part of an object is taken as the objects position. The magnitude of the average position error depends on the objects size and on the perspective. Figure 5 illustrates the result of such a test.

In a second series of experiments we tested the motion detection and tracking algorithms under more difficult and realistic conditions. The environment chosen for these experiments was the waiting hall of a train station during the

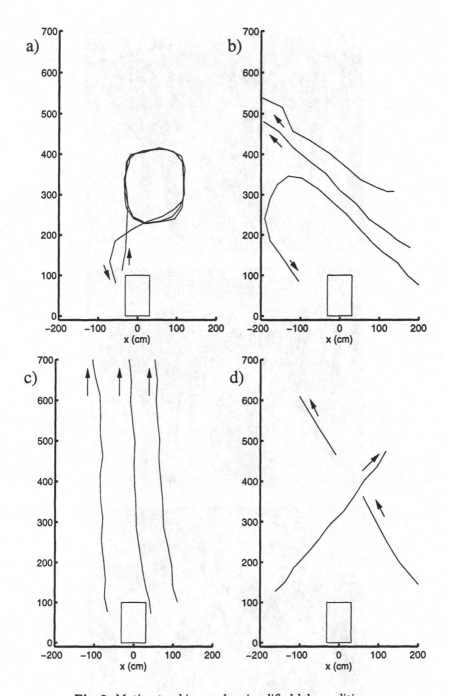

Fig. 2. Motion tracking under simplified lab conditions.

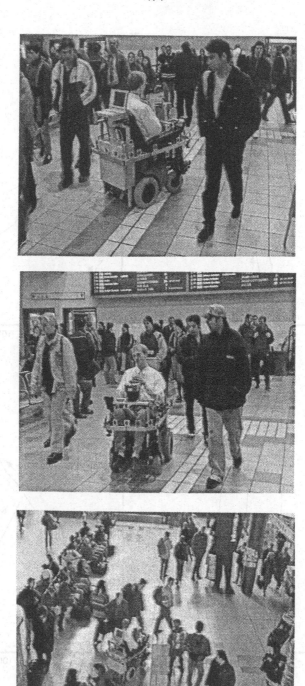

Fig. 3. MAid traveling in the concourse of a railway station.

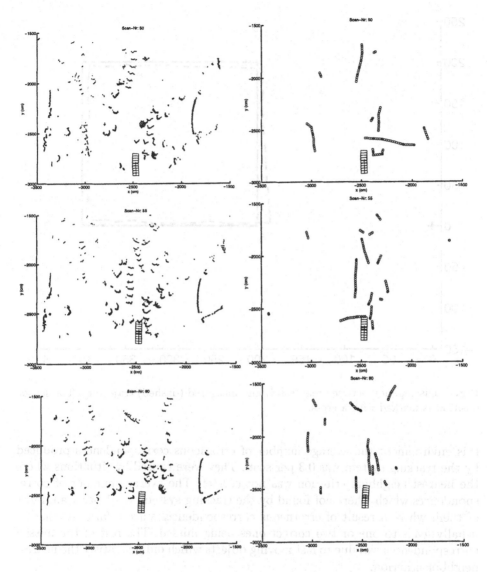

Fig. 4. Tracking moving objects in the concourse of a railway station.

morning rush-hour. Snapshots of the environment are shown in Fig. 3 a) - d). The pictures show the wheelchair which was manually steered through the test environment in the experiment. The sensor is mounted on the front side of the wheelchair and is not visible in the pictures. The number of people staying and moving in the waiting hall varied between 50 and 200. The average number of objects (not only persons) visible to the sensor per scan was 20. This includes moving objects as well as stationary objects. As a result of the clustering algorithm which sometimes splits objects if they have a very rough surface the average number of objects per scan recognized by the tracking system was 22. In

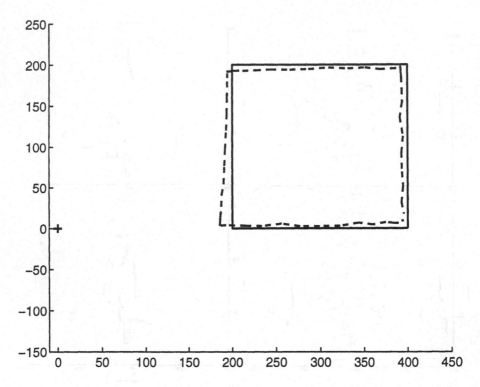

Fig. 5. Discrepancy between real (solid) and measured (dashed) trajectory. The sensor position is marked with a cross.

this environment the average number of errorneous correspondences produced by the tracking system was 0.3 per scan. They were caused by situations where the nearest neighbors criterion was not correct. The average number of correspondences which where not found by the tracking system was 1 per scan. Most of them where a result of errorneous correspondences since a false association usually leads to one or two correct ones being missed. The rest of the missed correspondences was due to fast moving objects which did not satisfy the nearest neighbor criterion.

The results of one of the experiments are shown in Fig. 4. The left column there shows a sequence of superimposed range images. Each superimposed range image actually consists of six subsequent plain range images. Next to each superimposed range image we show in the right column the trajectories of the moving objects which were tracked in these six range images. Stationary objects which appear as bold point sets in the superimposed range images are not shown in the pictures on the right side.

It should be noted that effects such as temporary occlusion of objects, crossing trajectories and alike, which we already faced in the lab experiments, occur far more often in the waiting hall experiment. Also, people often stopped all of a sudden in front of a counter or a display to study departure times, for example, or even in front of our wheelchair to express their sympathy with the driver of this strange vehicle. This explains why some tracks shown in the pictures in the right column appear quite erratic while others describe more or less smooth straight motions. Especially because of occlusion, most of the objects could only be tracked for a short period of time without interuption. For moving objects the average time of visibility was about two seconds. Anyhow, some of the moving objects could be tracked for up to ten seconds.

5 MAid's navigation system

MAid has a hierarchical control architecture consisting of three levels: a basic control level, a tactical level and a strategic level.

On the basic control level the motion commands calculated in the tactical level are provided to the vehicle's hardware. A velocity control loop observes the actual values provided by the vehicle's dead-reckoning system and adjusts the speed of the wheels to match with the given motion commands.

The tracking system is a part of the tactical level, which forms the core of the control system. It works hand in hand with a module which computes evasive maneuvers. The tracking system gets the range data form the laser scanner and the position/orientation data from the odometry and produces a list of those objects, which are currently in the robots field of view. The module for the evasive maneuvers analyzes this list and checks for possible collisions with objects. For each object a so-called *collision cone* [5] is calculated. A collision cone describes a set of motion commands which would lead to a collision with the corresponding object. Subtracting the collision cones for all objects detected by the tracking system from the set of steerable motion commands results in a set of motion commands which do not lead to a collision. Out of this set a command leading as close to MAid's goal as possible is chosen.

Since on the tactical level MAid tries to find a collision free and as direct as possible path to the goal, its the responsibility of the strategic level to provide appropriate goal points. In the current design the selection of goal points is left to the user. Accordingly the strategic level is just a user interface. At a later point, the strategic level will be expanded by a path planner, for example, which will provide the tactical level with a sequence of intermediate goals.

6 Conclusion

We presented an approach to tracking a large number of moving objects in crowded environments, such as waiting halls in train stations, airport terminals, or shopping malls. The approach uses the range data provided by a 2D laser rangefinder. This sensor was chosen to facilitate the real-time capability of the tracking system. By using a laser rangefinger our approach differs from the majority of known methods for motion detection and tracking which are based on visual information.

The time-variance of an environment is captured by a sequence of tempo- ral maps, which we denoted as time stamp maps. A time stamp map is simple projection of a range image onto a two-dimensional grid, where each cell which coincides with a specific range value is assigned a time stamp. The major advantage of this representation is that it is very efficient. The assimilation of a range image in a 200×200 grid does not take more than 1.5 ms on a Pentium 166MHz.

Based on this representation we have further devised two very simple algorithms for motion detection and motion tracking, respectively. One complete cycle involving both motion detection and tracking takes 6 ms. The approach was successfully applied to a set of range images recorded in the waiting hall of a train station during the morning rush-hour. In the experiments we tracked between 5 and 30 moving objects at a time.

Our approach, the underlying representation as well as the algorithms for motion detection and tracking, does not presuppose the existence of kinematic and dynamic models of purposive human locomotion. Those models are not available in the environments which we consider in our work. With a cycle time of 6 ms, however, our approach is definitely "quick" and assures the required real-time capability.

Due to occlusion effects, our tracking method may temporarily loose a moving object. Occlusion effects, crossing tracks, or splitting of objects, however, are very general problems in motion tracking and not specific to our approach.

Future work will address issues such as the integration of fast matching methods into the approach to disambiguate moving objects based on their shape. Also we will extend the approach by a motion prediction algorithm to cope with problems which are caused by occlusion or by crossing tracks but also to facilitate motion planning in time-varying environments.

Acknowledgment

This work was supported by the German ministry for education, science, research, and technology (BMB+F) under grant no. 01 IN 601 E 3 as part of the project INSERVUM.

References

1. H. Alt, B. Behrends, J. Blömer. Approximate Matching of Polygonal Shapes. In *Proc. of the 7th Ann. ACM Sypm. on Computational Geometry*, 1991.
2. Y. Bar-Shalom, T.E. Fortmann. *Tracking and Data Association*. Academic Press, 1987.
3. Q. Cai, A. Mitiche, J. K. Aggarwal. Tracking Human Motion in an Indoor Environment. In *Proc. Int. Conf. on Image Processing*, 1995.
4. A. Elfes. *Occupancy Grids: A Probabilistic Framework for Robot Perception and Navigation*. PhD thesis, Electrical and Computer Engineering Department/Robotics Institute, Carnegie-Mellon University, 1989.
5. P. Fiorini, Z. Shiller. Motion planning in Dynamic Environments Using the Relative Velocity Paradigm. In *Proc. of the 1993 IEEE Int. Conf. on Robotics and Automation* , Atlanta, 1993.

6. B.K.P. Horn, B.G. Schunck. Determining Optical Flow. *Artificial Intelligence*, 17, pp. 185-203, 1981.

7. Y. Mae, Y. Shirai, J. Miura, Y. Kuno. Object Tracking In Cluttered Background Based On Optical Flows And Edges. In *Proc. of the Int. Conf. on Pattern Recognition*, pp. 196-200, 1996.

8. D. Murray, A. Basu. Motion Tracking with an Active Camera. *IEEE Trans. on Pattern Analysis and Machine Intelligence*, 16(5), pp. 449-459, 1994.

9. P. Nordlund and T. Uhlin. Closing the Loop: Detection and Pursuit of a Moving Object by a Moving Observer. *Image and Vision Computing*, 14, pp. 265-275, 1996.

10. N.P. Papanikolopoulos, P.P. Khosla, T. Kanade. Visual Tracking of a Moving Target by a Camera Mounted on a Robot: A Combination of Vision and Control. *IEEE Trans. on Robotics and Automation*, 9(1), pp. 14-35, 1993.

11. E. Prassler, J. Scholz, M. Strobel. MAid: Mobility Assistance for Elderly and Disabled People. In *Proc. of the 24th Int. Conf. of the IEEE Industrial Electronics Soc. IECON'98* (to appear), 1998.

12. Y. Rong Li, Y. Bar-Shalom. Tracking clutter with nearest neighbor filters: analysis and performance. *IEEE Trans. Aerospace and Electronic Systems*, 32, pp. 995-1010, 1996.

13. P. Wunsch, G. Hirzinger. Echtzeit–Lagebestimmung dreidimensionaler Objekte aus Bildsequenzen zur Lagebestimmung eines Industrieroboters. In B. Mertsching: *Proceedings in Artificial Intelligence*, pp. 169-173, 1996.

Active Knowledge–Based Scene Analysis

D. Paulus, U. Ahlrichs, B. Heigl, J. Denzler, J. Hornegger, H. Niemann

Lehrstuhl für Mustererkennung (LME, Informatik 5)
Martensstr. 3, Universität Erlangen–Nürnberg, 91058 Erlangen
http://www5.informatik.uni-erlangen.de
Ph: +49 (9131) 85–7894 Fax: +49 (9131) 303811
email: paulus@informatik.uni-erlangen.de

Abstract We present a modular architecture for image understanding and active computer vision which consists of three major components: Sensor and actor interfaces required for data–driven active vision are encapsulated to hide machine–dependent parts; image segmentation is implemented in object–oriented programming as a hierarchy of image operator classes, guaranteeing simple and uniform interfaces; knowledge about the environment is represented either as a semantic network or as statistical object models or as a combination of both; the semantic network formalism is used to represent actions which are needed in explorative vision.

We apply these modules to create two application systems. The emphasis here is object localization and recognition in an office room: an active purposive camera control is applied to recover depth information and to focus on interesting objects; color segmentation is used to compute object features which are relatively insensitive to small aspect changes. Object hypotheses are verified by an A^*–based search using the knowledge base.

1   Introduction

Autonomous mobile systems with visual capabilities are a great challenge for computer vision systems since they require skills for the solution of complex image understanding problems, such as driving a car [36] or exploring a scene. The system presented in this contribution provides mechanisms for knowledge–based image understanding and active computer vision. It combines and links various modules for low–level image processing, image segmentation, and high–level image analysis. We combine data–driven and knowledge–based techniques in such a way that a goal–directed exploration guided by the explicitly represented knowledge is possible. The major goal here is to explore a scene with an active camera device. This can also be used in autonomous mobile systems which navigate and act based on visual information. Such systems need an explicit representation of actions and search strategies. A literature review in [5] on the topic of

This work was funded partially by the *Deutsche Forschungsgemeinschaft* (DFG) under grants number SFB 182 and SFB 603. Only the authors are responsible for the contents.

knowledge–based image analysis gives a comprehensive discussion of the state of the art. Image analysis systems have also been reported for example in [21, 22]. In [21] as well as here, semantic networks are used as a formalism for knowledge representation. We now use this formalism for the unified representation of objects, scenes, actions, and strategies in order to provide flexible and exchangable strategies for active vision and scene exploration.

A software system for image understanding usually has a considerable size. The major problem in software design of general imaging systems is that on the one hand highly run–time efficient code and low–level access to hardware is required, and that on the other hand a general and platform–independent implementation is desired which provides all data types and functions also for at least intermediate–level processing, such as results of segmentation. Today's software engineering is closely coupled with the ideas of object–orientation which can help simplifying code reuse; if applied properly, it unifies interfaces and simplifies documentation by the hierarchical structure of classes. Genericity provides an alternative solution to software engineering problems. Both concepts are available in C++. Object–oriented programming has been proposed for image processing and computer vision by several authors, in particular for the image understanding environment [15]; this approach is mainly used to represent data. We also use object–oriented programming for operators, devices, and actions.

In Sect. 2 we outline the general structure of our system and the object–oriented implementation. In Sect. 3 we describe some of the modules which are provided by the system; special emphasis is layed on the knowledge representation for computer vision and on the extension of the semantic network formalism to represent strategies and actions. We apply these modules in Sect. 4 to two problems in computer vision.

The goal of our example application in Sect. 4.1 is to explore an office room. Objects are hypothesized in the image based on their color. Their 3–D position is estimated from a coarse 3–D map computed from trajectories of colored points which are tracked during during a translational motion of the active camera. The objects are chosen in such a way that they cannot be distinguished by their color solely. Close–up views are captured and segmented into color regions. Features of these regions are subject to matching with the knowledge base. If objects are not found in the scene, the camera is moved based on action descriptions found in the knowledge base.

In Sect. 4.2 we describe a recent research project in the area of visual guided autonomous mobile systems. Many of the algorithms described in Sect. 3 and Sect. 4.1 are involved. First results for visual self–localization based on color histograms in natural office scenes are presented.

We conclude with a summary and future directions in Sect. 5.

2 System Architectures

The need for a flexible, knowlededge–based computer vision system with real–time capabilities lead to "**An image analysis system**" (ANIMALS, [1, 26, 25]) which is implemented in C++. It provides modules for the whole range of algorithms from low–level sensor control up to knowledge–based analysis and actions. For a unified documentation and description of the numerous modules, the notation as introduced in [23] has been used.

2.1 Data Flow for Knowledge–Based Analysis

The general problem of image analysis is to find the *optimal* description of the input image data which is appropriate to the current problem. Sometimes this means that the most precise description has to be found, in other cases a less exact result which can be computed faster will be sufficient. For active exploration, the goal is to fulfill the task which is described in the knowledge base.

These problems can be divided into several sub–problems. After an initial preprocessing stage, images are usually segmented into meaningful parts. Various segmentation algorithms create so called segmentation objects [25] which can be matched to models in a knowledge base containing expectations of the possible scenes in the problem domain. This is achieved best if the formalism for the models is similar to the structure of segmentation results, as it is the case for semantic networks and segmentation objects [23].

An overview of the main components of our image analysis system is shown in Figure 1; data is captured and digitized from a camera and transformed to a description which may cause changes in camera parameters or tuning of segmentation parameters. Models which are collected in the knowledge base are created from segmentation results (in Sect. 3.3) or at least have similar structure (in Sect. 3.6). These models are used for the analysis. Image processing tasks are shown in oval boxes; data is depicted as rectangles.

The dotted lines in Figure 1 indicate that a control problem has to be solved in active vision or active exploration resulting in a closed loop of sensing and acting. Information is passed back to the lower levels of processing and to the input devices; this way, parameters of procedures can be changed systematically, or the values of the camera and lens can be modified. Changes to the param-

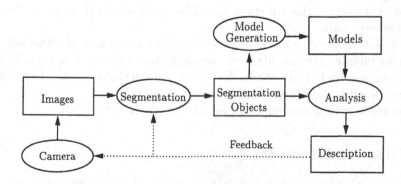

Figure 1. Data flow in an image analysis system after [25]

eters of the image input process, selection of the appropriate algorithms, and parameter control for both are summarized under the term *action*.

2.2 Examples of Other Software Environments

From the variety of software systems for image processing and analysis, we choose two well known examples.

A group of leading experts in image analysis joint their efforts for a common image understanding environment [15]. The system was planned as a basis for image processing, computer vision, and knowledge based image analysis. The system covers all areas of imaging with many applications; due to the many contributors, a variety of ideas has to be united into a hierarchy of classes. The design goals are: object–oriented programming with graphical interaction, extensibility, program exchange and a common performance evaluation platform for image processing. Real–time processing was explicitly excluded from the original goals [15, p. 160]. In the present version, no classes are provided for devices such as cameras. This environment is applied for example in [18] to the analysis of satellite images.

The other widely used system is Khoros [28] which provides a nice graphical user interface for image processing systems. Data structures beyond images and matrices are not available to the user. Therefore, knowledge–based processing is not integrated in the system. The interface to the large function library is compatible to C and does not provide object–oriented features.

Real–time processing as well as symbolic data structures are crucial for active exploration. Both systems have thus to be modified or extended to be used for our purpose.

2.3 Object–Oriented Design for Image Analysis

The algorithms and data structures of our system are implemented in a **Hierarchy** of **Picture Processing ObjectS** (HIPPOS, written as ἵππος [26, 25]), an object–oriented class library designed for image analysis which is based on the commonly used NIHCL C++ class library. In [26], the data interfaces were defined as classes for the *representation* of segmentation results. The *segmentation object* [26] provides a uniform interface between low–level and high–level processing. In [16], this system is extended to a hierarchical structure of *image processing and analysis classes* and *objects* (cmp. [4]). Objects are the actual algorithms with specific parameter sets which are also objects (OperatorOpt in Figure 2, [16]). Classes as implementation of algorithms are particularly useful, when operations require internal tables which increase their efficiency since tables can then be easily allocated and handled. The basic structure of the class hierarchy for line–based image segmentation is shown in Figure 2. On a coarse level, operators for line–based segmentation can be divided into edge detection, line following, gap closing, and corner and vertex detection. For each processing step, which is implemented here as a class, there exists a large variety of choices in the literature. When the whole sequence of operations is subjected

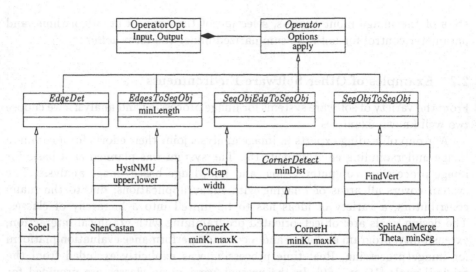

Figure 2. Part of a class hierarchy for image operators from [16] in UML notation

to optimization, either manually or automatically, it is crucial to have similar interfaces to exchangeable single processing steps, such as several corner detection algorithms. This is greatly simplified by object–oriented programming and polymorphic interfaces as shown here. Only the type of input and output data has to remain fixed for such a system. This is guaranteed by the abstract classes directly derived from the class **Operator**; for example the *EdgesToSegObj* defines the interface for the conversion of edge images to segmenation objects.

Several segmentation algorithms are implemented in our system which operate on gray–level, range, or color images using the interfaces provided by the segmentation object. To give an example, the application in Sect. 4.1 works on color images and applies a split–and–merge algorithm extended to color images. The result is represented as a segmentation object containing chain code objects for the contours of the regions. The major advantages of operator–classes for segmentation and image processing are threefold:

- Algorithms can be programmed in an abstract level referencing only the general class of operations to be performed; extensions of the system by a new derived special operator will not require changes in the abstract algorithm.
- Such an extension cannot change the interface which is fixed by the definition in the abstract base class. This guarantees reusable, uniform, and thus easy–to–use interfaces.[1] In Figure 2, this is shown for the edge detectors (Sobel and ShenCastan) and for two different corner detectors (from [16]).
- Dynamic information about the operator which is actually used, is available. For example, a program may just reference a filter object; during run time it will be decided which concrete filter should be used.

---

[1] Of course, this is not *always* possible to achieve.

In Sect. 2.4 we argue that these advantages produce no additional run–time overhead. Similar hierarchies as the one in Figure 2 exist for filters and for region–based segmentation.

2.4 Software Experiments

Our system is compiled and tested for various hardware platforms, including HP (HPUX 9.07 and HPUX 10.20, 32 bit and 64 bit Versions), PC (Linux), SGI (IRIX 6.20), Sun (Solaris), etc.

The NIHCL class library served as a tool for most general programming problems, such as dictionaries, lists, and external data representation. It is available for all platforms listed above. STL was not available when the system was initiated but has now been used as well.

Operator classes are invoked by virtual function calls. This overhead in comparison to direct function calls is negligible, as long as the operation to be performed is non–trivial (as it is the case in the examples given). Pixel access — of course — may not be programmed by virtual function calls. This would slow down processing too much. Instead, the concept of genericity is used here (provided by templates in C++). Safe and efficient pixel access without any run–time overhead is provided as described in [25]. The application in Sect. 4.2 shows that real–time processing is possible using this approach.

3 Modules of ANIMALS

Various modules are provided in ANIMALS which were implemented for several applications. Since all segmentation algorithms use the common interface by segmentation objects, the compatiblity is high. This flexibility first requires additional effort for portable software. On the long run it reduces the effort of software maintenance.

3.1 Sensors and Actors

Due to the variability of the used hardware, several frame grabbers, cameras, lenses, stereo devices, etc. are connected to the system. In order not to burden the programs by a large number of switches, all these devices are encapsulated as classes. Whereas the internal implementation may be sophisticated and thereby provides the required performance, the user interfaces for these classes are simple in C++. To give an example, the stepper motor objects can all be assigned the desired position by the assignment operator in C++; thus, the vergence axis of the stereo head has the same software interface as the pan axis of a surveillance camera.

Calibration of zoom lenses is a complex problem since the motors used in consumer cameras will not always lead to accurate postitions. For the object localization system in Sect. 4.1 we need the enlargement factor related to a given position of the zoom stepper motor. The calibration according to [39] is

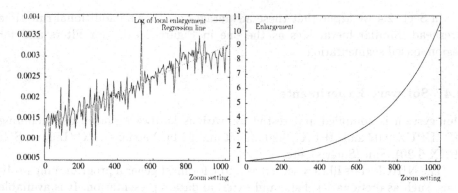

Figure 3. Logarithm of local enlargement factors and estimated enlargement factors

hard to do fully automatically, since a calibration pattern has to be chosen that is visible and that provides stable segmentation data for all possible focus and zoom settings.

In a simple approach we investigated the enlargement for two slightly different zoom settings for arbitrary lines in an image which are defined by two corresponding points, each. The corresponding points are found by tracking color points (Sect. 3.5) during zooming. To compute the factor from the smallest focal length to a given position, all intermediate results have to be multiplied. Naturally, this approach is not very stable since local errors accumulate. We took the logarithm of the factors and approximated these values by a regression line (Figure 3 (left)). The enlargement factors are computed by the exponential function (Figure 3 (right)). This provided reasonable accuarcy in the experiments in Sect. 4.1.

The results of this algorithm are recorded together with the camera object. Persistent storage of this object records all available calibration information.

3.2 Color

Most algorithms in ANIMALS operate on color images as well as gray–level images. Color provides simple cues for object localization since it is not very sensitive to aspect changes. Color histograms are used in [35] to form hypotheses for the position of an object in the two–dimensional projection in an image. A color image $[f_{ij}]_{1 \leq i \leq M, 1 \leq j \leq N}$ is searched for an object which is characterized by its histogram $T = [T_l]_{l=1...L}$ in some quantization L. In addition, the approximate size of the object in the image is needed for the algorithm; this size is represented by a mask. D_r covering the object. The function h maps a color vector f to an index $l = 1...L$ in the histogram and thus permits to use arbitrary quantizations. The principle of the algorithm is shown in Figure 4. The histogram H of the image is used to produce an output image B of the size of the input image; internally, an intermediate image A of the same dimension is used.

Given: image histogram $T = [T_l]_{l=1...L}$ of an object,
Wanted: object position (i_t, j_t)
Compute color histogram $H = [H_l]_{l=1...L}$ of given image
FOR Each bin $l \in \{1, \ldots, L\}$
$\quad R_l = \min\{\frac{T_l}{H_l}, 1\}$ (compute ratio histogram $R = [R_l]_{l=1...L}$)
FOR All positions (i, j) in the image
$\quad A_{i,j} := R_{h(f_{i,j})}$, where $f_{i,j}$ denotes the color vector at position (i, j)
$B := D_r \star A$, where $\star$ denotes convolution
$(i_t, j_t) := \mathrm{argmax}_{i,j}(B_{i,j})$

Figure 4. Localization of objects by histogram backprojection according to [35].

Color histograms for different color spaces are again represented as classes. Backprojection is a method of a common base class for these histograms. This means that the algorithm in Figure 4 can mostly be programmed as it is shown in the mathematical notation, which does not mention any particular color space.

3.3 Statistical Object Recognition

In a Bayesian framework for 3–D object recognition using 2–D images [1, 19], statistical model generation, classification, and localization is based on projected feature vectors O. We assume that the image $[f_{i,j}]_{1 \leq i \leq M, 1 \leq j \leq N}$ is transformed into a segmentation object of two–dimensional feature vectors $O = \{o_k \in \mathbb{R}^2 | 1 \leq k \leq m\}$ consisting of points (e.g. corners or vertices) or lines which can be detected by several combinations of segmentation operators from the class hierarchy shown in Figure 2, e.g. by the operator EdgeToSegObj. Results are shown in Figure 5. Model densities of 3–D objects appearing in images embody three principal components: the uncertainty of segmented feature vectors, the dependency of features on the object's pose, and the correspondence between image and model features. Due to the projection of the 3–D scene to the 2–D image plane, the range information and the assignment between image and model features is lost. The statistical description of an object belonging to class Ω_κ is defined by the density $p(O|B_\kappa, R, t)$, and discrete priors $p(\Omega_\kappa)$, $1 \leq \kappa \leq K$, if only single objects appear, or $p(\Omega_{\kappa_1}, \Omega_{\kappa_2}, \ldots, \Omega_{\kappa_q})$ for multiple

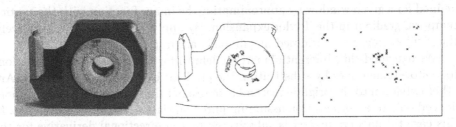

Figure 5. Object (left) segmented to lines and vertices (center) and points (right)

object scenes; the priors for the occurrences of an object are estimated by their relative frequencies in the training samples. The parameter R denotes rotation and projection from the model space to the image plane; t denotes translation. The parameter set B_κ contains the model–specific parameters which model the statistical behavior of features as well as the assignment. In the special case of segmented point features, B_κ statistically models the accuracy and stability of the object points.

Let us now assume that the parametric density of the model feature c_{κ,l_k} corresponding to o_k is given by $p(c_{\kappa,l_k}|a_{\kappa,l_k})$, where a_{κ,l_k} are the paramters for the density function of the feature c_{κ,l_k}. A standard density transform results in the density $p(o_k|a_{\kappa,l_k}, R, t)$ which characterizes the statistical behavior of the feature o_k in the image plane dependent on the object's pose parameters.

Using the robot or a camera mounted on some actor we record a set of images where the parameters R and t are known from calibration. For a segmented point it can be tested statistically, that a Gaussian distribution adequately models the features. The unknown parameters of the model density can be estimated by a maxium likelihood estimator. For object recognition and pose estimation, the parameters R and t are unknown as well and have to be estimated. Optimization classes (Sect. 3.8) were developed for this application [19].

Experimental evaluations compared standard methods for pose estimation with the introduced statistical approach. The statistical pose estimation algorithm requires 80 sec. using global optimization; to compare, the alignment method [37] needs 70 sec. in average on an HP 735. On a smaller sample of 49 images, the correct pose is computed for 45 images with the statistical approach; the alignment method failed for 11 images. In a test based on 1600 randomly chosen views of objects, the recognition rates for the statistical approach were in the range of 95% for 2–D recognition.

In another approach [27] we recognize objects directly by appearance–based statistical models of the image data. The approach can handle gray–level, color, and depth images as well as combinations of them.

3.4   Point Tracking

The basic idea in [34] is to select those points in a sequence of gray–level images, which exhibit features for stable tracking. Thereby the two questions which were formerly posed independently, are now combined to one problem: the question which points to select and how to track. The method minimizes a residue defined for a given window by approximating the image function with the spatio–temporal gradient in the Taylor expansion. By applying this method iteratively, the displacement is determined in sub–pixel accuracy.

We extended this differential method defined for real–valued image functions to vector–valued ones by substituting the gradient by the Jacobian matrix. Another extension to the original method is to restrict the search space of correspondenced only to an orientation assuming pure translational camera movement. In this case the Jacobin matrix is substituted by the directional derivative for the orientation vector of the epipolar line; this line links each pixel to the epipole.

For both extensions the criterion for tracking has been adapted. The use of color values shows, that more points can be selected and the tracking is more stable. In the case of restricted search space, the criterion results in a large gradient in the search direction. Therefore a huge number of points can be selected. We found that better and more robust tracking is possible in RGB than in an perceptually motivated color space or in gray–level image sequences; the number of points lost during tracking in RGB is more then 20% smaller than for gray–level images [1].

3.5 3–D Reconstruction

The module in Sect. 3.4 can be used to recover 3–D information. A camera mounted on a linear sledge is moved horizontally to record a sequence of images. Since points are tracked, no such correspondence problem as in stereo vision has to be solved explicitly. Instead, the regression line through the trajectory of a point determines its disparity. The regression error can be used as a measure for the certainty of the disparity value. The reliability of the range value is proportional to the disparity multiplied by the reliability of the disparity. The algorithm accepts an abstract point tracking operator (object), i.e., the same algorithm can be used for gray–level as well as color images.

3.6 Knowledge Base

In Sect. 3.3 we represented single objects by model densities. Alternatively, structural knowledge about scenes, object, as well as actions and strategies can be represented in a semantic network. Semantic networks have been applied successfully e.g. in [21, 22, 24] to pattern analysis problems. They provide an intuitive formalism for the representation of objects and facts which are required for computer vision. Our goal is to continue the work on knowledge representation concerning the semantic network formalism ERNEST [1, 24] by the integration of camera actions into the knowledge base. We also re–use the existing control algorithms for the semantic network. Alternative solutions for the explicit representation of actions are e.g. and–or trees [14] or Bayesian networks [32].

Using the notation and structure defined in [23, 33], a semantic network is a directed acyclic graph consisting of nodes and labeled edges. The nodes are concepts composed of attributes. They are used for the representation of objects and camera actions. The edges denote specialization which implies inheritance of attributes, part–of relations, and the concrete link which links entities of a different level of abstraction. Since image processing is never exact, all entities in the semantic network have an attached judgment which measures the degree of certainty. The judgment values are used to guide an A* graph search algorithm. The expansion of nodes in the search tree during analysis follows six inference rules [33], i.e. the control works independently of judgment functions and of the particular semantic network used in an application. Alternative possibilities for control strategies such as Markov decision processes are discussed in [12]; we also provide a second control algorithm called "parallel iterative control" [13].

Computer vision can be seen as an optimization problem which searches for the best match of segmentation data to the objects in the knowledge base and chooses optimal camera actions. A state search by A* thus is appropriate to solve this problem.

Figure 6 shows a typical semantic network. The lower part of the network contains objects which are used in the application in Sect. 4.1. The gray–shaded ovals represent different camera actions where each competing action (direct_search for a search without intermediate object [14], punch_besides_gluestick for a search for a punch using the intermediate object glue stick, ...) is linked to the concept explOfficeScene by competing part links; the control resolves these alternatives which are collected in so–called sets of modality (see [24] for details), i.e. for each alternative a new node in the search tree is generated during analysis. Concrete links relate the camera actions such as e.g. direct_search to the knowledge on objects. An instantiation of the concept direct_search calculates a new value for the attribute "pan position". The same holds for punch_besides_gluestick. Both instances have associated judgments, which are now used by the control in combination with the judgments of the scene knowledge to select the next search tree node for expansion. A subsequent instantiation of explOfficeScene using the higher judged camera action yields a camera movement to the position stored in the pan attribute. After this movement, new instances for the concepts representing the scene knowledge (colorRegion, punch ...) are generated. If the judgments of these concepts get worse, the search tree node which contains the instance of the other camera movement becomes the node with the highest judgment in the search tree. Therefore this node is selected by the control for expansion, which causes a second instantiation of the concept explOfficeScene. During this instantiation the other camera movement is performed.

The implementation, naturally, provides classes for all major items in the semantic network. A formal language definition is used to generate a parser and code generator which creates C++ code from the knowledge–base definition. Two control strategies can be tested on only one (unchanged) knowledge base definition. The classes involved here are an abstraction of the analysis procedure which is seen as a sequence of analysis states.

3.7 Active Contours and Active Rays

A simple and thereby powerful method for fast object detection and tracking is based on active contours or snakes [20]. A number of control points has to be chosen which define a parametric curve around an object. From an initial estimate, an energy minimization process contracts the contour to the object. To track moving objects, this step is repeated over time, in combination with some prediction mechanism to introduce some coherence of the contour movement in time [7].

In [1, 7] we proposed the notion of active rays which can also be used for the description of an object's contour; this reduces the 2–D contour extraction problem of active contours to a 1–D one. In this case, rays are cast in certain directions from an initial reference point inside the contour. The image is sampled

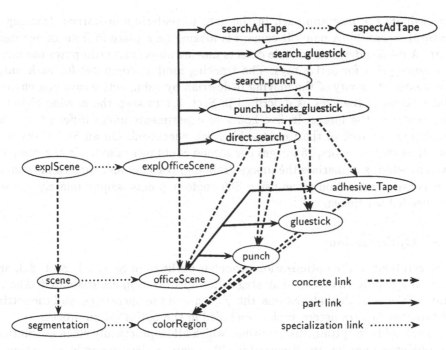

Figure 6. Combined representation of actions and objects in a knowledge base

along each ray. The contour points are now located in 1–D signals, i.e. the sampled image date on each ray. Similar to active contours, an internal and external energy is defined. The contour is extraced by minimizing the sum of these energies. In contrast to active contours, the energy minimization now takes place only along 1–D rays to attract points on each ray to the estimated object contour. The coherence in space of the contour is forced by the internal energy. Both ideas, active contours and active rays, are naturally represented as classes and share many lines of code.

Compared to active contours, there are several advantages of active rays for real–time applications: first, due to the representation of the contour points, parameterized by an angle defining the direction of each ray, neither any crossing can occur in the contour nor the contour points can move along the contour of the objects. Thus, prediction steps can be robustly applied. Second, an any–time algorithm can be defined which allows for an iterative refinement of the contour depending on the time which is available for each image. This is an important aspect for real–time applications. Third, textural features can be efficiently defined on 1–D signals, to locate changes in the gray–value statistics, identifying borders between two textured areas. This is a computational expensive task for active contours due to the independent search in the 2–D image plane [31]. Finally, an efficient combination with a 3–D prediction step is possible by using a similar radial representation of 3–D objects [8]

A complete object tracking system, called COBOLT (contour based localization and tracking, [7]) has been implemented in the ANIMALS framework to evaluate the new approach in the area of real–time pedestrian tracking in natural scenes [9]. A pan–tilt camera is looking on a place in front of our institute. A motion detecion module detects moving objects and computes the initial reference point for active rays. The tracking module computes for each image the center of gravity of the moving pedestrian by using active rays and changes the settings of the axes as described in Sect. 3.1 to keep the moving object in the center of the image. In five hours of experiments under different weather conditions, in 70% of the time tracking was successful. On an SGI Onyx with two R10000 processors, 25 images per second could be evaluated in the complete system which summarizes the image grabbing, tracking and camera movement. For contour extraction alone using 360 contour points, approximately 7 msec. are needed per image.

3.8 Optimization

The solutions of the optimization problems outlined in Sect. 2.1, Sect. 3.3, and Sect. 3.7 require that several strategies for optimization are evaluated. The results of the individual algorithms, the sequence of the operations, and the setting of the camera parameters, each is included in the optimization process.

Probabilistic optimization routines which allow practically efficient solutions for object recognition are discussed in [19]. Again, a class hierarchy for optimization strategies similar to the operator hierarchy above simplifies the experiments.

The basic idea of the implementation is to program the algorithms independently from the function which is to be optimized. An abstract base for all optimization strategies has an internal variable which is the function to be optimized; the class provides a method for minimization or maximization to all derived classes.

All optimization algorithms can be divided into global and local procedures; additional information may be present such as e.g. the gradient of the function which yields another class in the hierarchy. Procedures which use the function directly are e.g. the combinatorial optimization, the simplex algorithm, or the continuous variant of the simulated annealing algorithm. The gradient vector can be used for the optimization of first order. Examples are the iterative algorithms implemented in [19], the algorithm of Fletcher und Powell, and the well known Newton–Raphson iteration. The interface to the optimization classes simply accepts vector objects of real numbers and does not impose any other constraints on the parameters other than an interval in the case of global optimization. The computation times measured in [19] for the optimization classes were around one minute for 10000 calls to the function to be optimized.

4 Examples and Applications

4.1 Active Object Recognition

The goal of our major example in the context of this article is to show that a selection of the modules presented in Sect. 3 can be combined to build a system that locates objects in an office room. In [38] colored objects are located without prior knowledge; the image is partitioned and searched in a resolution hierarchy. The system here actively moves the camera and changes the parameters of the lens to create high resolution detail views. Camera actions as well as top–level knowledge are explicitly represented in a semantic network; the control algorithm of the semantic network used to guide the search is independent of the camera control. Knowledge on objects is represented in [11] by a hierarchical graph which could as well be formulated as a semantic network; the viewpoint control described there is part of the control algorithm for evaluating the graph. In contrast, [30] uses Bayesian networks to represent scenes and objects. Evidence gathered during analysis determines the next action to be performed which can be either a camera action or a new segmentation.

Real–world objects (e.g. a tape roller Figure 5, a glue stick and a punch Figure 7 right) are used in our experiments. The objects occupy only few pixels in the wide–angle views captured initially (Figure 7 left); they are presented to the system first isolated from the background; their color histogram for the current lighting is recorded. The approximate size of the object is stored in the semantic network manually in advance. This simple object model is sufficient to discriminate the objects in this example. The formalism used as well as the control structure allows for arbitrary other object models, such as for example aspects as applied in [11]; such a model will be simple for the object Figure 5 (left) but will be complex in the case of objects such as the punch in Figure 7 (right). Hypotheses for object locations in the scene are generated based on color using the algorithm outlined in Sect. 3.2. Results are shown below in Figure 9 for the object from Figure 5. An evalutation of six color normalization algorithms in [6] on 20 objects including those in Figure 5 and Figure 7 (right) revealed that the choice of the best color normalization algorithm with respect to object localization depends on the particular object. In most cases, UV histograms performed better than RGB.

The pan–tilt unit mounted on the linear sledge is moved to estimate 3–D information using the ideas outlined in Sect. 3.5; we compute a set of scattered 3–D points. The focal length is known from calibration (Sect. 3.1). A result is shown in Figure 8; neither the accuracy nor the number of points is sufficient to estimate 3–D surfaces of the objects.

The subsequent goal now is to fovealize each object hypothesis and to generate close–up views. This is required since for the object's size in the overview image no stable features based on segmented regions can be detected. Figure 7 shows an overview of the scene captured with minimal focal length. Figure 7 shows three hypotheses in the close–up view. First, the pan–tilt unit is rotated such that the optical axis of the zoom lens points to the hypothesized object position estimated from the backprojection. From the 3–D information and the approximate size stored in the knowledge–base we can now estimate the zoom position which is appropriate for a close–up view of the object. In [40, p. 45] three methods are listed to do fovealization technically. The method above using a pan–tilt device on a linear sledge adds a new fourth method to this list.

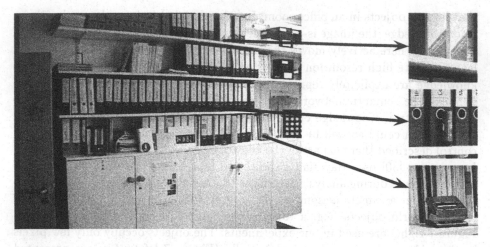

Figure 7. Scene overview and hypotheses for objects

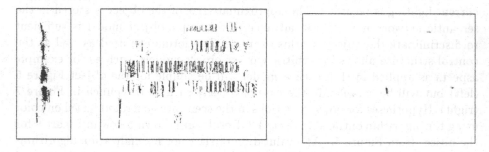

Figure 8. Two projections of 3–D points for **Figure 9.** Backprojection of red ob-
Figure 7   ject

The segmentation of color regions on the detail view of the scene now uses
the color segmentation mentioned in Sect. 2.3 and passes these regions to the
knowledge–based analysis module; they are collected in a segmentation object
attributed by the focal length, distance to the camera, and reliability of the
depth value. Results are shown in Figure 10.

The goal of the module for object verification is to find an optimal match
of segmented regions in the color close–up views and the gray ovals in Figure 6.
The search is directed by the judgment of the concept officeScene which is the
goal concept for the subgraph of gray ovals in Figure 6. For the computation
we use the attributes, relations, and their judgments in the parts and concrete
concepts. In the concept colorRegion we use the Euclidian distance of the mean
color vector to a prototype of the color red which is determined by the mean of a
histogram, previously. The color space is the intensity–normalized RGB-space.

The similarity of regions for the concepts punch, adhesive_Tape, and gluestick
is computed by the attributes height and width of the objects and thus — in the
current implementation — depends on the aspect. An extension is envisaged in

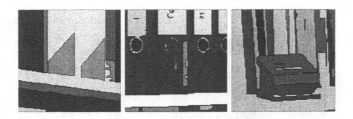

Figure 10. Segmentation of object hypotheses; shown in Figure 7 (right).

combination with the project in Sect. 3.3. The actual scale is determined by the 3–D information computed in Sect. 3.5.

For the search during matching of the regions we use an A^* control [23] for the graph search which computes an instantiation path through the network. The concepts are then instantiated bottom–up in the order determined by the path. This means, that no restrictions are propagated during the analysis. The judgment of the nodes in the search tree is equal to the judgment of the goal concept; all judgments of non–instantiated parts are set to one as long as the goal concept is not reached, in order to guarantee an optimistic estimate. The computation of the judgment is deferred to computations of judgments for concepts which in turn use their attributes. The similiarity measure for color regions influencing the judgment is part of the task specific knowledge and can thus be exchanged easily.

In 17 experiments for evaluation of this application we used the punch, glue stick and two tape rollers of identical shape but different size; thus object identification based only on color was not possible. The data driven hypotheses located 77 of 97 objects correctly. To restrict the size of the search tree to 300–600 nodes, we presently use a heuristic judgment function which weights regions of the object's color higher than regions of other colors. The rate of correct verifications of the hypotheses is around 70%. This figure includes the frequent confusions of stapler with the large tape. If we leave this object out, the recognition rate is around 80%. The total time for processing is around 2 min. for one scene on an SGI O2 (R10000, 195 MHz). Large parts of this time are spent for the color segmentation, backprojection, and waiting for the camera to reach a stable position. The convolution in Figure 4 was replaced by a 21×21 median filter to obtain good local maxima which needs several seconds per image to be computed.

4.2 Autonomous Mobile Systems

Autonomous mobile systems ideally can be used to integrate different aspects of computer vision into one common application. In the project DIROKOL[2] a service robot will supply employees in hospitals by so–called fetch and carry services. The system is equipped with a couple of classical robotic sensors (sonar,

[2] The project is funded by the Bavarian Research Foundation (Bayerische Forschungsstiftung).

 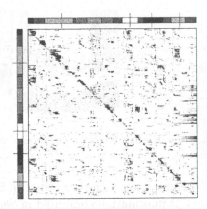

Figure 11. Left: Sample landmark defintion. Right: Confusion matrix of the positions during a movement through our lab showing the quality of self–localization. Dark areas indicate high correspondence between two positions. Bars indicate turning points.

infrared, etc.), a four finger hand [3] mounted on a robot arm, and with a stereo camera system for visual navigation, object recognition and active knowledge–based scene exploration. Similar to the application described in Sect. 4.1 semantic networks are used. The complexity of dynamic scenes in autonomous mobile systems applications makes it necessary, to apply probabilistic knowledge representation schemes (Markov models, dynamic Bayesian networks) as well. For these approaches it is more natural, to acquire knowledge during a training step automatically. The goal for the future is, to combine the classical approach of semantic networks with probabilistic representation schemes to have both, a hard–wired explicit knowledge base and an adjustable, trainable part, especially for the active components in an active vision system.

Actual work on probabilistic methods in this context has been performed on automatic natural landmark definition and localization with application to visual self–localization based on stochastic sampling [10]. The landmark definition is based on color histograms (Sect. 3.2) which has been extended to contain additional information on the distribution of the pixels position of a certain color bin as in [17]. The extented color histogram is implemented by re–using code of the classical histogram by deriving a new class with additional information about the distribution in the image plane of pixel falling into a certain histogram bin.

The experiments have shown, that on average 4.2 landmarks (variance: 11.19) have been automatically defined for each position (see Figure 11, left). With these landmarks self–localization by a stochastic sampling have been evaluated. The computation time for landmarks definition and self–localization is 230 msec. and 14 msec. for 100 samples, respectively. In Figure 11, right, results are shown by using a confusion matrix of the positions in our laboratory. As expected, the diagonal of the matrix has many entries, indicating a good self–localization ability. Also, similar positions seen during the movement are recognized (dark entries on certain side diagonal elements). It is worth noting, that these results are only based on color histograms without any 3D knowledge or other active sensors. Actually neither dependencies between landmarks seen at a certain position nor context in time is taken into account. This is done in our actual work.

5 Conclusion and Future Work

Most knowledge–based systems in computer vision represent only objects or scenes in the knowledge base. Here, an approach to represent actions and strategies in the same formalism was presented. This will be most important in active vision and for autonomous systems.

We described our system architecture for active image understanding which is implemented in an object–oriented fashion. Classes and objects encapsulate data, devices, and operators as well as the knowledge base. The applications presented make use of a subset of the modules and prove that the approach is feasible for knowledge–based analysis as well as real–time processing. We argued that this programming paradigm simplifies solving image analysis tasks. Object–oriented programming is preferred to genericity for hierarchies of operator classes; assuming that the task of an operator is not trivial, the overhead imposed by this implementation scheme is negligible. Genericity is used for regular data structures such as for pixel access in image matrices.

In our application for active object recognition and scene exploration, we used a knowledge base represented as a semantic network of camera actions and object models. In our application for autonomous mobile systems, color was used for landmark detection as a first stage of knowledge–based navigation and operation. Both applications share various modules for image processing and analysis.

More modules exist in our system which can be combined with the systems described in Sect. 4. To give an example, one of the color normalization algorithms described in [6] will be selected for each object in the application in Sect. 4.1; this selection will be annotated to the object in the knowledge base. Moving objects in an object room will be tracked using the methods of Sect. 3.7 after they have been localized. An integration of statistical models (Sect. 3.3) and semantic networks (Sect. 4.1 [19, 27]) will be used for holistic object recognition as in [21]. These models are invariant of the aspect. To apply our appearance based statistical method (Sect. 3.3 [27]), a fixed size of the object within the image is required. Therefore, we need exact knowledge about depth to zoom to the appropriate size. The changing perspective distortions at different object distances are neglected.

References

1. More references to our own work can be found in the publication section of our web site.
2. R. B. Arps and W. K. Pratt, editors. *Image Processing and Interchange: Implementation and Systems*, San Jose, CA, 1992. SPIE, Proceedings 1659.

3. J. Butterfass, G. Hirzinger, S. Knoch, and H. Liu. Dlr's multisensory articulated hand. In *IEEE International Conference on Robotics and Automation*, pages 2081–2086, Leuven, Belgium, 1998.

4. I. C. Carlsen and D. Haaks. IKS^{PFH} — concept and implementation of an object–oriented framework for image processing. *Computers and Graphics*, 15(4):473–482, 1991.

5. D. Crevier and R. Lepage. Knowledge-based image understanding systems: A survey. *Computer Vision and Image Understanding*, 67(2):161–185, August 1997.

6. L. Csink, D. Paulus, U. Ahlrichs, and B. Heigl. Color Normalization and Object Localization. In Rehrmann [29], pages 49–55.

7. J. Denzler. *Aktives Sehen zur Echtzeitobjektverfolgung*. Infix, Aachen, 1997.

8. J. Denzler, B. Heigl, and H. Niemann. An efficient combination of 2d and 3d shape description for contour based tracking of moving objects. In H. Burkhardt and B. Neumann, editors, *Computer Vision - ECCV 98*, pages 843–857, Berlin, Heidelberg, New York, London, 1998. Lecture Notes in Computer Science.

9. J. Denzler and H. Niemann. Real–time pedestrian tracking in natural scenes. In G. Sommer, K. Daniliidis, and J. Pauli, editors, *Computer Analysis of Images and Patterns, CAIP'97, Kiel 1997*, pages 42–49, Berlin, Heidelberg, New York, London, 1997. Lecture Notes in Computer Science.

10. J. Denzler and M. Zobel. Automatische farbbasierte Extraktion natürlicher Land-marken und 3D-Positionsbestimmung auf Basis visueller Information in indoor Umgebungen. In Rehrmann [29], pages 57–62.

11. S.J. Dickinson, H.I. Christensen, J.K. Tsotsos, and G. Olofsson. Active object recognition integrating attention and viewpoint control. *Computer Vision and Image Understanding*, 67(3):239–260, September 1997.

12. B. Draper, A. Hanson, and E. Riseman. Knowledge-directed vision: Control, learn-ing and integration. *Proceedings of the IEEE*, 84(11):1625–1637, Nov 1996.

13. V. Fischer and H. Niemann. A parallel any–time control algorithm for image un-derstanding. In *Proceedings of the 13th International Conference on Pattern Recog-nition (ICPR)*, pages A:141–145, Vienna, Austria, October 1996. IEEE Computer Society Press.

14. T. Garvey. Perceptual strategies for purposive vision. Technical report, SRI AI Center, SRI International, Menlo Park, 1976.

15. R. M. Haralick and V. Ramesh. Image understanding environment. In Arps and Pratt [2], pages 159–167.

16. M. Harbeck. *Objektorientierte linienbasierte Segmentierung von Bildern*. Shaker Verlag, Aachen, 1996.

17. B. Heisele, W. Ritter, and U. Kreßel. Objektdetektion mit Hilfe des Farbflecken-flusses. In V. Rehrmann, editor, *Erster Workshop Farbbildverarbeitung*, volume 15 of *Fachberichte Informatik*, pages 30–35, Universität Koblenz–Landau, 1995.

18. A. Hoogs and D. Hackett. Model-supported exploitation as a framework for image understanding. In *ARPA*, pages I:265–268, 1994.

19. J. Hornegger. *Statistische Modellierung, Klassifikation und Lokalisation von Ob-jekten*. Shaker Verlag, Aachen, 1996.

20. M. Kass, A. Wittkin, and D. Terzopoulos. Snakes: Active contour models. *Inter-national Journal of Computer Vision*, 2(3):321–331, 1988.

21. F. Kummert, G. Fink, and G. Sagerer. Schritthaltende hybride Objektdetektion. In E. Paulus and F. Wahl, editors, *Mustererkennung 1997*, pages 137–144, Berlin, September 1997. Springer.

22. C.-E. Liedtke, O. Grau, and S. Growe. Use of explicit knowledge for the reconstruction of 3-D object geometry. In V. Hlavac and R. Sara, editors, *Computer analysis of images and patterns — CAIP '95*, number 970 in Lecture Notes in Computer Science, Heidelberg, 1995. Springer.

23. H. Niemann. *Pattern Analysis and Understanding*, volume 4 of *Springer Series in Information Sciences*. Springer, Heidelberg, 1990.

24. H. Niemann, G. Sagerer, S. Schröder, and F. Kummert. Ernest: A semantic network system for pattern understanding. *IEEE Transactions on Pattern Analysis and Machine Intelligence (PAMI)*, 9:883–905, 1990.

25. D. Paulus and J. Hornegger. *Pattern Recognition of Images and Speech in C++*. Advanced Studies in Computer Science. Vieweg, Braunschweig, 1997.

26. D. Paulus and H. Niemann. Iconic–symbolic interfaces. In Arps and Pratt [2], pages 204–214.

27. J. Pösl, B. Heigl, and H. Niemann. Color and depth in appearance based statistical object localization. In H. Niemann, H.-P. Seidel, and B. Girod, editors, *Image and Multidimensional Digital Signal Processing '98*, pages 71–74, Alpbach, Austria, July 1998. Infix.

28. J. R. Rasure and M. Young. Open environment for image processing and software development. In Arps and Pratt [2], pages 300–310.

29. V. Rehrmann, editor. *Vierter Workshop Farbbildverarbeitung*, Koblenz, 1998. Föhringer.

30. R. Rimey and C. Brown. Task–oriented Vision with Multiple Bayes Nets. In A. Blake and A. Yuille, editors, *Active Vision*, pages 217–236, Cambridge, Massachusetts, 1992.

31. R. Ronfard. Region-based strategies for active contour models. *International Journal of Computer Vision*, 13(2):229–251, 1994.

32. S. J. Russell and P. Norvig. *Artificial Intelligence. A Modern Approach*. Prentice-Hall, Englewood Cliffs, NJ, 1995.

33. G. Sagerer and H. Niemann. *Semantic Networks for Understanding Scenes*. Advances in Computer Vision and Machine Intelligence. Plenum Press, New York and London, 1997.

34. J. Shi and C. Tomasi. Good features to track. In *Proceedings of Computer Vision and Pattern Recognition*, pages 593–600, Seattle, Washington, Juni 1994. IEEE Computer Society Press.

35. M. J. Swain and D. H. Ballard. Color indexing. *International Journal of Computer Vision*, 7(1):11–32, November 1991.

36. F. Thomanek and E.D. Dickmanns. Autonomous road vehicle guidance in normal traffic. In *Second Asian Conference on Computer Vision*, pages III/11–III/15, Singapore, 1995.

37. S. Ullman. *High-Level Vision: Object Recognition and Visual Cognition*. MIT Press, Cambridge, MA, 1996.

38. V.V. Vinod and H. Murase. Focused color intersection with efficient searching for object extraction. *Pattern Recognition*, 30(10):1787–1797, October 1997.

39. R.G. Willson. *Modeling and Calibration of Automated Zoom Lenses*. PhD thesis, Carnegie Mellon University, Pittsburgh, 1994.

40. Y. Yeshurun. Attentional mechanisms in computer vision. In V. Cantoni, editor, *Artificial Vision, Human and machine perception*, pages 43–52. Plenum Press, New York, 1997.

Experience in Integrating Image Processing Programs

M. Thonnat, S. Moisan, and M. Crubézy

Projet ORION, INRIA – B.P. 93 F-06902 Sophia Antipolis Cedex, France
Monique.Thonnat, Sabine.Moisan, Monica.Crubezy@sophia.inria.fr

Abstract. This paper describes experience we have gained in using program supervision techniques for integration and control of image processing programs. The role of these knowledge-based techniques is to handle high level knowledge about the use of programs together with their effective execution and control. First, the main concepts of program supervision techniques are introduced. Then we present three major classes of application domains where we have applied program supervision techniques: road obstacle detection, medical imaging and astronomy. From these experiments, we conclude that program supervision techniques are good candidates to perform a semantical integration of image processing programs. These techniques are independent of any particular application domain or image processing programs. We propose a general architecture for such systems, which can be slightly tuned for specific purposes. For code designers, semantical integration implies to think from the beginning about how their image processing programs can be integrated and controlled.

1 Introduction

We are interested in knowledge-based techniques for integration and control of image processing programs, called *program supervision*. The role of program supervision is to select programs in an existing library, to run them for particular input data and to eventually control the quality of their results. Various knowledge-based systems have been developed for this purpose in the domain of image processing. We first present our motivations and objectives, then we define more precisely what program supervision is and its importance in vision applications. The heart of the paper describes some prototype applications we have developed for image processing problems. We present three major classes of application domains where we have applied program supervision techniques: road obstacle detection, medical imaging and astronomy. Then, an architecture for program supervision systems and a platform for developing them are presented. We finally conclude that program supervision techniques are adapted to semantical integration of various image processing programs for different applications, at the price of a minimal effort from the beginning of the code design.

2   Motivation

The field of image processing has produced a large number of powerful programs and many different program libraries have been developed. In such libraries the individual programs are integrated from a low-level point of view. But no support is provided to users who need to solve practical image processing problems. Every end-user cannot have a deep understanding of program semantics and syntax. Inexperienced ones may only have a basic understanding of the field of image processing and its terminology. On the other hand, programs implement more and more complex functionalities and their use is equally difficult. If it is too demanding for an end-user to catch the complexity of new programs, these programs will never be widely applied. Our objective is to help users in application fields manage image processing techniques that are needed for their applications. From the analysis of the task of an image processing expert who processes data using a set of programs, we have derived knowledge models related to this task. Based on these models, we propose to support users of image processing libraries, by providing a knowledge-based system for program supervision that takes in charge the management of the library use, freeing the user of doing it manually. This aid can range from an advisory guide up to fully automatic program monitoring systems. The basic idea is to automate the choice and execution of programs from a library to accomplish a user's processing objective. This is done by encapsulating the knowledge of program use in a knowledge base and by emulating the strategy of an expert in the use of the programs. We can summarize our motivation by saying that we are interested in a semantical integration of programs which can also take in charge the control of the quality of their execution.

3   Program Supervision

Program Supervision aims at facilitating the (re)configuration of data processing programs. Such a configuration may involve the chaining of many different programs. It is to note that the program codes usually pre-exist (in a library, for example) and the goal is not to optimize the program themselves, but their *use*. A program supervision knowledge-based system helps a non-specialist user apply programs in different situations as shown in figure 1. It is composed of a program supervision engine and a knowledge base.

The role of the program supervision *engine* is to exploit knowledge about programs in order to produce a plan of programs, that achieves the user's goal. It emulates the strategy of an expert in the use of programs. The final plan that produces satisfactory outputs is usually not straightforward, it often results from several trials and errors. The reasoning engine explores the different possibilities and computes the best one, with respect to expert criteria, available in the knowledge base. The reasoning of a program supervision system consists of different phases, that can be completely or only partly automated: *planning* and *execution* of programs, *evaluation* of the results, and *repair*.

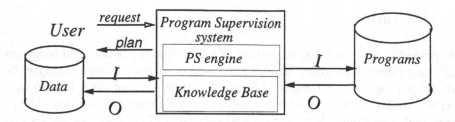

Fig. 1. A knowledge-based program supervision system helps a user (re)use a set of programs for solving a request on input data $\mathcal{I}$ to obtain output data $\mathcal{O}$, as the result of the execution of a plan of programs. It is composed of a program supervision engine and a knowledge base.

The *knowledge base* contains *operators* which are representations of programs (with descriptions of their data and parameters) and of typical combinations of programs, as well as criteria to guide the reasoning process. There are two types of operators: primitive and complex ones. A *primitive operator* represents a particular program and a *complex operator* represents a particular combination of programs. Program combinations correspond to decompositions into more concrete programs, at different levels of abstraction, either by specialization (alternatives) or composition (sequences, parallel, loops, etc.). Moreover, abstract processing functionalities are represented by *goals*. Various criteria, implemented by rules, play an important role during the reasoning, e.g. to choose between different alternatives (*choice criteria*), to tune program execution (*initialization criteria*), to diagnose the quality of the results (*evaluation criteria*) and to repair a bad execution (*adjustment* and *repair criteria*). The contents of the knowledge base should be sufficient for the engine to select the programs, to initialize their parameters, to manage non trivial data-flow and to combine the programs to produce a satisfactory plan of programs, depending on the input data and user's request.

Program supervision is a research domain with an increasing number of work coming from many applicative and technical domains [17]. These research activities are often motivated by a particular application domain (as image processing, signal processing or scientific computing). On the contrary to knowledge-based systems for image interpretation which have been studied for about 20 years, knowledge-based systems for image processing program supervision are more recent. In Japan, numerous teams, belonging both to the research and to the industrial sector, have spent an important effort to this problem (see [18], [14] and [10]). In Europe work has been developed either as research on general tools (as OCAPI [6]) or as industrial tools for a particular application (as the VIDIMUS Esprit project [4]). In the United States early work has been done by Johnston [9] and by Bailey [1]. Recently [8] and [5] have used planning techniques for composing image analysis processes.

4 Prototype Applications

This section shows examples of program supervision systems for image processing in very different application domains.

4.1 Road Obstacle Detection

In the framework of the European Eureka project PROMETHEUS we have done two different experiments using our program supervision techniques for road image analysis.

Stereovision-based Road Obstacle Detection The first example concerns a module performing the detection of objects (such as road, cars, and posts) in road scenes and urban scenes using stereovision data. This module is difficult to use due to the existence of a lot of technical parameters to tune. The data come from two cameras fixed on the top of a moving car. A pyramidal stereovision algorithm based on contour chain points [11] is used to reconstruct the 3D environment in front of the vehicle. Obstacles are detected using 3D as well as 2D information. Integration of the knowledge on the use of this module is needed for robustness, and above all to manage the great variety of the scenes. This integration has been done through a knowledge base, named PROMETHEE. More precisely, a lot of contextual values in the scenes may vary. The luminosity depends on the weather conditions and on the moment in the day, the complexity of the scene depends on the number of objects in front of the car, and the velocity of objects depends on the location of the scene: highway, countryside road or urban street. Due to this variety, it is not possible to fix once and for all the values of the different parameters involved in the processing.

The initial request is the processing of a particular pair of images (taken by two cameras) for object detection. Figure 2 shows an example of such images in the case of an urban scene. First, a 3D reconstruction of the scene is made using a pyramidal stereovision process. Then the 3D reconstruction, together with 2D information (the straight line segments), are used to detect the road, the cars, and the posts. The detected cars are shown in figure 3.

The user needs to take numerous decisions to manage the usage of these programs. A full processing chain contains about 15 different programs to run. Some programs are run several times with different input data; it is the case for instance for the primitive extraction which is made both on left and right images and for different image resolutions. The complete processing contains about 70 program executions. For some steps there are different alternative methods the user can select; for instance there are two different matching techniques each one having several implementations with slight differences. There are a total of 54 values to set to initialize numerical parameters. Among these values several are correlated and there are numerous sensitive parameters.

We have developed a knowledge base to express the knowledge of the usage of these programs. This knowledge base works with the OCAPI [6] engine. Here follow some examples of goals, operators and criteria in this base.

Fig. 2. Stereo images corresponding to an urban scene

Fig. 3. Detected cars in an urban scene

Goals and Operators The knowledge base contains several *goals*, e.g.: *object-detection, pyramidal-stereovision, primitive-extraction, stereo-matching, contour-detection, 2D-3D-cooperation*. For instance, the goal *stereo-matching* corresponding to the actual matching of two images (as part of the pyramidal stereovision process) has 6 input arguments (three pairs of images, with respectively the contour chains, the gradients, and the gradient orientations). The output arguments are an image containing the matched primitives (3D information), and an image containing disparity information. Four choice criteria and one evaluation rule are attached to this goal.

Several primitive and complex *operators* have also been defined in the knowledge base: each of them corresponds to a particular abstract goal. The operator *O-detect-objects* is an example of a complex operator. It corresponds to the goal *object-detection*. It is decomposed into several substeps: first pyramidal stereovision, then a polygonal approximation and finally an object detection using both 2D and 3D information. An example of a primitive operator is the operator *O-meygret-stereo-match* that corresponds to the goal *stereo-matching*. Besides the input and output arguments of its corresponding goal, it also has some additional parameter arguments: two threshold values, respectively on the magnitude and the orientation of the gradient. This operator also contains three initialization criteria and three adjustment criteria.

Criteria The criteria, expressed as production rules, often use information stored in the knowledge base describing the context of use, e.g. information about the physical environment: the type of camera used, the distance from the camera to the front of the car, and whether there is motion or not (motion of the cameras and/or motion of the objects). Some other information concerns the user constraints such as the level of detail that must be extracted from the image (compared to the amount of information in the scene), the desired stereo matching adaptability and quality, or if the processing has to be performed automatically (without possibility of asking a human user to validate the results) or in an interactive way.

- *Choice criteria* contain knowledge on how to select the pertinent operator according to the context of use and to operator characteristics, when several operators are available to solve the same goal. For instance, several operators are available to satisfy the goal *pyramidal-stereovision*. Among them the two operators *O-stereo-pyr1* and *O-stereo-pyr2* perform stereovision using a pyramidal technique and are based on contour chain points. The first operator directly implements this algorithm, while the second one first separates the two interlaced acquisition frames by sampling the lines. The second operator is thus well-adapted when motion is present and when two consecutive lines are not taken consecutively, but at time t and $t + T/2$ (if t is the time, and T is the acquisition period). The rule presented below, attached to the goal *pyramidal-stereovision*, implements such a choice criterion.

    if   *context.motion* $==$ *present*
    then   use-operator-with-characteristic *with-sampling-for-motion*
    comment "only 1 of the 2 interlaced frames if motion"

- *Evaluation criteria* are most of the time very difficult to express to assess the results of low level goals (like thresholding) since, for example, results are matrices of pixels. But for higher level goals which produce descriptions or object interpretations as results, they are easier to express for experts. For example, the intermediate-level goal *stereo-matching* produces as output matched pairs of primitives which can be counted and compared to a required value. Here follows an automatic evaluation rule of the goal *stereo-matching*:

> if $xyz.primitives.number < (imchains.primitives.number) / 3$
> then   assess $number\text{-}primitives\ insufficient$
> comment "insufficient matched pairs"

This rule tests the ratio between the number of matched primitives (stored in the data description of the image input data xyz of the goal $stereo\text{-}matching$) and the number of input primitives (stored in the data description of the argument $imchains$). If this ratio is below the value of 1/3 the rule qualifies the number of matched pairs of primitives as insufficient. Once this problem is diagnosed, it can be repaired later.

– *Initialization criteria* are used to set the parameters of an operator, the value of which depends strongly on the context. For instance, the operator *O-thres-hysteresis* which performs a thresholding by hysteresis (as part of the primitive extraction process) needs the initialization of two input parameters: a high threshold and a low threshold. These thresholds are defined as numerical parameters. The initialization of these values is usually performed in two reasoning phases. In a first phase only symbolical information is used. For example if the user only wants *few* details to be extracted, the threshold should be *high,* as shown in the rule:

> if $context.user\text{-}constraints.details == few$
> then $threshold := high$
> comment "few details implies high threshold"

In a second reasoning phase the symbolical values are translated to concrete numbers, as in the rule:

> if $threshold == average$
> then $heuristic\text{-}value := 25$
> comment "average threshold implies 25 as heuristic value"

This second phase of translation into numbers can be done by selecting a static heuristic value (as shown in the previous rule) or by dynamically computing a value using a calculation method (e.g. probability calculations based on the image histogram).

– When an operator fails because the results are not satisfactory, *adjustment criteria* provide knowledge on how to modify its parameters w.r.t. the type of the failure. For example, we have seen that the evaluation of the goal *stereo-matching* can assess that the number of matched pairs of primitives is insufficient; in such a case, it is possible to adjust the input parameters of the corresponding operator *O-meygret-stereo-match* which are a threshold on the magnitude of the gradient (*thr-m*), and a threshold on the orientation of the gradient (*thr-o*). Below, we show two adjustment rules for this operator. The first one states that the adjustment method for the parameter (*thr-o*) is a technique by percentage:

> if   ...
> then adjust-by percentage *thr-o*,
>   adjustment-step *thr-o* $:= 0.3$

The second rule states that if the number of matched pairs of primitives is insufficient, the two parameters *(thr-m)* and *(thr-o)* have to be increased:

> if   assessed? *number-primitives insufficient*
> then increase *thr-m*,
>   increase *thr-o*

The PROMETHEE knowledge base [16] contains the representations of 24 programs and 15 combinations of programs. There are 120 criteria among which 64 parameter initializations, 15 choices between operators, 20 result evaluations, and 21 parameters adjustments. Thanks to this knowledge base, all numerical parameters are automatically set. Moreover, all decisions for method selection are fully automated. In the same way all repairs are automatic: they are achieved by adjustment of numerical parameters. The image processing module is general and can be applied to very different images corresponding to various application domains. Two types of problems are automatically detected: a bad primitive extraction and a bad matching. Two other types of thresholding problems can be detected interactively.

Real-time Road obstacle Detection After this positive experiment, we decided to use these techniques to facilitate the integration and control of various image processing programs which have been developed by three external laboratories within the framework of the Eureka European PROMETHEUS project. Thus, a real-time program supervision system, named PLANETE [12], has been embarked on a demonstrator vehicle for traffic safety [13]. It managed the use of a 3-D obstacle detector using telemetry [19], of a mathematical morphology-based obstacle detector [3], and of a motion segmenter [2]. The aim was to provide a system for driving assistance (or copilot) to help the driver in detecting obstacles (cars, pedestrians, etc.) in realistic traffic situations. The demonstration vehicle was equipped with several sensors: 5 CCD cameras, 1 linear stereo camera pair and one telemetry-camera combination, in addition to a number of proprioceptive sensors. The copilot was an intelligent real-time system which processed the information flowing into it from the sensors, used this information to interpret the traffic situation in the vicinity of the vehicle, and communicated its analysis to the driver by means of several interfaces. The total duration of such a cycle was 200ms. In such a real-time real-life application the task of a program supervision system is made more difficult by the stringent requirements of efficiency and speed, and by limited computational (hardware and software) resources. The copilot was composed of a situation interpreter, a data manager, and the real-time program supervision system PLANETE (see figure 4).

The high-level analysis of the traffic scene was done by the situation interpreter, that emitted a request. This request, expressed in terms of zones, obstacles, etc., was then translated by PLANETE into a series of low-level commands—expressed in terms of sensors, program names, data flow, etc.—to the perception programs. The results of the processing done by these programs were then communicated via the data manager to the situation interpreter for further analysis. The role of PLANETE was to make the perceptual processing optimal in the sense of efficiency, timeliness and responsiveness to the rapidly-varying informational requirements of the copilot. PLANETE supervised the running of perception pro-

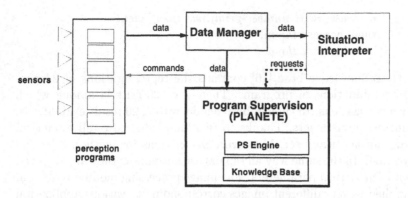

Fig. 4. The copilot architecture.

grams (selection of programs, setting of parameters, etc.) on the one hand, and the efficient management of the computational resources on the other. The prototype vehicle was designed to detect obstacles in different traffic scenarios, such as driving on a city street, crossing an intersection or driving on a highway.

The PLANETE program supervision system succeeded in being fully automated. It was able to manage different types of events: switching from normal driving to overtaking (in that case detection of possible obstacles in the left lane and the status of the blinkers of possible cars in the rear was checked), arrival at a crossing area (a motion detection in both left and right front areas was checked), switching back to normal driving (detection and tracking of obstacles in the front area). It has been demonstrated in October 1994 at the end of the PROMETHEUS project. Unfortunately, the validation of PLANETE has been partial because it has only been tested on several occurrences of a one hour driving scenario in one test circuit.

4.2 Medical Imaging

The third example falls in the medical imaging domain. The objective is to provide clinical users with wider access to evolving medical image processing techniques. In this context, better than fully automating the use of programs, program supervision works in collaboration with users, leaving them with their interpretation (e.g. diagnosis) competence (e.g. for many evaluation criteria). We have developed two applications: Factor Analysis of Medical Image Sequences [7] and Brain Anatomic Segmentation. We detail here our study concerning brain segmentation on 3D MRI images, based on spatial characteristics (e.g. anatomic)[1]. The segmentation process uses computer vision methods, mainly mathematical morphology. First, it binarizes and isolates the informative area (i.e. brain) in images, merely by thresholding methods, then it eliminates the small uninteresting connexities (by means of erosion method) and extracts the

---

[1] In collaboration with the EPIDAURE team at INRIA, Sophia Antipolis, France.

greatest connected component in the image, assumed to be the brain. Third, lost information is reconstructed thanks to a dilation and an intersection with thresholded image. Last, the segmented brain is presented with superimposition to initial image (see figure 5).

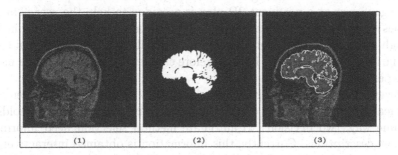

Fig. 5. Example of a segmentation process on 3D MRI brain images: first image is part of initial acquisition, second image shows a slice of the result of segmentation and third image presents a superimposition of the segmented area on initial image, for better visualisation. (Courtesy of Grégoire Malandain, INRIA)

The exact process performed depends on image characteristics, and is solved by its run-time adaptation by the supervision engine. The user needs to take numerous decisions to manage the usage of these programs; a full processing chain contains between 10 and 15 programs to run. There are a total of 27 values to set to initialize numerical parameters. Among these values several are correlated; for instance the size of the structural element for erosion and the one for dilation. The user needs also to take 7 decisions to select between alternative methods.

Medical knowledge important for supervision is not included in programs, but involved in expert's mental process when applying them. We have developed a knowledge base to explicit this process. We have expressed pre-defined high-level combinations of processing steps using symbolic formulation of this knowledge. In particular, medical-related knowledge is stored at an abstract level of the knowledge base, on top of general image processing methodological knowledge. This separation enables the effective supervision of programs and prepares their re-use for other purposes. Another hallmark of this application is that expert's reasoning is highly based on a trial process. Program parameters are difficult to initialize appropriately at once, as they are very sensitive to image quality. The repair phase of program supervision takes here its whole importance, implemented by a mechanism that enables to store the history of problems and transmit them to operators that hold corresponding repair knowledge. Decisions also consider the global objective of the processing as constraints on its realization e.g. to determine the precision with which the brain must be extracted.

The knowledge base contains one goal, 21 primitive operators and 16 complex ones. There are 231 criteria among which 81 parameter initializations, 24 choices between operators, 38 result evaluations, 36 parameters adjustments and 52 repair strategies. Thanks to this knowledge base, 25 values for numerical parameters are automatically set. Moreover, all decisions for method selection are fully automated. For remaining interactive steps an automatic positioning of the 3D image viewer at a pertinent 2D plan is provided to help the user. There are 11 types of problems that are automatically repaired when detected (for instance too high value for binarization threshold, too small brain size, and brain shape irregularity). This knowledge base therefore enables the programs to be used by non-expert users.

However, this program supervision system can be improved. Two remaining numerical parameters must be set interactively (2 binarization thresholds). In the same way, two decisions to automate method selection need information on image descriptions. Currently, this information is obtained interactively. For instance, to choose the right thresholding method information concerning the presence of a gradient of intensity in the image background is needed. Last, all the evaluations are still interactive and their automation requires to develop more image processing programs. For instance, to detect that the brain is too small the automatic computation of the size of the segmented region is necessary. It can then be compared with a reference size.

4.3 Astronomy

The last example is an application in astronomy, where the role of the program supervision system is to automate a complete processing in order to cope with possible variations in the input data (images of galaxies) [15], [20]. The processing aims at analysing astronomical images containing a galaxy. The long term goal is to classify the galaxy contained in the image as astronomical experts do. As astronomical observing systems provide a great amount of high quality data, it is necessary to fully automate their processing.

Galaxy Morphology Description In this case, the image processing objective is to describe the morphology of the galaxy in terms of pertinent numerical parameters. In the current version 45 numerical parameters are computed: 3 global morphological parameters (size, orientation, excentricity) of the galaxy, 2 global photometrical parameters (measuring the errors made by approximating the projected profile with a linear and a $r^{\frac{1}{4}}$ model) and 8 local parameters describing the morphology of 5 different regions of the galaxy (orientation, perimeter, area, coordinates of the center of gravity, length on the major axis and on the minor axis and distance to an elliptical shape). So for each image, the goal of the image processing is the same: detection of the galaxy and computing of these global and local parameters. The programs were already a modular set of 37 image processing programs. The corresponding program supervision knowledge base is a rich one with many of abstraction levels. The criteria are numerous and fully automatic: there are 20 choices between operators, 16 parameter initializations, 11 result evaluations, 14 repair strategies, and 7 parameter adjustments. Thanks to all those criteria, the complete image processing for morphological galaxy description is fully automated and directly provides inputs for an automatic galaxy classification system.

Automatic Galaxy Classification A current requirement in image processing applications is the cooperation between image processing techniques for object description and data interpretation techniques for object recognition. This is the case for the recognition of complex natural objects such as galaxies. Automation of object recognition requires a great amount of knowledge in both image processing and data interpretation. This knowledge corresponds to two different kinds of expertise, this is the reason why we use a distributed approach that separates the two sources of knowledge into two knowledge-based systems (see figure 6).

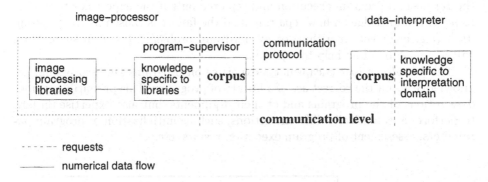

Fig. 6. Two knowledge-based systems (in program supervision and data interpretation) cooperate to automate galaxy classification.

Each system is highly specialized for a task, and they communicate by message sending. The two systems share a common vocabulary, by means of a corpus of typical terms used in vision. The first knowledge-based system is specialized in image processing program supervision. It computes from the image numerical parameters describing the galaxy morphology, as described in previous section. The second one is specialized in data interpretation. It classifies the galaxy described by the numerical parameters. Its engine is based on a taxonomy of galaxy classes and uses a fuzzy mechanism. The complete system provides as output the morphological type plus a detailed symbolic description of the galaxy. The cooperation between these two sub-systems leads to an increasing quality of the results.

5 Architecture of Program Supervision Systems

From these experiments, we can draw a general system architectural framework, that all the previously presented systems conform to. A program supervision system is composed of a reusable program supervision engine, a knowledge base capturing the expert's knowledge about the use of programs, and the library itself as shown in figure 7.

The reasoning of a program supervision *engine* can coarsely be divided into four steps. An initial planning step determines the best (partial) plan to reach the processing goals defined by the user's request. Then the execution of the (partial) plan is triggered, i.e. the individual programs in the plan are executed. The results of the program execution are passed on to an evaluation step that assesses their quality. This evaluation can be performed either automatically by using the expertise in the knowledge base, or interactively by the user. If the assessment on results is negative, it is considered as a failure and a repair step activates the appropriate corrective action. Otherwise the process continues with the planning step for the remaining (sub)goals, if there are any. It is to note that the failure detection and repair mechanisms stay at the level of program supervision expertise. That is to say that a failure is detected only when assessing the *results* of a program execution and repaired only if the expert has been able to provide knowledge on how repairing it. If the failure is caused by the program itself (e.g. incorrect algorithm) or by hardware problems, program supervision will of course be of no help to repair it.

The *knowledge base* encapsulates expertise on programs and processing, i.e. knowledge about the correct use of a library of programs. This primarily includes descriptions of the programs and of their arguments, but also expertise on how to perform automatically different actions, such as initialization of program parameters, assessment of program execution results, etc.

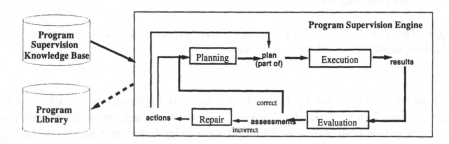

Fig. 7. General program supervision system architecture.

We offer a software platform to develop program supervision knowledge-based systems following this general architecture. This platform, named LAMA, provides knowledge-based system development facilities and different program supervision engines. This generic environment can be used as is, since it is general enough to support the needs of most application domains. As we have stated in the examples, slight differences may exist depending on the particular domain needs. These differences concern both engine capacities and program description details. That is why we offer both a very general set of structures that covers most of the application needs in term of knowledge description and some variants of engines, all based on the same general model (described in figure 7). The platform has already been used to design several systems in program supervision, e.g. most of the examples presented in this paper.

The platform first supplies different engines to run particular reasoning strategies. For example, the planning phase of the engine can be based on either hierarchical-task planning (HTN) techniques, or on operator-based ones, or on a combination of those two techniques. In the same way, the repair phase can be more or less sophisticated. We distinguish two levels of repair: local repair, which means re-execution of the current operator (program) with different parameter values, and global repair, which consists of transmitting a bad assessment to other operators in the plan, until the offending one is found. Local repair may be sufficient when assessment of results is easy to express for almost all the programs of the library. Since problems are detected as soon as their appear they can thus be repaired locally. On the contrary, in other libraries it is possible to assess only few program results. So the detection of failure after the execution of a program often comes from an undetected failure of another. In such cases global repair is necessary to transmit the problem diagnosed and to backtrack in the plan until the faulty program can be re-run. Repair mechanisms are present in all engines, they allow a kind of reactive planning, i.e. the plan can be automatically adapted in reaction to specific problems in the contents of the processing results. This reactivity is part of the knowledge base and the expert should have foreseen the different problems that may occur. Only PLANETE was reactive in the real-time sense to events derived from sensor information.

Concerning the knowledge representation, even if the proposed representation is general and homogeneous, it may be adapted to experts' wishes. Indeed, the experts cannot always express a complete information for every knowledge base piece. Depending on the available knowledge, some parts of the representations may be left empty, without affecting the operationalization of the final system. For instance, each program description must not contain all types of criteria. The organization of program combination into complex operators may also be more or less sophisticated. The only important point is to choose an engine able to cope with the available knowledge (with only some loss of performance if there is too few knowledge). The platform provides domain experts with a representation framework to guide them in expressing their knowledge at the expertise level. This framework is implemented by structures representing the main general concepts of program supervision (such as processing goals, operators, data and parameters, rules, etc.) that will constitute the contents of the knowledge base. Experts describe their knowledge bases using a readable language that includes general templates for all these concepts. Knowledge base verification facilities are attached to this language, to help the experts during the design of a new knowledge base for a particular library.

Vision experts hence have at their disposal a generic environment, composed of common tools that can be shared for designing different knowledge-bases systems. Even if a specific domain demands focused adaptation, the platform also allows us to easily tailor an engine to take into account characteristics of target application domains or particular end-users' needs.

6 Conclusion

As we have seen through the examples shown in section4, program supervision techniques can be good candidates –once the low-level program integration has been done– to perform a semantical integration of image processing programs. These techniques are independent of any particular application domain: even if this paper is not exhaustive, we have shown program supervision systems applied to robotics for road scene analysis, to medical imagery, and to astronomy. These techniques are also independent of any particular image processing programs or library of programs. All the program supervision systems presented in the examples were based on the same general model of program supervision for knowledge representation and engine reasoning, that has been derived and adapted with respect to the particular needs of each application.

Semantical integration of image processing programs is needed in two cases: first to develop fully automated systems (as shown in the second example of real-time road obstacle detection and in the last one for automatic galaxy classification), second to develop intelligent help for an end-user (as shown in medical imagery, where the end-user is a clinician).

As a general advice to image processing developers we can suggest from this experience to think from the beginning about how their image processing programs can be integrated and controlled. It can be done by adding to the code information on their functionality, performance, limitations, etc. In particular evaluation and repair knowledge is very important to control the execution of the programs and to adapt the reasoning process. The building of a knowledge base for program supervision is still a big effort for an expert. However, once the knowledge base has been written, program supervision techniques allow code developpers to widely distribute packages of their programs to non-expert end-users.

References

1. D. G. Bailey. Research on Computer-assisted Generation of Image Processing Algorithms. In *Workshop on Computer Vision - Special Hardware and Industrial Applications*, Tokyo, October 1988. IAPR.
2. A. Bellon, J-P. Dérutin, F. Heitz, and Y. Ricquebourg. Real-Time Collision Avoidance at Road Crossing On Board the Prometheus Prolab2 Vehicle. In *Intelligent Vehicles'94 Symposium*, pages 56–61, Paris, (France), October 1994.
3. S. Beucher and M. Bilodeau. Road Segmentation and Obstacle Dectection by a Fast Watershed Transformation. In *Intelligent Vehicles'94 Symposium*, pages 296–301, Paris, (France), October 1994.

4. British-Aerospace. VIDIMUS Esprit Project Annual Report. Technical report, Sowerby Research Centre, Bristol, England, 1991.
5. S. A. Chien and H. B. Mortensen. Automating image processing for scientific data analysis of a large image database. *IEEE Transactions on Pattern Analysis and Machine Intelligence*, 18(8):854–859, August 1996.
6. V. Clément and M. Thonnat. A Knowledge-based Approach to the Integration of Image Processing Procedures. *Computer Vision, Graphics and Image*, 57(2):166–184, March 1993.
7. M. Crubézy, F. Aubry, S. Moisan, V. Chameroy, M. Thonnat, and R. Di Paola. Managing Complex Processing of Medical Image Sequences by Program Supervision Techniques. In *SPIE Medical Imaging'97*, volume 3035, pages 614–625, February 1997.
8. L. Gong and C. A. Kulikowski. Composition of Image Analysis Processes Through Object-Centered Hierarchical Planning. *IEEE Transactions on Pattern Analysis and Machine Intelligence*, 17(10), October 1995.
9. M.D. Johnston. An Expert System Approach to Astronomical Data Analysis. In *Proceedings, Goddard Conf. on Space Applications of Artificial Intelligence and Robotics*, pages 1–17, 1987.
10. T. Matsuyama. Expert systems for image processing: Knowledge based composition of image analysis processes. *Computer Vision Graphics Image Processes*, 48:22–49, 1989.
11. A. Meygret, M. Thonnat, and M. Berthod. A pyramidal stereovision algorithm based on cont our chain points. In *European Conference on Computer Vision*, Antibes, April 1990.
12. S. Moisan, C. Shekhar, and M. Thonnat. Real-Time Perception Program supervision for Vehicle Driving Assistance. In Okyay Kaynak, Mehmed Ozkan, Nurdan Bekiroglu, and Ilker Tunay, editors, *ICRAM'95 International Conference on recent Advances in Mechatronics*, pages 173–179, Istanbul, Turkey, August 1995.
13. Groupe PROART. Rapport de fin de contrat de recherche PROMETHEUS-PROART. Technical report, Projet PROMETHEUS, December 1994.
14. H. Sato, Y. Kitamura, and H. Tamura. A Knowledge-based Approach to Vision Algorithm Design for Industrial Parts Feeder. In *Proceedings, IAPR Workshop on Computer Vision, Special hardware and industrial applications*, pages 413–416, Tokyo, 1988.
15. M. Thonnat, V. Clément, and J. C. Ossola. Automatic galaxy description. *Astrophysical Letters and Communication*, 31(1-6):65–72, 1995.
16. M. Thonnat, V. Clement, and J. van den Elst. Supervision of perception tasks for autonomous systems: the OCAPI approach. *Journal of Information Science and Technology*, 3(2):140–163, Jan 1994. Also in Rapport de Recherche 2000, 1993, INRIA Sophia Antipolis.
17. M. Thonnat and S. Moisan. Knowledge-Based Systems for Program Supervision. In *Proceedings of KBUP'95*, pages 3–8, Sophia Antipolis, France, November 1995. INRIA.
18. T. Toriu, H. Iwase, and M Yoshida. An Expert System for Image Processing. *FUJITSU Sci.Tech.Journal*, 23.2:111–118, 1987.
19. L. Trassoudaine, J. Alizon, F. Collange, and J. Gallice. Visual Tracking by a Multisensorial Approach. In *First IFAC International Workshop on Intelligent Autonomous Vehicles*, pages 111–116, Southampton, (UK), April 1993.
20. R. Vincent, M. Thonnat, and J.C. Ossola. Program supervision for automatic galaxy classification. In *Proc. of the International Conference on Imaging Science, Systems, and Technology CISST'97*, Las Vegas, USA, June 1997.

Integration of Vision and Decision-Making in an Autonomous Airborne Vehicle for Traffic Surveillance

Silvia Coradeschi*, Lars Karlsson*, Klas Nordberg[+]

*Department of Computer and Information Science
[+]Department of Electrical Engineering
Linköping University, Sweden
E-Mail: silco@ida.liu.se, larka@ida.liu.se, klas@isy.liu.se

Abstract. In this paper we present a system which integrates computer vision and decision-making in an autonomous airborne vehicle that performs traffic surveillance tasks. The main factors that make the integration of vision and decision-making a challenging problem are: the qualitatively different kind of information at the decision-making and vision levels, the need for integration of dynamically acquired information with a priori knowledge, e.g. GIS information, and the need of close feedback and guidance of the vision module by the decision-making module. Given the complex interaction between the vision module and the decision-making module we propose the adoption of an intermediate structure, called Scene Information Manager, and describe its structure and functionalities.

1 Introduction

This paper reports the ongoing work on the development of an architecture for Unmanned Airborne Vehicles (UAVs) within the WITAS project at Linköping University. One of the main efforts within the project has been to achieve an efficient integration between a vision module, dedicated to tasks such as object recognition, velocity estimation, camera control, and an autonomous decision-making module which is responsible for deliberative and reactive behaviors of the system. A critical issue in such a system is to handle the fact that the vision module represents an object in terms of coordinates in some reference frame, whereas the decision-making module represents the same object in relational and qualitative terms. For example, the vision module can represent a car as a point in the image together with some parameters that describe its shape. The decision-making module, on the other hand, will represent the same car in terms of its relation to some road, or to other cars, and describe its shape in terms of symbolic attributes rather than as estimated parameters.

A second issue to be handled in the project is the integration of a priori information, here referred to as static information, and dynamically acquired information, e.g., produced by the vision module. An example of this integration is how to combine information about the shape and topology of a road network, stored in a conventional GIS (Geographic Information System), and descriptions about cars (position, shape, etc) produced by the vision system, assuming that these cars are moving along the roads.

Section 2 presents a more thorough discussion on these and other issues. The general conclusion is that we need an intermediate structure, the Scene Information Manager (SIM), located between the vision and the decision-making module. The SIM solves both the problem of translating object references, e.g, from image coordinates to symbolic road labels, and vice versa, as well as manages the linkage of dynamic to static information and high-level prediction. The structure and functionalities of the SIM are described in more detail in section 3.

The resulting architecture has been implemented and tested on a number of scenarios. Section 4 briefly presents some of them and describes how the SIM is used to solve the above integration issues, thereby allowing the system to maintain a suitable distinction in abstraction level between the task driven vision module, mainly devoted to low-level vision processing, and the decision-making module which operates on symbolic information.

1.1 The WITAS project

The WITAS project, initiated in January 1997, is devoted to research on information technology for autonomous systems, and more precisely to unmanned airborne vehicles (UAVs) used for traffic surveillance. The first three years with focus on basic research will result in methods and system architectures to be used in UAVs. Because of the nature of the work most of the testing is being made using simulated UAVs in simulated environments, even though real image data has been used to test the vision module. In a second phase of the project, however, the testing will be made using real UAVs.

The WITAS project is a research cooperation between four groups at Linköping University. More information about the project can be found at [14].

1.2 General system architecture

The general architecture of the system is a standard three-layered agent architecture consisting of

- a deliberative layer mainly concerned with planning and monitoring,
- a reactive layer that performs situation-driven task execution, and
- a process layer for image processing and flight control.

Of particular interest for this presentation is the interaction between the reactive layer (currently using RAPS [5] [6]) and the process layer. This is done in terms of *skills*, which are groups of reconfigurable control processes that can be activated and deactivated from the reactive layer, and *events* that are signals from the process layer to the reactive layer. Events can both carry sensor data and status information. In the rest of the paper, we will refer to the deliberative and reactive layers as the decision-making module.

Besides vision, the sensors and knowledge sources of the system include:

- a global positioning system (GPS) that gives the position of the vehicle,
- a geographical information system (GIS) covering the relevant area of operation, and
- standard sensors for speed, heading and altitude.

Currently, the system exists as a prototype implementation operating in a simulated environment, and some functionalities, e.g., GIS and deliberation, only exist in simplified forms.

1.3 Related Work

The areas in which most work has been produced with relevance to the issues presented in this document are event/episode recognition and active vision.

Pioneering work in the event/episode recognition has been done by Nagel [11] and Neumann [12]. The aim of their work was to extract conceptual descriptions from image sequences and to express them in a natural language. As the focus of the work is on the natural language aspect, all vision processing up to a complete recovery of the scene geometry including classified objects was done by humans.

The Esprit project VIEWS by Buxton, Howarth and Gong is one of the most interesting works on episode recognition in the traffic domain [8][2][9]. In this work, video sequences of the traffic flow in a roundabout are examined and events such as overtaking and cars following each other are recognized. A stationary and precalibrated camera is used, and the system presupposes an intermediate-level image processing that detects moving objects and estimates various properties of these objects. Given this information, and the ground-plane representation, the system can recognize simple events, e.g., a car turning left, and episodes, e.g., a car overtaking another car, which are composed of simple events using a Bayesian belief network. Focus of attention and deictic pointers are used to increase the performance of the system.

Active or *animate vision* is currently an active area of research in computer vision. One of the pioneers of this area is Ballard [1] who has pointed out that vision is an active process that implies gaze control and attentional mechanisms. In contrast to traditional computer vision, active vision implies that the tasks direct the visual processing and establish which parts of the image are of interest and which features should be computed. By reducing the complexity and accelerating scene understanding, active vision opens up the possibility of constructing continuously operating real-time vision systems. Our approach is fully within the active vision paradigm since the executing tasks at the decision-making level select what part of the image the vision module processes and what features are computed. Deictic pointers are also created to objects of interest and the vision module is focused on these objects.

Our aim is to create an integrated vision and decision-making component capable of complex behaviors. This was a goal also for the Esprit project VISION

As PROCESS [3]. It integrated a stereo camera head mounted on a mobile robot, dedicated computer boards for real-time image acquisition and processing, and a distributed image description system, including independent modules for 2D tracking and description, 3D reconstruction, object recognition, and control. This project has similarity with our project even if the application domain is different. In particular, both projects include active vision, focus of attention, scene manipulation and the need of real-time performance. We intend to use some of the methods developed during the VISION As PROCESS project and reconsider them in the context of our application.

Reece and Shafer [13] have investigated how active vision can be used for driving an autonomous vehicle in traffic. They address techniques for requesting sensing of objects relevant for action choice, decision-making about the effect of uncertainty in input data, and using domain knowledge to reason about how dynamic objects will move or change over time. Autonomous vehicles have been investigated also by Dickmanns [4].

A project for autonomous take-off and landing of an aircraft is currently under development by Dickmanns [7]. Conventional aircraft sensors are combined with data taken from a camera mounted on a pan and tilt platform. The camera data is mainly used during the final landing approach to detect landmarks and possible obstacles on the runway. Regarding vision, this work is mainly focused on object recognition.

The RAPS system used in our reactive layer has been employed previously to control a vision module [6]. Similar to our approach, the executing tasks call visual routines that execute specific image processing routines. The added difficulty in our case lies in the fact that the anchoring between symbolic and visual information is complicated by the dynamics of the objects in the scene. Anchoring between symbolic and perceptual information has been considered in the Saphira architecture [10], but also in this case mainly for static objects.

To summarize, the aspects that are more extensively studied in the above projects are event/behavior recognition, active selection of vision processing algorithms, and focus of attention. Not so widely explored are general methods for integration of static and dynamic knowledge, continuous support of the vision module by the decision-making module on the basis of short term prediction, and general methods for anchoring of symbolic to visual information in dynamic scenes.

2 Integration of vision and decision-making systems

In this section we discuss several important issues related to the integration between the vision module and the decision-making module. As a result of this discussion we propose the intermediate structure called Scene Information Manager, elaborated in the next section.

2.1 From image domain to symbolic information

The data required by the decision-making module is mainly about the road network and about moving objects and their position with respect to the road network. For example, if the airborne vehicle is pursuing a car, it needs to know in which road the car is, where along the road it is, and in which direction the car is moving (dynamic information). It also needs to predict future actions of the car based on the structure of the road network (static information). Typically, the static information is retrieved from a GIS, and the dynamic information is produced by the vision module.

The integration of static and dynamic information can be done in several ways, but the solution implies in general that symbolic data, e.g., the label of the road on which the car is traveling, has to be accessed by means of information derived from the image domain, e.g., image coordinates of the car. This task depends on low-level parameters from the camera calibration and, therefore, does not fit the abstraction level of the decision-making module. However, to access the static information image coordinates have to be transformed into some absolute reference system, using the information in the GIS. Database access is not a typical image processing task, and therefore the solution does not fit the abstraction level of the image processing module.

2.2 From symbolic information to image domain

The above description also applies to the information flow which goes from the decision-making module to the vision module. For example, if the decision-making module decides to focus its attention on a specific car (which can be outside the current field of view), the knowledge about this car is represented in symbolic form, e.g., that the car is located at a certain distance from an end point of a specific road. To solve this task, however, the vision module must know the angles by which the camera has to be rotated in order to point the camera at the car. Hence, there is a need for translating symbolic information (road/position) to absolute coordinates from which the camera angles can be derived given the absolute position of the UAV.

2.3 Support and guidance of visual skills

Knowledge about the road network should help the vision processing and give hints as to what the vision module is expected to find in the image. For example, knowledge about roads and landmarks that are expected to be found in the image can greatly facilitate the vision module in recognizing objects in the image that correspond to road network elements. Knowledge about the road network structure and its environment can also avoid failures in the image processing. For example, if the vision module is tracking a car and the car disappears under a bridge or behind a building, the vision module can get confused. However, this situation can be avoided by giving information to the vision module about the presence of the occluding objects and the coordinates of the next position where the car is expected to reappear.

The basic mechanism of this support is prediction. Prediction, e.g. of future positions of a car, or of whether the car will be occluded by another object, is usually a high-level processing which relies on an understanding of the concepts of cars, roads, and occlusions. On the other hand, the final result of this prediction will be used directly in the low-level parts of the vision module. This implies that the prediction processing has to be made by some type of decision-making and image processing hybrid.

2.4 Support of decision making

The vision system delivers information in the same rate as camera images are processed, and on a level of detail which is not always relevant to the decision-making module. Thus, there is often a need to filter and compile information from the vision module before it is presented to the decision-making module. For instance, some vision skills compute uncertainty measures continuously, but these measures are only relevant to decision-making when they pass some threshold.

2.5 Discussion

From the above presentation we can conclude that by employing an intermediate structure, located between the high-level decision-making module and the low-level vision module, some important issues related to the integration between the two module can be handled. This structure is dedicated to translating symbolic references, e.g., in terms of labels, to either absolute or image coordinates, and vice versa. To do so it needs access to a GIS in order to retrieve information about the road network, both in terms of the connection topology and the shapes and positions of each road segment. By means of this information it can make links between static information (the roads) and dynamic information (the cars). In order to translate between absolute world coordinates and image coordinates it needs to have access to a reliable positioning system which continuously measures the position and orientation of the UAV and its image sensors, e.g., using GPS and inertial navigation.

Using the information which it stores, this structure can provide support to the vision module based on high-level prediction of events such as occlusion. It can also act as a filter and condense the high frequent low-level information produced by the vision module into low frequent high-level information which is sent to the decision-making module.

The intermediate structure proposed above is here called the Scene Information Manager (SIM), and it is presented in the following section.

3   The Scene Information Manager

Given the complex interaction between vision processing and decision-making, it is apparent that there is a need for a structure that can store static and dynamic information required, and that also satisfies the needs of vision and decision-making as described in the previous section. The Scene Information Manager (SIM), figure 1, is part of the reactive layer and it manages sensor resources: it receives requests for services from RAPS, in general requests for specific types of information, it invokes skills and configurations of skills [1] in the vision module (and other sensor systems), and it processes and integrates the data coming from the vision module. Currently, a standard color camera is the only sensor resource present, but one can expect the presence of additional types of sensors in the future. In the following sections, we present the functionalities of the SIM.

3.1   World model and anchoring

The SIM maintains a model of the current scene under observation, including names and properties of elements in the scene, such as cars and roads, and relations between elements, e.g., a car is in a position on a specific road, or one car is behind another car. What is stored is mainly the result of task-specific service requests from the decision-making levels, which implies that the model is partial;

---

[1] A configuration of skills is a parallel and/or sequential execution of skills.

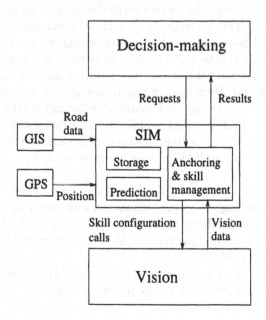

Fig. 1. Overview of the Scene Information Manager and its interactions with decision-making and vision.

with some exceptions, information that has not been requested is not registered. The SIM also maintains a correlation between the symbolic elements and image elements (points, regions). This correlation (anchoring) is done in terms of shape and color information, and reference systems which are independent of the position and orientation of the camera. For instance, if a service request refers to a specific car by its name, the SIM looks up its coordinates and signature and provides these as parameters to the vision module. The vision module is then responsible for performing the processing required to find the car in the actual image. Likewise, the SIM is also capable of finding the symbolic name of an object given its position in the image, and of assigning names to objects that are observed for the first time.

Finally, the SIM contains mappings from symbolic concepts to visual representations and vice versa. For instance, colors, e.g., "red", are translated to color data, e.g, RGB values, and car models, e.g., "Mercedes", can be translated to geometrical descriptions.

3.2 Skill management

The SIM is responsible for managing service requests from the decision-making levels such as looking for a car with a certain signature and calling the appropriate configuration of skills with the appropriate parameters. These parameters can include cars, which are are denoted with symbolic names in the request and translated ("de-anchored") when passed on to vision routines, and concepts, which go through appropriate translations. The SIM is also responsible for returning the results produced by the vision skills to the task that requested the service, and to update its information about the relevant objects. In order to do this, it has to keep track of the identities of relevant objects. For instance, if a service is active for tracking a specific car, then the SIM must maintain information about what car is being tracked (indexical referencing).

Furthermore, skill management involves combining the results of different visual processes, or adapting or compiling the output of visual processes to a form which is more suitable for decision making. In particular, it involves reducing the amount of information sent to the decision-making module by detecting and notifying when certain events occur, such as when a given threshold is passed. For instance, the visual data include certainty estimates, and the SIM determines whether to notify the decision-making module that the certainty is too low or to confirm that it is good enough. This treatment of uncertainty supports making decisions about taking steps to improve the quality of data when necessary, without burdening the decision-making module with continuous and detailed information about measurement uncertainties.

3.3 Identification of roads

The information stored in the SIM is mainly the result of active skills; objects that are not in the focus of some skills will simply not be registered. The only "skill-independent" processing going on is the identification of roads and crossings, based on information about the positions and geometries of roads extracted from the GIS. This information is used to find the parts of the image corresponding to specific roads, which enables determining the position of cars relative to the roads. This is the most important example of integration of static and dynamic knowledge in the system.

This functionality can be implemented in several ways, and two quite different approaches have been tested. One is based on tracking landmarks with known world coordinates and well-defined shapes which are easily identified in an aerial image. From the world coordinates and the corresponding image coordinates of all landmarks, a global transformation from image to world coordinates (and vice versa) can be estimated assuming that the ground patch which is covered by the image is sufficiently flat. A second approach uses the shape information about each static object, e.g., roads, and measurements of the position and orientation of the UAV's camera to generate a "virtual" image. This image "looks" the same as the proper image produced by the camera, but instead of intensity values each pixel contains symbolic information, e.g., road names, position along the road, etc. The virtual image works as a look-up table which is indexed by image coordinates.

Since it relies on tracking of several landmarks, the first approach is more robust but less effective and versatile than the second approach which, on the other hand, is less robust since it depends on having enough accurate measurements of the camera's position and orientation.

3.4 Prediction

The information stored in the SIM is not just what is obtained from the most recently processed image, but includes the near past and a somewhat larger region than the one currently in the image. Past information such as the position of a car two seconds ago, are extrapolated to find the car again after being temporally out of focus, thereby increasing the robustness of the system and extending its functionality. Such extrapolation might involve formulating alternative hypotheses, like a number of possible positions of the car. In this case, vision is directed to check one hypothesis after the other until either the presence of the car is confirmed in one of the positions or there are no more hypotheses to consider. Likewise, prediction can also aid in determining if a newly observed car is identical to one observed a short time ago.

3.5 Conclusions

In conclusion, the SIM has a number of functions, ranging from storage and parameter translation to supportive prediction. In addition, the SIM provides a flexible interface between the vision system and the decision-making levels, which supports modifying concept definitions and exchanging visual processing techniques with preserved modularity. In the next section we present two specific tasks implemented in our system, namely looking for and tracking a car of a specific signature.

4 Examples

In this section we illustrate the most significant points of the current implementation of our system by means of some examples which include looking for cars of a specific signature and tracking a car. For the case of tracking a car, it is shown how the vision module can be supported during the tracking procedure with high-level information regarding occlusion. The examples have been simulated on an SGI machine using MultiGen and Vega software for 3D modelling and animation.

4.1 Looking for and tracking a car

The goal of the UAV is here to look for a red Mercedes that is supposed to be near a specific crossing and, once found, follow the car and track it with the camera. During the simulation sequence, the UAV flies to the crossing and, once there, the decision-making module requests the SIM to look for the car. Rather than sending the service request directly to the vision module, it is first processed by the SIM which invokes a skill configuration and translates the symbolic parameters of the skills to what they mean in vision terms. In this case, color values, e.g., RGB-values, are substituted for the symbolic name of the color, and the width and length of the car are substituted for the name of the car model. Furthermore, the absolute coordinate of the crossing is substituted for its symbolic name. The vision module then directs the camera to that point, and reports all cars its finds which fit the given signature within a certain degree of uncertainty. In this particular case, two cars are found, see figure 2, and their visual signature (color/shape) together with their image position are sent to the SIM. Here, image coordinates are translated into symbolic names of roads and positions along these roads. For each of the two cars, a record is created in the memory part of the SIM, and each record is linked to the corresponding road segment already present in the memory. These records also contain information about the actual shape and color which can be used later, e.g., for reidentification. Once established, the linkage between cars and roads can be used by the decision-making module for high-level reasoning.

So far, most of the activities has been taking place in the SIM and in the vision module. However, since more than one car has been reported to fit the description, the decision-making module has to decide on which of the two cars it will follow or, alternatively, to make more measurements in order to obtain a better support for its actions. In this case, it chooses to follow one of the two cars, and it requests that the chosen car is to be reidentified (since it may have moved since last seen) and then tracked. However, since the decision-making module only has a symbolic references to the car, the SIM must translate this reference to a world coordinate which the vision module, in turn, can translate

Fig. 2. Two cars of the right shape and color are found at the crossing.

Fig. 3. The camera is zooming in on one of the two cars in the previous image.

into camera angles. The SIM also provides the previously measured signature (color/shape) of the specific car to be reidentified. Assuming that the car is sufficiently close to its latest position it can now be reidentified and the tracking can start. Figure 3 shows the situation where the camera is zooming in on the car just prior to starting the tracking. In the case when there are ambiguities about which car to track, or if none can be found, the vision module reports this directly to the decision-making module.

If the chosen car turns out to be wrong, e.g., an integration of measurements shows that it does not match the shape of a Mercedes, this is reported back to the decision-making module. In this example, there is one more car which fits the given signature, but it is out of sight from the camera and some time has elapsed from when it was last seen. However, using the information stored in the memory of the SIM, the prediction component of the SIM can make high-level predictions on the whereabouts of the second car. Consequently, upon receiving a report on the tracking failure of the first car, the decision-making module sends a request to reidentify and track the second car, this time based on high-level prediction of the car's current position. This is solved in the same way as for the first car, with the exception that there are several options regarding the car's position, since it was approaching a crossing when last seen. Each of the positions is tested using the reidentification skill of the vision module until a matching car is found or none can be found.

It should be mentioned that during the tracking operation, the vision module is not just responsible for the camera motion. The image position of the car is constantly being measured and then translated by means of the SIM into symbolic links relative to the road network.

4.2 High-level support during tracking

In the second example we illustrate another use of the prediction component of the SIM. During tracking the prediction component uses information about the tracked car and of the surrounding road network to perform high-level predictions about the position of the car, as was mentioned above. However, the prediction functionality is also used in case of occlusion of the car, e.g., by large buildings or bridges.

The prediction module regularly estimates the expected position of the car and, in case the car disappears or there is a significant difference between the expected and measured positions, it checks the presence of occluding objects by consulting the geographical information system. If the presence of an occluding object (e.g. bridge or tunnel) is confirmed, the vision module receives information about where the object is going to reappear. If there is no record of an occluding object, the vision module uses predicted information about the car's position for a pre-specified amount of time. If the car reappears, normal tracking is continued, and if it does not reappear, a failure message is sent to the decision-making module.

Figure 4 shows two identical cars, one traveling along a road which makes a bend under a bridge, and one which travels on the bridge. In this example,

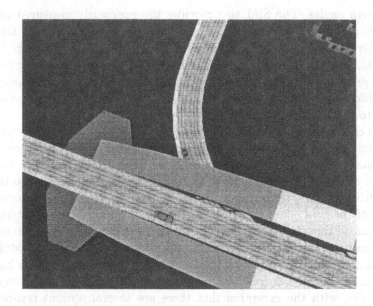

Fig. 4. The UAV is tracking a car which soon will disappear under the bridge. A second car is on the bridge.

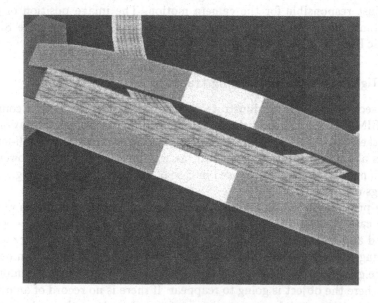

Fig. 5. The tracked car is occluded by the bridge and is therefore likely to be confused with the second car.

Fig. 6. The car reappears from under the bridge and can therefore be tracked again.

the UAV is tracking the first car which soon will disappear under the bride and, even worse, a few moments later the second car will be a position in the image where the first car would have been, had it not be occluded, figure 5. Using the high-level prediction provided by the SIM, the vision module reidentifies the correct car when it reappears from under the bridge, figure 6.

5 Conclusion

This paper presents a system which integrates vision and decision-making in an autonomous UAV for traffic surveillance. A number of issues related to the integration have been considered: integration of a priori and dynamically acquired knowledge, anchoring of symbolic data into visual data, focus of attention, supporting the execution of visual skills by decision-making, and handling of uncertainty.

A structure, the Scene Information Manager, where these issues are addressed has been presented. Integration of a priori knowledge and dynamically acquired knowledge is achieved by continuously matching elements in the GIS and corresponding elements in the current image. Anchoring is performed during service requests and transmission of visual data to the decision-making module, using stored data and short term prediction. Certainty of visual data is reported to the SIM where it is elaborated and transmitted when necessary to the decision-making module. Uncertainty due to extrapolation of data is handled by the SIM by guiding the vision in checking one hypothesis after the other. Finally, short term prediction is used to support the vision module and anticipate failures.

6 Acknowledgment

The simulation data presented here is the result of a teamwork in which participated, besides the authors, Johan Wiklund, Thord Andersson, Gunnar Farnebäck, Tommy Persson, and John Olsson. The WITAS project is fully sponsored by the Knut and Alice Wallenberg Foundation.

References

1. D. H. Ballard. Animate vision. *Artificial Intelligence*, 48:57–87, 1991.
2. H. Buxton and Shaogang Gong. Visual surveillance in a dynamic and uncertain world. *Artificial Intelligence*, 78:431–459, 1995.
3. J. L. Crowley and H. I. Christensen, editors. *Vision as Process*, Esprit Basic Research Series, Berlin, 1995. Sringer-Verlag.
4. E. D. Dickmanns. Vehicles Capable of Dynamic Vision. *IJCAI-97*, Nagoya, Japan, 1997.
5. J. Firby. Task Networks for Controlling Continuous Processes. Proceedings of the Second International Conference on AI Planning Systems, 1994.
6. J. Firby. The RAP language manual. Technical Report AAP-6, University of Chicago, 1995.
7. S. Fürst, S. Werner, D. Dickmanns, and E. D. Dickmanns. Landmark navigation and autonomous landing approach with obstacle detection for aircraft. In *AereoSense97*. Orlando, FL, 1997.
8. R. Howarth. *Spatial representation, reasoning and control for a surveillance system*. PhD thesis, Queen Mary and Westfield College, 1994.
9. R. Howarth. Interpreting a dynamic and uncertain world: task-based control. *Artificial Intelligence*, 100:5–85, 1998.
10. K. Konolige, K. L. Myers, E. H. Ruspini, and A. Saffiotti. The Saphira architecture: A design for autonomy. *Journal of Experimental and Theoretical Artificial Intelligence*, 9(1):215–235, 1997.
11. H. H. Nagel. From image sequences towards conceptual descriptions. *Image and vision computing*, 6:59–74, 1988.
12. B. Neumann. Natural language description of time varying scenes. In *Semantic Structures*, pages 167–206. Lawrence Erlbaum associates, Hillsdale, NJ, 1989.
13. D. A. Reece and S. A. Shafer. Control of perceptual attention in robot driving. *Artificial Intelligence*, 78:397–430, 1995.
14. http://www.ida.liu.se/ext/witas/eng.html

Multilevel Integration of Vision and Speech Understanding Using Bayesian Networks

Sven Wachsmuth, Hans Brandt-Pook, Gudrun Socher[*1],
Franz Kummert, Gerhard Sagerer

University of Bielefeld, Technical Faculty, P.O. Box 100131, 33501 Bielefeld, Germany
[*]Now with Vidam Communications Inc.,2 N 1st St.,San Jose,CA 95113
Tel.: +49 521 106 2937, Fax: +49 521 106 2992
e-Mail: swachsmu@techfak.uni-bielefeld.de

Abstract The interaction of image and speech processing is a crucial property of multimedia systems. Classical systems using inferences on pure qualitative high level descriptions miss a lot of information when concerned with erroneous, vague, or incomplete data. We propose a new architecture that integrates various levels of processing by using multiple representations of the visually observed scene. They are vertically connected by Bayesian networks in order to find the most plausible interpretation of the scene.

The interpretation of a spoken utterance naming an object in the visually observed scene is modeled as another partial representation of the scene. Using this concept, the key problem is the identification of the verbally specified object instances in the visually observed scene. Therefore, a Bayesian network is generated dynamically from the spoken utterance and the visual scene representation. In this network spatial knowledge as well as knowledge extracted from psycholinguistic experiments is coded. First results show the robustness of our approach.

1 Introduction

Human machine interfaces are one of the major bottlenecks when using computer systems in real environments. One possibility to overcome these drawbacks is using multiple modalities in the communication between humans and machines which is a quit natural concept for human communications. In this case, we distinguish different perceptive channels by which the system is connected with the environment. The consequence is that we have to generate a common interpretation of the transmitted information on all channels or modalities instead of analysing them in an isolated way. In order to combine different perceptive channels, they have to be connected by an internal knowledge representation. In this paper, we concentrate on the integration of image and speech processing in a situated environment.

We developed a system for the following concrete scenario. A human has to instruct a robot in a construction task. Therefore, both communication partners perceive an arrangement of building parts on a table (fig. 1). These can be assembled by screwing or

[1] The work of G. Socher has been supported by the German Research Foundation (DFG).

232

245

user: "Take the bar."
system: "I have found two bars. Should I take the long one or the short one?"
user: "Take the long one."
system: "O.k., I will take the five-holed-bar."

Figure1. Example dialogue of the domain.

plugging. The human speaker has to specify the objects in the scene verbally by describing properties of these objects without knowing the exact terms. Therefore, the system has to interpret mostly vague descriptions. The system is capable to view the objects in the scene and has a speech recognition and speech understanding unit. Because we use our system in a real environment and it has to interpret vague descriptions, the mapping of the verbal object descriptions and the visually perceived objects is a very tough task. In figure 1, we present an example dialogue which may happen in our domain. The user views the scene on a table and instructs the robot which object it should grasp.

A rather easy way to combine results of the vision and speech understanding processes is shown in figure 2a. Both processes analyze their input signals separately through different levels of abstraction and generate some high level description using common logical predicates. Afterwards, logical inferences can be drawn to get a consistent interpretation of the input data. When applying such an approach in real noisy environments any decision in lower processing levels results in a loss of information on higher levels. Thereby, logic inferences on the top level of description may fail even when the separate interpretations are only slightly incorrect.

We propose a new architecture (fig. 2b) which integrates multi-modal processing on several levels of abstraction. A careful approach to uncertainty is needed to get a

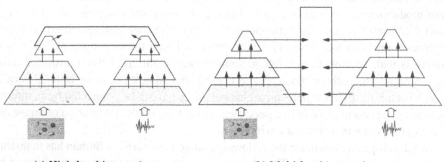

(a) High-level integration.   (b) Multi-level integration.

Figure2. Integration of vision and speech understanding.

consistent interpretation of the input data which takes respect to several layers and the dependencies between them. Therefore, we use Bayesian networks as a decision calculus which can handle uncertainties, erroneous data, and vague meanings in a very comfortable way.

Many persons which were asked to identify an object in our domain use spatial relations in order to specify the location of the intended object. Therefore, an important issue in our system is the modeling of space. Based on the definition of projective relations between two objects in three dimensions we show how to approximate these when data is available only in two dimensions and how to integrate context information about the topology of the presented scene.

The paper is organized in the following sections. In section 2 we will briefly review some related approaches dealing with the problem of vision and speech integration. Then we will describe some important aspects of the image and speech processing components (section 3) and the spatial model (section 4) in our system. Afterwards, we will propose a new approach that integrates these two modalities using multiple representation layers (section 5). We emphasize that the spatial modeling is an important aspect in this interaction scheme. Finally, we will give some experimental results of the implemented system (section 6) showing the robustness of our approach and a short conclusion (section 7).

2 Related Work

In literature the topic of integrating vision and speech understanding is referenced from different viewpoints [21]. The construction of mental pictures [7] can be induced by verbal descriptions or previously seen objects. They are used to reason about scenes which are currently not visible. This is an important aspect in language understanding when spatial knowledge is involved [29, 1, 16]. Other systems [13, 6, 28] try to generate verbal descriptions from images or image sequences. They realize an automatic generation of qualitative representations from image data which is fundamental for integration of vision and speech understanding and use various approaches to modeling spatial relations. Lastly, there has been a lot of work to incorporating both linguistic and pictorial inputs concerning the interpretation of textual annotated pictures [22], lip-reading [9, 2] or multimedia systems [12]. In the following we concentrate on systems which visually observe the scene to enable natural human-computer interaction.

The PLAYBOT project [23, 24] was started to provide a controllable robot which may enable physically disabled children to access and manipulate toys. The robot possesses a robotic arm with a hand, a stereo color vision robot head, and a communication panel. The child gives commands on the communication panel which displays actions, objects, and locations of the objects. The command language consists of verbs, nouns, and spatial prepositions. The child selects the 'words' by pointing on the communication panel. While language processing is simplified by using the communication panel most attention is given to processing of visual data. Object recognition [3] is performed by fitting deformable models to image contours. Object tracking [25] is done by perspective alignment. The event perception [17] is based on an ontology suitable for describing object properties and the generation and transfer of forces in the scene. To find instances of a target object in the image, a Bayesian network approach is employed which exploits the probabilities in the aspect hierarchy of modeled objects which is used in object recognition.

The Ubiquitous Talker [15] was developed to provide its user with some information related to a recognized object in the environment. The system consists of an LCD display that reflects the scene at which the user is looking as if it is a transparent glass, a CCD camera for recognizing real world objects with color-bar ID codes, and a microphone for recognizing a human voice. The main aspect of the system is the integration of the linguistic and non-linguistic contexts to interpreting natural language utterances which becomes much easier when the situation is fixed by nonverbal information. The system basically consists of two subsystems, the subsystem which recognizes a number of real world situations that include objects with color-bar ID codes and another subsystem which recognizes and interprets user speech inputs. The image (color-code) recognizer triggers the speech recognizer and send a message to it in order to select the appropriate vocabulary and grammar for analyzing the spoken utterance. There are two connections between linguistic and non-linguistic contexts. User's intentions are abductively inferred by using a plan library [14]. This process is initially triggered by introducing a new non-linguistic context. Another connection is deictic centers [30] that are possible referents of deictic expressions. The object and the location in a non-linguistic context can be current deictic centers. The preferences on possible deictic centers as a referent are based on dialogue information.

Two aspects of the mentioned systems are important for the integration of vision and speech understanding in our domain. Firstly, in PLAYBOT a Bayesian network is used to calculate the most plausible interpretation of an aspect hierarchy which describes possible target objects on different levels. Secondly, the ubiquitous talker uses specific vocabularies and grammars for speech recognition which are selected by the situative context and uses detected objects and locations as referents for deictic expressions. In our domain we have also a non-linguistic context because the speaker is confronted with a scene of building parts and has to specify an intended object.

Both mentioned systems simplify the task of matching the interpretation of the visually observed scene and the instruction of the user. Recognized objects are visualized on a screen and are directly accessible via a communication panel (PLAYBOT) or some textual information about them is shown on a display and can directly be refered to by speech (ubiquitous talker). Another difference is that our system has to deal with uncertainties on both modalities while PLAYBOT is only concerned with uncertainty in vision processing and the ubiquitous talker only with uncertainty in speech recognition.

3 System Components

In order to motivate the interaction scheme of image and speech processing we will briefly introduce some important aspects of the components of our systems.

3.1 Hybrid Object Recognition

The vision component is based on a hybrid approach [8] which integrates structural and holistic knowledge about the real world objects in a semantic network formalism. An HSV camera image is segmented into homogeneously colored regions. Every region is characterized by some shape features and its center point is classified by a special artificial neural network [5] — the Local Linear Map (LLM) — using a 16 dimensional feature vector. By this classification, we get a holistic 2D-object hypothesis which is verified by the structural knowledge of the semantic net using the features of the colored regions.

Because precise spatial reasoning is only possible in three dimensions and the robot needs the three dimensional position and orientation to grasp an object, we calculate a reconstruction in space for all 2D-hypothesis based on simple geometric object models [19, 18]. Geometric features like points, lines and ellipses are fitted to detected image features [11] using an iterative optimization technique.

3.2 Integrated Speech Recognition and Understanding

The speech component of our system consists of two subcomponents, the recognizer and the understanding component, which are tightly coupled . The understanding component is realized in a semantic network which models both linguistic knowledge and knowledge about the construction task. Both knowledge types are incorporated into the recognition process using an LR(1)-grammar [27]. An important aspect in the interaction of vision and speech is extracting object descriptions from spoken utterances. These are especially modeled by the used grammar so that the understanding component gets structured hypotheses from the recognition component. On a higher level in the understanding component, feature structures are generated specifying an intended object by type, color, size and shape attributes and by spatial relations using reference objects. Attributes, such as "color:red", can be instantiated even on word level using a lexicon while instantiating reference objects, such as "ref:{rel:left,{type:cube,color:blue}}", needs more structural analysis.

4 Spatial Model

Human object localization via spatial relations, such as "take the object left to the long one", is qualitative, vague, and context sensitive. When we try to build up a spatial model of our scene there are various aspects which are involved. Firstly, there are inherent properties of the two objects mentioned with a binary spatial relation e.g. direction, relative distance, orientation, and extension of the reference object [26]. Secondly, we have a large influence of the local configuration of the other objects when considering scenes with collections of objects. Therefore, an important concept is neighborhood that we use to define the topology of the visible scene. The neighborhood of two objects can not be defined only by inherent properties of an object pair. Additional objects in the scene can strongly influence this property (fig. 3).

Figure3. Topological influence of additional objects. If we add a bar between the cube, the bolt, and the rhomb-nut, two neighborhood relations vanish and three other neighborhood relations are newly introduced.

4.1 Topological Representation

As we will see later, the topological representation of the scene plays a fundamental role in integrating vision and speech understanding. We have to define it on different levels of abstraction if we want to expand the interaction scheme. The concept of neighborhood is basically defined on local separation of objects. Using 3D data, we model relations between closed object volumes — using 2D data, we model relations between object regions. For simplicity, we only present the 2D model in this section. But the whole concept can be expanded to 3D data in a similar way. The object regions used in the 2D neighborhood relations are projections of the 3D objects in the scene (fig. 4). We get a special projection from camera view if we use the segmented regions from 2D object recognition. This can be interpreted as an approximation of the local configuration of the objects in the scene.

One object region is 'separated' from the other if the area between them is overlapped by other object regions in the scene more than a specified percentage (fig. 5). The term *neighbor* is applied to every pair of object regions which are not 'separated'.

The hole set of neighborhood relations defines the topology of the visual scene. 3D data may provide a more precise topology using the 3D object volumes or other views of

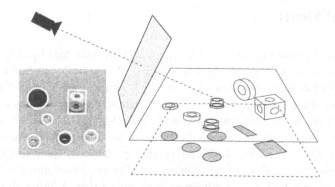

Figure4. Approximation of the 3D scene using 2D regions of objects.

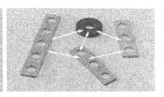

| (a) Area between objects. | (b) Degree of 'separation' of the left and right bar. | (c) Neighborhood relations in the scene. |

Figure5. Definition of neighborhood based on object regions. (a) The rectangled area between two objects is defined by the shortest path between the two region boundaries and the expansion of them in the orthogonal direction. (b) The dark colored sections of the area between the left and right bar define the percentage by which they are 'separated'. (c) The left and right bar are not neighbors because their object regions are 'separated' by regions of two other objects.

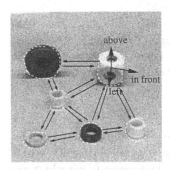
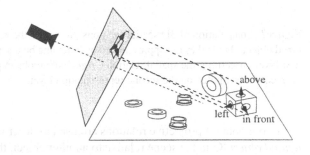

Figure6. The direction vectors from the 2D spatial model can be interpreted using the projection of the reference-frame of the user to the 2D-image.

the objects in the scene, like the top-view. But all we need to construct an approximate version of the neighborhood relations are some segmented regions from vision, which are a kind of low level information with respect to an abstraction hierarchy.

4.2 Projective Relations

Since we are living in a three dimensional world, precise spatial reasoning can only be done using a 3D model of space. The system can not disambiguate all directions if it only knows one 2D view of the scene. Especially if you consider arbitrary locations of objects — which may be not on the planar table — and overlapping regions of objects, the system needs a 3D spatial model in order to resolve the description of an intended object. Nevertheless, we can observe that humans use sometimes projective relations like 'above' or 'below' in an 2D manner as they were looking at a picture and do not imagine the 3D scene [26].

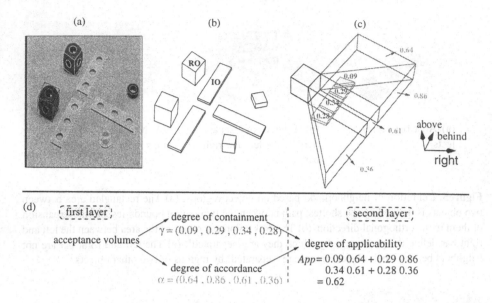

Figure7. Computation of 3D spatial relations. (a) shows the adapted CAD-models of the recognized objects. In (b) they are approximated by bounding boxes. (c) shows the representation of the first layer concerning the spatial relation (*'right'*) of an object pair. (d) A degree of applicability *App* can be computed on the second representation layer.

In our domain projective relations are used to describe the spatial location of an *intended object* IO in the scene relative to another object, the *reference object* RO. Which relation is named by the user depends on the currently used reference-frame which can change in every utterance. The user may look on the scene from different view points. Our computational model for spatial relations is designed to compute the binary relations left, right, above, below, behind, and in-front. They are defined on different levels.

On the 2D-level spatial relations between two objects are represented by a vector which describes the orientation of the shortest path between both regions associated with the objects. In a second step, the reference-frame is projected into the image (fig. 6) and a *degree of applicability* is computed in regard to the angle between the 2D-vector of the spatial relation and the vector of the mentioned projective relation.

The 3D-level is much more complex. The computational model is able to cope with different frames of reference, represents vague and overlapping meanings of projective relations, and considers the influence of the objects' shape on the applicability of prepositions. A detailed description can be found in [4]. The rough idea of the model is presented in figure 7.

Instead of detailed geometric models of the objects, we use surrounding boxes as abstractions that are collinear to the objects inertia axes (fig. 7b). A finite number of acceptance volumes is associated with each object (fig. 7c). These are infinite open polyeders bound to the sides, edges, and corners of the object. They partition the 3D space surrounding the object. A direction vector corresponds to each acceptance volume. It roughly models the direction to which an acceptance volume extends in space.

The computation of spatial relations from objects is a two-layered process (fig. 7d). In the first layer, a reference-independent spatial representation is computed. It can be expressed by a set of acceptance relations which are associated with each acceptance volume. They are judged by the *degree of containment* $\gamma(IO, RO)$ with regard to the intended object. Also reference-dependent meaning definitions of relations rel (e.g. 'right') with regard to certain reference objects and a given reference frame ref of the user are calculated in the first layer. The membership of an acceptance relation is judged by its *degree of accordance* which is computed using the angle between the direction vector of the acceptance volume and the direction of the relation rel. These two judged symbolic reference-independent and reference-dependent descriptions are the basis for the computation of reference-dependent relational expressions for IO-RO-pairs in the second layer. We get a *degree of applicability App* by calculating the scalar product:

$$App(ref, rel, IO, RO) = < \alpha(ref, rel, RO) | \gamma(IO, RO) >$$

In order to apply this computational model to a spatial relation both objects must be reconstructed in three dimensional space. In many cases we do not need precise 3D relations to identify an indented object which was denoted by a spoken utterance. In these cases, we are able to reason about spatial descriptions using the 2D spatial model even if there is no 3D information available according to time constraints or recognition or segmentation failures.

4.3 Multilevel Representation of the Scene

In the preceding sections we described how we model different aspects of the visual scene, like topology and spatial relations. If we want to use this information plus the results from object recognition in an integrated way, we need a comprising representation of these aspects.

For this purpose, we define a labeled graph

$$\mathcal{G}_{vision} = (\mathcal{V}, \mathcal{E}), \quad \mathcal{E} \subseteq \mathcal{V} \times \mathcal{V}$$

which we call *neighborhood graph* because the edges in this graph represent neighborhood relations between objects. The nodes $v \in \mathcal{V}$ are labeled with object hypotheses $Obj(v)$ from vision. The edges $e = \{v_1, v_2\} \in \mathcal{E}$ are labeled with reference-independent representations of the 2D and 3D spatial relations $Rel(Obj(v_1), Obj(v_2)), Rel(Obj(v_2), Obj(v_1))$.

The labels of this graph are defined on different levels of abstraction (fig.8). They are connected by the common concept of neighborhood which defines the connectivity in the graph.

- If an object is detected but classified as unknown we can represent it on the lowest level using region information and 2D spatial relations.
- If an object was classified to a specific object class we can label the graph node on an intermediate level with this object class.
- If an object has been reconstructed in the 3D space, we can label the nodes on the higher level with the adapted CAD-model including the features used for the adaptation, e.g. contour ellipses, and the edges with 3D spatial relations.

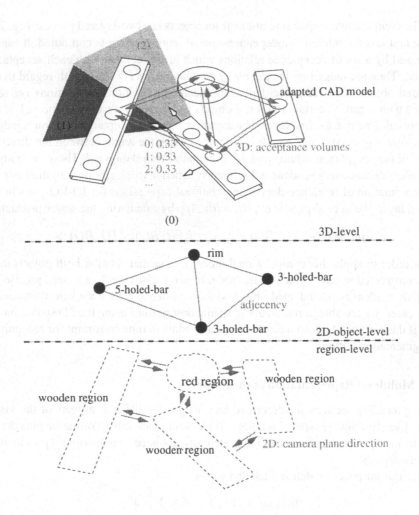

Figure8. Multilevel representation of the scene.

If we label the graph on a higher level, the lower labels still remain because we can use them to get a more probable interpretation of the scene which takes failures into account that happen on a higher level processing stage.

5 Interaction Scheme

Any verbal description which denotes an object in the scene can be interpreted as a partial representation of this scene (fig. 9). If we look at an utterance, e.g. "Take the object in front of these two cubes", we know about the scene that there are three objects in neighborhood and that one object lies in front of two cubes. This information can be represented similar to the neighborhood graph which represents the visual information. In order to compute the object which was denoted by the speaker, we have to find the correspondence between the visual and the verbal representation.

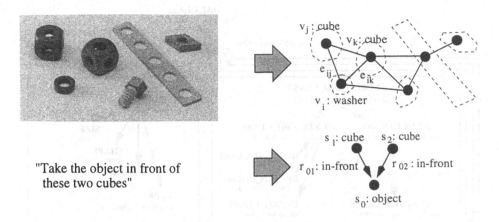

Figure9. Visual and verbal neighborhood graph of the observed scene.

5.1 From Verbal Descriptions to Visual Abstraction Hierarchy and vice versa

If a naive user describes an object in the scene by using attributes he will typically use another vocabulary than the fixed vocabulary appropriate for processing of visual data without point to point correspondence. But, if we want to compare representations generated by vision and by interpreting verbal descriptions of an object, we need a common concept to connect these two representations. In our domain that is the object class which is indented by the speaker and hypothesized by the vision component. Instead of using this concept as a symbolic predicate like classical systems would do, we model a probability distribution which integrates the abstraction hierarchies an vocabularies on both sides and connects them. Reasoning on this probability distribution is realized by a Bayesian network. A first approach to identifying objects using this network is described in [20].

Verbal descriptions of an intended object class consist of some specified attributes which are partly defined on word level, such as "red","long" or "bolt", and partly defined on simple grammatical attachments, such as "the bar with three holes". Currently we distinguish four types of features which are mentioned in order to specify an intended object class:

– type information: bar, bolt, rim, cube, 3-holed-bar, etc.
– color information: white, red, dark, light, etc.
– size information: small, big, short, long, etc.
– shape information: round, hexagonal, elongated, etc.

All feature types are interpreted as random variables and are modeled as nodes in the Bayesian network. Conditional probabilities $P(\text{feature}_i = f | \text{object\_class} = o)$ connecting these features with an object class are estimated from results of two experiments described in [20]. In the first case, type and color features were extracted from utterances which name a marked object from a scene which was presented on a computer screen. In the second case, size and shape features were collected from a questionnaire

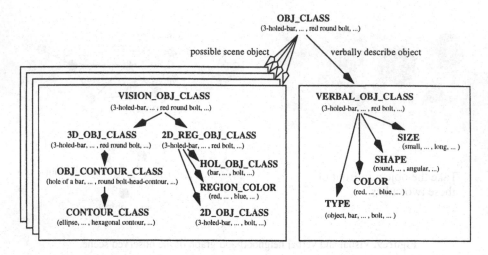

Figure 10. Bayesian network used to connect speech and vision data.

in the World Wide Web (WWW). We estimated the conditional probabilities by counting the uttered type and color features and the selected size and shape features for each object class.

The visual abstraction hierarchy of an object hypothesis consists of several graduated results generated by the vision component. Some components directly hypothesize object classes or subclasses, others generate results which are related to an object class, such as the color of a region or an ellipse which is the contour of an object. In our system we distinguish the following visual evidences:

– HOL_OBJ_CLASS (holistic classification results): object classes or subclasses generated by the holistic component using the special artificial network 'linear local maps'.
– REGION_COLOR: color information associated with a segmented region.
– 2D_OBJ_CLASS (2D-classification results): object classes or subclasses, generated by the semantic network.
– CONTOUR_CLASS (contours found in an object region): ellipses, concentric pairs of ellipses, parallel lines, rectangular closed contours, hexagonal closed contours, etc. which are part of the input of the 3D reconstruction.
– OBJ_CONTOUR_CLASS (contours used in the 3D reconstruction process): these contours are assigned to features of the geometric object model. Therefore, the possible values of this random variable are features of these geometric models, such as hole-contour of a bar, head-contour of a bolt, body-contour of a bar, etc.

All types of evidences are modeled as nodes in the Bayesian network. The conditional probabilities are estimated using a labeled test set of 156 objects on 11 images and the recognition results on this test set.

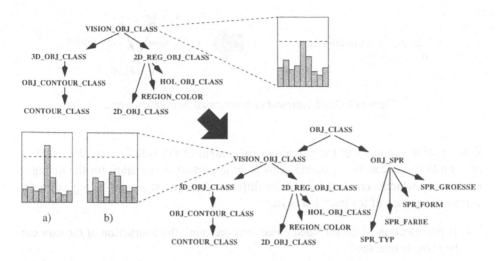

Figure11. Effects on the belief of an object class considering verbal descriptions.

The whole Bayesian network is shown in figure 10. Currently only region color information and 2D-classification results are used in the vision subnet. The network provides us with useful information for speech, dialogue and vision components.

Comparison of Verbal Descriptions and Representations from Vision

If evidence has been instantiated in the 'verbal' ($\mathcal{B}_{speech}$) and 'vision' ($\mathcal{B}_{vision}$) subnets of the Bayesian network and a bottom up propagation is started we can compare both diagnostic influences on the top object class node in order to measure the correspondence between these two representations. If the two diagnostic influence vectors δ_{speech} and δ_{vision} describe different object classes they are orthogonal to each other. If they describe the same class they are in parallel. This is measured by calculating the scalar product of the influence vectors:

$$Cmp(\mathcal{B}_{speech}, \mathcal{B}_{vision}) = \alpha \sum_{i=1}^{\#obj\_classes} \delta_{speech}[i]\,\delta_{vision}[i]$$

where $\delta_{speech}[i]$ is the diagnostic support for an object class i in the subnet $\mathcal{B}_{speech}$,
  $\delta_{vision}[i]$ is the diagnostic support for an object class i in the subnet $\mathcal{B}_{vision}$,
  α is a normalizing constant.

After bottom up and top down propagation of evidences has been finished and the network is in equilibrium state we get a common belief upon the membership of a scene object to an object class. Two effects can result from considering the mentioned verbal description.

  – the gain of information results in an increasing belief in one object class (fig. 11a).
  – the gain of information results in a lower belief in an object class (fig. 11b).

244

"Take the object in front of
these two cubes"

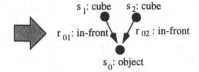

Figure12. Graph representation generated from an utterance.

If we note the changes of the maximum component of the belief vector the certainty of a node match can be measured. This is an important information for the dialogue component which may switch between different dialogue strategies in regard to the certainty measure of the intended object:

- If the selection of the intended object was 'certain', the instruction of the user can be directly executed.
- If the selection of the intended object was not 'certain', the system can ask for confirmation.
- If the system selects a set of different objects which all had an increasing belief component, the system can ask for a more specific description or otherwise can reject the instruction.

Using the weighted description comparison and the certainty measure of a selected object, we get a very flexible scoring scheme which integrates evidences from different abstraction levels and offers very detailed informations to a dialogue component. The first score measures a kind of 'distance' between the visual and the verbal description of an object. The second one — the certainty measure — describes a gain of information. The scoring scheme is based on a probability distribution which was estimated from results of psycholinguistic experiments [20] and from recognition results generated by the vision component.

5.2 Linking Verbal Descriptions and Vision Processing Results by Subgraph Matching

If spatial relations are included in an utterance, the comparison between the verbal description and the visual abstraction hierarchy is expanded to a weighted graph matching problem. Typically the graph representation of an utterance which denotes an object in the scene is star-shaped (fig. 12). It consists of a description of the localized object which is the intended object and a list of reference objects plus associated spatial relations. There are several uncertainties which have to be considered if we search for the best match of the verbal description and the description of the scene generated by the vision component.

We chose a probabilistic approach, Bayesian networks, to cope with these problems. The structure of the Bayesian network is generated from the graph representation of the verbal description $\mathcal{G}_{speech} = \{\mathcal{S}, \mathcal{R}\}$, the possible labels of the random variables and the conditional probabilities are generated from the graph representation of the vision processing results $\mathcal{G}_{vision} = \{\mathcal{V}, \mathcal{E}\}$ (fig. 13):

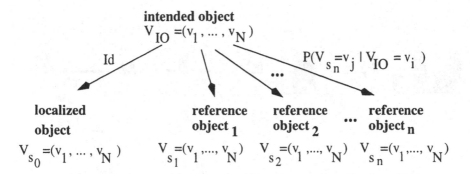

Figure13. Bayesian network for identifying the intended object.

$V_s :: \mathcal{V}$ is a random variable which denotes the node of the vision graph which should be assigned to the node s of the verbal graph. The diagnostic support from evidence ϵ^- that the nodes $v \in \mathcal{V}$ and $s \in \mathcal{S}$ are identical is defined as:

$$P(\epsilon^-_{V_s=v}|V_s = v) = Cmp(\mathcal{B}_{speech}(s), \mathcal{B}_{vision}(v))$$

where $\mathcal{B}(v)$ is one of the Bayesian networks $\mathcal{B}_{speech}$ or $\mathcal{B}_{vision}$ which is instantiated with the information attached with a node v.

Another uncertainty which is modeled in the Bayesian network is the probability that $V_{s_k} = v_j$ is the reference object if the user mentions a spatial relation $Rel(r_{0k})$ and we assume that $V_{IO} = v_i$ is the intended object:

$$P(V_{s_k} = v_j|V_{IO} = v_i) = App(Ref, Rel(r_{0k}), Rel(e_{ij}))$$

where $Rel(e_{ij}) = Rel(Obj(v_i), Obj(v_j))$ is the representation of the spatial relation between the objects $Obj(v_i)$ (IO) and $Obj(v_j)$ (RO).
Ref is the current reference frame of the speaker.
$App(.,.,.)$ denotes the applicability function of the spatial model.

If we want to propagate the evidences to the top node there are some constraints which we have to consider. One particular node $v \in \mathcal{V} = \{v_0 \ldots v_N\}$ can only be assigned to one of the nodes $s \in \mathcal{S} = \{s_0 \ldots s_n\}$ and all assignments must be injective. This is concerned by a search algorithm which finds the most plausible assignment of nodes for all values of $V_{IO} = v_{io=1\ldots N} \in \mathcal{V}$ which is defined by

$$(v_{s_0} \ldots v_{s_n})^* = \underset{(v_{s_0} \ldots v_{s_n})}{argmax} \, Bel(V_{IO} = v_{io})$$

$$= \underset{(v_{s_0} \ldots v_{s_n})}{argmax} \, P(\epsilon^-_{V_{s_0}=v_{s_0}} \ldots \epsilon^-_{V_{s_n}=v_{s_n}}|V_{IO} = v_{io})$$

$$= \underset{(v_{s_0} \ldots v_{s_n})}{argmax} \, \prod_{i=0\ldots n} P(\epsilon^-_{V_{s_i}=v_{s_i}}|V_{s_i} = v_{s_i})P(V_{s_i} = v_{s_i}|V_{IO} = v_{io})$$

where $(v_{s_0} \ldots v_{s_n}) \in \mathcal{V}^n$ are injective node assignments for $(s_0 \ldots s_n)$

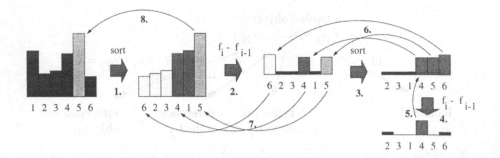

Figure14. Example presenting the partitioning of the plausibility vector.

Propagating down gives us some expectations about an object which would be consistent with the rest of our instantiated evidence.

Evaluating the Bayesian network provides us a plausibility for all objects in the scene. The components of this *plausibility vector* rate which object was denoted by the spoken utterance. If we have to chose a particular object in order to generate a system answer, many times the decision can not be definite. There are several reasons why this will happen:

- The user intended to specify a group of objects.
- The user did not realize that his naming was not specific enough.
- Some attributes the user mentioned were not recognized by speech processing.
- The vision component classified an object to the wrong class.

The ambiguity remained in the set of selected objects can only be resolved by a dialog component which is able to consider the dialog context of the utterance. Therefore, the answer of the component which interprets the utterance only in scene context has to include all objects which are plausible.

Partitioning the plausibility vector U_{IO} into one group of elements which defines the system answer and one group with plausibility below a threshold is a difficult task because we have no information about a distribution of these values on which such decision could be based. Often, we intuitively split such vectors into more than two groups, e.g. one with low, one with middle, and one with high plausibility.

Therefore, we use differences of values in order to partition the plausibility vector (fig. 14). In a first step the plausibility values are sorted (1.) so that we get a monotonic discretizised function. The biggest jumps in this function are hypothetical boundaries of partitions. In order to get the right number of partitions the differences of each jump are sorted (2.+3.). The maximum jump in this new monotonic function (4.) provides us all differences which are significant for partitioning the original sorted plausibility vector (5.+6.+7.). Finally, the system answer is generated including all objects which are member of the partition with maximal plausibility (8.).

The partitioning scheme can be influenced by varying the 'zero-partitioning-line'. This value defines the difference which is assigned to the minimum component of the plausibility vector. If it is set to zero, there is a tendency to selecting all objects in context. If it is set to the value of the minimum component there are more differences

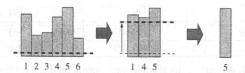

Figure15. Increasing the 'zero-partitioning-line' in different focus contexts. If the maximum component of the example in fig. 14 is slightly less, three components are selected. If we focus on these and raise the 'zero-partitioning-line', the maximum component can be selected.

which are classified as significant (fig. 15). This may be useful if the scene context is varied by the dialogue component relative to a set of objects which may be in focus.

6 Results

In this section we will concentrate on some aspects concerning the interaction scheme of the speech understanding and vision component. Given an instruction, the system has to identify the objects which were denoted by the utterance. Firstly, we mention some aspects concerning the results of the system components. After that, we compare the identification results of our system under different conditions using speech and transcribed (NL) input, uncertain and perfect vision. We stated that the topology of the visual scene has a great impact on the verbal description of an object. In another experiment we will measure this impact on identification results of our system. Finally, the identification results are compared to former results described in [20]. These did not consider topological information and a slightly different criterium was used in order to select a set of intended objects.

6.1 Experimental Data

Two different test sets were used evaluating our system. In a first psycholinguistic experiment 10 subjects named objects verbally which were presented on a computer screen. In each image, one object was marked and the subjects were told to name this object using an instruction, such as "give me the big yellow object" or "take the long bar". From this experiment, 453 verbal object descriptions were collected. These descriptions were partly used to estimate some conditional probabilities concerning type and color information in the Bayesian network used for node comparison (section 5.1). This test set is called 'FEATURE'-set. In a second experiment under the same conditions 6 persons were asked to name the marked object by using spatial relations, such as "take the red object in front of the long one". 144 utterances were collected using 5 different scenes. This test set is called 'SPATIAL'-set.

The instructions were transcribed orthographically in order to exclude speech recognition errors. This input is labeled as 'NL' (natural language). Instead of a set of labeled images, we use a subset of utterances which denote a correctly recognized object. This input is labeled as 'PV' (perfect vision).

Former results described in [20] were generated on subsets of these two test sets which are called 'FEATURE^{old}' and 'SPATIAL^{old}'.

	#utt	WA	FA	NL ∪ S
FEATURE_S	325	66.4%	79.3%	90%
SPATIAL_S	123	67.1%	72.3%	64%

Table1. Results of the speech components on different test sets.

	#utt	perfect vision	wrong color	wrong object class	none
FEATURE	352	88.6%	5.1%	2.0%	4.3%
FEATURE_NL	325	88.9%	5.2%	2.2%	3.7%
SPATIAL	133	70.7%	18.0%	4.5%	6.8%
SPATIAL_NL	123	71.5%	20.3%	4.1%	4.1%

Table2. Results of the vision component on different test sets.

6.2 Component Results

In order to interpret the identification results correctly, we have to analyse the partial results of the system components. On the speech side, the quality of the recognition component is measured by the word accuracy (WA) [10]. A similar measure can be defined for feature structures which counts substitutions, insertions, and deletions of feature entries. For that, we use the feature structures, which are generated by the speech understanding component using NL-input, as reference data. This measure is called feature accuracy (FA) and can be interpreted as the influence of speech recognition errors on the speech understanding component for object specifications. Even for NL-input, there are some failures which happen in the understanding component, due to unknown words or language structures which were not modeled in the grammar or in the semantic network. In these cases the understanding component generated none or more than one object specification. These utterances were left out when computing the identification results. Thereby, we get slightly different test sets for speech- and NL-input. The word and feature accuracy for both speech test sets is given in table 1.

On the vision side, there are three different kinds of errors: wrong object class, wrong color classification, no object hypothesis at all. In some scenes, there was an object which was unknown to the vision component. These objects caused most wrong object classifications. We measured these failures for all marked objects of the different test sets (tab. 2).

6.3 Classification of System Answers

Given an instruction, the system generates a set of objects which were hypothetically denoted by the instruction. The system answer is classified into different classes in regard to the marked object which was intended.

– **precise:** the marked object is the only one the system selected.
– **included:** the system selected more objects beside the marked one which have the same object class as the marked object.

	#utt	correct	additional	false	nothing
NL+PV	312	94.6%	6.4%	5.4%	0.0%
NL+UV	352	87.8%	6.5%	10.5%	1.7%
S+PV	289	94.1%	9.0%	5.5%	0.4%
S+UV	325	87.1%	8.6%	11.1%	1.8%

Table3. Identification results for the FEATURE-set using text (NL), speech (S), perfect vision (PV), and uncertain vision (UV) as input.

- **additional:** the marked object is member of the selected subset of objects but some selected objects have a different object class than the marked object.
- **correct:** the marked object is member of the selected subset. Note that 'correct' is the union of 'precise','included', and 'additional'.
- **false:** the system has selected some objects but the marked object is not a member of the subset.
- **nothing:** the system rejected the instruction because the system did not find an appropriate object.

The class 'precise' is only relevant if the intended object is localized by specifying some reference objects and spatial relations. Otherwise the system can not distinguish objects of the same object class.

6.4 Results using the FEATURE-Set

In table 3 we present the identification results using the FEATURE-set of instructions. In all cases the percentage of correct system answers is quit high ($> 87\%$). This is a very important aspect for the acceptance of the system with regard to a user. Even if additional objects are selected, a dialog strategy can disambiguate the instruction by a precise request.

If we compare the results for different inputs, we examine the expected ordering from the best result with 'text'- and 'perfect vision'-input to the lowest identification result with 'speech'- and 'uncertain vision'-input. It is remarkable that the impact of 'speech'-input is very low even though the word accuracy (66.4%) was quit worse and the feature accuracy (79.3%) is far from that of text-input.

6.5 Results using the SPATIAL-Set

In the previous section we presented identification results from utterances which did not mention spatial relations. Therefore, only the Bayesian networks for verbal feature descriptions and the visual abstraction hierarchy, and the partitioning scheme of the plausibility vector are evaluated. In the SPATIAL-set, we have to consider more influences on the identification results, e.g. spatial model and topology. The results are presented in table 4.

We can examine the same tendencies as mentioned for the FEATURE-set. The influence of the usage of speech-input instead of text-input is quit low and in the case of

	#utt	precise	correct	additional	false	nothing
NL+PV	94	70.2%	90.4%	12.9%	9.6%	0.0%
NL+UV	133	54.9%	79.7%	10.5%	20.3%	0.0%
S+PV	88	68.2%	86.4%	10.2%	13.6%	0.0%
S+UV	123	56.1%	79.7%	8.1%	20.3%	0.0%

Table4. Identification results for the SPATIAL-set using text (NL), speech (S), perfect vision (PV), and uncertain vision (UV) as input.

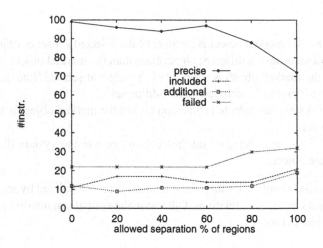

Figure16. Influence of the neighborhood graph.

uncertain vision we get nearly equal results. The biggest impact is introduced by uncertain vision. The rates of 'false'-identifications are nearly doubled. This is due to the fact that the user does not specify many features when using spatial relations. Therefore, the node comparison in the subgraph-matching procedure is not very restrictive and sensitive for uncertain vision results.

Influence of the Neighborhood Graph

In order to measure the influence of topology introduced by the neighborhood graph on the system answers we used the SPATIAL test set and NL-/UV-input. The neighborhood of objects in the scene is defined by overlapping regions (section 4.1). We varied the threshold which defines the percentage two object regions are allowed to be separated without loosing their neighborhood. 100% means that all objects are neighbors. The classification of the system answers are shown in figure 16. We observe that above 60% separation, system answers are much more sloppy and that 'additional' and 'false' system answers increase. On the other side we nearly did not loose any 'precise' system answer if the threshold is defined very rigorously. This provides us a high evidence that the assumptions on which we defined the neighborhood hold. The concept of defining neighborhood relations by separations seems to model an important aspect when humans specify intended objects using spatial relations.

source	#instr.	correct	additional	false	nothing
FEATURE_NL_UV^{old}	417	86.3%	8.1%	9.6%	4.0%
FEATURE_NL_UV	352	87.8%	6.5%	10.5%	1.7%
FEATURE_NL_PV^{old}	412	92.5%	8.3%	7.5%	0.0%
FEATURE_NL_PV	312	94.6%	6.4%	5.4%	0.0%
SPATIAL_NL_UV^{old}	84	78.6%	8.3%	21.4%	0.0%
SPATIAL_NL_UV	133	79.7%	10.5%	20.3%	0.0%
SPATIAL_NL_PV^{old}	98	83.5%	2.0%	16.5%	0.0%
SPATIAL_NL_PV	94	90.4%	12.9%	9.6%	0.0%

Table5. Comparison to former results.

6.6 Comparison to Former Results

In table 5 we compare results of our system to those of an earlier version of the system. Results generated using speech input are not compared because the speech recognition and understanding components are different. For results of the earlier system, the NL-input was adapted to the grammar used in speech understanding component in order to avoid errors in this component. While results of the earlier system show that speech recognition errors have the greatest impact on the overall results (FEATURE_S_UV^{old} correct: 70%, SPATIAL_S_UV^{old} correct: 76%), our system has nearly the same performance using speech input as using NL input. In nearly all cases we could improve the correct system identifications. By using the described partitioning scheme of the plausibility vector (sec. 5.2), we could slightly increase the number of 'correct' system answers and reduce the number of system answers classified as 'additional' (FEATURE-set). The percentage of system answers for SPATIAL_NL_PV which were classified as 'correct' increased significantly by 7.8% while 'false' classifications could be reduced by 41.8%. The main reason for this gain in system performance is the introduction of the neighborhood graph.

There are many aspects of the system which had not been evaluated so far. Most attention will be paid to a more detailed analysis of the system if it is concerned with more extreme erroneous data. We plan some tests by changing the color and type information of marked objects randomly and will evaluate the performance of the speech understanding component using hand labeled feature structures as a reference set.

7 Conclusion

We presented a new approach to integrating vision and speech understanding. As we work in real environments, we are typically concerned with erroneous, vague or incomplete data. We cope with these problems by using multiple representations on different levels of abstraction. In order to find the most plausible interpretation of the scene the graduated results of the vision components are connected by Bayesian networks.

The interpretation of a spoken utterance concerning the visual scene is modeled as another partial representation of the scene. Verbal descriptions often use qualitative features of the object instead of the exact name and specify spatial relations only vague.

We model the coherence between these features and the object classes used in vision in a Bayesian network. The conditional probabilities were estimated using results of psycholinguistic experiments.

We showed that the topology of the scene is an important aspect if a speaker localizes an intended object by using spatial relations. We introduced this influence by the definition of a neighborhood graph which is used on all representation layers. The nodes of this graph are labeled with the graduated results generated by the vision components respectively with mentioned features of a verbal object description. The edges are labeled with spatial relations which are represented numerically (vision) or by name (verbal).

The identification of the object which was indented by the speaker is modeled as a weighted subgraph match between the graph representation generated by vision and the verbally specified graph representation. It is realized by using a Bayesian network which is dynamically constructed from both graph representations and provides us a plausibility vector which components rate the plausibility that the object related the component was denoted by the utterance. In order to select a set of objects which are hypothetically denoted by the utterance, we developed a partitioning technique which does not need a pre-specified threshold and does not suppose a specific distribution of the values. Secondly, we defined an additional confidence measure which provides a dialogue component some information concerning the uncertainty of the selection.

We demonstrated the effectiveness of our approach on real data in which naive users were asked to name objects in a visual scene. We could improve former results on this test set especially by the introduction of the neighborhood graph. Because of the hierarchical modeling we obtain first results with drastically reduced computational complexity. As computation continues, results will be more precise. Thereby, an anytime behavior is realized.

Further research will concentrate the expansion of the vision abstract hierarchy, the modeling of an increased set of spatial relations, and the integration of hand gestures pointing at an intended object. Secondly, we will use the plausibility measure from object identifications as a scoring scheme in the understanding component in order to weight alternative interpretations of the utterance.

Acknowledgements

This work has been supported by the German Research Foundation (DFG) in the project SFB 360 "Situated Artificial Communicators".

References

1. G. Adorni, M. D. Manzo, and F. Giunchiglia. Natural language driven image generation. In *COLING*, pages 495–500, 1984.
2. L. E. Bernstein. For speech perception by humans or machines, three senses are better than one. In *International Conference on Spoken Language Processing*, pages 1477–1480, 1996.
3. S. Dickenson and D. Metaxas. Integrating qualitative and quantitative shape recovery. *International Journal of Computer Vision*, 13(3):1–20, 1994.

4. T. Fuhr, G. Socher, C. Scheering, and G. Sagerer. A three-dimensional spatial model for the interpretation of image data. In P. Olivier and K.-P. Gapp, editors, *Representation and Processing of Spatial Expressions*, pages 103–118. Lawrence Erlbaum Associates, 1997.

5. G. Heidemann and H. Ritter. Objekterkennung mit Neuronalen Netzen. Technical Report 2, Situierte Künstliche Kommunikatoren, SFB 360, Universität Bielefeld, 1996.

6. H. Kollnig and H.-H. Nagel. Ermittlung von begrifflichen Beschreibungen von Geschehen in Straßenverkehrsszenen mit Hilfe unscharfer Mengen. In *Informatik Froschung und Entwicklung*, 8, pages 186–196, 1993.

7. S. M. Kosslyn. Mental imagery. In D. A. O. et al., editor, *Visual Cognition and Action*, pages 73–97, Cambridge, Mass, 1990. MIT Press.

8. F. Kummert, G. A. Fink, and G. Sagerer. Schritthaltende hybride Objektdetektion. In *Mustererkennung 97*, 19, pages 137–144, Berlin, 1997. DAGM-Symposium Braunschweig, Springer-Verlag.

9. F. Lavagetto, S. Lepsoy, C. Braccini, and S. Curinga. Lip motion modeling and speech driven estimation. In *Proc. Int. Conf. on Acoustics, Speech and Signal Processing*, pages 183–186, 1997.

10. K. Lee. *Automatic Speech Recognition: The Development of the SPHINX System*. Kluwer Academic Publishers, 1989.

11. A. Maßmann, S. Posch, and D. Schlüter. Using markov random fields for contour-based grouping. In *Proceedings of International Conference on Image Processing*, volume 2, pages 207–242, 1997.

12. T. Maybury, editor. *Intelligent Multimedia Interfaces*. AAAI Press/The MIT Press, 1993.

13. D. McDonald and E. J. Conklin. Salience as a simplifying metaphor for natural language generation. In *Proceedings of AAAI-81*, pages 49–51, 1981.

14. K. Nagao. Abduction and dynamic preference in plan-based dialogue understanding. In *International Joint Conference on Artificial Intelligence*, pages 1186–1192. Morgan Kaufmann Publishers, Inc., 1993.

15. K. Nagao and J. Rekimoto. Ubiquitous talker: Spoken language interaction with real world objects. In *International Joint Conference on Artificial Intelligence*, pages 1284–1290, 1995.

16. P. Olivier, T. Maeda, and J. ichi Tsujii. Automatic depiction of spatial descriptions. In *Proceedings of AAAI-94*, pages 1405–1410, Seattle, WA, 1994.

17. W. Richards, A. Jepson, and J. Feldman. Priors, preferences and categorial percepts. In W. Richards and D. Knill, editors, *Perception as Bayesian Inference*, pages 93–122. Cambridge University Press, 1996.

18. G. Socher. *Qualitative Scene Descriptions from Images for Integrated Speech and Image Understanding*. Dissertationen zur Künstlichen Intelligenz (DISKI 170). infix-Verlag, Sankt Augustin, 1997.

19. G. Socher, T. Merz, and S. Posch. 3-D Reconstruction and Camera Calibration from Images with Known Objects. In D. Pycock, editor, *Proc. 6th British Machine Vision Conference*, pages 167–176, 1995.

20. G. Socher, G. Sagerer, and P. Perona. Baysian Reasoning on Qualitative Descriptions from Images and Speech. In H. Buxton and A. Mukerjee, editors, *ICCV'98 Workshop on Conceptual Description of Images*, Bombay, India, 1998.

21. R. K. Srihari. Computational models for integrating linguistic and visual information: A survey. In *Artificial Intelligence Review*, 8, pages 349–369, Netherlands, 1994. Kluwer Academic Publishers.

22. R. K. Srihari and D. T. Burhans. Visual semantics: Extracting visual information from text accompanying pictures. In *Proceedings of AAAI-94*, pages 793–798, Seattle, WA, 1994.

23. J. K. Tsotsos and et al. The PLAYBOT Project. In J. Aronis, editor, *IJCAI'95 Workshop on AI Applications for Disabled People*, Montreal, 1995.

24. J. K. Tsotsos, G. Verghese, S. Dickenson, M. Jenkin, A. Jepson, E. Milios, F. Nuflo, S. Stevenson, M. Black, D. Metaxas, S. Culhane, Y. Yet, and R. Mann. Playbot: A visually-guided robot for physically disabled children. *Image and Vision Computing*, 16(4):275–292, 1998.

25. G. Verghese and J. K. Tsotsos. Real-time model-based tracking using perspective alignment. In *Proceedings of Vision Interface'94*, pages 202–209, 1994.

26. C. Vorwerg, G. Socher, T. Fuhr, G. Sagerer, and G. Rickheit. Projective relations for 3D space: computational model, application, and psychological evaluation. In *Proceedings of the 14th National Joint Conference on Artificial Intelligence AAAI-97*, Rhode Island, 1997.

27. S. Wachsmuth, G. A. Fink, and G. Sagerer. Integration of parsing and incremental speech recognition. In *Proceedings EUSIPCO-98*, 1998.

28. W. Wahlster. One word says more than a thousand pictures. on the automatic verbalization of the results of image sequence analysis systems. In *Computers and Artificial Intelligence*, 8, pages 479–492, 1989.

29. D. L. Waltz. Generating and understanding scene descriptions. In B. Webber and I. Sag, editors, *Elements of Discourse Understanding*, pages 266–282, New York, NY, 1981. Cambridge University Press.

30. M. Zancanaro, O. Stock, and C. Strapparava. Dialogue cohension sharing and adjusting in an enhanced multimodal environment. In *International Joint Conference on Artificial Intelligence*, pages 1230–1236. Morgan Kaufmann Publishers, Inc., 1993.

A Bayesian Computer Vision System
for Modeling Human Interactions

Nuria Oliver[1], Barbara Rosario[1] and Alex Pentland[1]

[1] Vision and Modeling. Media Laboratory, MIT,
Cambridge, MA 02139, USA
{nuria,rosario,sandy}@media.mit.edu
http://nuria.www.media.mit.edu/~nuria/humanBehavior/humanBehavior.html

Abstract. We describe a real-time computer vision and machine learning system for modeling and recognizing human behaviors in a visual surveillance task. The system is particularly concerned with detecting when interactions between people occur, and classifying the type of interaction. Examples of interesting interaction behaviors include following another person, altering one's path to meet another, and so forth.
Our system combines top-down with bottom-up information in a closed feedback loop, with both components employing a statistical Bayesian approach. We propose and compare two different state-based learning architectures, namely HMMs and CHMMs, for modeling behaviors and interactions. The CHMM model is shown to work much more efficiently and accurately.
Finally, to deal with the problem of limited training data, a synthetic 'Alife-style' training system is used to develop flexible prior models for recognizing human interactions. We demonstrate the ability to use these a priori models to accurately classify real human behaviors and interactions with no additional tuning or training.

1 Introduction

We describe a real-time computer vision and machine learning system for modeling and recognizing human behaviors in a visual surveillance task. The system is particularly concerned with detecting when interactions between people occur, and classifying the type of interaction.

Over the last decade there has been growing interest within the computer vision and machine learning communities in the problem of analyzing human behavior in video ([10],[3],[21], [8], [17], [14],[9], [11]). Such systems typically consist of a low- or mid-level computer vision system to detect and segment a moving object — human or car, for example —, and a higher level interpretation module that classifies the motion into 'atomic' behaviors such as, for example, a pointing gesture or a car turning left.

However, there have been relatively few efforts to understand human behaviors that have substantial extent in time, particularly when they involve interactions between people. This level of interpretation is the goal of this paper, with the intention of building systems that can deal with the complexity of multi-person pedestrian and highway scenes.

This computational task combines elements of AI/machine learning and computer vision, and presents challenging problems in both domains: from a *Computer Vision* viewpoint, it requires real-time, accurate and robust detection and tracking of the objects of interest in an unconstrained environment; from a *Machine Learning and Artificial Intelligence* perspective behavior models for interacting agents are needed to interpret the set of perceived actions and detect eventual anomalous behaviors or potentially dangerous situations. Moreover, all the processing modules need to be integrated in a consistent way.

Our approach to modeling person-to-person interactions is to use supervised statistical learning techniques to teach the system to recognize normal single-person behaviors and common person-to-person interactions. A major problem with a data-driven statistical approach, especially when modeling rare or anomalous behaviors, is the limited number of examples of those behaviors for training the models. A major emphasis of our work, therefore, is on efficient Bayesian integration of both prior knowledge (by the use of synthetic prior models) with evidence from data (by situation-specific parameter tuning). Our goal is to be able to successfully apply the system to any normal multi-person interaction situation without additional training.

Another potential problem arises when a completely new pattern of behavior is presented to the system. After the system has been trained at a few different sites, previously unobserved behaviors will be (by definition) rare and unusual. To account for such novel behaviors the system should be able to recognize such new behaviors, and to build models of the behavior from as as little as a single example.

We have pursued a Bayesian approach to modeling that includes both *prior* knowledge and *evidence* from data, believing that the Bayesian approach provides the best framework for coping with small data sets and novel behaviors. Graphical models [6], such as Hidden Markov Models (HMMs) [22] and Coupled Hidden Markov Models (CHMMs) [5, 4, 19], seem most appropriate for modeling and classifying human behaviors because they offer dynamic time warping, a well-understood training algorithm, and a clear Bayesian semantics for both individual (HMMs) and interacting or coupled (CHMMs) generative processes.

To specify the priors in our system, we have developed a framework for building and training models of the behaviors of interest using *synthetic agents*. Simulation with the agents yields synthetic data that is used to train *prior models*. These prior models are then used recursively in a Bayesian framework to fit real behavioral data. This approach provides a rather straightforward and flexible technique to the design of priors, one that does not require strong analytical assumptions to be made about the form of the priors[1]. In our experiments we have found that by combining such synthetic priors with limited real data we can easily achieve very high accuracies of recognition of different human-to-human interactions. Thus, our system is robust to cases in which there are only a few examples of a certain behavior (such as in interaction type 2 described in section

---

[1] Note that our priors have the same form as our posteriors, namely they are Markov models.

5.1) or even no examples except synthetically-generated ones.

The paper is structured as follows: section 2 presents an overview of the system, section 3 describes the computer vision techniques used for segmentation and tracking of the pedestrians, and the statistical models used for behavior modeling and recognition are described in section 4. Section 5 contains experimental results with both synthetic agent data and real video data, and section 6 summarizes the main conclusions and sketches our future directions of research. Finally a summary of the CHMM formulation is presented in the appendix.

2 System Overview

Our system employs a static camera with wide field-of-view watching a dynamic outdoor scene (the extension to an active camera [1] is straightforward and planned for the next version). A real-time computer vision system segments moving objects from the learned scene. The scene description method allows variations in lighting, weather, etc., to be learned and accurately discounted.

For each moving object an appearance-based description is generated, allowing it to be tracked though temporary occlusions and multi-object meetings. A Kalman filter tracks the objects location, coarse shape, color pattern, and velocity. This temporally ordered stream of data is then used to obtain a behavioral description of each object, and to detect interactions between objects.

Figure 1 depicts the processing loop and main functional units of our ultimate system.

1. The real-time computer vision input module detects and tracks moving objects in the scene, and for each moving object outputs a feature vector describing its motion and heading, and its spatial relationship to all nearby moving objects.
2. These feature vectors constitute the input to stochastic state-based behavior models. Both HMMs and CHMMs, with varying structures depending on the complexity of the behavior, are then used for classifying the perceived behaviors.

Note that both *top-down* and *bottom-up* streams of information are continuously managed and combined for each moving object within the scene. Consequently our Bayesian approach offers a mathematical framework for both combining the observations (bottom-up) with complex behavioral priors (top-down) to provide expectations that will be fed back to the perceptual system.

3 Segmentation and Tracking

The first step in the system is to reliably and robustly detect and track the pedestrians in the scene. We use 2-D *blob features* for modeling each pedestrian. The notion of "blobs" as a representation for image features has a long history in computer vision [20, 15, 2, 26, 18], and has had many different mathematical

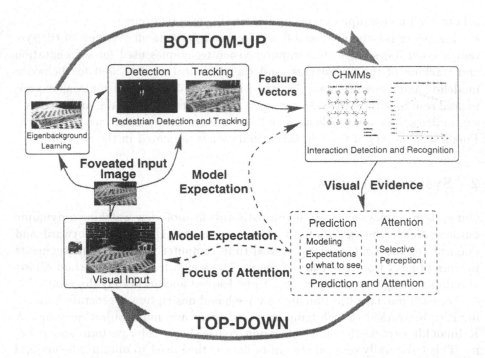

Fig. 1. Top-down and bottom-up processing loop

definitions. In our usage it is a compact set of pixels that share some visual properties that are not shared by the surrounding pixels. These properties could be color, texture, brightness, motion, shading, a combination of these, or any other salient spatio-temporal property derived from the signal (the image sequence).

3.1 Segmentation by Eigenbackground subtraction

In our system the main cue for clustering the pixels into blobs is motion, because we have a static background with moving objects. To detect these moving objects we adaptively build an eigenspace that models the background. This eigenspace model describes the range of appearances (e.g., lighting variations over the day, weather variations, etc.) that have been observed. The eigenspace can also be generated from a site model using standard computer graphics techniques.

The eigenspace model is formed by taking a sample of N images and computing both the mean μ_b background image and its covariance matrix C_b. This covariance matrix can be diagonalized via an eigenvalue decomposition $L_b = \Phi_b C_b \Phi_b^T$, where Φ_b is the eigenvector matrix of the covariance of the data and L_b is the corresponding diagonal matrix of its eigenvalues. In order to reduce the dimensionality of the space, in principal component analysis (PCA) only M eigenvectors (eigenbackgrounds) are kept, corresponding to the M largest eigenvalues to give a Φ_M matrix. A principal component feature vector $I_i - \Phi_{M_b}^T X_i$ is then formed, where $X_i = I_i - \mu_b$ is the mean normalized image vector.

Note that moving objects, because they don't appear in the same location in the N sample images and they are typically small, do not have a significant contribution to this model. Consequently the portions of an image containing a moving object cannot be well described by this eigenspace model (except in very unusual cases), whereas the static portions of the image can be accurately described as a sum of the the various eigenbasis vectors. That is, the eigenspace provides a robust model of the probability distribution function of the background, but not for the moving objects.

Once the eigenbackground images (stored in a matrix called Φ_{M_b} hereafter) are obtained, as well as their mean μ_b, we can project each input image I_i onto the space expanded by the eigenbackground images $B_i = \Phi_{M_b} X_i$ to model the static parts of the scene, pertaining to the background. Therefore, by computing and thresholding the Euclidean distance (distance from feature space DFFS [16]) between the input image and the projected image we can detect the moving objects present in the scene: $D_i = |I_i - B_i| > t$, where t is a given threshold. Note that it is easy to *adaptively* perform the eigenbackground subtraction, in order to compensate for changes such as big shadows. This motion mask is the input to a connected component algorithm that produces blob descriptions that characterize each person's shape. We have also experimented with modeling the background by using a mixture of Gaussian distributions at each pixel, as in Pfinder [27]. However we finally opted for the eigenbackground method because it offered good results and less computational load.

3.2 Tracking

The trajectories of each blob are computed and saved into a *dynamic track memory*. Each trajectory has associated a first order Kalman filter that predicts the blob's position and velocity in the next frame. Recall that the Kalman Filter is the 'best linear unbiased estimator' in a mean squared sense and that for Gaussian processes, the Kalman filter equations corresponds to the optimal Bayes' estimate.

In order to handle occlusions as well as to solve the correspondence between blobs over time, the appearance of each blob is also modeled by a Gaussian PDF in RGB color space. When a new blob appears in the scene, a new trajectory is associated to it. Thus for each blob the Kalman-filter-generated spatial PDF and the Gaussian color PDF are combined to form a joint (x, y) image space and color space PDF. In subsequent frames the Mahalanobis distance is used to determine the blob that is most likely to have the same identity.

4   Behavior Models

In this section we develop our framework for building and applying models of individual behaviors and person-to-person interactions. In order to build effective computer models of human behaviors we need to address the question of how

Fig. 2. Background mean image, blob segmentation image and input image with blob bounding boxes

knowledge can be mapped onto computation to dynamically deliver consistent interpretations.

From a strict computational viewpoint there are two key problems when processing the continuous flow of feature data coming from a stream of input video: (1) Managing the computational load imposed by frame-by-frame examination of all of the agents and their interactions. For example, the number of possible interactions between any two agents of a set of N agents is $N * (N - 1)/2$. If naively managed this load can easily become large for even moderate N; (2) Even when the frame-by-frame load is small and the representation of each agent's instantaneous behavior is compact, there is still the problem of managing all this information over time.

Statistical directed acyclic graphs (DAGs) or probabilistic inference networks (PINs) [7, 13] can provide a computationally efficient solution to these problems. HMMs and their extensions, such as CHMMs, can be viewed as a particular, simple case of temporal PIN or DAG. PINs consist of a set of random variables represented as nodes as well as directed edges or links between them. They define a mathematical form of the joint or conditional PDF between the random variables. They constitute a simple graphical way of representing causal dependencies between variables. The absence of directed links between nodes implies a conditional independence. Moreover there is a family of transformations performed on the graphical structure that has a direct translation in terms of mathematical operations applied to the underlying PDF. Finally they are modular, i.e. one can express the joint global PDF as the product of local conditional PDFS.

PINs present several important advantages that are relevant to our problem: they can handle incomplete data as well as uncertainty; they are trainable and easy to avoid overfitting; they encode causality in a natural way; there are algorithms for both doing prediction and probabilistic inference; they offer a framework for combining prior knowledge and data; and finally they are modular and parallelizable.

In this paper the behaviors we examine are generated by pedestrians walking in an open outdoor environment. Our goal is to develop a generic, compositional analysis of the observed behaviors in terms of states and transitions between states over time in such a manner that (1) the states correspond to our common sense notions of human behaviors, and (2) they are immediately applicable to a wide range of sites and viewing situations. Figure 3 shows a typical image for our pedestrian scenario.

Fig. 3. A typical image of a pedestrian plaza

4.1 Visual Understanding via Graphical Models: HMMs and CHMMs

Hidden Markov models (HMMs) are a popular probabilistic framework for modeling processes that have structure in time. They have a clear Bayesian semantics, efficient algorithms for state and parameter estimation, and they automatically perform dynamic time warping. An HMM is essentially a quantization of a system's configuration space into a small number of discrete states, together with probabilities for transitions between states. A single finite discrete variable indexes the current state of the system. Any information about the history of the process needed for future inferences must be reflected in the current value of this state variable. Graphically HMMs are often depicted 'rolled-out in time' as PINs, such as in figure 4.

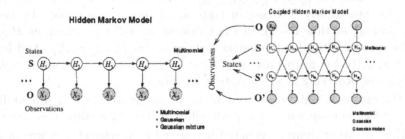

Fig. 4. Graphical representation of HMM and CHMM rolled-out in time

However, many interesting systems are composed of multiple interacting processes, and thus merit a compositional representation of two or more variables. This is typically the case for systems that have structure both in time and space. With a single state variable, Markov models are ill-suited to these problems. In order to model these interactions a more complex architecture is needed.

Extensions to the basic Markov model generally increase the memory of the system (durational modeling), providing it with compositional state in time. We are interested in systems that have compositional state in *space*, e.g., more than one simultaneous state variable. It is well known that the exact solution of extensions of the basic HMM to 3 or more chains is intractable. In those cases approximation techniques are needed ([23, 12, 24, 25]). However, it is also known that there exists an exact solution for the case of 2 interacting chains, as it is our case [23, 4].

We therefore use two Coupled Hidden Markov Models (CHMMs) for modeling two interacting processes, in our case they correspond to individual humans. In this architecture state chains are coupled via matrices of conditional probabilities modeling causal (temporal) influences between their hidden state variables. The graphical representation of CHMMs is shown in figure 4. From the graph it can be seen that for each chain, the state at time t depends on the state at time $t - 1$ in both chains. The influence of one chain on the other is through a causal link. The appendix contains a summary of the CHMM formulation.

In this paper we compare performance of HMMs and CHMMs for maximum *a posteriori* (MAP) state estimation. We compute the most likely sequence of states $\hat{S}$ within a model given the observation sequence $O = \{o_1, \ldots, o_n\}$. This most likely sequence is obtained by $\hat{S} = argmax_S P(S|O)$.

In the case of HMMs the posterior state sequence probability $P(S|O)$ is given by

$$P(S|O) = P_{s_1} p_{s_1}(o_1) \prod_{t=2}^{T} p_{s_t}(o_t) P_{s_t|s_{t-1}} \tag{1}$$

where $S = \{a_1, \ldots, a_N\}$ is the set of discrete states, $s_t \in S$ corresponds to the state at time t. $P_{i|j} \doteq P_{s_t=a_i|s_{t-1}=a_j}$ is the state-to-state transition probability (i.e. probability of being in state a_i at time t given that the system was in state a_j at time $t - 1$). In the following we will write them as $P_{s_t|s_{t-1}}$. The prior probabilities for the initial state are $P_i \doteq P_{s_1=a_i} = P_{s_1}$. And finally $p_i(o_t) \doteq p_{s_t=a_i}(o_t) = p_{s_t}(o_t)$ are the output probabilities for each state, (i.e. the probability of observing o_t given state a_i at time t).

In the case of CHMMs we need to introduce another set of probabilities, $P_{s_t|s'_{t-1}}$, which correspond to the probability of state s_t at time t in one chain given that the other chain — denoted hereafter by superscript ' — was in state s'_{t-1} at time $t-1$. These new probabilities express the causal influence (coupling) of one chain to the other. The posterior state probability for CHMMs is given by

$$P(S|O) = \frac{P_{s_1}p_{s_1}(o_1)P_{s'_1}p_{s'_1}(o'_1)}{P(O)} \times \prod_{t=2}^{T} P_{s_t|s_{t-1}}P_{s'_t|s'_{t-1}}P_{s'_t|s_{t-1}}P_{s_t|s'_{t-1}}p_{s_t}(o_t)p_{s'_t}(o'_t)$$

(2)

where $s_t, s'_t; o_t, o'_t$ denote states and observations for each of the Markov chains that compose the CHMMs. We direct the reader to [4] for a more detailed description of the MAP estimation in CHMMs.

Coming back to our problem of modeling human behaviors, two persons (each modeled as a generative process) may interact without wholly determining each others' behavior. Instead, each of them has its own internal dynamics and is influenced (either weakly or strongly) by others. The probabilities $P_{s_t|s'_{t-1}}$ and $P_{s'_t|s_{t-1}}$ describe this kind of interactions and CHMMs are intended to model them in as efficient a manner as is possible.

5 Experimental Results

Our goal is to have a system that will accurately interpret behaviors and interactions within almost any pedestrian scene with little or no training. One critical problem, therefore, is generation of models that capture our prior knowledge about human behavior. The selection of priors is one of the most controversial and open issues in Bayesian inference. To address this problem we have created a synthetic agents modeling package which allows us to build flexible prior behavior models.

5.1 Synthetic Agents Behaviors

We have developed a framework for creating synthetic agents that mimic human behavior in a virtual environment. The agents can be assigned different behaviors and they can interact with each other as well. Currently they can generate 5 different interacting behaviors and various kinds of individual behaviors (with no interaction). The parameters of this virtual environment are modeled on the basis of a real pedestrian scene from which we obtained (by hand) measurements of typical pedestrian movement.

One of the main motivations for constructing such synthetic agents is the ability to generate synthetic data which allows us to determine which Markov model architecture will be best for recognizing a new behavior (since it is difficult to collect real examples of rare behaviors). By designing the synthetic agents models such that they have the best generalization and invariance properties possible, we can obtain flexible prior models that are transferable to real human behaviors with little or no need of additional training. The use of synthetic agents to generate robust behavior models from very few real behavior examples is of special importance in a visual surveillance task, where typically the behaviors of greatest interest are also the most rare.

In the experiments reported here, we considered five different interacting behaviors: (1) Follow, reach and walk together (inter1), (2) Approach, meet and go on separately (inter2), (3) Approach, meet and go on together (inter3), (4) Change direction in order to meet, approach, meet and continue together (inter4), and (5) Change direction in order to meet, approach, meet and go on separately (inter5).

Note that we assume that these interactions can happen at any moment in time and at any location, provided only that the precondititions for the interactions are satisfied.

For each agent the position, orientation and velocity is measured, and from this data a feature vector is constructed which consists of: $\dot{d}_{12}$, the derivative of the relative distance between two agents; $\alpha_{1,2} = sign(< v_1, v_2 >)$, or degree of alignment of the agents, and $v_i = \sqrt{\dot{x}^2 + \dot{y}^2}, i = 1, 2$, the magnitude of their velocities. Note that such feature vector is invariant to the absolute position and direction of the agents and the particular environment they are in.

Figure 5 illustrates the agents trajectories and associated feature vector for an example of interaction 2, i.e. an 'approach, meet and continue separately' behavior.

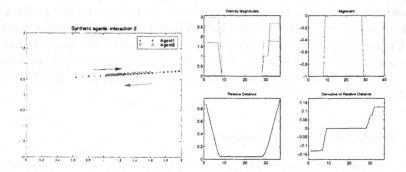

Fig. 5. Example trajectories and feature vector for interaction 2, or approach, meet and continue separately behavior.

Comparison of CHMM and HMM Architectures We built models of the previously described interactions with both CHMMs and HMMs. We used 2 or 3 states per chain in the case of CHMMs, and 3 to 5 states in the case of HMMs (accordingly to the complexity of the various interactions). Each of these architectures corresponds to a different physical hypothesis: CHMMs encode a spatial coupling in time between two agents (e.g., a non-stationary process) whereas HMMs model the data as an isolated, stationary process. We used from 11 to 75 sequences for training each of the models, depending on their complexity, such that we avoided overfitting. The optimal number of training examples, of states for each interaction as well as the optimal model parameters were obtained by a 10% cross-validation process. In all cases, the models were set up with a full state-to-state connection topology, so that the training algorithm was responsible for determining an appropriate state structure for the training data. The feature vector was 6-dimensional in the case of HMMs, whereas in the case of CHMMs each agent was modeled by a different chain, each of them with a 3-dimensional feature vector.

To compare the performance of the two previously described architectures we used the best trained models to classify 20 unseen new sequences. In order to find the most likely model, the Viterbi algorithm was used for HMMs and the N-heads dynamic programming forward-backward propagation algorithm for CHMMs.

Table 5.1 illustrates the accuracy for each of the two different architectures and interactions. Note the superiority of CHMMs versus HMMs for classifying the different interactions and, more significantly, identifying the case in which there are no interactions present in the testing data.

Table 1. Accuracy for HMMs and CHMMs on synthetic data. Accuracy at recognizing when no interaction occurs ('No inter'), and accuracy at classifying each type of interaction: 'Inter1' is follow, reach and walk together; 'Inter2' is approach, meet and go on; 'Inter3' is approach, meet and continue together; 'Inter4' is change direction to meet, approach, meet and go together and 'Inter5' is change direction to meet, approach, meet and go on separately

Accuracy on synthetic data					
	No inter	Inter1	Inter2	Inter3	Inter4	Inter5
HMMs	68.7	87.5	85.4	91.6	77	97.9
CHMMs	90.9	100	100	100	100	100

Complexity in time and space is an important issue when modeling dynamic time series. The number of degrees of freedom (state-to-state probabilities+output means+output covariances) in the largest best-scoring model was 85 for HMMs and 54 for CHMMs. We also performed an analysis of the accuracies of the models and architectures with respect to the number of sequences used for training. Figure 5.1 illustrates the accuracies in the case of interaction 4 (change direction for meeting, stop and continue together). Efficiency in terms of training data is specially important in the case of on-line real-time learning systems -such as ours would ultimately be-, specially in domains in which collecting clean labeled data is difficult.

The cross-product HMMs that result from incorporating both generative processes into the same joint-product state space usually requires many more sequences for training because of the larger number of parameters. In our case, this appears to result in a accuracy ceiling of around 80% for any amount of training

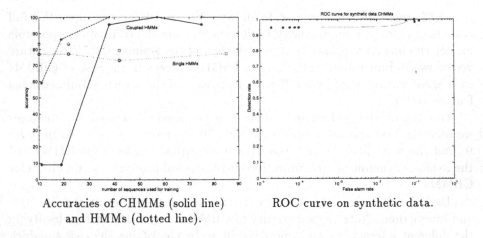

Accuracies of CHMMs (solid line)   ROC curve on synthetic data.
and HMMs (dotted line).

Fig. 6. *First figure:* Accuracies of CHMMs (solid line) and HMMs (dotted line) for one particular interaction. The dashed line is the accuracy on testing without considering the case of no interaction, while the dark line includes this case. *Second figure:* ROC curve on synthetic data.

that was evaluated, whereas for CHMMs we were able to reach approximately 100% accuracy with only a small amount of training. From this result it seems that the CHMMs architecture, with two coupled generative processes, is more suited to the problem of the behavior of interacting agents than a generative process encoded by a single HMM.

In a visual surveillance system the *false alarm* rate is often as important as the classification accuracy. In an ideal automatic surveillance system, all the targeted behaviors should be detected with a close-to-zero false alarm rate, so that we can reasonably alert a human operator to examine them further. To analyze this aspect of our system's performance, we calculated the system's ROC curve. Figure 5.1 shows that it is quite possible to achieve very low false alarm rates while still maintaining good classification accuracy.

5.2 Pedestrian Behaviors

Our goal is to develop a framework for detecting, classifying and learning generic models of behavior in a visual surveillance situation. It is important that the models be generic, applicable to many different situations, rather than being tuned to the particular viewing or site. This was one of our main motivations for developing a virtual agent environment for modeling behaviors. If the synthetic agents are 'similar' enough in their behavior to humans, then the same models that were trained with synthetic data should be directly applicable to human data. This section describes the experiments we have performed analyzing real pedestrian data using both synthetic and site-specific models (models trained on data from the site being monitored).

Data collection and preprocessing Using the person detection and tracking system described in section 3 we obtained 2D blob features for each person in several hours of video. Up to 20 examples of *following* and various types of *meeting* behaviors were detected and processed.

The feature vector $\bar{x}$ coming from the computer vision processing module consisted of the 2D (x, y) centroid (mean position) of each person's blob, the Kalman Filter state for each instant of time, consisting of $(\hat{x}, \dot{\hat{x}}, \hat{y}, \dot{\hat{y}})$, where $\hat{\cdot}$ represents the filter estimation, and the (r, g, b) components of the mean of the Gaussian fitted to each blob in color space. The frame-rate of the vision system was of about 20-30 Hz on an SGI R10000 O2 computer. We low-pass filtered the data with a 3Hz cutoff filter and computed for every pair of nearby persons a feature vector consisting of: d_{12}, derivative of the relative distance between two persons, $|v_i|, i = 1, 2$, norm of the velocity vector for each person, $\alpha = sign(< v_1, v_2 >)$, or degree of alignment of the trajectories of each person. Typical trajectories and feature vectors for an 'approach, meet and continue separately' behavior (interaction 2) are shown in figure 7. This is the same type of behavior as the one displayed in figure 5 for the synthetic agents. Note the similarity of the feature vectors in both cases.

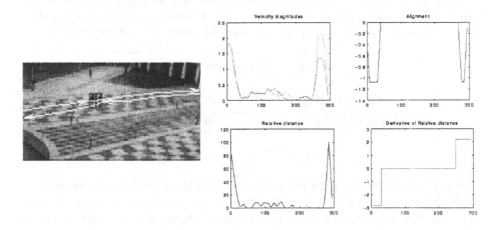

Fig. 7. Example trajectories and feature vector for interaction 2, or approach, meet and continue separately behavior.

Behavior Models and Results CHMMs were used for modeling three different behaviors: meet and continue together (interaction 3); meet and split (interaction 2) and follow (interaction 1). In addition, an *interaction* versus *no* *interaction* detection test was also performed. HMMs performed much worse than CHMMs and therefore we omit reporting their results.

We used models trained with two types of data:

1. Prior-only (synthetic data) models: that is, the behavior models learned in our synthetic agent environment and then directly applied to the real data with *no additional training or tuning of the parameters.*
2. Posterior (synthetic-plus-real data) models: new behavior models trained by using as starting points the synthetic best models. We used 8 examples of each interaction data from the specific site.

Recognition accuracies for both these 'prior' and 'posterior' CHMMs are summarized in table 5.2. It is noteworthy that with only 8 training examples, the recognition accuracy on the real data could be raised to 100%. This results demonstrates the ability to accomplish extremely rapid refinement of our behavior models from the initial prior models.

Table 2. Accuracy for both untuned, a priori models and site-specific CHMMs tested on real pedestrian data. The first entry in each row is the interaction vs no-interaction detection accuracy, the remaining entries are classification accuracies between the different interacting behaviors. Interactions are: 'Inter1' follow, reach and walk together; 'Inter2' approach, meet and go on; 'Inter3' approach, meet and continue together.

Testing on real pedestrian data				
	No-inter	Inter1	Inter2	Inter3
Prior CHMMs	90.9	93.7	100	100
Posterior CHMMs	100	100	100	100

Finally the ROC curve for the posterior CHMMs is displayed in figure 8.

One of the most interesting results from these experiments is the high accuracy obtained when testing the a priori models obtained from synthetic agent simulations. The fact that a priori models transfer so well to real data demonstrates the robustness of the approach. It shows that with our synthetic agent training system, we can develop models of many different types of behavior — avoiding thus the problem of limited amount of training data — and apply these models to real human behaviors without additional parameter tuning or training.

Parameters sensitivity In order to evaluate the sensitivity of our classification accuracy to variations in the model parameters, we trained a set of models where we changed different parameters of the agents' dynamics by factors of 2.5 and 5. The performance of these altered models turned out to be virtually the same in every case except for the 'inter1' (follow) interaction, which seems to be sensitive to people's relative rates of movement.

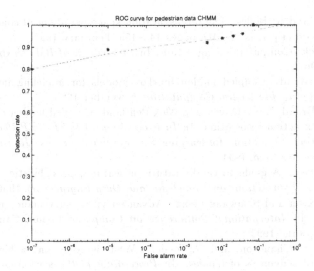

Fig. 8. ROC curve for real pedestrian data

6 Summary, Conclusions and Future Work

In this paper we have described a computer vision system and a mathematical modeling framework for recognizing different human behaviors and interactions in a visual surveillance task. Our system combines top-down with bottom-up information in a closed feedback loop, with both components employing a statistical Bayesian approach.

Two different state-based statistical learning architectures, namely HMMs and CHMMs, have been proposed and compared for modeling behaviors and interactions. The superiority of the CHMM formulation has been demonstrated in terms of both training efficiency and classification accuracy. A synthetic agent training system has been created in order to develop flexible and interpretable prior behavior models, and we have demonstrated the ability to use these a priori models to accurately classify real behaviors with no additional tuning or training. This fact is specially important, given the limited amount of training data available.

Acknowledgments

We would like to sincerely thank Michael Jordan, Tony Jebara and Matthew Brand for their inestimable help and insightful comments.

References

1. R.K. Bajcsy. Active perception vs. passive perception. In *CVWS85*, pages 55–62, 1985.

2. A. Bobick and R. Bolles. The representation space paradigm of concurrent evolving object descriptions. *PAMI*, pages 146–156, February 1992.

3. A.F. Bobick. Computers seeing action. In *Proceedings of BMVC*, volume 1, pages 13–22, 1996.

4. Matthew Brand. Coupled hidden markov models for modeling interacting processes. *Submitted to Neural Computation*, November 1996.

5. Matthew Brand, Nuria Oliver, and Alex Pentland. Coupled hidden markov models for complex action recognition. In *In Proceedings of IEEE CVPR97*, 1996.

6. W.L. Buntine. Operations for learning with graphical models. *Journal of Artificial Intelligence Research*, 1994.

7. W.L. Buntine. A guide to the literature on learning probabilistic networks from data. *IEEE Transactions on Knowledge and Data Engineering*, 1996.

8. Hilary Buxton and Shaogang Gong. Advanced visual surveillance using bayesian networks. In *International Conference on Computer Vision*, Cambridge, Massachusetts, June 1995.

9. C. Castel, L. Chaudron, and C. Tessier. What is going on? a high level interpretation of sequences of images. In *Proceedings of the workshop on conceptual descriptions from images, ECCV*, pages 13–27, 1996.

10. T. Darrell and A. Pentland. Active gesture recognition using partially observable markov decision processes. In *ICPR96*, page C9E.5, 1996.

11. J.H. Fernyhough, A.G. Cohn, and D.C. Hogg. Building qualitative event models automatically from visual input. In *ICCV98*, pages 350–355, 1998.

12. Zoubin Ghahramani and Michael I. Jordan. Factorial hidden Markov models. In David S. Touretzky, Michael C. Mozer, and M.E Hasselmo, editors, *NIPS*, volume 8, Cambridge, MA, 1996. MITP.

13. David Heckerman. A tutorial on learning with bayesian networks. Technical Report MSR-TR-95-06, Microsoft Research, Redmond, Washington, 1995. Revised June 96.

14. T. Huang, D Koller, J. Malik, G. Ogasawara, B. Rao, S. Russel, and J. Weber. Automatic symbolic traffic scene analysis using belief networks. pages 966–972. Proceedings 12th National Conference in AI, 1994.

15. R. Kauth, A. Pentland, and G. Thomas. Blob: An unsupervised clustering approach to spatial preprocessing of mss imagery. In *11th Int'l Symp. on Remote Sensing of the Environment*, Ann Harbor MI, 1977.

16. B. Moghaddam and A. Pentland. Probabilistic visual learning for object detection. In *ICCV95*, pages 786–793, 1995.

17. H.H. Nagel. From image sequences towards conceptual descriptions. *IVC*, 6(2):59–74, May 1988.

18. N. Oliver, F. Berard, and A. Pentland. Lafter: Lips and face tracking. In *IEEE International Conference on Computer Vision and Pattern Recognition (CVPR97)*, S.Juan, Puerto Rico, June 1997.

19. N. Oliver, B. Rosario, and A. Pentland. Graphical models for recognizing human interactions. In *To appear in Proceedings of NIPS98, Denver, Colorado, USA*, November 1998.

20. A. Pentland. Classification by clustering. In *IEEE Symp. on Machine Processing and Remotely Sensed Data*, Purdue, IN, 1976.

21. A. Pentland and A. Liu. Modeling and prediction of human behavior. In *DARPA97*, page 201–206, 1997.

22. Lawrence R. Rabiner. A tutorial on hidden markov models and selected applications in speech recognition. *PIEEE*, 77(2):257–285, 1989.

23. Lawrence K. Saul and Michael I. Jordan. Boltzmann chains and hidden Markov models. In Gary Tesauro, David S. Touretzky, and T.K. Leen, editors, *NIPS*, volume 7, Cambridge, MA, 1995. MITP.

24. Padhraic Smyth, David Heckerman, and Michael Jordan. Probabilistic independence networks for hidden Markov probability models. AI memo 1565, MIT, Cambridge, MA, Feb 1996.

25. C. Williams and G. E. Hinton. Mean field networks that learn to discriminate temporally distorted strings. In *Proceedings, connectionist models summer school*, pages 18–22, San Mateo, CA, 1990. Morgan Kaufmann.

26. C. Wren, A. Azarbayejani, T. Darrell, and A. Pentland. Pfinder: Real-time tracking of the human body. *In* Photonics East, SPIE, volume 2615, 1995. Bellingham, WA.

27. C.R. Wren, A. Azarbayejani, T. Darrell, and A. Pentland. Pfinder: Real-time tracking of the human body. *IEEE Transactions on Pattern Analysis and Machine Intelligence*, 19(7):780–785, July 1997.

Appendix: Forward (α) and Backward (β) Expressions for CHMMs

In [4] a deterministic approximation for maximum *a posterior* (MAP) state estimation is introduced. It enables fast classification and parameter estimation via expectation maximization, and also obtains an upper bound on the cross entropy with the full (combinatoric) posterior which can be minimized using a subspace that is linear in the number of state variables. An "N-heads" dynamic programming algorithm samples from the $O(N)$ highest probability paths through a compacted state trellis, with complexity $O(T(CN)^2)$ for C chains of N states apiece observing T data points. For interesting cases with limited couplings the complexity falls further to $O(TCN^2)$.

For HMMs the forward-backward or Baum-Welch algorithm provides expressions for the α and β variables, whose product leads to the *likelihood* of a sequence at each instant of time. In the case of CHMMs two state-paths have to be followed over time for each chain: one path corresponds to the 'head' (represented with subscript 'h') and another corresponds to the 'sidekick' (indicated with subscript 'k') of this head. Therefore, in the new forward-backward algorithm the expressions for computing the α and β variables will incorporate the probabilities of the head and sidekick for each chain (the second chain is indicated with '). As an illustration of the effect of maintaining multiple paths per chain, the traditional expression for the α variable in a single HMM·

$$\alpha_{j,t+1} = [\sum_{i=1}^{N} \alpha_{i,t} P_{i|j}] p_i(o_t) \tag{3}$$

will be transformed into a pair of equations, one for the full posterior α^* and another for the marginalized posterior α:

$$\alpha^*_{i,t} = p_i(o_t) p_{k_{i',t}}(o_t) \sum_j P_{i|h_{j,t-1}} P_{i|k_{j',t-1}} P_{k_{i',t}|h_{j,t-1}} P_{k_{i',t}|k_{j,t-1}} \alpha^*_{j,t-1} \tag{4}$$

$$\alpha_{i,t} = p_i(o_t) \sum_j P_{i|h_{j,t-1}} P_{i|k_{j',t-1}} \sum_g p_{k_{g',t}}(o_t) P_{k_{g',t}|h_{j,t-1}} P_{k_{g',t}|k_{j',t-1}} \alpha^*_{j,t-1} \quad (5)$$

The β variable can be computed in a similar way by tracing back through the paths selected by the forward analysis. After collecting statistics using N-heads dynamic programming, transition matrices within chains are re-estimated according to the conventional HMM expression. The coupling matrices are given by:

$$P_{s'_t=i,s_{t-1}=j|O} = \frac{\alpha_{j,t-1} P_{i'|j} p_{s'_t=i}(o'_t) \beta_{i',t}}{P(O)} \quad (6)$$

$$\hat{P}_{i'|j} = \frac{\sum_{t=2}^{T} P_{s'_t=i,s_{t-1}=j|O}}{\sum_{t=2}^{T} \alpha_{j,t-1} \beta_{j,t-1}} \quad (7)$$

Action Reaction Learning: Automatic Visual Analysis and Synthesis of Interactive Behaviour

Tony Jebara and Alex Pentland

Vision and Modeling
MIT Media Laboratory, Cambridge, MA 02139, USA
{jebara,sandy}@media.mit.edu
http://jebara.www.media.mit.edu/people/jebara/arl

Abstract. We propose Action-Reaction Learning as an approach for analyzing and synthesizing human behaviour. This paradigm uncovers causal mappings between past and future events or between an action and its reaction by observing time sequences. We apply this method to analyze human interaction and to subsequently synthesize human behaviour. Using a time series of perceptual measurements, a system automatically discovers correlations between past gestures from one human participant (action) and a subsequent gesture (reaction) from another participant. A probabilistic model is trained from data of the human interaction using a novel estimation technique, Conditional Expectation Maximization (CEM). The estimation uses general bounding and maximization to monotonically find the maximum conditional likelihood solution. The learning system drives a graphical interactive character which probabilistically predicts a likely response to a user's behaviour and performs it interactively. Thus, after analyzing human interaction in a pair of participants, the system is able to replace one of them and interact with a single remaining user.

1 Introduction

The Action Reaction Learning (ARL) framework is an automatic perceptual machine learning system. It autonomously studies the natural interactions of two humans to learn their behaviours and later engage a single human in a synthesized real-time interaction. The model is fundamentally empirical and is derived from what humans do externally, not from underlying behavioural architectures or hard wired cognitive knowledge and models.

Earlier models of human behaviour proposed by cognitive scientists analyzed humans as an input-output or stimulus-response system [Wat13] [Tho98]. The models were based on observation and empirical studies. These *behaviourists* came under criticism as cognitive science evolved beyond their over-simplified model and struggled with higher order issues (i.e. language, creativity, and attention) [Las51]. Nevertheless, much of the lower-order reactionary behaviour was still well modeled by the stimulus-response paradigm. To a casual observer, these simple models seem fine and it is only after closer examination that one realizes that far more complex underlying processes must be taking place.

We propose Action-Reaction Learning for the recovery of human behaviour by making an appeal to the behaviourists' stimulus response (input-output) model. By learning correlations between gestures that have been observed perceptually, it is possible to imitate simple human behaviours. This is facilitated by the evolution of computer vision beyond static measurements to temporal analysis and dynamic models. For instance, Blake and others [BY92] discuss active vision beyond static imagery via Kalman filters and dynamical systems. More recently, visual tracking of human activity and other complex actions has included some learning algorithms and behavioural machinery that describe higher order control structures. Isaard describes how multiple hypothesis dynamical models can learn complex hand dynamics and exhibit better tracking [IB98]. Bobick and Wilson use hidden Markov models in a state space [WB98] to recognize complex gestures. Models which combine dynamics with learned Markov models are discussed by Pentland [PL95], and Bregler [Bre97] for predicting and classifying human behaviour. Johnson [JGH98] utilizes learning techniques to predict and synthesize interactive behaviour. Thus, an important transition is taking place as automatic perception allows the acquisition of behavioural models from observations.

Once behavioural models are acquired, the ARL framework uses them to synthesize interactive behaviour with humans (again using real-time visual tracking). Important contributions in behaviour synthesis arise in robotics and animation. In the ALIVE system[MDBP96], body tracking allows users to interact with Silas, a graphical dog based on ethological models and competing behaviours. Terzopolous [TTR94] describes an animated environment of synthetic fish based on dynamical models. In robotics, Brooks [Bro97] points out the need for bottom-up robotics behaviour with perceptually grounded systems. Pirjanian [PC97] discusses objectives and decision making in robotic behaviour. Uchibe [UAH98] trains robots to acquire soccer playing interactions using reinforcement learning. Mataric [Mat98] presents interacting multi-agent robots inspired from biology, cognitive models and neuroscience. Large [LCB97] describes multiple competing dynamic models for synthesizing complex robotic behaviour.

We consider the *integration* of both behaviour acquisition and interactive synthesis. The Action-Reaction Learning framework is initially presented. The approach treats past activity as an input and future activity as an output and attempts to uncover a probabilistic mapping between them (a prediction). The system performs imitation learning [DH98] automatically by observing humans and does not require manual segmentation, supervised training or classification. In particular, by learning from a time series of interactions, one can treat the past interaction of two individuals as input and predict a likely output reaction of the participants. The probabilistic model is estimated using, *Conditional Expectation Maximization* which recovers a conditional density of the input-output relationship between the two participants.

We also discuss the details of some of the perceptual inputs[1] into the learning system. Subsequently, there is a description of the processing of temporal information and the use of a probabilistic model for inferring reactions to a past interaction. This drives the output of the system which is realized as a graphical character. An example application as well as some results illustrating the technique are then shown as the system learns to behave with simple gestural interactions. Effectively, the system learns to play or behave not by being explicitly programmed or supervised but simply by observing human participants.

2 System Architecture

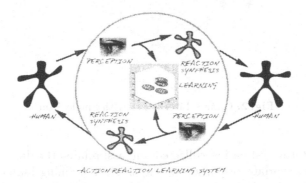

Fig. 1. Offline: Learning from Human Interaction

The system is depicted in Figure 1. Three different types of processes exist: perceptual, synthesis and learning engines interlinked in real-time with asynchronous RPC data paths. Here, the system is being presented with a series of interactions between two individuals in a constrained context (i.e. a simple children's game). The system collects live perceptual measurements using a vision subsystem for each of the humans. The temporal sequences obtained are then analyzed by a machine learning subsystem to determine predictive mappings and associations between pieces of the sequences and their consequences.

On the left of the diagram, a human user (represented as a black figure) is being monitored using a perceptual system. The perception feeds a learning system with measurements which are then stored as a time series. Simultaneously, these measurements also drive a virtual character in a one-to-one sense (gray figure) which mirrors the left human's actions as a graphical output for the human user on the right. A similar input and output is generated in parallel from

---

[1] Only constrained visual behaviours and gestures will be considered. It is not essential that the input be visual or even perceptual. However, perceptual modalities are rich, expressive, intuitive and non-obtrusive. One could take other measurements if they help infer behaviour, internal state or intentionality.

the activity of the human on the right. Thus, the users interact with each other through the vision-to-graphics interface and use this virtual channel to visualize and constrain their interaction. Meanwhile, the learning system is 'spying' on the interaction and forming a time series of the measurements. This time series is training data for the system which is attempting to learn about this ongoing interaction in hopes of modeling and synthesizing similar behaviour itself.

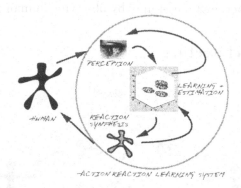

Fig. 2. Online: Interaction with Single User

In Figure 2, the system has collected and assimilated the data. At this point it can infer appropriate responses to the single remaining human user. Here, the perceptual system only needs to track the activity of the one human (black figure on the left) to stimulate the learning or estimation system for real-time interaction purposes (as opposed to learning). The learning system performs an estimation to generate a likely response to the user's behaviour. This is manifested by animating a computer graphics character (gray figure) in the synthesis subsystem. The synthesized action is fed back into the learning subsystem so that it can remember its own actions and generate self-consistent behaviour. This is indicated by the arrow depicting flow from the reaction synthesis to the learning + estimation stage. Thus, there is a continuous feedback of self-observation in the learning system which can recall its own actions. In addition, the system determines a likely action of the remaining user and transmits it as a prior to assist tracking in the vision subsystem. This flow from the learning system to the perception system (the eye) contains behavioural and dynamic predictions of the single observed user and should help improve perception.

2.1 A Typical Scenario

Action-Reaction Learning (ARL) involves temporal analysis of a (usually multi-dimensional) data stream. Figure 3 displays such a stream (or time series). Let us assume that the stream is being generated by a vision algorithm which measures the openness of the mouth [OPBC97]. Two such algorithms are being run simultaneously on two different people. One person generates the dashed line and the other generates the solid line.

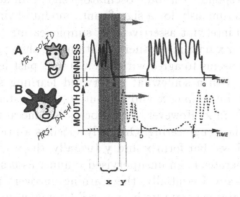

Fig. 3. Dialog Interaction and Analysis Window

Now, imagine that these two individuals are engaged in a conversation. Let us also name them Mr. Solid (the fellow generating the solid line) and Mrs. Dash (the lady generating the dashed line). Initially (A-B), Mr. Solid is talking while Mrs. Dash remains silent. He has an oscillatory mouth signal while she has a very low value on the openness of the mouth. Then, Mr. Solid says something shocking, pauses (B-C), and then Mrs. Dash responds with a discrete 'oh, I see' (C-D). She too then pauses (D-E) and waits to see if Mr. Solid has more to say. He takes the initiative and continues to speak (E). However, Mr. Solid continues talking non-stop for just too long (E-G). So, Mrs. Dash feels the need to interrupt (F) with a counter-argument and simply starts talking. Mr. Solid notes that she has taken the floor and stops to hear her out.

What Action-Reaction Learning seeks to do is discover the coupling between the past interaction and the next immediate reaction of the participants. For example, the system may learn a model of the behaviour of Mrs. Dash so that it can imitate her idiosyncrasies. The process begins by sliding a window over the temporal interaction as in Figure 3. The window looks at a small piece of the interaction. This piece is the short term or iconic memory the system will have of the interaction and it is highlighted with a dark rectangular patch. The consequent reaction of Mrs. Dash and Mr. Solid is highlighted with the lighter and smaller rectangular strip. The first strip will be treated as an input **x** and the second strip will be the desired subsequent behavioural output of both Mr. Solid and Mrs. Dash (**y**). As the windows slide across the interaction, many such (**x**, **y**) pairs are generated and presented to a machine learning system. The task of the learning algorithm is to learn from these pairs to later generate predicted **ŷ** sequences which can be used to compute and play out the future actions of one of the users (i.e. Mrs. Dash) when only the past interaction **x** of the participants is visible.

Thus, the learning algorithm should discover some mouth openness behavioural properties. For example, Mrs. Dash usually remains quiet (closed mouth) while Mr. Solid is talking. However, after Solid has talked and then stopped briefly, Mrs. Dash should respond with some oscillatory signal. In addition, if Mr. Solid has been talking continuously for a significant amount of time, it is more likely that Mrs. Dash will interrupt assertively. A simple learning algorithm could be used to detect similar **x** data in another situation and then predict the appropriate **y** response that seems to agree with the system's past learning experiences.

We are dealing with a somewhat supervised learning system because the data has been split into input **x** and output **y**. The system is given a target goal: to predict **y** from **x**. However, this process is done automatically without significant manual data engineering. One only specifies a-priori a constant width for the sliding windows that form **x** and **y** (usually, the **y** covers only 1 frame). The system then operates in an unsupervised manner as it slides these windows across the data stream. Essentially, the learning uncovers a mapping between *past and future* to later generate its best possible prediction. Interaction can be learned from a variety of approaches including reinforcement learning [UAH98]. The objective here is primarily an *imitation*-type learning of interaction.

3 Perceptual System

A key issue in the visual perceptual system is the recovery of action parameters which are particularly expressive and interactive. In addition, to maintain real-time interactiveness and fast training, the input/output parameters should be compact (low dimensional). The tracking system used is a head and hand tracking system which models the three objects (head, left and right hand) as 2D blobs with 5 parameters each. With these features alone, it is possible to engage in simple gestural games and interactions.

The vision algorithm begins by forming a probabilistic model of skin colored regions [AP96]. During an offline process, a variety of skin-colored pixels are selected manually, forming a distribution in rgb space. This distribution can be described by a probability density function (pdf) which is used to estimate the likelihood of any subsequent pixel ($\mathbf{x}_{rgb}$) being a skin colored pixel. The pdf used is a 3D Gaussian mixture model as shown in Equation 1 (with $M = 3$ individual Gaussians typically).

$$p(\mathbf{x}_{rgb}) = \sum_{i=1}^{M} \frac{p(i)}{(2\pi)^{\frac{3}{2}} \sqrt{|\Sigma_i|}} \; e^{-\frac{1}{2}(\mathbf{x}_{rgb}-\mu_i)^T \Sigma_i^{-1}(\mathbf{x}_{rgb}-\mu_i)} \qquad (1)$$

The parameters of the pdf ($p(i), \mu_i$ and Σ_i) are estimated using the Expectation Maximization [DLR77] (EM) algorithm to maximize the likelihood of the training rgb skin samples. This pdf forms a classifier and every pixel in an image is filtered through it. If the probability is above a threshold, the pixel belongs to the skin class, otherwise, it is considered non-skin (see Figures 4(a) and (d)).

To clean up some of the spurious pixels misclassified as skin, a connected components algorithm is performed on the image to find the top 4 regions in the image, see Figure 4(b). We choose to process the top 4 regions since sometimes the face is accidentally split into two regions by the connected components algorithm. Note, however, that if the head and hands are touching, there may only be one non-spurious connected region as in Figure 4(e).

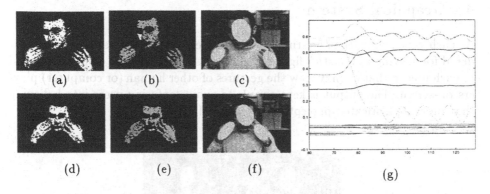

(a)   (b)   (c)

(d)   (e)   (f)

(g)

Fig. 4. Head and Hand Blob Tracking with Time Series Data

Since we are always interested in tracking three objects (head and hands) even if they form a single connected region, it is necessary to invoke a more sophisticated pixel grouping technique. Once again, we use the EM algorithm to find 3 Gaussians that this time maximize the likelihood of the *spatially* distributed (in xy) skin pixels. This Gaussian mixture model is shown in Equation 2.

$$p(\mathbf{x}_{xy}) = \sum_{j=1}^{3} \frac{p(j)}{2\pi\sqrt{|\Sigma_j|}} \; e^{-\frac{1}{2}(\mathbf{x}_{xy}-\mu_j)^T \Sigma_j^{-1}(\mathbf{x}_{xy}-\mu_j)} \tag{2}$$

The update or estimation of the parameters is done in real-time by iteratively maximizing the likelihood over each image. Our implementation of EM here has been heavily optimized to run at 50ms per iteration on images of 320x240 pixels. The resulting 3 Gaussians have 5 parameters each (from the 2D mean and the 2D symmetric covariance matrix) and are shown rendered on the image in Figures 4(c) and (f). The covariance (Σ) is actually represented in terms of its square root matrix, Γ where $\Gamma \times \Gamma = \Sigma$. Like Σ, the Γ matrix has 3 free parameters ($\Gamma_{xx}, \Gamma_{xy}, \Gamma_{yy}$) however these latter variables are closer to the dynamic range of the 2D blob means and are therefore preferred for representation. The 5 parameters describing the head and hands are based on first and second order statistics which can be reliably estimated from the data in real-time. In addition, they are well behaved and do not exhibit wild non-linearities. More complex measurements could be added if they have similar stability and smoothness. The 15 recovered parameters from a single person are shown as a well behaved continuous time series in Figure 4(g). These define the 3 Gaussian blobs (head, left hand and right hand).

The parameters of the blobs are also smoothed in real-time via a Kalman Filter with constant velocity predictions. In addition, the same system can be used to track multiple colored objects and if colored gloves are used, the system handles occlusion and tracking more robustly.

4 Graphical System

At each time frame, the 15 estimated parameters for the Gaussians can be rendered for viewing as the stick figure in Figure 5. This is also the display provided to each user so that he may view the gestures of other human (or computer) players on-screen. The output is kept simple to avoid confusing users into believing that more sophisticated perception is taking place.

Fig. 5. Graphical Rendering of Perceptual Measurements

5 Temporal Modeling in the ARL System

The Action-Reaction Learning system functions as a server which receives real-time multi-dimensional data from the vision systems and re-distributes it to the graphical systems for rendering. Typically during training, two vision systems and two graphics systems are connected to the ARL server. Thus, it is natural to consider the signals and their propagation as multiple temporal data streams. Within the ARL server, perceptual data or tracked motions from the vision systems are accumulated and stored explicitly into a finite length time series of measurements.

For head and hand tracking, two triples of Gaussian blobs are generated (one triple for each human) by the vision systems and form 30 continuous scalar parameters. Each set of scalar parameters forms a 30 dimensional vector $\mathbf{y}(t)$ at time t. The ARL system preprocesses then trains from this temporal series of vectors to later forecast the parameters of the 6 blobs in the near future.

An account of the Santa Fe competition is presented in [GW93] where issues in time series modeling and prediction are discussed. We consider the connectionist representation due to its explicit non-linear optimization of prediction accuracy and its promising performance against hidden Markov models, dynamic models, etc. in the competition. One of its proponents, Wan [Wan93], describes a nonlinear time series auto regression which computes an output vector from its T previous instances. The mapping is approximated via a neural network function $g()$ as in $\mathbf{y}(t) = g\left(\mathbf{y}(t-1), ..., \mathbf{y}(t-T)\right)$. In our case, each $\mathbf{y}$ is a 30 dimensional vector of the current perceptual parameters from two humans.

However, since T previous samples are considered, the function to be approximated has a high dimensional domain. For head and hand tracking data (15Hz tracking), values of $T \approx 120$ are required to form a meaningful short term memory of a few seconds (≈ 6 seconds). Thus, the dimensionality ($T \times 30$) is very large. A dimensionality reduction of the input space is accomplished via Principal Components Analysis (PCA) [Bis96]. Consider the input as vector $Y(t)$, the concatenation of all T vectors that were just observed $\mathbf{y}(t-1), ... \mathbf{y}(t-T)$. Each vector Y is a short term memory window over the past 6 seconds. In a few minutes of training data, many such vectors Y are observed and form a distribution. Its principal components (most energetic eigenvectors) span a compact subspace of Y. The eigenvalues of this distribution are shown in decreasing order in Figure 6(a). Over 95% of the energy of the Y vectors (short term memories) can be represented using linear combinations of the first 40 eigenvectors. Thus the distribution of Y occupies only a small sub manifold of the original 3600 dimensional embedding space and 40 dimensions span it sufficiently. We call the low-dimensional subspace representation of $Y(t)$ the immediate past short term memory of interactions and denote it with $\mathbf{x}(t)$. In Figure 6(b) the first mode (the most dominant eigenvector) of the short term memory is rendered as a 6 second evolution of the 30 head and hand parameters of two interacting humans. Interestingly, the shape of the eigenvector is not exactly sinusoidal nor is it a wavelet or other typical basis function since it is specialized to the training data.

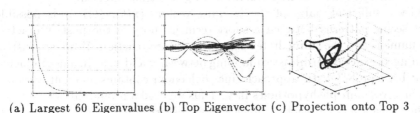

(a) Largest 60 Eigenvalues (b) Top Eigenvector (c) Projection onto Top 3

Fig. 6. Top Eigenvectors and Eigenvalues and 3D Projection onto Eigenspace

It should be noted that the above analysis actually used weighted versions of the Y vectors to include a soft memory decay process. Thus, an exponential decay ramp function is multiplied with each Y window. This reflects our intuition that more temporally distant elements in the time series are less relevant for prediction. This decay agrees with some aspects of cognitive models obtained from psychological studies [EA95]. Once the past T vectors ($y(t)$) have been attenuated, they form a new 'exponentially decayed' short term memory window $\hat{Y}(t)$. The process is shown in Figure 7. The eigenspace previously discussed is really formed over the $\hat{Y}$ distribution. $\hat{Y}$ is represented in a subspace with a compact $\mathbf{x}(t)$. This is the final, low dimensional representation of the gestural interaction between the two humans over the past few seconds.

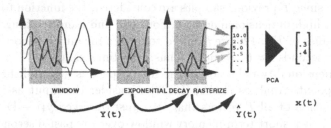

Fig. 7. Exponential Decay and Pre-Processing

5.1 Probabilistic Time Series Modeling

Of course, immediately after the time window over the past, another observation $\mathbf{y}(t)$ (of the near future) is also obtained from the training data. The $\mathbf{x}(t)$ vector represents the past action and the $\mathbf{y}(t)$ represents the consequent reaction exactly at time t. For a few minutes of data, we obtain thousands of pairs of $\mathbf{x}$ and $\mathbf{y}$ vectors (i.e. action-reaction pairs) by sliding the attentional window over the training time series. Figure 6(c) shows the evolution of the dominant 3 dimensions of the $\mathbf{x}(t)$ vectors as we consider an interaction between two participants over time t of roughly half a minute. This represents the evolution of the short term memory of the learning system during this time interval.

Given sufficient pairs of the training vectors $(\mathbf{x}(t),\mathbf{y}(t))$, it is possible to start seeing patterns between a short term memory of the past interaction of two humans and the immediate subsequent future reaction. However, instead of learning an exact deterministic mapping between $\mathbf{x}$ and $\mathbf{y}$, as in a neural network, we utilize a probabilistic approach since behaviour contains inherent randomness and involves multiple hypotheses in $\mathbf{y}$. Thus we need a probability density $p(\mathbf{y}|\mathbf{x})$ or the probability of a reaction *given* a short history of past action. We are not, for instance, interested in the conditional pdf $p(\mathbf{x}|\mathbf{y})$, which computes the probability of the past ($\mathbf{x}$) given the future. Mostly, we will query the system about what future result should follow the actions it just saw. Probabilistic techniques are also interesting since they can generate behaviour that is correlated with the user's past actions but is *also* not entirely predictable and contains some pseudo random choices in its space of valid responses.

6 Conditional Expectation Maximization

To model the action-reaction space or the mapping between $\mathbf{x}$ and $\mathbf{y}$ we estimate a conditional probability density. The conditioned mixture of Gaussians is selected since it is tractable and can approximate arbitrary non-linear conditional densities given enough components. The model can be interpreted as a mixture of experts with multiple linear regressors and ellipsoidal basis gating functions [JJ94]. Equation 3 depicts the model where $\mathcal{N}$ represents a normal distribution.

$$p(\mathbf{y}|\mathbf{x}) = \frac{p(\mathbf{x},\mathbf{y})}{p(\mathbf{x})} = \frac{\sum_m^M p(\mathbf{x},\mathbf{y},m)}{\sum_m p(\mathbf{x},m)} = \frac{\sum_m^M p(m)\mathcal{N}(\mathbf{x},\mathbf{y}|\mu_m^x,\mu_m^y,\Sigma_m^{xx},\Sigma_m^{yy},\Sigma_m^{xy})}{\sum_m^M p(m)\mathcal{N}(\mathbf{x}|\mu_m^x,\Sigma_m^{xx})} \quad (3)$$

Traditionally, estimating probabilistic models is done by maximizing the likelihood (L) of a model (Θ) given the data as in $L = \prod_{i=1}^N p(\mathbf{x}_i,\mathbf{y}_i|\Theta)$. Techniques like EM [DLR77] can be used to optimize the parameters of a pdf such that its joint density is a good model of the data. In clustering, for instance, data is treated homogeneously without special considerations for the distinction between input $\mathbf{x}$ and output $\mathbf{y}$. If the data is split as aforementioned into response ($\mathbf{y}$) and covariate ($\mathbf{x}$) components, this indicates that the covariate components will always be available to the system. Thus, when fitting a probabilistic model to the data, we should optimize it only to predict $\mathbf{y}$ using $\mathbf{x}$ ($\mathbf{x}$ is always measured). This forms a more discriminative model that concentrates modeling resources for the task at hand.

We recently developed a variant of the EM algorithm called Conditional Expectation Maximization (CEM) for specifically optimizing conditional likelihood [JP98]. It essentially fits a pdf that maximizes the conditional likelihood of the response given the covariates. CEM is an iterative technique which uses fixed point solutions (as opposed to gradient descent) to converge the parameters of a conditional density to a local maximum of conditional likelihood, $L_c = \prod_{i=1}^N p(\mathbf{y}_i|\mathbf{x}_i,\Theta)$.

Applying CEM to the pdf optimizes its $p(\mathbf{y}|\mathbf{x})$ over the data. EM, on the other hand, typically optimizes $p(\mathbf{x},\mathbf{y})$, the ability to model the data as a whole. Since resources (memory, complexity) are sparse and training examples are finite, it is preferable here to directly optimize the model's conditional likelihood [Pop97] using CEM. In other words, we want the learning system to be good at figuring out what Mrs. Dash will do next (i.e. use $\mathbf{x}$ to predict $\mathbf{y}$). We are not as interested in asking the system what past event would have provoked Mrs. Dash to do what she just did (i.e. use $\mathbf{y}$ to get $\mathbf{x}$).

Consider the 4-cluster (x,y) data in Figure 8(a). The data is modeled with a conditional density $p(y|x)$ using only 2 Gaussian models. Estimating the density with CEM yields $p(y|x)$ as in Figure 8(b) with monotonic conditional likelihood growth (Figure 8(c)) and generates a more conditionally likely model. In the EM case, a joint $p(x,y)$ clusters the data as in Figure 8(d). Conditioning it yields the $p(y|x)$ in Figure 8(e). Figure 8(f) depicts EM's non-monotonic evolution of conditional log-likelihood. EM produces a good joint likelihood (L) but an inferior conditional likelihood (L_c). Note how the CEM algorithm utilized limited resources to capture the multimodal nature of the distribution in y and ignored spurious bimodal clustering in the x feature space. These properties are critical for a good conditional density $p(y|x)$. In regression experiments on standardized databases, mixture models trained with CEM outperformed those trained with EM as well as conventional neural network architectures [JP98].

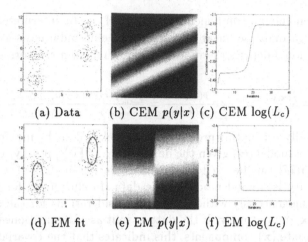

(a) Data　　(b) CEM $p(y|x)$　(c) CEM $\log(L_c)$

(d) EM fit　　(e) EM $p(y|x)$　(f) EM $\log(L_c)$

Fig. 8. Conditional Density Estimation for CEM and EM

Thus, CEM is used to estimate the conditional probability density (cpdf) relating past time series sequences ($\mathbf{x}$) to their immediate future values ($\mathbf{y}$) from training data (thousands of $\mathbf{x}, \mathbf{y}$ pairs). A total of M Gaussians are fit to the data as a conditioned mixture model. This is ultimately used to regress (predict) the future values of a time series for a single forward step in time. Once the probabilistic behavioural model is formed from training data, it is possible to estimate an unknown $\hat{\mathbf{y}}$ from observed $\mathbf{x}$. When $\hat{\mathbf{x}}$ is measured from the past time series activity and inserted into the conditional probability density, it yields a marginal density exclusively over the variable $\mathbf{y}$ (the prediction or reaction to the past stimulus sequence). This density becomes a 30 dimensional, M-component Gaussian mixture model.

However, we need to select a single reaction, $\hat{\mathbf{y}}$ from the space of possible reactions over $\mathbf{y}$. It is customary in Bayesian inference to use the expectation of a distribution as its representative. Using the pdf over $\mathbf{y}$, we integrate as in Equation 4 to obtain the predicted $\hat{\mathbf{y}}$, a likely reaction according to the model (we have also considered arg max and sampling methods for choosing $\hat{\mathbf{y}}$).

$$\hat{\mathbf{y}} = \int \mathbf{y} p(\mathbf{y}|\hat{\mathbf{x}}) d\mathbf{y} = \frac{\sum_m^M \hat{\mathbf{y}}_m p(\hat{\mathbf{y}}_m|\hat{\mathbf{x}})}{\sum_m^M p(\hat{\mathbf{y}}_m|\hat{\mathbf{x}})} \quad \& \quad \hat{\mathbf{y}}_m = \mu_m^y + \Sigma_m^{yx} \Sigma_m^{xx-1} (\hat{\mathbf{x}} - \mu_m^x) \quad (4)$$

7　Integration

At this point, we discuss the integrated system. The flow between perceptual input, graphical output, time series processing and the learning system are presented as well as some of the different modes of operation they can encompass.

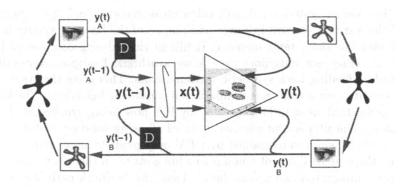

Fig. 9. Training Mode

7.1 Training Mode

For training, two humans interact while the system accumulates information about the actions and reactions (see Figure 9). The learning system is being fed $\mathbf{x}(t)$ on one end and $\mathbf{y}(t)$ on the other. Once many pairs of data are accumulated, the system uses CEM to optimize a conditioned Gaussian mixture model which represents $p(\mathbf{y}|\mathbf{x})$. We note the role of the integration symbol which indicates the pre-processing of the past time-series via an attentional window over the past T samples of measurements. This window is represented compactly in an eigenspace as $\mathbf{x}(t)$. Note, that the $\mathbf{y}$ vector can be split into $\mathbf{y}_A(t)$ and $\mathbf{y}_B(t)$, where each half the vector corresponds to a user.

7.2 Interaction Mode

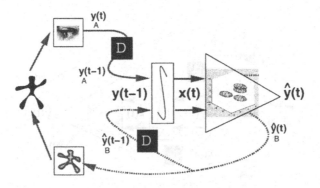

Fig. 10. Interaction Mode

In Figure 10, the system is synthesizing interactive behaviour with a single user. User A is given the illusion of interacting with user B through the ARL system. The vision system on A still takes measurements and these integrate and feed the learning system. However, the output of the learning system is *also* fed back into the short term memory. It fills in the missing component (user B) inside **x**. Thus, not only does user A see synthesized output, continuity is maintained by feeding back synthetic measurements. This gives the system the ability to see its own actions and maintain self-consistent behaviour. The half of the time series that used to be generated by B is now being synthesized by the ARL system. The $\mathbf{x}(t)$ is continuously updated allowing good estimates of $\hat{\mathbf{y}}$. In fact, the probabilistic model trained by CEM only predicts small steps into the future and these 'deltas' do not amount to a full gesture on their own unless they are fed back, integrated and accumulated. Thus, the feedback path is necessary for the system to make continuous predictions. Since the attentional window which integrates the **y** measurements is longer than a few seconds, this gives the system enough short term memory to maintain consistency over a wide range of gestures and avoids instability [2]. Simultaneously, the real-time graphical blob representation is used to un-map the predicted perceptual (the $\hat{\mathbf{y}}_B(t)$ action) for the visual display. It is through this display that the human user receives feedback in real-time from the system's reactions.

7.3 Perceptual Feedback Mode

Of course, the CEM learning system generates *both* a $\hat{\mathbf{y}}_B(t)$ and a $\hat{\mathbf{y}}_A(t)$. Therefore, it would be of no extra cost to utilize the information in $\hat{\mathbf{y}}_A(t)$ in some way while the system is interacting with the user. Instead of explicitly using Kalman filters in the vision systems (as described earlier), we also consider using the predicted $\hat{\mathbf{y}}_A(t)$ as an alternative to filtering and smoothing. The ARL system then emulates a non-linear dynamical filter and helps resolve some vision tracking errors.

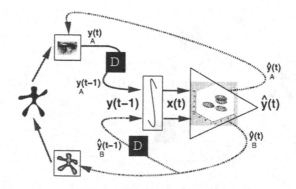

Fig. 11. Perceptual Mode

---

[2] For the initial seconds of interaction, the system has not synthesized actions and user A has yet to gesture but the feedback loop automatically bootstraps and stabilizes.

Typically, tracking algorithms use a variety of temporal dynamic models to assist the frame by frame vision computations. The most trivial of these is to use the last estimate in a nearest neighbor approach to initialize the next vision iteration. Kalman filtering and other dynamic models [BY92] involve more sophistication ranging from constant velocity models to very complex control systems. Here, the the feedback being used to constrain the vision system results from dynamics *and* behaviour modeling. This is similar in spirit to the mixed dynamic and behaviour models in [PL95]. In the head and hand tracking case, the system continuously feeds back behavioural prediction estimates of the 15 tracked parameters (3 Gaussians) in the vision system for improved tracking.

More significant vision errors can also be handled. Consider the specific case of head and hand tracking with skin blobs. For initial training, colored gloves were used to overcome some correspondence problems when heads and hands touched and moved by each other. However, the probabilistic behavioural model can also accomplish this task. It recognizes a blob as a head or hand from its role in a gesture and maintains proper tracking. In the model, a coarse estimate of $p(\mathbf{x})$ is evaluated to determine the likelihood of any past interaction (short term memory). Different permutations of the tracked blobs are tested with $p(\mathbf{x})$, and any mislabeling of the blob features is detected and corrected. The system merely tests each of the 6 permutations of 3 blobs to find the one that maximizes $p(\mathbf{x})$ (the most likely past gesture). This permutation is then fed back in $\hat{\mathbf{y}}$ to resolve the correspondence problem in the vision module. Instead of using complex static computations or heuristics to resolve these ambiguities, a reliable correspondence between the blobs is computed from temporal information and a top-down strategy.

8 Interaction Results

It is prudent to train the ARL system in a constrained context to achieve learning convergence from limited data and modeling resources. Thus, users involved in training are given loose instructions on the nature of the interactions they will be performing (as in Figure 12(a)). The humans (A and B) randomly play out these multiple interactions. The learning algorithm is given measurements of the head and hand positions of both users over several minutes of interaction. Once the training is complete, the B gesturer leaves and the single user remaining is A. The screen display for A still shows the same graphical character but now user B is impersonated by synthetic reactions in the ARL system (or, by symmetry, the system can instead impersonate user A).

More specifically, the training contained 5 to 10 examples of each of the above interactions and lasted 5 minutes. This accounts for ≈ 5000 observations of the 30 dimensional $\mathbf{y}(t)$ vectors. These were then processed into $(\mathbf{x}, \mathbf{y})$ pairs. The dimensionality of $\mathbf{x}$ was reduced to only 22 eigenvectors and the system used $M = 25$ Gaussians for the pdf (complexity was limited to keep real-time operation). The learning took ≈ 2 hours on an SGI OCTANE for a 5 minute training sequence (see Figure 13(a)).

Inter-action	User	Corresponding Action
1	A	Scare B by raising arms
	B	Fearfully crouch down
2	A	Wave hello
	B	Wave back accordingly
3	A	Circle stomach & tap head
	B	Clap enthusiastically
4	A	Idle or Small Gestures
	B	Idle or Small Gestures

(a) Instructions

(b) Perceptual Training

Fig. 12. Instructions and Perceptual Training

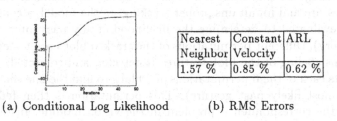

Nearest Neighbor	Constant Velocity	ARL
1.57 %	0.85 %	0.62 %

(a) Conditional Log Likelihood

(b) RMS Errors

Fig. 13. Conditional Log Likelihood on Training and RMS Errors on Test Data

8.1 Quantitative Prediction

For a quantitative measure, the system was trained and learned a predictive mapping $p(\mathbf{y}|\mathbf{x})$. Since real-time is not an issue for this kind of test, the system was permitted to use more Gaussian models and more dimensions to learn $p(\mathbf{y}|\mathbf{x})$. Once trained on a portion of the data, the system's ability to perform prediction was tested on the remainder of the sequence. Once again, the pdf allows us to compute an estimated $\hat{\mathbf{y}}$ for any given $\mathbf{x}$ short term memory. The expectation was used to predict $\hat{\mathbf{y}}$ and was compared to the true $\mathbf{y}$ result in the future of the time series. For comparison, RMS errors are shown against the nearest neighbor and constant velocity estimates. The nearest neighbor estimate merely assumes that $\mathbf{y}(t) = \mathbf{y}(t-1)$ and the constant velocity assumes that $\mathbf{y}(t) = \mathbf{y}(t-1) + \Delta_t \dot{\mathbf{y}}(t-1)$. Figure 13(b) depicts the RMS errors on the test interaction and these suggest that the system is a better instantaneous predictor than the above two methods and could be useful in Kalman filter-type prediction applications.

8.2 Qualitative Interaction

In addition, real-time online testing of the system's interaction abilities was performed. A human player performed the gestures of user A and checked for the system's response. Whenever the user performed one of the gestures in Table 12, the system responded with a (qualitatively) appropriate animation of the synthetic character (the gesture of the missing user B). By symmetry, the roles could be reversed such that the system impersonates user A and a human acts as user B.

Fig. 14. Scare Interaction

In Figure 14, a sample interaction where the user 'scares' the system is depicted. Approximately 750ms elapse between each frame and the frames are arranged lexicographically in temporal order. The user begins in a relaxed rest state and the synthetic character as well. Then, the user begins performing a menacing gesture, raising both arms in the air and then lowering them. The synthetic character responds by first being taken aback and then crouching down in momentary fear. This is the behaviour that was indicated by examples from the human-to-human training. Moreover, the responses from the system contain some pseudo random variations giving them a more compelling nature.

A more involved form of interaction is depicted in Figure 15. Here, the user stimulates the character by circling his stomach while patting his head. The system's reaction is to clap enthusiastically for this slightly tricky and playful gesture. Once again, the system stops gesturing when the user is still (as is the case at the beginning and at the end of the sequence). The oscillatory gesture the user is performing is rather different from the system's response. Thus, there is a higher-level mapping: oscillatory gesture to different oscillatory gesture[3].

The user produces complex actions and the system responds with complex reactions in a non 1-to-1 mapping. The response depends on user input as well as on the system's previous internal state. The mapping associates measurements over time to measurements over time which is a high dimensional learning problem.

9 Online Learning and Face Modeling

It is also feasible to continue an online training of the CEM algorithm while the system is performing synthesis with a single user. The system merely looks at the

---

[3] Please consult the web page for video animation and interaction examples.

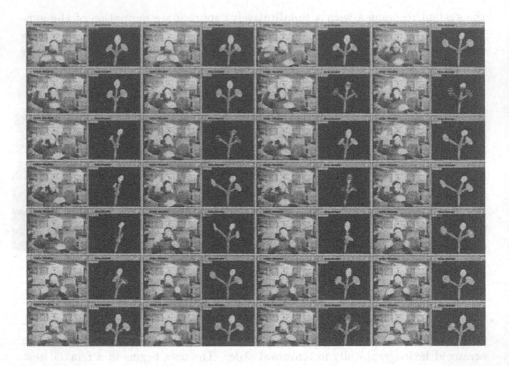

Fig. 15. Clapping Interaction

reactions produced by the user from the past interaction sequence between user and synthetic character. The window of mutual interaction and its immediate consequence form the same input-output data pair $(\mathbf{x}, \mathbf{y})$ as was initially processed offline. The system could thus dynamically learn new responses to stimuli and include these in its dictionary of things to do. This makes it adaptive and its behaviour will be further tuned by the engagement with the single remaining user. This process is currently under investigation.

Face modeling is also being considered as an alternate perceptual modality. A system which automatically detects the face and tracks it has been implemented [JRP98]. It tracks 3D rotations and motions using normalized correlation coupled with structure from motion. In addition, it continuously computes an eigenspace model of the face's texture which is used to infer 3D deformations. Thus, the system generates a real-time temporal sequence including XYZ translations, 3D rotations and texture/deformation coefficients (see Figure 16). To synthesize an output, a 3D renderer reconstructs a facial model in real-time using the recovered deformation, texture and pose (see Figure 16(d)). The data representing each static frame is a 50 dimensional time series which is suitable for ARL analysis.

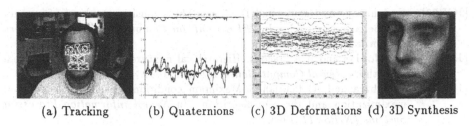

(a) Tracking (b) Quaternions (c) 3D Deformations (d) 3D Synthesis

Fig. 16. 3D Face Modeling and Tracking

10 Conclusions

We have demonstrated a perceptual real-time system which learns two-person interactive behaviour automatically by modeling the probabilistic relationship between a past action and its consequent reaction. The system is then able to engage in real-time interaction with a single user, impersonating the missing person by estimating and synthesizing likely reactions. The ARL system is data driven, autonomous, and perceptually grounded and it learns its behaviour by looking at humans.

11 Acknowledgments

The authors thank Nuria Oliver for help with RPC data communications.

References

[AP96]   A. Azarbayejani and A. Pentland. Real-time self-calibrating stereo person tracking using 3-d shape estimation from blob features. In *International Conference on Pattern Recognition (ICPR)*, 1996.

[Bis96]   C. Bishop. *Neural Networks for Pattern Recognition*. Oxford Press, 1996.

[Bre97]   C. Bregler. Learning and recognizing human dynamics in video sequences. In *IEEE Conf. on Computer Vision and Pattern Recognition*, 1997.

[Bro97]   R.A. Brooks. From earwigs to humans. *Robotics and Autonomous Systems*, 20(2-4), 1997.

[BY92]   A. Blake and A. Yuille. *Active vision*. MIT Press, 1992.

[DH98]   K. Dautenhahn and G. Hayes, editors. *Agents in Interaction - Acquiring Competence through Imitation*. Inter. Conf. on Autonomous Agents, 1998.

[DLR77]   A.P. Dempster, N.M. Laird, and D.B. Rubin. Maximum likelihood from incomplete data via the em algorithm. *Journal of the Royal Statistical Society*, B39, 1977.

[EA95]   S. Elliott and J. R. Anderson. The effect of memory decay on predictions from changing categories. *Journal of Experimental Psychology: Learning, Memory and Cognition*, 1995.

[GW93]   N. Gershenfeld and A. Weigend. *Time Series Prediction: Forecasting the Future and Understanding the Past*. Addison-Wesley, 1993.

[IB98]   M. Isaard and A. Blake. A mixed-state condensation tracker with automatic model-switching. In *International Conference on Computer Vision 6*, 1998.

[JGH98]   N. Johnson, A. Galata, and D. Hogg. The acquisition and use of interaction behaviour models. In *IEEE Conf. on Computer Vision and Pattern Recognition*, 1998.

[JJ94]   M.I. Jordan and R.A. Jacobs. Hierarchical mixtures of experts and the em algorithm. *Neural Computation*, 6:181–214, 1994.

[JP98]   T. Jebara and A. Pentland. Maximum conditional likelihood via bound maximization and the cem algorithm. In *Neural Information Processing Systems (NIPS) 11*, 1998.

[JRP98]   T. Jebara, K. Russel, and A. Pentland. Mixtures of eigenfeatures for real-time structure from texture. In *Proceedings of the International Conference on Computer Vision*, 1998.

[Las51]   K.S. Lashley. The problem of serial order in behavior. In L.A. Jefress, editor, *Cerebral Mechanisms in Behavior*, pages 112–136, New York, 1951. The Hixon Symposium, John Wiley.

[LCB97]   E. W. Large, H. I. Christensen, and R. Bajcsy. Scaling dynamic planning and control: Cooperation through competition. In *IEEE International Conference on Robotics and Automation*, 1997.

[Mat98]   M.J. Mataric. Behavior-based robotics as a tool for synthesis of artificial behavior and analysis of natural behavior. *Trends in Cognitive Science*, 2(3), 1998.

[MDBP96] P. Maes, T. Darrel, B. Blumberg, and A. Pentland. The alive system: Wireless, full-body interaction with autonomous agents. *Multimedia and Multisensory Virtual Worlds, ACM Multimedia Systems*, 1996.

[OPBC97] N. Oliver, A. Pentland, F. Berard, and J. Coutaz. Lafter: Lips and face tracker. In *Computer Vision and Pattern Recognition Conference '97*, 1997.

[PC97]   P. Pirjanian and H.I. Christensen. Behavior coordination using multiple-objective decision making. In *SPIE Conf. on Intelligent Systems and Advanced Manufacturing*, 1997.

[PL95]   A. Pentland and A. Liu. Modeling and prediction of human behavior. In *IEEE Intelligent Vehicles 95*, 1995.

[Pop97]   A.C. Popat. Conjoint probabilistic subband modeling (phd. thesis). Technical Report 461, M.I.T. Media Laboratory, 1997.

[Tho98]   E.L. Thorndike. Animal intelligence. an experimental study of the associative process in animals. *Psychological Review, Monograph Supplements*, 2(4):109, 1898.

[TTR94]   D. Terzopoulos, X. Tu, and Grzeszczukm R. Artificial fishes: Autonomous locomotion, perception, behavior, and learning in a simulated physical world. *Artificial Life*, 1(4):327–351, 1994.

[UAH98]   E. Uchibe, M. Asada, and K. Hosoda. State space construction for behaviour acquisition in multi agent environments with vision and action. In *Proceedings of the International Conference on Computer Vision*, 1998.

[Wan93]   E.A. Wan. Time series prediction by using a connectionist network with internal delay lines. In A.S. Weigend and N.A. Gershenfeld, editors, *Time Series Prediction*, 1993.

[Wat13]   J.B. Watson. Psychology as the behaviorist views it. *Psychological Review*, 20:158–17, 1913.

[WB98]   A. Wilson and A. Bobick. Recognition and interpretation of parametric gesture. In *International Conference on Computer Vision*, 1998.

A Generic Model for Perception-Action Systems. Analysis of a Knowledge-Based Prototype

D.Hernández-Sosa, J.Lorenzo-Navarro, M.Hernández-Tejera, J.Cabrera-Gámez, A.Falcón-Martel, J.Méndez-Rodríguez *

Grupo de Inteligencia Artificial y Sistemas
Dpto. Informática y Sistemas, Campus de Tafira
Universidad de Las Palmas de Gran Canaria
35017 Las Palmas de Gran Canaria, Spain
dhernandez@dis.ulpgc.es

Abstract. In this paper we propose a general layered model for the design of perception-action system. We discuss some desirable properties such a system must support to meet the severe constrains imposed by the expected behaviour of reactive systems. SVEX, a knowledge-based multilevel system, is used as a test prototype to implement and evaluate those considerations.
Additionally two aspects of the system are analyzed in detail in order to prove the benefits of the design criteria used in SVEX. These aspects refer to learning and distribution of computations. Finally, the results of some SVEX applications are shown.

1 Introduction

A layered approach is a resource commonly used in the analysis and synthesis of complex systems. We consider this alternative to be also valid in the design of an active Computer Vision system, that is, a system conceived as an element that is tightly coupled with its environment in a closed loop control cycle of perception and action [1] [2]. In order to preserve system reactivity, however, several aspects must be taken into account. Since system processes may run at very different frequencies we must enable asynchronous communication mechanisms and flow control policies that can cope with the unbalances generated during system operation. System reactivity can also be conditioned by slow perception-action loops involving all system levels. We need then to permit the co-existence of control loops at different levels. The same question leads to the convenience that symbolization mechanisms should be present at each system level to allow multilevel decision making.

The ideas of parallelization and distribution of computations appear as intuitive solutions when we face the severe time limitation problems these systems suffer. The architecture of the system should then be flexible enough to meet this posibility.

---

* This research is sponsored in part by Spanish CICYT under project TAP95-0288. The authors would also like to thank reviewers for their comments.

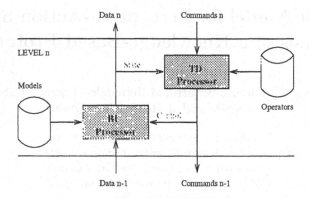

Fig. 1. BUTD Module

A modular architecture is also highly desirable. In this way, a structure derived from a basic building block includes several advantages such as simplification of design and clear identification of data and control paths. Additionally, this conception will permit the construction of different architectures and their performance evaluation in a common frame. From the system interface point of view, a multilevel system can take advantage of the generalized sensors and generalized effectors concept to promote the use of homogeneous level design guidelines.

Another fundamental aspect of the system must be the facilities it offers for the development of different applications in terms of modularity, legibility or software reusability. System programming should provide encapsulation of low level implementation and easy manipulation of high level problem solution knowledge. Here, automatic tuning capabilities and learning methods will need to be considered to improve system robustness and autonomy.

System should combine several data sources in order to enable multiple interpretation reinforcement mechanisms. This characteristic would allow a certain level of independence between system design and the available physical sensors, favouring thus system portability.

Along this paper, we will describe SVEX, a knowledge-based vision system prototype showing many of the ideas stated above. SVEX constitutes a multilevel perception-action system conceived around the information grain each level processes. To illustrate the system we will relay on a current two-level implementation based on images, thus the information units considered are pixels and segments. The system includes perception or data processing paths fed by generalized sensors, and action or command generation paths directed to generalized effectors. Each system level share a common internal organization based on a generic BU-TD module. An object-oriented language has been developed for programming the system using a reduced set of objects. The declarative nature of the language makes explicit all the knowledge involved in the solution of a given vision problem.

First we will describe in detail SVEX's levels and its internal structure. For each level, the programming language and its data and operator types are presented. Then we will focus in two important aspects of the system: a learning scheme for induction of classifiers, and a distribution of computation mechanism. Finally, a set of image processing applications will illustrate SVEX's perception capabilities.

2 Levels of Organization and System Architecture

SVEX is a multilevel knowledge-based system for perception-action operation. Both numerical and symbolic computations take place at each level, and the transition between these two domains is clearly and consistently defined by the computational structure. SVEX is made up of two levels, characterized by the nature of the "information grain" that is numerically and symbolically described within each of them. These units are the pixels at the lower level named Pixel Processor, and the segments or aggregations of pixels at the upper level named Segment Processor. We consider this data-based problem partition a simple opportunistic approach that contributes to maintain and homogeneous level structure design and eases knowledge acquisition.

The primary control of both levels is goal oriented, so that computational processes are started by the reception of a computation request from an upper level. Accordingly, data flows in two directions across each level. In a first top-down processing, upper level requests are received and transformed into the corresponding commands for satisfying them. This commands can be directed to the physical world, through physical effectors, or to a virtual lower level world by means of virtual effectors. In the opposite bottom-up direction, each level processes data coming from a lower level, transforms them and sends results to the upper level. Data can be sensed from the physical world through physical sensors or from a lower level virtual world using virtual sensors. For the processing of both data flows, each level has a TD unit (for control, planning and decoding) and a BU unit (for diagnosis, codification or abstraction). On a second internal control the system can generate control actions directed to the same level the stimulus come from.

Each level can be seen as a machine or "virtual processor" that interacts with a certain "virtual world" [5] from which it receives data. This element is called the BU-TD module (Figure 1), the basic structural unit of the system. Such an organization permits, on one hand, to provide a clearly defined and scalable computational structure (in terms of the complexity of the problem to be solved) and, on the other, to keep the same organization inside each level.

Conceived also as a tool for the construction of computer vision applications, SVEX is programmed by means of a special purpose object-oriented language developed on the basis of a reduced set of level objects described below. The declarative nature of this language makes explicit all the knowledge involved in the solution of a given computer vision problem. This property speeds up application design and implementation times, making easier maintenance tasks.

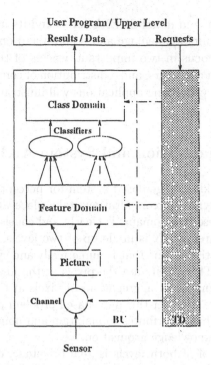

Fig. 2. Architecture of the Pixel Processor

2.1 The Pixel Processor

Starting from the source image, the first level of SVEX, the Pixel Processor [21], produces diagnostic maps in terms of membership degrees of each pixel to certain symbolic classes [23]. The BU unit receives images as input data from camera sensors and produces symbolic diagnostic images as output data. The TD unit receives requests for computing pixel diagnoses and transforms these requests into execution orders addressed to the BU unit. Figure 2 shows the internal organization of the Pixel Processor.

At the pixel level, the numerical representation consists of feature maps (gradient, color, ...) obtained using image processing algorithms, and the symbolic representation handles symbolic images or maps ('HighGradientPixel', ' Green-Pixel', ...) [32] generated from features using fuzzy symbolization processes for evidence combination and uncertainty control.

At this level, we consider the following elements as necessary to define a symbolic processing methodology:

a) **Numerical Features.** A feature is a numeric property of a pixel, obtained by means of Procedures (see below) applied to raw source data or to other features. A set of features defines a numerical domain where each pixel can be described numerically using measures related to its properties and those of its neigbours.

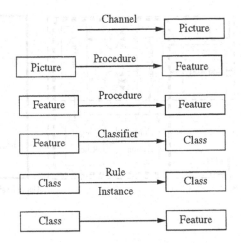

Fig. 3. Objects of the Pixel Processor

b) **Transformation Operators**. There are three types of operators: Procedures, Classifiers and Rules. Procedures and Classifiers operate in the numeric domain defined by the features with different objectives. As stated above, Procedures are used to compute pixel features, trying to avoid complex computations that we consider not very useful at this level. The Classifiers allow to define symbolic classes from features, projecting the numeric domain of features into a symbolic domain where the classes of pixels are defined. The Rules constitute the third type of operator and permit the definition of new classes imposing logical conditions in terms of other defined classes.

c) **Classes of pixels**. They represent a visual category in a symbolic domain. The degree of membership of each pixel to a certain class as being 'green' or 'low-variance' is expressed by a value in the interval [0-100].

The relationships between these elements are shown in Figure 3 in a datatypes (inside boxes) vs. transformation-operators (over arrows) organization. The object Picture identifies the input image. The Classifiers, as stated, carry out the transformation of a numerical description into another of symbolic nature. This transformation comprises two consecutive processes. The first process defines the features that are used and how they are combined (lineally, quadratically) to generate a descriptor. The second process maps the value of the descriptor into a fuzzy logic range [0-100] according to a certain decision function model (sigmoid, threshold, exponential, ...).

SVEX's language at pixel level is based on the objects described formerly. Application's code takes the form of declarative description of object and its dependencies. The system can be easily extended in several aspects such as sensor descriptions, library of procedures, classifier methods, etc. However we have not focused our efforts on developing a large set of processing alternatives (other systems, like Khoros, offer a greater variety in this concern).

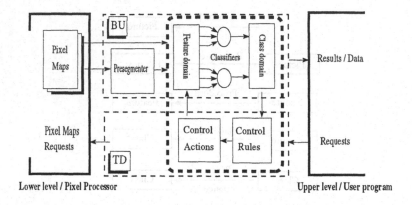

Fig. 4. Architecture of the Segment Processor and Domains at this Level

2.2 The Segment Processor

The second level of SVEX is conceived around the segments (connected aggregation of pixels defined by shape and/or property criteria). The output of this level is an image partition constituted by segments by shape along with their corresponding assignment to symbolic segment classes, their spatial localizers and the spatial relations among neighbors. The BU unit receives data pixel diagnostic maps (pixel classes), previously requested by the TD unit to the Pixel Processor, and produces symbolic diagnoses for the segments of the partition. As in the pixel level, symbolization process uses the measures obtained in the numerical domain to derive the segment's degree of membership symbolic classes. These classes are normally fuzzy, so the symbolic descriptions must have an associated uncertainty factor [9]. The achievement of a final segmentation of an image is not a one-stop process, but it is better formulated as a refinement process guided by the current state of the segmentation. A control strategy for this process can be implemented using fuzzy control rules that are evaluated over a segment and its neighbors (see [6] for a more detailed description of this aspect).

Compared to the Pixel Processor, the Segment Processor imposes two specific requirements. The first one, the need for a definition of the segments from the pixel maps, is met by means of a special module (see below), that generates the initial image partition. The second one is the desirability of having a refinement or control mechanism over the partition. For this purpose the control actions make possible the modification of the spatial definition of the segments using different operations (merge, split, include, ...).

From the point of view of functionality, the Segment Processor's architecture (Figure 4) is organized in three blocks, each one addressing a specific objective.

The first of these blocks is charged with the obtaining of the initial partition. This is the mission of the presegmenter module that is part of the Bottom-Up (BU) processor. Different methods can be used to achieve this goal so the presegmenter module has been conceived as an interchangeable part within the Segment Processor, currently this module is based on the Watershed transform [31]. The second functional block has the goal of computing the segment diagnoses. This block is structured by the distinction between a numerical domain, where the segments are described by features, and another symbolic domain based on classes. The third functional block is located at the Top-Down (TD) processor and manages the diagnostics requests and controls the Segment Processor. This control includes evaluating the state of the partition from a set of rules that may trigger actions to modify the spatial definition of the segments.

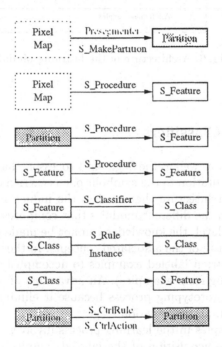

Fig. 5. Objects of the Segment Processor

The objects used in the programming of the Segment Processor are shown in Figure 5. The S_MakePartition object controls the presegmenter action. S_Procedure, S_Classifier, S_Class and S_Rule objects are equivalent to their homonyms in the Pixel Processor, but being now applied to segments instead of pixels. The S_Condition object permits to express premises for the rules that may include spatial relations (below, left, contains, ...). S_CtrlRuleSet, S_CtrlRule and S_CtrlAction objects can be used to define control actions over the partition. The S_Interface object determines which segment diagnoses are visible to the upper level (typically an user-provided program module) and the P_Interface object indicates which pixel classes are to be requested to the Pixel Processor.

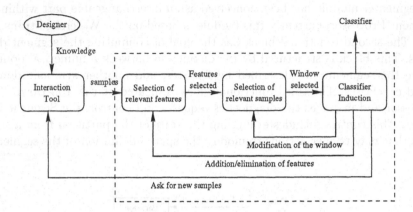

Fig. 6. Architecture of the Learning Module

3 Learning of Classifiers

In the Pixel Processor as well as the Segment Processor, the transformation from the numerical representation to the symbolic one is carried out by the classifiers. In this section, an architecture that realizes the induction of the classifiers is shown (Figure 6) and the different modules that composes it are explained.

At the numerical level, the knowledge can not be made explicit properly due to the lack of symbolism of the associated concepts. In these cases a widely used approach is starting from labeled examples to accomplish the learning process of the classes (learning from examples). An advantage of this approximation is that speeds up the prototyping process because it eliminates the existence of knowledge acquisition and verification stages.

The need of examples in the learning process involves the development of a tool that permits the acquisition of the labeled samples (Figure 7). This tool constitutes the element of interaction of the designer with the learning module, so the handling easiness is its main characteristic. Each sample is made up of a feature vector corresponding to an instance of the information grain, and a label assigned by the designer that gives the membership degree of the instance to the class.

The two main tasks in any induction process are to identify which features to use in describing the class and deciding how to combine them. The first task, the feature selection, has been studied in other fields like Statistical Inference, Pattern Recognition and Machine Learning. Many of the solution given in these fields are not useful in the framework of the Knowledge Based Vision Systems because they realize a transformation of the initial feature space [10, 8] into a

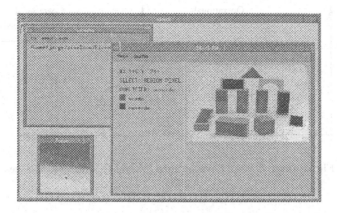

Fig. 7. Tool of Samples Acquisition

new one with a lower dimensionality, losing the features their meaning in this transformation. Other solutions consider all the combinations of the features as a search space and carry out a search in this space looking for the most relevant subset of features. A critical element in the previous approach is how to measure the relevance of a feature subset. In Pattern Recognition there are some measures as divergence, Matsusita distance or interclass distances that gives the dependence of the class with respect to a feature set. A drawback of the previous measures arises because they establish some probability distributions of the samples and treat each feature of the subset independent one from each other. In Machine Learning some authors have tackled the feature selection problem using concepts of the Information Theory like entropy or mutual information [26, 14]. The use of these concepts is motivated because they measure information and the most relevant feature subset is the one that gives more information about the class. A measure based on Information Theory that tries to select the most relevant features taking into account the interdependence among the features, is the GD measure [19,20]. The GD measure collects the dependence among features defining a matrix, called Transinformation matrix, that holds a conceptual resemblance with the covariance matrix used in the Mahalanobis distance.

Just as some features are more useful than others, so many some examples better aid the learning process than others. This suggests a second broad type of selection that concerns the examples themselves. There are several reasons to select examples [3]. In the context of this work, it is desirable to get a prototype of a vision system in a brief period of time, so reducing the number of examples the time of the learning process is decreased. The selection of examples must take into account the relevance of the examples [7] to select the most informative examples. Apart from the sample selection, an incremental learning scheme can be introduced to avoid the presentation to the learning process of all the samples. With this scheme the system establishes the number of samples

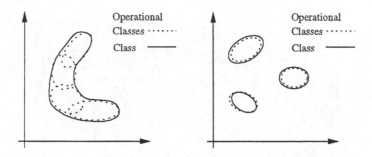

Fig. 8. Two Classes Divided into Several Operational Classes

that the learning process utilizes in each iteration of the learning process [35] and the over-fitting problem disappears giving as result a classifier with a better generalization capability.

The induction of the classifiers have to deal with the lack of explicit knowledge above mentioned. In this case, the artificial neural networks framework for the induction of the classifiers is a valid approach [4].

For the sake of the efficiency, we differentiate the process of the induction of classifiers for linearly separable classes and for nonlinearly ones. So in a first phase of the induction process it is necessary to detect the separability of the classes. For linearly separable classes, the combination rule is a linear combination followed by a nonlinear discriminant function [10]. In the artificial neural networks framework, the induction of the previous classifiers can be achieved with the single-layer perceptron [28, 30].

For nonlinearly separable classes, a class corresponds to a generic region of the feature space, including a set of non connected regions. Due to the generality of the region form is useful to define a intermediate concept called 'operational class'. An operational class is a region of the feature space that can be isolated with a linear of quadratic discriminant. In this way, a class is composed of several operational classes (Figure 8) whose number is unknown a priori and the degree of membership of samples is a combination of the degree of membership to the different operational classes.

A well suited artificial neural networks to induce classifiers that fulfill the previous class model, are the Radial-Basis Function Networks (RBFN) [18, 27, 25]. The structure of these artificial neural networks consists of a input layer, a hidden layer and an output layer. The hidden layer is composed of units whose activation function is a radial-basis function, normally Gaussian functions. The units of the output layer combine linearly the outputs of the units of the hidden layer and then with a non linear function gives the output of the network. The induction process determines the number of units in the hidden layer, which corresponds to the operational classes, and the weights of the output combination.

As a part of the induction process, it is included the feedback of the designer to validate the learning process results (Figure 6) given to the designer the possibility of introducing more examples or adjust some parameters (features selected) to try to improve the results.

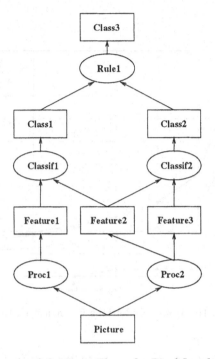

Fig. 9. Example of the Data Flow of a Pixel Level Application

The learning module yields as result a set of features and the induced classifier. This result can be translated directly into a program of the Pixel or Segment Processor object-oriented language, because the Classifier object (Figure 3) as well as the S_Classifier object (Figure 5) permit linear and quadratic combinations of the features.

4   Distribution of Processing

The reduction of execution times has also been addressed in the development of SVEX system. This aspect becomes especially important when dealing with reactive systems that must give a response to perceived stimulus in a limited period of time. On this subject computation distribution is a natural solution that fits in SVEX design. In this work several distribution schemes have been tested, including load-balancing procedures and prediction models for execution times [16].

The experiments have been performed on a hardware environment composed by several workstation with different characteristics. On the software side, the message passing tool PVM [12] is in charge of hiding data transference and synchronization complexity, turning the set of machines into a heterogeneous network of computational resources [22] [24]. This environment has been chosen in order to take advantage of the availability and frequent infra-utilization of this type of resources.

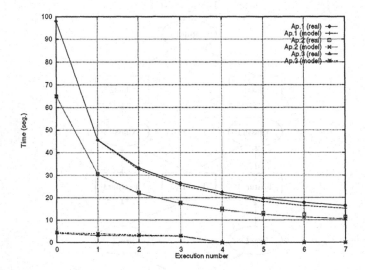

Fig. 10. Model predictions vs. measured times

Considering the levels of processing in SVEX and its internal structure, the distribution involves first the Pixel Processor and, especially the BU unit. Here is where most intense computation resources are demanded.

There are several alternatives for distributing the computations associated with an image-processing application (see Fig.9 for an example). Among these we have: functional or task-based distribution (each time an operator is invoked), data flow distribution (identifying parallel processing lines) or distribution based on the data (partitioning the image to be processed).

The operators considered at the level of pixels are local and not recursive, and there are no restrictions in their assignation to the different machines, physical sensor and actuator location apart. These characteristics have favoured the selection of the third implementation option, resulting in a SIMD paradigm implemented by means of a principal process (data distribution, results gathering) and several secondary processes (actual processing). This method offers several advantages such as a reduction of communications, a high level of reachable parallelism, simplification of the workload distribution, etc.

Two factors must be taken into account when partitioning the image for the data-based distribution. Firstly, most of the applicable procedures at the level of pixels involve convolution-type operations, computed over a window whose width is defined by the user. This requires the distribution of image regions with an overlap in order to avoid the possibility of areas going unprocessed in the interior section of the image. The consequences are inefficiencies generated in both the image distribution and computation, which are minimized by using squared regions. The second factor is the unequal workload assignment to each secondary process, as it must depend on factors associated with the machine it is being executed on (relative power and load, bandwidth and network load, etc.).

Fig. 11. Building source image

Fig. 12. Road source image

4.1 Load Balancing, Time Execution Model and Experiments

Both static and dynamic load balancing mechanisms have been implemented. Static ones perform an initial distribution of the load that it is not modified throughout all the time of execution. The work assigned to each machine depends on a parameter of capacity that considers factors such as nominal machine power, machine load, nominal network bandwidth, network load or distribution list order. The dynamic schemes vary the assigning of the workload to each machine throughout the entire execution time on a demand serve basis.

The processing of sequences with the Pixel Processor incorporates two factors that are especially critical from the computational distribution perspective. The first factor is the minor computational load per frame that generally involve these applications. The second factor is the possibility of performing operations that need data from previous instants of time, which requires the maintenance of temporal data-storage.

The prediction of the execution times in a heterogeneous environment such as the one considered is essential to analyze resource utilization, for example to measure speedup, define some machine-selection criteria, etc. A simple model must include several terms reflecting initial delay, reception of data, processing and results gathering.

Fig. 13. House A source image

Fig. 14. House B source image

Fig. 15. Initial Partition (House B)

Fig. 16. Final Partition (House B)

307

In the experiments, diverse applications of the PP have been used on RGB color images with different processing window sizes. Execution times have been measured with the UNIX command timex, and transference and processing times by inserting calls to gettimeofday function in the application's code. In Fig. 10, the execution times predicted by the model are compa red with measured times for three different applications, showing the time evolution as new machines are added to the computational network.

In situations approaching zero load, the static balance scheme based on the estimation of the computational capacity is that which offers better results as expected. However, the dynamic scheme presents an acceptable behaviuor, despite conditions being clearly unfavourable. The variable load environment constitutes the normal operation conditions of the computational network, that is, many users debugging programs, displaying images, reading documents, etc. In this situation the dynamic load-balancing scheme clearly surpasses the static one. The reason lies in the ratio between load variation frequency and typical execution times, which makes difficult for the static scheme to obtain precise load estimations.

Fig. 17. Segment Class Road (Building)

Fig. 18. Segment Class Road (Road)

The execution times in the case of sequences follow the same guidelines as those for a single image. In zero load situations the best results are obtained by the static scheme because the number of blocks can be reduced to the minimum. For variable load environments, the efficiency obtained depends on the relationship between the improvements in the balance due to relocation and the setbacks produced for having carried it out.

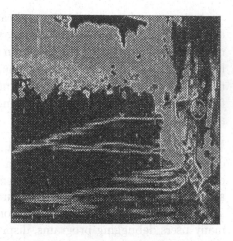

Fig. 19. Segment Class Green (Building)

Fig. 20. Segment Class Green (Road)

5 SVEX Applications Examples

In this section we will illustrate SVEX's perception capabilities by means of two specific applications. The first one (Figures 13 to 22) presents the results obtained in the segmentation of several outdoor images. Both images have been processed with the same programs set, without computing complex or costly features.

Fig. 21. Segment Class Window (House A)

Fig. 22. Segment Class Front (House B)

The pictures include source images, the initial partition obtained from the Pixel Processor and the presegmenter, the final partition as a result of the refinement process applied to the initial partition, and a selection of some segment classes (front, window, road) from this final partition.

The second application has been taken from a real sedimentology problem which is illustrated by Figure 23. Given a back-lighted sample of sand grains (see upper left image) the objective is to detect the particles that are approximately round.

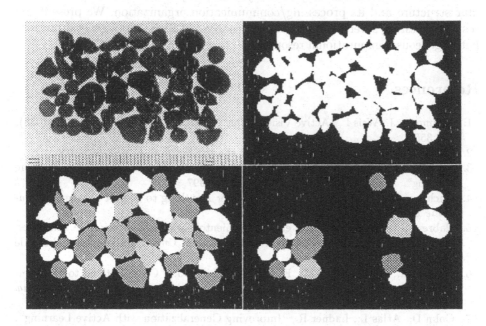

Fig. 23. Top) Original Image and Initial Partition. Bottom) Final Partition and Selected Round Particles.

6 Conclusions

We have presented a layered model for the design of perception-action systems suited for the incorporation of several desirable characteristics such as asynchronous communication, multilevel control loops, virtual sensing and acting and modular architecture. We analyze the effects of these properties on system global performance.

We describe an implementation (SVEX) on the basis of the generic system model to show the benefits of this approach. SVEX knowledge-based system exhibits several interesting characteristics inherited from its modular design. From a structural point of view, the system offers clearly defined computation and control paths. Considered as a tool for the development of compute vision applications it permits a significative reduction in prototyping and maintenance costs.

Two important aspects of the system have been studied in detail. Learning of classifiers speeds up the development of prototypes because it takes care of selecting the most relevant features and permits to induce the classifier from labeled examples of instances of each level information grain. The layered structure of SVEX with similar objects in each level favours the learning process, allowing the use of the same learning paradigm in both levels. Computation distribution solutions are easy to analyze and implement due to system modular structure and its processing/communication organization. We present the results of testing several distribution alternatives of SVEX on a general-purpose heterogeneous computational resource.

References

1. Aloimonos J., Weis I., "Active Vision", *Int. Journal of Computer Vision*, 2, (1988), 333-356.
2. Bajcsi R., "Active Perception", Proc. of the IEEE, 76, 8, (1988), 996-1005.
3. Blum A. L., Langley P., "Selection of relevant features and examples in machine learning", *Artificial Intelligence*, 97:245–271, 1997.
4. Buchanan B., "Can Machine Learning Offer Anything to Expert Systems?", *Machine Learning*, 4, pp. 251-254, 1989.
5. Cabrera J., "Sistema Basado en Conocimiento para Segmentación de Imágenes. Desarrollos y Aplicaciones", Doctoral Dissertation, Universidad de Las Palmas de Gran Canaria, 1994.
6. Cabrera J., Hernández F.M., Falcón A., Méndez J., "Contributions to the symbolic processing of segments in computer vision", *Mathware and Soft Computing*, III(3):403–413, 1996.
7. Cohn D., Atlas L., Ladner R., "Improving Generalization with Active Learning", *Machine Learning*, 15, pp. 201-221, 1994.
8. Devijver P. A., Kittler J., *Pattern Recognition: A Statistical Approach*. Prentice-Hall, Englewood Cliffs, New Jersey, 1982.
9. Dubois D., Prade H., Yager R. R., Introduction in *Readings in Fuzzy Sets for Intelligent Systems*, Morgan Kaufmann Pub., (1993), 1-20.
10. Duda R., Hart P., *Pattern Classification and Scene Analysis*, Wiley, 1973.
11. Fukunaga K., *Introduction to Statistical Pattern Recognition*. Academic Press Inc., 2nd edition, 1990.
12. Geist A., *PVM: Parallel Virtual Machine - A Users' Guide and Tutorial for Networked Parallel Computing*, The MIT Press, 1994.
13. Gordon J., Shortliffe E.H., "The Dempster-Shafer Theory of Evidence", in *Rule-Based Expert Systems*, Buchanan and Shortliffe (Eds.), (1984), 272-292.
14. Koller D., Sahami M., "Toward optimal feature selection", Proc. of the 13th Int. Conf. on Machine Learning, pages 284–292. Morgan Kaufmann, 1996.
15. Krisnapuram R., Keller J.M., "Fuzzy Set Theoretic Approach to Computer Vision: An Overview", in *Fuzzy Logic Technology and Applications*, IEEE Tech. Activities Board, (1994), 25-32.
16. Hernández D., Cabrera J., "Distribution of Image Processing Application on a Heterogeneous Workstation Network. Modeling, Load-balancing and Experimental Results", SPIE-97 Parallel on Distributed Methods for Image Processing, vol. 3166, pp. 170-179,July 1997, San Diego.

17. Huntsberger T.L., Rangarajan C., Jayaramamurthy S.N., "Representation of Uncertainty in Computer Vision using Fuzzy Sets", *IEEE Trans. Comput.*, 35, 2, (1986), 145-156.
18. Lee. S., Kil R. M., "Multilayer Feedforward Potential Function Network", Proc. of 2nd. Int. Conf. on Neural Networks, vol I, pp. 161-171, 1988.
19. Lorenzo J., Hernández M., Méndez J., "An information theory-based measure to assess feature subsets", Preprints of the VII National Symposium on Pattern Recognition and Image Analysis (AERFAI'97), volume 2, pages 38–39, 1997.
20. Lorenzo J., Hernández M., J. Méndez. "A measure based on information theory for attribute selection", (IBERAMIA-98) 6th Ibero-American Conference on Artificial Intelligence, Lisbon, Portugal, Lectures Notes in Artificial Intelligence, Springer Verlag, October 1998.
21. Méndez J., Falcón A., Hernández F.M., Cabrera J., "A Development Tool for Computer Vision Systems at Pixel Level", *Cybernetics & Systems*, 25, 2, (1994), 289-316.
22. Munro D., "Performance of Multiprocessor Communications Networks", Doctoral Dissertation, Dep. of Electronics, University of York, 1994.
23. Niemann H., Brünig H., Salzbrunn R., Schröder S., "A Knowledge-Based Vision System for Industrial Applications", *Machine Vision and Applications*, 3, (1990), 201-229.
24. Pennington R., "Distributed and Heterogeneous Computing", Cluster Computing Lecture Series, Pittsburg Supercomputing Center 1995.
25. Poggio T., Girosi F., "Networks for approximation and learning", *Proceedings of the IEEE*, 78:1481–1487, 1990.
26. Quinlan J. R., "Induction of decision trees", *Machine Learning*, 1:81–106, 1986.
27. Renals S., Rohwer R., "Phoneme Classification Experiments using Radial Basis Functions", Proc. Int. Conf. on Neural NetworksI, pp. 416-467, 1989.
28. Rosenblatt F., "On the Convergence of Reinforcement Procedures in Simple Perceptrons", Cornell Aeronautical Report VG-1196-G-4, Buffalo, NY, 1960.
29. Risemann E.M., Hanson A.R., "A Methodology for the Development of General Knowledge-Based Vision Systems", in *Vision, Brain and Cooperative Computation*, MIT Press, Cambridge Mass., (1987), 285-328.
30. Rumelhart D. E., Hinton G. E., Williams R. J., "Learning Representations by Back-Propagating Errors", *Nature*, 323, pp. 533-536, 1986.
31. Vincent L., Soille P., "Watersheds in Digital Spaces: An efficient algorithm based on immersion simulations". *IEEE Trans. on Pattern Anal . and Mach. Intell.*, Vol 13, n 6, pp. 583-598, 1991.
32. Wilson R., Spann M., *Image Segmentation and Uncertainty*, Research Studies Press Ltd., 1988.
33. Zadeh L.A., "PRUF- A meaning representation language for natural languages", in *Fuzzy Reasoning and its Applications*, Academic Press, London, (1981), 1-39.
34. Zadeh L.A., "Commonsense Knowledge Representation based on Fuzzy Logic", *IEEE Computer*, 16, 10, (1983), 61-65.
35. Zhang B., "Accelerated Learning by Active Example Selection", *International Journal of Neural Networks*, vol. 5 (1), pp. 67-75, 1994.

A Hierarchical Vision Architecture for Robotic Manipulation Tasks

Zachary Dodds[1], Martin Jägersand[1], Greg Hager[1], and Kentaro Toyama[2]

[1]Department of Computer Science, Yale University, New Haven, CT 06520
[2]Microsoft Research, Redmond, WA 98052

Abstract. Real world manipulation tasks vary in their demands for precision and freedoms controlled. In particular, during any one task the complexity may vary with time. For a robotic hand-eye system, precise tracking and control of full pose is computationally expensive and less robust than rough tracking of a subset of the pose parameters (e.g. just translation). We present an integrated vision and control system in which the vision component provides (1) the continuous, local feedback at the required complexity for robot manipulation and (2) the discrete state information needed to switch between control modes of differing complexity.

1 Introduction

In *robotic hand-eye tasks* (which we will also refer to as *visual servoing* or *vision-based manipulation*), the rote motions of classical industrial robotics are replaced by a flexible control strategy which is robust to deviations in camera positioning, robot calibration, and placement of objects in the robot workspace. In large part, this robustness is due to feedback from vision systems which observe a robot action in progress, allowing for continual adaptation of robot motion.

Despite the importance of vision in these tasks, vision systems which support hand-eye robot coordination have generally been developed *ad hoc*, designed specifically for particular tasks. In this paper, we present a principled approach to vision and control system design which supports complex vision-based manipulation.

Robotic systems need to integrate a broad spectrum of sensor information to accomplish their tasks. Often, tasks decompose into manipulation skills of varying levels of specificity. In particular, there is a continuum of control motions ranging from simple, coarse motions to refined, precise movements. Likewise, there is an associated range of vision algorithms from observations that are low-dimensional and approximate to those which are multi-dimensional and precise. A key to solving robotic hand-eye tasks efficiently and robustly is to identify how precise control is needed at a particular time during task execution, and then match that with appropriately precise visual tracking, Fig. 1. For instance during the reach motions of a basic pick-and-place task simple vision and control suffices, while for the pickup and place typically precise fine manipulation and visual estimation of full 6D pose are needed.

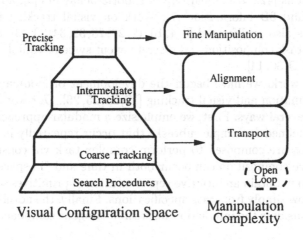

Fig. 1. The vision hierarchy and corresponding supported manipulation skills. As the set of possible target configurations narrows, the control system can perform more complex actions.

In this paper, we claim that an effective vision-system architecture for hand-eye coordination can be distilled into three key ideas:

- A control framework for hand-eye manipulation which manages the complexity of tasks through the composition of a few simple primitives that can be intuitively manipulated.
- A complementary set of fast image-processing primitives which can be combined to support the requirements of hand-eye tasks.
- Integration of the control and vision frameworks in such a way that both planned and exogenous events are handled by discrete transitions among the servoing and vision modules. Because hand-eye tasks are dependent on vision, failure of the vision system to deliver certain observations will affect the choice of robot action.

In Section 2, we briefly review related work and present background for visual servoing and vision-based tracking. Section 3 extends these low-level capabilities through temporal composition to construct more sophisticated tasks which adapt to visual events. Finally, an implementation of the system and some experimental results are presented in Section 4.

2 Background

Rapid strides in technology and a great deal of research interest have yielded progress on both theoretical and applied aspects of robotic hand-eye coordination [1, 6, 8, 13, 15, 22, 9, 24, 31, 37, 33, 41, 40, 45, 47, 46]). For a recent survey see [11]. Notable recent advances include the manipulation of automotive parts under realistic conditions [42], visual learning of robotic behaviors [3], and techniques for fusing 2D and 3D information [7]. Work on visual tracking for real-time applications has also proliferated [2, 4, 10, 12, 27, 28, 32, 34, 39, 43]. Some of this work considers task composition and discrete event systems to link active-vision modules, *e.g.*, [29, 30, 14].

In our own work, we have begun the development of modular systems for hand-eye coordination and visual tracking [19, 21, 25, 26]. Our work differs from other work in several ways. First, we emphasize a modular approach where task primitives are defined for simple subtasks that occur repeatedly in the domain. These primitives are composed to perform complex task via consistent design principles, where composition can occur both in time and "in space." Throughout, we strive to maintain an intuitive representation of primitives so that implementations follow simply from task specifications. Finally, the novel contribution of this paper considers the interaction between analogous components of control and vision.

In this section, we review our approach to visual servoing and visual tracking. We will consider task primitives for each domain and explain non-temporal compositions of primitives.

2.1 Visual Servoing

An Example Task Consider a gluing task: a robot must manipulate a glue-filled syringe such that the nozzle reaches a designated application point and the syringe is at a prescribed orientation. Both constraints must be satisfied within a given error tolerance before the actual gluing can begin. Because the exact geometric relationships between the robot, tool, and surface may be unknown, rote actions by the robot are not acceptable. One option is to continually reconstruct the 3D scene using vision, and proceed until the reconstruction fits the goal configuration. For computational efficiency, however, we consider another approach whereby the task is described as a set of sensor constraints which *imply* the desired goal. In our example, the goal configuration may be described as one in which the nozzle tip appears to coincide with the glue-application point simultaneously in two cameras.

As the example illustrates, the fundamental goal of visual servoing is to achieve a set of constraints on the configuration of an actuated system. Constraints can be described in terms of a set of salient features in the robot workspace – that is, by an equation

$$T(p) = 0,$$

where p is a list of observable features on the robot or in its environment and T is a *task function* [38]. In the example above, p could contain the 3D coordinates

315

of the nozzle and the target point. T measures a configuration's error, vanishing when the task is complete.

The information available to perform a task are the observations of the features, p, by one or more cameras. Let $\mathbf{y} \in \Re^m$ denote the available observations of the features p. Assuming $\mathbf{y}$ is the only information available for performing a task $T(p) = 0$, then if the task can be performed at all, it must be the case that there is an equation of the form

$$\mathbf{E}(\mathbf{y}) = 0$$

such that

$$\mathbf{E}(\mathbf{y}) = 0 \Leftrightarrow T(p) = 0. \tag{1}$$

We refer to $\mathbf{E}(\mathbf{y}) = 0$ as an *image-based encoding* of the task $T(p) = 0$ and we say that $\mathbf{E}(\mathbf{y}) = 0$ *verifies* the task $T(p) = 0$ if Equation 1 holds [23].

Carrying out a given visual servoing task involves finding a robot configuration which achieves the encoded task. Let $\mathbf{x} \in \Re^n$ represent the robot state, and let $\mathbf{f}$ be the *visual-motor model*, which expresses image-feature values as a function of the robot's state: $\mathbf{y} = \mathbf{f}(\mathbf{x})$. In a precisely calibrated system one can solve the equation

$$\mathbf{E}(\mathbf{f}(\mathbf{x}^*)) = \mathbf{E}(\mathbf{y}^*) = 0$$

for a goal position $\mathbf{x}^*$. In an uncalibrated system, $\mathbf{f}$ is not known, but a rough estimate of the Jacobian, $\mathbf{J}(\mathbf{x})$, of $\mathbf{E}(\mathbf{f}(\cdot))$ is sufficient to perform a set of static positioning skills accurately. Intuitively, $\mathbf{J}(\mathbf{x})$ maps small changes in robot state about the point $\mathbf{x}$ to changes in the error measurement. Thus, the following control law can be used to determine the robot's image velocity, $\dot{\mathbf{x}}$:

$$\dot{\mathbf{x}} = -\mathbf{W}\mathbf{J}^+(\mathbf{x})\mathbf{E}. \tag{2}$$

This drives the observed error, $\mathbf{E}$, to zero under certain assumptions, even in the presence of calibration error [21]. Here, $\mathbf{W}$ is a positive definite gain matrix and $^+$ denotes the generalized matrix inverse (simple matrix inverse, when $\mathbf{J}$ is invertible, and the pseudo-inverse, $(\mathbf{J}^T\mathbf{J})^{-1}\mathbf{J}^T$, when it is not).

A crucial aspect of this framework is that task specifications exist in *task space* while the command encoding exists in *image space*. Thus, by developing a set of primitive task-space constraints with corresponding image-space encodings, we can support intuitive specification of tasks in the "natural" geometry of the robot workspace and still issue image-space commands directly from observations *without having to perform an explicit scene reconstruction.*

In addition, if the primitive tasks are chosen carefully, they can be combined to form new tasks which meet each of the constituent contraints. For example, Equation 2 expresses a primitive task defined by a single image constraint. A common method for building more complex tasks is to "stack" such constraints:

$$\dot{\mathbf{x}} = -\mathbf{W}\begin{pmatrix}\mathbf{J}_1\\ \vdots\\ \mathbf{J}_k\end{pmatrix}^+\begin{pmatrix}\mathbf{E}_1\\ \vdots\\ \mathbf{E}_k\end{pmatrix}. \tag{3}$$

We refer to this composition of servoing tasks as *parallel composition*.

In general, one can define any number of primitive servoing operations using one or more cameras. In this article, we consider two cameras and only two primitive skills: point-to-point and point-to-line servoing. In the former, a point rigidly attached to the robot's end effector is positioned to a fixed reference point; in the latter, the manipulated point is brought to lie on a fixed reference line. Detailed explanations of these and related primitives are provided in the appendix and in [16, 18].

As suggested, even these simple primitives are sufficient for performing relatively complex tasks. Returning to the gluing task, for example, assume that the syringe must be aligned vertically at the point where gluing begins. A point-to-point constraint will bring the nozzle tip to the target point. A point-to-line constraint which moves the top of the syringe to a vertical line through the target point will ensure the desired orientation. These constraints can be met simultaneously by composing them as in Equation 3.

Notice that typically there are multiple ways to choose $\mathbf{E}$ for a particular task. The choice we make can affect the convergence and convergence rate of the servoing (related to how well the lineararization $\mathbf{J}(\mathbf{x})$ approximates $\mathbf{E}(\mathbf{f}(\mathbf{x}))$), the accuracy with which the goal can be achieved, and how robust the servoing will be with respect to disturbances and loss of data. We will take advantage of this in Section 3.

2.2 Vision System Primitives

In order to support the vision-based control architecture described above, we have developed a corresponding set of visual tracking primitives. This system, called "XVision," also incorporates a notion of primitive tracking composition similar in spirit to parallel composition. Here, we highlight XVision's fundamental features; [17, 19, 36, 35] contain more detailed descriptions.

Every tracking primitive returns a parameter vector – the vector of parameters it observes. Tracking algorithms follow a cyclic process consisting of three phases: In the *predict* phase, an initial guess is made for the parameter vector of the primitive. The default prediction is that features remain at their last observed location, but other prediction schemes (*e.g.*, Kalman filters) have been incorporated. Although in practice, the prediction is a single parameter vector, implicitly, the prediction represents a set of parameter vectors over which the *search* phase searches. Using the notation introduced for visual servoing, if $\mathbf{y} \in \mathcal{Y}$ represents the space of possible parameter vectors, then a prediction that an observation is expected at $\hat{\mathbf{y}}$ can be thought to represent a compact region, $\mathbf{Y}$, in parameter space, where $\hat{\mathbf{y}}$ and, hopefully, the ground-truth observation are in $\mathbf{Y}$. A final *update* phase adjusts the optimal result from search based on higher-level constraints.

Currently, XVision supports the following primitive tracking types:

- "Blobs" of classified pixels which provide the centroid and area of a set of pixels classified according to intensity, color, motion, or texture.

- Contrast edges, which are fixed in length and return center position and orientation parameters.
- Textured image regions based on iterative sum-of-squared-differences (SSD) minimization, which return up to six parameters corresponding to the affine deformations an image region can undergo.
- Arbitrarily-shaped contours based on image gradients, which can return either the positions of contour control points or the centroid of the circuscribed region.

In addition to the tracked parameters, each tracking primitive returns a confidence value in its tracking estimate. For example, for the edge tracker, this value is greater for higher-contrast edges; for the SSD region tracker, the value is proportional to the negative of the sum-of-squared-difference residual between the template and the image.

Tracking primitives are organized according to a type system; each feature type provides a state vector with characteristic component values. Analogous to the servoing primitives, the elemental types are `PointFeature` and `LineFeature`.

Primitive features are composed by placing constraints on their joint state vector. In addition, a composition function C may be used to compute the state of a composite tracker in terms of its constituent parts. For example, tracking two edges, l_1 and l_2, as a corner, y_{cor}, exemplifies the composition of a `PointFeature` from two `LineFeatures`: $y_{cor} = C_{l \to p}(l_1, l_2)$.

Similar geometric constructions, such as affine transformations $C_{tr}(l)$ and midpoint constructions $C_{mp}(y_1, y_2)$, can likewise be represented as compositions or state transformations of visible image primitives. In addition to features of a geometric type, more general scalar and vector states are possible, $e.g.$, cross ratios $C_{cr}(y_1, y_2, y_3, y_4)$, componentwise differences $C_{pp}(y_1, y_2)$, and scalar products $C_{pl}(y, l)$. The latter two provide exactly the error information required for the point-to-point and point-to-line servoing primitives. In this way, the vision system can provide a single, composite tracker whose state is the encoded task error, $\mathbf{E}$, needed for robot control in Equation 3.

3 Task Decomposition

Parallel composition alone cannot solve whole manipulation tasks. A principal challenge is the creation of temporal manipulation sequences from simpler servoing actions. In order to distinguish this type of task composition in time from the parallel composition of tasks, we will use the term *task chain* to denote a temporal sequence of servoing tasks, and *task link* to denote a single task in time. We note that a task link may itself be a parallel composition of primitive tasks. There are obvious extensions to tasks in tree structures for multi-robot or multi-threaded tasks, but they will not be discussed here.

3.1 Task Chaining

In image space, a single task link can be described by an action specification as follows:

$$ A = (\mathbf{E}^{init}(\cdot), \mathbf{M}, \mathbf{E}^{final}(\cdot)). \tag{4} $$

Here, $\mathbf{E}^{\text{init}}(\cdot)$ expresses the perceptual precondition for the task: $\mathcal{Y}^{\text{init}} = \{\mathbf{y} : \mathbf{E}^{\text{init}}(\mathbf{y}) = 0\}$ represents the set of observations, of which one must be observed before the task can begin. Similarly, $\mathbf{E}^{\text{final}}(\cdot)$ expresses the desired final configuration, and the set of allowable observations is $\mathcal{Y}^{\text{final}} = \{\mathbf{y} : \mathbf{E}^{\text{final}}(\mathbf{y}) = 0\}$. For explicit trajectory control $\mathbf{E}^{\text{init}}$ and $\mathbf{E}^{\text{final}}$ can be extended to a one parameter family of encodings: $\mathbf{E}^{\text{traj}}(y, t) = 0$, for $t \in [0, 1]$, $\mathbf{E}^{\text{traj}}(\cdot, 0) = \mathbf{E}^{\text{init}}(\cdot)$ and $\mathbf{E}^{\text{traj}}(\cdot, 1) = \mathbf{E}^{\text{final}}(\cdot)$. For t between 0 and 1, $\mathbf{E}^{\text{traj}}(y, t) = 0$ defines the intermediate points (or sets thereof) on the trajectory.

M describes any (visual or motor) constraints that must maintained during the manipulation, e.g., restricting the movement of a redundant arm, avoiding joint limits and singularities, and maintaining grasp [25]. Here we simply use M to maintain the pose of the not explicitly controlled freedoms e.g. for a 3 DOF translatory movement we maintain $(x_4 \ldots x_6)$ constant in motor space.

A task chain is then a sequence of actions, $\{A_0 \ldots A_{K-1}\}$, such that the potential final observations of task $k - 1$ satisfy the required initial observations for task k. More precisely, $\mathcal{Y}_{k-1}^{\text{final}} \subseteq \mathcal{Y}_k^{\text{init}}$ for $0 < k < K$. $\mathbf{E}_{K-1}^{\text{final}}(\mathbf{y}^{final}) = 0$ verifies task completion.

In many cases the purpose of a task is to go from a loosely-defined initial state to a highly constrained final state; typically, $\mathcal{Y}^{\text{init}}$ is large whereas $\mathcal{Y}^{\text{final}}$ contains a smaller set of observations. For example, in the gluing task, the robot may start almost anywhere in the workspace, allowing $\mathcal{Y}^{\text{init}}$ to be the set of all of the possible observations that might occur with the robot holding the syringe. On the other hand, there is only a single observation vector (together with some small margin of error) that forms the set $\mathcal{Y}^{\text{final}}$ of goal observations. The purpose of the sequence $\{A_0 \ldots A_{K-1}\}$ is to break down this overall task into manageable and robust task links, where each subgoal is defined by smaller and smaller sets of possible final states.

As long as each subtask succeeds, the system will achieve its overall goal. In Section 3.4, we consider the possibility of subtask failure due to failures in vision.

3.2 Manipulation Hierarchy

How should large tasks be broken into task links? One natural division establishes task links based on changes in the features, dimensionality, or precision of the constraints that occur during a complex task. This happens, for instance, (i) when more precise movement is needed and more features need to be incorporated, (ii) when the salient part of an object changes (e.g., from the head to the claw of a hammer) and (iii) whenever an object is grasped or regrasped, changing its geometry with respect to the robot end effector.

A general principle for system design is to use the simplest possible servoing movement which suffices for each step in a manipulation task. In other words, we use the set of primitives which accomplish the task with contraints on the fewest degrees of freedom (DOF). Our experimental evaluations of control level visual servoing in [26] show that smaller and simpler manipulation models result in more robust model estimation and servoing. Also, controlling fewer DOF requires fewer visual measurements and a smaller task description. Simpler and more robust tracking can be used for coarse movements, and sensitive, computationally expensive tracking is only needed during fine manipulation.

Consider again the gluing task. The system begins with a movement to bring the syringe from some arbitrary initial configuration to some point near the target. This is naturally solved as a 3-DOF translational movement, accomplished by a coarse point-to-point primitive ("coarse" means that E^{final} accepts a fairly large volume of observations as end goals). To align the syringe, orientation must be controlled, *e.g.*, through parallel composition of two point-to-line primitives. Finally, to bring the nozzle to the application point, an additional point-to-point constraint must be added. One possible decomposition of this task, therefore, involves three separate task links. Discontinuities in control complexity such as these provide natural breakpoints for many tasks.

To solve typical coarse-to-fine tasks, we define three classes of servoing movements: *transportation, alignment* and *fine manipulation*, summarized in Figure 2. The transportation movement is a coarse primitive for long motions, such as reaching to bring a tool near the site of a task. The movement is typically 3 DOF, but can be lower (it is 2 DOF when pushing something on a surface). This means that for m visual measurements the visual-motor Jacobian is of size $m \times 3$. When using stereo vision, simple centroid tracking of the moving object giving a 4×3 Jacobian is sufficient to complete a transportation subtask.

Fine manipulation movements adjust translation and orientation precisely in up to 6 DOF for a rigid object. A visual-motor Jacobian of size $m \times 6$, $m \geq 6$ is required, based on tracking m image feature values. For example, centroid tracking is, in general, insufficient for controlling both position and orientation. More sensitive estimation of several object features must be used.

When switching between transportation and fine manipulation modes, the appropriate preconditions $E^{init}(y)$ of the higher DOF fine manipulation must be satisfied, and to perform accurate fine manipulation a reasonably accurate model is needed. The alignment movement is a high DOF movement whose goal $E^{final}(y)$ is the precondition of the subsequent fine manipulation, but whose precondition $E^{init}(y)$ specifies fewer DOF. 3-DOF transportation as defined above can deliver an object to a specific location, but typically, at an unspecified, arbitrary orientation. The alignment move accepts this arbitrary orientation in $E^{init}(y)$, but delivers the object at a specific position and orientation for fine-manipulation.

Other variations are possible. For instance, a guarded move (useful in grasping tasks) can be created by servoing along some visually defined direction until an external contact condition is met. Open-loop movements can be performed using the visual-motor model, but without continuous visual feedback.

Composition Example We now describe the construction of a mid-level skill from the chaining of low-level task links. The example in Fig. 3 shows a system in which the task is similar to the gluing application: insertion of a piece of

Basic visual servoing movements

1. **Transportation**
    - A coarse primitive for large movements.
    - < 3 DOF control of object centroid.
    - Robust to disturbances.
2. **Alignment**
    - For switching modes between coarse and fine manipulation.
    - Moves from 3D control coarse final pose to satisfy the 6D defined initial pose of the fine manipulation.
3. **Fine manipulation**
    - For high precision control of both translational and angular position.
    - 6 DOF control based on several object features.
    - Adaptive to environment changes if on-line model estimation is used, but not as robust as the 3 DOF control.

Fig. 2. Visual space task planning and decomposition. Typical tasks have coarse and fine movements. We decompose movements into transportation, alignment and fine manipulation.

packing foam into a box of similar size using direct joint control on a PUMA robot arm. The visual goal is to align the white dots $p = p_1 \ldots p_6$ on the foam with the corresponding white dots p^* on the box, so $T(p) = p - p^*$. The insertion naturally decomposes into a coarse transportation to the vicinity of the box and an alignment to make the foam plane parallel with that of the box. Lastly, a 6-DOF fine manipulation movement is used to bring the foam into the box.

To switch between the different movement types, intermediate goals are constructed in free space. In this example the cameras are uncalibrated, but by using object structure in each image separately, consistent (stereo) goal points can be constructed as follows. The vertical lines around the box are extracted and labeled l_1, l_2, l_3. The average of their lengths is $\|l\|$. Using l_1, l_2, l_3 the two visible sides of the box are reconstructed projectively at $\|l\|$ and $2\|l\|$ above the real target in each frame.

For the 3-DOF long range transportation, only one of the feature points is needed in each image. A point-to-point constraint, $\mathbf{E}^{\text{final}} = [y_1 \ y_2 \ y_3 \ y_4]^T - [y_1^* \ y_2^* \ y_3^* \ y_4^*]^T$ is used to position this feature on the corresponding reconstructed point at height $2\|l\|$. For the fine manipulation a redundant description based on 14 feature values are used $\mathbf{y} = [y_1 \ldots y_{14}]^T$ by tracking the row and column pixel location of 7 points between the two cameras (Figure 3). To satisfy initial constraint of the fine manipulation, $\mathbf{y} = [y_1 \ldots y_{14}]^T$ are aligned with the corresponding reconstructed points at $\|l\|$; at the end of the fine manipulation, they coincide with the real feature points on the box. This alignment forces the foam to be directly above the box in a plane parallel to it.

The box-packing example demonstrates the varying demands on a visual tracking system during the execution of a manipulation task. Even as task-specific demands for information increase, exogenous events can degrade sensing and inhibit progress. A hierarchical vision system can tailor its processing to

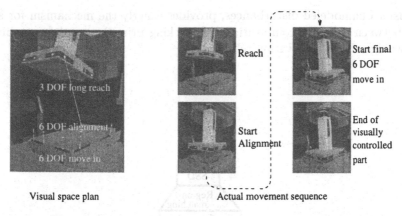

Fig. 3. Left: Planning the different phases of an insert type movement consisting of reaching and fine manipulation movements. Right: Performing the planned insertion.

the changing requirements of a manipulation task and can inform a supervisory controller as to whether sensing requirements are being met.

3.3 Vision Hierarchy

Consider a vector of visual observations, $\mathbf{y}$. A key question is how much of the vector $\mathbf{y}$ must be known for a particular task. Often, a partial observation vector suffices for transport, while more observations are needed for alignment or manipulation. Due to non-optimal tracking conditions, the system may obtain only a partial estimate of $\mathbf{y}$ at any given moment. That is, elements of $\mathbf{y}$ may be only approximately estimated or altogether unreliable.

In general, it is difficult to determine exactly what part of an observation vector is reliable. Nor is it clear what should happen when an observation is inaccurate. In practice, one can imagine different strategies to construct encodings, $\mathbf{E}$, with varying tolerance to data loss:

- If $\mathbf{E}$ is a minimal encoding the loss of any visual data will render the task T impossible.
- If $\mathbf{E}$ is a paralell composition $\mathbf{E} = (\mathbf{E}_0 \ldots \mathbf{E}_{I-1})^T$ of several "blocks" $\mathbf{E}_i$, each independently verifying T, then the dropping of features could be tolerated as long as at least one block $\mathbf{E}_i$ can be computed reliably from the observations. This situation arises when the vision system provides a great deal of redundant information, *e.g.*, many tracked points.
- An on-line strategy involves analyzing $\mathbf{J}$, the linear estimate of the visual-motor model. If a n-DOF task is being performed, but the decimated $\mathbf{J}$ has an effective rank less than n, the task cannot be completed.

Ultimately, however, it is necessary that the vision system be aware of its ability to support a particular task. We, therefore, choose a vision system architecture which parallels that of the manipulation hierarchy. The *Incremental Focus of Attention* framework [43] (IFA), developed to make object tracking robust to unmodeled disturbances, provides exactly the mechanism for switching between different compositions of tracking primitives and for maintaining knowledge about observation reliability.

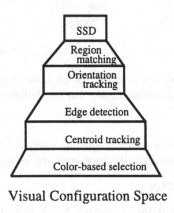

Visual Configuration Space

Fig. 4. The IFA vision hierarchy used for the task in Section 4.

As suggested in Figure 4, layers in the hierarchy represent different sets of tracking primitives (singly or in composition, as described in Section 2.2), and each layer fills in the observation vector, y, to varying degrees, with higher layers offering more complete observations. At any moment, execution occurs only in a single layer. Tracking takes place at the highest layer possible, given good visual circumstances, but if tracking is lost for whatever reason (fast object motion, lighting changes, clutter, occlusions, etc.), the system falls to lower layers to perform partial observation and recovery.

Integration of the trackers is managed through explicit handling of failures and tracking re-initialization. Layers of tracking (rectangular layers in Figure 4) are interspersed with search layers (trapezoids) which narrow the set of possible configurations of objects of interest.

Layers can be interpreted as operating on the space of observations, where each layer consumes and produces sets of observations vectors. A color-based blob tracking layer, for example, would be given an initial set of possible observations, y^{in}, corresponding to a prediction range about where the blob might be, and return an observation set, y^{out}, representing its estimate together with a small margin of error. In this particular example, the y's might specify the position of the target feature, but leave the orientation observations undefined. A color-based search layer, on the other hand, might take the full observation space as its input set $\mathcal{Y}^{\text{in}}$, and return a smaller output set, $\mathcal{Y}^{\text{out}}$, that could serve as the input to color-based tracking. In this case, $\mathcal{Y}^{\text{out}}$ specifies observation vector elements that are unspecified in $\mathcal{Y}^{\text{in}}$. This difference between a tracking layer and a search layer is typical (though not necessary) – tracking layers will tend to preserve the dimensionality of the observations, whereas search layers will tend to provide additional dimensions of observation.

Transition to another layer occurs based on the success of the current layer. Tracking failures, as determined by the failure of the tracking primitives or failure to maintain a geometrical constraint among primitives cause transitions downward. In all other cases, execution proceeds to the next higher layer (when one exists). For example, in Figure 4, consider the case where the orientation tracking layer is invoked. This layer may be using two parallel edge tracking primitives to determine the orientation of a robot tool. Should one of the tracking primitives return low confidence values, or should the two edges appear sufficiently non-parallel, the layer would signal failure and drop down to the edge detection layer in an attempt to re-initialize the edges. On the other hand, if tracking is successful, exeuction would continue with region matching and SSD tracking, where observations are made with greater precision.

Finally, we emphasize the natural correspondence between the task decomposition paradigm and IFA. In particular, where tasks are decomposed according to the types of observations required to perform them, the vision system is organized based on the observations it can provide. Moreover, although the transitions between layers in the IFA hierarchy are controlled by visual events, the layers themselves encode the degree of observational information provided by the vision system. In short, the layer of execution immediately determines which visual servoing tasks can execute.

3.4 Integrating Vision and Manipulation

If vision-based tracking operated perfectly (and barring physical obstacles), task chains as defined in Section 3.1 would run one link after the other without difficulty. Section 3.3's hierarchy for the vision component would be entirely unnecessary, since tracking would remain at the top layer throughout the task.

In reality, tracking is imperfect, so movement up and down IFA layers is inevitable. When vision runs at a lower layer, some observations are unavailable, and so certain task links are effectively prohibited. This model for vision-action interaction is sufficiently flexible that it can be integrated with a number of robot control models – robots are free to plan, react, backtrack, learn, and do otherwise, just as long as they do not execute prohibited actions.

The simplest approach for a system which is prohibited from proceeding with a subtask due to inadequate vision is to wait for vision to recover. In this case, the task chain is followed in order, with occasional pauses in robot execution.

If actions have a strict ordering of preference, reactive control through action prohibition enables a more proactive approach. Assume that A_i is always preferred over A_j for $i < j$. Then, given an observation, $\mathbf{y}$, the action to execute is the one indexed by $\arg\min_k \left(A_k : \mathbf{E}_k^{\text{init}}(\mathbf{y}) = 0 \right)$. That is, the most preferred task allowed by sensing should be performed. For example, if the manipulated object remains partly visible even if some features are lost, the robot may still continue with a coarse positioning task. This can be seen as a type of reactive behavior [5], where sensory input deterministically triggers one (or more) motor actions.

One can also incorporate open-loop actions which trigger upon entry to a particular layer of the vision system. Open-loop movements are a detour from the task chain. In order to continue, the sensors must observe the results of the open-loop action, y_{ol} and then find a task link for which $\mathbf{E}^{init}(y_{ol}) = 0$. At that point, the system can merge onto the original task chain. Disturbances to the system can be handled similarly.

Finally, classical planning and robot control can be integrated with this paradigm by adding run-time checks and additional preconditions into the planning framework. Run-time checks simply require accurate sensing of relevant portions of the world prior to operation execution. The additional preconditions state that particular perceptual inputs must be available for certain operations to be legal. Initially, planning would proceed as normal, with assumptions that all perceptual conditions are met. Then, at run-time, certain actions may fail because of faulty sensing and enforced prohibitions. At that point the agent may replan, first eliminating those operations which have the failed sensing as preconditions. Under these paradigms, task chains are constantly revised and reconstructed, based on the observables and the planning algorithm.

4 Implementation

This section presents an implementation of the gluing task. Information from the vision system provides the only sensing used in these experiments. Briefly, the workcell setup consists of an IMI Zebra manipulator, and a variety of cameras which supply images to Sun Sparc 10 or Sparc 20 and SGI Indigo workstations running Solaris and Irix.

The task chain for the gluing task consists of three links: (i) a transport motion which brings the syringe from its starting location to within a neighborhood of the target surface, (ii) an alignment to achieve a desired orientation, and (iii) a movement to bring the tip of the applicator to the surface while maintaining vertical alignment.

The vision modules are arranged in layers paralleling these three links. At the bottom of the attentional hierarchy lies a centroid-tracker, based on the color and intensity of the syringe, sufficient for coarse 3 DOF control. Above this, a pair of edge trackers extract the occluding contours of the applicator. With the edge information, two corner trackers can lock onto the top of the syringe. Finally, an SSD region tracker is used to monitor the location of the lower tip of the syringe. Figure 4(right) outlines this hierarchy. Search procedures build up the vision system's set of tracked image fatures from lower-level information. For example, when tracking at the lowest level, the system only searches for parallel edges which are approximately equidistant from the syringe's centroid. The goal point, an arm of a small fastener, is also tracked using an SSD tracker.

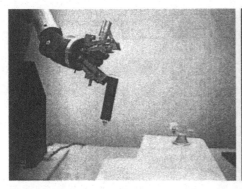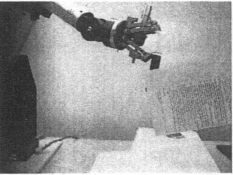

Fig. 5. Left: The starting configuration of the robot and the syringe in an adhesive-application task. **Right:** A 3 DOF reaching motion continues, even without complete state information (the applicator tip and edges are occluded), because partial information (the centroid of the syringe) is available.

Initially, the syringe, grasped by the robot end-effector, is held steady while tracking bootstraps itself through IFA's layers. Figure 5(left) shows the starting position of the robot. Once both cameras supply consistent estimates of the syringe's centroid, the prerequisites for the first level in the manipulation hierarchy are satisfied, and transport motion begins. A setpoint constructed above the goal point (using pixel columns, rather than an external cue to indicate vertical alignment) with a coarse tolerance serves as the goal of the reaching motion. As the syringe approaches the fastener, the vision system continues to try to improve its estimation of its state, *i.e.*, searching to initialize the edge and SSD trackers. Even if the edges and tip are found and subsequently lost through temporary occlusion (Figure 5(right)), the motion proceeds because the vision system is providing sufficient information (a centroid estimate) to perform the current subtask.

When the syringe is above the target surface, the manipulation system checks to be sure that the central axis of the applicator is being estimated. If not, motion stops and visual search proceeds until the edges are found. When the central axis (as the average of the occluding contours [21]) is found, the manipulation enters the alignment phase, in which the syringe is servoed to an upright position. The final approach to the fastener is prohibited until both images provide the additional visual information of the target point (via SSD trackers) and applicator tip (with corners). Figure 6(left) shows the locations of the blob tracker and the two SSD trackers before descent begins; the tracker of the applicator tip has slid slightly to the left. If one of the trackers fails entirely, the action ceases until visual recovery occurs. When the final configuration is reached (Figure 6 (right)), the manipulation system switches state and waits. At this point an open-loop motion to apply adhesive to the surface would be executed.

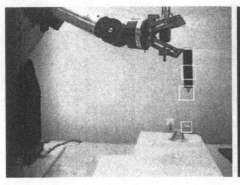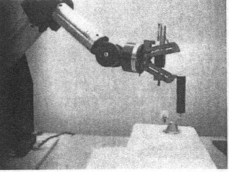

Fig. 6. Left: The states of the SSD trackers of the syringe tip and goal point are shown after the alignment phase of the task. The upper square is centered at the current centroid estimate provided by the syringe's blob tracker. **Right:** The final configuration.

Nonmanipulative Applications One of the benefits of designing a component-based real-time vision system is its ability to transfer to disparate applications. XVision and the IFA framework have been successfully applied to such pure tracking tasks as robust face localization [43], robot navigation [20], and six DOF pose estimation for human-computer interaction through a known calibration object (the "surfball") [44]. These examples testify to the flexibility and ease-of-use of the vision system architecture.

5   Conclusions

We have presented a vision system which enables robust hand-eye manipulation tasks. Both the vision and control frameworks abstract low-level processing away from algorithmic details. The vision hierarchy explicitly incorporates on-line performance assessment, and the control hierarchy allows efficient planning and replanning of tasks based on available observation. The compositional structure balances the need for performance, gained through task-specialization, with the generality of a tool kit based on primitive components that support reuse and modularity. The result is a powerful tool with built-in handling of unmodeled disturbances which can be applied to a variety of tasks.

The XVision system and IFA framework are part of an ongoing project to create a lean, portable vision system for a variety of real-time applications. This research intereacts closely with continuing work on manipulator control, robot navigation, and task specification. Additional functionality currently being investigated includes a probabilistic model for combining trackers based on different modalities (color and contour, for example). Broader problems include autonomous learning of tracking hierarchies, possibly in conjunction with learning a particular manipulation task, and incorporation of algorithms for image-to-model feature matching to link 2D and 3D *a priori* information.

As demands for flexible and powerful actuation systems grow, the demands on the sensing systems which inform them will likewise increase. In order to handle the spectrum of system concerns – from low-level servoing to control in the face of unmodeled events – vision architectures must balance task-specificity and domain-generality. The principles of composition of primitive components and continuous performance evaluation and adjustment lay a necessary foundation for a vision system which supports practical and general hand-eye tasks.

Acknowledgements This work was supported by National Science Foundation grant IRI-9420982 and EIA-9805817, ARPA grant DAAE07-98-C-L031, and by funds provided by Yale University.

References

1. P.K. Allen, B. Yoshimi, and A. Timcenko. Hand-eye coordination for robotics tracking and grasping. In K. Hashimoto, editor, *Visual Servoing*, pages 33–70. World Scientific, 1994.
2. R. L. Anderson. Dynamic sensing in a ping-pong playing robot. *IEEE Trans. Robot. Automat*, 5(6):723–739, December 1989.
3. M. Asada, K. Hosoda, and S. Suzuki. Vision-based learning and development for emergence of robot behaviors. In *Proc. of Symp. on Emergent Systems*, pages 16–22, 1997.
4. A. Blake, R. Curwen, and A. Zisserman. Affine-invariant contour tracking with automatic control of spatiotemporal scale. In *Proc. Internal Conf. on Computer Vision*, pages 421–430. IEEE Computer Society Press, 1993.
5. R. A. Brooks. Intelligence without representation. *Artificial Intelligence*, 47:139–159, 1991.
6. A. Castano and S. A. Hutchinson. Visual compliance: Task-directed visual servo control. *IEEE Trans. Robot. Automat*, 10(3):334–342, June 1994.
7. F. Chaumette, E. Malis, and S. Boudet. 2-D 1/2 visual servoing with respect to a planar object. In *Workshop on New Trends in Image-Based Robot Servoing*, pages 45–52, 1997.
8. F. Chaumette, P. Rives, and B. Espiau. Classification and realization of the different vision-based tasks. In K. Hashimoto, editor, *Visual Servoing*, pages 199–228. World Scientific, 1994.
9. W.Z. Chen, U.A. Korde, and S.B. Skaar. Position control experiments using vision. *Int. J. of Robot Res.*, 13(3):199–208, June 1994.
10. Jiyoon Chung and Hyun S. Yang. Fast and effective multiple moving targets tracking method for mobile robots. In *IEEE Int. Conf. Robotics Automat.*, pages 2645–2650, Nagoya, Japan, May 1995.
11. P. I. Corke. Visual control of robot manipulators—a review. In K. Hashimoto, editor, *Visual Servoing*, pages 1–32. World Scientific, 1994.
12. M. W. Eklund, G. Ravichandran, M. M. Trivedi, and S. B. Marapane. Adaptive visual tracking algorithm and real-time implemenation. In *IEEE Int. Conf. Robotics Automat.*, pages 2657–2662, Nagoya, Japan, May 1995.
13. B. Espiau, F. Chaumette, and P. Rives. A New Approach to Visual Servoing in Robotics. *IEEE Trans. on Robotics and Automation*, 8:313–326, 1992.
14. J. Faymann, E. Rivlin, and H. I. Christensen. A system for active vision driven robotics. pages 1986–1992, April 1996.
15. J.T. Feddema, C.S.G. Lee, and O.R. Mitchell. Weighted selection of image features for resolved rate visual feedback control. *IEEE Trans. Robot. Automat*, 7(1):31–47, February 1991.

16. G. D. Hager. A modular system for robust hand-eye coordination. DCS RR-1074, Yale University, New Haven, CT, June 1995. Accepted to appear in IEEE Trans. on Robotics and Automation.

17. G. D. Hager and P. N. Belhumeur. Efficient region tracking of with parametric models of illumination and geometry. To appear in IEEE PAMI., April 1997.

18. G. D. Hager and Z. Dodds. A projective framework for constructing accurate hand-eye systems. In *Proc. IROS Workshop on New Trends in Image-based Robot Servoing*, pages 71–82, 1997.

19. G. D. Hager and K. Toyama. The "XVision" system: A general purpose substrate for real-time vision applications. *Comp. Vision, Image Understanding.*, 69(1):23–27, January 1998.

20. G. D. Hager, K. Toyama, W. Feiten, and B. Magnussen. Modeling and control for mobile manipulation in everyday environments. Technical Report TR-1137, Yale University, New Haven, CT, 1997.

21. G. D. Hager, J. Wang, and K. Toyama. Servomatic: A modular approach to robust positioning using stereo visual servoing. In *Proc. Conf. on Robotics and Automation*, pages 2636–2641, 1996.

22. K. Hashimoto. LQ optimal and nonlinear approaches to visual servoing. In K. Hashimoto, editor, *Visual Servoing*, pages 165–198. World Scientific, 1994.

23. J. Hespanha, Z. Dodds, G. D. Hager, and A. S. Morse. What tasks can be performed with an uncalibrated stereo vision system? Submitted for review to IJCV, November 1997.

24. K. Hosoda and M. Asada. Versatile visual servoing without knowledge of true jacobian. In *IEEE Int. Workshop on Intelligent Robots and Systems*, pages 186–191. IEEE Computer Society Press, 1994.

25. M. Jagersand, O. Fuentes, and R. Nelson. Acquiring visual-motor models for precision manipulation with robot hands. In *Proc., ECCV*, 1996.

26. M. Jagersand, O. Fuentes, and R. Nelson. Experimental evaluation of uncalibrated visual servoing for precision manipulation. In *Proc., ICRA*, pages 2874–2880, 1997.

27. H. Kass, A. Witkin, and D. Terzopoulos. Snakes: Active contour models. *Int. Journal of Computer Vision*, 1:321–331, 1987.

28. D. Koller, J.W. Weber, and J. Malik. Robust multiple car tracking with occlusion reasoning. In *Proc. European Conf. on Computer Vision*, pages A:189–196, 1994.

29. J. Kosecka, H. Christensen, and R. Bajcsy. Discrete event modeling and visually guided behaviors. *IJCV*, 14:179–191, 1995.

30. Demian M. Lyons. Representing and analyzing action plans as networks of concurrent processes. *IEEE Transactions on Robotics and Automation*, 9(7):241–256, 1993.

31. N. Maru, H. Kase, A. Nishikawa, and F. Miyazaki. Manipulator control by visual servoing with the stereo vision. In *IEEE Int. Workshop on Intelligent Robots and Systems*, pages 1866–1870. IEEE Computer Society Press, 1993.

32. D. Murray and A. Basu. Motion tracking with an active camera. *IEEE Trans. Pattern Anal. Mach. Intelligence*, 16(5):449–459, May 1994.

33. B. Nelson and P. K. Khosla. Increasing the tracking region of an eye-in-hand system by singularity and joint limit avoidance. In *Proc. IEEE Int. Conf. Robot. and Automat.*, pages 418–423. IEEE Computer Society Press, 1993.

34. P. Prokopowicz, M. Swain, and R. Kahn. Task and environment-sensitive tracking. Technical Report 94-05, University of Chicago, March 1994.

35. C. Rasmussen and G. D. Hager. Joint probabilistic techniques for tracking multi-part objects. to appear in CVPR 98, November 1998.

36. C. Rasmussen, K. Toyama, and G. D. Hager. Tracking objects by color alone. In *Proceedings of the Workshop on Applications of Computer Vision*, 1996. Submitted.

37. A.A. Rizzi and D. E. Koditschek. Further progress in robot juggling: The spatial two-juggle. In *Proc. IEEE Int. Conf. Robot. and Automat.*, pages 919–924. IEEE Computer Society Press, 1993.

38. C. Samson, M. Le Borgne, and B. Espiau. *Robot Control: The Task Function Approach.* Clarendon Press, Oxford, England, 1992.

39. J. Shi and C. Tomasi. Good features to track. In *Proc. IEEE Conf. Comp. Vision and Patt. Recog.*, pages 593–600, 1994.

40. S. B. Skaar, W. H. Brockman, and W. S. Jang. Three-dimensional camera space manipulation. *Int. J. of Robot Res.*, 9(4):22–39, 1990.

41. C.E. Smith, S.A. Brandt, and N.P. Papnikolopoulos. Controlled active exploration of uncalibrated environments. In *Proc. IEEE Conf. Comp. Vision and Patt. Recog.*, pages 792–795. IEEE Computer Society Press, 1994.

42. M. Tonko, K. Schafer, F. Heimes, and H.-H. Nagel. Towards visually servoed manipulation of car engine parts. In *IEEE Proc. Int. Conf. on Robotics and Automation*, 1997.

43. K. Toyama. *Robust Vision-based Object Tracking.* PhD thesis, Yale University, 1997.

44. K. Toyama. The surfball. Technical report, Yale University, http://www.cs.yale.edu/ HTML/ YALE/ CS/ HyPlans/ toyama/ surfball/ surfball.html, 1997.

45. L.E. Weiss, A.C. Sanderson, and C.P. Neuman. Dynamic sensor-based control of robots with visual feedback. *IEEE J. Robot. Automat.*, RA-3(5):404–417, Oct. 1987.

46. S.W. Wijesoma, D.F.H Wolfe, and R.J. Richards. Eye-to-hand coordination for vision-guided robot control applications. *Int. J. of Robot Res.*, 12(1):65–78, 1993.

47. W.J. Wilson. Visual servo control of robots using kalman filter estimates of robot pose relative to work-pieces. In K. Hashimoto, editor, *Visual Servoing*, pages 71–104. World Scientific, 1994.

Appendix

Servoing Primitives

Point-to-Point Positioning Given a fixed reference point p^* and a point p rigidly attached to the end-effector, we want to develop a regulator that positions the end-effector so that $p = p^*$. The corresponding feature-based task error function is

$$T_{pp}(p; p^*) = p - p^*. \tag{5}$$

Because two points not on the camera baseline are coincident in space if and only if their stereo projections are coincident, an image-based encoding which verifies the point-to-point task function (outside of singular configurations) is

$$\mathbf{E}_{pp}(\mathbf{y}) = \mathbf{y} - \mathbf{y}^*, \tag{6}$$

where $\mathbf{y} = (y_{lx}, y_{ly}, y_{rx}, y_{ry})$, the row and column coordinates in the left and right camera and $\mathbf{y}^*$ is the similarly-parametrized observation of the designated reference point.

Point-to-Line Positioning Suppose we are given a reference line in Cartesian space, L, specified by a point on the line, L_d, and a vector in the direction of the line, L_v. With a point p rigidly on the robot end-effector, we want to develop a regulator that positions the arm so that $p \in L$. The corresponding task error function is given by

$$T_{pl}(p; L) = (p - L_d) \times L_v. \tag{7}$$

We let $\mathbf{y} = (l; y)^T$, $l = (l_l\ l_r)^T$, and $y = (y_l\ y_r)^T$ represent the image projections of L and p, respectively, where l_l and l_r represents the line by the normal vector to a plane defined by the line and the camera center, and the points in y are in homogeneous coordinates. Then, an image-based encoding verifying T_{pl} results from the observation that for arbitrary L (not in the epipolar plane containing p), $l_l \cdot y_l = l_r \cdot y_r = 0$ if and only if $p \in L$. Thus, we define $\mathbf{E}_{pl}$ as:

$$\mathbf{E}_{pl}(y; l) = \begin{bmatrix} y_l \cdot l_l \\ y_r \cdot l_r \end{bmatrix}. \tag{8}$$

An equivalent image encoding can be defined by representing the line as 2 points and expressing Eq. 7 directly in left and right image coordinates.

A composition example Now, consider the gluing example from Section 2.1. Let the observation of the nozzle tip be denoted by y_{tip}, the target point by y^*, and the top of the syringe by y_{top}. A line in a known relative pose (perhaps observed on a nearby object), l_{vis}, can be used to hallucinate a target line, l^*, should no vertical cue exist at y^*. The resulting image encoding of the composite task is

$$\mathbf{E}(y_{\text{tip}}; y_{\text{top}}; y^*; l_{\text{vis}}) = \begin{bmatrix} y_{\text{tip}} - y^* \\ y_{\text{top}} \cdot tr(l_{\text{vis}}) \end{bmatrix} \tag{9}$$

Here, tr is an affine translation of its argument in image space; its use is justified so long as an affine visual approximation is valid.

Optimal Image Processing Architecture for Active Vision Systems

Peter Krautgartner, Markus Vincze

Institute of Flexible Automation, Vienna University of Technology
Gusshausstrasse 27-29, 1040 Vienna, Austria
{pk, vm}@flexaut.tuwien.ac.at

Abstract. *In this paper the tracking performance of visual fixation control systems is evaluated in terms of the image processing architecture applied. The configurations evaluated are serial or parallel image acquisition and processing, and pipeline processing. The performance measure is the maximum change in velocity of the target in the image that can be tracked within the window observed. The basis of the evaluation is the design of an optimal controller with respect to a performance metric. This controller yields an equivalent transient response behavior for different latencies within the visual feedback system. Applying this controller a relation between system latency and maximum pixel error is derived. This maximum pixel error defines the window size necessary for not loosing the target. The window size, in turn, is directly related to the processing time. This dependence is used to find the dynamic performance for all the system configurations. The final comparison shows that processing in a pipeline obtains highest velocity due to high cycle rate of the system. The parameters for the point of maximum velocity of the pipeline structure are derived.*

1. Introduction

Vision-based control has been a challenging discipline for the last two decades. Vision and robotics researchers have constructed several active vision [3], [12] and *visual servoing* systems [8], [10]. In such *vision-based control* systems the goal is to control the pose of a mechanism, i.e., the end-effector of a robot manipulator or a pan/tilt unit, according to the target pose using visual feedback information. One or more cameras can either be fixed within the working space or mounted at the end-effector of the robot or at a pan/tilt unit. The basic difference to the conventional control of motion is the additional latency in the feedback loop. Latency is introduced due to frame time, necessary to obtain and transfer an image or parts of an image, and by processing the image to obtain relevant data which has to be provided for the motion controller.

Latency, arising from the time inevitably necessary for acquiring and processing an image, has great impact on system dynamics. The dynamic performance of *vision-based control* of motion is denoted by the dynamic properties which can be reached.

Within *active vision*, these properties are the velocity the target can have and the acceleration it can make without getting lost. In *visual servoing* tasks the dynamics of steering the robot towards a pre-defined goal are significant.

Processing the entire image is possible for simple tasks such as tracking a region of high contrast [2[, [6]. Most tasks need sophisticated image processing to extract the target, and research in robust vision will add to this additional request for computing power. To utilize these techniques within *vision-based control*, the general approach is to limit processing to small windows [9], [13] or to subsample the entire image to obtain less data which has to be evaluated [7]. The standard method to obtain a high dynamic performance is to reduce processing time, and therefore latency, by applying efficient image processing algorithms and by using powerful computer hardware. A common procedure to compensate for the still remaining latency introduced by the vision system is prediction of the target locations, e.g. after Kalman [14], [15]. The combination of these measures, that is, taking care of time-efficient image processing and overcoming latency by predicting the future target location, usually yields good results.

Various conceptional design cases of the vision system are known, which differ in the processing configuration. A commonly applied configuration is parallel processing, e.g., [15], where image acquisition and image processing are performed in parallel as opposed to a simple sequential treatment when applying a serial processing configuration. Another approach makes use of a pipeline for processing visual data, which nests several loops and leads to a small cycle time of the control system even though at the cost of large latencies, e.g., [1], [11].

However, there still remains a lack of generally applicable rules for the design of *vision-based control* systems, that is, both *active vision* systems and *visual servoing* approaches. As a consequence, the motivation arises to provide 'recipes' for the optimal design of *vision-based control* systems in order to reach the best overall system performance. The optimality concerns the controller design and the selection of the optimal image processing configuration. The term controller design comprises the classical control theory and the inclusion of state estimators and predictors, if needed.

Within *active vision*, the task of gazing at an object of interest by directing a camera towards its centroid will further on be considered and referred to as *fixation*. The systematic investigation of the dynamic performance of *vision-based control* of motion was started in the excellent work of Corke [4]. Corke investigated the demands on a controller for turning the wrist axes of a Puma robot in a *fixation* task. The dynamic performance of *visual tracking* (the vision processing in itself) has been investigated for the first time in [16]. In *visual tracking* the object of interest is tracked by permanently shifting a window of defined size within the entire image. [16] shows that there exists a relationship between the tracking velocity and the window size which, in turn, defines the time needed to interpret the data. This relationship is used to derive the window size for maximum tracking performance.

Starting out from Corke's work, the result of *visual tracking* regarding performance will be extended to the system design of *visual fixation control* systems. It is the aim of this work to formalize the parameters of visual *fixation* systems and to find the system design which gives the best dynamic performance. The systematic analysis of maximum performance relies on careful control loop design with respect to stability and dynamics which can be reached. The basic design cases investigated are serial or parallel image acquisition and image processing, and the effect of a pipeline. Additionally, the case of processing vision data on-the-fly, as, e.g., Corke did [4], is taken into account and compared to the other system architectures.

The paper starts by describing the basic control loop (Section 2) for visual feedback systems. The difference between these vision processing strategies is discussed in Section 3 with respect to the resulting sampling time of the discrete control system. The sampling time affects the dynamic properties of the visual feedback system essentially. A performance metric for fixation tasks is defined in Section 4 and the controller designed accordingly (Section 5). Applying this controller the relation between maximum pixel error and latency is derived (Section 6). By including the relationship between window size and processing time, the different system designs are then compared in order to find the optimal architecture (Section 7). Sofar the mechanism was dynamically considered as a simple unit delay. The effect of treating the dynamics of the controlled mechanism as a second order system is investigated in Section 8. The paper closes with a conclusion and further perspectives in Section 9.

2. Visual feedback System

The goal of fixation is to keep the target in the center of the image plane. As the target motion x_t is not directly measurable it has to be treated as a non-measurable disturbance input [5]. In fixation tasks just 2-DOF[1] of the mechanism have to be controlled. In his thesis [4] Corke realized fixation by turning the wrist axis of a Puma robot. Fixation can also be achieved by simply mounting a camera on a commercially available pan/tilt unit and then directing gaze at the object of interest. In either case the rotation of the two axes can be decoupled[2]: a deviation of the image plane location of the target from the image plane center in x-direction causes the horizontal gaze direction to be adapted (pan), whereas an error in y-direction requires the second rotational axis to be turned (tilt). Therefore we will further examine just the 1-DOF visual feedback control and expand the results obtained to the 2-DOF fixation task. Fig. 1 shows the block diagram of the 1-DOF fixation control.

The controlled variable is the image plane pixel error ΔX which should approach zero. The blocks marked by $V(z)$, $C(z)$, and $R(z)$ constitute the discrete transfer functions of the vision system, the feedback controller, and the mechanism (robot or pan/tilt unit), respectively. As the vision system $V(z)$ provides a position error ΔX which is transformed to a velocity demand $\dot{x}_d$ by the controller $C(z)$, an integrator

---

[1] DOF: degree(s) of freedom.

[2] Provided that the target is fixated in the center of the image plane. Otherwise second order terms will slightly affect the idealization of decoupling.

must generate a position setpoint x_d for the control of the axis. This integration is performed in Cartesian space where Cartesian velocity is integrated and the corresponding joint position is obtained by inverse kinematics.

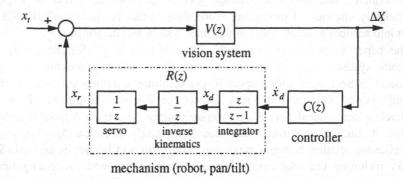

mechanism (robot, pan/tilt)

Fig. 1. Detailed block diagram of the 1-DOF control.

The servo unit of the mechanism is ideally treated as a unit delay. This is justified by the assumption that the underlying position loop has a higher sampling rate than the vision system and therefore an interpolation of the position setpoint is possible. Assuming, e.g., that the servo rate of the mechanism is 10 times the sampling rate of the discrete control system depicted in Fig. 1, the servo controller linearly interpolates between successive position setpoints tenfold. Under the assumption that the interpolated motion requests remain within the velocity and acceleration limits of the axis, the servo will reach the position setpoint within one sampling interval and may thus be modeled as pure unit delay. Corke showed [5] that this simplification is appropriate and gives good results. One further unit delay represents the time needed for the integration, inverse kinematics, and eventual transfer times inherent in the feedback loop of the vision-based control system. These additional delays are combined in the block *'inverse kinematics'* of Fig. 1. When assigning these further delays to the mechanism, it results in a latency of the mechanism of two unit delays.

Generally speaking, the vision system introduces n unit delays, one for acquiring the image and the other $n-1$ for processing the data. Thus the transfer function of the vision system is

$$V(z) = \frac{k_v}{z^n} \qquad (1)$$

where k_v constitutes the gain which relates the target pose to an image plane displacement. This gain describes the projection rule from 3D-space onto the image plane including the inter pixel scaling factor of the camera array.

The resulting closed-loop transfer function of the image plane error as a reaction to the target motion can be written as

$$F_w(z) = \frac{\Delta X(z)}{x_t(z)} = \frac{k_v \cdot z \cdot (z-1)}{z^{n+1} \cdot (z-1) + k_v \cdot C(z)}. \qquad (2)$$

The transfer behavior stated in eq. (2) will be the basis for the subsequent performance investigation of visual fixation control. The main objective is tracking an object, referred to as *pursuit* or *pursuing*, ideally assuming that the target is initially identified in the center of the image and then fixated. The case of turning the camera in order to compensate for any deviation from the center of the image at the beginning of the fixation process (*saccading*) is not taken into account here.

3. Comparison of Different Vision Strategies

To be able to compare different system configurations with each other, the resulting differences regarding the sampling time T of the discrete control system of Fig. 1 must be investigated. The four different configurations which will be considered are parallel, serial, pipeline processing, and processing vision data on-the-fly as, for example, [4] did. Fig. 2 shows the four cases pointing out image acquisition time t_{ac} and image processing time t_p.

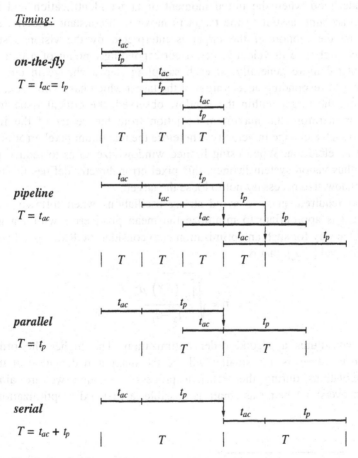

Fig. 2. On-the-fly, parallel, serial, and pipeline processing system.

In each case arises a corresponding sampling time T of the discrete control system. Apart from processing data on-the-fly, where processing time is defined to last as long as the image acquisition takes, in Fig. 2 processing time is assumed to be twice as long as acquisition time. For the latter three cases this results in a latency introduced by the vision system of three times the acquisition time. The arrows mark the time instant when the processed data is available for further use, e.g., for placing a window of defined size within the entire image depending on the computed feature location.

4. Performance Metrics

Performance metrics often applied to dynamic control design are, for example, settling time or overshoot of unit step responses. In case of fixation control, a more appropriate metric to evaluate the performance of following a target is to consider a ramp input, i.e., a constant velocity motion profile of the target. The rationale can be easily understood when the initial moment of target identification and fixation is taken into account: assuming the target to move with constant velocity, at the first time instant the motion of the target is interpreted by the vision system as an instantaneous change in velocity, i.e., a corresponding amount of acceleration (see Fig. 3). Stated more generally, at each sampling step a change in target velocity stands for a corresponding acceleration of the target which has to be tracked. In order not to loose the target within the window observed, the critical issue for fixation behavior is therefore the maximum deviation from the center of the image as a reaction to such a change in velocity. Therefore the maximum pixel error is a measure for target acceleration. When using limited window size so as to reduce processing time and thus vision system latency, this pixel error directly defines the lower limit for the window size necessary not to loose the target.

Another requirement is to avoid strong oscillations when following the target. Therefore it is appropriate to minimize the mean pixel error within a given time interval. One way for such an optimization is to consider the RMS[1] pixel error η over the time interval $[t_1, t_2]$, that is

$$\eta = \sqrt{\frac{\int_{t_1}^{t_2} (\Delta X)^2 \, dt}{t_2 - t_1}} \tag{3}$$

which constitutes a second order optimization. The higher the order of the performance criteria is, the smaller will be the maximum deviation at the cost of larger oscillations during the transient process. Although we are aiming at a maximum overshoot being as small as possible, a first order optimization, i.e., the

---

[1] RMS: random least square.

absolute value of the mean deviation over a given time interval,

$$\eta = \frac{\int_{t_1}^{t_2} |\Delta X| \, dt}{t_2 - t_1}, \tag{4}$$

seems to be more appropriate. The main advantage of the latter metric is the much smoother oscillation behavior than resulting from that one given by eq. (3). Therefore we choose to design the controller with respect to the mean performance metric given by eq. (4).

Fig. 3 shows the difference between these two performance metrics when reacting to a ramp input signal x_r, that is, a constant velocity of the target, which is taken as input to the visual feedback system depicted in Fig. 1. The image plane pixel error ΔX shall approach zero as soon as possible. The controllers applied are designed according to the considerations which will be made in the subsequent Section 5. These controllers are tuned in a way so as to optimize the dynamic response curves with respect to the corresponding performance metric.

The latency introduced by the mechanism itself is assumed as 2 unit delays (see Fig. 1), i.e., *40ms* for a sampling time of *20ms*. The vision system is assumed to introduce 2 unit delays, one for acquiring and one for processing the image.

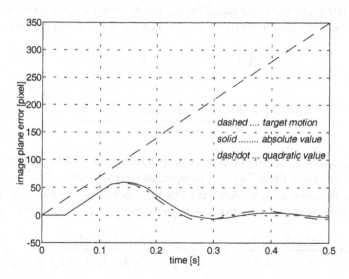

Fig. 3. Dynamic response to a ramp input depending on performance metric for controller design. Vision system: $V(z)=700/z^2$.

One can clearly observe that the system optimized with respect to the RMS performance metric given in eq. (3) shows less overshoot, that is, a smaller maximum pixel error in the image plane. However, this is reached at the cost of stronger oscillations as already theoretically stated before.

5. Controller Design

In Section 4 we have derived a performance metric appropriate for our task of dynamic performance investigation in visual fixation tasks. Now this metric will be used to find the optimal controller for the visual feedback system which has been derived in Section 2.

In Section 5.1 we will first choose an appropriate control structure for the 1-DOF control circuit depicted in Fig. 1. With respect to the performance metric selected, this controller will then be optimized for different latencies in the visual feedback system in Section 5.2.

5.1. Theoretical Considerations

A constant velocity motion profile of the target was defined for the evaluation of dynamic performance of visual fixation control systems. In order to provide a ramp following behavior without any steady-state error, a double integrator in the open-loop transfer function is necessary, referred to as a Type 2 system in classical control theory. This can be accomplished by adding open-loop integrators to the consisting controlled system. Since the visually controlled system consists of just one integrator one further integrator has to be added for the steady-state tracking error of zero. This can be achieved by a classical PID-controller with the discrete transfer function

$$C(z) = k_P + k_I \frac{zT}{z-1} + k_D \frac{z-1}{zT} \tag{5}$$

$$= \frac{z^2\left(k_P T + k_I T^2 + k_D\right) - z\left(k_P T + 2k_D\right) + k_D}{z(z-1)T} \tag{6}$$

where k_P, k_I, and k_D are the proportional, integral and derivative gains respectively and T is the sampling time. The two compensator zeros can be chosen according to the dynamic behavior desired. Applying this PID-controller, the closed-loop transfer function of the vision-based control task depicted in Fig. 1 can be written now as

$$F_W(z) = \frac{\Delta X(z)}{x_t(z)} = \frac{V(z)}{1 + F_O(z)} = \frac{k_V \cdot z^2 \cdot (z-1)^2}{z^{n+2} \cdot (z-1)^2 + k_C \cdot k_V \cdot (z-z_1) \cdot (z-z_2)}. \tag{7}$$

k_C is the compensator gain, that is,

$$k_C = \frac{k_P \cdot T + k_I \cdot T^2 + k_D}{T} \tag{8}$$

and z_1 and z_2 constitute the compensator zeros which can be chosen freely within certain limits.

Another way to obtain a Type 2 system would be the addition of one simple open-loop integrator. This method fails because of the inherent tendency of a double

339

integrator to become unstable without any further compensation. The application of more sophisticated controllers such as Smith's predictor or state feedback controllers with integral action for arbitrary pole placement is also possible. These techniques are thoroughly investigated in [4] for their application in visual feedback systems.

5.2. Parameter Optimization

The optimal free parameters of a PID-controller, i.e., the compensator gain and the zeros, are investigated now for different latencies in the control loop. The controller design is carried out with the aid of the root-locus method by Evans. The problem with a double integrator in the open-loop transfer function is the inherent tendency to become unstable. On the other hand this double integrator is necessary for ramp following behavior with a steady-state error to become zero. Directly applying the root-locus method in the discrete-time domain, the two zeros of the PID-compensator can be used to bend the root locus inside the unit circle which corresponds to the stability of the closed-loop system. A proper selection of the open-loop gain then yields the optimality of the closed-loop system with respect to the performance metric of eq. (4). To demonstrate the optimization process for a given vision system $V(z)=k_v/z^2$, Fig. 4 shows the resulting root-locus arms for different combinations of the two controller zeros.

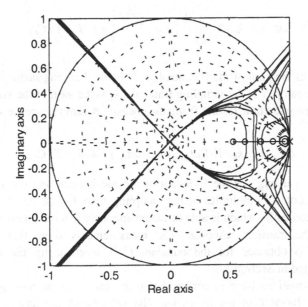

Fig. 4. Root-locus plot of the fixation control; vision system $V(z)=k_v/z^2$; mechanism: 2 unit delays; PID-controller: $z_1=0.53$, _0.63_, $z_2=0.76$, _0.86_, 0.96.

The stars and the circles mark the poles and the zeros of the open-loop transfer function, respectively. The crosses indicate the optimal open-loop gain $k_O = k_v \cdot k_C$ for this setup. The transient disturbance behavior of the closed-loop system using this optimized controller has been shown in Fig. 3. In contrast to the work in [5] the controller is designed to obtain a closed-loop system without a dominant pole pair. This yields a better maximum dynamic performance, that is, a smaller maximum pixel error at the expense of small oscillations.

6. Image Plane Error vs. Latency

Now we want to derive an optimality criterion for the dynamic performance as a reaction to a given latency in the visual feedback loop. Therefore it is necessary to find a mathematic relation between latency and measured (optimal) image plane error.

Two different approximations have been investigated:

- The first approximation is based on the assumption that a P-controlled system leads to the same dynamic behavior, i.e., maximum image plane error ΔX as reaction to a ramp input, as the PID-controlled system, provided that the damping factors D of both systems are the same. The difference between a P- and a PID-controlled system is that when using a P-controller there remains a steady-state error. The image plane pixel error ΔX_I is a result of the steady-state error and the amount of overshoot of a P-controlled system and can be written as

$$\Delta X_I = k \cdot k_V \cdot T \cdot \frac{1}{k_C} \cdot \left(1 + e^{-\frac{\pi \cdot D}{\sqrt{1-D^2}}} \right) = k \cdot k_V \cdot T \cdot C_I ; \tag{9}$$

where k_C is the gain of the P-controller, D is the damping factor, k is the rising factor of the ramp, T is the sampling time, and k_V is the gain of the vision system.

- Another approximation results from the measured ramp response curves and is given by

$$\Delta X_{II} = k \cdot k_V \cdot T \cdot \left(lat_{Mech} + C \cdot lat_{Vis} \right) = k \cdot k_V \cdot T \cdot C_{II} ; \tag{10}$$

where lat_{Mech} and lat_{Vis} are the latencies of the mechanism and the vision system, respectively, denoted as multiples of the sampling time T. The constant factor C is ideally 1 for a controller which is able to instantaneously react to an error without any overshoot in the transient response. The measurements show that a very good approximation is obtained for the constant $C = \frac{9}{8}$ when using the optimal PID-controller selected in Section 5.

Both approximations have in common that the image plane error grows linearly with the rising factor k of the ramp, i.e., the velocity of the target, and with the sampling time T. The terms C_I and C_{II} denote the dependence on latency in the visual control loop. But these two approximations differ in the boundary conditions:

If there exists one dominant closed-loop pole pair the first approximation is well suited (Fig. 5). When using this approximation for the estimation of the dynamic behavior, it has to be guaranteed that this assumption is met. If there does not exist one dominant pole pair the second approximation with the constant $C=^9/_8$ is very precise (Fig. 6). In case of one dominant pole pair this approximation fits well when the factor C is changed to $^{12}/_8$. This means that maximum ΔX is larger, too (see eq. (4)). The two different approximations are depicted in Figs. 5 and 6, where the measured and the approximated ΔX are shown for varying latency in the control loop.

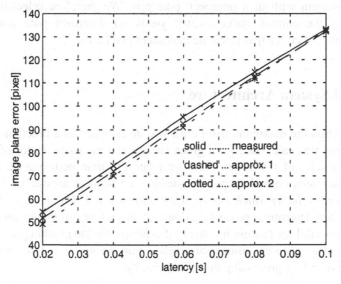

Fig. 5. Measured and calculated image plane error for a system with one dominant pole pair; $k_v=700$, $C=^{12}/_8$.

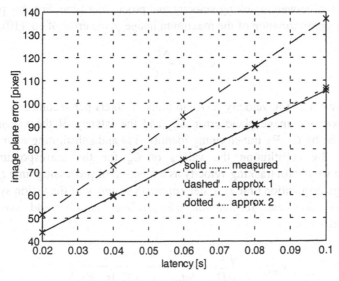

Fig. 6. Measured and approximated image plane error for a system without dominant poles; $k_v=700$, $C=^9/_8$.

The controller applied in Fig. 5 yields one dominant pole pair of the closed-loop system. Therefore approximation 1 yields better results than approximation 2. The results for the case with no dominant pole pair are depicted in Fig. 6. Here approximation 2 is very exact, whereas approximation 1 yields large deviations from the real values. By comparing the measured curves (solid lines) in Figs. 5 and 6, we observe that the image plane error is much smaller for a controller which yields a closed-loop system without a dominant pole pair. We therefore select the optimal controller for the control system which yields no dominant pole pair and the approximation 2 of eq. (10) to calculate maximum pixel error.

7. Optimal System Architecture

In the last section the maximum pixel error was investigated as a function of latency. The pixel error was calculated for a given latency and the rising factor of the ramp, that is the velocity of the target. Now we relate dynamic performance to a given latency in the visual control loop. The question we want to answer is: *What is the maximum target velocity which can be tracked for a given window size?* Remember that window size determines processing time and thus latency of the vision system.

An estimate valid for processing time t_p of common tracking techniques [16] states, that t_p is proportional to the number of pixels within the window. For a window size with the side length $2r$ processing time t_p is given by

$$t_p = 4 \cdot D_{pix} \cdot r^2, \tag{11}$$

where D_{pix} describes the time necessary to evaluate one pixel. The goal is now to derive a relation between tracking velocity and processing time. For this purpose we transform the approximation of the maximum image plane error of eq. (10),

$$k \cdot k_V = \frac{\Delta X_{II}}{T \cdot C_{II}} \tag{12}$$

which shows tracking velocity $k \cdot k_V$ in units of pixels per second as a function of both the maximum image plane error ΔX_{II} and the latency of the visual feedback system denoted by C_{II}. By transforming identity (11) and substituting r for ΔX_{II} in eq. (12), further by substituting the values of C_{II} for the corresponding system configuration we obtain tracking velocity as a function of processing time t_p. Together with the image acquisition time t_{ac}, t_p determines the latency of the vision system. Eqs. (13) to (15) show the results for the pipeline, parallel and serial system configurations.

$$v_{pipe} = \frac{\sqrt{t_p}}{2 \cdot \sqrt{D_{pix}}} \cdot \frac{1}{lat_{Mech} \cdot t_{ac} + C \cdot \left(t_{ac} + t_p\right)} \tag{13}$$

$$v_{par} = \frac{\sqrt{t_p}}{2 \cdot \sqrt{D_{pix}}} \cdot \frac{1}{lat_{Mech} \cdot t_p + C \cdot \left(t_{ac} + t_p\right)}$$

(14)

$$v_{ser} = \frac{\sqrt{t_p}}{2 \cdot \sqrt{D_{pix}}} \cdot \frac{1}{lat_{Mech} \cdot \left(t_{ac} + t_p\right) + C \cdot \left(t_{ac} + t_p\right)}$$

(15)

A special case is processing vision data on-the-fly, where processing time t_p equals acquisition time t_{ac} and image processing is executed during image acquisition. This processing strategy can be attributed to each of the aforementioned cases by just setting processing time t_p to zero (see Fig. 2). To compare this strategy to the other ones, window size must be computed from eq. (11) according to the given processing time. The latter results directly from the constant D_{pix} which constitutes the time required to evaluate one pixel. Further keeping in mind that vision system latency is just one unit delay, together with the resulting factor C_{II} the tracking velocity for the on-the-fly (OTF) processing strategy can be concluded,

$$v_{OTF} = \frac{\sqrt{t_p}}{2 \cdot \sqrt{D_{pix}}} \cdot \frac{1}{\left(lat_{Mech} + C\right) \cdot t_p},$$

(16)

which is twice as large as the tracking velocity of the serial case if processing time equals acquisition time, $t_p = t_{ac}$.

Fig. 7 shows tracking velocity as a function of processing time in all four cases. The image acquisition time is $20ms$ and the entire latency of the mechanism is assumed to be two unit delays as derived in Section 2.

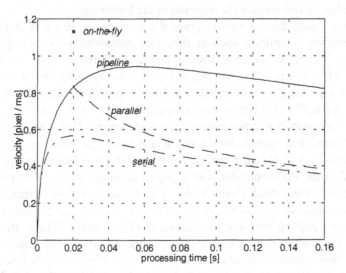

Fig. 7. Tracking performance vs. processing time.
$t_{ac} = 20ms, lat_{Mech} = 2; k_v = 700, D_{pix} = 10^{-6} s.$

When assuming the ideal case that all transfer times and trajectory computation times can be neglected (block 'inverse kinematics' in Fig. 1), the mechanism introduces only one unit delay. The effects on the dynamic performance are depicted in Fig. 8.

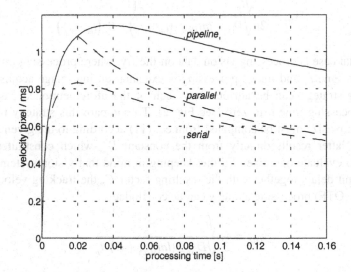

Fig. 8. Tracking performance vs. processing time.
$t_{ac}=20ms$, $lat_{Mech}=1$; $k_v=700$, $D_{pix}=10^{-6}s$.

Obviously the velocity here is higher than in Fig. 7, since the overall latency is smaller. Figs. 7 and 8 are examples of system configurations. Many similar systems can be realized depending on their mechanism and vision latencies. Concerning the various configurations we can always observe the following:

Processing vision data on-the-fly gives the best results. But it is limited to very simple processing algorithms such as threshold operations with subsequent gravity computation. The performance is twice as high as for serial processing which can be easily derived from eqs. (15) and (16) or Fig. 2. The sampling time T of the control circuit in a pipelining system equals the time required for taking one image, t_{ac}, whereas in a parallel or serial system sampling time is a function of the processing time t_p or of acquisition and processing time, respectively. This leads to a completely different dynamic behavior. Although vision latency in a pipeline system is very high, the vision data is available each sampling instant, thus providing an image plane pixel error signal to the PID-controller with a high sampling rate. As a consequence the system is able to react much earlier to an image plane error than comparable parallel or even serial processing systems. In the latter two cases the performance is reduced by the lower sampling rate due to processing of the image. These effects are the reason for the different curves of tracking velocities shown in Figs. 7 and 8. If processing time equals acquisition time, i.e., $t_p=t_{ac}=20ms$, or t_p is becoming even smaller, the parallel case coincides with the pipeline case (see also Fig. 2). For very large processing times the performance of the parallel system comes close to the serial case. This is due to the fact that processing time is rather large in relation to acquisition time.

As demonstrated in Figs. 7 and 8, the maximum tracking velocity is obtained for the pipeline structure. After the differentiation of eq. (13) with respect to t_p we obtain the maximum of tracking velocity when

$$t_{p,opt} = t_{ac} \cdot \frac{lat_{Mech} + C}{C}, \tag{17}$$

which can be verified in Figs. 7 and 8. It shows that best dynamic performance expressed as maximum tracking velocity is obtained when using a pipeline structure with this processing time.

The optimal tracking velocity for both the serial and the parallel processing strategy is obtained when processing time equals acquisition time, that is, $t_p=t_{ac}$. In the serial case this result can be computed directly from eq. (15) as in the pipelining case, whereas for the parallel configuration the resulting optimum of eq. (14) would appear for a processing time which is smaller than the acquisition time. As new data being processed is dependent on the repetition rate of taking new pictures, the lower limit for the sampling time T is defined by the image acquisition time t_{ac}.

8. Mechanism Treated as PT$_2$-System

Sofar, all the investigations make the assumption that the dynamic behavior of the mechanism can be regarded as a simple unit delay (see Fig. 1). If an interpolation of the setpoint (see Section 2) cannot be realized the real dynamics of the servo unit to be controlled have to be considered. Normally, the dynamics of a closed-loop control system can be approximated by a second order system (PT$_2$-system).

In order to introduce the effects of the transient response of such a system into the investigation of dynamic performance of fixation tasks, we have to adapt the identity of eq. (10) which relates the maximum image plane error to the latency in the visual feedback loop. The latency of the mechanism, lat_{Mech}, will be divided now into one unit delay, lat_{InvKin}, and another delay. lat_{InvKin} is still arising from computation and transfer times whereas the other delay is coming from the transient response of the servo unit treated as PT$_2$-element. It seems obvious to consider the output of the servo unit after one sampling period, that is, the value of step response $h(t)|_{t=T}$, for further investigation. The approximation of the image plane error given in eq. (10) can be adapted now to

$$\Delta X_{II} = k \cdot k_V \cdot T \cdot \left(lat_{InvKin} + (2 - h(t)|_{t=T}) + \frac{9}{8} \cdot lat_{Vis} \right). \tag{18}$$

Proceeding as in Section 7, we observe very similar results as obtained when treating the mechanism as a unit delay. The only difference is that the performance curves of all vision strategies are slightly shifted and distorted according to the dynamics of the PT$_2$-system given. Pipeline processing leads again to the best dynamic performance of all visual processing configurations, with the point of maximum tracking velocity computed as

$$t_{p,opt} = t_{ac} \cdot \frac{lat_{InvKin} + \left(2 - h(t)|_{t=T}\right) + C}{C}. \tag{19}$$

The deduction of the effects of dynamically treating the mechanism as a second order system is based on the assumption that the required actuating variable calculated by the underlying axis controller never exceeds the limit given by the power supply unit. If this requirement is not met the axis of the controlled mechanism will have to be modeled exactly by also considering a power limit of the actuating variable.

9. Conclusion and Perspectives

The main objective of this work has been to find the optimal system layout for *visual fixation* control systems. First we have discussed a method of optimal controller design using a performance metric. An RMS optimization has been applied, as well as a simple optimization of the absolute value of the control deviation, that is, the fixation error when tracking a target moving with constant velocity. The maximum tracking velocity has been proven to be definitely related to the overall latency of the visual feedback system. The relationship found has been used to derive the optimal processing architecture for visual fixation tasks. Among all configurations investigated, the pipeline configuration has yielded the best tracking performance, that is, the highest target velocity which can be tracked. Not only the optimal processing strategy but also the point of optimal performance has been determined.

When building visual fixation systems researches should follow the guidelines given in this work concerning the optimal processing strategy in order to obtain best system performance:

⇨ **Pipeline processing gives best performance**

⇨ **A certain number of pipeline steps gives optimal performance**: processing time fixes the window size in which the target is searched for at each cycle.

⇨ **This optimum is independent of processing power**: higher computing power increases window size and thus performance.

⇨ **Optimal system architecture is fixed**: adding computer power for image processing increases the performance without changing the optimal architecture.

The procedure of the performance evaluation proposed is completely independent of the controller applied, as well as of the performance metric defined. In other words, any arbitrary more or less sophisticated controller can be designed without changing the results obtained regarding the optimal visual processing strategy. The same applies to the use of different performance metrics.

As future extension of this work, mainly one further issue needs to be tackled. Sofar, just the visual fixation tasks has been considered. The results obtained with respect to the optimal processing strategy have already been adapted theoretically to the general visual servoing problem in a straight forward fashion. The practical evaluation of the performance of visual servoing will be carried out in the near future.

Acknowledgments

This work is supported by the Austrian Science Foundation (FWF) in the Research Project PORTIME, contract number P11420-MAT.

References

[1] Allen, P.K., Timcenko, A., Yoshimi, B., Michelman, P.: Automated Tracking and Grasping of a Moving Object with a Robotic Hand-Eye System; IEEE Trans. RA Vol.9(2), pp.152-165, 1993.

[2] Anderson, R.L.: Dynamic Sensing in a Ping-Pong Playing Robot; IEEE Trans. RA 5(6), pp.728-739, 1989.

[3] Bajcsy, R.: Active Perception; IEEE Proceedings 76(8), pp. 996-1006, 1988.

[4] Corke, P.I: High-Performance Visual Closed-Loop Robot Control; PhD thesis, Department of Mechanical and Manufacturing Engineering, University of Melbourne, 1994.

[5] Corke, P. I.: Visual Control of Robots: High Performance Visual Servoing, Research Studies Press (John Wiley), 1996.

[6] Corke, P.I., Good, M.C.: Dynamic Effects in Visual Closed-Loop Systems; IEEE Trans. on RA Vol.12(5), pp.671-683, 1996.

[7] Grosso, E., Metta, G., Oddera, A., Sandini, G.: Robust Visual Servoing in 3D Reaching Tasks; IEEE Trans./RA Vol.12(5), pp.671-683, 1996.

[8] Hashimoto, K.: Visual Servoing; World Scientific, 1993.

[9] Hager, G.D., Toyama, K.: XVision: Combining Image Warping and Geometrical Constraints for Fast Visual Tracking, Proc. ECCV, pp. 507-517, 1996.

[10] Hutchinson, S., Hager, G.D., Corke, P.I.: A Tutorial on Visual Servo Control; IEEE Trans. on RA Vol.12(5), pp.651-670, 1996.

[11] Li, F., Brady, M., Hu, H.: Visual Guidance of an AGV; 7th Int. Symp. on Robotics Research, pp.403-415, 1995.

[12] Olson, T.J., Coombs, D.J.: Real-Time Vergence Control for Binocular Robots; Int. J. of Computer Vision Vol.7(1), pp.67-89, 1991.

[13] Rizzi, A.A., Koditschek, D.E.: An Active Visual Estimator for Dexterous Manipulation; IEEE Trans. RA Vol.12(5), pp.697-713, 1996.

[14] Wilson, W.J., Williams Hulls, C.C., Bell, G.S.: Relative End-Effector Control Using Cartesian Position Based Visual Servoing; IEEE Trans. RA Vol.12(5), pp.684-696, 1996.

[15] Wunsch, P., Hirzinger, G.: Real-Time Visual Tracking of 3-D Objects with Dynamic Hand-ling of Occlusion; ICRA, pp.2868-2873, 1997.

[16] Vincze, M., Weiman, C.: On Optimising Window Size for Visual Servoing; ICRA, April 22-24, 1997.

Reactive Computer Vision System with Reconfigurable Architecture

Domingo Benitez and Jorge Cabrera

University of Las Palmas G.C. Dept. Informatica y Sistemas
Campus Universitario de Tafira. 35017 Las Palmas. Spain
{dbenitez,jcabrera}@dis.ulpgc.es

Abstract. In this paper we propose a system architecture which is hardware/software reconfigurable, modular, and intended to be a generic approach to partitioning reactive visual algorithms for implementation on high-performance multiprocessing systems integrated in robotic environments. We present a configurable and flexible parallel perception system that provides a platform for developing applications which allows for experimenting with real-time computer-vision algorithms. An automatic target recognition application using our reconfigurable architecture have been implemented successfully. The paper describes how this reactive application is implemented in a pair of boards based on different technology: a reconfigurable board and a general purpose Pentium board.

1 Introduction

A challenge in the development of reactive vision systems where the same processing is not carried out at any time is to incorporate an optimized technology solution while achieving the highest performance/cost relation. Different technologies have been applied to reactive systems with high demands of processing. These technologies can be grouped in: (a) function specific, (b) programmable, and (c) configurable computing.

The first offers high silicon efficiency with low flexibility and achieves high performance as for example custom VLSI chips or specialized structure modules [14]. Custom pipelined hardware systems implement several fixed processes which, once set up for a particular algorithm, do not allow any change in architecture or connectivity to be made ([8], [11]). These systems usually are very rigid and it is difficult to implement any change in their activity. VLSI solutions may be efficient but are costly and require highly skilled developers in hardware systems.

The programmable technology has high flexibility with low silicon efficiency. It is characterized by its low performance so applications are based on software development, as for instance when used general purpose processors or Digital Signal Processors (DSPs) ([2], [14]).

Many developers of computer-vision applications program multiprocessor systems to achieve high throughput and efficient multiprocessor execution. This technology is less costly when a high level language is exclusively used but reactive response is difficult to achieve for many algorithms. There are several reasons why a multiprocessor system may not achieve required performance on a given application ([16], [1], [2]):

- Mismatch between the parallelism in the algorithm and the multiprocessor architecture.
- Synchronization bottleneck when processors must wait for results from other processors.
- Resource contention when two or more processors need to simultaneously use the same functional resource.
- Clock skew and clock distribution limit the expandability of the system.
- High performance can only be achieved by laborious manual optimization of the code.

Configurable computing systems combine reconfigurable hardware like, for instance, Field Programmable Gate Arrays (FPGAs) or Complex Programmable Logic Devices (PLDs), in conjunction with general purpose programmable processors to capitalize on the strengths of hardware and software. Reconfigurable devices achieve high performance by using massive fine-grain parallelism, fast static communication, and high throughput, and can be configured to user specification. Configurable computing technology includes hardware description languages (for instance VHDL, Verilog, etc.), hardware synthesis tools, and software development tools. These software facilities allow hardware to be configured [3]. Thanks to these advances, some developments previously made on custom VLSI chips have been efficiently developed by using the flexible reconfigurable technology [10].

However, computing models need to be refined into reusable frameworks. Thus far, the abstraction generally exists in the developer's mind and is implemented through ad hoc mechanisms based on local experience and available technology [12]. This could be one of the reasons why configurable technology is costly. So, efficient application development frameworks must be created that allow the developer to quickly and clearly describes the desired organization, function and performance constrains.

Fig. 1 illustrates qualitatively the relationship between performance and flexibility of all mentioned technologies. This model allows a wide range of design choices and one of our research goals is to determine the best resource allocation for active computer-vision applications.

This paper provides an architectural model for reactive computer-vision systems which is based on taking a technological choice which accommodates best to application constrains and moreover, tries to achieve the best performance/cost ratio. Our solution is based on partitioning a "Technological Computer-Vision Space" which is depicted in fig. 2.

The Technological Computer-Vision Space is a general framework for qualitatively depicting the interaction between temporal constrains and functional operations of computer-vision systems in correspondence with possible technological choices used in the implementation as mentioned above. Temporal constrain for real-time applications determines the time for performing an algorithmic operation. These constrains may be classified into: pixel clock, blank interval, image period, and some frames.

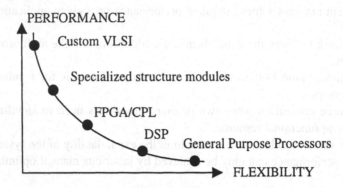

Fig. 1. Performance vs. Flexibility in technologies used by computer-vision systems.

Functional operations are grouped into three levels of algorithmic complexity: low, intermediate, and high. Each operation could be implemented using exclusively either hardware or software. Real-time low-level algorithms are characterized by processing raw input images in order to extract primitive features. These algorithms are easily parallelized because most of the pixel operations are very regular and can be performed using image data in the neighborhood of the pixels. Another main feature is that the image after processing has the same array structure as the input image. Low-level tasks are better adapted to pipeline hardware organization than software procedures [10]. However, this hardware solution imposes an additional system cost which is the result of designing and integrating various methods and recourses to configure all the system.

Intermediate-level algorithms groups low-level features into a hierarchy of increasingly complex and more abstract descriptions. High-level algorithms interpret the intermediate-level descriptions for finding semantic attributes of an image. Both types of algorithms are not regular and are very different from one application to another [16]. Software solutions on Multiple Instruction Multiple Data (MIMD) architectures seems to be adopted extensively. They have also a high cost and do not offer the performance levels demanded by interactive or real-time modes of execution. Larger parallel systems do not automatically yield higher speed ups for vision applications as they do for many of the scientific applications. High processor efficiency for the irregular vision tasks is difficult to achieve and some hardware solution could be adopted.

We propose here an architectural model of computer-vision systems which is intended to be a generic approach to partitioning algorithms for parallel implementation on high-performance multiprocessing platforms integrated in robotic environments. The next section describes this reconfigurable architecture. Section 3 gives a description of the algorithmic operators which are finer-grained representations of the parallel processing. In section 4, it is shown how the architectural model is applied to an automatic target recognition application, and finally some concluding remarks are provided.

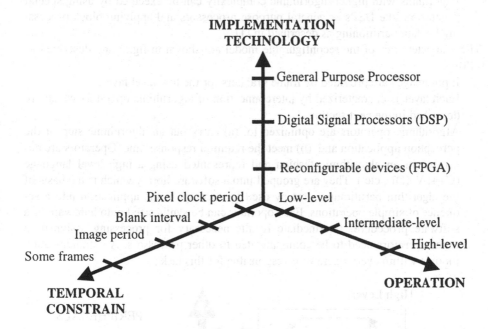

Fig. 2. The Technological Computer-Vision Space.

2 Reconfigurable Architectural Model

We have developed a systematic approach to solving the algorithm partitioning problem for many computer-vision algorithms. Our architectural solution aims at exploiting the flexibility provided by configurable computing and for overcoming the difficulties of using some parallel systems as described in previous section. This architecture is based on the following principles:

- The visual processing can be partitioned into three levels of algorithmic complexity: Low level, Intermediate level, and High level. This is done with the aim of technological mapping the application algorithm onto the Technological Computer Vision Space.
- System structure is hardware/software configured by the algorithm with purpose of reducing software overhead. This inefficient code could be generated by standard compilers in data intensive applications such as those belonging to the computer-vision domain.

- Low level and some intermediate level algorithms are executed by optimized operators that are synthesized onto reconfigurable hardware (CPLD or FPGA). This strategy implements parallelism using concurrence and pipelining.
- Algorithms with higher algorithmic complexity can be executed by using special processors like DSPs or general purpose processors and applying block processing by data partitioning as described in [1].

The characteristics of the reconfigurable model are shown in fig. 3 and described as follows:

- Input images are provided by frame grabbers for the low level layer.
- Each layer is characterized by interconnection of algorithmic operators which are described in the next section.
- Algorithmic operators are optimized to: (a) carry out an algorithmic step of the perception application and, (b) meet the required response time. Operators are described in an algorithmic fashion and represented using a high level language (C++, VHDL, etc.). They are grouped into a software library which is the basis of the algorithm partitioning strategy used to decompose the application into a sequence of simple operations. Each operator can be synthesized onto hardware or a software procedure. Intermediate results necessary for processing assigned to other operators need to be communicated to other processors. A communication module within every operator is responsible for this task.

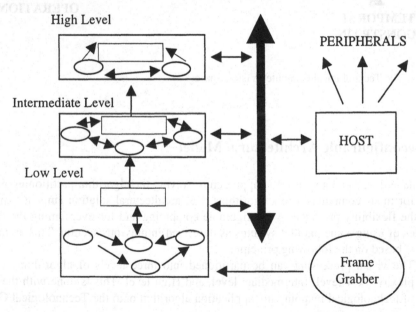

Fig. 3. The reconfigurable architectural model of a computer-vision system.

- There are two different communication protocols between layers and the host. The first one allows the results of processing assigned to each layer to be stored in a shared memory which can be accessed by two adjacent layers. The second protocol allows data to be distributed among layers and host.

- The host is responsible for controlling the peripherals attached to the robotic system.

Block Data Parallel Architecture (BDPA) represents a flexible and high-performance approach to parallel processing used in many digital signal and image processing algorithms [1]. Our reconfigurable architectural model may integrate the BDPA as an algorithmic operator in the low level because BDPA consists of one input module that serves as a buffer, an interconnected array of processors which provides the computational power, and one output module that collect results from the array. Our approach tries to be more general than BDPA extending the partitioning to other algorithmic levels.

As other approaches, our architecture exposes the hardware low-level details to the software which determines the best resource allocation for each approach [15]. However, the reconfigurable architecture is better suited to computer-vision applications because hardware is divided into different levels of algorithmic complexity. This may allow the performance/cost relation to be improved.

3. Algorithmic Operators

Each architectural level is composed of a multi-operator system which is implemented using a technological choice that provides the needed performance for running at the demanded rate. We use the term Algorithmic Operator to denote a set of blocks where all the computations assigned to an algorithmic process are performed. Each operator is characterized by producing whatever result corresponding to its assigned algorithmic process at a constrained execution time. So, we can associate functional operation with temporal constrain within the Technological Computer-Vision Space during a first step in the synthesis process of the architecture (see fig.2). This form of association depending on application is a fundamental part of the reconfigurability principle on which our architecture is based.

The structure of each algorithmic operator evolved from our research on developing computer-vision architectural models [7]. Previously, we proposed an architecture called DIPSA for implementing real-time image processing algorithms [6], and low level algorithmic operators are extensions of this model to accommodate to configurable computing technology. Furthermore, we have experienced that this model can be applied to algorithms of higher complexity. Each algorithmic operator is composed of (see fig.4):

- *Processing Network*. This corresponds to the data path of the algorithmic operator which in turn is composed of a set of processing elements designed and optimized in advance. These elements are parameterized, so their structures are dimensioned in the synthesis process. The processing elements has no control, so the processing network is locally controlled by the control unit. A simple interconnection network with point-to-point connection is sufficient.
- *Control Unit* (C.U.). This module provides the necessary resources for scheduling operations executed in the processing network and the communication port. The control unit is configured by a control program which is described as a finite state

machine using a high level language: VHDL for a reconfigurable platform, and
C++ for general-purpose processors. This module can manage the configuration
process of the processing network by initialising the modules stored in the library
of models. The configuration process is depicted in fig. 4 by dashed lines.

Input and Output Memories. Modules used whenever it is necessary to store input
data to the processing network and intermediate or final results are needed to be
stored. For instance, to be read by the host when the specific real-time processing
has finished, or to execute an algorithm that needs another input data format.

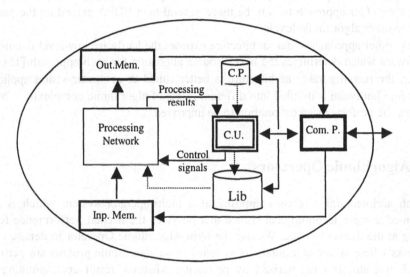

Fig. 4. Structure of an algorithmic operator.

- *Library of Models* (Lib). These parameterized models are described in a high
  level language (C++, VHDL, etc) and are necessary when the processing network
  is set up. This set up process can be both, static before real-time processing or
  dynamic during run time.
- *Control Program* (C.P.). Set of orders needed for the control unit. The specifications of these orders is done during the system set-up phase.
- *Communication Port* (Com.P.). This module allows data and commands to be
  exchanged asynchronously among algorithmic operators and host.

4. Application to Automatic Target Recognition

Automated target recognition (ATR) is a computer-vision application area where
reconfigurable platforms can provide high level of performance [7]. This section
describes a hardware/software mapping experiment using the reconfigurable architectural model of vision system described above. A systolic implementation of an
ATR algorithm is mapped onto a reconfigurable platform from Altera called RIPP10

and a Pentium-based system. The configurable computing board operation is synchronized with other computer-vision system components by software.

The ATR algorithm uses a matching-based technique where an image pattern is detected by its chromatic features as described in [4] and [5]. This pattern is tracked using the coordinates of the corresponding image segment center.

We are based on the assumption that objects are characterized by homogeneous colors. So, given a N x M color digital image provided by the frame grabber, the ATR algorithm has the following steps:

1. Chromatic coordinates of pixels are transformed from R-G-B to I2-I3 [13].
2. Detection of pixels with coordinates I2 and I3 in a specific range.
3. X and Y coordinates and the number of pixels (NCOLOR) with detected color are added.
4. The center of mass is obtained. The sums of X and Y are divided by NCOLOR.
5. Object movement detection by sensing any change in the coordinates of the center of masses.
6. Camera movement control. Direction and velocity of the pan and tilt camera movements are transmitted through the RS-232 serial interface.

Table 1 shows the results of the temporal analysis applied to each algorithm step. Temporal constrains of the operations and the RISC-like instructions [9] needed to execute them generate a performance demand as a function of Millions of Instructions executed Per Second (MIPS).

After analyzing the ATR algorithm we proceed with its implementation by using a computer-vision development system which is shown in fig. 5. It contains the above mentioned reconfigurable board from Altera called RIPP10 with 100.000 gates and 2 MB of SRAM, a Pentium-based personal computer, a color frame grabber from Imaging Technology, and a color video camera with pan and tilt movement control by a serial link from Sony. The frame grabber, the reconfigurable board and the Pentium-board are interconnected through the ISA bus.

Table 1. Analysis of the computational performance required by the real-time ATR algorithm.

Algorithm Step	Temporal constrain	Instructions	Required performance
1	Pixel clock (66,7 ns.)	2 SUB, 1 ADD, 1 SHR	60 MIPS
2	Pixel clock (66,7 ns.)	1 LD	15 MIPS
3	Pixel clock (66,7 ns.)	3 ADD	45 MIPS
4	Blank period (4 µs.)	1 DIV	3 MIPS
5	Image period (40 ms.)	2 IN, 2 ADD, 2 MUL, 2 SUB, 1 ABS, 1 SLT	2475 IPS
6	Image period (40 ms.)	4 DIV, 9 OUT	

Operations from 1 to 4 are executed by Altera's reconfigurable platform. The key to achieving an implementation with real-time performance using the reconfigurable platform is to carefully partition the design into modules. So, our reconfigurable architectural model is suited for this and other stream-based signal-processing applications. The technique used has been to look at the chromatic features by pixel and sum up the spatial coordinates (X,Y) of the detected pixels. After the image has been processed completely, the sum for X and Y are divided by the number of detected pixels (NCOLOR).

In this implementation, each pixel processing is performed in parallel and the final division is carried out during the vertical synchronism interval. This application is actually running with 768 x 512 images at 50 Hz. of frame frequency and 15 MHz. of pixel frequency.

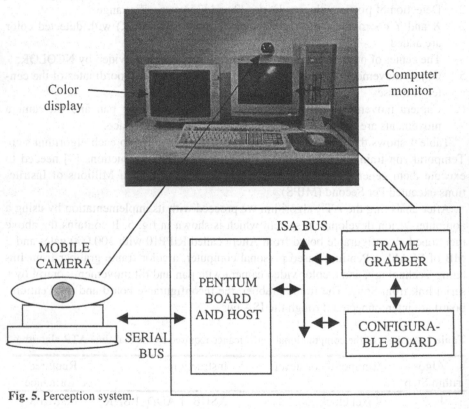

Fig. 5. Perception system.

Fig. 6 depicts the implementation results of the ATR algorithm using the reconfigurable architecture. As can be seen, it is needed two algorithmic operators (P1 and P2). P1 performs a linear chromatic transformation, from the R-G-B color system to I2-I3 (algorithm step 1) followed by a pixel codification in 256 chromatic classes (algorithm step 2). A chromatic code extends in a range within the bi-dimensional I2-I3 space. A Look-Up-Table memory (LUT) stores these codes which are generated in a learning phase using a Radial Basis Function neural network [5]. In a previous set-up phase of the system, the codes are introduced in the LUT. A chromatic code is specified in the set-up phase of the application. In this way, the user can determine the color for target recognition and tracking.

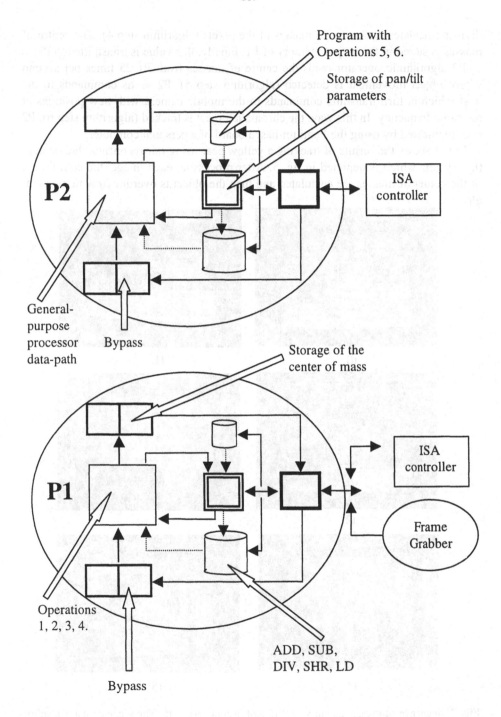

Fig. 6. Implementation of the ATR application using the reconfigurable architecture.

Following these steps, an arithmetic unit calculates the sum of X and Y coordinates coming from the LUT module with a chromatic code (algorithm step 3), and then, a divisor calculates the centre of masses of the pixels (algorithm step 4). The centre of masses is stored in the output memory of P1. Finally, this value is transmitted to P2.

P2 algorithmic operator reads the centre of masses from P1 25 times per second where object movement is detected (algorithm step 5). P2 sends commands to the host which in turn transmits commands to the mobile camera with new positions at the same frequency. In this way, the chromatic object is tracked (algorithm step 6). P2 is implemented by using the Pentium-based board of a personal computer.

Fig. 7 shows the results of tracking a yellow pear using our reconfigurable perception system which is depicted in fig. 5. After processing each image, the coordinates of the center of masses are calculated and then the object is overdrawn with a rectangle.

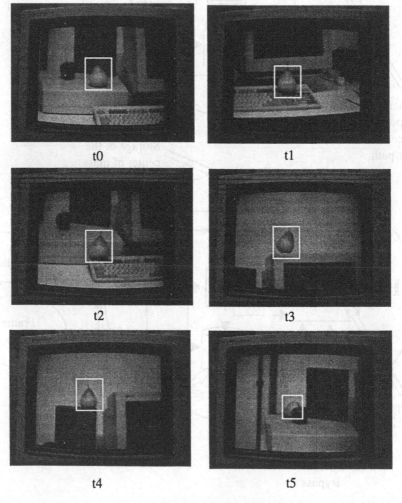

t0 t1

t2 t3

t4 t5

Fig. 7. Sequence of images acquired at different instants: t0, ...,t5. The scene contains a yellow pear which is tracked. This object is overdrawn with a rectangle.

Other computer-vision algorithms can be mapped onto our reconfigurable architecture. For example, convolution algorithms like 2-D FIR filters require only one algorithmic operator and can be implemented in our reconfigurable platform. The input data stream comes from the frame grabber and is stored in the input memory which serves as a FIFO between the input device and the processing network. The specification of the convolution is used to configure the parallel processing network. Individual tasks are described by models grouped into the library of models. Results from processing are collected into the output memory. Finally, the communication port routes synchronously the output data flow out of the algorithmic operator to the host for displaying.

5. CONCLUSIONS

In this paper we focus on refining specialized architectures for synthesizing visual reactive applications in multi-platform computing systems. Experimental results show that the required performance for a computer-vision system may be obtained at a reasonable cost by adapting algorithms and hardware to each other. Our specialized reconfigurable architecture tries to configure different technology-based boards to fulfill computing requirements measured in MIPS. This strategy has been proved to be feasible by explaining how a real-time ATR application is implemented while using the reconfigurable architectural model.

As result of our experience we can conclude that:

- A configurable FPGA/CPLD-based coprocessor presents a flexibility that enables different applications on the same board while ASIC design and configurable hardware development have nearly the same design difficulty.
- VHDL high level language was used for design capture and it permits the narrowing of the gap between software developer and hardware designer but it has been found that the low level abstraction used in configurable devices is still difficult to work with.
- Commercial success of configurable computing systems applied to computer-vision applications could be based on a standard high level programming interface with programmable hardware maintaining performance.
- The architecture presented in this paper can be used as intermediate level between software and configurable hardware.

Acknowledgments

This research was supported in part by the Spanish "Comisión Interministerial de Ciencia y Tecnología" under projects TIC95-0230-C02-01 and TIC98-0322-C03-02 and in part by ALTERA Corporation. The authors thank the reviewers for their comments.

References

1. Alexander, W.E., Reeves, D.S., Gloster Jr., C.S.: Parallel Image Processing with the Block Data Parallel Architecture. Proceedings of the IEEE **84**, 7 (1996) 947-968
2. Baglietto, P., Maresca, M., Migliardi, M., Zingirian, N.: Image Processing on High-Performance Risc Systems. Proceedings of the IEEE **84**, 7 (1996) 917-930
3. Buell, D.A., Arnold, J.M., Kleinfelder, W.J.: Splash 2. IEEE Computer Society Press (1996)
4. Benítez-Díaz, D., Carrabina, J.: Modular Architecture for Custom-Built Systems Oriented to Real-Time Artificial Vision Tasks. EUROMICRO 95. IEEE Computer Society Press (1995) 639-646
5. Benítez-Díaz, D.: Real-Time Vision Processor System with Neural Network for Color Recognition. EUROMICRO 95. IEEE Computer Society Press (1995) 541-547
6. Benitez-Diaz, D.: Modular Architecture for Custom-Built Systems Oriented to Real-Time Computer Vision: Application to Color Recognition. Journal of System Architecture **42**, 8, (1996/97) 709-723
7. Cabrera, J., Hernandez, F.M., Falcon, A., Mendez, J.: Contributions to the symbolic processing of segments in computer vision. Mathware and Soft Computing **3** (1996) 403-413
8. Gilbert, J.M., Yang, W.: A Real-Time Face Recognition System Using Custom VLSI Hardware. Proceedings of the IEEE Workshop on Computer Architecture for Machine Perception. IEEE Computer Society Press (1993) 58-66
9. Hennessy, J.L., Patersson, D.: Computer Architecture. A Quantitative Approach. 2nd edn. Morgan Kaufmann Publishers (1996)
10. Hou, K.M., Belloum, A., Yao, E., Méribout, M., Trihandoyo, A., Li, K., Park, Y.H., Mayorquim, J.L.: Perception Sensor for a Mobile Robot. Real-Time Imaging **3** (1997) 379-390
11. Kubota, H., Okamoto, Y., Mizoguchi, H., Kuno, Y.: Vision Processor System for Moving-Object Analysis. Machine Vision and Applications **7** (1993) 37-43
12. Mangione-Smith, W.H., Hutchings, B., Andrews, D., DeHon, A., Ebeling, C., Hartenstein, R., Mencer, O., Morris, J., Palem, K., Prasanna, V.K., Spaanenburg, H.A.E.: Seeking Solutions in Configurable Computing. Computer (December 1997) 38-43
13. Ohta, Y.: Knowledge-Based Interpretation of Outdoor Natural Color Scenes. Pitman Advanced Publishing Program (1985)
14. Pirsch, P., Demassieux, N., Gehrke, W.: VLSI Architectures for Video Compression-A survey. Proceedings of the IEEE, **83**, 2 (1995) 220-246
15. Waingold, E. , Taylor, M. , Srikrishna, D., Sarkar, V., Lee, W., Lee, V., Kim, J., Frank, M., Finch, P., Barua, R., Babb, J., Amarasinghe, S., Agarwal, A.: Baring It All to Software: Raw Machines. Computer. (September 1997) 86-93
16. Wang, C., Bhat, P.B., Prasanna, V.K.: High-Performance Computing for Vision. Proceedings of the IEEE **84**, 7 (1996) 931-946

MEPHISTO
A *M*odular and *E*xtensible *Path* Planning *Sys*tem Using *O*bservation

Peter Steinhaus, Markus Ehrenmann and Rüdiger Dillmann

Institute of Process Control and Robotics, University of Karlsruhe, Geb. 40.28,
Kaiserstr. 12, 76128 Karlsruhe, Deutschland
{steinhaus,ehrenman,dillmann}@ira.uka.de,
WWW Home Page: http://wwwipr.ira.uka.de/~{steinhau,ehrenman,dillmann}

Abstract. In this paper a scalable architecture with a computer vision subsystem as an integrated part to achieve a fast and robust navigation for almost autonomous mobile systems in dynamic environments is presented. The principal approach is not only using the robots' mobile sensor systems but also some fixed external vision sensors to build the required environment models. The measurements of the mobile and external sensors are fused to improve the quality of the input data. This sensor fusion is done by an active dynamic environment model that also provides an optimised data layer for different path planning systems. To achieve the required system's scalability a distributed approach is followed. Instead of using one big global environment model a distributed redundant environment model is employed to allow easier local path planning and to reduce bottlenecks in data transmission. Thus the path planning system is split to a local path planner and a global planning system.

1 Introduction

Autonomous mobile systems are topic of intensive research projects. Many existing prototypes proved that the principal approach of building mobile systems moving autonomously way in static, changing and really dynamic environments is not a dead end. But at a closer look to all the application fields where these machines could be used like transportation and guidance in airports, railway stations, hotels, malls, factories it can be found that there do not exist many industrial products that really work autonomous. In many factory environments with almost no human interaction or never changing transport ways there are guided vehicles that work stable in these environments but they are not flexible enough to work in dynamic environment like the ones mentioned above. The main problem of the state of the art autonomous mobile systems is that their local sensor systems are not able to acquire enough information about the surrounding environment in a time in which this information is valid. But this kind of information is needed to generate fast plans to guide the machines in dynamic environments where configurations change fast and plans are not valid for a long time. There exist some machines that find their way to their destination by exploring the changed environment. These methods are just effective for building maps of almost never changing environments.

There are innumerable scientific approaches that try to cope with the specific problems of navigating mobile robots through known and unknown environment models. As representatives for these different approaches [4] for potential fields methods, [8] for stochastic planning, [3] for visibility graphs should be mentioned. All of these methods are using the entire global environment for planning and have therefore problems with large scale applications. Another disadvantage of this methodologies is that they do not use currently acquired sensor data. That means they just try to find a path in an environment without having information about the current environment configuration.

As a representative for the set of local path planners working with sensor data [1] is quoted. Mobile visual based navigation as well as laser scanner methods cope with current changes of environment configurations. Unfortunately they are not able to make useful decisions in a global sense because they do not have the required global configuration information.

To solve the problem of navigating in dynamic environments a human behaviour model is needed. A human acquires information about his environment with their biological sensor systems. This means classifying obstacles as static or dynamic, estimating their speed and direction of movement, maybe their destination, but reducing the data just to an extent that is necessary for reaching the goal. In the next step they plan their way using all the gathered information as constraints and then they move, adapting their plan as long as possible.

There do not exist yet any technical sensor systems that can compete with the biological examples, additionally there do not exist any sensor data processing methods as effective as the brain of living beings. However, our work will be oriented at the given example. This means it is tried to acquire just the required information about the environment with technical sensor systems. It is tried to estimate speed and direction of moving obstacles in a short interval of time in the future and search for a good (not optimal) path to the destination.

A solution to this problem can possibly be provided by the use of global or so called external sensor systems that acquire additional information about the whole area in which the mobile system has to operate.

The only existing work known to the authors that takes these ideas into account is the MONAMOVE system, developed until 1995 in Braunschweig, Germany. This navigation concept solves some of the mentioned problems (like to be seen in [2], [6] and [7]) by using ceiling cameras to track mobile systems and obstacles. However the acquired information is just used to build statistics for stochastic path planning algorithms, not for dynamic navigation. Additionally, their system architecture is not scalable, because all the collected sensor data is inserted into one global environment model. This causes bottlenecks and is not very useful for fast planning.

Our approach supposes an architecture that integrates the data of several external sensors and the mobile sensor systems of the robot to improve the quality of the measured sensor data. However, the main advantage of our architecture is its scalability that prevents bottlenecks in communication, data acquisition, processing, environment modelling and planning. In principal the choice of the sensor type and position in this architecture is free but we suppose the use of ceiling mounted color cameras as external sensors and laser scanners as mobile vision sensors.

The general scalable architecture is described in detail in the next section. Section 4 explains some details about the prototype implementation of the system, especially the used robots, cameras and vision systems.

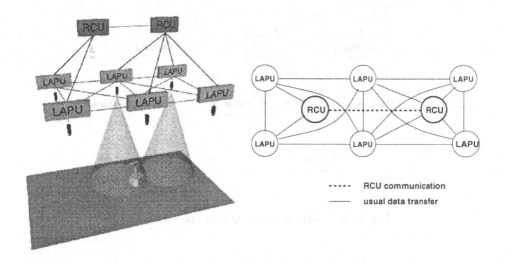

Fig. 1. GAPU with 6 LAPUs and the corresponding topology

2 General Architecture

To fulfil the introduced tasks like acquiring only the needed data, processing the sensor data and finding paths to the destination in a speed that is high enough to get valid paths we have to use parallel processing methods. The use of specialised local area processing units (LAPUs) is proposed that realize the observation of their local area, the update of their local environment model, the short time prediction and the short way planning. Every LAPU is connected to exactly one robot control unit (RCU) that contacts the robots via a radio interface to send commands and receive status messages and preprocessed sensor data. The combination of the LAPUs with their dedicated RCUs is called global area processing unit (GAPU). Figure 1 shows an example of a GAPU with 6 LAPUs and 2 RCUs. There do also exist connections between certain LAPUs.

These are used for global and local planning, environment model enhancement and sensor data fusion. By this parallel approach bottlenecks in sensor data transmission, processing and slow planning in unnecessary big environments is avoided. Additionally the system becomes more redundant and data quality is improved by data fusion.

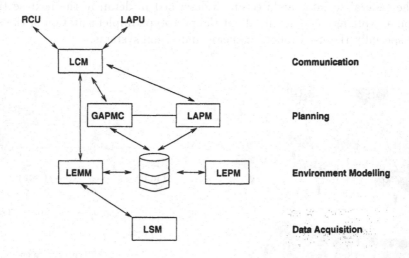

Fig. 2. Architecture of a local area processing unit

2.1 Global Area Processing Unit

The GAPU is characterised by five parameters. The first parameter is the origin and orientation of a 3D global coordinate system like shown in figure 1. But as we talk about navigation of mobile systems we usually project things down to the XY-plane and speak of areas. The second parameter consists of the description of all static objects like for example walls or heavy furniture that never change their position. The third parameter is the array of positions of the LAPUs in this global coordinate system in combination with their sensor area entry regions. The entry regions are small areas that any object has to pass to enter or leave the sensor area. These sensor positions have to be chosen in a way that the union of the observed areas of the LAPUs includes the area that has to be controlled by the GAPU. The last parameter is the communication topology of the LAPUs and RCUs. This topology is represented by an indirected graph with two kinds of vertices, LAPUs and RCUs. An example can be seen in figure 1. Parts of these components are known to every LAPU.

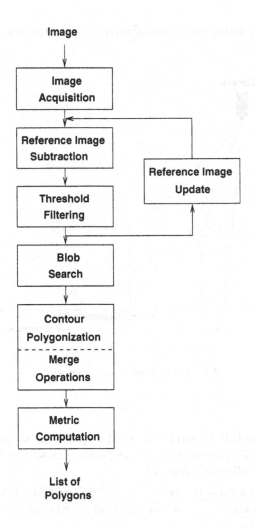

Fig. 3. Object detection algorithm

2.2   Local Area Processing Unit

Figure 2 shows the complex architecture of a LAPU. Beginning in the sensor layer the local sensor module (LSM) tracks the positions of obstacles and robots during their way through the sensor area. The resulting data is given to the local environment modelling module (LEMM) and the local environment prediction module (LEPM) in the environment layer. These build up the current and short time future environment representations for the local area planning module (LAPM) and the global planning module component (GPMC) in the planning layer. The LEPM is responsible for choosing a good path inside the local sensor area while the GPMC is planning a good path to the destination LAPU. The local communication module (LCM) is responsible for handling incoming and

outgoing sensor, planning and administrative data to the other LAPUs and the
dedicated RCU.

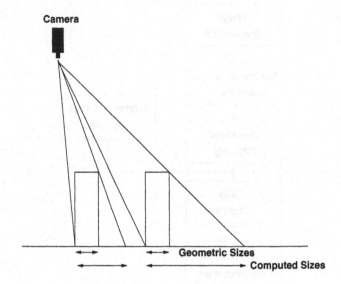

Fig. 4. Error in size computation

Local Sensor Module (LSM) The LSM acquires the sensor data by the use
of digital RGB CCD-cameras with $n \times m$ pixels. The sensor data acquired at a
time t_i can be modelled as a function

$$img_i : [n-1] \times [m-1] \longrightarrow \qquad [255] \times [255] \times [255]$$
$$(x,y) \qquad \mapsto \quad image_i(x,y) = (r_i(x,y), g_i(x,y), b_i(x,y))$$

The process of finding obstacles and robots in the sensor area is shown in
figure 3. After image acquisition a difference image d_img is computed by absolute subtraction of a reference image ref_i and application of a threshold filter
on each color component:

$$ref_i : [n-1] \times [m-1] \longrightarrow \qquad [255] \times [255] \times [255]$$
$$(x,y) \qquad \mapsto \quad ref_i(x,y) = (r\_ref_i(x,y), g\_ref_i(x,y), b\_ref_i(x,y))$$

$$d\_img_i : [n-1] \times [m-1] \longrightarrow \qquad [255] \times [255] \times [255]$$
$$(x,y) \qquad \mapsto \quad \begin{cases} d = |img_i(x,y) - ref_{i-1}(x,y)| & \text{, if } d \geq thresh. \\ (0,0,0) & \text{, else.} \end{cases}$$

This difference image is used to build the new reference image ref_i from the old
ref_{i-1} and the current image img_i by

$$ref_i : [n-1] \times [m-1] \longrightarrow \qquad [255] \times [255] \times [255]$$
$$(x,y) \qquad \mapsto \quad \begin{cases} ref_{i-1}(x,y) & \text{, if } d\_img_i(x,y) \neq (0,0,0) \\ img_i(x,y) & \text{, else.} \end{cases}$$

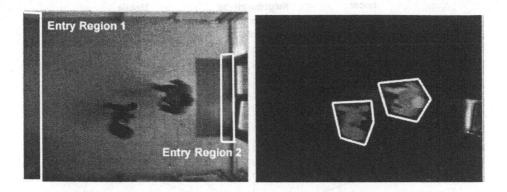

Fig. 5. Ceiling camera: original and difference image

The difference image is used to find the blobs that represent the objects in the sensor area. To find a blob, that is a connected area of pixels where the color is different from (0,0,0), we follow boundaries of objects and build a convex polygon that includes the blob with a recursive add and split algorithm. As it can happen that objects are represented by more than one blob we try to merge polygons by a distance criterion. At the end of this process we have an array of pixel polygons $(pP_{1,i}, \ldots, pP_{p,i})$ at time t_i with

$$pP_{j,i} = ((x_1, y_1), \ldots, (x_{p_j}, y_{p_j}))$$

Figure 5 shows an example of an input image and the desired result.

To compute metric distances from pixel coordinates a calibrated camera system is needed. The pinhole camera model is usually used to calibrate camera systems but as we have to work with lenses that have very short focal lengths (< 8mm) we are using a "lookup and interpolate with least squares" strategy like the one described in [5]. During the calibration process we build a table of correspondences between many pixel coordinates and global coordinates and in the application we interpolate the global coordinates by using the table values. We are implementing the least squares method for creating the lookup table and the bilinear method for interpolating points not in the table. Lookup and interpolation gives us a function

$$to\_metric : [n-1] \times [m-1] \longrightarrow R \times R$$
$$(x, y) \longmapsto to\_metric(x, y) = (gx, gy)$$

that maps pixel positions to global coordinates. So we can compute an array of polygons with global coordinates $gP_{j,i}$ by mapping the *to_metric* function on the pixel values:

$$gP_{j,i} = (to\_metric(pP_{j,i}[1]), \ldots, to\_metric(pP_{j,i}[p_j]))$$

These gP are given to the LEMM. Usually the resulting polygons include an oversized area. This is an effect that can't be eliminated as long as there is no

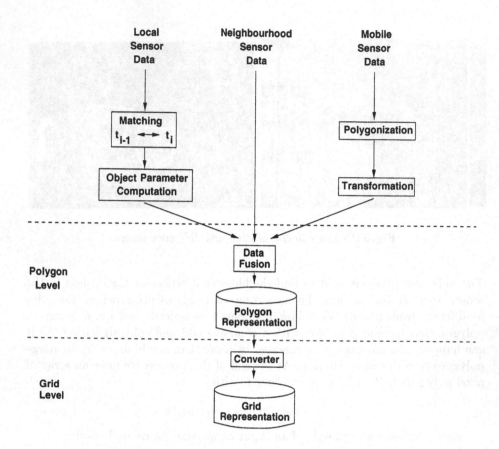

Fig. 6. Local environment modelling module

3D object information available and just a single image is used. It is described in [5] and can be seen in figure 4. As there is no height information for an observed object, the smallest possible height has to be taken for computing the object size.

Local Environment Model Module (LEMM) The LEMM is an active component that receives and integrates new data from different sources, namely data from the own sensor layer, data from connected LAPUs and data from mobile systems driving through the own area. Figure 6 gives an overview over the different tasks that have to be performed by the LEMM.

An array of polygons $gP_{j,i}$ at time t_i of the own sensor array has to be matched to an array of polygons $gP_{j,i-1}$ at time t_{i-1}. The matching relation is many to many. The matching is necessary to compute the velocity (v_x, v_y) of every polygon. These values are needed in the prediction module to predict future events.

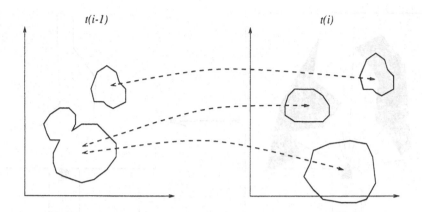

Fig. 7. Many to many relations in matching process

To obtain a match we estimate the current position of the polygons $gP_{j,i-1}$ at time t_i by linear interpolation and use a distance criterion to decide whether a certain match is valid or not (example in figure 7). The resulting data sets are written to the internal environment representation model and to the send queue of the local communication module to be sent to the connected LAPUs.

The LEMM also has to integrate sensor data received from other LAPUs via the local communication module. In this case the data is already preprocessed so all required parameters exist. Thus the data has just to be put to the internal representation model.

The third source of sensor data is the mobile system. The data is received via the LCM, too, but has a completely different type. We suppose the use of laser scanners on mobile robots and therefore we shortly explain how to handle this kind of data.

A laser scanner measures the distance of an object to the internal origin of the scanner. The scan can be modelled as a function

$$localscan_i : [0..180] \longrightarrow [0..max]$$
$$\alpha \quad \mapsto \quad scan_i(\alpha)$$

that gives the distance of an object by the angle α of the light ray.

As we have the position and orientation of the robot in the global coordinate system given by the RCU via the LCM it is possible to compute the global coordinates of every obstacle point of the scan. So based on this global data set the scan *localscan* can be transformed to a polygon *globalscan* like in figure 8. This polygon does not represent the area where an obstacle is expected like in the other cases but an area that is certainly free.

So we can combine the data of all three sources to improve the results in the environment model like seen in figures 9 and 10. The first figure shows data fusion in two overlapping sensor areas. Here we have the intersection of the two polygon areas as an estimation better than the original sensor data. The

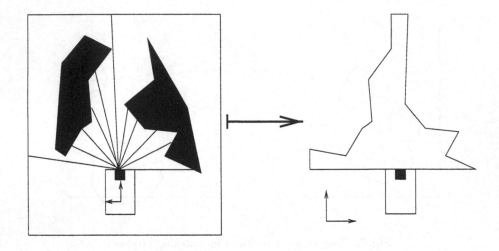

Fig. 8. Transformation of local scan to global polygon

second figure shows data fusion of a LAPU and a mobile system, where we use a difference operation to get a better estimation for the real object area.

The internal representation of the environment model consists of three components. The first component holds all the acquired object (blob) information like for example identifier or velocity. The second component is a polygonal representation for data improvement and the third component is a grid based representation useful for the planners. The grid based representation is computed from the polygonal data and we link polygons and grid fields to the corresponding object information for fast access.

Local Environment Prediction Module (LEPM) The local environment prediction is based on the polygonal representation of the environment. The prediction is done by extrapolation of historic positions.

In this module we want to try out different methods like neuronal nets or stochastic movement models that avoid collisions of the polygons and find a good prediction by estimating the destination of every dynamic obstacle.

The result of a prediction is again a grid representation of the environment at time $t_{i+k}, k = 1, 2, \ldots$ that can be used by the planners.

Local Area Planning Module (LAPM) The local area planning module gets orders from the corresponding global area planning module component. An order can be to plan a short path for the mobile system to reach the destination in the same sensor area or to a certain entry region in the sensor area where the robots leaves the area and drives into the next LAPU-region. To plan the path the LAPM can use the current environment and additionally the predicted environments. As the local environment does not only include information from

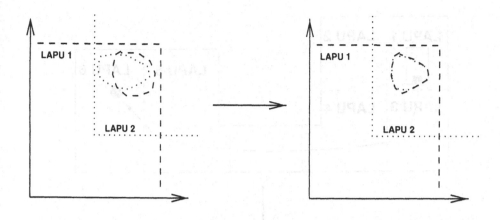

Fig. 9. Data fusion by two LAPUs

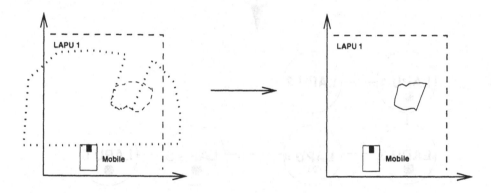

Fig. 10. Data fusion by a LAPU and a mobile system

the local sensor area but also from connected areas, there is enough information to plan a way without being surprised by unknown objects.

The results of the planning process are given back to the mobile system via LCM and RCU, but the planner adapts its path continuously and transmits new results if there are significant changes.

As planning algorithms all fast grid based planners can be used. At the moment we prefer gradient descent methods.

Global Area Planning Module Component (GAPMC) The global area planning module component is informed via the local communication module by the robot control unit that a mobile system in its area wants to have a path to a specific destination. If the destination point exists in its own sensor area the GAPMC starts the local area planning module to do the job, else it plans a path over several LAPU-regions by the use of a connection map that corresponds to

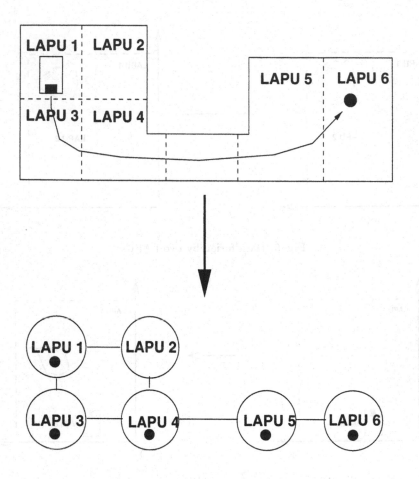

Fig. 11. Global planning as graph search

the communication topology but also includes the local identifiers of the entry regions that connect two connected LAPUs.

With this map, given by initialisation, the planning process is reduced to a graph search (figure 11). After having found a path the GAPMC gives again order to the LAPM to find a path to the specific entry region and if this goal is reached the control is given to the GAPMC of the next LAPU.

Local Communication Module (LCM) During initialisation of the system the LCM has to connect the specific neighbour LAPUs as specified in the topology graph. The RCU is connected at that time, too. Starting with one component all LAPUs, RCUs and the mobile systems have to synchronise their timestamp functionality. This job is done recursively by the first LAPU in a depth first search strategy. It sends its time to a neighbour, that is not yet marked as synchronised, receives an acknowledge message and computes a correction term from the measured transmission time. These correction term is sent back again to the neighbour that adapts its timer. The neighbour marks itself as synchronised and starts the same job with an unmarked neighbour. The LCM of the RCU offers the same synchronisation protocol and can therefore be synchronised like a LAPU. Synchronising the mobile systems is done by the RCUs.

After initialisation the LCM has to do transfer jobs for the local environment modelling module and the global area planning module component. These jobs are sending and receiving sensor data from local sensors, neighbour sensors and mobile systems (via the RCU).

2.3 Robot Control Unit (RCU)

The robot control unit is the representative for all mobile systems in the network of LAPUs. It is equipped with a fast radio interface and connects to all mobile systems in its area. Its area is given by initialisation data and includes the sensor areas of all connected LAPUs. A RCU holds connections to neighbour RCUs and gives control to them, if mobile systems leave the RCUs area.

During initialisation the already synchronised RCU is synchronising every mobile robot in its area with the same "set and correct" algorithm.

The RCU is sending the sensor data of the mobile system just to one LAPU, namely the one that is responsible for the robot.

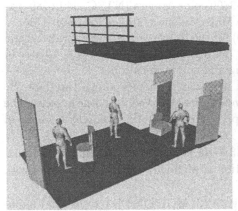
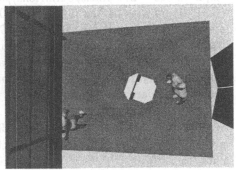

Fig. 12. Total view and ceiling camera

3 Prototype System

Our prototype implementation of the above described architecture consists of two local area processing units and one robot control unit. The area that has to be observed can be seen in figure 12. It has a length of 7.75 m and a width of 4.05 m.

Fig. 13. Mobile systems VIPER and MORTIMER

A LAPU consists of a Pulnix TMC-9700 color camera (NTSC, 640×480 pixels, used 320 × 240 pixels, 6 mm lens), a Matrox Genesis Image Processing Board (DSP-Board with 64 MB RAM, TI-C80) for the image processing operations and a standard dual-pentium 200 MHz PC (64 MB RAM, Windows NT, 10BaseT) for the environment modelling, planning and communication.

Both sensor systems are fixed in a height of 4 meters above the floor. So approximately $5.50m \times 4.20m = 23.10m^2$ can be observed with one system. The sensor areas are overlapping. So one pixel represents (in average) an area of $1.7cm \times 1.7cm = 2.89cm^2$.

The RCU consists of a standard 133 MHz pentium PC running with linux, an analog radio modem (ISDN-connection is planned) and a standard network card.

Our mobile systems can be seen in figure 13. MORTIMERs (right side) application area is the hotel environment where it is used for transport and guidance. MORTIMER has an easy to use differential drive that allows to turn on place and drive any curves. It is equipped with ultra sonic sensors and a Sick laser scanner. These sensors allow MORTIMER to drive with collision avoidance.

VIPER (left side) is designed for industrial transport. It has a new complex drive system that allows switching between curve and lateral mode. Equipped with this drive VIPER is able to connect to docking stations or to move into (un-)loading areas. Like MORTIMER VIPER uses a Sick laser scanner for navigation and collision avoidance.

MEPHISTOs state of implementation allows to acquire image data, to detect the objects, to compute the polygon lists in pixel and metric coordinates and to visualize the results in a simple environment model. The next implementation steps consist of connecting the isolated LAPUs and the RCU via the LCM, reorganizing the environment model and starting with the sensor fusion.

4 Conclusion

In this paper we have presented a scalable navigation system for mobile robots in dynamic environments. It was shown that the distributed approach is able to

- avoid communication bottlenecks as there are only local transmissions necessary,
- accelerate planning, as the environment model includes only the important data

Additionally it is possible to improve the environment data by fusion of overlapping LAPU sensor data and mobile sensor data.

This paper should be seen as an overview over the whole architecture of the MEPHISTO project, where many parts are not implemented yet. More details about algorithms and implementation of the modules will follow in future publications.

References

1. Clint Bidlack, Arun Hampapur, and Arun Katkere. Visual robot navigation using flat earth obstacle projection. In *IEEE International Conference on Robotics and Automation*.
2. R. Gutsche, C. Laloni, and F.M. Wahl. Navigation und Überwachung fahrerloser Transportfahrzeuge durch ein Hallen-Sensorsystem. In *Autonome Mobile System, 7. Fachgespräch*.
3. Jason A. Janet, Ren C. Luo, and Michael G.Kay. The essential visibility graph: An approach to global motion planning for autonomous mobile robots. In *IEEE International Conference on Robotics and Automation*.
4. K.J. Kyriakopoulos and N.J. Krikelis P. Kakambouras. Navigation of nonholonomic vehicles in complex environments with potential fields and tracking. In *IEEE International Conference on Robotics and Automation*.
5. C. Laloni. *Globales Monitoring System zur Steuerung und Überwachung Fahrerloser Transportsysteme in Fabrikationsumgebungen*. PhD thesis, Technische Universität Braunschweig, 1995.
6. C. Laloni, R. Gutsche, and F.M. Wahl. A factory-floor monitoring system for mobile robot guidance. In *International Conference on Automation, Robotics and Computer Vision*.
7. C. Laloni, R. Gutsche, and F.M. Wahl. Factory floor monitoring system with intelligent control for mobile robot guidance. In *JSME International Conference on Advanced Mechatronics*.
8. Aleksandar Timcenko and Peter Allen. Probability-driven motion planning for mobile robots. In *IEEE International Conference on Robotics and Automation*.

DESEO: An Active Vision System for Detection, Tracking and Recognition

M. Hernández, J. Cabrera, M. Castrillón, A. Domínguez, C. Guerra,
D. Hernández, and J. Isern *

Grupo de Inteligencia Artificial y Sistemas
Departamento de Informatica y Sistemas
Edificio de Informatica y Matematicas
Campus Universitario de Tafira
Universidad de Las Palmas de Gran Canaria
35017 Las Palmas - SPAIN
Phone: +34 928 458758/00
Fax: +34 928 458711
emailmhernandez@dis.ulpgc.es

Abstract. In this paper, a basic conceptual architecture aimed at the design of Computer Vision System is qualitatively described. The proposed architecture addresses the design of vision systems in a modular fashion using modules with three distinct units or components: a processing network or diagnostics unit, a control unit and a communications unit. The control of the system at the modules level is designed based on a Discrete Events Model. This basic methodology has been used to design a real-time active vision system for detection, tracking and recognition of people. It is made up of three functional modules aimed at the detection, tracking, recognition of moving individuals plus a supervision module. The detection module is devoted to the detection of moving targets, using optic flow computation and relevant areas extraction. The tracking module uses an adaptive correlation technique to fixate on moving objects. The objective of this module is to pursuit the object, centering it into a relocatable focus of attention window (FOAW) to obtain a good view of the object in order to recognize it. Several focus of attention can be tracked simultaneously. The recognition module is designed in an opportunistic style in order to identify the object whenever it is possible. A demonstration system has been developed to detect, track and identify walking people.

1 Introduction

The design of Computer Vision Systems (CVS) has experienced diverse evolutions and reorientations during its almost thirty five years of existence. These have gone from the most naive approaches, that tried the design of general CVS in a technologically poor framework, to more actual trends aimed at the design

* This research is sponsored in part by Spanish CICYT under project TAP95-0288.

of CVS capable of solving specific tasks in a robust manner showing continuous operation and real-time performance.

During the last decade, the design and construction of CVS has been largely influenced by the Active Vision paradigm, initiated by the seminal works [1, 3]. It is actually understood as a methodological framework [18] in which the design of artificial vision systems is based on elaborated mechanisms for the control of sensors parameters and processing with the aim of achieving a more robust operation, sometimes exploiting the restrictions of the environment in a Gibsonian or ecological sense.

Many systems have been built within the active vision paradigm, contributing new ideas and powerful techniques to solve specific problems. Andersen [2] includes an extensive survey of vision systems developed using robotic heads up to 1996. However few of them have considered the problem of extending the designed systems to new contexts other than those initially considered at design time or connecting the system to higher level modules [8].

Crowley [7] describes the methodological foundations for the integration of several reactive continuous processes in a Discrete Event Model with a supervisory control scheme. Using this approach, a system for detection, fixation and tracking is implemented. This system employs a combination of visual processes that rely on blink detection, color histogram matching and normalized cross correlation for face detection and tracking [9]. XVision [12] is a modular portable framework for visual tracking designed as a programming environment for real-time vision. It consist in a set of image-level tracking primitives and a framework for combining tracking primitives to form complex tracking systems. Perseus [13]is an architecture developed for the purposive visual system of a mobile robot and lets it to interact visually with the environment. It is based on object representation obtained from certain feature maps and in the use of visual rutines [21] paradigm. In order to perform person detection in the scene, Perseus uses an oportunistic strategy. Kosecka [14] proposes an approach for systematic analysis and modelling visually guided behaviours of agents, modelling behaviours as finite state machines and resolving the conflicts of parallel execution of them via supervisory control theory of Discrete Event Systems [19].

In this paper we describe DESEO (acronym of Detection and Tracking of Objects in Spanish), a development based on a modular conceptual architecture for the design of perception-action systems, using active vision for the detection and tracking of mobile objects. Its modular nature eases the mapping of complex activities over a network of modules that implement more simple behaviors. DESEO integrates a commercial binocular head, a DSP-based motor controller board and a TI TMS320C80 (C80) parallel DSPs on a Dual Pentium II PC running Windows NT 4.0. The system is able of real-time continuous operation and made up of several modules that perform different operations but share a common internal structure. Due to the modular nature, the system can be tailored to perform different tasks. As an experimental development, a system aimed at the detection, tracking and recognition of individuals is described.

The organization of this paper is as follows. Section 2 is devoted to introduce the main ideas underlying the design of DESEO. Section 3 describes its architecture and provides a description of the modules developed for the demonstration system. The internal organization of a generic module is presented in Section 4. The last sections are dedicated to the description of some experiments and conclusions.

2   Considerations for the Design of CVS

Actually Computer Vision seems to lack a common approach for the design of Vision Systems, situation which is extensible in general to the design of more complex robotic systems [7]. This lack of methodology normally provokes that CVS are designed as closed systems that are hardly reusable for solving other vision problems than those originally considered. When designing a CVS is necessary to consider the system within the framework of a conceptual methodology that assumes the a priori considerations, goals and design criteria. In this scenario the availability of a conceptual architecture has the mission of closing the gap between the resources provided by the affordable technology and the design restrictions and requirements. Pursuing these ideas we are trying to develop vision systems in a systematic way using for design the following three simple considerations:

1. Computer Vision systems should be programmed to be built in an incremental and modular way. So the concept of module, as the minimum logical entity that performs something useful, is a basic element. Also to cope with this objective and favor the reconfigurability of the system in terms of its modules, these should share a common structure and interface.
2. Internal details of each module, regarding specifically what that module computes, are going to vary between modules. However, all of them are going to share some common aspects. Most modules will exhibit three distinguishable functional parts respectively dedicated to perform the computations to obtain results from the data, to evaluate the results and to control the performance of the algorithms.
3. For sake of versatility, a control scheme which combines data driven and objective driven mechanisms supplies a powerful tool in order to obtain diverse and complex behaviors.

These three ideas are the basement of the proposed Bottom-Up/Top-Down Module (BU-TD). It is basically a percepto-effector unit with the following main functions:

- The obtainment of a description or computational result from some input data. Its objective is to derive results or descriptions from the analysis of the input data in a bottom-up or data driven fashion. This is the task of the bottom-up (BU) unit depicted in Figure 1. In general, a BU unit is conceived as an interpreter that operates cyclically.

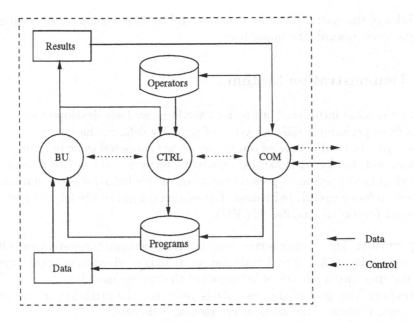

Fig. 1. Conceptual Architecture of a BU-TD Module.

- There is normally a need to evaluate the results obtained by the operation of the BU unit and control its operation through available parameters. This is performed by the top-down control unit (CTRL) to close a first control loop. This unit has also the task of decoding incoming events and messages into the control actions (Operators in Figure 1) meaningful to the module.
- Distribution of computations is normally a necessity, in terms of required computational power as well as in terms of functional modularity, so we normally do not want to design systems where the different parts executes synchronously in a single thread. The tasks in the system should be assigned to dedicated modules that exchange events and messages but that may run at different frequencies. The communication unit (COM) allows for sending or receiving data to other modules without interrupting the operation of the module. This capacity of modules to operate asynchronously is a essential characteristic in the design of reactive perception-action systems.

The state of each module is controlled at different levels. At the lowest level, the control unit of the module is monitoring its own operation through the evaluation of the results achieved. This internal control loop lets the module adapt its operation parameters and react to changes in the environment in a reactive way. At a second level, control is modeled using a Discrete Event System (DES) paradigm [19, 15]. Thus modules can receive and send events to other modules to share results or signal certain circumstances. Aside from these two bottom-up control mechanisms, there is a top-down control which is arbitrated by a supervisor module. The main goal of this module is to decode complex commands received from an upper layer into commands that are issued to the modules of the system to set its behavior and to serve results obtained from the lowest levels towards the upper layer.

3 Demonstration System

Using the ideas introduced in previous sections, we have developed a prototype capable of performing different types of task. By default, the system can scan a zone trying to localize moving objects which are supposed to be upright position walking individuals. After fixating on moving objects, it tries to localize the head and identify the person. A possible variation of this behavior is to command the system to find a specific individual. The system comprises the following set goal-oriented functional modules (GOFM):

Supervisor: This module serves as an interface between the system and outside and its basic task is to decode the commands received from upper layers or the user into a pattern of behaviors of the system modules.

Detector: The goal of this module is to direct the attention of the system towards areas of the scene where motion is detected.

Tracker: As its name suggests this module is responsible of controlling the active vision system which is made up of a Helpmate Robotics' BiSight binocular head, a motor controller board and a PCI board containing a C80 parallel DSP. The prototype uses only one camera so that movement is performed on that camera's vergence and head tilt angles. Image acquisition is done using the frame grabber available on the C80 board. The tracking of moving targets is done at frame- rate in the C80 DSP as is explained bellow.

Recognizer: The recognition of known individuals is the task of this module. It operates in two steps. At a first stage, it analyzes the small window returned by the Tracker module to determine if this image corresponds to a head or not and its pose (front, lateral or rear) if it is the case. At the second stage, zones identified as heads in frontal pose are analyzed in order to attempt the identification of the person.

The behavior of the whole system is the resulting pattern of conmmutation between the GOFM modules as is dictated by Supervisor module.

3.1 Detection Module

This module is really a pipeline of two modules, respectively devoted to detect areas exhibiting coherent movement, and to produce an estimate of the head position within the selected area. The movement detection acts as the basic mechanism for capturing the attention of the system towards potentially inter-esting areas. For the sake of simplicity, in the context of this application it is assumed that moving areas a priori correspond to walking individuals. This hy-pothesis is later confirmed or unconfirmed based on evidences, as is explained bellow.

The detection of movement is done first computing the optical flow and then segmenting it to select areas that exhibit a coherent movement. The optical flow is computed according to the technique presented in [5]. This technique approximates the flow field by estimating the optical flow only at the center of the rectangular patches in which the image is divided. The basic assumption of the technique is that within the rectangular patches a linear approximation of the flow field holds. Clearly, the computed optical flow is an approximation to the "real" flow field. In order to compute the optical flow at points other than the center of the patches, a linear interpolation can be used.

This technique provides a flexible solution that allows to balance numerical accuracy with computational requirements by varying the size of the patch. This makes possible to compute the optical flow at different levels of accuracy, for example at high resolution in the FOAW for fine tracking and at a coarser in the periphery of the visual field for detecting large moving objects [17].

This module can account for the egomotion of the robotic head. Using the known kinematics of the head it is possible to subtract the component of the optical flow due to the egomotion of the head [17]. This allows for detection of moving objects even when the head is moving.

The second stage of this module uses thresholding of the computed optical flow and blob detection to extract "patches" showing coherent movement. These patches are ranked according to their size and an area centered on top of the best ranked blob is extracted as a potential area of interest. This area is expected to contain the head of the individual if any. Its size and position inside the blob are determined using knowledge about normal width and height proportions of human heads and the measured mean velocity of the that zone. A similar strategy is used in many other systems as in the Perseus system [13].

3.2 Tracking Module

The tracking process is capable of tracking several targets on a sequential manner. Each target is an element in a list of focus of attention built from high saliency areas returned by the detection module. For the focus of attention that is active at each time, the tracking is performed first commanding a saccade to the predicted location of the target in the static frame of reference of the head, and then proceeding with a normal tracking until the next focus of attention is scheduled for visual control. The tracking is performed by the correlation procedure explained below. For the sake of real-time performance, this procedure is restricted to a relocatable window of $m \times m$ pixels (80×80). This FOAW can be placed anywhere in the visual field [11] to rapidly follow a moving object, somehow alleviating the latencies introduced by the electromechanical system of the head. In parallel, the head is commanded to the expected target's position using an alfa-beta predictive filter, that takes into account all the latencies of the tracking process. The head is commanded to new positions every 40 ms.

Another interesting feature of the FOAW is that it can switch to a new focus of attention at frame rate if the new and old focus are visible within the same visual field. The switching policy between focus of attention is based on priority queue. The length of the queue, just the number of focus of attention that the system can track simultaneously, can be variable but in our experiments has been fixed to 2 or 3. Initially, the list of focus of attention is empty until the supervisor or the detection module start sending high saliency areas to the tracker to fix on them. The management of the focus of attention is carried out by a simple scheduler that assigns a priority to each focus of attention. This priority is computed on the basis of the estimated velocity of the target and the error in the predicted position. This means that even if there are other focus of attention pending for visual attention, the system may not be able to attend them if the active focus of attention moves very fast or in an unpredictable manner. In practice, tracking several targets is only feasible if they move slowly and with constant velocity. Switching between focus of attention is made by means of a saccade followed by fixation. The tracker must assign the active focus of attention a time slice enough for performing the saccade and stabilizing on the target to update the estimates of position and velocity.

The basis of the tracking module is the determination of the new target location using a real-time correlation operator that returns the best match position between a series of patterns and the current FOAW image. This correlation process must accomplish two constraints: temporal constraints, it must return a new position estimate every new frame, and it should accommodate the evolution of the object's view appearance. This is a need if the object is moving in an unrestricted manner (change of scale, rotations, deformations, ...) in an unstructured environment where the illumination is non uniform or may change during the tracking process.

Several iconic correlation algorithms can be implemented for real-time performance on a parallel DSP like the C80. However, its performance is very limited if the object being tracked change its appearance while the model is kept constant. This is due, both to the characteristics of the matching measure [10] and to the static nature of the model that does not track the variations in the visual appearance of the area being tracked. Obviously, to accomplish with the second condition a mechanism is needed to update the model. To deal with this problem, we have developed a new algorithm based in the assumption that if the update is performed frequently enough, literally at frame-rate, the change in the visual appearance of the object with respect to the observer is expected to be smooth. The algorithm uses several patterns corresponding with different views of the object of interest. This set of iconic models constitutes a stack of L elements that may be assimilated to a short-term visual memory. This model of visual memory is created, used and updated autonomously by the algorithm through a function that evaluates its relevance both in terms of difference or error with the model and its perdurability and obsolescence.

Every focus of attention object has an associated stack (STK), whose first element, $STK(0)$, represents the most recent model of the object. Every model in the stack is represented by: an array $m(i)$ of $n \times n$ pixels, that stands for the i-th iconic model of the object, the obsolescence (t_s) of that model or the time when this model was recalled last time, the persistence time (t_p) or the amount of time that this model has been actived stack (STK), whose first element, $STK(0)$, represents the most recent model of the object as the identified model, and finally, a flag that can be used to lock a model in memory so that it can not be removed by another model, either because it corresponds to a view of the object that has been previously recognized or because it corresponds to a view of an object that has been uploaded from a model database to be searched. With this data and for each model $STK(i)$, an utility index (U) can be computed as $U(t_a, i) = t_p(i)/[1 + t_a - t_s(i)]$, where t_a represents the actual time. This utility measure takes into account the stability or persistency of a model and the time interval since it was recalled form the stack. Using this measure it is possible to quantify the relative "liveness" of the different models in the stack. Thus a model with a low utility measure is a candidate for being removed from the stack when refreshing the memory. Three type of processes act over the stack of models: stack creation, tracking by comparison and model updating.

A. Stack creation: A stack is created whenever a tracking is initiated for a new focus of attention. This may result from a detection process or due to an executive order received from the supervisor module. In this moment the data space is allocated and the memory allocating process begins with the first element, $STK(0)$, corresponding to the active model of the object being tracked. The memorization of new models in the stack is done by transferring the active model, $STK(0)$, to a new position, $STK(j)$, whenever the active model is going to be updated and certain conditions hold. For the active model to be memorized, its persistence (t_p) must be long enough or, equivalently, it needs to have been active for a sufficiently long period of time (actually 5 frames, or 200 ms). In order to avoid introducing weak models in the memory, the candidate model must also contain certain level of variability or structure. This is checked by computing the mean of the absolute value of the gradient over every pixel of the model, which must be larger than a threshold. Finally, it must be somehow different to models already present in the memory, this being measured directly as the Sum of Absolute Differences (SAD) between the candidate and the rest of models. To determine a sufficiently large difference a threshold is employed.

B. Tracking by comparison and updating the model. The process is controlled by two limits, corresponding respectively to a lower (E_{min}) and upper (E_{max}) limits for the minimum correlation error. Given a minimum or best match error at current time, $E(t_a)$, between the active model $STK(0)$ and the FOAW, if $E(t_a) < E_{min}$ the active model remains unchanged and only its persistence is incremented. Else, if $E(t_a) > E_{max}$, this means that possibly the object has been lost and a search mode is triggered. Within this mode every model in the memory, starting with the model with largest persistence (t_p), is tried as the active model and the best match point is searched with the FOAW located at different positions until a good match is found. Otherwise, $E_{min} < E(t_a) < E_{max}$, the active model is updated through substitution by the $n \times n$ image window centered on the best match position. After this, a correlation is repeated for each of the models present in the memory over an area centered in the best match position whose size is a fraction of the FOAW. Actually, this is a window of $(m/2) \times (m/2)$ pixels, being m the side length of the FOAW. From this correlation the model providing minimum error is selected, and if this error is less than the value obtained with the previous active model, it is taken as the new active model and its persistence (t_p) and obsolescence (t_s) are updated. This process is carried out to compensate the drift on the location in the image of the best match that is observed when the active model is updated.

Thus the system has its "memory" structured at three levels depending on its function and persistence. The active model used for the tracking can be considered as a very short term memory that needs to be refreshed frequently. The collection of models associated with a focus of attention object act as a semi-permanent working memory with a medium degree of persistence. Finally, the face database used by the recognition module constitutes the long term or permanent memory of the system.

3.3 Recognition

The recognition module operates over a small window returned by the tracking module, centered at the point of best match in the image. Given the complex characteristics of the recognition process and its inherent limitations, the recognition is tried as a chain of opportunistic classifications. Some preprocessing is done at the beginning, basically to locate the center of the head in the window returned by the tracker. At the present implementation this is done exploiting the context at our lab, where the background appearing in the images is normally uniform and lighter than people appearing in the image. Also the area of the image containing a face presents a higher variance than the rest of the window. Thus we use a combination of gray level and variance thresholding to select points likely belonging to a head/face to compute the centroid and size of the head. Actually, our prototype is restricted to operate at short range around a predetermined distance so that we don't take care of changes of scale. Clearly, the approach followed for locating the subject's head is rather simplistic and exploits the conditions present at a particular escenario. We plan to utilize the skin color as the basic mechanism for head/face detection as in [23],[9].

After this preprocessing, the rectangular area enclosing the selected points is extracted and warped to a predetermined size using Fant's resampling algorithm [22]. This image is supplied to a two steps classification process. At the first step in the recognition process, the selected area is classified to determine the pose of the head. If the selected pose is not frontal the recognition process stops and awaits a new image. When a view is classified as a front view of the head, a second classifier is used to determine the identity of the person. Normally, several positive identifications are accumulated before a recognition is considered definitive.

Both classifiers use the Fisherfaces method, a recognition procedure based on linear projections in the space defined by the eigenvectors of the image [4], a technique conceived as a derivation of the Eigenfaces method [20]. These methods are based on subspace classification in the vector space obtained as a lexicographical ordering of the image pixels. The Eigenfaces method strongly degrades when, as in our case, there are changes in illumination conditions or slight changes in pose or gestures. In many situations, also in our case, the variations between the images of the same face due to illumination and viewing direction are almost always larger than image variations due to change in the face identity [16]. Both techniques have been tested in the context of our application, having obtained with the Fisherfaces method a substantial increase in the quality of recognitions in different conditions of illumination.

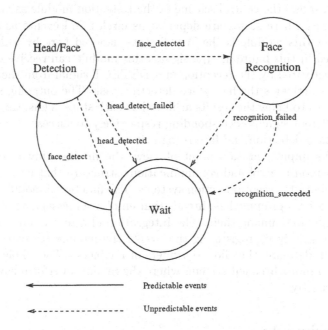

Fig. 2. Detection module control.

4 Module Design

The modules that integrate the DESEO system share a common conception that follows the methodological considerations exposed in section 2. Internally, each module is modeled as a nondeterministc automata comprising a set of states and events. Each state is assimilated to an elementary computational task that is carried out using the module's computational network. Associated with each computational task there is a control program that allows the control unit to evaluate the output of the bottom-up unit and trigger the corresponding control actions which may provoke a transition to a new state or select a new parameter set to perform a new cycle in the current state.

Adopting the BU-TD model as a valid model for the design of a generic module, several desiderable properties emerge. First, a clear separation is introduced between diagnostics and control what makes facilitates the reusability of diagnostics code and clarifies the control scheme. The existence of a control unit for every module allows for closing tight and reactive control loops without dening the existence of a control at a higher level. At the same time, the BU-TD model may serve as a basis element to articulate a distributed system approach. Even more, the existence of a communications unit in the model permits the system to cope with modules with different latencies so that communications are carried out asynchronously.

Figure 2 shows the control scheme of the Detection module as an illustration of these ideas, where states are depicted as circles and events as arrows. The init state for this module is the WAIT state denoted here by a double circle. Not included in this figure are the signals this module can receive or send. The module is activated by the reception of a DETECT signal from the TRACKER module that activates the head/face detection task. The outgoing signals allow other modules to know the results achieved at each state. Thus, this module can send six different signals corresponding respectively to success or failure in head detection, face detection and face recognition.

From the implementation point of view, the modules involved in DESEO share a common control and communications structure that ease the engineering of distributed perception-action systems. The functional modules comprising the system are programmed as threads that employ a message passing paradigm for event signaling among them. The integration of a new module into the system is done simply by registering the events the module (thread) may receive and/or send, detailing the allowed senders or recipients. The whole system then behaves as a multithreaded system, where the modules perform asynchronously and concurrently.

5   Experiments

As an experimental application of DESEO, a system oriented to detect, track and identify people in real time has been developed. The recognition process is made based on facial information. Within the last several years, numerous algorithms have been proposed for face recognition [6] and, although much progress has been made towards recognition of faces under small variations, there are not still reliable solutions for recognition under more extreme variations, for example, on illumination or in pose.

Due to the complex nature of person recognition by face, in our system an opportunistic solution to recognition has been implemented, based on a cascade scheme of confirmations. As the system is real time, its first objective is the detection of moving blobs (Figure 3), confirming that this is a person and detecting and isolating his head.

While the person is moving in the environment, the system will track him/her, centering the FOAW in what is supposed to be the head (Figure 4), waiting

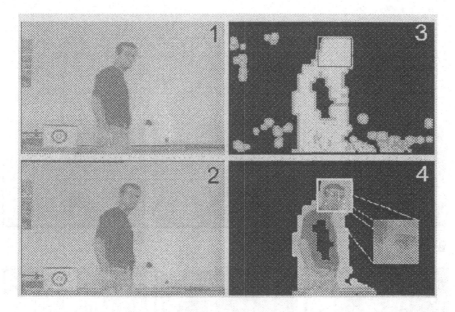

Fig. 3. Data images from optical flow analysis stage. Images 1 and 2 represent two consecutive frames that are the input to moving detection module. Image 3 shows a blob image provided by the optical flow algorithm. Image 4 represents the located head and the extracted pattern for the correlation algorithm.

opportunistically to obtain a good front view to identify the individual and confirming it while being tracked.

Once the person has been identified (Figure 5), the identity and an image on his/her face are sent to the supervisor. Depending on the supervisor policy, the tracking process can be continued, or in other case, its activity is shiffted towards other focus of attention areas. Due to the design of the system, several focus of attention can be tracked and followed simultaneously.

At this moment, an advanced prototype is being evaluated. An element which will be modified in order to obtain a more robust global behavior is related to the head detection procedure. At short term our objective is to modify it in order to obtain a better and more general head detection technique to more accurately locate the face, which in fact will result in a more robust face recognition. Another aspect of the system that will deserve further work is the immunity of the recognition procedure to scale variations due to different separations between the sensor and the individual. In the present implementation it is only partially solved through image warping.

The current prototype of the system runs in real-time on a Dual 350 MHz Pentium II PC, equipped with a PCI board containing a C80 DSP that are used as a slave processor for the tracking module.

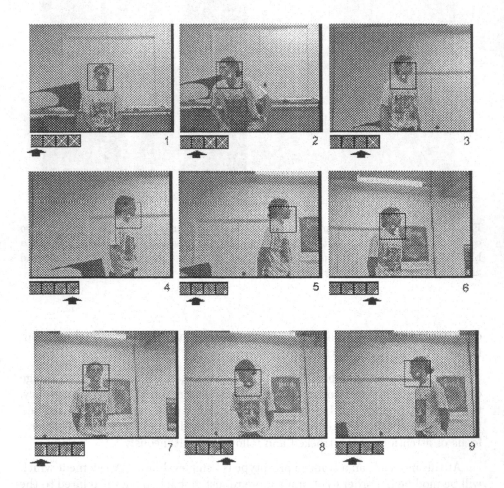

Fig. 4. A set of frames selected from a sequence where a person is tracked by the correlation algorithm exclusively. Several automatically chosen patterns can be observed under the images (crossed boxes are still empty patterns). The black rectangle represents the position of the FOAW. Note that in absence of higher level information, the correlation module tries to keep in the pattern database the most stable views of the target. This explains the shift of the FOAW towards the neck of the subject.

Fig. 5. Some examples from the database with heads at different views, including frontal, lateral, back and no-head samples.

6 Conclusions

A methodology or approach may be termed as superior to others as the systems implemented following its guidelines tend to be easier to build, easier to maintain or simply show a better performance in some sense. However the benefits or drawbacks of using a certain methodology or approach in the design of perception-action systems can only be stated a posteriori, arising from the lessons learned after extensive experimentation. While we don't make definitive claims about the methodology used in the development of DESEO, we think we can draw two different types of conclusions.

On one side are the basic considerations, which permits the conception, design and development of perception-action systems in general and CVS in particular. It provides a versatile though conceptually simple architecture, conceived in a modular fashion in order to facilitate the incremental development and updating of the system. The generic BU-TD module promotes a clear separation of diagnostics and control, what facilitates code reusability and usually makes control simpler. On the other side is the application developed as a preliminary experimental evaluation of this approach. This has allowed us to solve a real-world complex problem as is the detection, tracking and recognition of individuals in indoor environments using an active vision approach. The system built as prototype, although still in development, shows real-time continuous operation using mainstream technology. The experimental results achieved so far are promising and seem to validate the design considerations on which DESEO has been based.

390

References

1. J.Y. Aloimonos, I. Weiss, and A. Bandyopadhay. Active vision. *Inter. Journal of Computer Vision*, pages 333–356, 1988.
2. C.S. Andersen. *A Framework for Control of a Camera Head.* PhD thesis, Laboratory of Image Analysis, Aalborg University, Denmark, 1996.
3. R. Bajcsy. Active perception. *Proceedings of IEEE*, 76:996–1005, 1988.
4. P.N. Belhumeur, J.P. Hespanha, and D.J. Kriegman. Eigenfaces vs. fisherfaces: Recognition using class specific linear projection. *IEEE Trans. on PAMI*, 19(7):711–720, 1997.
5. M. Campani and A. Verri. Motion analysis from first-order propierties of optical flow. *CVGIP: Image Understanding*, 56(1):90–107, July 1992.
6. R. Chellappa R., C. Wilson, and S. Sirohey. Human and machine recognition of faces: A survey. *Proceedings IEEE*, 83(5):705–740, 1995.
7. J.L. Crowley and J.M. Bedrune. Integration and Control of Reactive Processes. *Proc. ECCV'94*, 47-58, Springer-Verlag, 1994.
8. J.L. Crowley and H.I. Christensen, editors. *Vision as Process.* ESPRIT Basic Research Series. Springer, 1995.
9. J.L. Crowley and F. Berard. Multi-Modal Tracking of Faces for Video Communications. *Proc. IEEE Conf. on Comput. Vision Patt. Recog.*, Puerto Rico, June 1997.
10. F.R.Hampel, E.M. Ronchetti, P.J. Rousseeuw, and W.A. Stahel. *Robust Statistics. The Approach Based on Influence Functions.* John Wiley & Sons Inc., New York, 1986.
11. C. Guerra, F.M. Hernandez, and J. Molina. A space-variant image structure for real-time purposes. implementation in a c80-based processing architecture. In J. Vitria A. Sanfeliu, editor, *Proc. VII National Simposium of the Spanish Assoc. Of Pattern Recognition and Imge Analysis (AERFAI)*, Barcelona, 1995.
12. G.D. Hager and K. Toyama. The XVision System: A General-Purpose Substrate for Portable Real-Time Vision Applications. *Computer Vision and Image Understanding*, 69(1):23–37, 1998.
13. R.E. Kahn, M.J. Swain, P.N. Prokopowicz, and R.J. Firby. Gesture Recognition Using the Perseus Architecture. *Proc. CVPR'96*, 1996.
14. J. Kosecka, R. Bajcsy and M. Mintz. Control of Visually Guided Behaviors GRASP Lab Tech Rep., num 367, Univ. of Pensilvania, 1993.
15. J. Kosecka. *A Framework for Modelling and Verifying Visually Guided Agents: Design, Analysis and Experiments.* PhD thesis, GRASP Lab, University of Pennsylvania, 1996.
16. Y. Moses, Y. Adini, and S. Ullman. Face recognition: The problem of compensating for changes in illumination direction. In *Proc. European Conf. on Computer Vision*, pages 286–296, 1994.
17. D. W. Murray, K. J. Bradshaw, P. F. McLauchlan, I. D. Reid, and P. M. Sharkey. Driving saccade to pursuit using image motion. *International Journal of Computer Vision*, 16(3):205–228, 1995.
18. K. Pahlavan, T. Uhlin, and J.O. Eklundh. Active vision as a methodology. In Y. Aloimonos, editor, *Active Vision*, Advances in Computer Science. Lawrence Erlbaum, 1993.
19. P.J. Ramadge and W.M. Wonham. The control of discrete event systems. *Proceedings of IEEE*, 77(1):81–97, January 1989.

20. M. Turk and A. Pentland. Eigenfaces for recognition. *J. Cognitive Neuroscience*, 3(1):71–86, 1991.
21. S. Ullman. Visual Routines, *Cognition*, 18:97–159, 1984.
22. G. Wolberg. *Digital Image Warping.* IEEE Computer Society Press, 1990.
23. J. Yang and A. Waibel. A Real Time Face Tracker, *IEEE Workshop on Appl. Comput. Vision*, 142–147, Los Alamitos (CA), USA, 1996.

Playing Domino: A Case Study for an Active Vision System

Maik Bollmann, Rainer Hoischen, Michael Jesikiewicz, Christoph Justkowski,
and Bärbel Mertsching

University of Hamburg, Department of Computer Science, AG IMA, Vogt-Kölln-Str. 30
D-22527 Hamburg, Germany
{bollmann,hoischen,4jesikie,2justkow,mertschi}@informatik.uni-hamburg.de
http://ima-www.informatik.uni-hamburg.de

Abstract. We introduce a mobile robot playing at dominoes. The robot is
equipped with a pan-tilt unit and a CCD camera and is solely guided by the
vision system. Besides the mobile robot the overall system is distributed on a
general-purpose workstation. The communication is realized by three radio links
transmitting the video signal and two serial data streams for the pan-tilt and the
robot controller respectively. Two client/server connections enable a bidirectional data exchange between the image processing software and the robot control and navigation software. The protocol includes requests for certain actions
to be performed by the opposite module and the transmission of domino coordinates. The robot identifies the dominoes, collects them, and deposits them in
form of a straight chain where two adjacent domino halves possess the same
digit. Several iterations of a perception action cycle have to be executed to fulfill
this task: The first cycle starts with a visual exploration of the robot's environment and a subsequent explicit foveation of detected domino point clusters.
After a coordinate transformation the dominoes are identified by template
matching followed by a comparison with a knowledge base to eliminate ambiguities. The positions of the dominoes are registered into the global map space of
the robot which position is continuously updated while it is moving. When the
robot has reached a so-called virtual point in front of a specified domino the
robot requests a control view towards this domino to verify its position. After
feedback from the vision system the robot grips the target, moves to the appropriate position in front of the already formed chain, again verifies its position,
and deposits the domino. Afterwards the robot returns to its initial position
where the cycle starts again with the selection of the next target domino.

1 Introduction

With the increased demand for flexible and largely autonomous robot systems research
is focussed more and more on active vision systems. From the well-established active
vision paradigm going back to [1] and [2] it is obvious that vision is not an isolated
process, but is instead part of a complex system interacting with its environment.
Visual attention, gaze control, data selection from multiple sources, cues from motion,
depth cues from binocular disparities, and hand-eye coordination belong to the key-

aspects of active vision (see also [7]). All these techniques are highly task-dependent and require real-time solutions. In order to achieve this functionality several camera platforms have been developed since the late eighties (e.g. [11], [3], [19], [16]).

Robot vision is not only useful for navigation assistance but is also a tool for high-level tasks. Robot systems provided with vision sensors are able to acquire additional information about geometric and haptic characteristics of objects which are hardly obtained with non-visual sensors. However, the integration of vision into robot architectures opens a door to many new applications (e.g. [5], [6], [4], [17], [12], [15], [18]).

Comprehensively, mobile active vision systems should be capable to fulfill the following requirements:

- localization of possibly task-relevant objects,
- recognition and priorization of these objects,
- autonomous navigation to the task-relevant objects in order to perform a desired manipulation.

Additionally, a high degree of adaptability to similar domains or changing conditions is desirable for any system. The implementation of the above constraints in an integrated system is a challenging task solved in a special case study: playing domino. Figure 1 shows the applied experimental platform. The robot identifies the dominoes in its environment and collects them in the right order to form a chain. Details are described in the following sections.

Fig. 1. A Pioneer1 robot serves as the mobile experimental platform. The basic robot consists of a differential wheel drive, seven sonars, an onboard controller, and a one DoF gripper. Additionally, the robot is equipped with a pan-tilt unit and a CCD camera

2   System Architecture

2.1   Overall Configuration

The system is divided into several modules which run on a general-purpose workstation and a mobile robot respectively. The Pioneer1 robot consists mainly of a differential wheel drive with incremental encoders, seven sonars, an onboard controller, and a one DoF gripper. Additionally, we mounted a pan-tilt unit with a single CCD color camera on the robot. For the application described in this paper we disabled the sonar sensors so that the system was solely supplied with information stemming from the CCD sensor. For communication with the modules running on the workstation three radio links were added transmitting the camera's analogous video signal and two serial data streams for the pan-tilt unit and the robot controller respectively (see Fig. 2).

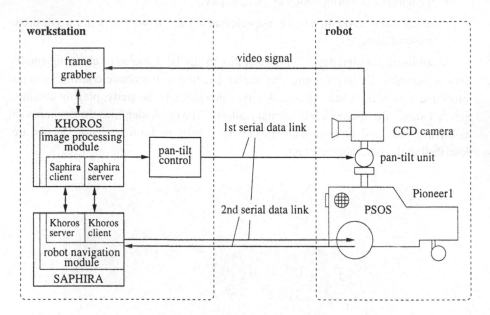

Fig. 2. The hybrid system architecture can be divided into modules running on a general-purpose workstation (frame grabber, KHOROS image processing module, pan-tilt control, and SAPHIRA robot navigation module) and a hardware platform (mobile robot Pioneer 1, pan-tilt unit, and CCD camera)

The video signal is digitized by a frame grabber and sent to the image processing and software development environment KHOROS via a socket connection (whenever requested by a KHOROS routine). The image processing module necessary to solve the domino task was embedded in this environment because of its well-supported extension facilities. The robot controlling and navigation module is implemented under the robotics application development environment SAPHIRA. To enable a bidirectional communication link, each module has an interface for data exchange consisting of an independent server and client process. In conjunction both processes and their counterparts in the opposite module maintain a full duplex connection between the image processing and robot navigation module. KHOROS sends the identifier, position, and orientation of all recognized dominoes or of a specified domino to SAPHIRA while SAPHIRA requests those services by triggering certain actions of the image processing system required by the current task. The implemented client/server architecture is described in the next subsection.

More details on the Pioneer1 robot and SAPHIRA can be found e.g. in [8], [9], and under http://www.activmedia.com/robots/. For information about KHOROS look at http://www.khoral.com.

2.2   Module Interface

In this section the interface for data exchange between single modules of the system is described in more detail because it is essential to the synchronization of the different modules (and development environments respectively).

The implementation of the client/server block varies between both modules according to different task scheduling mechanisms. Under KHOROS, running on a standard UNIX workstation, they can be build up in a normal fashion leaving the task of the parallel execution of both processes to the operating system. However, the SAPHIRA environment has its own task scheduling strategy under special consideration of real-time execution aspects, which has to be applied here to implement a compliant client/server block. To show how the module interface is integrated into the SAPHIRA environment some important aspects of the mechanisms provided are presented here (for the complete manual see [10]).

The SAPHIRA architecture comes with a synchronous, interrupt-driven OS. Each so-called micro-task is implemented as a finite-state machine (FSM) and registered with the OS. The SAHIRA OS cycles through all registered FSMs every 100 ms and performs a single step (state transition) in each of them. This mechanism guarantees full synchronization between all FSMs since the whole system state is being updated before a certain FSM, which may depend on the state of other FSMs, is being executed. On the other hand, the 100 ms timeslot for a complete cycle requires a relatively short execution time of the code associated with a certain state of an FSM. Naturally, this depends on the number of FSMs running simultaneously and on the speed of the host machine SAPHIRA is running on.

Considering the above mentioned criterions our server and client micro-tasks had to be mapped to finite-state machines. The FSMs for both tasks are shown in Fig. 3. The number of states a complete server or client cycle is divided into has been heuristically determined. The messages exchanged between an assigned KHOROS client / SAPHIRA server or SAPHIRA client / KHOROS server pair respectively base on a proprietary protocol. It includes requests for certain actions to be performed by the opposite module and the transmission of domino coordinates (for details about the protocol format see section 2.3).

After initialization most of the time the server and client FSMs are waiting for some event triggering a working cycle. In case of the server a client connection request (client_request == true) causes the server to collect and interpret a client message. The client FSM is waked up by an external event (trigger == true) which is generated by the robot navigation module.

(a) Server FSM   (b) Client FSM

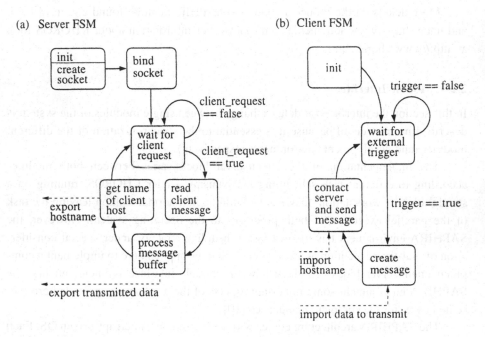

Fig. 3. (a) The SAPHIRA server FSM creates a socket and binds it to the hostname in Internet domain name space. When a client requests a connection the server reads and processes its message, retrieves the hostname the client has connected from, and exports the transmitted data and the retrieved hostname. (b) The SAPHIRA client FSM is activated by an external event generated by the robot navigation module. It imports data provided by this module, creates a message, and sends these data to the KHOROS server using the already retrieved hostname

Another welcome feature arising from the client/server concept is the possibility to run the modules on different hosts and let them communicate over the network. Thus, there is no need to run the time-consuming image processing module on the same host as the robot control. The latter requires the retrieval of the host name the vision module is running on by the SAPHIRA server FSM because the image processing shall not be restricted to a certain host. However, the SAPHIRA module controls the robot over a serial line and therefore has to run on the same machine the robot is connected to. The remaining problem was to enable the image acquisition over the network since the frame grabber itself is installed in a selected host. The problem was solved by another client/server combination where only the server process is allowed to access the frame grabber hardware and on demand delivers images to the client which can be started on any host.

2.3 Message Protocol

Messages exchanged between servers and clients conform to a simple proprietary protocol. Basically, a message is a string of arbitrary length containing all necessary information to perform a certain step within a superior task. Such a string is divided into several sections. Each section is marked by a special tag which carries the information about the type of data in the corresponding section (see section 5 for a short overview about naming conventions and space representations used by SAPHIRA). Currently, four tags are supported which contain information about

- the type of artifacts (e.g. point, line, wall, corridor etc.),
- the action to be performed (e.g. moving to a target, verifying the current position),
- the primary target's coordinates,
- and additional coordinates (for other artifacts than the primary target).

The *type-of-artifact tag* specifies a so-called artifact which is used by SAPHIRA to represent the properties of certain objects in the perceptual space of the robot, including coordinates and orientation. Each domino can be represented uniquely by the ordinary 2D coordinates of its center of gravity, its orientation and an identifier. Thus, there is no need to use more complex artifact types than points. However, it may be useful for other applications to exploit the special attributes of more complex artifact types, so this is the reason why the tag was introduced.

The *action tag* specifies the type of service a client can request from the server when it needs support to successfully solve a task step. For example, the navigation module running within the SAPHIRA environment needs to verify the robot's exact position before picking up a domino (see section 3). Therefore, it sends an appropriate action request to the KHOROS vision module including the target's current position and orientation which are not known exactly due to errors introduced by robot motion. This enables the vision module to direct its gaze to the domino and determine its exact position in the robot's local perceptual space. After sending back this coordinates the robot is able to update its internal map before gripping the domino.

The *primary-target tag* selects the artifact for the specified action. All artifacts currently known by the robot are labelled with unique numerical IDs and logically the data area following this tag contains the ID of the target. For example, if the robot receives an action command like „GotoDomino", the primary target field contains the identifier of this domino.

The *additional-coordinates tag* allows the transmission of other artifact coordinates. At present it is used in the first step of the perception action cycle (see section 3) by the KHOROS vision module to transmit the coordinates of all detected dominoes to the SAPHIRA navigation module, which now can initialize or update its internal map properly.

3 Processing Scheme

Goal of the robot domino game is to deposit the pieces close together in such a way that adjacent halves of two dominoes possess the same digit. To facilitate the navigation the robot has to arrange the dominoes in form of a chain. Several iterations of a perception action cycle have to be executed to collect all dominoes.

The perception action cycle starts with a visual exploration of the frontal half-field of the robot's environment. Dominoes are found and identified (described in the following section) and the first domino which fits to the defined beginning of the domino chain is selected. Subsequently, the robot drives to a position, which we named virtual point, 50 cm in front of this domino. The virtual point depends on the orientation of the selected domino and on the half of the domino which has to fit the end of the chain (see Fig. 4).

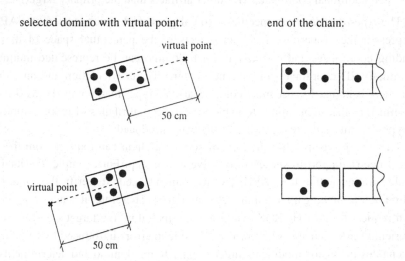

Fig. 4. The robot verifies its position from a virtual point 50 cm in front of the domino which has to be manipulated. The virtual point depends on the orientation of the selected domino and on the half of the domino which has to fit the end of the chain

If the robot has reached the virtual point the perception unit verifies the position of the domino. We decided not to drive directly to the domino because of possible position errors (differences between external and internal coordinates) caused by gearbox play, wheel imbalance, and slippage. The distance between the virtual point and the goal of the desired manipulation was heuristically determined. The distance has to be large enough to correct the position error calculated from the visual verification and short enough that a new position error on the way to the target coordinates will remain small. If the internal coordinates are adapted to the real-world the robot grips the domino, drives to a virtual point in front of the chain, again verifies its actual position, deposits the domino, drives back to its initial position, and finally verifies its position. Subsequently, the next cycle starts with the selection of the new target domino which fits to the chain of already deposited dominoes (compare to Fig. 5).

During the phases of perception the robot stands still while it is blind during the phases of navigation.

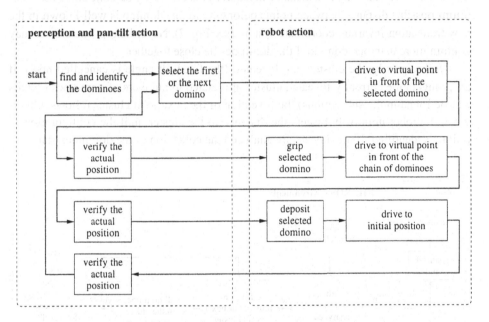

Fig. 5. The perception action cycle starts with the search for the dominoes and their identification, both performed solely by the vision system (perception and pan-tilt action). Subsequently, the robot selects a domino which fits to the chain of already deposited dominoes, drives to a virtual point in front of this domino (robot action) and verifies its position (perception and pan-tilt action). The robot grips the selected piece and drives to a virtual point in front of the chain of dominoes (robot action). When the robot has reached this point it again verifies its position (perception and pan-tilt action), deposits the domino, and drives to its initial position (robot action). Consequently, the robot verifies its position from the initial position and selects the next domino whereby a new perception action cycle begins

4 Visual Search and Identification of the Dominoes

The search strategy for the detection of dominoes can be characterized as systematic because the robot possesses only little a priori knowledge about the positions of the dominoes. We only assume the dominoes to be in front of the initial position of the robot in a pan range of -90° to 90°. Furthermore, the robot expects the dominoes to be no more than 2 m away from its starting position. Otherwise, it would not be able to detect the domino points because of the small elevation of the camera. With these assumptions we determined a fixed tilt angle of -20° and a pan interval of 30° resulting in 7 pan angles. By a 48° wide field of view we obtain an overlap between consecutive images.

In the first iteration loop possible domino points are detected by applying the described systematic search (see Fig. 6). The images are smoothed and segmented where segments unlikely to represent domino points are eliminated. The centers of gravity of the remaining segments are transformed into a bird-eye view and separated into clusters by introducing a distance measure. This can easily be done since the maximum possible distance between points belonging to one domino is well-known in the new translation-invariant coordinate system (see Fig. 7). Nevertheless, one cluster may contain more than one domino if the dominoes lie close together.

Subsequently, the clusters are foveated (the fixed tilt angle is cancelled now). If all points in the currently foveated cluster are related to numbers of dominoes (details can be found in the subsections) the foveation of the next point cluster follows. Otherwise, the robot iteratively bisects the distance to the cluster until the configuration of points is identified. If all clusters are analyzed the collection of the dominoes starts.

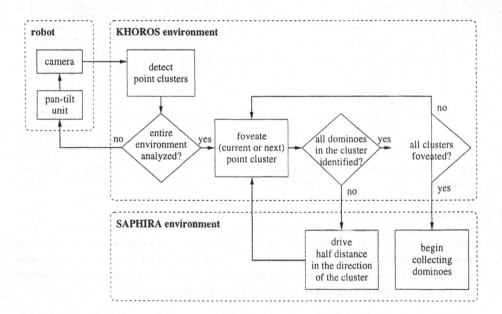

Fig. 6. Identification of the dominoes: All point clusters in the frontal half-field of the robot's initial position are detected in a systematic search. In a following foveation of these clusters all dominoes are identified by template matching. If the identification fails the robot successively bisects the distance to the cluster until all dominoes are recognized

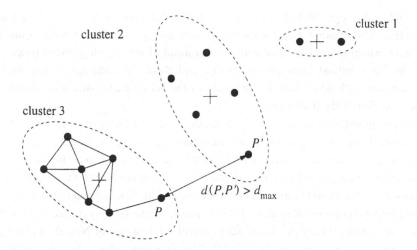

Fig. 7. The domino points detected in the systematic search are separated into clusters and successively foveated (*the crosses mark the fixation points*). After the projection of the domino points into a bird-eye view the clustering is simply done by supplying a distance measure $d(P,P')$ to each pair of points P, P' and comparing those measures with d_{max}, where d_{max} denotes the maximum over all distances between two arbitrary points of a template (half of a domino)

The following subsections deal with details of the recognition process.

4.1 Detection of the Domino Points

In the course of the domino game images are analyzed in three different defined states requested by the navigation module:

- during the systematic search for point clusters from the initial position
- if a point cluster is foveated from the initial position or from following shorter distances
- during the verification of the actual position from a virtual point

Each state starts with a request for a gray-level image which is supplied by a frame grabber and smoothed in KHOROS to reduce noise and disturbances resulting mainly from reflections of the radio waves. Subsequently, the smoothed images are segmented based on gradient images. The gradient images are obtained from a filter operation with horizontally and vertically oriented Sobel kernels. The segmentation is a region growing procedure with a static threshold synchronously performed on both gradient images. After segmentation those segments are removed which are too small or large to represent domino points. The remaining segments are smoothed during several dilation cycles. Moreover, geometrical properties like size, center of gravity, orientation, and compactness are calculated and updated for each segment during the region growing and merging process respectively.

402

Goal of the segmentation is the detection of the domino points and not the pieces themselves. The reason for that is the nearly constant contrast between the points and the pieces which is used to determine the threshold of the region growing procedure. Whereas, the contrast between the pieces and their surroundings varies strongly depending on the kind of floor and (because of the 3D characteristic of the dominoes) on the direction of the illumination.

The segmentation process is not faultless. Some domino points are not detected while other disturbing segments arise. Consequently, a test is required to separate the desired domino points from other segments. We use the compactness and the orientation of the segments as the relevant criteria. For the domino points we assume a compactness near two (ellipse) and a horizontal alignment. The orientation is calculated from a principal component analysis (PCA). The segmentation procedure and the PCA are borrowed from the attention and gaze control mechanisms of NAVIS, a more general active vision system (see [13], [14]). The segments which does not fulfill the above criteria are removed from the segmentation image.

4.2 Transformation of the Domino Points' Coordinates

After the segmentation procedure the domino points' centers of gravity are available in sensor-centered coordinates. Such a variant representation of the domino points is not suited for a template matching which is the easiest way to recognize the digits of domino points, a limited number of well-known point configurations. Additionally, we need the position of the dominoes in the egocentric coordinate system of the robot to perform the desired manipulations. The first step towards a transformation of the domino points' centers of gravity into a robot-centered coordinate system (bird-eye view) is the measurement of the geometry of the vision system. The fundamental parameters of the vision system's geometry are depicted in fig. 8. OC denotes the origin of the camera-centered coordinate system, O denotes the origin of the robot-centered coordinate system (LPS, see section 5). The transformation between both coordinate systems depends on the distances a, b, c, and s as well as the pan and tilt angles h and v respectively.

The current pan and tilt angles are maintained by the gaze control and directly available in the image processing module. The projection properties of the camera were experimentally investigated with several test images. The deduced camera parameters were again experimentally validated. A comparison between known coordinates of a dot raster and those coordinates which were calculated from the determined camera parameters show a relative position error of 1.5 %.

(a)

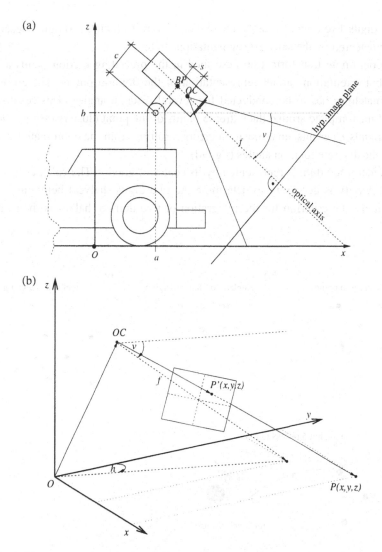

(b)

Fig. 8. (a) The fundamental parameters of the vision system's geometry: OC denotes the origin of the camera-centered coordinate system while O denotes the origin of the robot-centered coordinate system. The transformation between both coordinate systems depends on the distances a, b, c, and s as well as the pan and tilt angles h and v. (b) The projection properties of the camera were experimentally investigated with several test images

4.3 Template Matching

After the transformation of the domino points (strictly speaking, their centers of gravity) into a robot-centered coordinate system the domino digits have to be extracted from the point clusters. Each domino digit is represented by a reference model with ideal point distances. The foveated point clusters are searched with all admitted templates, the digits 1 to 6. In contrast to the real domino rules digit 0 is omitted because it can not be detected by the selected segmentation strategy.

The coordinate transformation described in the preceding section yields a size-invariant but orientation-variant representation of the domino points. Therefore, the template matching has to be conducted for several discrete angles. This results in a rotation of the template around the extreme points of the point clusters (see fig. 9c). A tolerance radius r permits small position errors resulting from the coordinate transformation or the discrete rotation angles (fig. 9d).

Each identified digit is represented by its center of gravity. The calculation of the centers of gravity is necessary to determine the two digits (halves) belonging to the same domino. The criterion for the integration of two domino halves is their known distance.

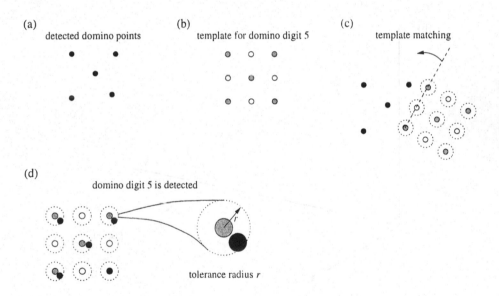

Fig. 9. The coordinate transformation of the domino points into a bird-eye view leads to a size-invariant but orientation-variant representation. Therefore, the template matching results in a rotation of the template around the extreme points of the point clusters (*top-right*). A tolerance radius r permits small position errors resulting from the coordinate transformation or the discrete rotation angles (*bottom*)

The identification of the domino digits is not faultless as well. Main problems are missing points of a domino digit caused by segmentation errors and misclassifications produced by unfavorable arrangements of the dominoes (a digit may possess more than one neighboring digit in a distance pointing to a unity of the digits). Most of these problems can be solved by a comparison of the supposed dominoes with a knowledge base (see fig. 10a). Currently, each domino is unique and the absolute number of dominoes is very small. Further investigations with a larger set of dominoes will be done in the future. However, this requires a more sophisticated implementation of the knowledge base. Nevertheless, we believe that the vision system is able to cope with larger quantities of dominoes because in our experiments we have observed only a small influence of the knowledge base on the recognition results.

After the adaptation of the supposed dominoes to the knowledge base the dominoes' orientations and centers of gravity, which are necessary for the navigation of the robot, are calculated from the centers of gravity of the corresponding domino halves. The orientation of the dominoes is defined in a coordinate system in compliance with the global and local map of the robot (see fig. 10b). Therefore, no further coordinate transformations are necessary in the robot navigation module.

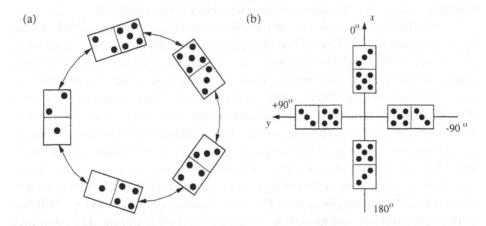

Fig. 10. (a) We use a small set of five dominoes in our experiments. Each piece has two neighbors so that the knowledge base can be depicted as a ring structure. (b) The orientation of the dominoes is defined in a coordinate system which corresponds with the internal representations used in the robot environment

5 Robot Navigation

The active part of the domino game is performed by the Pioneer1 robot. Since its exploration of the real-world depends at present solely on information from the image processing system, the interface between the image processing and the robot control and navigation module must be capable of carrying out all required information and passing over different requests depending on the current situation.

5.1 SAPHIRA Terminology and Mechanisms

SAPHIRA provides an abstract representation of the robots actual state called the *state reflector*. It contains information about various state variables like translational and rotational speed and position, motor stall detection, sonar readings, and control structures to directly command robot motions. The state reflector allows a user routine to easily access appropriate control variables and the SAPHIRA communication routines will send the proper commands to the robot.

There are different schemes for motion control under SAPHIRA. The simpler one uses *direct motion control* to turn or move the robot to a certain location, to set speed parameters, etc. The second method enables more complex motion control by facilitating the implementation of *behaviors*. They base on fuzzy control rules, provide additional state variables like priorities or activity levels which enable their interaction with other behaviors, and have a certain goal. To coordinate more complex *activities* SAPHIRA provides a control language named *Colbert* which allows to schedule action sequences of the robot. *Activity schemes* build up from activities are executed as micro-tasks after passing the Colbert interpreter. They are able to spawn child activities and behaviors and coordinate actions among concurrently running activities.

SAPHIRA maintains two major representations of space: a fixed global one for larger perspectives called the *Global Map Space* (GMS) and an egocentric coordinate system centered on the robot denoted as *Local Perceptual Space* (LPS). The GMS offers the possibility to add representations of certain objects found in the environment. Structures in the GMS are called *artifacts*. There exist many types of artifacts for the representation of different real-world objects, e.g. point, line, or wall artifacts. For the representation of dominoes the point artifact is sufficient since its implementation provides predefined variables for the spatial coordinates, an orientation, and an identifier. Thus, the domino representation chosen in the image processing module can directly be used to create or change a point artifact in the GMS. After adding an artifact to the GMS it also exists in the LPS and is automatically registered by SAPHIRA with respect to the robot's movement obtained from motion sensing. The robot uses dead-reckoning to permanently update its position. Thus, the errors arising during the movement of the robot let the accuracy of the robot's global position decay continuously. On the other hand, gripping a domino or depositing it at the right place at the end of a chain requires rather accurate position information. Therefore, it is necessary to align the robot with stationary artifacts representing real-world objects. This process, called *registration*, is used to update the robot's location in an internal map to compensate for position errors. Since sensory input from the environment is provided only by the vision system there must exist a close link between both modules.

5.2 Domino Activity Scheme

As shown in Fig. 5, a whole perception action cycle starts with the activation of the vision module. Its first task is to determine the location and orientation of all dominoes in its environment. Since the camera is mounted ontop of the robot and the relationship between the camera- and robot-centered coordinate system is well-known the transformation from camera to robot coordinates of all detected dominoes is performed by the vision system. After contacting the Saphira Server FSM and transmitting all domino coordinates they can directly be used to create initial point artifacts in the robot's GMS (which appear also in the LPS). In detail, the first contact of the server instantiates a superior activity scheme which is responsible for the execution of further robot actions controlled by activities, behaviors, and direct motion control.

By using the coordinates and orientation of the specified target domino the robot computes the virtual point in front this domino and creates an additional point artifact which serves only as a temporary target for the predefined GoToPos behavior. Once the behavior has achieved its goal by reaching the virtual point, the corresponding artifact is removed and the robot requests a control view from the vision system. The message sent to it includes the positional parameters of the target domino to enable the vision module shifting its gaze directly to the selected target. We assume here that the accumulated position error at this time is not as great as it causes the object to lie outside the field of view after pointing the camera towards the transmitted coordinates. As soon as the feedback from the vision system arrives, the robot updates its position by registration from the artifact associated with the target domino and starts gripping it by first opening the gripper, moving to the target position by direct motion control, and finally closing the gripper.

Afterwards the robot moves to the appropriate position in front of the already formed chain by applying the same method described above. After the mandatory control view it deposits the domino at the end of the chain and returns to its initial position where the cycle starts again.

6 Results and Conclusion

The domino scenario was developed as a case study for an active vision system. Despite the fact that many algorithms could be borrowed from the already existent (and more general) active vision system NAVIS, several algorithms had to be modified for playing domino. Main limitations arise from the small elevation of the camera since this reduces the maximum distance by which domino points are detectable to 2 m. Hence, the space for navigation is small which influences also the number of allowed dominoes. What we have learned from the domino scenario is that foveation of possibly interesting regions is essential to recognition. By establishing the foveation of point clusters between the systematic search and the template matching we could increase the recognition rate dramatically.

Figure 11 shows results from major steps during the visual part of the perception action cycles: The domino points are detected by a systematic search and a subsequent foveation of point clusters. Afterwards their centers of gravity are back-projected into a robot-centered coordinate system. The domino digits are identified in the resulting reference frame by template matching with regard to a knowledge base.

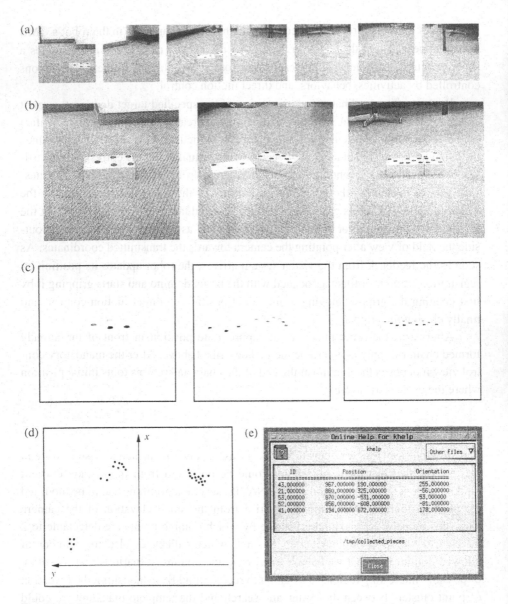

Fig. 11. (a) Clusters of domino points are detected by a systematic search within the frontal half-field of the robot. (b) Subsequently, the point clusters are foveated to facilitate the recognition of the dominoes. (c) The domino points are segmented and (d) their centers of gravity are back-projected into a bird-eye view. (e) A template matching performed in this new coordinate system results in a list of identified dominoes transmitted to the navigation module

Figure 12 shows the main window of the SAPHIRA environment after the map has been initialized with the domino coordinates as detected by the vision module. It depicts the scene in fig. 11 from the robot's point of view.

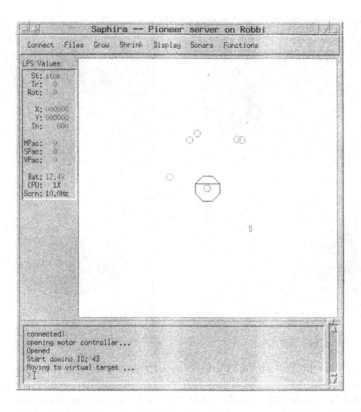

Fig. 12. The SAPHIRA main window: The left side contains status information like the current position and battery power. The symbol in the middle of the workspace area represents the robot while the small circles around belong to point artifacts in its LPS corresponding with dominoes

Some snapshots from the domino scenario are shown in fig. 13. The robot foveates on point clusters detected through a systematic search, identifies the dominoes, collects them in the right order, and deposits them in form of a chain. Several control views (in front of the target domino or the chain of dominoes) are necessary during the successive perception action cycles to verify the position of the robot. A demonstration of the closed domino scenario was presented on the Hannover Messe 1998.

Presently we are working on the integration of a blob detector into the vision module to speed up the detection of domino points and on route planning to avoid collisions with not-selected dominoes. Furthermore, it is desirable to have a more flexible knowledge base which is able to maintain an arbitrary set of dominoes.

Acknowledgments. The Deutsche Forschungsgemeinschaft has partly supported this work (grant Me 1289/3-1).

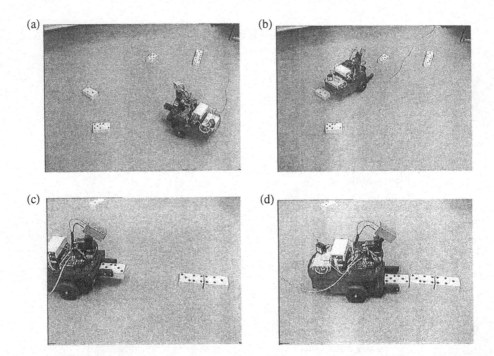

Fig. 13. : (a) The robot performs the systematic search for all dominoes from its initial position. (b) The robot has reached the virtual point in front of the target domino and verifies its position. (c) The robot has reached the virtual point in front of the already deposited chain of dominoes and verifies its position once more. (d) The robot deposits the current target domino

References

1. Aloimonos, Y., Weiss, I., Bandopadhay, A.: Active vision. Proc. 1st Int. Conf. on Computer Vision (1987) 35-54
2. Bajcsy, R.: Active perception. Proc. of the IEEE 76(8) (1988) 996-1005
3. Ballard, D. H.: Animate vision. Artificial Intelligence 48 (1991) 57-86
4. Bayouth, M., Thorpe, C.: An AHS concept based on an autonomous vehicle architecture. Proc. of the 3rd Annual World Congress on Intelligent Transportation Systems (1996)
5. Becker, C., Gonzalez-Banos, H., Latombe, J. C., Tomasi, C.: An intelligent observer. 4th Int. Symposium on Experimental Robotics, Stanford (1995)
6. Buhmann, J., Burgard, W., Cremers, A. B., Fox, D., Hofmann, T., Thrun, S.: The mobile robot rhino. AI Magazin 16(1) (1995)
7. Eklundh, J.-O., Nordlund, P., Uhlin, T., Issues in active vision: attention and cue integration/selection. Proc. British Machine Vision Conference (1996) 1-12
8. Guzzoni, D., Cheyer, A., Julia, L., Konolige, K.: Many robots make short work. AI Magazine 18(1) (1997) 55-64
9. Konolige, K., Myers, K., Saffiotti, A., Ruspini, E.: The Saphira architecture: a design for autonomy. J. of Experimental and Theoretical Artificial Intelligence 9 (1997) 215-235
10. Konolige, K.: Saphira Software Manual, Version 6.1, Stanford Research International (1998) http://robots.activmedia.com/docs/all_docs/sman61f.pdf

11. Krotkov, E. P.: Active Computer Vision by Cooperative Focus and Stereo. Springer-Verlag, Berlin Heidelberg New York (1989)

12. Maurer, M., Dickmanns, E.: A system architecture for autonomous visual road vehicle guidance. IEEE Conf. on Intelligent Transportation Systems, Boston (1997)

13. Mertsching, B., Bollmann, M.: Visual attention and gaze control for an active vision system. In: Kasabov, N. et al. (eds.): Progress in Connectionist-Based Information Systems. Vol. 1. Springer-Verlag, Singapore et al. (1997) 76-79

14. Mertsching, B., Bollmann, M., Hoischen, R., Schmalz, S.: The neural active vision system NAVIS. To appear in: Jähne, B.; Haußecker, H.; Geißler, P. (eds.): Handbook of Computer Vision and Applications. Vol. 3. Academic Press, San Diego et al. (1998)

15. Oswald, N., Levi, P.: Cooperative vision in a multi-agent architecture. In: Image Analysis and Processing. Springer-Verlag, Berlin Heidelberg New York (1997) 709-716

16. Pahlavan, K.: Designing an anthromorphic head-eye system. In: Zangemeister, W. H. et al. (eds.): Visual Attention and Vision. Elsevier, Amsterdam et al. (1996)

17. Vestli, S., Tschichold, N.: MoPS, a system for mail distribution in office-type buildings. Service Robot: An International Journal 2(2) (1996) 29-35

18. Vetter, V., Zielke, T., von Seelen, W.: Integrating face recognition into security systems. In: Bigün, J. et al. (eds.): Audio- and Video-based Biometric Person Authentication. Springer-Verlag, Berlin Heidelberg New York (1997) 439-448

19. Vieville, T., Clergue, E., Enriso, R., Mathieu, H.: Experimenting with 3-D vision on a robotic head. Robotics and Autonomous Systems 14 (1995) 1-27

Improving 3D Active Visual Tracking

João Barreto, Paulo Peixoto, Jorge Batista, and Helder Araujo

Institute of Systems and Robotics, Dept. Electrical Engineering, University of
Coimbra, 3030 Coimbra, Portugal,
jpbar,peixoto,batista,helder@isr.uc.pt,
WWW home page: http://www.isr.uc.pt/

Abstract. Tracking in 3D with an active vision system depends on the
performance of both motor control and vision algorithms. Tracking is
performed based on different visual behaviors, namely smooth pursuit
and vergence control. A major issue in a system performing tracking is
its robustness to partial occlusion of the target as well as its robustness
to sudden changes of target trajectory. Another important issue is the
reconstruction of the 3D trajectory of the target. These issues can only
be dealt with if the performance of the algorithms is evaluated. The
evaluation of such performances enable the identification of the limits and
weaknesses in the system behavior. In this paper we describe the results
of the analysis of a binocular tracking system. To perform the evaluation
a control framework was used both for the vision algorithms and for the
servo-mechanical system. Due to the geometry changes in an active vision
system, the problem of defining and generating system reference inputs
has specific features. In this paper we analyze this problem, proposing
and justifying a methodology for the definition and generation of such
reference inputs. As a result several algorithms were improved and the
global performance of the system was also enhanced. This paper proposes
a methodology for such an analysis (and resulting enhancements) based
on techniques from control theory.

1   Introduction

Tracking of moving 3D targets using vision can be performed either with passive
or active systems. Active systems facilitate tracking and the reconstruction of
3D trajectories if specific geometric configurations of the system are used [1, 2].
In the case of active systems robust 3D tracking depends on issues related both
to vision processing and control[3, 4]. Robustness of a specific visual behavior is a
function of the performance of vision and control algorithms as well as the overall architecture[5]. The evaluation of the global performance of both vision and
control aspects should be done within a common framework. For example, when
dealing with the problem of uncertainties and coping with varying environments
(which are difficult or impossible to model) one can, in principle, choose to use
more complex vision algorithms and/or more robust control algorithms. Good
decisions and choices can only be made if all the aspects can be characterized

in a common framework [6].Improvements in performance as well as the identification of less robust elements in the system strongly benefit from a common approach[7].

Many aspects related to visual servoing and tracking have been studied and several systems demonstrated [8,9]. One of these aspects is the issue of system dynamics. The study of system dynamics is essential to enable performance optimization [10,11]. Other aspects are related to stability and the system latencies [12,13]. In [13] Corke shows that dynamic modeling and control design are very important for the improved performance of visual closed-loop systems. One of his main conclusions is that a feedforward type of control strategy is necessary to achieve high-performance visual servoing. Nonlinear aspects of system dynamics have also been addressed [14,15]. In [14] Kelly discusses the nonlinear aspects of system dynamics and proves that the overall closed loop system composed by the full nonlinear robot dynamics and the controller is Lyapunov stable. In [15] Hong models the dynamics of a two-axis camera gimbal and also proves that a model reference adaptive controller is Lyapunov stable. In [16] Rizzi and Koditschek describe a system that takes into account the dynamical model of the target motion. They propose a novel triangulating state estimator and prove the convergence of the estimator. In [17,18] the control performance of the Yorick head platform is also presented. They pay careful attention to the problem of dealing with image processing inherent delays and in particular with variable delays. Problems associated with overcoming system latencies are also discussed in [19,20]. Optimality in visual servoing was studied by Rivlin in [21]. Recently, in the GRASP laboratory, the performance of an active vision system has also been studied [22].

Fig. 1. The MDOF binocular system

414

2 Control of the MDOF Binocular Tracking System

In most cases visual servoing systems are analyzed as servo systems that use vision as a sensor [23, 24]. Therefore the binocular tracking system should be considered as a servomechanism whose reference inputs are the target coordinates in space and whose outputs are the motor velocities and/or positions. However in the case of this system, and as a result of both its mechanical complexity and its goal (tracking of targets with unknown dynamics), we decided to relate the system outputs with the data measured from the images. Thus this system can be considered as a regulator whose goal is to keep the target in a certain position in the image (usually its center). As a result of this framework target motion is dealt with as a perturbation. If the perturbation affects the target position and/or velocity in the image it has to be compensated for.

2.1 Monocular Smooth Pursuit

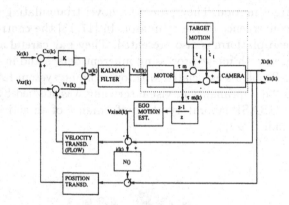

Fig. 2. Monocular smooth pursuit block diagram. The dotted box encloses the analog components of the structure. Block $N(i(k))$ represents a non-linear function. $V_{xf}(k)$ is the command sent to the motor, obtained by filtering $u(k)$, the sum of the estimated velocity with the position error multiplied by a gain $K.V_{xind}(k)$ is the velocity induced in image by camera motion

Each camera joint has two independent rotational degrees of freedom: pan and tilt. Even though pure rotation can not be guaranteed we model these degrees of freedom as purely rotational. A schematic for one of the these degrees of freedom is depicted in Fig 2 (both degrees of freedom are similar and decoupled). Notice that 2 inputs and 2 outputs are considered. Both position and velocity of the target in the image are to be controlled or regulated. Even though the two quantities are closely related, this formal distinction allows for a better evaluation of some aspects such as non-linearities and limitations in performance.

$$\begin{cases} i(k) = V_{xt}(k) - V_{xind}(k) \\ N(i(k)) = 1 \impliedby i(k) \neq 0 \\ N(i(k)) = 0 \impliedby i(k) = 0 \end{cases} \qquad (1)$$

Considering that the motion computed in the image is caused by target motion and by camera motion, the computation of the target velocity requires that the effects of egomotion are compensated for. The egomotion is estimated based on the encoder readings and on the inverse kinematics. Once egomotion velocity $(V_{xind}(k))$ is compensated for, target velocity in the image plane is computed based on an affine model of optical flow. Target position is estimated as the average location of the set of points with non-zero optical flow in two consecutive frames (after egomotion having been compensated for). This way what is actually computed is the center of motion instead of target position. The estimated value will be zero whenever the object stops, for it is computed by using function $N(i(k))$ (equation 1) .

2.2 Vergence Block Diagram

In this binocular system, pan and tilt control align the cyclopean Z (forward-looking) axis with the target. Vergence control adjusts both camera positions so that both target images are projected in the corresponding image centers. Retinal flow disparity is used to achieve vergence control. Vergence angles for both cameras are equal and angular vergence velocity is computed in equation 2 where Δv_{xf} is the horizontal retinal motion disparity and f the focal length.[25]

$$\frac{\partial \beta}{\partial t} = \frac{\Delta v_{xf}}{2f} \qquad (2)$$

A schematic for vergence control is depicted in Fig.3. Horizontal target motion disparity is regulated by controlling the vergence angle.

Both in smooth pursuit and vergence control, target motion acts as a perturbation that has to be compensated for. To study and characterize system regulation/control performance usual control test signals must be applied. Two problems have to be considered:

– The accurate generation of perturbation signals;
– The generation of perturbation signals functionally defined, such as steps, ramps, parabolas and sinusoids;

3 Reference Trajectories Generation Using Synthetic Images

To characterize the system ability to compensate for the perturbations due to target motion, specific signals have to be generated. Instead of using real targets, we decided to use synthetic images so that the mathematical functions corresponding to reference trajectories could be accurately generated. These images

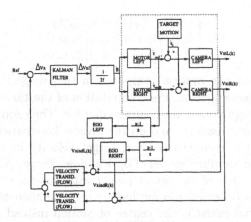

Fig. 3. Vergence block diagram. Egomotion is estimated for each camera. After that target velocities in both left and right images are computed using differential flow. Estimated horizontal disparity (Δv_{xf}) is obtained by filtering the difference of measured velocities in both images

are then used as inputs in the binocular active vision system. Given a predefined motion, captured frames will depend, not only on the target position, but also on the camera orientation. Due to the change on the system geometry as a result of its operation, images have to be generated on line to take into account the specific geometry at each time instant. Therefore at each time instant both target position and camera orientation have to be known in the same inertial coordinate system. The former is calculated using a specific motion model that enables the computation of any kind of motion in space. Camera orientation is computed by taking into account the motor encoders readings and the inverse kinematics. The inertial coordinate system origin is placed at optical center (monocular case) or at the origin of the cyclopean referential (binocular case).

To accurately describe the desired target motion in space the corresponding equations are used. Motion coordinates are converted into inertial cartesian coordinates by applying the suitable transformation equations[26]. Target coordinates in the inertial system are converted in camera coordinates. This transformation depends on motor positions that are known by reading the encoders. Perspective projection is assumed for image formation. These computations are performed at each frame time instant.

4 Perturbation Signals. The Reference Trajectories Equations.

To characterize control performance, target motion correspondent to a step, a ramp, a parabola and a sinusoid should be used to perturb the system.

4.1 The Monocular Tracking System

Reference Trajectories Defined for the Actuators Consider the perturbation at actuator/motor output. The reference trajectories are studied for both a rotary and a linear actuator.

In the former the actuator is a rotary motor and the camera undergoes a pure rotation around the Y (pan) and X (tilt) axis. Consider target motion equations defined in spherical coordinates (ρ, ϕ, θ), where ρ is the radius or depth, ϕ the elevation angle and θ the horizontal angular displacement. The target angular position $\theta(t)$ at time t is given by one of:

$$\theta(t) = \begin{cases} Const \Longleftarrow t > 0 \\ 0 \Longleftarrow t = 0 \end{cases} \tag{3}$$

$$\theta(t) = \omega.t \tag{4}$$

$$\theta(t) = \frac{\gamma}{2}.t^2 \tag{5}$$

$$\theta(t) = A\sin(\omega.t) \tag{6}$$

Equations 3, 4, 5 and 6 describe a step, a ramp, a parabola and a sinusoid for the pan motor. For instance, if the target moves according to equation 4, the motor has to rotate with constant angular velocity ω to track the target. These definitions can be extended to the tilt motor by making $\theta = 0$ and varying ϕ according to equations 3 to 6.

Assume now a linear actuator and camera moving along the X axis. Cartesian equations 7 to 10 are the equivalent to spherical equations 3 to 6. In all cases the depth z_i is made constant.

$$x_i(t) = \begin{cases} Const \Longleftarrow t > 0 \\ 0 \Longleftarrow t = 0 \end{cases} \tag{7}$$

$$x_i(t) = v.t \tag{8}$$

$$x_i(t) = \frac{a}{2}.t^2 \tag{9}$$

$$x_i(t) = A\sin(v.t) \tag{10}$$

Reference Test Signals Defined in Image To relate the system outputs with the data measured from the images, control test signals must be generated in the image plane. Thus a step (in position) is an abrupt change of target position in image. A ramp/parabola (in position) occurs when the 3D target motion generates motion with constant velocity/acceleration in the image plane. And a sinusoid is generated whenever the image target position and velocity are described by sinusoidal functions of time (with a phase difference of 90 degrees).

Assume the camera is static. Target motion described by equations 7 to 10 generates the standard control test signals in image. This result is still true if camera moves along a linear path.

418

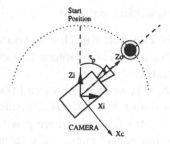

Fig. 4. Monocular tracking. $\alpha_p(t)$ is motor angular position and $\theta(t)$ the target angular position

$$\omega_i = f \cdot \frac{d\theta}{dt} \cdot \frac{1}{\cos^2(\theta - \alpha_p)} \tag{11}$$

$$\gamma_i . t = f \cdot \frac{d\theta}{dt} \cdot \frac{1}{\cos^2(\theta - \alpha_p)} \tag{12}$$

$$A\omega_i \cos(\omega_i . t) = f \cdot \frac{d\theta}{dt} \cdot \frac{1}{\cos^2(\theta - \alpha_p)} \tag{13}$$

However MDOF system eye cameras perform rotations. For this situation the reference trajectories that generate a perturbation in ramp, parabola and sinusoid are derived by solving the differential equations 11, 12 and 13 in order to $\theta(t)$ (ω_i, γ_i and A are the desired induced velocity, acceleration and amplitude in image plane).[27] The difficulty is that the reference trajectories ($\theta(t)$) will depend on the system reaction to the perturbation ($\alpha_p(t)$). Thus to induce a constant velocity in image during operation, target angular velocity must be computed at each frame time instant in function of the the tracking error.

Consider the case of perfect tracking. The tracking error will be null and $\alpha_p(t) = \theta(t)$. With this assumption the solutions of differential equations 11 to 13 are given by equations 4 to 6 (making $\omega = \frac{\omega_i}{f}$ and $\gamma = \frac{\gamma_i}{f}$). These are the reference trajectories that we use to characterize the system. While is true that, for instance, trajectory of eq.4 (the ramp) only induces a constant velocity in image if tracking error is null (small velocity variation will occur otherwise), the test signal becomes independent of the system reaction and the generated perturbation allows the evaluation of system ability to recover from tracking errors.

4.2 The Vergence Control System

Taking into account the considerations of last section, the reference trajectories for vergence control characterization of the binocular system depicted in Fig. 5 are presented.

$$2fb \cdot \frac{d\rho}{dt} + v.\rho^2 = -v.b^2 \tag{14}$$

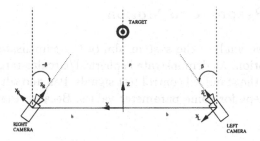

Fig. 5. Top view of binocular system. The distance between the cameras is $2b$ and symmetric vergence is assumed. $\rho(t)$ is the target Z coordinate.

$$a = -\frac{2fb}{\rho^2 + b^2} \cdot \frac{d^2\rho}{dt^2} + \rho \cdot \frac{4fb}{(\rho^2 + b^2)^2} \cdot (\frac{d\rho}{dt})^2 \tag{15}$$

$$2fb. \frac{d\rho}{dt} + Aw\cos(wt).\rho^2 = -Aw\cos(wt).b^2 \tag{16}$$

Assume perfect tracking. The target motion equation $\rho(t)$ that generates a motion corresponding to a ramp in image target position (constant velocity disparity v) is determined solving equation 14. For a parabola (constant acceleration disparity a) equation 15 must be solved. In the case of a sinusoidal stimulus, the relevant target motion equation $\rho(t)$ can be computed by solving equation 16.[27] Test signals obtained solving diferential equations 14 and 16 are depicted in

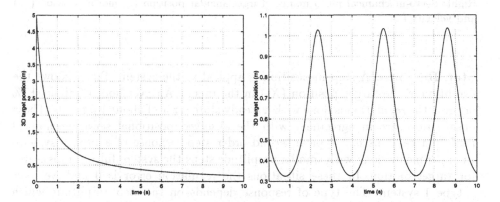

Fig. 6. Left: Ramp perturbation. Target motion to generate a constant disparity of 1 pixel/frame ($\rho(0) = 5(m)$).Right: Sinusoidal Perturbation. Target motion that generates a sinusoidal velocity disparity in images($A = 2$(pixel), $\omega = 2$(rad/s) and $\rho(0) = 1$(m))

Fig.6. Notice that to induce a constant velocity disparity in images the 3D target velocity increases with depth. This is due to the perspective projection.

5 System Response to Motion

In this section we analyze the system ability to compensate for perturbations due to target motion. As demonstrated spherical/circular target motion must be used to generate the standard control test signals. Pan and tilt control algorithms are identical except for some parameter values. Because that we only consider the pan axis.

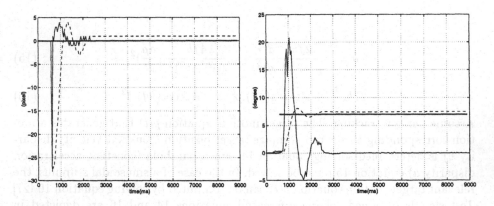

Fig. 7. Left: Regulation performance. Target position (- -) and velocity (-) in image. Right: Servo-mechanical performance. Target angular position (.), motor position (- -) and velocity (-)

Step Response A step in position is applied to the system. Fig. 7 shows the evolution of the target position (X_t) in the image. An overshoot of about 10% occurs. The regulation is done with a steady state error of about 1.5 pixels. These observations are in agreement with the observed positional servo-mechanical performance. This is a typical second order step response of a type 0 system. In experiments done with smaller amplitude steps the system fully compensates for target motion. In these situations the regulation error is 0 and we have a type 1 system. The type of response depends on the step amplitude which clearly indicates a non-linear behavior. One of the main reasons for the non-linear behavior is the way position feedback is performed. After compensating for egomotion, target position is estimated as the average location of the set of points with non-zero optical flow in two consecutive frames. Thus the center of motion is calculated instead of the target position. If the target stops, any displacement detected in the image is due camera motion. In that case target velocity $(V_{xt}(k))$ is equal to induced velocity $(V_{xind}(k))$ and the position estimate C_x will be 0. Therefore target position would only be estimated at the step transition time instant. Only with egomotion as a pure rotation would this occur. In practice sampling and misalignment errors between the rotation axis and the center of projection introduce small errors.

A step in position corresponds to an impulse perturbation in velocity. Fig 7 shows the ability of the system to cancel the perturbation. Note that only the first peak velocity is due to real target motion.

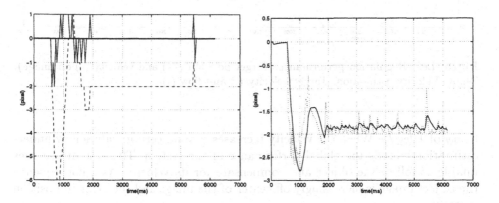

Fig. 8. Left:Regulation performance.Target position (- -) and velocity (-) in the image. Right: Kalman filtering. Kalman input $u(k)$ (.) and output $V_{xf}(k)$(-)

Ramp Response Fig.8 exhibits the ramp response for a velocity of 10 deg/s (1.5 pixel/frame). The target moves about 6 pixels off the center of image before the system starts to compensate for it. It clearly presents an initial inertia where the action of the Kalman filter plays a major role. The Kalman filtering limits the effect of measurement errors and allows smooth motion without oscillations.

Considering the motor performance we have a type 1 position response to a ramp and a second order type 1 velocity response to a step. The position measurement error

$$e(k) = X_t(k) - C_x(k) \tag{17}$$

will be directly proportional to the speed of motion.

The algorithm for velocity estimation using optical flow only performs well for small velocities (up to 2 pixels/frame). For higher speeds of motion the flow is clearly underestimated. This represents a severe limitation that is partially compensated for by the proportional position error component on the motor commands. Experiments were performed that enabled us to conclude that the system only follows motions with constant velocities of up to 20 deg / s.

Parabola Response The perturbation is generated by a target moving around the camera with a constant angular acceleration of 5 deg /s^2 and an initial ve-

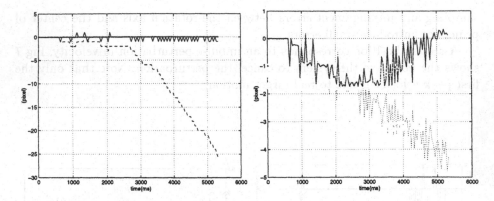

Fig. 9. Left: Regulation performance. Target position (- -) and velocity (-) on image). Right: Velocity estimation. Target velocity (.) and flow (-)

locity of $1 \deg/s$. When the velocity increases beyond certain values flow underestimation bounds the global performance of the system. The system becomes unable to follow the object and compensate for its velocity. As a consequence the object image is increasingly off center of the image and the error in position increases.

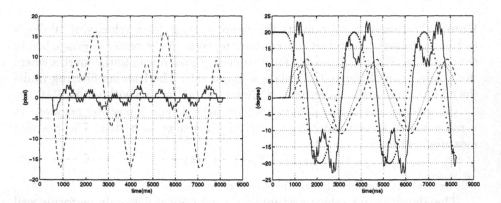

Fig. 10. Left: Regulation Performance–Target position(- -) and velocity (-) in the image. Right: Servo-mechanical performance in position. Motor position (- -) and velocity (-). Target position (:) and velocity (.)

Sinusoidal Response System reaction to a sinusoidal perturbation of angular velocity $2 rad/s$ is studied. Fig. 10 shows target position X_t and velocity V_x in the image. Non-linear distortions, mainly caused by velocity underestimation, can be observed. Notice the phase lag and the gain in position motor response in Fig. 10.

6 Motor Performance and Its Implication in Global System Behavior

During system response analysis non-linear behaviors were observed. Despite that, linear approximations can be considered for certain ranges of operation. Therefore we have estimated the transfer functions of some of the sub-systems depicted in Fig. 2 using system identification techniques. [26].

$$M(z) = 0.09z^{-3} \cdot \frac{1 + 0.38z^{-1}}{(1 - z^{-1})(1 - 0.61z^{-1} + 0.11z^{-2})} \qquad (18)$$

Equation 18 gives the obtained motor transfer function. $M(z)$ relates the computed velocity command ($V_{xf}(k)$) in $pixel/sec$, with motor angular position in degrees. The pole in $z = 1$ is due to the integration needed for velocity-position conversion. A pure delay of 3 frames (120ms) was observed. There is a consid-

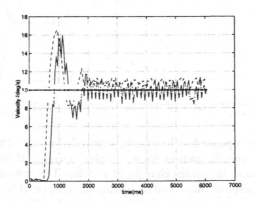

Fig. 11. Motor input and output for a ramp perturbation of 1.5pixel/frame (10deg/s). Velocity command sent to DCX board controler (–) and motor velocity measured by reading the encoders (-). Sampling period of 40ms (each frame time instant)

erable inertia from motor input to output (see Fig.11). Such a delay certainly interferes with global system performance. In the MDOF robot head actuation is done using DC motors with harmonic drive controlled by Precision Microcontrol DCX boards. The implemented control loop is depicted in Fig.12. Motor position is controlled using a classic closed-loop configuration with a digital PID controller running at 1KHz. For velocity control the reference inputs (in position) are computed by a profile generator. This device integrates the velocity

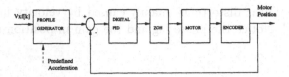

Fig. 12. Motor control loop. A PID is used to control motor position. The sampling frequency in the closed-loop is 1KHz. A profile generator allows to control the motor in velocity

commands sent by the user process. Acceleration and deacceleration values can be configured to assure more or less smoothness in velocity changes. Due to the fact that each board controls up to six axis, the user process can only read the encoders and send commands for 6ms time intervals.

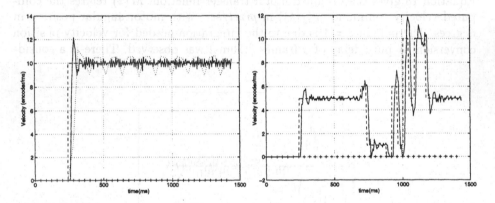

Fig. 13. Left: Step response for the velocity controlled motor. The velocity command (–) and the motor velocity output for a sampling interval of 6ms (-) and 40ms (:). Right: Motor response to sudden changes in velocity. The velocity command (–) and the motor velocity response measured for a sampling interval of 6ms (-). In both figures, the dashes along zero axis mark the frame time instants (40ms)

$$V_\alpha[kT] = \frac{1}{T} \int_{(k-1)T}^{kT} v_\alpha(t).dt \tag{19}$$

As shown in Fig.2, at each frame time instant (40ms), the velocity command $V_{xf}[k]$ is sent to motor and camera position is read at the encoders. These readings are used to estimate motor velocity. Assuming that $v_\alpha(t)$ is the continuous time motor velocity, the measured value $V_\alpha[kT]$ will be given by equation 19, where T is the sampling period. Therefore, at each sampling instant, we are estimating the average velocity along the period instead of the velocity at that instant. Fig.13 shows the same step response measured for two different sampling rates. we can therefore conclude that $T = 40ms$ is too large to correctly estimate instantaneous velocity. We can also conclude that the delay of 3 frames as well as the ripple observed in Fig.11 results from different sampling rates. As a matter of fact such delay as well as ripple do not occur.

Notice that the delay observed in transfer function $M(z)$ is correct (velocity input and position output). It means that the motor takes about 3 frame time instants to get to the same position that it would reach in 1 frame time instant for an ideal velocity response. from the standpoint of position regulation this value is important. It interferes with the tracking steady state error. However, to achieve high performance visual tracking the system must perform velocity regulation. The rise time of motor velocity response is the crucial parameter to achieve responsive behaviors.

The DCX board turns a position controlled axis in a velocity controlled axis using an additional integrator (the profile generator). The PID of the inner position loop must be "tight" in order to minimize the position error and guarantee small velocity rise times. Fig.13 exhibits the motor response for successive velocity commands. The rise time is about 1 frame time instant. The overshoot is not constant (non-linear behavior) and the global performance decreases for abrupt changes in input. So, during operation, abrupt changes in velocity commands must be avoided to maximize motor performance. A decrease in processing time

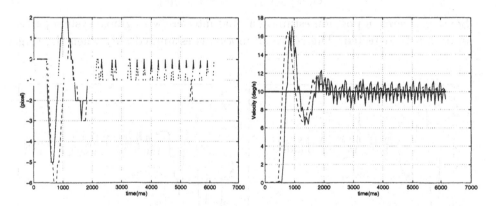

Fig. 14. Response for a ramp perturbation of 1.5pixel/frame (10deg/s).Left: Regulation performance. Processing time of 38ms (–) and 8ms(-).Right: Velocity command sent to DCX board controller (–) and motor velocity measured by reading the encoders (-). In both figures the sampling interval is 40ms

from 38ms to 9ms was achieved by improving the used hardware (processor upgrade). The effects in global performance can be observed in Fig.14. In the first implementation, the frame was captured and the actuating command was sent just before the following frame grabbing. Considering a rise time of 1 frame time instant, the motor only reached the velocity reference 80ms after the capture of the corresponding frame. By decreasing the image processing time the reaction delay is reduced to almost half the value and the system becomes more responsive. When the second frame is grabbed, the camera is approximately moving with the target velocity estimated in the previous iteration.

7 Improvements in the Visual Processing

The characterization of the active vision system allows the identification of several aspects that limit the global performance. In this section improvements in visual processing are discussed as a way to overcome some of the problems.

7.1 Target Position Estimation in Image

The input velocity sent to the motor is obtained by filtering the sum of the estimated target velocity with the estimated target position multiplied by a gain K(equation 20). This is a simple control law that will probably be changed in future developments. However, the position component is always fundamental to keep the position regulation error small and to reduce the effects of occasional velocity misprediction.

$$u(k) = V_x(k) + K.C_x(k) \tag{20}$$

$$C_x[k] = C_x[k-1] + V_{xind}[k] \tag{21}$$

Some problems in position estimation, that interfere with global system performance, were detected. The center of motion is estimated only when the target

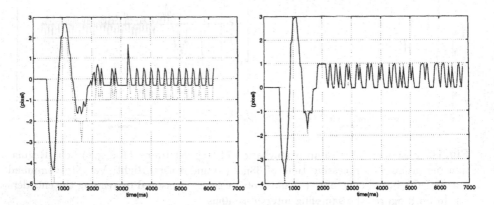

Fig. 15. Response for a ramp perturbation of 1.5pixel/frame (10deg/s). Left: Position estimation using the original method. Target position (:) and target position estimation(-). Right: Position estimation using the improved method. Target position (:) and target position estimation (-)

induces motion in image. When no target motion is detected (after egomotion compensation) it can be assumed that the target did not move. Thus the new position estimate should be equal to the previous estimate compensated for the induced velocity due to camera motion(equation 21). Another problem is that the center of motion is computed instead of the target position. The position estimate is computed as the average location of the set of points with non-zero optical flow in two consecutive frames. If this set is restricted to the points of the last grabbed frame that have non-zero brightness partial derivatives with respect to X and Y, the average location will be near the target position. The improvements in position estimation can be observed in Fig.15. The improvements on

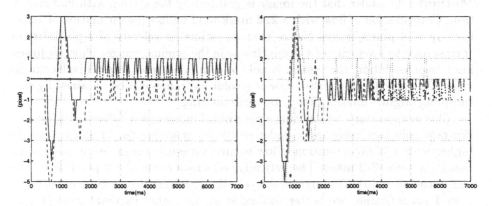

Fig. 16. Response for a ramp perturbation of 1.5pixel/frame (10deg/s). Left: Regulation performance. Original (–) and improved (-) position estimation method. Right: Regulation performance. Improved position estimation method for a K=0.2 (:), 0.3 (-) and 0.4 (–)

global system performance can be observed in Fig.16. The selected value for the gain K was 0.3. This value decreases the time of reaction and the position error without leading to oscillatory behaviors.

7.2 Target Velocity Estimation in Image

To estimate target velocity in image, the brightness gradient $(grad_I(I_x, I_y, I_t)$ is calculated in all pixels of the grabbed frame. Considering the flow constraint and assuming that all points in image move with the same velocity, the velocity vector (u, v) is estimated using a least squares method.

$$I_x.u + I_y.v + I_t = 0 \qquad (22)$$

The flow constraint 22 is true for a continuous brightness function. However our brightness function $I(x, y, t)$ is discrete in time and space. Aliasing problems in partial derivatives computation can compromise a correct velocity estimation.

When the target image moves very slowly high spatial resolution is needed in order to correctly compute the derivatives Ix and Iy and estimate the velocity. On the other hand, if the the target image moves fast, there are high frequencies in time and I_t must be computed for small sampling periods. However the sampling frequency is limited to 25Hz. One solution to estimate high target velocities is to decrease the spatial resolution. The drawback of this approach is that high frequencies are lost, and small target movements will no longer be detected. We tried two methods to increase the range of target velocities in image that the systems is able to estimate.

Method 1 Consider that the image is grabbed by the system with half resolution. Computation of flow with a $2x2$ mask would allow the estimation of velocities up to 4 pixels/frame. Notice that an estimated velocity of 2 pixels/frame corresponds to a velocity of 4 pixels/frame in the original image. Thus, by lowering image resolution, the system is able to compute higher target displacements using the same flow algorithm. Lower resolution frames can be obtained by subsampling original images after a low-pass filtering.

This method starts by building a pyramid of images with different resolutions. For now only two levels are considered: the lower with a $64x64$ image, and the higher with a $32x32$ resolution. Flow is simultaneously computed in both levels using the same 2x2 mask. Theoretically, velocities below the 2 pixel/frame are well estimated in the low pyramid level (V_{low}). Higher displacements (between 2 to 4 pixels/frame) are better evaluated at the higher pyramid level (V_{high}). At each frame time instant the algorithm must decide which estimated velocity (V_{low} or V_{high}) is nearest to real target velocity in image.

$$\sum_{i=1}^{N} (I_x^i.u + I_y^i.v + I_t^i)^2 = 0 \tag{23}$$

Consider N data points where brightness gradient is evaluated. The velocity (u, v) is computed as the vector that minimizes the quadratic error of 23. Most of times the "fitting" is not perfect and each data point has a residue associated with it. The mean residue of the N points can be used as a measurement of the estimation process performance. Our algorithm chooses the velocity estimation with the smaller mean residue.

Method 2 As in method 1 a similar two-level pyramid is computed. The flow is computed at the high level using a $2x2$ mask. The result of this operation (V_{high}) controls the size of the mask that is used to estimate target velocity in the 64x64 level (V_{low}). The mask can have the size of 2,3 or 4 pixels depending on the value of V_{high} at each time instant. Notice that in this approach the final velocity is always given by V_{low}. The decision is not about which level has the best velocity estimation, but about changing the mask size for flow computation in the low level frame.

The law that controls mask size is based on intervals between predefined threshold values. To each interval corresponds a certain mask size that it is chosen if the value of V_{high} belongs to that interval. For a two level pyramid two threshold values are needed. The threshold values are determined experimentally.

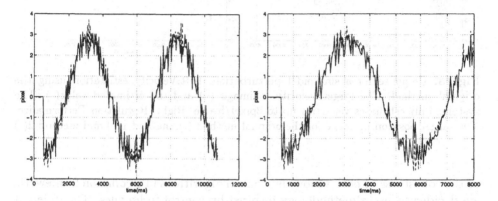

Fig. 17. Response for a sinusoidal perturbation. Right: Velocity estimation using method 1. Left: Velocity estimation using method 2. The target velocity in image (−) and the estimated value(-). Both methods perform a correct estimation of velocity

Experimental Results The original implementation is unable to estimate velocities above 2pixel/frame (see Fig18). With the new methods the system becomes able to estimate velocities up to 4pixel/frame.

The improvements in system performance can be observed in Fig18. In both methods the range of estimated velocities can be increased by using more levels in the pyramid. In method 2 the choice of the threshold values is critical for a good performance. Method 2 has the advantage of decoupling the velocity estimation in X and Y. For instance, consider that target velocity in the image is very high in X direction (horizontal) and small in Y direction (vertical). With method 1 it is not possible to have a good velocity estimate in both directions. If V_{high} is chosen then vertical velocity estimation will be affected by a great error; if V_{low} is chosen the horizontal velocity will be underestimated. Method 2 deals with this case by computing the flow in the 64x64 image with a rectangular mask 2x4.

8 Summary and Conclusions

In this paper we address the problem of improving the performance of tracking performed by a binocular active vision system. In order to enable the evaluation

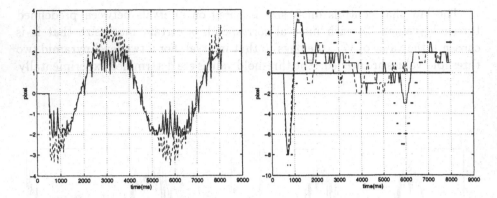

Fig. 18. Response for a sinusoidal perturbation. Left: Velocity estimation using the original method. The target velocity in image (–) and the estimated value(-). The systems only estimates velocities up to 2pixel/frame. Right: Regulation Performance. The target position in image for the original method (.), method 1(–) and method 2(-)

of the robustness of both vision and control algorithms in a common framework, we decided to use a methodology inspired by control techniques. The different subsystems were characterized by their responses to test inputs. Due to the specific features of an active vision system several questions related to the definition of system reference inputs had to be addressed. As a result we propose and justify a methodology for the definition and generation of such reference inputs.

System identification of some modules of the system, including the visual processing routines (which required their linearization), was also done. The results enabled us to identify elements that should be improved. Specifically, in this paper, we described the improvements in the visual processing algorithms. These improvements enable the system to track targets in a much larger range of depths.

References

1. Ruzena Bajcsy. Active perception vs. passive perception. *Third Workshop on Computer Vision: Representatin and Control*, pages 55–59, October 1985.
2. Y. Aloimonos, I. Weiss, and A. Bandyopadhay. Active vision. *International Journal of Computer Vision*, 1(4):333–356, January 1988.
3. H. I. Christensen, J. Horstmann, and T. Rasmussen. A control theoretic approach to active vision. *Asian Conference on Computer Vision*, pages 201–210, December 1995.
4. J. L. Crowley, J. M. Bedrune, M. Bekker, and M. Schneider. Integration and control of reactive visula processes. *Third European Conference in Computer Vision*, 2:47–58, May 1994.
5. J. O. Eklundh, K. Pahlavan, and T. Uhlin. The kth head-eye system. In *Vision as a Process*, pages 237–259, 1995.

6. T. Vieville. A few steps towards 3d active vision. *Springer-Verlag*, 1997.
7. A. Bernardino and J. Santos-Victor. Sensor geometry for dynamic vergence: Characterization and performance analysis. *Workshop on Performance Characterization of Vision Algorithms*, pages 55–59, 1996.
8. G. Hager and S. Hutchinson. Special section on vision-based control of robot manipulators. *IEEE Trans. on Robot. and Automat.*, 12(5), October 1996.
9. R. Horaud and F. Chaumette, editors. *Workshop on New Trends in Image-Based Robot Servoing*, September 1997.
10. E. Dickmanns. Vehicles capable of dynamic vision. *in Proc. of the 15th International Conference on Artificail Intelligence*, August 1997.
11. E. Dickmanns. An approach to robust dynamic vision. *in Proc. of the IEEE Workshop on Robust Vision for Vision-Based Control of Motion*, May 1998.
12. P. I. Corke and M. C. Good. Dynamic effects in visual closed-loop systems. *IEEE Trans. on Robotics and Automation*, 12(5):671–683, October 1996.
13. P. I. Corke. *Visual Control of Robots: High-Peformance Visual Servoing*. Mechatronics. John Wiley, 1996.
14. R. Kelly. Robust asymptotically stable visual servoing of planar robots. *IEEE Trans. on Robot. and Automat*, 12(5):697–713, October 1996.
15. W. Hong. Robotic catching and manipulation using active vision. Master's thesis, MIT, September 1995.
16. A. Rizzi and D. E. Koditschek. An active visual estimator for dexterous manipulation. *IEEE Trans. on Robot. and Automat*, 12(5):697–713, October 1996.
17. P. Sharkey, D. Murray, S. Vandevelde, I. Reid, and P. Mclauchlan. A modular head/eye platform for real-time reactive vision. *Mechatronics*, 3(4):517–535, 1993.
18. P. Sharkey and D. Murray. Delays versus performance of visually guided systems. *IEE Proc.-Control Theory Appl.*, 143(5):436–447, September 1996.
19. C. Brown. Gaze controls with interactions and delays. *IEEE Trans. on Systems, Man and Cybern.*, 20(2):518–527, 1990.
20. D. Coombs and C. Brown. Real-time binocular smooth pursuit. *International Journal of Computer Vision*, 11(2):147–164, October 1993.
21. H. Rotstein and E. Rivlin. Optimal servoing for active foveated vision. *in Proc. of the IEEE Conf. on Computer Vision and Pattern Recognition*, pages 177–182, June 1996.
22. Ulf M. Cahn von Seelen. Performance evaluation of an active vision system. Master's thesis, University of Pennsylvania, Philadelphia, USA, May 1997.
23. B. Espiau, F. Chaumette, and P. Rives. A new approach to visual servoing in robotics. *IEEE Trans. on Robot. and Automat.*, 8(3):313–326, June 1992.
24. P. Allen, A. Timcenko, B. Yoshimi, and P. Michelman. Automated tracking and grasping of a moving object with a robotic hand-eye system. *IEEE Trans. on Robot. and Automat.*, 9(2):152–165, 1993.
25. J. Batista, P. Peixoto, and H. Araujo. Real-time active visual surveillance by integrating peripheral motion detection with foveated tracking. In *Proc. of the IEEE Workshop on Visual Surveillance*, pages 18–25, 1998.
26. J. Barreto, P. Peixoto, J. batista, and H. Araujo. Evaluation of the robustness of visual behaviors through performance characterization. *in Proc. of the IEEE Workshop on Robust Vision for Vision-Based Control of Motion*, 1998.
27. J. Barreto, P. Peixoto, J. Batista, and H. Araujo. Performance characterization of visula behaviors in an active vision system. *In 6th International Symposium on Intelligent Robotic Systems*, pages 309–318, July 1998.

Surveillance System Based on Detection and Tracking of Moving Objects Using CMOS Imagers

J. E. Santos Conde[1], A. Teuner[1], S.-B. Park[2], and B. J. Hosticka[1]

[1] Fraunhofer Institute of Microelectronic Circuits and Systems,
Finkenstr. 61, D-47057 Duisburg, Germany, santos@ims.fhg.de
[2] Bayerische Motoren Werke AG,
Knorrstr. 147, D-80788 München, Germany

Abstract. The present contribution presents a novel stand-alone surveillance system based on detection and tracking of moving objects using CMOS imagers. The system fuses the acquisition and processing task, so that a flexible, low-cost, and highly efficient image processing system for home and industrial applications can be realised. The surveillance system consists of a CMOS camera mounted on a multi-functional module (MfM) using a PCMCIA 10 Mbit Ethernet card. The acquired images can be transmitted directly via Internet protocol to the requesting workstations. The surveillance camera system is capable of suppressing extraneous illumination effects caused for example by day light variations. The detection of moving objects in the image sequence is carried out using a novel adaptive image processing algorithm. The required parameters are adapted automatically to the observed scene. The apparent shapes of independently moving objects are extracted with high accuracy even for objects that are stationary for certain time periods. The approach also takes into account slowly changing illuminations, and does not detect them as moving objects. It works very well with severely image sequences corrupted by noise. The presented simulation results highlight the performance of the proposed method using synthetic and real video data.

1 Introduction

The main aim of a surveillance system is to detect scene changes by evaluating apparent shapes of moving objects in an image sequence regardless of their speed, direction, or texture. This task can be solved using a great variety of image processing methods. Image sequence processing is, in general, computationally exhaustive due to high data volume typical for 2-D signal processing. For real-time applications most of the known methods require special hardware and complex software which prevent them from being used in low cost surveillance systems. In our contribution we propose a novel method, which exhibits a high performance at low cost.

In the past detection of scene changes has been usually considered regarding either only the algorithmic or the sensory part. In contrast with this we will consider both parts of a surveillance system in order to obtain an efficient solution. In Section 2, we will discuss the sensory part. We present some advantages of the CMOS imager used in our camera system and will discuss this in more details. In Section 3, we describe the surveillance system consisting of the CMOS camera. The algorithmic part is described in Section 4. Several approaches to detection of scene changes are presented and compared with our method. Afterward we present some simulation results that verify the superior performance of the proposed method and give a short summary.

2 CMOS Camera

The mainstream technology for image sensors is based on the principle of charge-coupled devices called CCDs. At present this technology is the best for high-quality image sensors for video applications. But there are some limitations to the use of CCD technology in vision applications which will be discussed in the following. The major drawbacks are the relatively high costs of these imagers and the lack of possibility to include readout circuitry and control logic on the CCD imager chip.

An alternative for the CCDs are image sensors based on CMOS technology. As an example we want to demonstrate our camera which contains a 128×128 pixel photosensor array chip based on standard CMOS technology which will be used in the proposed surveillance system. The chip also contains readout electronics and control logic. The CMOS image sensor used provides a high dynamic range, which is necessary to cope with large illumination variations which, for instance, occur in automotive applications [10]. The variation of the average illumination level in outdoor scenes is extremely high: it can vary from very bright light on sunny days (>10 klx) to poor illumination at night (<100 mlx). Moreover, the illumination level can also vary within a single image. To characterize the maximal intensity variation in an image which can be processed, we define a so called dynamic range which is the ratio created by the maximum and minimum intensities. The dynamic range of CCD imagers is usually below 80 dB, which is too low for many applications. In addition, CCD photosensors show two more serious problems connected with high illumination variations in a scene. Vertical columns under and above the pixels exposed to high intensity irradiance may appear *white* owing to the illumination of these columns during the transfer of the photocharges. This phenomenon is called smearing. The second phenomenon is called blooming. Blooming results in an enlargement of the region of saturated pixels. The charges generated under a saturated pixel will be detected by the neighbours until also these pixels saturate. The result is an enlargement of the saturated region of pixels. In extreme situations the entire image is saturated. Modern commercial CCDs with an anti-blooming-function can reduce the blooming effect, but not eliminate it. Moreover, the photoresponsivity of the CCD imagers is somewhat reduced due to these measures. Another problem of CCD based imagers is their limited temperature range: the maximum operating temperature is below 60°C. The effect of the temperature is an increase in dark current, which doubles every 8°C. Especially in poor illuminated scenes, the dark current, which is added to the photocurrent, can be seen as a random temperature dependent pattern which is superimposed to the image. Due to the variation of the dark current from pixel to pixel, it cannot be distinguished from the photo signal. In the following we sumarize a few advantages to the use of CMOS technology [10].

- One significant advantage is the possibility to integrate on-chip readout and control. Intelligent vision algorithms can be implemented to perform low-level vision tasks [16].
- At present CCDs are still superior for high-quality imaging, like scientific applications. But for vision and consumer applications, the image quality of CMOS sensors is satisfactory.
- The power consumption of CMOS image sensors is low.
- CMOS imagers have a high optical dynamic range and a high maximum operating temperature.
- CMOS sensors offer flexibility in the pixel design. The pixel can be optimised for high-dynamic range, image quality, and responsivity. Besides, a truly random addressable pixel is only possible in CMOS technology.

The CMOS photosensor array used in our camera provides a logarithmic pixel readout and random pixel access. The array was designed to implement a fast 2-D CMOS imager which exhibits 3 dB pixel cut-off frequency of 1 MHz, 0 dB pixel frequency well above 3 MHz, and an optical dynamic range of 140 dB with a signal-to-noise ratio of 56 dB. The 128 × 128 pixel imager has been integrated in a standard 1 μm double-metal CMOS process. A hexagonal structure has been used to provide a good circular symmetry [5].

Fig. 1. Acquisition unit of the CMOS camera.

Fig. 2. Active surveillance camera system with the near-infrared LED array and the optical filter.

3   Surveillance System

The surveillance system consists of the CMOS camera mounted on a multifunctional module (MfM) using a PCMCIA interface card. This system includes an Ethernet interface that enables transmission of image sequences directly via Internet protocol to the requesting workstations. The multi-functional module used in our system consists of a Motorola 68332 μC with 1 MByte RAM and works on the real-time operation system VxWorks. The system offers the ability to program the read-out algorithm for the CMOS photosensor array in C or C++. Between the MfM and the CMOS camera an Ethernet connection has been realised using a common PCMCIA 10 Mbit Ethernet card. The system holds its own IP-address and can be connected immediately to the Internet or a LAN [12, 13]. A photograph of the acquisition unit of the CMOS camera is depicted in Fig. 1.

The optical part of the system has a viewing angle of 150° in an 1/3' image plane. The maximum frame rate of 10 frames/sec is limited by the μC. The achieved frame rate is sufficient for surveillance applications. The MfM has the task to capture the images and send them to the requesting station. It is also capable to process directly the images, which significantly reduces the amount of data needed to be transmitted for one image.

Beside the passive imaging the surveillance camera contains an array of near infrared light-emitting diodes (LEDs) (wavelength $\lambda \approx 950$ nm) for active scene illumination and an optical filter which attenuates light with wavelengths below 850 nm by about more than 90% and enables reduction of the effect of extrinsic light sources. In this way the camera system is capable to suppress extrane-

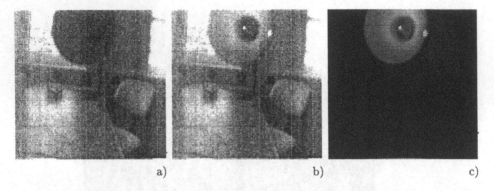

a)   b)   c)

Fig. 3. a) Image without infra-red light, b) image with active scene illumination, and c) IR image.

ous illumination effects caused for example by day light variations and other disturbing artefacts like shadows. The active scene illumination is mandatory when using the surveillance system in outdoor applications. A photograph of the surveillance system with the near-infrared LED array and the optical filter is depicted in Fig. 2. The so-called IR image, which results from the computing of the absolute difference of an image without and an image with active IR light, exhibits several benefits. By computing the IR images the system is capable to grab images including all objects illuminated by the IR light and independently of other light sources. Another advantage is the reduction of fixed-pattern-noise (FPN) caused by spatial nonuniformities of the CMOS photosensor array which can be clearly seen in Fig. 3. Therefore, no FPN correction is necessary.

4   Detection and Tracking of Moving Objects

The processing of image sequences has a broad spectrum of important applications including target tracking, robot navigation, cloud tracking, dynamic monitoring of industrial processes, highway traffic monitoring, and vehicle guidance [4]. Detection and tracking of moving objects in image sequences is a substantial prerequisite for the analysis of a scene. The first step in detection and tracking of objects towards a description of an environment is to separate the foreground from the background or to detect motion. The objective is to detect the apparent shapes regardless of their speed, direction, or texture [14].

The changes in an image sequence derive from three main causes. The first cause is called global motion or camera motion. Even if there is no object motion in the scene, the motion of the camera can induce a global motion in the captured scene. The second one can be caused by the intrinsic motions of the objects in the scene. These local motions usually do not affect the entire image. The third cause can be the variation of illumination caused by the lighting conditions changes while capturing the scene by the camera. In this contribution we assume that the images are taken by a stationary surveillance camera system with fixed focal length. Using this assumption, the changes in the captured images will be assumed to originate from the intrinsic motion of the objects and/or the variations of illumination.

Considering the fact that image sequence processing involves a large amount of data, the algorithms used in image processing are usually computationally exhaustive, especially for real-time applications. In order to realize low-cost stand-alone surveillance systems based on image processing a special care must be taken in order to keep costs down. A typical case of highly complex image processing hardware is represented by motion detection algorithms which are based on computing the *2-D motion field* or *optical flow* [2,3,6]. For real-time applications those methods require special highly expensive hardware which prevent them from being used in low cost surveillance applications. Also, optical flow methods must be used with care, since they are associated with the spatiotemporal variations of intensity. The 2-D motion field is the projection on the 2-D image plane of the 3-D motion scene. Ideally the optical flow will correspond to the 2-D motion field, but this will seldom be so.

In this contribution we present a novel algorithm which is able to detect independently moving objects and to indicate their instantaneous positions as well as apparent shapes with high accuracy, even for temporarily stationary objects. The approach is robust against temporal variations of the background illumination, and does not detect it as a moving object. It works also very well on noisy image sequences, as it will be shown in the simulation results. All algorithms for object detection which will be investigated in this contribution belong to the class of *reference image methods*. A reference image $b(x, y, t)$, designated as background, will be compared with the actual input image $g(x, y, t)$ to compute the binary mask image $\nu(x, y, t)$ which indicates the membership of each pixel in the image to one of the two classes, namely back- or foreground. The indices for horizontal, vertical, and temporal directions will be x, y, and t, respectively. Before introducing the proposed algorithm, we will discuss several algorithms known from the open literature.

4.1 Difference Method

The simplest traditional approach to the detection of moving objects is the so-called difference method which is based on computing the absolute difference of consecutive frames by forming

$$s(x, y, t) = |g(x, y, t) - b(x, y, t)| \tag{1}$$

$$= |g(x, y, t) - g(x, y, t - 1)| \tag{2}$$

and applying a suitably chosen constant threshold λ to this absolute difference in order to generate the binary mask $\nu(x, y, t)$

$$\nu(x, y, t) = \begin{cases} 1 & \text{if } s(x, y, t) > \lambda \ , \\ 0 & \text{else} \ . \end{cases} \tag{3}$$

This method is thus relying on the assumption that the variation of illumination is normally slow when compared to the intensity variations caused by moving objects and that the fast variations in the spatiotemporal intensity are due to local motions. A major drawback of this approach is that slowly moving or stationary objects cannot be detected as foreground. This is similar to the approaches based on computing the optical flow. Hence, the difference method produces an ambiguous mask image. The mask image may contain changes due to the object uncovering background, changes due to the object covering up background, and changes due to the object movement.

4.2   RTL-Filter Method

The ambiguity mentioned above can be avoided by estimating the *true* background image by using a recursive temporal lowpass filter (called RTL-filter) [1]

$$b(x, y, t) = \alpha g(x, y, t) + (1 - \alpha) b(x, y, t - 1) , \quad 0 \leq \alpha \leq 1 , \tag{4}$$

where α denotes the filter coefficient which controls the speed of the background image adaption to the changes of the input image. A recursive temporal filter (i.e. Infinite Impulse Response Filter) has the advantage that, in general, frame storage are quite relaxed. Furthermore, the control of a recursive temporal filter is rather simple. For $\alpha = 1$ the RTL-filter method yields the difference method. Thus the difference method is just a special case of the RTL-filter method. Another advantageous characteristic of this type of filter is that uncorrelated noise is suppressed.

The choice of α is critical for determining the performance of the algorithm. When considering the temporal direction of the 3-D image cube or image sequence two situations can be distinguished. First, in an inactive part of the sequence the temporal signals are stationary in wide sense and highly correlated. Second, in an active part of the sequence moving objects are passing, making the temporal signal highly nonstationary. Moving objects introduce intensity transitions or temporal edges. As nonstationarities in temporal signals are often due to object motion, a background extraction is achieved using a simply temporal lowpass filtering which removes temporal impulses and edges. A drawback of this approach is that objects exhibiting stop-and-go motion are adapted to the background which yields again ambiguities of the mask images. This dilemma can be avoided using the following approaches.

4.3   Kalman Method

The presented techniques for updating the background use only the limited amount of gray value difference to consider the illumination changes. In the following an algorithm is presented where the process of grey value changes in a background image is described as a signal processing system for each pixel. Equation (4) can be rewritten as

$$b(x, y, t) = b(x, y, t - 1) + \alpha \left(g(x, y, t) - b(x, y, t - 1) \right) . \tag{5}$$

In the framework of Kalman-filter theory [9] this equation can be interpreted as a recursive estimation of the background. The input image sequence can be regarded as a background image sequence contaminated by statistical noise and the moving objects. The estimation includes all system information about the past without storing all measured values. The system is controlled by a Kalman-Filter in order to adapt quickly to the illumination changes in the background, and to perform a slow adaption inside the regions including the moving objects. The new prediction is calculated by combining a prediction term which is given by the previous estimate and a correction term given by the measurement deviation.

In many applications where the illumination changes sensibly this first order recursion is not appropriate. Therefore, a dynamic model of the background is used that employs a state vector to improve the background estimation procedure. We will give a brief description of the Kalman-Filter method proposed in [7]. The estimation at time t is

$$
\begin{pmatrix} \hat{g}(x,y,t) \\ \hat{\dot{g}}(x,y,t) \end{pmatrix} = \begin{pmatrix} \tilde{g}(x,y,t) \\ \tilde{\dot{g}}(x,y,t) \end{pmatrix}
$$
$$
+ \mathbf{G}(x,y,t) \left(g(x,y,t) - \mathbf{H}(x,y,t) \begin{pmatrix} \tilde{g}(x,y,t) \\ \tilde{\dot{g}}(x,y,t) \end{pmatrix} \right) ,
$$
(6)

where the system state at time t is represented by $\hat{g}(x,y,t)$ corresponding to the estimated background intensity, $\hat{\dot{g}}(x,y,t)$ is the time rate of change of the estimated background intensity, $\mathbf{G}(x,y,t)$ is the Kalman gain matrix, and $\mathbf{H}(x,y,t)$ is the so-called measurement matrix. The predictive part is computed as

$$
\begin{pmatrix} \tilde{g}(x,y,t) \\ \tilde{\dot{g}}(x,y,t) \end{pmatrix} = \mathbf{A} \begin{pmatrix} \hat{g}(x,y,t-1) \\ \hat{\dot{g}}(x,y,t-1) \end{pmatrix} ,
$$
(7)

where the constant system matrix is given by

$$
\mathbf{A} = \begin{pmatrix} 1 & 0.7 \\ 0 & 0.7 \end{pmatrix}
$$
(8)

which represents the background dynamics. The measurement matrix, which expresses the linear relationship between state variables and measurements, is also constant, namely

$$
\mathbf{H} = (1\ 0) .
$$
(9)

The Kalman gain is computed using

$$
\mathbf{G}(x,y,t) = (k(x,y,t)\ k(x,y,t)) ,
$$
(10)

where $k(x,y,t)$ is set to

$$
k(x,y,t) = k_\alpha \nu(x,y,t-1) + k_\beta(1 - \nu(x,y,t-1)) , \quad 0 \le k_\alpha, k_\beta \le 1 .
$$
(11)

k_α and k_β are the fore- and background gains, respectively. These parameters determine the adaptive properties of the background extraction process.

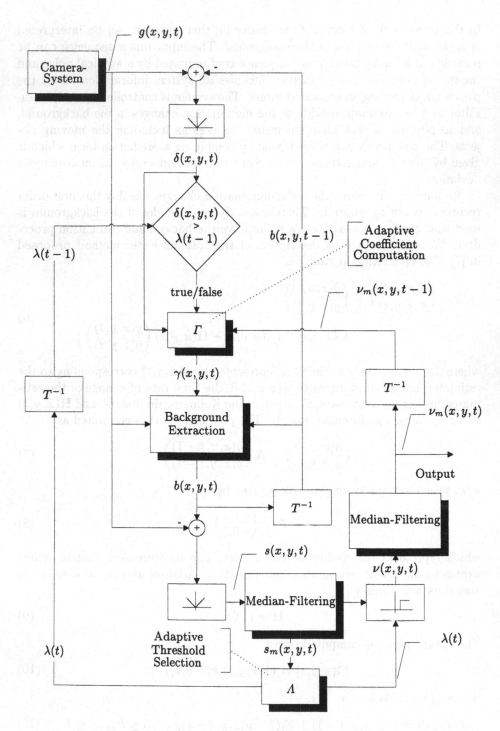

Fig. 4. Flowchart of the ARTL-filter method.

4.4 ARTL-Filter Method

The algorithms presented so far have the drawback that the required parameters are not adapted automatically to the observed scene. The parameters have to be set manually, which is not very useful for stand-alone surveillance systems. The performance of the algorithms is, for instance, essentially dependent on the choice of the threshold separating the foreground from the background. In most cases a fixed threshold is used, which yields unsatisfactory results. Furthermore, the filter gains are constant which is a bad trade.

We propose a novel method which adapts the required parameters automatically to the observed scene. The method is based on the use of a recursive temporal lowpass filter, as discussed above, but it employs an adaptive filter gain $\gamma(x, y, t)$. This depends on the location x, y and the time t

$$b(x, y, t) = \gamma(x, y, t)g(x, y, t) + (1 - \gamma(x, y, t)) \, b(x, y, t - 1) \ . \tag{12}$$

We shall call the proposed filter *adaptive recursive temporal lowpass filter* abbrevieted as ARTL-filter. The flowchart of the method employing the ARTL-filter is depicted in Fig. 4. The filter gain is computed as

$$\gamma(x, y, t) = \begin{cases} g_\beta \nu_m(x, y, t - 1) & \text{if } \delta(x, y, t) \geq \lambda(t - 1) \ , \\ g_\alpha \left(\delta(x, y, t) \right) \left(1 - \nu_m(x, y, t - 1) \right) & \\ + g_\beta \nu_m(x, y, t - 1) & \text{else} \ . \end{cases} \tag{13}$$

$\nu_m(x, y, t)$ is the filtered binary mask. The elimination of small regions that have not changed within changed regions and vice versa is performed using a 3×3 Median-filter. Alternatively a morphological operator can be used instead. $\delta(x, y, t)$ is the absolute difference of actual input image $g(x, y, t)$ and previous estimated background image $b(x, y, t - 1)$ which is defined as

$$\delta(x, y, t) = |g(x, y, t) - b(x, y, t - 1)| \ . \tag{14}$$

$g_\alpha(\delta(x, y, t))$ and g_β are the back- and foreground gain, respectively. The background gain depends on the absolute difference of the actual input image and the previous computed background image. The higher the absolute difference, the lower may be the background gain, assuming that the gray value changing in the background image is slow. The look-up table used for the background gain is depicted in Fig. 5. The foreground gain is constant and has to be sufficiently low. It allows the control over the foreground adaption. In our contribution we use a foreground gain of 0.001. A foreground gain too high would adapt objects exhibiting stop-and-go motion completely to the background.

$\lambda(t)$ is the adaptively computed threshold adjusted to the absolute difference image $s_m(x, y, t)$. In an ideal case the histogram of the gray levels of $s_m(x, y, t)$ is bimodal. In this case, a threshold can be chosen as the gray level that corresponds to the valley of the histogram [15]. In our situations the gray level histogram is not bimodal, as it is shown for an example in Fig. 6. Therefore, an optimal threshold is computed using the discriminant analysis [11]. The threshold selection method is nonparametric and unsupervised. In this method, the threshold

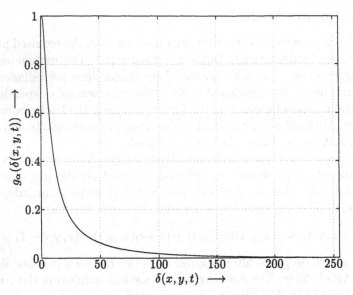

Fig. 5. Look-up table for the background gain.

operation is regarded as a separating of the pixels of the image $s_m(x, y, t)$ into two classes C_f and C_b, namely the fore- and background, at gray level ι. The optimal threshold ι_{opt} is determined by maximizing the following discriminant criterion measure, namely

$$\eta(\iota) = \frac{\sigma_B^2(\iota)}{\sigma_T^2} , \qquad (15)$$

where σ_B^2 and σ_T^2 are the between-class and the total variance, respectively. The procedure utilizes only the zeroth- and the first-order cumulative moments of the gray level histogram of $s_m(x, y, t)$. To ensure a stabile thresholding we set upper and lower ranges for the final threshold $\lambda(t)$ to

$$\lambda(t) = \begin{cases} \iota_{min} & \text{if } \iota_{opt}(t) < \iota_{min} , \\ \iota_{max} & \text{if } \iota_{opt}(t) > \iota_{max} , \\ \iota_{opt}(t) & \text{else} . \end{cases} \qquad (16)$$

In this contribution we used $\iota_{min} = 15$ and $\iota_{max} = 50$.

When taken the absolute difference $s(x, y, t)$

$$s(x, y, t) = |b(x, y, t) - g(x, y, t)| \qquad (17)$$

the borders between the subregions appear as cracks in the output mask. To avoid these cracks, the absolute values of the difference images are lowpass filtered. We have used a 5×5 Median-filter. However, other lowpass filters could be employed too. The lowpass filtering *fills* the cracks and makes the mask homogenous. It also suppresses uncorrelated noise in the difference image.

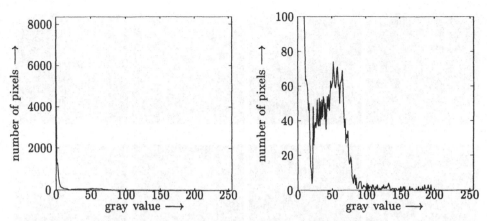

Fig. 6. Gray level histogram of the absolute difference image $s_m(x, y, t)$ of the indoor sequence in Fig. 11 (frame 55).

5 Simulation Results and Discussion

To evaluate the performance of the presented algorithms, we have used an artificial image sequence of 128 frames each exhibiting a size of 128×128 pixels consisting of natural textures that are moving at different velocities and accelerations as shown in Fig. 7. The sequence has been degraded using simulated additive white Gaussian noise up to a signal-to-noise ratio of 15 dB. The degradation model we are using here is given by

$$g(x, y, t) = f(x, y, t) + n(x, y, t) \, , \tag{18}$$

where $f(x, y, t)$ and $g(x, y, t)$ denote the original and degraded artificial image sequence, respectively, and $n(x, y, t)$ is the simulated independent, spatio-temporally additive Gaussian noise term. The expression used for calculation the SNR is given by

$$SNR = 10\log_{10} \left(\frac{\sum_{t=0}^{127} \sum_{y=0}^{127} \sum_{x=0}^{127} f^2(x, y, t)}{\sum_{t=0}^{127} \sum_{y=0}^{127} \sum_{x=0}^{127} (f(x, y, t) - g(x, y, t))^2} \right) \text{ (dB)} \, . \tag{19}$$

The algorithms were tested under Khoros/UNIX [8]. The simulation results are tabulated in Table 1 and shown in Figs. 8 and 9.

The results clearly indicate the superior performance of the ARTL-filter algorithm proposed in this work. In comparison to the conventional algorithms, the severe noise is not detected as foreground. Also, the generated object masks do not vary significantly if the object speed is subject to changes, and the object shapes are homogenous. Finally the troublesome ambiguity of the generated masks is completely avoided. In contrast to the difference method, the RTL-filter method, and the Kalman method the ARTL-filter method does not adapt objects moving at stop-and-go to the background. This is a necessary requirement for a surveillance system.

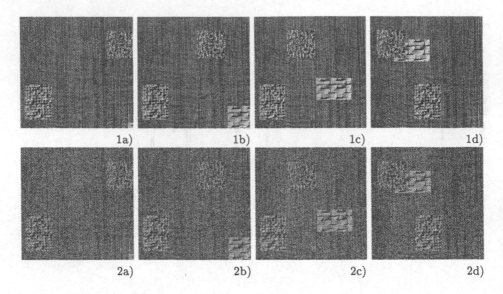

Fig. 7. 1) Frames 30, 60, 90, and 120 of the artificial image sequence. 2) Frames 30, 60, 90, 120 of the degraded artificial image sequence (SNR = 15 dB).

The proposed system can be for instance used for human body tracking systems, as the examples in Fig. 10 demonstrate. Here a person walks in the front of a wardrobe from the right to the left side. The whole sequence consists of 50 frames of size 128×128 pixels. The frame rate is of 5 frames/sec. The ARTL-filter method yields the best results. The shape of the moving person is nearly independent of slow illumination changes, and the shadow which originates from the person is not detected as foreground. As it can be seen in the results, the conventional change detection algorithms have the problems due to creation of double object boundaries. Besides, illumination changes are often detected as foreground.

The proposed system can be used for automotive applications as well. For instance, an intrusion protection system for the interior compartment protection can be realized, which offers significant advantages. Systems based on passive infra-red, vision or ultrasonic principles are sensitive to numerous nonidealities such as temperature, thermal air flow, traffic noises, and shadows of passing

Table 1. Simulation results.

	Total sum of foreground errors	Total sum of background errors
Difference method	546,307	2,317,195
RTL-Filter method	945,546	156,768
Kalman method	448,300	1,763,749
ARTL-filter method	227,551	23,621

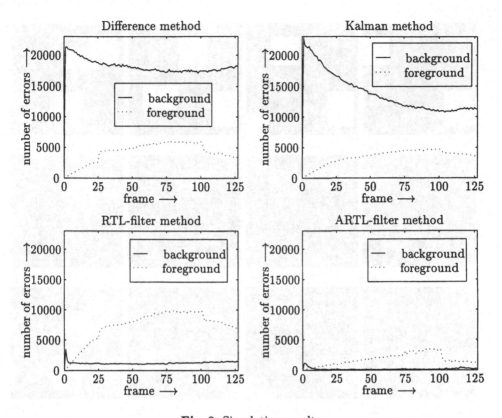

Fig. 8. Simulation results.

vehicles. These events must not activate the alarm [17]. Another automotive application of the proposed system is an occupancy detection system. It is shown, that our system is very effective for protection of car occupants because it allows optimization of air bag deployment. Fig. 11 shows the simulation results of a car compartment sequence with 170 frames of size 128 × 128 pixel.

6 Summary

In our contribution we have presented a surveillance system based on detection and tracking of moving objects which employs CMOS imagers and an enhanced change detection algorithm. The system fuses the image acquisition and processing task and thus enables a flexible image processing system for residential and industrial applications at low cost.

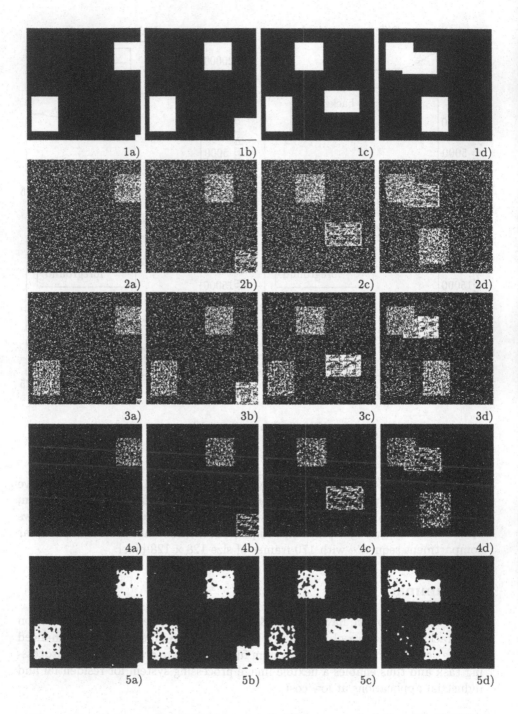

Fig. 9. Simulation results: 1) Ideal results, 2) difference method ($\lambda = 20$), 3) Kalman method ($\lambda = 20$, $k_\alpha = 0.001$, $k_\beta = 0.01$), 4) RTL-filter method ($\lambda = 20$, $\alpha = 0.5$), and 5) ARTL-filter method.

447

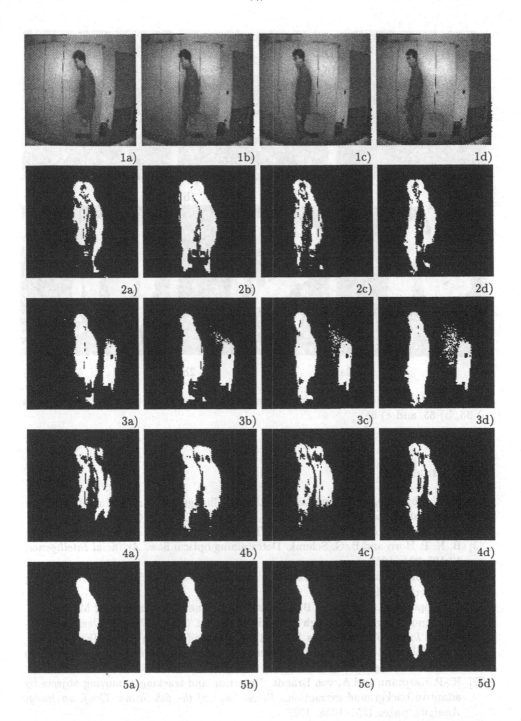

Fig. 10. A natural image sequence, a person walking in front of a wardrobe, and the simulation results are depicted. 1) Natural image sequence, resulting binary masks using 2) the difference method ($\lambda = 20$), 3) the Kalman method ($\lambda = 20$, $k_\alpha = 0.001$, $k_\beta = 0.01$), 4) the RTL-filter method ($\lambda = 20$, $\alpha = 0.5$), and 5) the ARTL-filter method. We show 4 consecutive frames of the test sequence, namely frames 18 to 21.

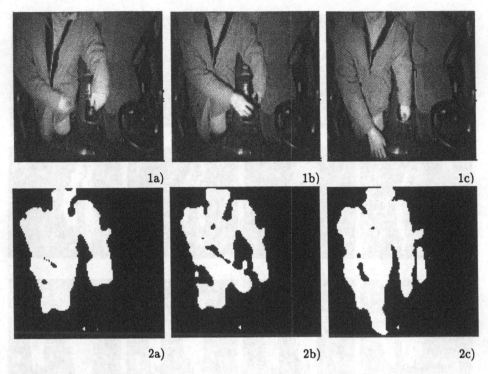

1a)   1b)   1c)

2a)   2b)   2c)

Fig. 11. Indoor sequence and simulation results using the ARTL-filter method (frames a) 35, b) 55, and c) 65).

References

[1] G. W. Donohoe, D. R. Hush, and N. Ahmed. Change detection for target detection and classification in video sequences. *Proc. ICASSP 1988*, 2:1084–1087, 1988.

[2] B. K. P. Horn. *Robot Vision*. The MIT Press, McGraw-Hill Book Company, 1986.

[3] B. K. P. Horn and B. G. Schunk. Determining optical flow. *Artificial Intelligence*, 17:185–204, 1981.

[4] T. S. Huang, editor. *Image Sequence Analysis*. Spinger-Verlag, Berlin Heidelberg New York, 1981.

[5] J. Huppertz, R. Hauschild, B. J. Hosticka, T. Kneip, S. Müller, and M. Schwarz. Fast cmos imaging with high dynamic range. In *Charge-Coupled Devices & Advanced Image Sensors*, pages R7-1–R7-4, Bruges (Belgium), 1997. IEEE.

[6] J. R. Jain and A. K. Jain. Displacement measurement and its application in interframe image coding. *IEEE Trans. Commun.*, COM-29:1799–1808, 1981.

[7] K.-P. Karmann and A. von Brandt. Detection and tracking of moving objects by adaptive background extraction. *Proceedings of the 6th Scand. Conf. on Image Analysis*, pages 1051–1058, 1988.

[8] K. Konstantinides and J. Rasure. The khoros software development environment for image and signal processing. *IEEE Transactions on Image Processing*, 3(3):243–252, May 1994.

[9] F. L. Lewis. *Optimal Estimation*. John Wiley & Sons, New York, 1986.

[10] G. Meynants, B. Dierickx, D. Scheffer, and J. Vlummens. A wide dynamic range cmos stereo camera. In D. E. Ricken and W. Gessner, editors, *Advanced Microsystems for Automotive Applications 98*, pages 173–181, Berlin Heidelberg New York, 1998. Springer-Verlag.

[11] N. Otsu. A threshold selection method from gray-level histograms. *IEEE Trans. Systems Man Cybernet.*, SMC-9(1):62–66, January 1979.

[12] S.-B. Park, A. Teuner, and B. J. Hosticka. A cmos photo sensor array based motion detection system. *1998 International Conference on Image Processing*, October 1998. IEEE Signal Processing Society.

[13] S.-B. Park, A. Teuner, B. J. Hosticka, and G. Triftshäuser. An interior compartment protection system based on motion detection using cmos imagers. *1998 IEEE International Conference on Intelligent Vehicles*, October 1998.

[14] C. Ridder, O. Munkelt, and H. Kirchner. Adaptive background estimation and foreground detection using kalman-filtering. *Proc. ICRAM'95*, pages 193–199, 1995.

[15] P. K. Sahoo, S. Soltani, A. K. C. Wong, and Y. Chen. A survey of thresholding techniques. *Computer Vision, Graphics, and Image Processing*, 41:233–260, 1988.

[16] M. Schanz, W. Brockherde, R. Hauschild, B. J. Hosticka, and M. Schwarz. Smart cmos image sensor arrays. *IEEE Transactions on Electron Devices*, 44(10):1699–1705, October 1997.

[17] J. Schriek. Interior compartment protection as an example of a microsystem. In *International Conference on Advanced Microsystems for Automotive Applications*, Berlin, December 1996.

3-D Modelling and Robot Localization from Visual and Range Data in Natural Scenes

Carlos Parra*, Rafael Murrieta-Cid**, Michel Devy, and Maurice Briot

LAAS-CNRS, 7 Av. du Colonel Roche, 31077 Toulouse Cédex 4,
France
{carlos, murrieta, michel, briot}@laas.fr

Abstract. This paper concerns the exploration of a natural environment by a mobile robot equipped with both a video camera and a range sensor (stereo or laser range finder); we focus on the interest of such a multisensory system to deal with the incremental construction of a global model of the environment and with the 3-D localization of the mobile robot. The 3-D segmentation of the range data provides a geometrical scene description: the regions issued from the segmentation step correspond either to the ground or to objects emerging from this ground (e.g. rocks, vegetations). The 3D boundaries of these regions can be projected on the video image, so that each one can be characterized and afterwards identified, by a probabilistic method, to obtain its nature (e.g. soil, rocks ...); the ground region can be over-segmented, adding visual information, such as the texture. During the robot motions, a slow and a fast processes are simultaneously executed; in the modelling process (currently 0.1Hz), a global landmark-based model is incrementally built and the robot situation can be estimated if some discriminant landmarks are selected from the detected objects in the range data; in the tracking process (currently 1Hz), selected landmarks are tracked in the visual data. The tracking results are used to simplify the matching between landmarks in the modelling process.

1 Introduction

This paper deals with perception functions required on an autonomous robot which must explore a natural environment without any a priori knowledge. From a sequence of range and video images acquired during the motion, the robot must incrementally build a model and correct its situation estimate.

The proposed approach is suitable for environments in which (1) the terrain is mostly flat, but can be made by several surfaces with different orientations (i.e. different areas with a rather horizontal ground, and slopes to connect these areas) and (2) objects (bulges or little depressions) can be distinguished from the ground.

---

* This research was funded by the PCP program (Colombia -COLCIENCIAS- and France -Foreign Office-)

** This research was funded by CONACyT, México

Our previous method [5] [4] dedicated to the exploration of such an environment, aimed to build an object-based model, considering only range data. An intensive evaluation of this method has shown that the main difficulty comes from the matching of objects perceived in multiple views acquired along the robot paths. From numerical features extracted from the model of the matched objects, the robot localization can be updated (correction of the estimated robot situation provided by internal sensors: odometry, compass, ...) and the local models extracted from the different views can be consistently fused in a global one. The global model was only a stochastic map in which the robot situation and the object features and the associated variance-covariance matrix were represented in a same reference frame; the reference frame can be defined for example as the first robot situation during the exploration task. Robot localization, fusion of matched objects and introduction of newly perceived objects are executed each time a local model is built from a newly acquired image [21]. If some mistakes occur in the object matchings, numerical errors are introduced in the global model and the robot situation can be lost.

In this paper, we focus on an improved modelling method, based on a multisensory cooperation; in order to make faster and more reliable the matching step, both range and visual data are used. Moreover, the global model has now several levels, like in [13]: a topological level gives the relationships between the different ground surfaces (connectivity graph); the model of each terrain area is a stochastic map which gives information only for the objects detected on this area: this map gives the position of these objects with respect to a local frame linked to the area (first robot situation when this area has been reached).

In the next section, an overview of our current method is presented. It involves a general function which performs the construction of a local model for the perceived scene; it will be detailed in section 3. The exploration task is executed by three different processes, which are detailed in the three following sections: the initialization process is executed only at the beginning or after the detection of an inconsistency by the modelling process; this last one is a slow loop (from 0.1 to 0.2 Hz according to the scene complexity and the available computer) from the acquisition of range and visual data to the global model updating; the tracking process is a fast loop (from 1 to 3 Hz), which require only the acquisition of an intensity image.

Then, several experiments on actual images acquired in lunar-like environment, are presented and analized.

2 The general approach

We have described on figure 1 the relationships between the main representations built by our system, and the different processes which provide or update these representations.

A 3-D segmentation algorithm provides a synthetic description of the scene. Elements issued from the segmentation stage are then characterized and afterwards identified in order to obtain their nature (e.g. soil, rocks ...).

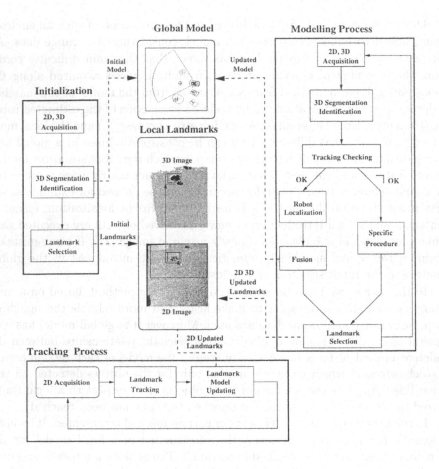

Fig. 1. The general approach

The nature of the elements (objects, ground) in the scene is obtained by comparing an attribute vector (computed from the shape and texture informations extracted from sensory data associated with this element) with a database. This database is function of the type of the environment. Here, we just have chosen 2 classes, which correspond to the principal elements in our environment: soil and rock. New classes inclusion as rocky soil and ground depressions (holes) are currently going on.

These phases allow us to obtain a local model of the scene. From this model, discriminant features can be extracted and pertinent objects for the localization tasks are selected as landmarks; according to some criteria which depend on higher decisional levels, one of these landmark is chosen as a tracked target; this same landmark could also be used as a goal for visual navigation. The tracking process exploits only a 2D image sequence in order to track the selected target while the robot is going forward. When it is required, the modelling process is executed: a local model of the perceived scene is built; the robot localization is performed from matchings between landmarks extracted in this local model, and those previously merged in the global model; if the robot situation can be updated, the models of these matched landmarks are fused and new ones are added to the global model.

The matching problem of landmark's representation between different perceptions is solved by using the result of the tracking process. Moreover, some verifications between informations extracted from the 2D and 3D images, allow to check the coherence of the whole modelling results; especially, a tracking checker is based on the semantical labels added to the extracted objects by the identification function.

3 Local scene modelling

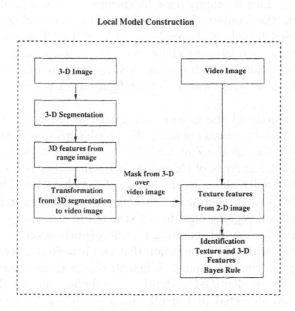

Fig. 2. The local model construction

The local model of the perceived scene is required in order to initialize the exploration task, and also to deal with the incremental construction of a global model of the environment.

The construction of this local model is performed from the acquisition of a 3D image by the range sensor, and of a 2D image from the video sensor (see figure 2), thanks to the following steps [18]:

- 3-D segmentation of the 3D image.
- Object characterization using the 3D and the 2D data.
- Object identification by a probabilistic method.

3.1 The 3-D Segmentation Algorithm

The main objective of the 3D segmentation step, is to extract the main scene components from the current 3D image. Two classes of components are considered: the ground and the obstacles. The ground corresponds to the surface on which the robot stands. This one is first identified, then the different obstacles are separated by a region segmentation of the 3D image. For more details about this segmentation algorithm, see [3].

To segment the ground, we must search in the scene the wider surface of uniform orientation which consequently corresponds to points having equivalent normal direction. This is mainly done by calculating a bi-variable histogram H which represents the number of points of the 3-D image having a given normal orientation, coded in spherical coordinates (θ, φ). The figure 3 (a) shows one video image; only correlated pixel by the stereovision module are displayed: white pixels correspond to occlusion or to distant 3-D points. The figure 3 (b) shows the range image (top view) and the figure 3 (c) presents the bi-variable histogram.

The predominance of the ground will appear as a peak in this bi-variable histogram even if the normals are noisy. This peak corresponds to points having normal direction close to the Z-axis of the robot frame; these points are essentially on the ground in front of the robot, but some other points can be linked to this peak: especially, the ones on the top of the obstacles. These points will be eliminated from the ground using the construction of a second histogram [3].

Once the ground regions have been extracted in the image, it remains the obstacle regions which could require a specific segmentation in order to isolate each obstacle. We make the assumption that an obstacle is a connected portion of matter emerging from the ground. Differents obstacles are separated by empty space which could be identified as depth discontinuities in the 3D image; these discontinuities are detected in a depth image, in which for each 3D point of the 3D image, the corresponding pixel value encodes the depth with respect to the sensor. Thus a classical derivative filter can be applied to obtain maxima of gradient corresponding to the depth discontinuities. Classical problems of edge closing are solved with a specific filter described in [3].

Finally the scene nature is deduced with a criterion based on:

- **number of peaks of H**: absence of a significative peak indicates that we could not easily differentiate the ground from the objects.
- **width of the peak**: if the peak is thin the ground is planar, otherwise the ground is very curved.
- **the mean error** caused by the approximation of the ground region with a given surface (plane or other shapes: paraboloid . . .): the smaller the error, the more even is the ground.

Image video   Image 3-D

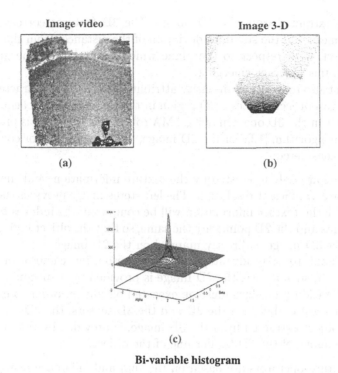

(a)   (b)

(c)

Bi-variable histogram

Fig. 3. (a) Video image (b) 3-D image (c) Bi-variable histogram

- **mean distance** of the 3D points along a common discontinuity line between two obstacle regions. If this distance is small the two obstacles are close to each other; they are grouped in a cluster, so that the mobile robot cannot move between them for example but, could easily perceive together these objects in multiple views.

The object-based representation we present in this paper, is only suitable when a peak is detected in the H histogram; in the other situation, a discrete representation (Digital Elevation Map) will be used in order to describe a ground region in an uneven terrain (see [11]). But in the more general situation, due to the high resolution of the range sensor close to the robot, our method detects only one peak, which corresponds to the ground area on which the robot is currently moving; a second peak is detected only when the robot comes near a slope discontinuity of the ground.

3.2   Object characterization

Each object of the scene is characterized by an attribute vector: the object attributes correspond either to 3D features extracted from the 3D image or to its texture extracted from the 2D image. The 3D features correspond to the statistical mean and the standard deviation of the distances from the 3-D points of the object, with respect to the plane which approximates the ground area from which this object is emerging.

We want also to associate intensity attributes to an object extracted from the 3D image; this object creates a 2D region in the intensity image acquired at the same time than the 3D one. On our LAMA robot, the 3D image is provided by a stereovision algorithm [12]; for the 2D image, two different sensor configurations have been considered:

- either we are only interested by the texture information, and the stereo images have a sufficient resolution. The left stereo image provides the 2D image on which the texture information will be computed; the indexes between the 3D points and the 2D points are the same, so that the object region extracted from the 3D image is directly mapped on the 2D image.
- or we want to take advantage of a high-resolution camera, or of a color camera. In such a case, the 2D image is provided by a specific camera, and an calibration procedure must be executed off line, in order to estimate the relative position between the 2D and the 3D sensors; the 2D region created by an object extracted from the 3D image, is provided by the projection on the 2D image of the 3D border line of the object.

The texture operators are based on the sum and difference histograms, this type of texture measure is an alternative to the usual co-occurrence matrices used for texture analysis. The sum and difference histograms used conjointly are nearly as powerful as co-occurrence matrices for texture discrimination. This texture analysis method requires less computation time and less memory requirements than the conventional spatial grey level dependence method.

For a given region of a video image $I(x, y) \in [0, 255]$, the sum and difference histograms are defined as [23]:

$$h_s(i) = Card(i = I(x, y) + I(x + \delta x, y + \delta y)) \quad i \in [0, 510]$$
$$h_d(j) = Card(j = |I(x, y) - I(x + \delta x, y + \delta y)|) \, j \in [0, 255]$$

The relative displacement $(\delta x, \delta y)$ may be equivalently characterized by a distance in radial units and an angle θ with respect to the image line orientation: this displacement must be chosen so that the computed texture attributes allow to discriminate the interesting classes; for our problem, we have chosen: $\delta x = \delta y = 1$. Sum and difference images can be built so that, for all pixel $I(x, y)$ of the input image, we have:

$$I_s(x, y) = I(x, y) + I(x + \delta x, y + \delta y)$$
$$I_d(x, y) = |I(x, y) - I(x + \delta x, y + \delta y)|$$

Furthermore, normalized sum and difference histograms can be computed for selected regions of the image, so that:

$$H_s(i) = \frac{Card(i = I_s(x, y))}{m} \quad H_s(i) \in [0, 1]$$
$$H_d(j) = \frac{Card(j = I_d(x, y))}{m} \quad H_d(j) \in [0, 1]$$

where m is the number of points belonging to the considered region.

Texture Feature	Equation
Mean	$\mu = \frac{1}{2}\sum_i i \cdot \hat{P}_{s(i)}$
Variance	$\frac{1}{2}\left(\sum_i (i - 2\mu)^2 \cdot \hat{P}_{s(i)} + \sum_j j^2 \cdot \hat{P}_{d(j)}\right)$
Energy	$\sum_i \hat{P}_{s(i)}^2 \cdot \sum_j \hat{P}_{d(j)}^2$
Entropy	$-\sum_i \hat{P}_{s(i)} \cdot \log \hat{P}_{s(i)} - \sum_j \hat{P}_{d(j)} \cdot \log \hat{P}_{d(j)}$
Contrast	$\sum_j j^2 \cdot \hat{P}_{d(j)}$
Homogeneity	$\frac{1}{1+j^2}\sum_j \cdot \hat{P}_{d(j)}$

Table 1. Texture features computed from sum and difference histograms

These normalized histograms can be interpreted as a probability. $\hat{P}_{s(i)} = H_s(i)$ is the estimated probability that the sum of the pixels $I(x,y)$ and $I(x + \delta x, y + \delta y)$ will have the value i. And $\hat{P}_{d(j)} = H_d(j)$ is the estimated probability that the absolute difference of the pixels $I(x,y)$ and $I(x + \delta x, y + \delta y)$ will have value j.

In this way we obtain a probabilistic characterization of the spatial organization of the image, based on neighborhood analysis. Statistical information can be extracted from these histograms. We have used 6 texture features computed from the sum and difference histograms, these features are defined in Table 1.

3.3 Object identification

The nature (class) of an object perceived in the scene is obtained by comparing its attribute vector (computed from the 3D features and from the texture) with a database composed by different classes, issued from a learning step executed off line.

This identification phase allows us to get a probabilistic estimation about the object nature. The label associated to an object, will be exploited in order to detect possible incoherences at two levels:

- at first, in the modelling process, a 3D segmentation error will be detected if the extracted objects cannot be labelled by the identification function.
- then, in the tracking process, the nature of the landmark could be used in addition to the partial Hausdorff distance to detect possible tracking errors or drifts.

A Bayesian classification is used in order to estimate the class membership for each object. The Bayesian rule is defined as [1]:

$$P(C_i \mid X) = \frac{P(X \mid C_i)P(C_i)}{\sum_{i=1}^{n} P(X \mid C_i)P(C_i)}$$

where:

- $P(C_i)$ is the *a priori* probability that an object belongs to the class (C_i).
- $P(X \mid C_i)$ is the class conditional probability that the object attribute is X, given that it belongs to class C_i.
- $P(C_i \mid X)$ is the *a posteriori* conditional probability that the object class membership is C_i, given that the object attribute is X.

We have assumed equal *a priori* probability. In this case the computation of the *a posteriori* probability $P(C_i \mid X)$ can be simplified and its value just depend on $P(X \mid C_i)$.

The value of $P(X \mid C_i)$ is estimated by using k-nearest neighbor method. It consists in computing for each class, the distance from the sample X (corresponding to the object to identify, whose coordinates are given by the vector of 3-D information and texture features) to $k - th$ nearest neighbor amongst the learned samples. So we have to compute only this distance (in common Euclidean distance) in order to evaluate $P(X \mid C_i)$. Finally the observation X will be assigned to the class C_i whose $k - th$ nearest neighbor to X is closest to X than for any other training class.

4 Initialization phase

The initialization phase is composed by two main steps; at first, a local model is built from the first robot position in the environment; then, by using this first local model, a landmark is chosen amongst the objects detected in this first scene. This landmark will be used for several functions:

- it will support the first reference frame linked to the current area explored by the robot; so that, the initial robot situation in the environment must be easily computed.
- it will be the first tracked target in the 2D image sequence acquired during the next robot motion (tracking process: fast loop); if in the higher level of the decisional system, a visual navigation is chosen as a way to define the robot motions during the exploration task, this same process will be also in charge of generating commands for the mobile robot and for the pan and tilt platform on which the cameras are mounted.
- it will be detected again in the next 3D image acquired in the modelling process, so that the robot situation could be easily updated, as this landmark supports the reference frame of the explored area.

Moreover, the first local model allows to initialize the global model which will be upgraded by the incremental fusion of the local models built from the next

3D acquisitions. Hereafter, the automatic procedure for the landmark selection is presented.

The local model of the first scene (obtained from the 3-D segmentation and identification phases) is used to select automatically an appropriated landmark, from a utility estimation based on both its nature and shape [19].

Localization based on environment features improves the autonomy of the robot. A landmark is defined first as a remarkable object, which should have some properties that will be exploited for the robot localization or for the visual navigation, for example:

- **Discrimination**. A landmark should be easy to differentiate from other surrounding objects.
- **Accuracy**. A landmark must be accurate enough so that it can allow to reduce the uncertainty on the robot situation, because it will be used to deal with the robot localization.

Landmarks in indoor environments correspond to structured scene components, such as walls, corners, doors, etc. In outdoor natural scenes, landmarks are less structured: we have proposed several solutions like maxima of curvature on border lines [8], maxima of elevation on the terrain [11] or on extracted objects [4].

In previous work we have defined a landmark as a little bulge, typically a natural object emerging from a rather flat ground (e.g. a rock); only the elevation peak of such an object has been considered as a numerical attribute useful for the localization purpose. A realistic uncertainty model has been proposed for these peaks, so that the peak uncertainty is function of the rock sharpness, of the sensor noise and of the distance from the robot.

In a segmented 3D image, a bulge is selected as candidate landmark if:

1. It is not occluded by another object. If an object is occluded, it will be both difficult to find it in the following images and to have a good estimate on its top.
2. Its topmost point is accurate. This is function of the sensor noise, resolution and object top shape.
3. It must be in "ground contact".

These criteria are used so that only some objects extracted from an image are selected as landmarks. The most accurate one (or the more significative landmark cluster in cluttered scenes) is then selected in order to support the reference frame of the first explored area. Moreover, a specific landmark must be defined as the next tracked target for the tracking process; different criteria, coming from higher decisional levels, could be used for this selection, for example:

- track the sharper or the higher object: it will be easier to detect and to match between successive images.
- track the more distant object from the robot, towards a given direction (visual navigation).

– track the object which maximizes a utility function, taking into account several criteria (active exploration).
– or, in a teleprogrammed system, track the object pointed on the 2D image by an operator.

At this time due to integration constraints, only one landmark can be tracked during the robot motion. We are currently thinking about a multi-tracking method.

5   The tracking process (fast-loop)

The target tracking problem has received a great deal of attention in the computer vision community over the last years. Several methods have been reported in the literature, and a variety of features have been proposed to perform the tracking [7, 16, 9].

Our method is able to track an object in an image sequence in the case of a sensor motion or of an object motion. This method is based on the assumption that the 3D motion of the sensor or the object can be characterized by using only a 2D representation. This 2D motion in the image can be decomposed into two parts:

– A 2D image motion (translation and rotation), corresponding to the change of the target's position in the image space.
– A 2D shape change, corresponding to a new aspect of the target.

The tracking is done using a comparison between an image and a model. The model and the image are binary elements extracted from a sequence of gray levels images using an edge detector similar to [6].

A partial Hausdorff distance is used as a resemblance measurement between the target model and its presumed position in an image.

Given two sets of points P and Q, the Hausdorff distance is defined as [20]:

$$H(P,Q) = \max(h(P,Q), h(Q,P))$$

where

$$h(P,Q) = \max_{p \in P} \min_{q \in Q} \| p - q \|$$

and $\| . \|$ is a given distance between two points p and q. The function $h(P,Q)$ (distance from set P to Q) is a measure of the degree in which each point in P is near to some point in Q. The Hausdorff distance is the maximum among $h(P,Q)$ and $h(Q,P)$.

By computing the Hausdorff distance in this way we obtain the most mismatched point between the two shapes compared; consequently, it is very sensitive to the presence of any outlying points. For that reason it is often appropriate to use a more general rank order measure, which replaces the maximization operation with a rank operation. This measure (partial distance) is defined as [14]:

$$h_k = K_{p \in P}^{th} \min_{q \in Q} \| p - q \|$$

where $K_{p \in P}^{th} f(p)$ denotes the K^{-th} ranked value of $f(p)$ over the set P.

5.1 Finding the model position

The first task to be accomplished is to define the position of the model M_t in the next image I_{t+1} of the sequence. The search for the model in the image (or image's region) is done in some selected direction. We are using the unidirectional partial distance from the model to the image to achieve this first step.

The minimum value of $h_{k1}(M_t, I_{t+1})$ identifies the best "position" of M_t in I_{t+1}, under the action of some group of translations G. It is possible also to identify the set of translations of M_t such that $h_{k1}(M_t, I_{t+1})$ is no larger than some value τ, in this case there may be multiple translations that have essentially the same quality [15].

However, rather than computing the single translation giving the minimum distance or the set of translations, such that its correspond h_{k1} is no larger than τ, it is possible to find the first translation g, such that its associated h_{k1} is no larger than τ, for a given search direction.

Although the first translation which $h_{k1}(M_t, I_{t+1})$ associated is less than τ it is not necessarily the best one, whether τ is small, the translation g should be quite good. This is better than computing all the set of valuable translation, whereas the computing time is significantly smaller.

5.2 Building the new model

Having found the position of the model M_t in the next image I_{t+1} of the sequence, we now have to build the new model M_{t+1} by determining which pixels of the image I_{t+1} are part of this new model.

The model is updated by using the unidirectional partial distance from the image to the model as a criterion for selecting the subset of images points I_{t+1} that belong to M_{t+1}. The new model is defined as:

$$M_{t+1} = \{q \in I_{t+1} \mid h_{k2}(I_{t+1}, g(M_t)) < \delta\}$$

Where $g(M_t)$ is the model at the time t under the action of the translation g, and δ controls the degree to which the method is able to track objects that change shape.

In order to allow models that may be changing in size, this size is increased whenever there is a significant number of nonzero pixels near the boundary and is decreased in the contrary case. The model's position is improved according to the position where the model's boundary was defined.

The initial model is obtained by using the local model of the scene previously computed. With this initial model the tracking begins, finding progressively the new position of the target and updating the model. The tracking of the model is successful if:

$$k1 > fM \mid h_{k1}(M_t, I_{t+1}) < \tau$$

and

$$k2 > fI \mid h_{k2}(I_{t+1}, g(M_t)) < \delta ,$$

in which fM is a fraction of the number total of points of the model M_t and fI is a fraction of image's point of I_{t+1} superimposed on $g(M_t)$.

5.3 Our contributions over the general tracking method

Several previous works have used the Hausdorff distance as a resemblance measure in order to track an object [15, 10]. This section enumerates some of the extensions that we have made over the general method [17].

- Firstly, we are using an automatic identification method in order to select the initial model. This method uses several attributes of the image such as texture and 3-D shape.
- Only a small region of the image is examined to obtain the new target position, as opposed to the entire image. In this manner, the computation time is decreased significantly. The idea behind a local exploration of the image is that if the execution of the code is quick enough, the new target position will then lie within a vicinity of the previous one. We are trading the capacity to find the target in the whole image in order to increase the speed of computation of the new position and shape of the model. In this way, the robustness of the method is increased to handle target deformations, since it is less likely that the shape of the model will change significantly in a small δt. In addition, this technique allows the program to report the target's location to any external systems with a higher frequency (for an application see [2]).
- Instead of computing the set of translations of M_t, such that $h_{k1}(M_t, I_{t+1})$ is no larger than some value τ, we are finding the first translation whose $h_{k1}(M_t, I_{t+1})$ is less than τ. This strategy significantly decreases the computational time.

5.4 Experimental results: tracking

The tracking method was implemented in C on a real-time operating system (Power-PC), the computation running time is dependent on the region size examined to obtain the new target position. For sequences the code is capable of processing a frame in about 0.25 seconds. In this case only a small region of the image is examined given that the new target position will lie within a vicinity of the previous one. Processing includes, edge detection, target localization, and model updating for a video image of (256x256 pixels).

Figures 4 show the tracking process. Figure 4 a) shows initial target selection, in this case the user specifies a rectangle in the frame that contains the target. An automatic landmark (target) selection is possible by using the local model of the scene. Figures 4 b), c), d), and e) show the tracking of a rock through an image sequence. The rock chosen as target is marked in the figure with a boundary box. Another boundary box is used to delineate the improved target position after the model updating. In these images the region being examined is the whole image, the objective is to show the capacity of the method to identify a rock among the set of objects.

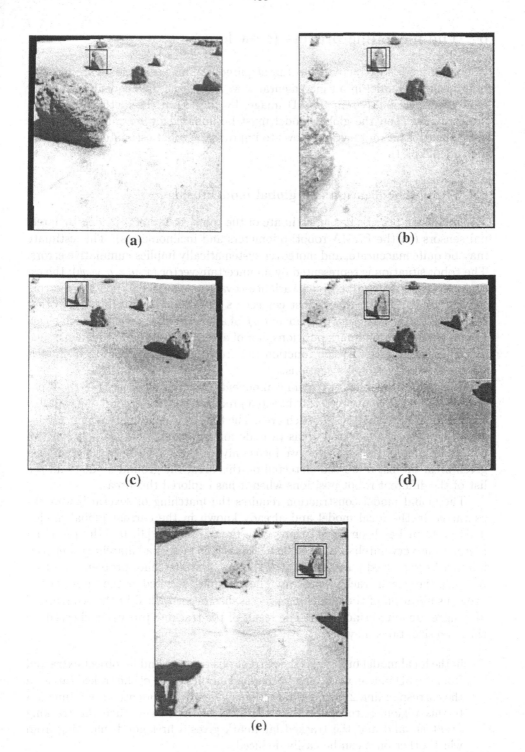

Fig. 4. Visual tracking

6 The modelling process (slow loop)

The local models extracted from the acquired 3D images are fused in order to build a global model in an incremental way. After each 3D acquisition, a local model is firstly built from the 3D image, by the use of the method described in section 3. Then the global model must be updated by merging it with the local one; this fusion function allows to improve the robot estimate position and attitude [22] [21].

6.1 Robot localization and global model fusion

The modelling process has an estimate of the robot situation provided by internal sensors (on the LAMA robot: odometers and inclinometers). This estimate may be quite inaccurate, and moreover systematically implies cumulative errors. The robot situation is represented by an uncertain vector $(x, y, z, \theta, \phi, \psi)$; the estimated errors is described by a variance-covariance matrix. When these errors become too large, the robot must correct its situation estimate by using other perceptual data; we do *not* take advantage of any *a priori* knowledge, such as artificial beacons or landmark positions, nor of external positionning systems, such as GPS. The self-localization function requires the registration of local models built at successive robot situations.

The global model has two main components; the first one describes the topological relationships between the detected ground areas; the second one contains the perceived informations for each area. The topological model is a connectivity graph between the detected areas (a node for each area, an edge between two connected areas). In this paper, we focus only on the knowledge extracted for a given area: the list of objects detected on this area, the ground model, and the list of the different robot positions when it has explored this area.

The global model construction requires the matching of several landmarks extracted in the local model and already known in the current global model. This problem has been solved using only the 3D images [4], but the proposed method was very unreliable in cluttered scenes (too many bad matchings between landmarks perceived on multiple views). Now, the matching problem is solved by using the visual tracking process. The landmark selected as the target at the previous iteration of the modelling process, has been tracked in the sequence of 2D images acquired since then. The result of the tracking process is checked, so that two situations may occur:

- in the local model built from the current position, we find an object extracted from the 3D image, which can be mapped on the region of the traked target in the corresponding 2D image. If the label given by the identification function to this region, is the same than the label of the target, then the tracking result is valid and the tracked landmark gives a first good matching from which other ones can be easily deduced.
- if some incoherences are detected (no mapping between an extracted 3D object and the 2D tracked region, no correspondance between the current

label of the tracked region and the previous one), then some specific procedure must be executed. At this time, as soon as no matchings can be found between the current local and global models, a new area is open: it means that the initialization procedure is executed again in order to select the best landmark in the local model as the new reference for the further iterations.

When matchings between landmarks can be found, the fusion functions have been presented in [4]. The main characteristics of our method is the uncertainty representation; at instant k, a random vector $\mathbf{X}_k = [\mathbf{x}_r^T \ \mathbf{x}_1^T \ ... \ \mathbf{x}_N^T]_k^T$ and the associated variance-covariance matrix represent the current state of the environment. It includes the current robot's situation and the numerical attributes of the landmark features, expressed with respect to a global reference frame. Robot situation and landmark feature updates are done using an Extended Kalman Filter (EKF).

6.2 Experimental results: modelling

The figure 5 shows a partial result of the exploration task, involving concurrently the modelling and the tracking processes. Figure 5 I.a shows the video image, Figure 5 I.b presents the 3-D image segmentation and classification, two grey levels are used to label the classes (rocks and soil). Figure 5 I.c shows the first estimation of the robot position. A boundary box indicates the selected landmark (see figure 5 I.a). This one was automatically chosen by using the local model. The selection was done by taking into account 3-D shape and nature of the landmark.

Figures 5 II and 5 III show the tracking of the landmark, which is marked in the figure with a boundary box. Another larger boundary box is used to delineate the region of examination.

Figure 5 IV.a presents the next image of the sequence, figure 5 IV.b shows the 3-D segmentation and identification phases used to build the local model. The visual tracking is employed here to solve the matching problem of landmark's representation between the different perceptions. Figure 5 IV.c presents the current robot localization, the local model building at this time is merged to the global one. In this simple example, the global model contains only one ground area with a list of three detected landmarks and a list of two robot positions.

The target tracking process goes on in the next images of the sequence (see figure 5 V and figure 5 VI.a). The robot motion between the image V and VI.a was too important, so the aspect and position of the target changes a great deal; it occurs a tracking error (see the in figure 5 VI.b, the window around the presumed tracked target). A new local model is built at this time (figure 5 VI.b). The coherence of the both processes (local model construction and target tracking) is checked by using the nature of the landmark. As the system knows that the target is a rock, this one is able to detect the tracking process mistake given that the model of the landmark (target) belongs to the class soil.

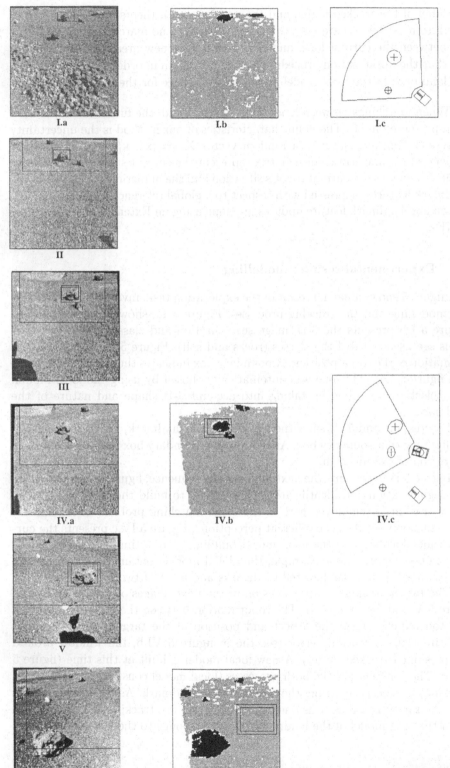

Fig. 5. 3-D robot localization

7   Conclusion and future work

The work presented in this paper concerns the environment representation and the localization of a mobile robot which navigates on a rather flat ground in a planetary environment.

A local model of the environment is constructed in several phases:

- region extraction: firstly, the 3-D segmentation gives a synthetic representation of the environment.
- object characterization: each object of the scene is characterized by using 3-D features and its texture. Having done the segmentation both texture and 3-D features are used to characterize and to identify the objects. In this phase, texture is taken into account to profit from its power of discrimination. The texture attributes are computed from regions issued from the 3D segmentation, which commonly give more discriminant informations than the features obtained from an arbitrary division of the image.
- object identification: the nature of the elements (objects and ground) in the scene is obtained by comparing an attribute vector with a database composed by different classes, issued from a learning process.

The local model of the first scene is employed in order to select automatically an appropriate landmark. The matching problem of landmark's is solved by using a visual tracking process. The global model of the environment is updated at each perception and merged with the current local model. The current robot's situation and the numerical attributes of the landmark features are updated by using an Extended Kalman Filter (EKF).

Some possible extensions to this system are going on: firstly, we plan to study image preprocessors that would enhance the extraction of those image features that are appropriate to the tracking method. Second, we plan to include new classes (e.g. rocky soil and ground depressions) to improve the semantic description of the environment. Finally, we would also like to consider other environments such as natural terrestrial environments (e.g. forests or green areas). In this case, the color information could be taken into account, like we have proposed in [18, 19].

References

1. H.C. Andrews. *Mathematicals Techniques in Pattern Recognition*. Wiley-Interscience, 1972.
2. C. Becker, H. González, J.-L. Latombe, and C. Tomasi. An intelligent observer. In *International Symposium on Experimental Robotics*, 1995.
3. S. Betgé-Brezetz, R. Chatila, and M. Devy. Natural Scene Understanding for Mobile Robot Navigation. In *Proceedings of the IEEE International Conference on Robotics and Automation (ICRA)*, California, USA, May 1994.
4. S. Betgé-Brezetz, P. Hébert, R. Chatila, and M. Devy. Uncertain Map Making in Natural Environments. In *Proceedings of the IEEE International Conference on Robotics and Automation (ICRA)*, West Lafayette, USA, April 1996.

5. S. Betgé-Brezetz, R. Chatila, and M. Devy. Object-based modelling and localization in natural environments. In *Proc. IEEE International Conference on Robotics and Automation, Osaka (Japon)*, May 1995.

6. J. Canny. A computational approach to edge detection. *I.E.E.E. Transactions on Pattern Analysis and Machine Intelligence*, 8(6), 1986.

7. P. Delagnes, J. Benois, and D. Barba. Adjustable polygons: a novel active contour model for objects tracking on complex background. *Journal on communications*, 8(6), 1994.

8. M. Devy and C. Parra. 3D Scene Modelling and Curve-based Localization in Natural Environments. In *Proceedings of the IEEE International Conference on Robotics and Automation (ICRA'98)*, Leuven, Belgium, 1998.

9. Yue Du. A color projection for fast generic target tracking. In *International Conference on Intelligent Robots and Systems*, 1995.

10. M. Dubuisson and A. Jain. 2d matching of 3d moving objects in color outdoors scenes. In *I.E.E.E. Computer Society Conference on Computer Vision and Pattern Recognition*, june 1997.

11. P. Fillatreau, M. Devy, and R. Prajoux. Modelling of Unstructured Terrain and Feature Extraction using B -spline Surfaces. In *Proc. International Conference on Advanced Robotics (ICAR'93),Tokyo (Japan)*, November 1993.

12. H. Haddad, M. Khatib, S. Lacroix, and R. Chatila. Reactive navigation in outdoor environments using potential fields. In *International Conference on Robotics and Automation ICRA'98*, pages 1332–1237, may 1998.

13. H.Bulata and M.Devy. Incremental construction of a landmark-based and topological model of indoor environments by a mobile robot. In *Proc. 1996 IEEE International Conference on Robotics and Automation (ICRA'96), Minneapolis (USA)*, 1996.

14. D.P. Huttenlocher, A. Klanderman, and J. Rucklidge. Comparing images using the hausdorff distance. *I.E.E.E. Transactions on Pattern Analysis and Machine Intelligence*, 15(9), 1993.

15. D.P. Huttenlocher, W.J. Rucklidge, and J.J. Noh. Tracking non-rigid objects in complex scenes. In *Fourth International Conference on Computer Vision*, 1993.

16. S. Jiansho and C. Tomasi. Good features to track. In *Conference on Computer Vision and Pattern Recognition*, 1994.

17. R. Murrieta-Cid. Target tracking method based on a comparation between an image and a model. Technical Report Num. 97023, LAAS CNRS, written during a stay at Stanford University, Toulouse, France, 1997.

18. R. Murrieta-Cid. *Contribution au développement d'un système de Vision pour robot mobile d'extérieur*. PhD thesis, INPT, LAAS CNRS, Toulouse, France, November 1998.

19. R. Murrieta-Cid, M. Briot, and N. Vandapel. Landmark identification and tracking in natural environment. In *Proceedings of the IEEE/RSJ International Conference on Intelligent Robots and Systems (IROS'98)*, Victoria, Canada, 1998.

20. J. Serra. *Image analysis and mathematical morphology*. Academic Press, London, 1982.

21. R. C. Smith, M. Self, and P. Cheeseman. Estimating Uncertain Spatial Relationships in Robotics. *Autonomous Robot Vehicles*, pages 167–193, 1990.

22. K. T. Sutherland and B. Thompson. Localizing in Unstructured Environments: Dealing with the errors. *I.E.E.E. Transactions on Robotics and Automation*, 1994.

23. M. Unser. Sum and difference histograms for texture classification. *I.E.E.E. Transactions on Pattern Analysis and Machine Intelligence*, 1986.

Ascender II, a Visual Framework for 3D Reconstruction*

Maurício Marengoni[1], Christopher Jaynes[2], Allen Hanson[1], and Edward
Riseman[1]

[1] University of Massachusetts, Amherst MA 01003, USA,
`marengon,hanson,riseman@cs.umass.edu`
[2] University of Kentucky, Lexington KY 40506, USA,
`jaynes@cs.uky.edu`

Abstract. This paper presents interim results from an ongoing project
on aerial image reconstruction. One important task in image interpretation is the process of understanding and identifying segments of an image.
In this effort a knowledge based vision system is being presented, where
the selection of IU algorithms and the fusion of information provided by
them is combined in an efficient way. In our current work, the knowledge
base and control mechanism (reasoning subsystem) are independent of
the knowledge sources (visual subsystem). This gives the system the flexibility to add or change knowledge sources with only minor changes in
the reasoning subsystem. The reasoning subsystem is implemented using
a set of Bayesian networks forming a hierarchical structure which allows
an incremental classification of a region given enough time. Experiments
with an initial implementation of the system focusing primarily on building reconstruction on three different data sets are presented.

1 Introduction

The typical knowledge-directed approach to image interpretation seeks to identify objects in unconstrained two-dimensional images and to determine the three-
dimensional relationships between these objects and the camera by applying
object- and domain-specific knowledge to the interpretation problem. A survey
of this line of research in computer vision can be found in [9].

Typically, a knowledge-based vision system contains a knowledge base, a
controller and knowledge sources. Knowledge representations range from semantic nets in the VISIONS system [8], and later schemas [7], to frames in
the ACRONYM system [2], and rules in the SPAM system [18], to relational
structures (generalized models) of objects in the MOSAIC system [10]. Controllers are typically a hybrid hierarchical system mixing bottom up and top
down reasoning. As an alternative, heterarchical control systems have been developed using blackboards as a global database. In this case knowledge sources

---

* Funded by the National Council for Scientific Research- CNPq, Brazil grant number
260185/92.2, by the APGD-DARPA project contract number DACA76-97-K-0005,
and by Army Research Office, contract number DAAG55-97-1-0188

are triggered if their preconditions have been met, placing their results in the blackboard for future use. Systems developed using this approach include the ABLS system [22] and the VISIONS schema system [7].

Recently, vision systems have been developed using Bayesian networks for both the knowledge representation and as the basis of information integration. The TEA1 system [20] was developed using a set of Bayesian networks that are combined to define where and what knowledge source should be applied in order to make scene interpretations at a minimum "cost". Although this system used selective perception [3] to reduce the number of knowledge sources called, the knowledge base (PART-OF net, Expected Area net, and IS-A net) encoded domain specific knowledge and was difficult to construct because of the level of detail required; it had to be re-engineered for a new domain. Although the classification results were satisfactory, it was slow and did not support "real-time" applications [20]. Binford [17] presented some ideas on how to generate bottom up inferences using geometric properties and Bayesian agregation, but the example used was simple and the environment well controlled. More recently Kumar [15] introduced a system with simple networks (each network has only 2 layers) for an aerial image interpretation. In this system, after an initial segmentation step, a Bayesian network is built and a set of features, related to each region or to pairs of neighbor regions, are computed from the image. These features are fed into the network and propagated to generate a label for each region. In general the features are simple to compute but a new network needs to be built for each image.

In most of these systems the controller and the vision algorithms are combined into a single system. One of the problems with this approach is that these systems can not be easily generalized to different domains from the ones for which they were developed and/or the amount of specific knowledge required to use the system in a different domain would be a burden in constructing it.

The system presented here (called Ascender II) was designed for aerial reconstruction of urban areas. In this system we introduce the idea of making the control and the visual operators completely independent, so it is divided into two major subparts: a reasoning subsystem and a visual subsystem. They are built separately and run on different machines. One advantage of this is that some changes in the reasoning subsystem or in the visual subsystem can be done independently, and available knowledge sources can be exchanged or augmented in the visual subsystem with no changes to the reasoning subsystem.

This paper discusses the Ascender II system and presents experiments on three different data sets. The results show that the system is robust across small changes in domain. The reasoning subsystem has a recognition rate of about 90% and the set of algorithms used in the visual subsystem produced reconstructions with an absolute error of less than 1.15 meters in the position of the 3D vertices. The system can easily be adapted to different environments of the same general type (i.e. aerial images). Section 2 presents the system, section 3 shows an example of 3D reconstruction, section 4 presents results obtained on three different data sets, and section 5 discusses directions for future work.

2 The Ascender II system

The original Ascender system (called Ascender I here) was developed for building detection and reconstruction from multiple aerial images of a site [4]. It used 2D image features and grouping operators to detect rooftop boundaries [13] and then matched these polygons under 3D constraints and across views to compute height and to build 3D volumetric models. The system used a fixed strategy and it detected nearly 90% of the buildings in controlled experiments on imagery from Fort Hood, Texas. However, a considerable number of false positives were generated due to scene clutter and the presence of buildings outside of the class for which the system was designed [5]. In order to address this problem of generality, the Ascender II system has been developed which incorporates AI mechanisms for dynamic control of a large set of IU processes, from simple T junction detectors to complex algorithms such as the Ascender I system for flat roof building detection.

The Ascender I system demonstrated that the use of multiple strategies and 3D information fusion can significantly extend the range of complex building types that can be reconstructed from aerial images [11]. The design approach for Ascender II is based on the observation that while many IU techniques function reasonably well under constrained conditions, no single IU method works well under all conditions. Consequently, work on Ascender II is focusing on the use of multiple alternative reconstruction strategies from which the most appropriate strategies are selected by the system based on the current context. In particular, Ascender II utilizes a wider set of algorithms that fuse 2D and 3D information and can make use of EO, SAR, IFSAR, and multi spectral imagery during the reconstruction process if available. We believe the system will be capable of more robust reconstruction of three dimensional site models than has been demonstrated in the past.

The system is divided into two independent components, running under different operating systems on different machines. The two subsystems communicate through sockets using a communication protocol specifically designed for this application; the system framework is shown in Figure 1.

Ascender II has been designed as a general purpose vision system, although our initial effort has focused primarily on recognizing and reconstructing building from aerial images. Less effort has gone into the knowledge networks and IU processes necessary for other objects, such as open fields, parking lots and vehicles.

Ascender II assumes that it has as input a set of focus of attention regions in the image data. These regions can be generated in a variety of ways, including human interaction and cues from other sources such as maps or other classified images. In the experiments described later, our primary goal was detecting and extracting buildings, so the initial regions were generated by using the Ascender I system to detect 2D building footprints. In one of the experiments described in Section 3, the regions were constructed using Ascender I and a classified SAR image. Once the regions are available, an intelligent control system based on Bayesian networks drives IU processes which extract and fuse 2D and 3D

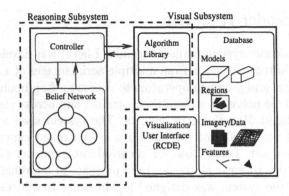

Fig. 1. Process overview. Control decisions are based on current knowledge about the site. Vision algorithms stored in the visual subsystem gather evidence, update the knowledge base and produce geometric models.

features into evidence for a specific set of class labels. Based on accumulated evidence, the system identifies regions as representing an instance of one of the generic object classes defined within the system and when possible constructs a coherent 3D model for each region [5, 12].

The reasoning subsystem is implemented as a server and is shown in Figure 2. It forks a process for each region and it is capable of processing regions in parallel. Each process forked by the reasoning subsystem has the structure presented in Figure 1. Note that the regions might not belong to the same image but they should belong to the same image domain. The next two subsections describe each of the subsystems in detail.

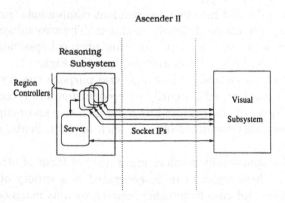

Fig. 2. The reasoning subsystem starts communication with the visual subsystem and makes a request to find regions in the image. For each returned region the reasoning subsystem forks a process to deal with that region.

2.1 The Reasoning Subsystem

The goal of the reasoning subsystem is to accumulate evidence sufficient to determine a plausible identity of the region in terms of the object classes represented within the system. A-priori knowledge about objects and their relationships is captured in a hierarchical Bayesian network (see below). Bayesian networks have been successfully used in systems required to combine and propagate evidence for and against a particular hypothesis [19, 14]. In the Ascender II system, we use these networks to determine what evidence to collect and what to do with the evidence once it has been obtained.

Evidence is obtained by using the network to select appropriate IU processes that obtain relevant feature information from the image(s). A-priori knowledge, in the form of initial prior probabilities associated with each object class, is used to select an IU process to use in the initial step. Generally, the process initially selected is fairly generic and measures simple features. In the case of a building, the kind of features measured might include the evidence for a center roof line, the number of L and T junctions on the boundary of the region, etc. As evidence accumulates for a particular hypothesis (e.g. a building), the IU process can become much more complex (and presumably return more consistent evidence). Once evidence has been obtained, it is combined with previous knowledge and the process is repeated until the system accumulates enough evidence to determine the region's most representative object class.

The problem with Bayesian networks is that propagation of evidence is, in general, an NP-hard problem [6] and the time for propagation is a function of the number of nodes, the number of links, the structure of the network and the number of states per node [14]. It is also known that if the network structure is a tree or a polytree (a structure in which a node can have multiple parents but there is no closed circuit in the undirected graph underneath) the propagation of evidence can be done in linear time [19]. In order to avoid the general propagation problem, the reasoning subsystem has been designed using a set of small Bayesian networks organized into a hierarchical structure according to levels of detail. This network structure is the system's knowledge base. A set of decision procedures uses the information inside the networks to decide what to do next. The idea of using a hierarchical set of networks is new; the drawback is that it is difficult to backtrack accross network boundaries. However, it is possible to implement backtracking strategies using an external control system (as we do with the multi-level network). It is also possible to implement an external data structure which returns the path through the hierarchy, or even use a message passing system between network structures when necessary. Our claim is that the system's ability to make local inference overcomes the drawback, but more studies need to be done.

Each network represents knowledge about a region at a particular scale of detail. Each object class is decomposed into subparts, similar to the work presented in [17]. The subparts are selected according to a natural decomposition of objects into parts which lend themselves to independent detection and reconstruction strategies.

The first level attempts to recognize that a region belongs to a generic class, like a building or a grass field or a parking lot. The second level assumes that the region belongs to the generic class found in the first level and attempts to recognize a subclass that the region can belong to; for instance if a region is recognized as a *parking lot* at one level, in the next level it might be recognized as a *full parking lot* using an IU process that counts vehicles in the region and compares this with the area covered. For consecutive levels the idea is the same, that is, a network at level i represents a refinement of a certain class represented in a network at level $i - 1$. This organization of networks is shown in Figure 3.

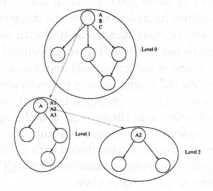

Fig. 3. The controller starts in level 0 and determines an outcome for the root node at that level (in this case A, B or C). If the outcome is A and time for further computation is available the controller loads the network for A in level 1 (the dotted line shows this inference call). The process can be repeated to subsequent level until the finest level is reached or there is no more time for computation.

The Bayesian networks were developed using the HUGIN system [1]. Our goal is to show that using small networks plus the hierarchical structure as suggested here increases performance and avoids propagation of evidence through variables that will not affect the overall classification process at a given level (see Section 3).

The knowledge in each network is structured as follows: each network has only one root node and each state of the root node represents a possible class label for a region. The other nodes in the network are random variables representing features that are expected to discriminate between two or more classes or to help confirm that a region belongs to a certain class. Each arc represents the relationship between features or between a feature and a certain class in the root node. Each feature has associated with it one or more knowledge sources (an IU process) in the visual subsystem which is responsible for computing and interpreting the corresponding feature.

Two types of knowledge are encoded in the network: general knowledge about the class (features that are expected to discriminate the class types), and domain specific knowledge in the form of prior probabilities for each possible class label. Changes in domain imply an adjustment in the set of prior probabilities used for each network in the reasoning subsystem. Because Bayesian networks utilize Bayes Rule for inferencing it is possible to reason in both directions. Thus, a feature can be measured in the image and its value propagated through the network, ultimately changing the beliefs in the root node for that region. In the other direction information about the frequency of objects in the image might be available and their change in the root node will change the expectations about the features in the image.

The hierarchical structure used in the reasoning subsystem can be used as a basic framework to implement an "anytime" recognition system. This topic will be explored in future work.

Selecting a feature and the recognition process: A selective perception system performs the minimum effort necessary to solve a specified task [3]. Thus a primary goal of the reasoning subsystem is to select a small subset of features that will allow a consistent identification of the region class.

A selection could be made in different ways, e.g., using a pre-defined static strategy where features are called independent of the evidence acquired or using a dynamic strategy where a different set of features is called depending on the feature values previously obtained. Even in a dynamic strategy there are many possible alternatives for selecting a feature, for example, we could simulate the network and select the node with the highest impact on the root node (impact here can be seen as the largest change in the belief distribution of the root node), or we could use utility theory as in the TEA1 system [20].

The reasoning subsystem as implemented here uses a simple dynamic strategy and introduces a selection process that selects the node which has the highest uncertainty. Maximum uncertainty is defined as the uniform distribution over the states in a random variable N. A measure for uncertainty, called the uncertainty distance, was defined which represents the difference between the value of the maximum belief in the node and the value of the belief if the node has an uniform distribution. This measure is computed as:

$$Uncertainty\ Distance\ = max(Belief(N)) - \frac{1}{S_N} \qquad (1)$$

where S_N represents the number of states in node N.

A more classical approach to measure uncertainty could be used, such as entropy. A simple empirical analysis comparing uncertainty distance and entropy was done. We simulated values for beliefs in a Boolean variable with states *Yes* and *No*. Initially we set the value of *Yes = 0* and *No = 1* and then incremented the values of *Yes* under the constraint that *Yes + No = 1*. For each step we measured entropy and uncertainty distance. The curves obtained for the *Yes* value using both measures are shown in Figure 4; the dotted line is the uncertainty distance and the continuous line is the entropy. One can see that both are symmetric and inversely related; while the entropy decreases (meaning that the uncertainty is reduced) the uncertainty distance increases (meaning that it is moving from the uniform distribution, thus reducing uncertainty as well). In some practical cases, the system using uncertainty distance performed slightly better than the system using entropy. Because we believe that it is more intuitively meaningful, we use this measure in the Ascender II system.

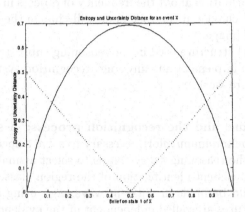

Fig. 4. The graph above shows entropy (solid line) and uncertainty distance (dotted line) for the state Yes in a Boolean variable (see discussion in text).

Given a network, the system computes the uncertainty distance for all nodes which have an IU process related to it and selects the node with the minimum uncertainty distance. As an example, consider the case where planar fit and line count are both Boolean variables. If the belief for a good planar fit in a region is 54% and the belief for a high number of lines inside the region is 67%, the uncertainty is higher for the planar fit variable, so this node will be selected.

Once a node is selected, a knowledge source is activated and performs an action on the image. The findings of this action are then returned to the controller, entered as evidence and propagated through the network. The process is repeated until the controller has enough evidence to recognize the class that the region belongs to.

Recognition within the system can be defined in a number of different ways. The simplest is to set a fixed threshold and every time a belief value reaches the threshold the region is identified as belonging to the class which has that belief value. This measure clearly has a problem: the threshold is fixed but the number of classes (states) in a node is not. If the threshold is too high and the node has many states, it might be difficult to reach the limit. Another approach is to define a relative threshold, say when a certain belief doubles from its initial value, or by using a relative comparison between the beliefs inside the node. A third possibility is to use a utility function [16] and keep acquiring evidence until it is not possible to increase the current utility.

The decision criteria for selecting a class label for a region in the root node used here is relative to the other classes at that node; that is, after each new piece of evidence is propagated through the network, the maximum belief and the second highest belief inside the root node are compared. If the maximum belief is at least k times the value of the second highest belief the controller stops and identifies the region as belonging to the class with the maximum belief. For our experiments the value of k was set to 2. The value was determined arbitrarily but the results obtained with it were both consistent and accurate; it is unclear how sensitive the performance is to changes in k.

Ascender II was developed mainly to build 3D models of buildings and to reconstruct their rooftop geometries. Because of this, finer levels of the network hierarchy were developed for the *building* outcome of the level 0 network. The networks implemented are presented in Figure 5 and Figure 6. The network at level 0 (Figure 5 left) attempts to recognize the class to which the region belongs. If the class identified is not *Building* the process is stopped and a generic 3D model is selected from the data base for visualization purposes. In the case where a building is identified the network at level 1 is called (Figure 5 right). This network is designed to identify single level buildings based on a simple set of features; if a single level building is identified the network shown in Figure 6 (left) is called to determine the rooftop class. If a multilevel building is identified, there is a possibility that the hypothesis is wrong (a multilevel building may have a line in the roof which looks very much like the center line of a peaked roof). Consequently the network shown in Figure 6 (right) is called to confirm a multilevel building or to backtrack to a single level building. If a multilevel building is identified the system breaks the region into two new subregions, based on the evidence gathered, and calls the network at level 1 for each subregion recursively.

Note that some knowledge sources can be called at different levels, but because each call is related to a specific region for which the feature values are stored in the visual subsystem, the system will not recompute values.

2.2 The Visual Subsystem

The visual subsystem is composed of two parts: a function library that stores the set of IU algorithms available to the system, and a geometric database that contains available data in the form of imagery, partial models, and other collateral information about the scene (such as classification of functional areas).

At the request of the controller, an algorithm is selected from the library and runs on a region that currently resides within the geometric database. New regions may be produced and stored in the database as a result of processing. In addition, the controller may request that regions be merged, split or eliminated.

The algorithm library contains information about each of the algorithms available to the system for selection as well as a definition of the contexts in which each algorithm can be applied. Contextual information, as well as sets of alternative algorithms gathering the same evidence, are stored in the form of an IU process. The IU process encodes the preconditions that are required for

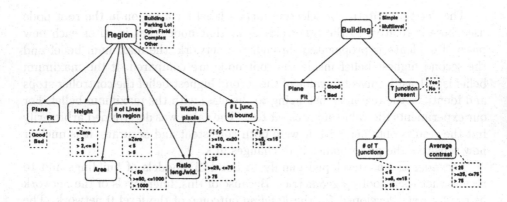

Fig. 5. The level 0 network at left determines if a region belongs to one of the possible classes. The level 1 network at the right is invoked for each building found in level 0 and tries to determine if it is a simple building or a multilevel building.

the algorithm to be executed, the expected type of data that the algorithm will produce, and the algorithm itself. If the preconditions for a particular algorithm are not met, then an alternative algorithm may be executed if it is available within the process. For instance, the system may obtain 3D information about a region from a DEM; if the DEM is not available the system uses a basic stereo processing algorithm to obtain the 3D feature requested. If there are no algorithms that can be run in the current context, then the corresponding belief value cannot be extracted by the visual subsystem and must be inferred from the Bayesian network.

The library of algorithms was developed to address aspects of the site reconstruction problem from aerial images. For example, finding regions that may contain buildings, classifying building rooftop shapes, and determining the position of other cultural features, are all important tasks for the model acquisition system. Some of the IU processes may be very "lightweight", be expected to perform only in a constrained top-down manner, and be usable in more than one context. Other algorithms may be very complex and may themselves contain multiple strategies and associated control; several of the algorithms used to generate the results presented here are sophisticated procedures. For a complete list of the Ascender II algorithms see [12].

If the framework is to be truly general, the cost of engineering a new IU processes must not be prohibitive, something that proved to be a problem in earlier knowledge-based vision systems [7, 18]. Only two components are necessary to convert an IU algorithm into a knowledge source that is usable by the system: the context in which the algorithm is intended to be run must be defined [21], and a method for deriving a certainty value from the output of the algorithm must

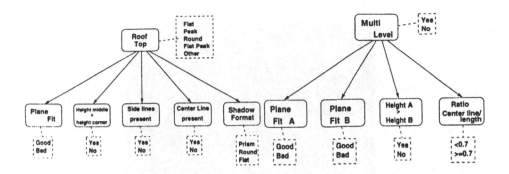

Fig. 6. Both networks are invoked at level 2. The network at left is called after a single building is detected and it is used to determine the rooftop type. The network at right is called when a multilevel building is detected. The reasoning system calls this network to confirm the recognition at level 1.

be defined. This certainty value is used by the system to update the knowledge base using Bayesian inference.

3 How the Ascender II system works - Snapshots

This section presents a sequence of snapshots taken when the system was running over a region in the Fort Benning, Georgia data set. The input image and the regions to be identified are shown in Figure 7; this set of regions were determined using optical images processed by the Ascender I system combined with a SAR classification provided by Vexcel Corp. The prior probabilities associated with the object classes in the level 0 network are shown in Table 1.

Consider the sequence of events which occurs when the system is processing region A in Figure 7. This region is shown in Figure 8 (top) with the network at level 0. The nodes with a thicker ellipse are the ones invoked by the reasoning subsystem; the evidence found and the class identification are shown in the figure. After deciding on a building class the system called the network at level 1, which checked for T junctions in the subregions shown in Figure 8 (middle). Evidence from level 1 identified the building as multilevel and the network to confirm multilevel building at level 2 is now called. At this point the system decomposed the region into two new subregions, as shown in Figure 8 (bottom), and recursively calls the network at level 1 for each of them.

The process is repeated on each of the two subregions, as shown in Figure 9 (top). Region A was also identified as a multilevel building and decomposed into two new subregions. The process is again repeated for the left most subregion (A1). This region was not identified as a multilevel building so the rooftop

Fig. 7. Regions to be identified by the Ascender II system from Fort Benning.

network is called for this particular region in an attempt to identify the type of roof. In this case, the system identifies it as a peaked roof, as shown in Figure 9 (middle). The process is now repeated for subregion A2, which is also identified as a peak roof building. The system then considers region B (Figure 9 top) and eventually identifies two peaked roof structures, as shown in Figure 9 (bottom), which is representative of the final result.

4 Experiments and Results

In all experiments described here, only the domain specific knowledge in the network at level 0 was changed from one experiment to the other (see Table 1). This knowledge represents expected frequency for each possible class in the root node and it is represented as prior probabilities. Experiments were performed on the Fort Hood data set (7 views with known camera parameters and corresponding DEM) shown in Figure 10 (left), on the Avenches data set (1 view and a DEM) shown in Figure 10 (right), and on the Fort Benning data set (2 views and a DEM) shown in Figure 7. The data sets have different number of images, different resolutions and different number of objects in each class.

There are seven knowledge sources available in the network at level 0 and three at level 1. Table 2 presents the average number of knowledge sources invoked by the reasoning subsystem for each data set and also the average calls by region type (object class). The recognition results obtained are summarized in Table 3.

The recognition results obtained for the regions (Fort Hood data) shown in Figure 10 (left) is shown in Figure 11 (top). The undecided region (region A) has

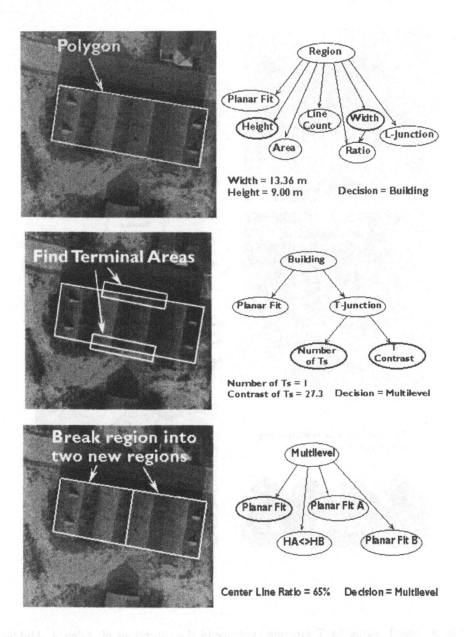

Fig. 8. Top: Region of discourse. The ground truth is a multilevel building with 4 peaked roofs. The building class was selected as the most probable because of the combination of the features Width = 12.36 m and Height = 9.0 m. Middle: The system used the fact that the region was identified as a building and that evidence of T junctions was found to identify it as a multilevel building. Bottom: The region was confirmed as a multilevel and it was broken into two new subregions.

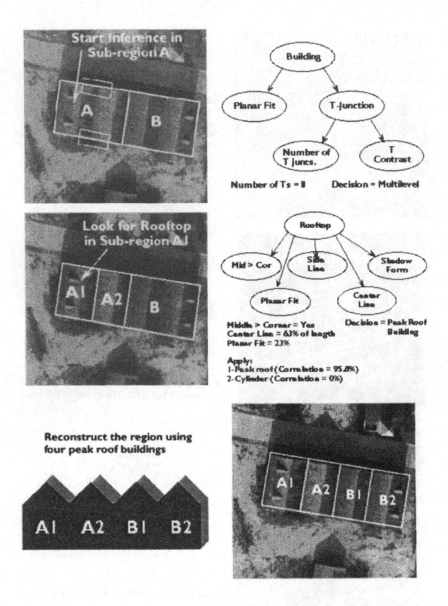

Fig. 9. Top: Looking for T junction evidence in the subregions of region A. Middle: Identified the region A1 as a peak roof building. Bottom: Reconstructed 3D model for the whole region.

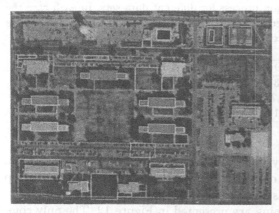

Fig. 10. At the left: the input regions from the Fort Hood data set. At the right: the input regions from Avenches data set. These regions were obtained by running the original Ascender I system constrained to detect two-dimensional building footprints.

Table 1. Probability distribution of beliefs in the root node for the level 0 network among the states Building, Parking Lot, Open Field, Single Vehicle and Other for all three data sets.

Knowledge	Build.	P.Lot	O.Field	S.Vehicle	Other
Fort Hood	0.35	0.2	0.2	0.15	0.1
Avenches	0.32	0.25	0.38	0.03	0.02
Fort Benning	0.35	0.2	0.2	0.15	0.1

a belief of 59% for the Parking Lot state and 31% for the Open Field state (the region is a parking lot). By the decision criteria discussed earlier, no decision is possible. The misclassified regions are a parking lot identified as building (region C) and 3 single vehicles identified as open fields.

The classification obtained for the regions in the Avenches site (Figure 10 right) is presented in Figure 11 (bottom). There is a set of small regions in the Avenches data set that were detected by the Ascender system as buildings and confirmed by the Ascender II system as single buildings with a flat roof; the correct identity of these objects is unknown. They look like big RV's or big containers, as one can see by their shadows and relative size. We considered these areas as RV's which could be identified as either flat roof building or a

Table 2. Average number of calls to knowledge sources for different data sets for all classes (Total column) and by specific classes (remaining columns).

Knowledge	Total	Build.	P.Lot	O.Field	S.Vehicle
Fort Hood	3.9	4.25	4.00	3.29	0
Avenches	4.7	5.22	5.00	4.0	0
Fort Benning	2.9	3.00	0	0	2.0

Table 3. Summary of the recognition process for different data sets. In each case the number of objects correctly identified is shown, followed by the total number of objects evaluated by the system (* - see text concerning identity of the RV regions).

Data set	Overall	Level 0	Level 1	Level 2
Fort Hood	37/41	37/41	21/21	21/21
Avenches	17/18*	18/18	16/16	15/16
Fort Benning	17/19	18/19	17/17	16/17

single vehicle. In this case the system correctly identified them. Region A is a parking lot for boats and it was correctly identified as parking lot. The rooftop of building B was misclassified as a peak instead of flat.

The results for the Fort Benning are presented in Figure 12. The only complete misclassification was a small peak roof building in front of the church that was classified as a single vehicle. The other problem found was a flat roof building classified as peak roof building due to a shadow that generates strong evidence for a center line in that building.

Notice that in all cases the misclassification was computed relatively to the initial focus of attention regions provided to the system and not against a complete ground truth model.

The final 3D reconstruction for the Fort Hood data and for the Fort Benning data are presented in Figure13. Geometric reconstruction of building models is based on a robust surface fit to the local DEM using the initial model and parameters generated by the recognition process. Error analysis was performed comparing hand constructed CAD models for the Fort Benning data and the 3D reconstruction obtained here; the errors are shown in Table 4 in Planimetric (horizontal), Altimetric (vertical) and Absolute distances, all in meters.

Table 4. Mean, maximum and minimum errors, in meters, for the 3D reconstruction in Fort Benning.

	IV Planimetric	IV Altimetric	IV Absolute
Mean	0.528	0.608	0.805
Maximum	0.848	0.892	1.112
Minimum	0.246	0.377	0.524

4.1 Evaluation

Our claim is that the Ascender II system can perform 3D reconstruction accurately and efficiently. In order to validate this claim the Fort Benning data was used to test the Ascender II system against a system that randomly selects a vision operator and also against a system that gets all available evidence prior to making a decision. The summary of these results are presented in Table 5. For the system with the random selector only the best performance is shown.

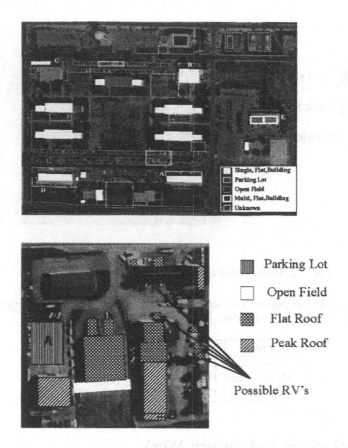

Fig. 11. At the left: recognition results on the Fort Hood data. Four regions were misclassified and for one region the system was not able to make a decision. At the right: recognition results on the Avenches data set.

Table 6 shows the average number of operators called by each method in the evaluation process. For the systems with best performance, Ascender II and All Evidence, the time required to process each region on average is shown in table 7.

The main difference between the Ascender II system and the All evidence system in terms of identification was that the small building in front of the church was classified as single vehicle by the Ascender II system. The system using all available evidence correctly identified it as a building, but misclassified its roof top as a cylinder and not a peak. The price paid by the All Evidence system was much higher in terms of time required for the correct classification. The random system generated a lot of misclassifications, exchanging buildings for parking lots and open fields. In the best case, three regions were misclassified in the first level.

Flat roof

Peak roof

Single Vehicle

Fig. 12. Recognition results on the Fort Benning data set.

Table 5. Number of regions correctly identified and total number of regions at each level for the Fort Benning data set.

Method	Overall	Level 0	Level 1	Level 2
Random	16/19	16/19	14/15	15/15
All Evidence	17/19	19/19	17/18	16/18
Ascender II	17/19	18/19	17/17	16/17

5 Conclusions and Future Work

A knowledge based vision system was presented where the reasoning subsystem and the visual subsystem were developed independently. The system is capable of performing incremental classification of regions. The overall performance is good: 90% correct recognition for the Fort Hood data, 94.4% for the Avenches data and 89.5% for the Fort Benning data. Although the data sets differ in the type of buildings present, image resolution, camera models, number of views available, imaging conditions, etc, the system correctly identified most of the regions in each site only changing the prior probabilities in the root node for each site. The hierarchical structure in the reasoning subsystem and the data

Table 6. Average number of operators called for each region for the Fort Benning data set.

Method	Level 0	Level 1	Level 2
Random	3.04	1.31	2.84
All Evidence	7	5	5
Ascender II	2	1.05	2

Fig. 13. At the left: 3D reconstruction on the Fort Hood data. At the right: 3D reconstruction on the Fort Benning data.

Table 7. Average time of processing on each region for Ascender II and All Evidence methods for the Fort Benning data.

Method	Level 0	Level 1	Level 2
All Evidence	39.6	24.8	1.68
Ascender II	11.3	24.6	0.89

base of IU algorithms in the visual subsystem allow new knowledge and new knowledge sources to be added with minor changes in the system.

The Ascender II system was compared with a system using a fixed strategy and a system using a random selector and in both cases the Ascender II performed either better or at the same level but always using less resources in terms of either operators or time.

The work presented here is an ongoing project. The system is being incrementally developed and new operators have been added continuously. In the future we plan to grow more branches of the hierarchy (i.e. add more object classes) and continue to develop new IU processes. We hope to examine the trade off between hand-coded IU strategies and the dynamic strategies provided by the Bayesian networks. We will also examine alternatives to the simple decision criteria used in the current system. In particular we plan to develop a utility theory approach to decision making and compare its performance with the current system.

References

1. Andersen, S., Olesen, K., Jensen, F., and F., J. Hugin - a shell for building bayesian belief universes for expert systems. In *Proceedings of the 11th International Congress on Uncertain Artificial Intelligence* (1989), pp. 1080–1085.
2. Brooks, R. Symbolic reasoning among 3-d models and 2-d images. *Artificial Intelligence 17* (1981), 285–348.

3. Brown, C., Marengoni, M., and Kardaras, G. Bayes nets for selective perception and data fusion. In *Proceedings of the SPIE on Image and Information Systems: Applications and Opportunities* (1994).

4. Collins, R., Cheng, Y., Jaynes, C., Stolle, F., Wang, X., Hanson, A., and Riseman, E. Site model acquisition and extension from aerial images. In *Proceedings of the Interantional Conference on Computer Vision* (1995), pp. 888–893.

5. Collins, R., Jaynes, C., Y. Cheng, X. W., Stolle, F., Hanson, A., and Riseman, E. The ascender system: Automated site modelling from multiple aerial images. *Computer Vision and Image Understanding - Special Issue on Building Detection and Reconstruction from Aerial Images* (1998), to appear.

6. Cooper, G. The computational complexity of probabilistic inference using bayesian belief networks. *Artificial Intelligence 42* (1990), 393–405.

7. Draper, B., Collins, R., Broglio, J., Hanson, A., and Riseman, E. The schema system. *International Journal of Computer Vision 2* (1989), 209–250.

8. Hanson, A., and Riseman, E. Visions: A computer system for interpreting scenes. In *Computer Vision Systems*, A. Hanson and E. Riseman, Eds. Academic Press, 1978.

9. Haralick, R., and Shapiro, L. *Computer and Robot Vision*. Addison-Wesley, 1993.

10. Herman, M., and Kanade, T. Incremental reconstruction of 3-d scenes from multiple complex images. *Artificial Intelligence 30* (1986), 289–341.

11. Jaynes, C., and et.al. Three-dimensional grouping and information fusion for site modeling from aerial images. *DARPA Image Understanding Workshop* (1996), 479–490.

12. Jaynes, C., Marengoni, M., Hanson, A., and Riseman, E. 3d model acquisition using a bayesian controller. In *Proceedings of the International Symposium on Engineering of Intelligent Systems, Tenerife, Spain* (1998), p. To appear.

13. Jaynes, C., Stolle, F., and Collins, R. Task driven perceptual organization for extraction of rooftop polygons. *IEEE Workshop on Applications of Computer Vision* (1994), 152–159.

14. Jensen, F. *An introduction to Bayesian networks*. Springer Verlag New York, 1996.

15. Kumar, V., and Desai, U. Image interpretation using bayesian networks. *IEEE Transactions on Pattern Analysis and Machine Intelligence 18(1)* (1996), 74–77.

16. Lindley, D. *Making Decisions: Second Edition*. John Wiley and Sons, 1985.

17. Mann, W., and Binford, T. An example of 3-d interpretation of images using bayesian networks. *DARPA Image Understanding Workshop* (1992), 793–801.

18. McKeown, D., Jr., A. W., and McDermott, J. Rule-based interpretation of aerial imagery. *IEEE Transactions on Pattern Analysis and Machine Intelligence PAMI-7* (1985), 570–585.

19. Pearl, J. *Probabilistic Reasoning in Intelligent System: Networks of Plausible Inference*. Morgan Kaufmann, 1988.

20. Rimey, R., and Brown, C. Task-oriented vision with multiple bayes nets. In *Active Vision*, B. A. and Y. A., Eds. The MIT Press, 1992.

21. Strat, T. Employing contextual information in computer vision. In *Proceedings of ARPA Image Understanding Workshop* (1993).

22. Wang, C., and Srihari, S. A framework for object recognition in a visually complex environment and its application to locating address blocks on mail pieces. *International Journal of Computer Vision 2* (1988), 125–151.

Hybrid Approach to the Construction of Triangulated 3D Models of Building Interiors[*]

Erik Wolfart,[1] Vítor Sequeira,[1] Kia Ng,[2] Stuart Butterfield,[2] João G.M. Gonçalves[1] and David Hogg[2]

[1] European Commission - Joint Research Centre, TP 270, 21020 Ispra (VA), Italy.
[2] School of Computer Studies, University of Leeds, Leeds LS2 9JT, UK.

E-mail: [erik.wolfart, vitor.sequeira, joao.goncalves]@jrc.it, [kia, stuart, dch]@scs.leeds.ac.uk

Abstract. This paper describes a system which integrates laser range data and video data to construct textured 3D models of building interiors. The system has been implemented in a prototype known as the AEST (Autonomous Environmental Sensor for Telepresence) - an autonomous mobile platform carrying a scanning laser range finder and video camera. The AEST is intended to fully automate the creation of models from building interiors by navigating automatically between positions at which range data and video images are captured. Embedded software performs several functions, including triangulation of the range data and registration of video texture, registration and integration of data acquired from different capture points, and optimal selection of these capture points. This paper concentrates on the triangulation algorithm of the system, which is a hybrid approach combining geometric surface extraction and a robust triangulation. It produces accurate geometric information and at the same time, a photo-realistic triangular mesh. This is important for graphical and visualisation applications such as virtual studios, virtualised reality for content-related applications (e.g., CD-ROMs), social tele-presence, architecture and others.

1 Introduction

The number of applications using augmented reality and virtual reality technologies are increasing rapidly. Whereas virtual reality is mostly used for entertainment and training, augmented reality is founding an increasing market niche for maintenance, remote verification and inspection. Both areas (augmented reality and virtual reality) require realistic 3D models to be successful.

---

[*] This work has been carried out as part of the EU-ACTS project RESOLV, involving partners from four countries.

In general, there are two techniques for 3D reconstruction of real objects and scenes that are commonly used. One is based on active range data (e.g. structured light, laser range finders), and the other is based on video images.

The extraction of high-quality models of small objects (e.g. museum artefacts) using high-resolution range cameras based on structured light is the main application active range sensing [12]. Recently, there have been attempts to use this technology for the reconstruction of large objects [7] and for creating virtual environments [8]. Commonly, the reconstruction of such systems is performed off-line with manual intervention to aid and correct the model during the processing cycle. To date, there has been no reported automatic detection of non-modelled parts or computation of the next best view. The existing systems are normally based on large and fixed set-ups and possess limited mobility.

Passive range techniques based on video images give good results in extracting a minimum structure from the scene (e.g. a wall made of four points) with video images to enhance 3D appearance. Examples of such reconstruction include building facets [9], [15], [16] and indoor environments [10], [11]. Normally, the full geometry of the scene is not available.

Automation in model building seeks to move away from the highly interactive and labour intensive process of existing systems for model building of large environments. Of paramount importance is the ability to fuse information acquired from different capture points into a unified model. Automation of this process requires registration between partial models and detection of occlusions between surfaces in the scene. The absence of automated occlusion handling is characteristic of current systems.

The work described in this paper aims at the provision of complete, high resolution and photo-realistic 3D reconstructed models from reality. To achieve this, we have implemented an integrated approach to the construction of textured 3D scene models that takes full advantage of the complementary nature of laser range data and digital images. This approach has been realised in a prototype device for 3D reconstruction known as the AEST (Autonomous Environmental Sensor for Telepresence). The AEST automates the creation of models from the interiors of buildings by incrementally building a model of its surroundings. Figure 2a shows the latest prototype system, and Figure 2b shows an earlier version of the prototype in the form of a manual trolley.

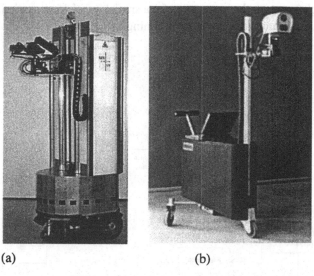

(a)   (b)

Figure 1: A picture of the AEST and EST.

The AEST has been developed to deal with large interiors for which many capture points may be required, such as one floor of an office block, factory or heritage site, and for hostile environments such as nuclear plants. Autonomous operation is required because a human operator cannot be used in hazardous locations and because offices and factories are best surveyed when they are empty and during the night when illumination can be controlled. The five principal components of the system are:

1. hardware, comprising the mobile platform, controlling computers, laser-range finder and camera;
2. software module for converting laser rangels (3D pixels) into a 3D triangulated model;
3. software module for mapping visual texture on to the 3D model;
4. navigation using the partially complete 3D model and ultrasonic sensors;
5. system software and human-computer interface;

In short, the embedded software performs several functions including data acquisition, triangulation of the range data, registration of video texture, registration and integration of data acquired from different capture points, and optimal selection of these capture points, ensuring that range data and video texture is acquired for all surfaces at the required resolution (see Figure 2). All these modules run on the host-PC, and communicate with each other via a Host Server (HS) module. In addition to controlling the flow of data and operations between software modules, the HS is also responsible for communication and remote-operation via the Internet. The on-board computer has a Web server installed, and is linked to the outside world by means of a wireless Ethernet link. Any authorised person (e.g. system's operator monitoring the acquisition session) using a standard computer can link to the computer's Web page, and, using Java applets, set-up the parameters for a spatial acquisition session (e.g., the area to be scanned, the spatial resolution, the zooming factor, etc.).

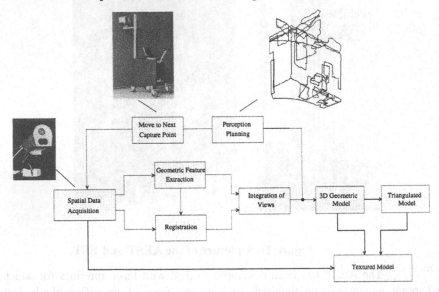

Figure 2: Paradigm for Photo-Realistic 3D Scene Reconstruction.

In Sections 2 and 3, this paper concentrates on the second component of the system, i.e. the triangulation module to build triangular piecewise planar meshes of arbitrary topology. Originally the system modelled a given scene by applying a surface fitting algorithm to the 3D data. For situations where the visual appearance rather than the surface structure is required, the surface fitting has now been combined with a robust triangulation to form a hybrid approach to scene modelling.

Section 4 summarises the algorithms needed to build a model from multiple viewpoints. For more detailed information on these components of the AEST see [3], [4], and visit the RESOLV web-page (http://www.scs.leeds.ac.uk/resolv/).

In Section 5 we briefly describe the texture mapping module which adds the colour information to the triangulated mesh and gives it the photo-realistic impression. Results of texture mapped models from single and multiple viewpoints can be seen in Section 6.

2 Scene Modeling

For each viewpoint, the laser scanner provides a set of two images, a range and a reflectance image (see Figure 3). The range value for each pixel is given by the distance to the object and the reflectance value by the intensity of the returned laser signal. As both values are measured from the same signal, the two images are perfectly registered. Knowing the geometry of the scanning system, we can compute the 3D position corresponding to each pixel in the 2D range image. Figure 4 shows a part of the 3D data produced from the range image in Figure 3 (the screen, parts of the desk and the wall) as a triangulated mesh. This 3D data, in itself, constitutes a 3D representation of the scene, but a higher level representation is required to interpret it. It is desirable that the reconstructed surface description is as simple as possible while preserving its precision. If a piece-wise surface representation is used, the number of reconstructed patches should be as small as possible, and if polynomial patches are used the degree of the polynomial should be as low as possible. The final representation should not depend on how the different views were taken and a single model for the whole scene should be built irrespective of the number of range images used to characterise the environment.

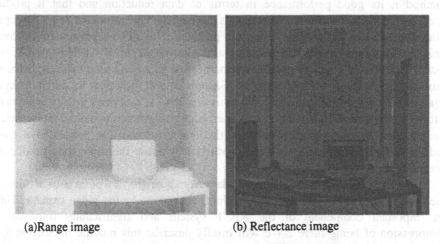

| (a)Range image | (b) Reflectance image |

Figure 3: 2D range and reflectance image as produced by laser scanner.

Figure 4: Segment of 3D points constructed from range image in Figure 3.

The way a reconstructed model is described depends crucially on the purpose for which the descriptions are intended. Two categories can be identified:

- those based on shape primitives, e.g. Constructive Solid Geometry (CSG), which are suitable for CAD-style applications, and
- those composed of polygonal meshes, more suitable for graphical and visualisation applications.

The initial version of the triangulation algorithm was based on extracting geometric features from the scene: polynomial surfaces of 1st or 2nd order are fitted to the raw data and the result is triangulated for visualisation. The advantage of this method is its good performance in terms of data reduction and that it produces accurate geometric information which is needed by later modules (e.g. Perception Planning and Navigation). However, the problem is that this representation provides only the dominant geometric description and does not accurately include small details that are present in a typical indoor environment (e.g., a book on a table, a thermostat box on the wall or a door handle). Section 3 will describe in detail a hybrid triangulation algorithm that overcomes this problem. It combines the original surface fitting with a robust triangulation that uses edge information to reduce noise and to model depth and orientation discontinuities that are frequently present in a typical indoor scene. It achieves a good data reduction while at the same time producing a complete and visually appealing model.

The final step in modelling the data from a single viewpoint is to texture map the triangulated mesh with the colour information given by the video camera. This is an important component of the AEST system and significantly improves the "impression of being there". We will briefly describe this module in Section 5, for more in depth information see [4].

3 Triangulation

As has been mentioned, the system originally modelled a scene by fitting polynomial surfaces to the 3D data. Although this provided accurate geometric information and allowed for modelling of the main features of a typical indoor scene, many of the details and smaller objects were not included in the model. A limited photo-realistic impression was the result. In order to increase the completeness of the model, it was decided to devise a triangulation algorithm that is directly applied to the raw 3D data. Given the nature of the scenes that we want to model, the algorithm faces the following problems:

- The amount of raw 3D data can be very high, especially if many viewpoints are required to model the entire scene. Therefore, the algorithm needs a high data reduction without losing too much detail.

- The scene may contain many scattered objects which introduce occlusions and depth discontinuities. The algorithm needs to reliably detect those depth discontinuities in the presence of a considerable amount of noise and make sure that they won't be connected by triangles.
- The scene may contain features at varying scales: large surfaces like walls, floors or columns as well as small objects with the size close to the noise level. Therefore, the resulting mesh must be multi-resolutional, using large triangles for smooth areas but keeping the detail of small features.

3.1 Multi-resolutional triangulation

The triangulation algorithm was devised to take account of the above constraints and also to take advantage of the fact that the 3D points are organised in a 2D grid (i.e. for each pixel in the 2D range image we know the corresponding 3D position in space).

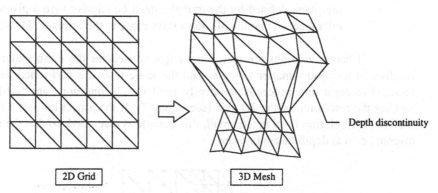

Figure 5: Triangulated range data in 2D grid and 3D space.

The algorithm starts by building a triangular mesh connecting all the valid pixels that are in adjacent rows and columns in the 2D grid, resulting in a mesh of regular triangles in the grid. Each pixel corresponds to a point in 3D space and each triangle on the grid has a corresponding triangle in space.

If the surface scanned by the system is perpendicular to the scanning direction, the triangle in 3D space will be isosceles. As the angle to the surface becomes smaller, the triangles get more elongated and depth discontinuities will produce very long and thin triangles (see Figure 5). To avoid joining portions of the surface that are separated by depth discontinuities (jump edges), a first test is performed for each triangle, based on the triangle aspect ratio, t, between the radius of the circumscribed circle, R, and the inscribed circle, r (see Figure 6).

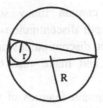

Figure 6: Triangle aspect ratio.

In order to decrease the number of triangles, the grid is divided in square blocks of a given size (e.g. 64x64 rangels) and each square is divided into two triangles, containing half of the points and triangles of the square block. Two condition are tested for each triangle:

1. The aspect ratio of the triangle and of all contained triangles must be larger than a pre-defined value. This ensures that depth discontinuities are not connected by the mesh.

$$t = \frac{r}{R} > \tau$$

2. The mean distance between the 3D points covered by the triangle and the plane defined by the triangle, must be smaller than a given distance tolerance, so that the 3D mesh stays close to the original 3D data.

If both conditions are met, the triangle is used for the mesh, otherwise it is subdivided into four smaller triangles and the same tests are performed for each of them. The algorithm proceeds iteratively until the 2 conditions are fulfilled or it reaches the resolution of the 2D grid (see Figure 7). If the aspect ratio of a triangle at the lowest resolution level is too small, this triangle is discarded, so that the surface is disconnected at depth discontinuities.

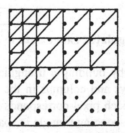

Figure 7: Example how a square 2D image area can be divided into regular triangles of varying size.

By applying this procedure it may be necessary to discard triangles that do not join depth discontinuities, but have been acquired with a small angle to the surface being scanned. These triangles are not reliable (the measurement noise increases exponentially with the angle between the surface normal and laser beam [3] and should also be discarded, and replaced with data acquired from another scanning position.

The result is a multi-resolutional triangular mesh, where edges are preserved, giving a very realistic representation of the 3D surface when textured with the laser reflectance or digital image data.

3.2 Triangulation using edge information

This first triangulation is an improvement over the previous algorithm using only surfaces in a sense that in principle all the objects in a scene are modelled regardless of their topology. However, some problems remain, mainly due to the noisy nature of the raw 3D data. The algorithm acts on a pixel-by-pixel basis, making it difficult to distinguish between noise and small objects. Hence, the data noise is often visible in the resulting model, some triangles might be lost if the aspect ratio gets too small due to the noise and the data reduction is not always as good as desired.

To further improve the algorithm and to make it more robust, the following steps were introduced:

1. The algorithm extracts depth and orientation discontinuities from the raw range.
2. The raw range data is smoothed using a median filter with the extracted discontinuities used as a mask.
3. Finally, the data is triangulated as before, but additionally using the extracted discontinuities to guide the triangulation parameters.

The remainder of this section explains these three steps in more detail. The depth discontinuity extraction works on the raw range image and is similar to the Canny edge detector [1]. It can be described as follows:

*   In order to make the depth discontinuity detection more robust, the image is first smoothed using a 3 by 3 median mask.
*   Then the edge strength and orientation is computed for each pixel location using a one dimensional differential mask in the horizontal and vertical direction.
*   A non-maximum suppression is applied: each edge value is compared with the edgels within a given range along a line perpendicular to the local edge orientation. If the value is not the maximum, it is set to zero. The result is an image where only the ridges of the original edge image have non-zero values.
*   Finally, the edgels are tracked in the image to obtain edge strings using a hysterisis threshold: only if an edge value exceeds an upper threshold the algorithm starts tracking, it then applies a second, lower threshold until it completely detected the current edge string. Edge strings under a certain length can then be removed thus further reducing noise in the image.

Additionally to the depth discontinuities, orientation discontinuities are extracted in a similar way. In this case, first the surface orientation for each pixel is computed by locally fitting a plane to the 3D data. Discontinuity values in the horizontal and vertical directions are extracted by computing the angles between the neighbouring surface orientations. Then the algorithm continues as for the depth discontinuities by applying non-maximum suppression and edge tracking.

The results of extracting depth and orientation discontinuities from the range image in Figure 3 can be seen in Figure 8. Since the surface orientation is sensitive to noise and can be unreliable in the vicinity of edges, the extracted orientation discontinuities are not as well localised as the depth discontinuities. However, the results are sufficient for our purposes.

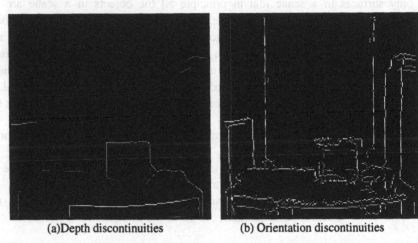

(a)Depth discontinuities   (b) Orientation discontinuities

Figure 8: Depth and orientation discontinuities of image in Figure 3.

In order to reduce the size of the resulting triangulated model and to improve its visible appearance, it was decided to decrease the noise in the raw range data prior to triangulation. This is done by applying a median filter to the original raw range data. The median was the preferred choice over other filters (e.g. mean), because it causes only little blurring at the edges and because the range data has a high content of non-gaussian noise. To maintain the high level of detail, the smoothing algorithm uses the depth and orientation discontinuities extracted in the previous step as a mask: if a pixel in the range image (or one of its 8-neighbours) was qualified as depth or orientation discontinuity, it maintains its original range value, only otherwise the value is replaced by the median of the local neighbourhood. This makes it possible to use a relatively large smoothing mask (usually 5 by 5 pixels) without losing too much information.

Finally the same triangulation algorithm as before is applied to the smoothed data. However, the thresholds for the aspect ratio and the distance tolerance for each triangle are guided by the output of the discontinuity detection:

- if any of the pixels that are covered by the triangle currently under investigation was classified as depth discontinuity, the triangle will be broken up (or discarded if it was already at the maximum resolution).
- each pixel covered by the triangle that was classified as orientation discontinuity, will cause the aspect ratio and distance tolerance tolerances to get tighter for this triangle, thus producing a better resolution at the orientation discontinuities.
- wider thresholds for aspect ratio and distance tolerance are applied when none of the pixels covered by a triangle was qualified as a discontinuity, thus resulting in less overall triangles and a more complete model.

These additional steps improve the resulting model, especially if the raw data has a high noise content. Due to the noise reduction and the relaxed thresholds inside a surface area, the model contains less triangles and at the same time the visual appearance is enhanced. Furthermore, the visible detail is higher along the discontinuities, as the parameters are tighter. The disadvantage of the pre-processing is, however, that features of which the size is smaller than the threshold used for detecting the depth discontinuities (i.e. the noise level) will be blurred during smoothing.

3.3 Hybrid 3D Modeling

Although the extended triangulation algorithm already produces a good model of the scene, it still can be possible to see the influence of noise in the 3D data, especially on large planar surfaces. This can have considerable negative affects on the photo-realistic appearance of the model and consequently it was decided to combine the original surface fitting algorithm with the best version of the triangulation.

The basic idea is the following: first the surface fitting algorithm is run over the raw 3D data and as many polynomial surfaces as possible are extracted [3]. During the fitting process the range image is segmented into distinct surfaces with most pixels in the image being assigned to one of the surfaces. The parameters of each surface are computed to minimise the mean distance between this surface and the points assigned to it. Any 3D point that was classified as being part of a surface is assigned a label unique to this surface and its coordinates are replaced with the projection of this point onto the plane. Thus, the resulting data set is perfectly smooth wherever a surface was extracted. Any point that could not be assigned to a surface remains unchanged. Thus, the surface fitting not only yields geometrical information about the scene, but it is also a more global method of removing noise from the data. Figure 9(a) illustrates the segmentation of the range image into polynomial surfaces, Figure 9(b) is a snapshot of the 3D wireframe model of the surfaces.

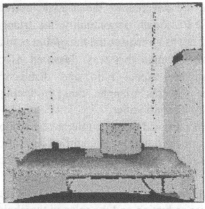 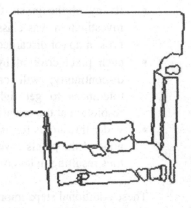

(a) Surface labels overlay on range image   (b) Snapshot of 3D wire-frame model

Figure 9: Result of fitting surfaces to the range image in Figure 3.

In a second step, the triangulation is applied to all points as before with the addition that also the surface labels are used to guide the parameters of the triangulation:

- if all pixels covered by a triangle have the same surface label (i.e. the triangle lies completely within one surface), the aspect ratio is ignored and the distance tolerance has a higher value.
- if the pixels have different labels or if some of the pixels were not assigned to any surface at all, the parameters are selected as described in the previous section.

The resulting model combines the advantages of both algorithms: large surface areas appear perfectly smooth with a maximum degree of data reduction. Since in a typical indoor scene, a large part of the surface area can be represented as a polynomial surface, the size of the overall model is fairly small. At the same time this method produces a representation for all valid 3D points in the raw data and maintains a high level of detail for objects not covered by the polynomial surfaces (e.g. books or other small objects on a desk). Another disadvantage of the original algorithm using only surfaces is that the 3D model often shows small gaps along the intersection of surfaces which can compromise the realistic impression considerably. This problem is overcome by the hybrid approach, as these gaps are closed by the triangulation.

Again, the problem is to distinguish between noisy data and small features in the scene during surface fitting. All points that lay within a certain threshold of a surface collapse onto this surface. Any feature smaller than this threshold will therefore disappear from the 3D data. However, since the 3D model is textured with video data (in which, of course, all features remain) the visual appearance of the model is not necessarily compromised.

Figure 10 and Figure 11 illustrate the results of applying the four different methods for the 3D scene reconstruction. Figure 10 shows the models texture mapped with the reflectance image obtained from the laser scanner whereas Figure 11 shows the same models using a wire frame representation. Figure 10(a) results from applying the original surface fitting algorithm to the raw data. Although the main features of the scene were reconstructed, the small details (e.g. the objects on the table) are missing. Also, intersecting surfaces do not connect in the model. In Figure 10(b) the 3D data was triangulated without any pre-processing. Now all objects are reconstructed, but the visual appearance is poor due to the noisy data. Figure 10(c) shows the triangulation of the pre-processed range data using the edge information. The noise is significantly reduced which yields a nicer and smaller model. The best model is obtained from combining surface fitting and triangulation (Figure 10(d)). It has a smoother appearance than Figure 10(c) and at the same time uses roughly half the amount of triangles. Table 1 lists the sizes of the models in Figure 10.

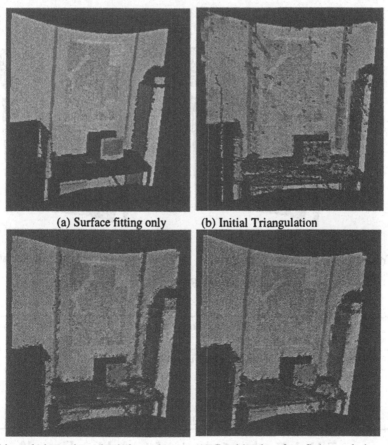

| (a) Surface fitting only | (b) Initial Triangulation |
| (c)Triangulation using edge information | (d)Combined surface fitting and triangulation |

Figure 10: 3D models using different triangulation approaches.

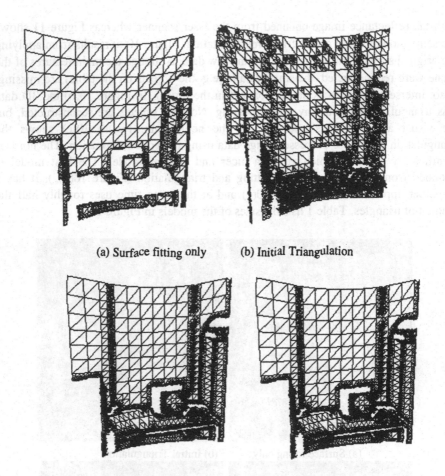

(a) Surface fitting only   (b) Initial Triangulation

c)   Triangulation using edge information (d)Combined surface and triangulation

Figure 11: Same data as Figure 12 as wire frame models.

Triangulation method	Number of triangles
Connecting all valid 3D points (see Figure 4)	73500
Surface fitting only (Model (a))	3660
Initial Triangulation (Model (b))	10900
Triangulation using edge information (Model c))	9640
Combined surface fitting and triangulation (Model (d))	4550

Table 1: Number of triangles of the models in Figure 10

4 Multiple Viewpoints

Normally it is not possible to have complete 3D representations from data acquired at a single viewpoint. To resolve occlusions in the scene or to reconstruct large scenes, it is necessary to acquire data from multiple viewpoints. Apart from resolving the ambiguities caused by occlusions, multiple range images may also be used to introduce higher resolution images in specific regions of interest. This section summarises the tasks performed by the AEST system in order to iteratively build a geometric model of the entire scene from multiple viewpoints. For more details see [3] and [4].

The initial step in each iteration is to detect the occlusions and gaps in the range data that was acquired so far and to plan a set of new viewpoints to resolve these occlusions. First, the occlusion detection is done by analysing the depth maps for surface discontinuities. During perception planning, the system computes a set of potential viewpoints that resolve all the occlusions, which are then optimised so that the number of required viewpoints is minimal, the acquisition conditions (e.g. distance and angle to objects) are optimal and the overlap between the scans is sufficient for the subsequent registration.

After perception planning, the AEST platform moves autonomously to the next computed viewpoint, acquires a new range image and computes the set of 3D points. The next step in the processing chain is to register the newly acquired with the existing 3D data. Our approach to registration is based on the *Iterative Closest Point (ICP)* algorithm [13] with some modification to cope with the specific kind of data and to speed up the process. The ICP algorithm first identifies the correspondences between two sets of 3D points and then computes a rigid 3D transformation based on those correspondences. It iteratively repeats this process until the stopping criteria is met. To work correctly the ICP algorithm requires an initial estimate of the 3D transformation between the two data sets which, in our case, is provided by the navigation module of the robot [14].

After registration, the different views are integrated, i.e. the overlapping data from different scans is combined to form one common representation of the entire scene. This is done by first identifying the overlapping areas for the new range image. Then, for each pixel, it is decided which scan is used to represent it in the final model based on a reliability measurement (a weighted sum of the distance between acquisition point and object, the local surface orientation, the returned intensity and the variance of the range measurement). This yields a *deletion map* for each range image which is used to mask out the redundant data during the subsequent triangulation. A triangular mesh is produced for each range image using the algorithm described in Section 3 together with the deletion masks and, in a final step, the different meshes are connected along the borders to form a single representation of the data.

The system repeats the entire cycle until all occlusions are resolved or the session is terminated by the user.

5 Visual Texture Mapping

The RESOLV project aims to generate computer models of scenes which are visually realistic. The Texture Mapping Module achieves this by texturing the 3D triangulated surfaces from the laser scan with pixel data from a set of video camera images. The camera and laser are mounted together on the sensor head of the AEST. Since the camera field-of-view is smaller than that of the laser, several images are acquired at different pan/tilt positions (typically 15 images in a 3´5 grid), in order to provide sufficient texture coverage. The triangulated data and camera images are processed to produce a texture-mapped VRML model.

In this section we present an overview of the components of the Texture Mapping Module, including the basic texture-mapping method and some techniques which improve efficiency and the quality of the resulting models.

5.1 The basic approach

In VRML, each 3D vertex is assigned a corresponding 2D texture map coordinate and the texture is interpolated between these vertices. To obtain these correspondences automatically requires *calibration* of the camera with respect to the 3D model.

The mapping between 3D points and a given 2D image is encapsulated in the *camera matrix* for a particular camera, denoted by M. M projects a model point in 3D laser co-ordinates, onto a 2D image point, $x = MX_L$.

Camera models vary in complexity, depending on how accurately they attempt to characterise the image formation process. This, in turn, determines the number and types of parameters in M. We use Tsai's camera model [5] which is based on the pin-hole model of perspective projection, and has eleven parameters. The six *extrinsic* parameters define the position and orientation of the camera with respect to the world co-ordinate system. Five *intrinsic* parameters describe the optical properties of the camera, including a 1st order approximation of a coefficient to correct for radial distortion [6].

The camera model parameters can be determined, if at least seven non-coplanar 3D points and their corresponding 2D image positions are known. Correspondence information is supplied by the system operator via a graphical user interface. When more than the minimum number of correspondences are known, we employ the RANSAC parameter estimation technique [2]. This attempts to identify and discard erroneous data, and thus use only the most accurate data to obtain a solution.

While acquiring the range data, the laser measures the reflectance properties of the surface at each scan location and generate a *reflectance image*. Thus each reflectance image pixel correspondence to a known 3D position. Hence, the operator needs only to match points in the reflectance and camera images to obtain the 2D/3D correspondences required for calibration.

Once calibrated, M can be used to obtain 2D texture coordinates by projecting any voxel to the camera image plane. These are stored in the VRML file and the texture-mapping process is completed. A number of texture-mapped models are presented in Section 6.

Although this *hand-calibration* process is normally done only once to calibrate the on-board video camera with the laser scanner, it is very flexible in that it allows the model to be texture-mapped using an image taken with any camera, at any time, from any location.

5.2 Enhanced techniques

In this section we briefly describe two extensions to the basic texture-mapping approach. For more details, see [4].

To texture-map a model composed of relatively large triangles, it is necessary to take account of perspective effects in the image formation process. In order for a VRML surface to look realistic from any viewpoint, it should be textured using data from a camera that is approximately orthogonal to that surface. Since this will not be possible for many surfaces, we have devised a method to recover the orthogonal view from an oblique view. The texture assigned to each triangle pixel is computed using a pipeline of transformations which maps between texture coordinates and original camera image coordinates, undoing the perspective effects.

Another problem is caused by the fact that the range data can be acquired from several different locations. Thus it is likely that some 3D model triangles will not be visible in one or more camera images. If this is because the triangle is *occluded* by other scene structure, it must not be texture-mapped using texture belonging to the occluding surface. The solution to the problem can be found by looking again at camera matrix, M, which projects each triangle into an image. Although two different 3D points can project onto the same 2D pixel, in homogeneous coordinates, the projective scale factor, λ, which is a function of the depth of the 3D point relative to the camera, will be different. Therefore, λ can be used to decide whether to texture-map a 3D triangle, or part thereof.

6 Results and Conclusions

This section presents a number of screen snapshots of reconstructed models. Other reconstructed models are available on-line and can be accessed via the RESOLV web-page (http://www.scs.leeds.ac.uk/resolv/).

Figure 12: Snapshots from 2 single view models of the lobby area at the Royal Institute of Chartered Surveyors, London.

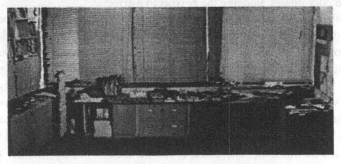

Figure 13: A multiple-view model of an office in the School of Computer Studies, University of Leeds.

The AEST system described in this paper allows to automatically reconstruct the 3D model of building interiors. The hybrid triangulation algorithm used by the system applies a surface fitting algorithm to the 3D data to recover dominant features like walls, floors and columns. It reconstructs small detailed objects (e.g. books on a desk) using a robust triangulation algorithm. The result is a 3D mesh that completely models the scanned data, reducing the noise content for large surfaces and providing high resolution where necessary. The number of triangles is significantly reduced over the original triangulation algorithm.

Combined with the texture mapping of the video data captured by the system, the algorithm considerably enhances the photo-realistic appearance of the resulting 3D.

Current work includes optimisation of the VRML file organisation and improving the accuracy and realism of the reconstructions. We are also experimenting with ways to augment the models to enhance the sense of "being there". For example, an animated movie texture could be superimposed on a virtual TV screen, or a video camera could track people in the real world scene and then representations of those people would mimic their movements in the reconstructed model.

References

1. Canny, J.F., 1986. A computational approach to edge detection, PAMI-8, No.6. pp. 679-698
2. Fischler, M.A., and Bolles, R.C., 1981. Random sample consensus: A paradigm for model fitting with applications to image analysis and automated cartography. Communications of the ACM, 24(6), pp. 381 — 395.
3. Sequeira, V., 1996. Active Range Sensing for Three-Dimensional Environment Reconstruction, PhD Thesis, Dept. of Electrical and Computer Engineering, IST-Technical University of Lisbon, Portugal.
4. Sequeira, V., Ng, K.C., Butterfield, S., Gonçalves, J.G.M., and Hogg, D. C., 1998. Three-dimensional textured models of indoor scenes from composite range and video images. In:

Proceedings of SPIE, Three-Dimensional Image Capture and Applications, edited by Ellson, R.N. and Nurre, J.H., vol. 3313.

5. Tsai, R.Y., 1987. A versatile camera calibration technique for high-accuracy 3D machine vision metrology using off-the-shelf TV cameras and lenses. IEEE Journal of Robotics and Automation, RA-3(4), pp. 323 — 344.

6. Weng, J., Cohen, P. and Herniou, M., 1992. Camera calibration with distortion models and accuracy evaluation. In: IEEE Trans. PAMI, vol. 14, pp 965 — 980.

7. Beraldin, J-A, Cournoyer, L., Rioux, M., Blais, F., El-Hakim, S. F. and Godin, G., 1997. Object model creation from multiple range images: Acquisition, calibration, model building and verification. Proc. Int. Conf. on Recent Advances in 3-D Digital Imaging and Modeling. Ottawa, Canada, pp. 326-333.

8. El-Hakim, S. F., Brenner, C., Roth, G., 1998. An approach to creating virtual environments using range and texture. Proc. ISPRS Int Symp. on "Real-Time Imaging and Dynamic Analysis", Hakodate, Japan, pp. 331-338.

9. Grau, O., 1997. A scene analysis system for the generation of 3-D models. Proc. Int. Conf. on Recent Advances in 3-D Digital Imaging and Modelling. Ottawa, Canada, pp. 221-228.

10. Johnson, A. E. and Kang, S. B., 1997. Registration and integration of textured 3-D data. Proc. Int. Conf. on Recent Advances in 3-D Digital Imaging and Modeling. Ottawa, Canada, pp. 234-241.

11. Kang, S.B. and Szeliski, R., 1996. 3-D scene data recovery using omnidirectional multibaseline stereo, Conf. on Computer Vision and Pattern Recognition. San Francisco, CA, pp. 364-370.

12. Soucy, M., Godin, G., Baribeau, R., Blais, F. and Rioux, M., 1996. Sensors and algorithms for the construction of digital 3D-colour models of real objects. Proc. IEEE Int. Conf. on Image Processing: Special Session on Range Image Analysis, ICIP'96, Lausanne, Switzerland, pp. 409-412.

13. Besl, P. J. and McKay, N. D., 1992. A method for registration of 3-D shapes. IEEE Trans. Pattern Analysis and Machine Intelligence, PAMI-14(2): 239-256.

14. Gomes-Mota, J. and Ribeiro, M. I., 1998. A multi-layer robot localisation solution using a laser scanner on reconstructed 3D models. Proc. 6th Int. Symp. on Intelligent Robotic Systems, SIRS'98, Edinburgh, Scotland, UK.

15. P.Beardsley, Phil Torr, Andrew Zisserman. 3D Model Acquisition from Extended Image Sequences. Proc. of European Conference on Computer Vision, 1996

16. Camillo J. Taylor, Paul E. Debevec, Jitendra Malik. Reconstructing Polyhedral Models of Architectural Scenes from Photographs, Proc. of European Conference on Computer Vision, 1996

On Camera Calibration
for Scene Model Acquisition and Maintenance
Using an Active Vision System

Rupert Young[1], Jiri Matas[1,2], and Josef Kittler[1]

[1] Centre for Vision, Speech and Signal Processing,
School of Electronic Engineering, Information Technology and Mathematics,
University of Surrey, Guildford GU2 5XH, United Kingdom.
R.Young,G.Matas,J.Kittler@surrey.ac.uk
[2] Centre for Machine Perception, Czech Technical University,
Karlovo náměstí 13, 12135 Praha, Czech Republic.
matas@cmp.felk.cvut.cz

Abstract. We present a fully integrated active vision system for interpreting dynamic scenes. We argue that even if the ego-motion of the mobile vision system is known, a single view camera calibration cannot adequately support scene model acquisition and maintenance. It is shown that stable camera/grabber chain calibration can be achieved using a multi-view calibration process. With such calibration, a predicted view of the scene from any arbitrary view point can successfully be used for object verification and scene model maintenance. Experimental results in scene interpretation confirm the benefits of the multi-view calibration approach.

1 Introduction

The recent research effort in computer vision, under the acronym VAP (vision as process) [4], clearly demonstrated the benefit of enhancing the commonly advocated active vision paradigm [3, 2, 1, 6] by the concept of continuous processing which facilitates the exploitation of temporal context to make the scene interpretation problem manageable. Accordingly, the vision system is not only able to control the camera to focus on regions of interest or to adopt a new view point to simplify a scene interpretation task, but most importantly, it is processing the input visual data on a continuous basis. The latter has the advantage that the degree of knowledge about the imaged scene (identity, location and pose of objects in the scene) is continuously maintained and this in turn simplifies the complexity of future visual tasks. This idea mimics the ability of the human vision system to build a model of the surrounding environment and use this model to generate visual expectations (even with closed eyes). In terms of machine perception, the capability to exploit temporal context translates into the requirement to build a symbolic scene model which is utilised in solving instantaneous visual tasks and is continuously updated.

We have developed a vision system which adheres to the VAP philosophy [7]. The scene is regularly sampled by visual sensing and the outcome of processing directed towards a particular visual task is entered into a scene model database. The database contains symbolic information about the types of objects detected, their position in the 3D world coordinate system defined for the environment in which the sensor operates, and their pose. The system has been shown to exploit multiple cues to generate object hypotheses and to verify the content of the scene model. It also has the capability to interpret dynamic scenes. In particular, it has been demonstrated how the combined use of temporal context and a grammatical scene evolution model enhance the processing efficiency of the vision system [10].

In the above studies the camera of the vision system acted as a static observer. We have recently extended the system capability by placing the camera on a robot arm with a view to performing scene model acquisition and maintenance experiments with an active observer. As the ego-motion of the active observer is known to sufficient accuracy, it should be possible to verify the presence of objects in the scene model database from any view point. However, a mobile camera raises the issue of accuracy and stability of calibration. If calibration is inaccurate, the prediction of the appearance of objects in the scene model will be rendered useless for efficient comparison with the observed data.

In the paper we investigate the influence of calibration errors on scene interpretation and scene model maintenance using an active observer. We show that a single view calibration does not yield calibration parameters which are sufficiently accurate. This leads to inaccurate estimates of object positions. Moreover, the positional estimates cannot be improved by viewing an object from several viewpoints, as the location estimates are biased towards the initial calibration viewpoint. We show that the problem can be effectively overcome by means of a multi-view calibration process. This avoids over-fitting the camera/grabber chain calibration parameters and facilitates reliable and computationally efficient scene model maintenance.

The paper is organised as follows. In the next section we present a brief overview of the calibration procedure used [20]. Section 3 describes the adopted approach to object recognition and verification which exploits the ground plane constraint [8, 13, 14, 16] and has been described in detail elsewhere [18, 19]. Section 4 describes the scene model maintenance experiments performed. The results of the experiments are presented and discussed in Section 5. Section 6 summarises the main results of the paper.

2 Camera Calibration

2.1 Camera Model

In our application the goal of camera calibration is to recover the projective transformation between image points and the corresponding 3D world points on a ground plane. Four coordinate systems need to be determined in order to compute the transformation, i.e. the world, camera, camera sensor plane and image coordinate systems respectively. Three sets of data are required, the extrinsic and intrinsic parameters and details concerning the camera sensor.

The extrinsic parameters define the position and orientation of the camera with respect to the world, and comprise the rotation matrix (R) and the translation vector (T), such that a point in world coordinates (x_w, y_w, z_w) can be defined in terms of its corresponding camera point (x_c, y_c, z_c) as,

$$\begin{bmatrix} x_c \\ y_c \\ z_c \end{bmatrix} = R \begin{bmatrix} x_w \\ y_w \\ z_w \end{bmatrix} + T. \tag{1}$$

The 3 x 3 rotation matrix can also be expressed as three parameters of rotation, the roll, pitch and yaw angles around the z, y, and x axes, respectively [5]. Together with the three elements of the translation vector T_x, T_y and T_z this gives six extrinsic parameters in the calibration implementation used in the procedure [17]. The transformation defined by the extrinsic parameters give the coordinates of a world point in terms of the camera coordinate system with the origin at the optical centre and the z axis along the camera's optical axis.

There are many possible intrinsic parameters, including different types of lens distortion, which could be modeled. For compatibility with other research and available software [17] we constrain ourselves to four intrinsic parameters, the focal length, f, the image centre C_x and C_y and a lens distortion factor κ are required for the remaining stages. The next step is to convert from the camera coordinate system to the plane of the CCD sensor.

$$X_u = f \frac{x_c}{z_c} \quad \text{and} \tag{2}$$

$$Y_u = f \frac{y_c}{z_c}, \tag{3}$$

where X_u and Y_u are the coordinates on the undistorted (ideal) sensor plane.

Due to geometric lens distortion the sensor coordinates require adjustment with the lens distortion factor giving the true sensor position of the point,

$$X_d = \frac{X_u}{(1 + \kappa \rho^2)} \quad \text{and} \tag{4}$$

$$Y_d = \frac{Y_u}{(1 + \kappa \rho^2)}, \tag{5}$$

where $\rho = \sqrt{X_u^2 + Y_u^2}$.

Finally, the image point is expressed by,

$$X_i = d_x^{-1} X_d s_x + C_x \quad \text{and} \tag{6}$$

$$Y_i = d_y^{-1} Y_d + C_y, \tag{7}$$

where d_x and d_y are the distances between the centres of the sensor elements and s_x is a scaling factor compensating for any uncertainty in the timing of the start of the image acquisition. These three camera sensor parameters are assumed to be constant, the values of d_x and d_y are given by the camera manufacturer and, for our present purposes, s_x is taken as 1.0.

The extrinsic parameters vary accordingly to pose, but are related through the camera movements, and the intrinsic parameters should be the same for any pose. The goal of the multi-view calibration procedure is to determine the intrinsic parameters, for any given camera, so that 3D information can be recovered by a mobile camera from any position and show that the results of our experimental procedure are repeatable, robust and stable.

2.2 Chart Detection

Successful camera calibration relies heavily on the accurate and consistent detection, in images, of precisely known world points. Points extracted from the image of conventional objects are notoriously unreliable. The object edges extracted from images at different poses may actually refer to different world points. There is also the added problem of finding the correspondence between points in different images.

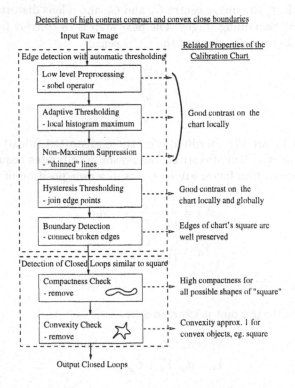

Fig. 1. Chart detection algorithm

To overcome these ambiguities we use as world registration markers points on a calibration chart (see figure 3b). In addition we apply a fast and robust technique for the accurate detection of the centres of the squares of the calibration chart. The chart detection technique is founded on the premise that the image gradient for pixels on the chart will be locally maximal and close to the global maximum. The resulting edge strings are closed, compact and convex.

The main stages of the method involve the processing of local image gradients, the feature extraction of the centre of gravity of each square and the linking of possible nodes to segment each individual chart. Figure 1 shows a block diagram of the entire process and more details can be found in Soh et al [12].

2.3 Multi-view Calibration

We pose camera calibration as the process of finding the optimal values for the parameters which correspond to the minimum error between the image points on a calibration object observed by the camera and the points obtained by re-projecting the corresponding calibration object points from the world coordinates onto the image plane.

Typically, calibration involves taking a single, static view of a set of points lying on a common plane (coplanar). However, there could be many variations of the calibration parameters which satisfy a specific view giving an acceptable re-projected error. If the world points are coplanar there can, particularly, be considerable ambiguity in the estimated f, T_z values. We have found that repeated calibration of the same scene, even without moving the camera gives unstable results. In our view the reason is parameter bias due to data over-fitting and, therefore, the parameters are only appropriate for the specific view from which they were determined.

To some degree the f, T_z ambiguity can be alleviated by using non-coplanar calibration points [15] (which requires some mechanism for moving the calibration points in space or for correlating points on different planes) and the intrinsic parameter bias can be alleviated by calibration from multiple poses [11]. We draw on these two concepts and derive a procedure which involves taking a series of views of a fixed calibration chart. The views are defined by known camera movements. All views are used jointly to determine the camera intrinsic parameters and the initial extrinsic parameters. By moving the camera in different planes (instead of the calibration points) and calibrating at a large number of positions which cover the desired working environment of the robot/camera system, we obtain very stable estimates of the calibration parameters [20].

3 Object Recognition

The object recognition approach used in the present system has been reported in detail elsewhere [18]. It uses a dedicated recognition engine for each type of object that can be found in a breakfast scenario. In particular we can cope

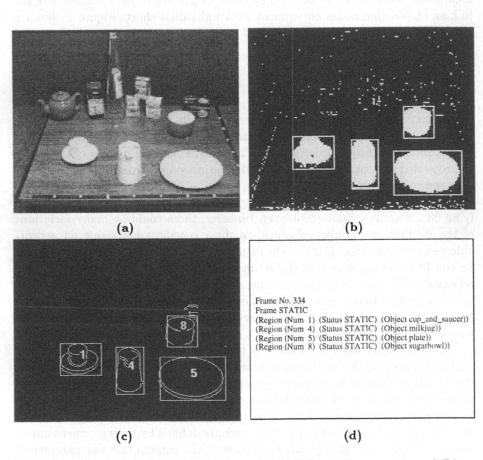

Frame No. 334
Frame STATIC
(Region (Num 1) (Status STATIC) (Object cup_and_saucer))
(Region (Num 4) (Status STATIC) (Object milkjug))
(Region (Num 5) (Status STATIC) (Object plate))
(Region (Num 8) (Status STATIC) (Object sugarbowl))

(a)

(b)

(c)

(d)

Fig. 2. Processing steps a) One image in sequence b) Colour difference regions c) Edges within regions of interest d) Symbolic interpretation of regions

with plates, saucers, sugar bowls, cups and milk jugs. The recognition scheme assumes some prior knowledge and constraints. All objects must be placed on a common, flat ground plane. The transformation between the camera coordinate system and the ground plane coordinate system must be known (established through calibration). The recognition procedure, for the initial pose, adheres to the processing steps shown in figure 2.

Regions of interest are determined by comparison of the current image with a background image of a static tabletop scene. Any areas which show a significant chromatic difference [9] are likely to represent new objects or events and are, therefore, deemed interesting. The outlines of objects within the regions of interest are extracted and compared with the projection of three-dimensional models onto the image plane. Thresholds for the object matches have previously defined experimentally [19]. The object is said to be recognised when a model match is found which falls below its corresponding threshold value.

4 Model Maintenance Experiments

4.1 Experimental Setup

All our experiments were carried out with a COSMICAR/PENTAX 25mm lens on a JVC TK1070E camera attached to a PUMA700 robot arm (figure 3a). All processing was performed on a Silicon Graphics Power Challenge machine.

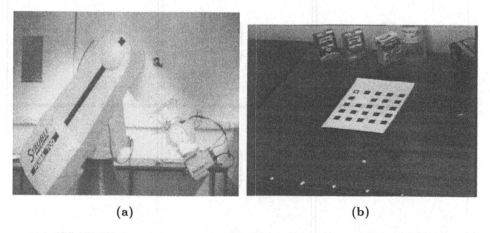

(a)   (b)

Fig. 3. a) Robot/camera system, b) Example view of calibration chart

4.2 Predicted World Position Experiments

Our hypothesis concerning the maintenance of models and calibration data is that the data derived from the multi-view procedure will produce a small variation in the predicted object positions from different poses, whereas the data from single-view calibration will not generalise well to new views, resulting in a large variation of predicted position. Having determined two sets of calibration data, from single and multiple camera poses [20], our next step was to determine the effect of the parameters on the predicted position of a recognised object.

The robot/camera system was successively positioned at 3D grid points 200mm apart, covering a 650x650x450 virtual 3D volume (barring the poses that were unreachable or violated the camera protection protocols). The direction of sight of the camera was always oriented towards the same point on the tabletop. In the initial position the object, a milk-jug, was recognised and its 3D position computed. At each subsequent position, using the known camera movement from the robot control system, the new image position of the object model was computed.

Fig. 4. The process of optimisation of the world object position as seen in the image position of the re-projected model.

Generally there would be some error between the new model position and the new edges. This discrepancy was resolved by optimising the x and y world position of the object such that the error between the re-projected model and the edges in the image was minimised. A typical example is shown in figure 4.

The first image indicates the initial re-projected error between the edges and the model (thick grey lines). The subsequent images show the minimisation process in action with the final image showing the ultimate match. With this process, a new world position of the object is determined at each new pose of the camera. Ideally, if the projective transformation is accurate, the computed position should be the same in each case.

To test the above hypothesis we performed the experiment as described with both sets of calibration data with the expectation that the more reliable the data the more precise the predicted position. As the results in section 5 indicate, our expectations were confirmed.

4.3 Occlusion Experiment

A further experiment demonstrates the application of the improved knowledge of the projective transformation by recovering from a situation where the detected object is occluded. In figure 6 the left hand column shows three successive scenes of the tabletop. The second shows objects occluding the target object from the first image. The robot is then moved to a new pose where the target is not occluded and an attempt is made to recover detection by utilising the predicted position from ground plane knowledge and the robot movement.

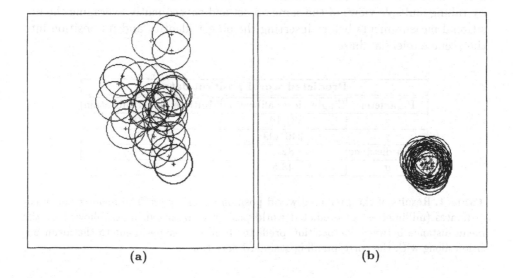

(a)   (b)

Fig. 5. Plan view of predicted positions from single view calibration (a) and from multiple view calibration. Each circle represents the base of the object, with the centre shown by a cross. The area of each image covers 600x600mm and the diameter of each circle is 100mm.

5 Results

The plot of the predicted object world positions at each pose of the camera is shown in figure 5. The circles represent the diameter of the base of the object on the tabletop seen in plan view with the cross indicating the centre. Figure 5a shows the predicted positions derived from the experiment using single view calibration data and 5b that for multiple view data. It is clear that the predicted positions derived from the multiple view calibration show a marked improvement over the single view, with a close clustering of points. Table 1 shows the mean and standard deviations of the distance of each point from the mean position of all the points, for both the single and multi-view calibration.

The predicted image positions derived from the single view calibration were, in fact, so poor that the regions allocated for edge detection were so far from the actual edges required that the position optimisation could not converge to the correct solution. This was resolved by manually indicating (with the cursor) an initial image location to start the position optimisation procedure.

A surprising outcome of this experiment is the finding that with the single view calibration the estimated camera parameters give rise not only to a larger variance in object position estimation but also to a bias. Thus the object pose cannot be refined merely by viewing it from several viewpoints and averaging the position estimates. However, the converse is true, provided the camera is calibrated using the multiple view calibration procedure. Thus with appropriately calibrated camera, an estimate of the position of an object can be refined by taking multiple views of the same object and subsequently averaging the positional measurements before inserting the object identity and its position into the scene model database.

Predicted world position data		
Parameter	Single view calibration	Multiple view calibration
x	331.105	442.728
y	240.409	391.170
Mean distance	82.2	15.4
σ	48.5	7.0

Table 1. Results of the predicted world position experiments. The mean x and y coordinates (millimetres) of predicted world positions are shown first, followed by the mean distance between the position predicted from each experiment to the mean position along with the corresponding standard deviation.

Given the confidence in position prediction derived from the previous experiments we are now able to show a benefit of the improved knowledge of the camera to ground plane transformation. The result of the experiment dealing with occlusion is shown in figure 6. Each row shows a different scene with the columns showing, from left to right, the grey-level image, the extracted edges and the edges with the region boundary and the superimposed model, if an object is detected.

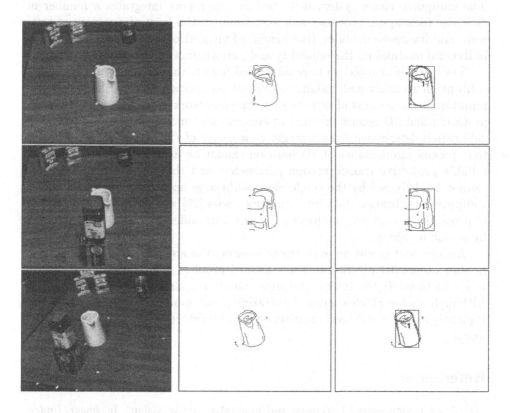

Fig. 6. Occlusion experiment. Each row shows a different scene from the robot. In the first scene an object, a milk-jug, is recognised. In the second the milk-jug is occluded and recognition fails. The robot is then moved to a new pose and the object is recovered.

In the first scene the milk-jug is detected (and its 3D world position recorded) as indicated by the thick grey outline in the right hand column, which matches the edges seen in the centre column. In the second scene the target object is occluded and no object is detected. In the final scene the camera is moved to a pose where the milk-jug is no longer occluded. From the world position derived from the first scene, the known robot movement and the precise knowledge of the projective transformation the image position of the object in the new scene is accurately determined, leading to successful matching of the re-projected model and the observed edges.

At present we only show how detection recovery is possible given a suitable new non-occluded pose and not how the choice of that pose is made. We leave for future work determination of appropriate positions of the camera relative to the target and occluding objects.

6 Conclusions

The computer vision system described in this report integrates a number of different techniques, processes and algorithms in the form of a variety of software and hardware modules. One benefit of integration is to show the effects of individual modules on the reliability and performance of the overall system.

The particular topic we have addressed here is the influence of the camera calibration accuracy and stability on object recognition and its 3D pose determination in the context of *active* vision. Previous work in the area of scene interpretation and 3D reconstruction has concentrated mainly on static poses with calibration determined from a single view image of the scene. We have shown that precise maintenance of 3D position cannot be achieved in the absence of reliable projective transformation parameters and that the required accuracy cannot be delivered by the single view calibration approach. The technique of computing calibration data from multiple views [20] was shown to significantly improve the predictions of object positions from different view points assumed by a mobile camera.

Also presented was an experiment showing the application of the ability to predict object 3D position to the standard problem of occlusion. The system was able to verify the initial interpretation after a target object was occluded. Although choice of view point facilitating scene model maintenance was not explicitly modelled, this will constitute a possible future extension of the reported work.

References

[1] J. (Y.) Aloimonos. Purposive and qualitative active vision. In *Image Understanding Workshop (Pittsburgh, Penn., Sep 11-13 1990)*, pages 816–828. Morgan Kaufmann, 1990.

[2] Y. Aloimonos. *Active Perception*. Lawrence Erlbaum Associates Ltd.,, 1993.

[3] D. H. Ballard. Reference frames for animate vision. In *Joint Conference on Artificial Intelligence*, pages 1635–1641, 1989.

[4] J Crowley and H I Christensen. *Vision as Process*. Springer-Verlag, Berlin, 1995.

[5] K.S. Fu, R.C. Gonzalez, and C.S.G. Lee. *Robotics*. McGraw-Hill, 1987.

[6] E. Grosso and D. Ballard. Head-centred orientation strategies in animate vision. In *International Conference Computer Vision*, pages 395–402, 1993.

[7] J. V. Kittler, J. Matas, M. Bober, and L. Nguyen. Image interpretation: exploiting multiple cues. In *IEE Conference Publication, 1995, 140, pp1-5*, 1995.

[8] D. Koller, K. Daniilidis, T. Thorhallson, and H.-H. Nagel. Model-based object tracking in traffic scenes. In *European Conference on Computer Vision*, pages 437–452, 1992.

[9] J. Matas. *Colour-based Object Recognition*. PhD thesis, University of Surrey, Guildford, Surrey GU2 5XH, 1995.

[10] J. Matas, J. Kittler, J. Illingworth, L. Nguyen, and H.I. Christensen. Constraining visiual expectations using a grammar of scene events. In I. Plander, editor, *Artificial Intelligence and Information-Control System of Robots '94 (Smolenice Castle, Slovakia)*, pages 81–93. World Scientific, 1994.

[11] P. Puget and T. Skordas. An optimal solution for mobile camera calibration. *European Conference on Computer Vision*, pages 187–198, 1990.

[12] L.M. Soh, J. Matas, , and J. Kittler. Robust recognition of calibration charts. In *IEE 6th International Conference on Image Processing and Its Applications*, pages 487–491, 1997.

[13] T. N. Tan, G. D. Sullivan, and K. D. Baker. Pose determination and recognition of vehicles in traffic scenes. In *European Conference on Computer Vision*, pages 501–506, 1994.

[14] A.F. Toal and H. Buxton. Spatio-temporal reasoning within a traffic surveillance system. In *European Conference on Computer Vision*, pages 884–892, 1992.

[15] Roger Y. Tsai. A versatile camera calibration technique for high-accuracy 3d machine vision metrology using off-the-shelf tv cameras and lenses. *IEEE Journal of Robotics and Automation*, 3:323–344, 1987.

[16] David Vernon. *Machine Vision: Automated visual inspection and robot vision*. Prentice Hall, 1991.

[17] R. Willson. Tsai camera calibration software. *http://www.cs.cmu.edu/People /rgw/TsaiCode.html*, 1995.

[18] D. Yang, J. V. Kittler, and J. Matas. Recognition of cylindrical objects using occluding boundaries obtained from colour based segmentation. In E Hancock, editor, *British Machine Vision Conference*, pages 439–448, 1994.

[19] R. Young, J. Kittler, and J. Matas. Hypothesis selection for scene interpretation using grammatical models of scene evolution. In *14th International Conference on Pattern Recognition (Brisbane, Australia, August 17–20, 1998)*, 1998.

[20] R. Young, J. Matas, and J. Kittler. Active recovery of the intrinsic parameters of a camera. In *International Conference Control, Automation, Robotics and Vision*, December 1998.

ADORE: Adaptive Object Recognition

Bruce A. Draper, Jose Bins, Kyungim Baek

Department of Computer Science
Colorado State University
Fort Collins, CO, USA. 80523
(draper|bins|baek)@cs.colostate.edu

Abstract. Many modern computer vision systems are built by chaining together standard vision procedures, often in graphical programming environments such as Khoros, CVIPtools or IUE. Typically, these procedures are selected and sequenced by an *ad-hoc* combination of programmer's intuition and trial-and-error. This paper presents a theoretically sound method for constructing object recognition strategies by casting object recognition as a Markov Decision Problem (MDP). The result is a system called ADORE (*Ad*aptive *O*bject *Re*cognition) that automatically learns object recognition control policies from training data. Experimental results are presented in which ADORE is trained to recognize five types of houses in aerial images, and where its performance can be (and is) compared to optimal.

1 Introduction

As the field of computer vision matures, fewer and fewer vision systems are built "from scratch". Instead, computer vision systems are built by chaining together standard vision procedures, including (but by no means limited to): image smoothing and enhancement, edge and corner extraction, region segmentation, straight line and curve extraction, grouping, symbolic model matching (including Hausdorf matching, key feature matching, and heuristic search), appearance matching, pose determination, and depth from stereo, motion or focus. Separately, each of these procedures addresses part of the computer vision problem. Sequenced together, they form end-to-end vision systems that perform specific tasks.

Computer vision software environments help users build end-to-end systems by providing procedure libraries and graphical user interfaces for sequencing them together. In Khoros, for example, programmers build applications by selecting procedures (called "glyphs") from menus and graphically connecting the output of one procedure to the input of another [27]. CVIPtools is a similar software environment intended primarily for academic use [33]. The Image Understanding Environment (IUE) is an object-oriented software developer's environment, but it also includes a GUI for sequencing procedures [23]. (The IUE is still under development at the time of writing, but a preliminary version is freely available at http://www.aai.com/AAI/IUE/IUE.html.)

Software tools such as Khoros, CVIPtools and IUE make it easier for programmers to form and test sequences of vision procedures. Unfortunately, they do not help programmers with the underlying problems of how to select procedures for a specific task, or how to compare one control strategy to another. Programmers are left to choose vision procedures based on intuition, and to refine sequences of procedures by trial and error.

The goal of the Adaptive Object Recognition (ADORE) project is to provide a theoretically sound mechanism for dynamically selecting vision procedures for specific tasks based on the current state of the interpretation. In the future, we hope to build systems that can adapt to any recognition task by dynamically selecting actions from among dozens (if not hundreds) of vision procedures. At the moment, however, this ambitious goal exceeds our grasp. This paper describes an initial prototype of ADORE that learns to find houses in aerial images using a library of ten vision procedures. While this system is clearly short of our ultimate goal, it is an example of an end-to-end system that adapts by dynamically controlling vision procedures. This paper describes two experiments with the prototype version of ADORE – one where ADORE succeeds in finding a nearly optimal recognition strategy, and one where it is less successful.

2 Examples of Static and Dynamic Control

Before describing ADORE in detail, let us first illustrate the problem it is supposed to solve. Figure 1 shows a nadir-view aerial image. The task is to find instances of specific styles of houses, such as the duplex in Figure 2. To accomplish this task, ADORE is given access to ten vision procedures and a template of the duplex. (Descriptions of all ten procedures can be found in Section 5.2.) ADORE is also given training images and training signals that give the position and orientation of each duplex. ADORE's role is to dynamically select and execute procedures so as to produce duplex (and only duplex) hypotheses.

ADORE finds duplexes by learning a control strategy that selects one vision procedure at each processing step. For example, ADORE can begin be selecting one of three procedures for producing regions of interest (ROIs) from images: a rotation-free correlation procedure [28], a statistical distribution test [25], and a probing routine. All three can be used to generate duplex hypotheses, but ADORE learns from the training data that for this task – where the duplexes are almost identical to each other, and lighting differences and perspective effects are minimal – pixel-level correlation outperforms the other two procedures. ADORE therefore learns a recognition strategy that begins with correlation.

The next step is more complex. Figure 3 shows three ROIs produced by correlation. The ROI on the left of Figure 3 matches the position and orientation of a duplex very well. In fact, none of the procedures in ADORE's procedure library can improve this hypothesis, so the best strategy for ADORE is to accept it. The ROI on the right in Figure 3, on the other hand, does not correspond to any duplex. The best strategy here is to reject it.

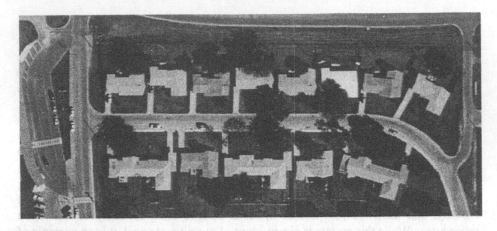

Fig. 1: A nadir-view image of a residential section of Ft. Hood, TX

The ROI in the middle of Figure 3, on the other hand, is more interesting. This ROI roughly matches a duplex, but the ROI is below and slightly rotated from the true position of the duplex, probably because the duplex is partially occluded in the image. In this case, the best strategy is to refine the hypothesis by resegmenting the image chip [10] and then applying a Generalized Hough Transform [5] to align the template with the extracted region boundary. Figure 4 shows the resulting hypothesis after these two procedures are applied.

Fig. 2. A Duplex

Examples like the one in Figure 3 demonstrate the importance of *dynamic control*. In all three cases, the first procedure was the same: correlation. The choice of the next procedure, however, depends on the quality of the data (in this case, ROI) produced by the previous step. In general, control strategies should choose procedures based not only on static properties of the object class and image domain, but also on properties of the data produced by previous procedures.

3 Related Work

Long before the appearance of software support tools like Khoros, researchers argued for specialized recognition strategies built from reusable low-level components. As far back as the 1970s, Arbib argued from psychological evidence for specialized visual "schemas" built from reusable procedures [4]. In the 1980's, Ullman developed a similar theory, in which primitive "visual routines" are combined to form specialized recognition strategies [32]. Later, Aloimonos [2] and Ikeuchi & Hebert [16] argued for specialized recognition strategies made from primitive vision operations in the context of visual robotics.

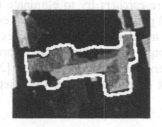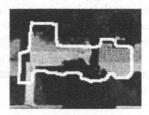

Fig. 3. A demonstration of dynamic control: the three ROIs above were all created by rotation-free correlation, yet the best strategy for refining these hypotheses depends on the quality of the ROIs, not the history of how they were created. In this case, the best strategy is to 1) accept the ROI on the left, 2) reject the ROI to the right, and 3) refine the ROI in the middle through segmentation [10] followed by the Generalized Hough Transform [5].

In practice, researchers have been building systems with special-purpose recognition strategies for twenty years. In the late '70s and early '80s, researchers built AI-style production and blackboard systems that selected and sequenced vision procedures to achieve specific tasks. Nagao & Matsuyama's production system for aerial image interpretation [24] was one of the first, and lead to several long-term development efforts, including SPAM [22], VISIONS/SCHEMA [11], SIGMA [15], PSEIKI [3] and OCAPI [9]. More recently, other researchers [8,17,19] have applied AI-style planning technology to infer control decisions from databases describing the task and the available procedures.

Fig. 4. The middle ROI from Figure 3 after refinement via segmentation [10] and the Generalized Hough Transform [5].

Unfortunately, knowledge-based systems are often *ad-hoc*. Researchers formulate rules for selecting procedures based on their intuition, and refine these rules through trial and error. (See [12] for a description of the knowledge engineering process in object recognition) As a result, there is no reason to believe that the control policies emerging from these heuristics are optimal or even good, nor is there any way to directly compare systems or to evaluate control policies.

Recently, researchers have tried to put the control of object recognition on a stronger theoretical foundation using Bayes nets (e.g. TEA1 [29] and SUCCESSOR [21]). Unfortunately, the design of Bayes nets can itself become an *ad-hoc* knowledge engineering process. Other researchers try to eliminate the knowledge acquisition bottleneck by learning control policies from examples. Researchers at Honeywell use genetic algorithms to learn target recognition strategies [1], while reinforcement learning has been used by Draper to learn sequences of procedures [13] and by Peng & Bhanu to learn parameters for vision procedures [26]. Maloof et. al. train classifiers to accept or reject data instances between steps of a static sequence of procedures [20].

4 Object Recognition as a Supervised Learning Task

The goal of the adaptive object recognition (ADORE) project is to avoid knowledge engineering by casting object recognition as a supervised learning task. Users train ADORE by providing training images and training signals, where a training signal gives the desired output for a training image. ADORE learns control strategies that dynamically select vision procedures in order to recreate the training signal as closely as possible. This control strategy can then be used to hypothesize new object instances in novel images.

To learn control strategies, ADORE models object recognition as a Markov decision problem. The state of the system is determined by data tokens produced by vision procedures. For example, the state of the system might be a region of interest (ROI), a set of 2D line segments, or a 2D contour. The actions are vision procedures that change the state of the system by producing new data tokens from the current data. A control policy is a function that maps states onto actions. In the context of ADORE, control policies map data tokens onto vision procedures, thereby selecting the next action in the recognition process.

At the software system level, ADORE is most easily thought of as two distinct components: a run-time execution monitor that applies vision procedures to data, and an off-line learning system. The connection between these two systems are the control policies that are developed by the learning system and applied by the execution monitor.

4.1 The Execution Monitor

The run-time execution monitor is a three-step loop that implements dynamic control policies. On each cycle, the execution monitor:

1. Measures properties of the current data token, producing a feature vector. The length and contents of the feature vector depend on the type of the data token; for example features measured of an image (average intensity, entropy, etc.) are different from features measured of a contour (length, curvature, contrast).

2. The control policy is a function that maps feature vectors onto vision procedures (see Section 4.2 below).

3. The selected procedure is applied to the current data token, thereby producing new data tokens.

The loop begins when an image is presented to the system as the first data token; the monitor then executes the loop above until a vision procedure fails to return any data, at which point the recognition process stops.

Of course, this simple description glosses over some important details. First, there are two special procedures – called *accept* and *reject* – that return no data, and therefore provide a stopping point. These are the procedures that interact with the user; the accept procedure signals that an object instance has been found, while the reject procedure indicates that the current data is a false hypothesis and should be abandoned. Second, the execution monitor also measures the run-time of each procedure, to be used in task statements (i.e. reward functions – see Section 4.2 below) that involve tradeoffs between time and accuracy. Finally, many vision procedures return multiple outputs. For example, the peak detection procedure (see Section 5.1) may detect several peaks corresponding to possible hypotheses. Similarly, many other detection, matching and grouping routine return multiple hypotheses. When this happens, we assume that the outputs do not overlap and consider each to be a separate hypothesis, forking as many new instances of the execution monitor as are needed to match the number of hypotheses.

In terms of software, the execution monitor is independent of the vision procedure library. Each vision procedure is an independent unix executable; a library file tells the execution monitor the number and type of input arguments for each procedure, the number and type of output arguments, and the unix pathname. The design goal is to allow vision procedures to be added or removed from the system by simply editing the library file. Similarly, the execution monitor is independent of particular data representations, since all data tokens are kept in files. For each data type, the library file tells the execution monitor 1) the name of the data type (so the monitor can match data tokens with arguments to vision procedures); 2) the length of the feature vector; and 3) the path of the unix executable for measuring features. Thus new data types, like new vision procedures, can easily be added to the system.

4.2 Control Policies

Control strategies are represented by *policies* that select vision procedures based on feature vectors. Since good control strategies depend on the target object class and image domain, a different strategy is learned for every object recognition task.

To learn theoretically justifiable control strategies, object recognition is modeled as a Markov Decision Problem (MDP). Although a general introduction to MDPs is beyond the scope of this article, they are structurally similar to finite state machines. The system begins in some a s_1 and applies an action a_1, thereby creating a transition to a new state s_2. This process repeats itself, creating a series of states and actions, s_1, a_1, s_2, a_2, s_3, ... Unlike a finite state machine, however, the state transitions in an MDP are probabilistic; when an action a_i is applied in state s_n, the resulting state is selected from a probability distribution associated with the state/action pair $<s_i, a_i>$. Because every state/action pair has a different probability distribution, the system has to select which action to apply at each state. This selection is made by a *control policy*, which is a mapping of states onto actions. Finally, every state transition has a *reward* (a.k.a. *penalty*) associated with it. The goal in a Markov decision problem is to find the control policy that maximizes the expected reward over time.

In ADORE, object recognition is cast as a Markov decision problem by equating actions with computer vision procedures (e.g. edge detection, region segmentation, grouping). These procedures produce and consume intermediate data tokens such as images, regions and line groups. The state of the Markov process is determined by a feature vector that describes the current data token. Vision procedures are probabilistic because even though we know the type of data they produce – for example, edge detection procedures create edges -- we do not know in advance what feature values that resulting data will have.

The reward/penalty function used for object recognition is task-specific. If the goal is to optimize recognition regardless of cost then the reward associated with every procedure other than *accept* is zero. When the system invokes *accept* it signals that it has found an instance of the object class, and it is rewarded or penalized according to how well that hypothesis matches the training signal. (The error function used to compare hypotheses to the training signal is also task-specific.) If the goal is to optimize a cost/quality tradeoff, every procedure other than *accept* and *reject* is penalized according to its runtime.

In this framework, a control policy is a function that maps feature vectors onto actions. (This mapping is limited by the practical constraint that every vision procedure can be applied to only one type of data). The control policy is built up from a set of Q-functions, one for every vision procedure. In Markov control theory, $Q(s,a)$ is the function that predicts the expected reward over time that follows from applying action a in state s. For example, in ADORE the off-line learning system trains a Q-function to predict the reward that results from segmenting ROIs (in the context of the current task), based on the features of the ROI. It also trains Q-functions for predicting the rewards that follow image correlation, curve matching, and every other procedure in the procedure library. The control policy evaluates these Q-functions on the current data and selects the procedure with the highest Q-value.

It is important to note that the Q-function predicts the total future reward that follows a procedure, not just the immediate reward. As described above, in most object recognition tasks the system does not get a positive reward until the final step when it accepts a (hopefully correct) hypothesis. As a result, Q-functions predict the quality of the hypothesis that eventually follows a procedure, even if it takes several additional steps to form that hypothesis.

4.3 Off-Line Learning

The control and artificial intelligence literatures contain many techniques for learning optimal Q-functions for control problems with discrete state spaces. If the transition probabilities associated with the actions are known (a so-called *process model*), dynamic programming will estimate Q-values and produce an optimal control policy.

In the absence of a process model, reinforcement learning (most notably the temporal difference [30] and Q-learning [34] algorithms) have been shown to converge to optimal policies in a finite number of steps.

Unfortunately, the object recognition problem as defined here depends on a continuous state space of feature vectors. Tesauro [31] and Zhang & Dietterich [35] have shown empirically that neural nets can approximate Q-functions for continuous feature spaces within a reinforcement learning system and still produce good control policies. Unfortunately, their method required hundreds of thousands of training cycles to converge. ADORE has a sequence of continuous feature spaces, one for each data representation (images, ROIs, contours, etc.) and would require getting a sequence of neural nets to converge on a single control policy. Although theoretically possible, we have not yet succeeded in making this work.

Instead, we train Q-functions by optimistically assuming that the best control policy always selects the action that yields the highest possible future reward for every data token. Strictly speaking, this assumption is not always true: a control policy maps points in feature space onto actions, and it is possible for two different tokens to have the same feature measurements and yet have different "optimal" actions. Nonetheless, the optimistic assumption is approximately true, and it breaks the dependence between Q-functions, allowing each neural net to be trained separately.

In particular, we approximate Q-functions by training backpropagation neural networks. The training samples are data tokens extracted from the training images. We apply all possible sequences of procedures to every training sample, in order to determine which procedure yields the maximum reward. A neural network Q-function is trained for every vision procedure using the data features as input and the maximum reward as the output. In this way, the neural net learns to approximate the future reward from an action under the optimistic control assumption. (Complicating the picture somewhat, we "bag" the neural nets to reduce variance; see [14].)

5 Experiments

5.1 Task #1: Duplex Recognition

To test ADORE in a tightly controlled domain, we trained it to recognize houses in aerial images like the one in Figure 1. In the first experiment, the goal is to find duplexes of the type shown in Figure 2. The training signal is a bitmap that shows the position and orientation of the duplexes in the training images; Figure 5 shows the training signal matching the image shown in Figure 1. The reward function is the size of the pixel-wise intersection of the hypothesis and the training signal, divided by the size of the union. This evaluation function ranges from one (perfect overlap) to zero (no overlap).

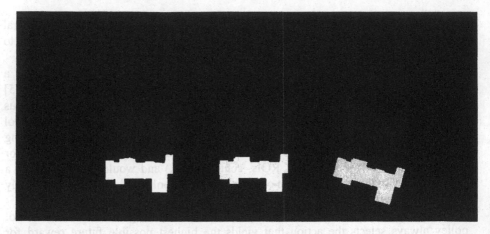

Fig. 5. The duplex training signal for the image shown in Figure 1.

5.2 The Vision Procedure Library

The vision procedure library contains ten 2D vision procedures, as depicted in Figure 6. Three of the procedures produce likelihood images (with orientation information) from intensity images and a template[1]. The rotation-free correlation procedure [28] correlates the template at each position in the image by first rotating the template until the direction of the edge closest to the center of the template corresponds to the edge direction at the center of the image window. The TAStat procedure is a modification of the algorithm in [25]. For every image window it also rotates a mask of the object until it aligns with the local edge data, and then measures the difference between the intensity distributions of the pixels inside and outside of the mask. The greater the difference between the intensity distributions, the more likely the mask matches an object at that location and orientation in the image. Finally, the probing procedure also uses edge information to rotate the template for each image window, and then samples pairs of pixels in the image window, looking for edges that match the location of edges in the template.

---

[1] In all of our experiments, we assume that a template of the object is available.

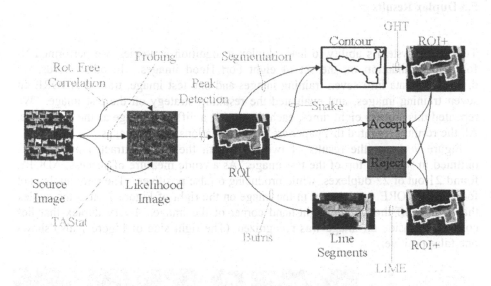

Fig. 6. A visual depiction of ADORE's vision procedure library. Note that the peak detection procedure produces approximately twenty ROIs each time it is called.

Regions of interest (ROIs) are chips from the original image that are hypothesized to correspond to object instances; each ROI also has a mask that details the hypothesized position and orientation of the object. ROIs can be extracted from likelihood images using a peak detection procedure, which finds the top N peaks in a likelihood image. For these experiments, the peak detection procedure was parameterized to extract twenty peaks from each likelihood image.

Five procedures can be applied to any ROI. Two of these actions are the special actions mentioned in Section 4.1, accept and reject. The other three options are: 1) an active contour procedure [18] that modifies the outline of an ROI mask until the contour lies along edges in the original image; 2) a segmentation procedure [10] that extracts the boundary of a new region (as a 2D contour) within the image chip; or 3) a straight line extraction procedure [7].

A Generalized Hough Transform procedure [5] matches 2D image contours to the contour of a template, thus creating a new ROI. A symbolic line matching procedure (LiME; [6]) finds the rotation, translation and scale that maps template (model) lines onto image lines, again producing an ROI. It should be noted that LiME transforms hypotheses in scale as well as rotation and translation, which puts it at a disadvantage in this fixed-scale domain.

5.3 Duplex Results

To test the system's ability to learn duplex recognition strategies, we performed N-fold cross-validation on the set of eight Fort Hood images. In other words, we divided the data into seven training images and one test image, trained ADORE on seven training images, and evaluated the resulting strategy on the test image. We repeated this process eight times, each time using a different image as the test image. All the results presented this paper are from evaluations of test images.

Figure 7 shows the results of two tests, with the ROIs extracted by ADORE outlined in white on top of the test image. As a crude measure of success, ADORE found 21 out of 22 duplexes, while producing 6 false positives. The only duplex not found by ADORE can be seen in the image on the right of Figure 7– it is the duplex that is half off the bottom right-hand corner of the image. Every duplex that lies completely inside an image was recognized. (The right side of Figure 7 also shows one false positive.)

Fig. 7. Duplexes extracted from two images. In the image on the left, all three duplexes were found. On the right image, a false positive appears on the upper right side. The half-visible duplex to the bottom right is the only false negative encountered during testing.

It would be incomplete to just analyzing ADORE in terms of false positives and false negatives, however. Much of the benefit of ADORE's dynamic strategies lies in their ability to refine imperfect hypotheses, not just make yes/no decisions. ADORE maximizes its reward function by creating the best hypotheses possible, given the procedure library. Table 1 gives a quantitative measure of ADORE's success. The left most entry in Table 1 gives the average reward across all 22 positive duplex instances from the optimal strategy, where the optimal strategy is determined by testing all sequences of procedures and taking the best result. The second entry gives the average reward generated by the strategy learned by ADORE. As further points of comparison, we implemented four static control strategies. The third entry in Table 1 gives the average reward for duplex instances if no further processing is applied after correlation and peak detection. The fourth entry gives the average reward if every duplex ROI is segmented and then repositioned by matching the region boundary to the duplex template boundary via a Generalized Hough Transform. The fifth entry gives the average reward if the active contour (i.e. snake) procedure is applied to every ROI, followed once again by the Generalized Hough Transform. Finally, the sixth entry is the average reward if straight lines are extracted from ROIs, and then the LiME geometric model matcher is applied to determine the position and rotation of the duplex.

	Optimal Policy	ADORE Policy	Accept or Reject	Segment	Active Contours	Line Extract
Avg Reward	0.8991	0.8803	0.7893	0.8653	0.7775	0.1807

Table 1. Comparison between the optimal policy, the policy learned by ADORE, and the four best static policies.

Two conclusions can be drawn from Table 1. First, the strategy learned by ADORE for this (admittedly simple) task is within about 98% of optimal. Second, the dynamic strategy learned by ADORE, although not perfect, is better than any fixed sequence of actions. As a result, our intuitions from Section 2 are validated: we achieve better performance with dynamic, rather than static, control strategies.

5.3 Task #2: Finding Smaller Houses

Having succeeded in finding a good strategy for recognizing duplexes, we changed the training signals and templates to recognize the four other styles of houses shown in Figure 8. The same procedure library and token features were used for these houses as for the duplex. After training, ADORE identified 18 of 19 instances of the house style *A* but generated 22 false positives. Combining the results from house styles A through D, ADORE found 47 out of 61 instances, while generating 85 false positives.

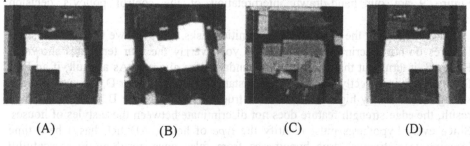

(A)   (B)   (C)   (D)

Fig. 8. Templates of four other styles of houses. Note that the boundaries of the templates are similar to each other

On the one hand, these results were encouraging. We had used the same procedure library and features to find five different classes of objects, by training five different control policies. On the other hand, these results were clearly not as good as the previous results with recognizing duplexes had been.

Why were these problems harder than finding duplexes? The most critical control decision (given our limited procedure library) occurs after ROIs are extracted from likelihood images. At this point, ADORE has a choice of five procedures: segmentation, active contours, line extraction, accept or reject. Of these five actions, line extraction is never optimal, but the other four actions are all optimal for some choice of ROI.

The control policy must select optimal actions based on ROI feature vectors. By inspecting the weights of the neural net Q-functions trained for duplex recognition, we discovered that two of the eleven ROI features dominated the control decision. One feature was the average edge strength along the boundary of the ROI. The second was the percent of pixels outside the mask that match the average intensity value of pixels under the mask. (We informally refer to these as "missing" pixels, since their intensities suggest that they were accidentally left out of the hypothesis.)

Based mostly on these two features, ADORE learned a strategy that worked well for duplexes. If we interpret the behavior of the Q-functions in terms of these two features, the duplex recognition strategy can be described as follows (see Figure 9): ROIs with very high boundary edge strength and very few "missing" pixels should be accepted as is. (The points in Figure 9 correspond to training samples, coded in terms of the optimal action for each ROI. Points marked with an open circle correspond to ROIs that receive approximately the same reward whether segmented or accepted as is.) If there is less edge strength but relatively few pixels are "missing", then the ROI should be segmented to adjust the boundary. Although many false hypotheses are segmented according to this rule, there is another control decision after segmentation where false hypotheses can be rejected and true ones accepted if the adjusted boundary still has low edge strength. There is also one small region in feature space where the active contour procedure is optimal. This is harder to explain and may result from the training set being a little too small, or it may be a decision triggered by some combination of the other nine features. Finally, if the missing pixel count is high or the edge strength is low, the ROI should be rejected. The solid boundaries in Figure 9 are our hand-drawn interpretation of the control policy's decision boundaries.

When we look at the other house recognition tasks, however, we find that the same features do not discriminate as well. If you overlay the four templates shown in Figure 8, it turns out that most of the boundaries are aligned. As a result, if an ROI for style A is incorrectly placed over an instance of styles B, C or D, the average edge strength is still very high. (The same is true for ROIs of style B, C and D). As a result, the edge strength feature does not discriminate between these styles of houses. Since every hypothesis must identify the *type* of house, ADORE has a hard time learning to distinguish true hypotheses from false ones, resulting in (gracefully) degraded performance. In effect, the difference *in feature space* between one style and another is too small to support a more reliably strategy. The policies learned by ADORE make the most of the feature set it is given and identify most instances correctly, but to improve performance on this task will require new and better features.

6 Conclusion

We have built a prototype adaptive object recognition system capable of learning object-specific recognition strategies, given a procedure library and features that describe intermediate hypotheses. When the intermediate-level features are descriptive enough to support intelligent control decisions, the result is a near-optimal object recognition system. When the intermediate-level features are less descriptive, ADORE still learns the best control policy relative to these (weak) features, but the resulting performance is naturally degraded.

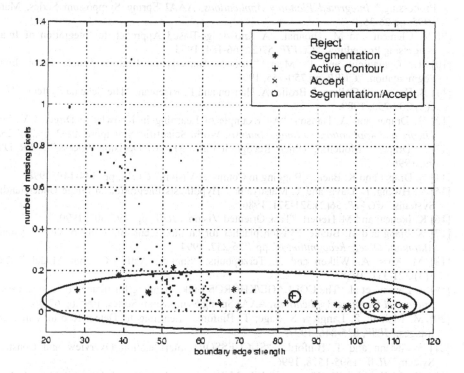

Fig. 9. ROIs plotted in two dimensions of the eleven dimensional feature space. The shape of the points indicates the optimal control decision for each ROI. (Open circles represent ROIs that receive roughly the same reward whether they are accepted as is or refined through segmentation.) The ellipses correspond to our interpretation of the decision boundaries learned by the neural networks.

References

[1] W. Au and B. Roberts. "Adaptive Configuration and Control in an ATR System," *IUW*, pp. 667-676, 1996.

[2] J. Aloimonos. "Purposive and Qualitative Active Vision", *IUW*, pp 816-828, Sept. 1990.

[3] K. Andress and A. Kak. "Evidence Accumulation and Flow of Control in a Hierarchical Spatial Reasoning System," *AI Magazine*, 9(2):75-94, 1988.

[4] M. Arbib. *The Metaphorical Brain: An Introduction to Cybernetics as Artificial Intelligence and Brain Theory*. Wiley Interscience, New York, 1972

[5] D. Ballard. "Generalizing the Hough Transform to Detect Arbitrary Shapes," *PR*, 13(2):11-122, 1981.

[6] R. Beveridge. *LiME Users Guide*. Technical report 97-22, Colorado State University Computer Science Department, 1997.

[7] B. Burns, A. Hanson and E. Riseman. "Extracting Straight Lines," *PAMI* 8(4):425-455, 1986.

[8] S. Chien, H. Mortensen, C. Ying and S. Hsiao. "Integrated Planning for Automated Image Processing," *Integrated Planning Applications*, AAAI Spring Symposium Series, March 1995, pp 26-35.

[9] V. Clement and M. Thonnat. "A Knowledge-Based Approach to Integration of Image Processing Procedures," *CGVIP*, 57(2):166-184, 1993.

[10] D. Comaniciu and P. Meer. "Robust Analysis of Feature Space: Color Image Segmentation," *CVPR*, pp.750-755, 1997.

[11] B. Draper, R. Collins, J. Brolio, A. Hanson and E. Riseman. "The Schema System," *IJCV*, 2(2):209-250, 1989.

[12] B. Draper and A. Hanson. "An Example of Learning in Knowledge Directed Vision," *Theory and Applications of Image Analysis*, World Scientific, Singapore, 1992. pp.237-252.

[13] B. Draper. "Modelling Object Recognition as a Markov Decision Process," *ICPR*, D95-99, 1996.

[14] B. Draper and K. Baek. "Bagging in Computer Vision," *CVPR*, pp. 144-149, 1998.

[15] V. Hwang, L. Davis and T. Matsuyama. "Hypothesis Integration in Image Understanding Systems," *CGVIP*, 36(2):321-371, 1986.

[16] K. Ikeuchi and M. Hebert. "Task Oriented Vision," *IUW*, pp. 497-507, 1990.

[17] X. Jiang and H. Bunke. "Vision planner for an intelligent multisensory vision system," *Automatic Object Recognition IV*, pp. 226-237, 1994.

[18] M. Kass, A. Witken and D. Terzopoulis. "Snakes: Active Contour Models," *IJCV* 1(4):321-331, 1988.

[19] A. Lansky, et al. "The COLLAGE/KHOROS Link: Planning for Image Processing Tasks," *Integrated Planning Applications*, AAAI Spring Symposium Series, 1995,pp 67-76.

[20] M. Maloof, P. Langley, S. Sage, T. Binford. "Learning to Detect Rooftops in Aerial Images," *IUW*, 835-846, 1997.

[21] W. Mann and T. Binford. "SUCCESSOR: Interpretation Overview and Constraint System," *IUW*, 1505-1518, 1996.

[22] D. McKeown, W. Harvey and J. McDermott. "Rule-Based Interpretation of Aerial Imagery," *PAMI*, 7(5);570-585, 1985.

[23] J. Mundy. "The Image Understanding Environment Program," *IEEE Expert*, 10(6):64-73, 1995.

[24] M. Nagao and T. Matsuyama. *A Structural Analysis of Complex Aerial Photographs*. N.Y.: Plenum Press, 1980.

[25] D. Nguyen. *An Iterative Technique for Target Detection and Segmentation in IR Imaging Systems*, Technical Report, Center for Night Vision and Electro-Optics, 1990.

[26] J. Peng and B. Bhanu. "Closed-Loop Object Recognition using Reinforcement Learning," *PAMI* 20(2):139-154, 1998.

[27] J. Rasure and S. Kubica. "The KHOROS Application Development Environment," In *Experimental Environments for Computer Vision*, World Scientific, New Jersey, 1994.

[28] S. Ravela, B. Draper, J. Lim and R. Weiss. "Tracking Object Motion Across Aspect Changes for Augmented Reality," *IUW*, pp. 1345-1352, 1996.

[29] R. Rimey and C. Brown. "Control of Selective Perception using Bayes Nets and Decision Theory," *IJCV*, 12(2):173-207.

[30] R. Sutton. "Learning to Predict by the Methods of Temporal Differences," *ML*, 3(9):9-44, 1988.

[31] G. Tesauro. "Temporal Difference Learning and TD-Gammon," *CACM*, 38(3):58-68, 1995.

[32] S. Ullman. "Visual Routines," *Cognition*, 18:97-156, 1984.

[33] S. Umbaugh. *Computer Vision and Image Processing: A Practical Approach using CVIPtools*, Prentice Hall, New Jersey, 1998.

[34] C. Watkins. *Learning from Delayed rewards*, Ph.D. thesis, Cambridge University, 1989.

[35] W. Zhang and T. Dietterich. "A Reinforcement Learning Approach to Job-Shop Scheduling," *IJCAI*, 1995.

Object Recognition for a Grasping Task by a Mobile Manipulator

Stéphanie Jonquières, Michel Devy, Flavien Huynh, and Maher Khatib

LAAS-CNRS, 7 Av. du Colonel Roche, 31077 Toulouse Cédex 4,
France
{jonqui, michel, huynh, maher}@laas.fr

Abstract. This paper presents the work currently done at LAAS/CNRS about scene interpretation required for manipulation tasks by a mobile arm. This task is composed of two steps : the approach of the mobile platform along the manipulation site and the grasping itself. The paper focuses on the object recognition and localization : the approach step is performed by a simple laser-based navigation procedure. For the grasping step, we use a CAD model of the object and discuss of the problems linked with such a representation : visibility informations must be added so that recognition and grasping strategies could be selected in a formal way. For the recognition, first matchings concerning discriminant patterns allow to generate a first prediction about the object situation; an optimal verification viewpoint can be computed. From this new camera position, we search for maximal sets of matched image features and model primitives; the best recognition hypothesis is determined by the best score. If no prediction can be determined, the system may switch to other discriminant patterns or move the camera respectfull to the arm and robot constraints.

1 Introduction

This paper presents some experimental methods required to deal with the recognition of 3D objects that must be grasped by a mobile manipulator. For such a perception task, a number of methods have been proposed; some interesting surveys on 3D object recognition [4] [13] [7] describe recognition strategies where sensory data are acquired by a single camera, or by a laser range finder (LRF), or by a multi-sensory system. In our lab, we have provided some contributions for different configurations of the sensory system (single camera [12] [8], LRF [1] or multi-sensory and mobile sensors [2] [9] [11]); in this paper, we address the problem of the selection of the best strategy for the recognition task of known objects, by the use of a single camera mounted close to the gripper of a mobile manipulator. (figure 15). The generic scenario we want to execute is represented on the figure 1 [10]; we are only concerned here with the perception module executed on board for the manipulation task.

In [6] [5], the authors present some variations around the classical interpretation-tree matching algorithm. The control process of our recognition task, follows

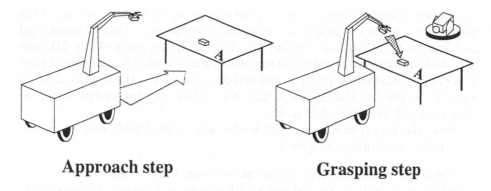

Approach step   **Grasping step**

Fig. 1. Grasping scenario

generally a classical "Hypothesise and Test" paradigm. But, in this work, we aim to develop a general method which could integrate :

– passive and active recognition procedures : a recognition based on one viewpoint if the result is unambiguous, or based on several images acquired from computed positions of the camera if several hypothesis can be considered,
– and different decisional processes : a depth-first approach if a discriminant visual cue can be searched at first, an exhaustive approach if the scene is very ambiguous.

Indeed, we can define discriminant visual cues from the model - cues that may be determined by the user or by comparison with a more general model of the class the object belongs to - that will help us to highlight the most interesting viewpoints, where such discriminant features are visible. We will try to get these particular viewpoints in so far as it is accessible to the arm and in so far as it doesn't lead to a great number of movements towards the robot.

However, these discriminant cues are sometimes not enough to make a decision. Their recognition is one step in a more complete decision process. In fact, we are led to make some hypothesis from our a priori knowledge and the recognition process is the search for the strongest pattern so that we start to search for some particular model primitives. Each time some visual features have been identified, we update our belief in the active hypothesis along the recognition process using Bayes nets [3] until we are able to determine the object.

2 Approach Step

Different control schemes could be used for the approach step; if the environment model is a priori known, a path planner could be used to generate a trajectory toward a required position of the mobile platform along the manipulation site (here, a simple table). This position could be computed in order to optimize the reachibility of the object put on the table.

A more complex functionality is presented here; we take advantage of the multisensory system mounted on our robot. The manipulation site is detected and located by a Sick laser sensor. On figure 2 are represented the 2D laser data and the figure 3 shows the 2D segments extracted from the previous figure. The manipulation site appears as two orthogonal segments the lengths of which are a priori known. This allows us to work without any knowledge about the localization of the manipulation site.

From the laser segments matched to the table sides, a table position is estimated. Two situations can occur :

- the object position on the table is approximatly known : an optimal position of the arm can be computed and a path is generated toward the corresponding platform position along the table.
- the object position is not a priori known. Before coming along the table, an active recognition procedure is executed from intermediate positions of the platform close to the table. These positions are computed from the aspect graph of the object, in order to detect some discriminant features and generate a good localization hypothesis.

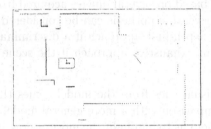
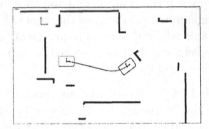

Fig. 2. 2D laser data acquired from the Sick sensor

Fig. 3. 2D laser data and extracted 2D segments

3 Object Recognition

Once the object is modelled, the main point is to match this representation with the visual data. The first topic we discuss here is the object modelling. Then we introduce the recognition process and mainly the hypothesis generation and verification.

3.1 Object modelling

The aim of this work is to be able to recognise a particular object. We don't need a general representation of the class the object belongs to, but on the contrary, we need a description of the object itself. That is why we built a CAD-model

with ROBMOD, a system developed by S. Cameron at Edinburgh. ROBMOD
is a CSG (Constructive Solid Geometry) modeller. The object is described by
3D-faces and 3D-segment loops. An interface has been developed to make this
description compatible with our data structure. All the work about the model
is done off-line.

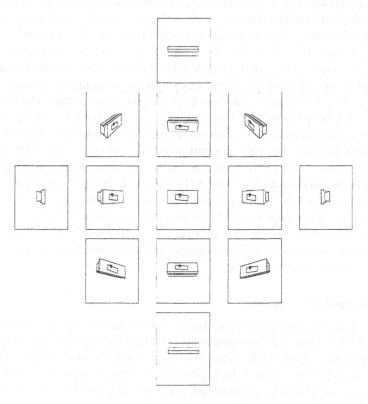

Fig. 4. Partial aspect table

This description is however insufficient in so far as all the segments are not
always visible. It depends on the viewpoint from which the object is observed.
This information about visibility can be gathered in aspect tables : each aspect
has a number and each segment of the model has an associated structure which
contains the numbers of the aspects where the segment is visible. Fig 4 shows a
part of our object's aspect table : the object we are working with is a blackboard
cleaner. The 3D-segments which happen to be only partially seen are not labelled
as visible. That is why some segments seem to miss on the figures. Aspects
concerning the other side of the object have not been represented : we only put
on fig 4 the aspects where a printed pattern with a kind of cross can be seen.

Among all the viewpoints, some are equivalent with respect to the visible segments. These viewpoints can be gathered in a structure including information about visible segments and an average viewpoint. Thus, we reduce the set of viewpoints we go through when we start the recognition process. Besides, it is particularly interesting to link such aspect graphs with highly discriminant cues.

Indeed, particular pattern can be extracted from the object model. They may be composed of parallel, collinear or connected segments, polygonal chains or particular patterns (trademark labels, colour cues, etc). These patterns can be defined by the user or automatically extracted from the object model. But these visual cues can't be considered at a same level : some of them have a higher discriminant value than other. That's why they are caracterized by an utility coefficient reflecting their likely importance in the recognition process. In order to determine a consistent value, we have to take into account the occurrence frequency of the pattern and how easy it is to highlight it among the other extracted visual patterns : we take into account the number of segments and the kind of segment patterns they are composed of (collinear or parallel segments, polygonal chains, etc). In the previous figure, the most discriminant pattern is the kind of box designed on a face of the object. It is not visible from the non-represented viewpoints. If this pattern can't be recognised, we try to work with the side views of the object, which are non only composed of parallel segments.

Thus, we start the recognition process with a 3D-model which contains information about the visibility of each segment and some particular object primitives useful to initiate the recognition.

3.2 Recognition Process

The aim of the process is to recognise an object using a 3D representation and 2D visual data from a gray-scaled picture. The first step consists in establishing a recognition hypothesis using the most discriminant features. Then, the recognition hypothesis is used to perform the verification process : this hypothesis provides us with a localization estimate which is used to project the whole model in the verification process.

Hypothesis Generation Fig 5 represents the scheme of the hypothesis generation process. According to what has been introduced previously, we start the process with information about discriminant cues. The most discriminant pattern is chosen and the search for this pattern in the picture data is performed.

The picture data are sorted so that we get sets of segments (parallel, collinear, connected, belonging to a chain). Then, we compare these structured sets with the one describing the selected pattern (number of parallel segments, connection types, etc) : we look for the occurrence of these specific sets of segments. Thus, some 2D points are matched with 3D points and we use Tsai's algorithm to compute the transformation between object and camera references.

If this search fails (non-visible pattern or non-recognised pattern), we can try with another pattern (less discriminant than the previous) or move the camera to get a new viewpoint (see section 3.3).

Hypothesis Verification The verification process is shown fig 6. We want here to check the localization hypothesis and, if necessary, we want to correct it.

The perception system provides us with a gray-scaled picture. It is treated to obtain 2D-segments. As the previous step has provided a localization estimation, it is used to project the 3D-model into a list of 2D-segments : we don't consider any longer particular sets of segments.

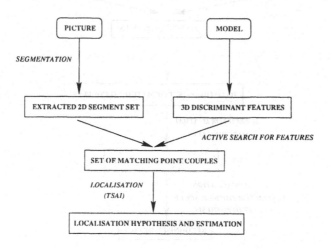

Fig. 5. Hypothesis generation scheme

From this localization, we can compute which segments are visible. Indeed, the initial localization allows us to determine an aspect which would lead to the same observation. We just have to label the 3D-segment which have this aspect number in their structure.

In the next step, matching is performed for each visible model segment. To determine how well the model primitive and the picture feature match we compute a score. Therefore, the couple of segments is submitted to a series of tests. After this, we get couples of segments with a score. Segments don't match if the score doesn't suit a final test. This is an exhaustive search for the machting couples of segments.

Sets of matching segments are built : their structure consists of lists of compatible couples of segments. These lists are kind of hypothesis in the verification process. Among those sets, we only keep those which have at least a certain number of couples. Then, we search for the maximum sets and we assign each hypothesis a new score. The best score determines the best hypothesis. From this result, the object is localized.

This method has been tested in several cases and it has also been made use of it in a static-look and move simulation. These applications are presented in a following section.

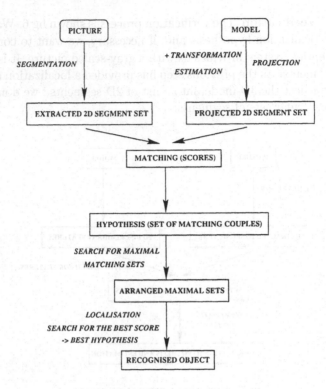

Fig. 6. Hypothesis verification scheme

3.3 Active Recognition

As mentionned in section 3.2, the most discriminant pattern may not be found. We can either keep on searching a less discriminant pattern or decide to get another viewpoint and to keep searching for the most discriminant pattern. To make this decision, the discriminant power of the pattern (how many aspects does it caracterize, how discriminant is it with respect to the other patterns, etc) but also the arm accessible domain and the robot movements must be taken into account. The pictures in fig 7 show what can be observed when the camera is moved in order to get different viewpoints until the most discriminant pattern is found.

What active recognition also means, is, for instance, to focus on a picture area, using eventually a priori knowledge. Thus, in our application, the object generally lies on a table and the soil is tiled so that the picture offers a lot of short connected segments on its borders. Thus, such areas with a lot of short segments can be rejected.

545

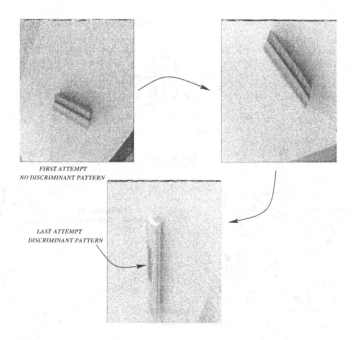

Fig. 7. Moving the camera to get different viewpoints

4 Grasping Step

Before any experiment, a lot of knowledge must be learnt. The final accuracy of the grasping, depends widely on the results of the calibration methods required to identify the model parameters for the mobile manipulator and for its environment. The figure 8 shows the different reference frames linked to the mobile robot (R_{robot}), the manipulator and the laser sensor (R_{arm} and R_{sick}, static w.r.t. R_{robot}), the end-effector (R_{eff}, dynamic), the gripper and the camera (R_{grp} and R_{cam}, static w.r.t. R_{eff}), the manipulation site, here a table (R_{table}, static) and the object that must be grasped (R_{obj}, static). The grasping process requires estimates for the following transformations:

- T_{ae} : end-effector in R_{arm}. Estimated from the internal sensors and from the geometrical model of the manipulator; this transformation must be used to request a manipulator movement towards a given position.
- T_{eg} : gripper in the end-effector frame. Constant.
- T_{to} : object in the table frame, unknown or approximatively given in the environment model (especially if this object has been placed here during a previous Pick and Place task).
- T_{grasp} : optimal grasping position for the gripper with respect to the object frame R_{obj}, it can be computed off-line from the gripper and the object models.

546

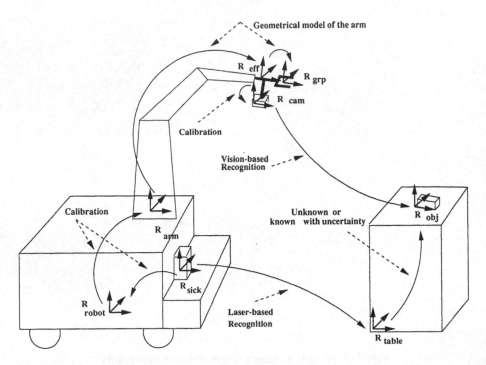

Fig. 8. Reference frames and transformations

If the object position on the table T_{to} is already in the model, as soon as the table has been located thanks to the laser data, an optimal placement of the robot along the table can be computed so that the grasping will be feasible without reaching any arm singularities or joint limits.

A trajectory can be generated so that the mobile platform is moved towards this goal defined as a known position of the table w.r.t the robot T_{rt}; at this time, this trajectory is executed by a closed loop on the odometer; so the actual robot position when coming along the table is not exactly known. The predicted object localization of the object w.r.t. the arm $\hat{T}_{ao}$ could be directly computed from the frame graph.

$$\hat{T}_{ao} = T_{ar}^{-1} * T_{rt} * T_{to}$$

If all transformations were perfectly known, the end-effector position T_{ae} - consequently, the manipulator movement- required in order to execute a perfect grasping operation, could be directly computed : unfortunately such a simple solution cannot be performed because $\hat{T}_{ao}$ is generally a too bad approximation according to ordinary accuracy requirements.

Nevertheless, if the object position on the table is already in the environment model, the vision-based recognition procedure can be simplified; by the use of the geometrical model of the arm and of the hand-eye calibration, the localization hypothesis $\hat{T}_{co}$ can be estimated. Only because of the need for $\hat{T}_{co}$ the hypothesis verification scheme (figure 6) is required.

A good grasping accuracy requires a final evaluation of T_{go} as precisely as possible, such as the cumulated error between the last relative movement (to reach the grasping position) and the last estimate of T_{go}, is less than the required tolerance.

The estimation of T_{go} by vision, can be based on either a static panoramic camera which localizes both the object and the gripper, or on a mobile wrist mounted camera which localizes only the object. For this paper, this last configuration has been chosen and a classical "Look and Move" strategy is proposed in order to guide the manipulator towards the object. Concerning R_{cam}, the frame linked to the camera, three transformations must be estimated :

- T_{ec} : camera in the end-effector frame. Constant.
- T_{eg} : gripper in the end-effector frame. Constant.
- T_{co} : object in the camera frame, given by the object localization.

By the use of the camera, the critical transformation T_{go} can be computed by :

$$T_{go} = T_{gc} * \hat{T}_{co} = T_{eg}^{-1} * T_{ec} * \hat{T}_{co}$$

T_{eg} and T_{ec} are constant : they must be evaluated off-line by specific calibrations. Then our accuracy requirements depend on the online localization procedure which provides $\hat{T}_{co}$.

In fact, an iterative strategy has been used, so that the grasping task can be controlled properly during the approach, and so that the errors due to the inaccuracies in the geometrical model of the manipulator or in the different off-line calibrations can be dynamically corrected. The last movement towards the grasp position will be undertaken only when the T_{go} estimation will be refined and when the length of this last movement will be short enough to insure that the grasp position will be reached with an error lower than the required tolerance.

5 Experimental Results

5.1 Recognition process

As said before, a gray-scale picture (fig 9) provides us with external information about the environment. This picture is segmented and we get about 290 segments. As said before, the picture can be divided into several areas caracterized by the length and the number of segments.

The extracted pattern is shown on fig 11. It is composed of two chains fitting into each other : the chain inside the other is also made of collinear segments.

The localization hypothesis is represented on fig 13. The result of the verification and recognition process is shown on fig 14. The hypothesis was quite accurate but this result has been improved by the exhaustive search of matched segments, only inside the window displayed on these figures.

Fig. 9. Recognition picture

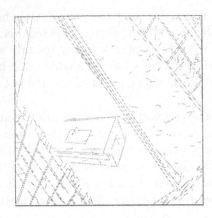

Fig. 10. Segmented picture

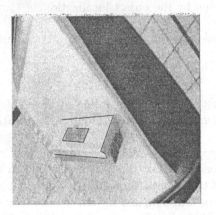

Fig. 11. Extracted pattern

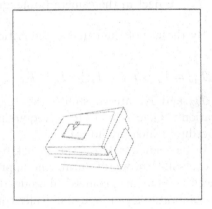

Fig. 12. Matching pattern with model

5.2 Grasping task

The grasping task is performed by an arm mounted on a mobile platform, as shown in fig 15. This task has been firstly simulated with a graphic system GDHE, developed in our lab (see fig 16), and, then, the real grasping has been successfully executed.

As described previously, the grasping is initiated with the computation of a localization hypothesis. Once the object has been recognised and localized, we compute the hypothesis using the transformation describing the arm movements. Indeed, the arm does not exactly reach the approach position. That's why the recognition process is performed all the grasping task long until it reaches the grasping position.

We have at this time some difficulties to estimate the error on the final grasp operation. The only result is visual; it seems we have less than 1 mm error, when the end-effector reaches the grasp position.

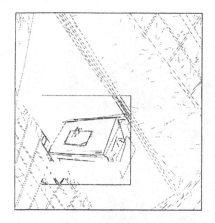 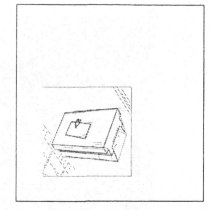

Fig. 13. Localization hypothesis   **Fig. 14.** Final recognition

This method provides good results, with satisfactory performances; with all the features extracted from one image, the sequence of prediction, localization and verification is executed in about 400 ms on a Sparcstation Ultra 10, without any software optimization.

6 Conclusion

We have described in this paper, a perception application related to visually guided Pick and Place task by a mobile arm. A multisensory system is mounted on our mobile robot : a Sick laser sensor allows to detect and locate the manipulation site, while a eye-in-hand camera allows to locate the object on the manipulation site.

This work is going on : we are implementing all the vision-based recognition procedure directly onboard, on the real time system on which the arm and the platform are controlled. We hope that a Dynamic Look and Move strategy could be tested, in order to avoid any arm stopped position between each iteration.

Other research works will be done in order to improve the different perceptual algorithms; especially, a tracking method will be integrated during object approach, in order to minimize the uncertainty and the time consumption of the object recognition algorithm.

References

1. M. Devy and J. Colly. Localisation of a multi-articulated 3D objet from a mobile multisensor system. In *The Second International Symposium on Experimental Robotics , Toulouse, (France)*, June 1991.
2. M. Devy, J. Colly, and R. Boumaza. Localization of a satellite by a multisensory perceptual system. *International Symposium Artificial Intelligence Robotics and Automation, in Space, Toulouse (France), 30 Septembre - 2 Octobre 1992, pp.117-128, Cépaduès Editions*, 1992.

Fig. 15. The real arm, mounted on a mobile platform.

3. D. Djian, P. Rives, and P. Probert. Training bayes nets for model-based recognition. In *4th Int. Conference on Control, Automation, Robotics and Vision, Singapore*, December 1996.
4. F.Arman and J.K. Aggarwal. Model-based object recognition in dense-range images - a review. *ACM Computing Surveys*, 25(1), March 1993.
5. R.B. Fisher. Performance comparison of ten variations on the interpretation-tree matching algorithm. In *3rd European Conference on Computer Vision,, Stockholm, Sweden*, 1994.
6. R.B. Fisher, A.W. Fitzgibbon, M. Waite, E. Trucco, and M.J.L. Orr. Recognition of Complex 3D Objects from Range Data. In *7th IARP International Conference on Image Analyses and Processing, Italy*, 1993.
7. P.J. Flynn and A.K. Jain. Cad-based computer vision : From cad models to relational graphs. *IEEE Transactions on Pattern Analysis and Machine Intelligence*, 13:114–128, February 1991.
8. V. Garric and M. Devy. Evaluation of calibration and localization methods for visually guided grasping. In *Proc. IEEE/RSJ International Conference on Intelligent Robots and Systems (IROS'95), Pittsburg (U.S.A.)*, August 1995.
9. P. Grandjean, M. Ghallab, and E. Dekneuvel. Multisensor Scene Interpretation : Model-Based Object Recognition. In *IEEE International Conference on Robotics and Automation, Sacramento, (USA)*, April 1991.
10. F. Huynh and M. Devy. Multi-View Vision Systems Cooperating for a Grasping Task. In *Proc. Fourth International Symposium on Intelligent Robotics Systems(SIRS'96), Lisbonne (Portugal), Rapport LAAS N.96180*, July 1996.

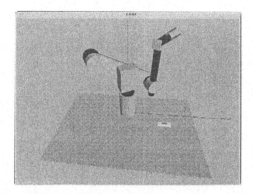

Fig. 16. The simulation display : the arm and the object.

Fig. 17. The simulated site.

11. S. Lacroix, P. Grandjean, and M. Ghallab. Perception Planning for a Multisensor Interpretation Machine. In *IEEE International Conference on Robotics and Automation, Nice, (France)*, May 1992.
12. L.H. Pampagnin and M. Devy. 3d Object Identification based on Matching between a Single Image and a Model. In *IEEE International Conference on Robotics and Automation, Sacramento, (USA)*, April 1991.
13. P. Suetens, P. Fua, and A. Hanson. Computational strategies for object recognition. *ACM Computing Surveys*, 24(1):5–61, March 1992.

Authors Index

Lecture Notes in Computer Science

For information about Vols. 1–1463
please contact your bookseller or Springer-Verlag

Vol. 1498: A.E. Eiben, T. Bäck, M. Schoenauer, H.-P. Schwefel (Eds.), Parallel Problem Solving from Nature – PPSN V. Proceedings, 1998. XXIII, 1041 pages. 1998.

Vol. 1499: S. Kutten (Ed.), Distributed Computing. Proceedings, 1998. XII, 419 pages. 1998.

Vol. 1501: M.M. Richter, C.H. Smith, R. Wiehagen, T. Zeugmann (Eds.), Algorithmic Learning Theory. Proceedings, 1998. XI, 439 pages. 1998. (Subseries LNAI).

Vol. 1502: G. Antoniou, J. Slaney (Eds.), Advanced Topics in Artificial Intelligence. Proceedings, 1998. XI, 333 pages. 1998. (Subseries LNAI).

Vol. 1503: G. Levi (Ed.), Static Analysis. Proceedings, 1998. IX, 383 pages. 1998.

Vol. 1504: O. Herzog, A. Günter (Eds.), KI-98: Advances in Artificial Intelligence. Proceedings, 1998. XI, 355 pages. 1998. (Subseries LNAI).

Vol. 1505: D. Caromel, R.R. Oldehoeft, M. Tholburn (Eds.), Computing in Object-Oriented Parallel Environments. Proceedings, 1998. XI, 243 pages. 1998.

Vol. 1506: R. Koch, L. Van Gool (Eds.), 3D Structure from Multiple Images of Large-Scale Environments. Proceedings, 1998. VIII, 347 pages. 1998.

Vol. 1507: T.W. Ling, S. Ram, M.L. Lee (Eds.), Conceptual Modeling – ER '98. Proceedings, 1998. XVI, 482 pages. 1998.

Vol. 1508: S. Jajodia, M.T. Özsu, A. Dogac (Eds.), Advances in Multimedia Information Systems. Proceedings, 1998. VIII, 207 pages. 1998.

Vol. 1510: J.M. Zytkow, M. Quafafou (Eds.), Principles of Data Mining and Knowledge Discovery. Proceedings, 1998. XI, 482 pages. 1998. (Subseries LNAI).

Vol. 1511: D. O'Hallaron (Ed.), Languages, Compilers, and Run-Time Systems for Scalable Computers. Proceedings, 1998. IX, 412 pages. 1998.

Vol. 1512: E. Giménez, C. Paulin-Mohring (Eds.), Types for Proofs and Programs. Proceedings, 1996. VIII, 373 pages. 1998.

Vol. 1513: C. Nikolaou, C. Stephanidis (Eds.), Research and Advanced Technology for Digital Libraries. Proceedings, 1998. XV, 912 pages. 1998.

Vol. 1514: K. Ohta, D. Pei (Eds.), Advances in Cryptology – ASIACRYPT'98. Proceedings, 1998. XII, 436 pages. 1998.

Vol. 1515: F. Moreira de Oliveira (Ed.), Advances in Artificial Intelligence. Proceedings, 1998. X, 259 pages. 1998. (Subseries LNAI).

Vol. 1516: W. Ehrenberger (Ed.), Computer Safety, Reliability and Security. Proceedings, 1998. XVI, 392 pages. 1998.

Vol. 1517: J. Hromkovič, O. Sýkora (Eds.), Graph-Theoretic Concepts in Computer Science. Proceedings, 1998. X, 385 pages. 1998.

Vol. 1518: M. Luby, J. Rolim, M. Serna (Eds.), Randomization and Approximation Techniques in Computer Science. Proceedings, 1998. IX, 385 pages. 1998.

1519: T. Ishida (Ed.), Community Computing and Support Systems. VIII, 393 pages. 1998. (Subseries LNAI).

Vol. 1520: M. Maher, J.-F. Puget (Eds.), Principles and Practice of Constraint Programming - CP98. Proceedings, 1998. XI, 482 pages. 1998.

Vol. 1521: B. Rovan (Ed.), SOFSEM'98: Theory and Practice of Informatics. Proceedings, 1998. XI, 453 pages. 1998.

Vol. 1522: G. Gopalakrishnan, P. Windley (Eds.), Formal Methods in Computer-Aided Design. Proceedings, 1998. IX, 529 pages. 1998.

Vol. 1524: G.B. Orr, K.-R. Müller (Eds.), Neural Networks: Tricks of the Trade. VI, 432 pages. 1998.

Vol. 1525: D. Aucsmith (Ed.), Information Hiding. Proceedings, 1998. IX, 369 pages. 1998.

Vol. 1526: M. Broy, B. Rumpe (Eds.), Requirements Targeting Software and Systems Engineering. Proceedings, 1997. VIII, 357 pages. 1998.

Vol. 1528: B. Preneel, V. Rijmen (Eds.), State of the Art in Applied Cryptography. Revised Lectures, 1997. VIII, 395 pages. 1998.

Vol. 1529: D. Farwell, L. Gerber, E. Hovy (Eds.), Machine Translation and the Information Soup. Proceedings, 1998. XIX, 532 pages. 1998. (Subseries LNAI).

Vol. 1530: V. Arvind, R. Ramanujam (Eds.), Foundations of Software Technology and Theoretical Computer Science. XII, 369 pages. 1998.

Vol. 1531: H.-Y. Lee, H. Motoda (Eds.), PRICAI'98: Topics in Artificial Intelligence. XIX, 646 pages. 1998. (Subseries LNAI).

Vol. 1096: T. Schael, Workflow Management Systems for Process Organisations. Second Edition. XII, 229 pages. 1998.

Vol. 1532: S. Arikawa, H. Motoda (Eds.), Discovery Science. Proceedings, 1998. XI, 456 pages. 1998. (Subseries LNAI).

Vol. 1533: K.-Y. Chwa, O.H. Ibarra (Eds.), Algorithms and Computation. Proceedings, 1998. XIII, 478 pages. 1998.

Vol. 1538: J. Hsiang, A. Ohori (Eds.), Advances in Computing Science – ASIAN'98. Proceedings, 1998. X, 305 pages. 1998.

Vol. 1540: C. Beeri, P. Buneman (Eds.), Database Theory – ICDT'99. Proceedings, 1999. XI, 489 pages. 1999.

Vol. 1541: B. Kågström, J. Dongarra, E. Elmroth, J. Waśniewski (Eds.), Applied Parallel Computing. Proceedings, 1998. XIV, 586 pages. 1998.

Vol. 1542: H.I. Christensen (Ed.), Computer Vision Systems. Proceedings, 1999. XI, 554 pages. 1999.

Vol. 1543: S. Demeyer, J. Bosch (Eds.), Object-Oriented Technology ECOOP'98 Workshop Reader. 1998. XXII, 573 pages. 1998.

Vol. 1544: C. Zhang, D. Lukose (Eds.), Multi-Agent Systems. Proceedings, 1998. VII, 195 pages. 1998. (Subseries LNAI).

Vol. 1546: B. Möller, J.V. Tucker (Eds.), Prospects for Hardware Foundations. Survey Chapters, 1998. X, 468 pages. 1998.

Vol. 1548: A.M. Haeberer (Ed.), Algebraic Methodology and Software Technology. Proceedings, 1999. XI, 531 pages. 1999.